This is No. 44 of a limited edition of 250 copies of the hard cover version of this book which have been signed by the author

[signature]

CLASSICAL
ARCHITECTURE

Some Other Published Writings by James Stevens Curl

English Victorian Churches: Architecture, Faith, & Revival with a Foreword by Barry Orford (London: John Hudson, 2022).

Freemasonry & the Enlightenment: Architecture, Symbols, & Influences with a Preface by Professor Andrew Prescott (Holywood: Nerfl, 2022).

St Michael's Kirkyard, Dumfries: A Presbyterian Valhalla with a Foreword by Roger Bowdler and an Epilogue by Robert L.D. Cooper (Holywood: Nerfl, 2021).

Introductory Essay and *Bibliography* in a fine, enlarged, numbered, limited, facsimile edn. of *On the Laying Out, Planting, and Managing of Cemeteries; and on the Improvement of Churchyards* by John Claudius Loudon (originally published 1843) with a Foreword by Ian Dungavell (Holywood: Nerfl, 2019).

Making Dystopia: The Strange Rise and Survival of Architectural Barbarism with a Prolegomenon by Timothy Brittain-Catlin (Oxford: Oxford University Press, 2018, 2019).

A Short History of the Cemetery Movement in *The Art of Memory: Sculpture in the Cemeteries of London* by Richard Barnes (Kirstead, Norfolk: Frontier, 2016).

The Oxford Dictionary of Architecture (with Susan Wilson) (Oxford: Oxford University Press, 2015, 2016).

Funerary Monuments & Memorials in the Church of Ireland (Anglican) Cathedral of St Patrick, Armagh with an Introit by The Most Reverend A.E.T. Harper, Archbishop of Armagh and Primate of All Ireland 2007–12, and a Foreword by Professor Janet Myles Spencer (Whitstable: Historical Publications, 2013).

Georgian Architecture in the British Isles 1714–1830 (Swindon: English Heritage, 2011).

Spas, Wells, & Pleasure-Gardens of London (London: Historical Publications, 2010).

Victorian Architecture: Diversity & Invention (Reading: Spire, 2007).

The Egyptian Revival: Ancient Egypt as the Inspiration for Design Motifs in the West with a Foreword by Peter Clayton (London and New York: Routledge, 2005).

The Victorian Celebration of Death (Thrupp, Stroud: Sutton, 2004).

'A Short History of the Cemetery Movement in Europe' in *Italian Memorial Sculpture 1820–1940: A Legacy of Love* by Sandra Berresford, with contributions by Fred S. Licht, Francesca Bregoli, Franco Sborgi, Robert W. Fichter, and Robert Freidus (London: Frances Lincoln, 2004).

Kensal Green Cemetery: The Origins & Development of the General Cemetery of All Souls, Kensal Green, London, 1824–2001 (ed., with contributions from several scholars) (Chichester: Phillimore, 2001).

The Honourable The Irish Society 1608–2000 and the Plantation of Ulster. The City of London and the Colonisation of County Londonderry in the Province of Ulster in Ireland. A History and Critique (Chichester: Phillimore, 2000).

The Londonderry Plantation 1609–1914. The History, Architecture, and Planning of the Estates of the City of London and its Livery Companies in Ulster (Chichester: Phillimore, 1986).

The Life and Work of Henry Roberts, 1803–76, Architect: The Evangelical Conscience and the Campaign for Model Housing and Healthy Nations (Chichester: Phillimore, 1983).

A Celebration of Death. An Introduction to Some of the Buildings, Monuments, and Settings of Funerary Architecture in the Western European Tradition (London: Constable, 1980).

The Erosion of Oxford (Oxford: Oxford Illustrated Press, 1977).

CLASSICAL ARCHITECTURE

Language, Variety, & Adaptability

JAMES STEVENS CURL

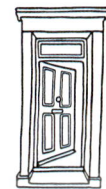

John Hudson Publishing

Published by
John Hudson Publishing
22 Stratford Grove
London SW15 1NU

© James Stevens Curl

First published by Batsford 1992
Second edition published by Batsford 2001
This edition published by John Hudson Publishing 2025

ISBN 978 1 7398229 2 7 (hardback)
ISBN 978 1 7398229 5 8 (paperback)
ISBN 978 1 7385400 2 0 (ebook)

British Library Cataloguing in Publication data
A CIP catalogue for this book is available from the British Library.

The right of James Stevens Curl to be identified as author of this work has been asserted by him
in accordance with the Copyright, Design and Patents Act 1988.

All rights reserved
No part of this publication may be reproduced or transmitted in any form or by any means, electronic
or mechanical, including photocopying, recording, or any information storage or retrieval system,
without permission in writing from the publisher.

Every effort has been made to trace the copyright holders and we apologise in advance for any unintentional omissions, which we would be pleased to correct in any subsequent editions of this book.

Typeset in Calluna

Indexed by Auriol Griffith-Jones
Page layout by Nicola Willmot (info@twoplusgeorge.co.uk)

Printed and bound in the United Kingdom by Short Run Press, Exeter

Front cover: the *Befreiungshalle* (Hall of Liberation) on the Michelsberg, near Kelheim, Bavaria (1842-63), commenced under the ægis of King Ludwig I of Bavaria (*r.*1825-48), and completed to designs by Leo von Klenze (1784-1864). *See* page 140 for a longer description (© *pwmotion – stock.adobe.com*).

Back cover: Bronze door and inventive Mannerist doorcase at the entrance to the baptistry
of the Chapel of Christ the Redeemer, Culham Court, Berkshire (2008-15), designed by
Craig Hamilton Architects (© *Paul Highnam*).

In Memoriam

Henry Hope Reed

who had the temerity to suggest that most contemporary American architecture by the 1950s was fraudulent, empty of intellectual content, ugly, and illiterate. Convinced that Classicism, possessing a rich architectural language, capable of infinite variations, offered salvation from dystopian barbarism and what he described as 'synthetic taste in architecture', he published his views in *The Golden City* (1959), and founded (1968) *Classical America* to promote it through exemplars and publications.

> *At one time, taste in the fine arts was acquired by the study of the best*
> *that man had created in the past. It called for severe discipline, systematic exercises for the eye,*
> *command of the art in the fullest sense, and self-control, which brings the only freedom.*
>
> HENRY HOPE REED:
> *The Golden City* (New York: Monacelli and the Institute of Classical Architecture and Art, 2020), 59.

> *Should you, my LORD,[1] a wretched Picture view;*
> *Which some unskilful Copying-*Painter *drew,*
> *Without Design, Intolerably bad,*
> *Would you not smile, and think the Man was mad?*
> *Just so a tasteless Structure; where each Part*
> *Is void of* Order, Symmetry, *or* Art:
> *Alike offends, when we the Mimick Place:*
> *Compare with* Beauty, Harmony, *or* Grace. ROBERT MORRIS:
> *The Art of Architecture, a Poem.*
> *In Imitation of HORACE's Art of Poetry* (London: R. Dodsley, 1742), 5.

---

[1] Richard Boyle, 3rd Earl of Burlington and 4th Earl of Cork (from 1704).

*Architecture cannot lie, and buildings, although inanimate,
are to that extent morally superior to men ...
Since the early nineteenth century we have depended
almost exclusively on what used to be called book learning,
so much so that we have become visually illiterate.*

JOHN EDWARDS GLOAG:
The Significance of Historical Research in Architectural and Industrial Design:
a Paper read to the Royal Society for the Encouragement of Arts,
Manufactures, and Commerce (20 March 1963).

*How truly admirable ... it is to preserve these time-honoured remains
for when a perishable manuscript is lost and all record gone,
a single capital or base of a column, a small fragment of foliage ...
may serve to fill up a hiatus on the page of history ...*

LEWIS NOCKALLS COTTINGHAM:
Report on the Present State of St James' Tower
for the Churchwardens at Bury St Edmunds, Suffolk (December 1842),
later published in the *Architect, Engineer, and Surveyor* **iv** (1843), 22–3, 57.

CONTENTS

Note on Illustrations ix

Preface and Acknowledgements xi

1 Introduction 1
What is Classical Architecture? A Few Definitions 1
Proportion 3
The Module 4

2 The Orders of Architecture and their Application 5
Introduction 5
The Greek Orders 6
The Roman Orders 17
Application of the Orders 32

3 The Græco-Roman Roots of Classical Architecture 35
Greek Architecture 35
Roman Architecture 36
Concluding Comparative Remarks 43

4 The Renaissance Period 45
Columns, Pilasters, Antæ, and Piers 45
A Lingering Presence of Antiquity 46
The 'Rediscovery' of Vitruvius 47
Key Buildings of the Early Renaissance 48
Later *Palazzi* 52
Venetian *Palazzi*, Sansovino, and Alberti 56
Centralised and Circular Plans 60
Michelangelo 64
Serlio and Vignola 67
Palladio 69

5 Classical Variations: Baroque, Rococo, Palladianism, and After 73
Introduction 73
Bernini, Borromini, Ellipses, and Western Façades 74
A Selection of French Examples 87
Classical Architecture in England 90
Some German Buildings 102
The Second Palladian Revival 106

6 Neo-Classicism and After 115
Neo-Classicism and Rome 115
Cordemoy and Laugier 115
The Rediscovery of Greece 116
The Greek Revival 118
The Move Away from Neo-Classicism 137

7 Aspects of a Continuing Classicism 151
Preliminary Remarks 151
The Survival of Classicism 153
Post-Modernism 158
New Urbanism and New Classicism 160

8 Epilogue 162
Some Practitioners of Classical Architecture in Recent Times 162
Conclusion 172

Select Glossary of Terms 175

Select Bibliography 241

List of Subscribers 245

Index 247

NOTE ON ILLUSTRATIONS

The author and publisher have endeavoured to ensure that full permission has been sought and given for all material used in this book. Every effort has been made to trace the copyright holders and we apologise for any unintentional omissions, which we will be pleased to correct in any subsequent edition. Sources are given in brackets after each caption, with the abbreviated form of the publication or collection indicated in either the caption or the source in parentheses. Abbreviations indicate the collections from which the illustrations derive, with the reference number or shelf-mark (if appropriate) after the abbreviation. Drawings are by the author unless indicated otherwise. Sketch-plans and sections are at differing scales. The key to abbreviations is as follows:

AA	© ADAM Architecture	F&S	© Fairfax & Sammons Architects
ACWM	© Anthony C.W. Merrick	GB	Geoff Brandwood
AH	© Angelo Hornak, London	GBM	Georg Böttger, Munich, photographer
AFK	Photograph by Anthony Kersting, © Conway Library, Courtauld Institute of Art. Distributed under a Creative Commons CC-BY-NC-4.0 license	Gibbs (1728)	Gibbs, James: *A Book of Architecture, Containing Designs of Buildings and Ornaments* (London: Innys & Manby, 1728)
Alinari	© Alinari Archives, Florence: Courtesy of Fondazione Alinari per la Fotografia	HES	© Historic Environment Scotland
		HPM	Hirmer Photoarchiv Munich
Ap	© Apollodorus Architecture	JOD	© James O. Davies
AvE	© Andreas von Einsiedel	JSA	© John Simpson Architects
BP	© Ben Pentreath	JSC	© James Stevens Curl: drawing or photograph by him
Brindley & Weatherley (1887)	Brindley, William, & Weatherley, W. Samuel: *Ancient Sepulchral Monuments* (London: Vincent Brooks, Day & Son, 1887)	Kent (ed.) (1727)	Kent, William (ed.): *Designs of Inigo Jones* (London: William Kent, 1727)
		Langley (1745)	Langley, Batty: *The CITY and COUNTRY BUILDER'S and WORKMAN'S TREASURY of DESIGNS: Or the ART of DRAWING and WORKING The Ornamental PARTS of ARCHITECTURE* (London: S. Harding, 1745)
BSGKW	© *Benediktinerabtei St Georg Kloster Weltenburg*, Bavaria		
BTB	By kind permission of Batsford Books		
Campbell (1725)	Campbell, Colen: *Vitruvius Britannicus, or The British Architect* iii (London: The Author, 1725)	Lloyd (1925)	Lloyd, Nathaniel: *A History of English Brickwork* (London: H. Greville Montgomery, 1925)
CC	Crown Copyright	LOC	© Liam O'Connor
CHA	© Craig Hamilton Architects	MC/RIBAC	© Martin Charles/Royal Institute of British Architects Collections
Chamoust (1783)	Chamoust, Charles-François Ribart de: *L'Ordre François Trouvé dans la Nature* (Paris: The Author, 1783)	MK	© Mark Kirby
		MvS	© Morley von Sternberg
CL	Country Life Picture Library	MW	© Mark Watson
coll.	Collection	MWJ	© Mark Wilson Jones
CSB	© C. Stadler/Bwag; CC-BY-SA-4.0	NB	Collections held in the Palace of Nieborów
D&A	© Davison & Associates, Dublin	NCP	© Nick Carter Photography
D&C	By kind permission of Duckworth & Co. Ltd., 2974-363	NMA	© Muzeum w Nieborowie i Arkadii
		Normand (1852)	Normand, Charles: *NOUVEAU PARALLÈLE des ORDRES D'ARCHITECTURE des GRECS, des ROMAINS et des AUTEURS MODERNES* (Paris: Normand Aîné, and Carillian, Goeury & Dalmont, 1852)
DS	© Durston Saylor		
DT	© Dylan Thomas		
EW	© Ewen Wetherspoon		

Osborne (1954)	Osborne, A.L.: *A Dictionary of English Domestic Architecture* (London: Country Life, 1954)
PA	© Peter Aaron/OTTO
PH	© Paul Highnam
Plaw (1782)	Plaw, John: *Rural Architecture; or Designs, from the Simple Cottage to the Decorated Villa* (London: J. Taylor, 1782)
PorA	© Porphyrios Associates
publ.	published
RCHME	Royal Commission on the Historical Monuments of England
RCAHMS	Royal Commission on the Ancient and Historical Monuments of Scotland
RCR	Rodney C. Roach
RHB	© Roger Bowdler
RIBAC	© Royal Institute of British Architects Collections
Richardson (1914)	Richardson, Albert Edward: *Monumental Classic Architecture in Great Britain and Ireland during the Eighteenth & Nineteenth Centuries* (London: B.T. Batsford, 1914)
Rosengarten (1893)	Rosengarten, A.: *A Handbook of Architectural Styles*, W. Collett-Sandars (trans.) (London: Chatto & Windus, 1893)
Schinkel (1866)	Schinkel, Karl Friedrich: *Sammlung Architektonischer Entwürfe* (Berlin: Ernst & Korn, 1866)
SB/JFCH	© Sue Barr, image kindly provided by the Jencks Foundation at The Cosmic House
SNBR	© Scottish National Buildings Record
Spiers (1893)	Spiers, R. Phené: *The Orders of Architecture, Greek, Roman, and Italian. Selected from Normand's Parallel and Other Authorities* (London: B.T. Batsford, 1893)
Stuart and Revett (1762–1816)	Stuart, James, and Revett, Nicholas: *The Antiquities of Athens* (London: Haberkorn, Nichols, & J. Taylor, 1762–1816)
Troost (ed.) (1942–3)	Troost, Gerdy (ed.): *Das Bauen im Neuen Reich* (Bayreuth: Gauverlag Bayreuth GmbH, 1942–3)
TR-S	© Terence Reeves-Smyth
UGLE	© United Grand Lodge of England, which granted permission to reproduce the image
Woolfe and Gandon (1767)	Woolfe, John, and Gandon, James: *Vitruvius Britannicus, or The British Architect* (London: The Authors, 1767)
WP	Image kindly supplied by Włodzimierz Piwkowski

PREFACE AND ACKNOWLEDGEMENTS

I finde great occasion … to use a certaine Forewarnyng and Præface.

JOHN DEE:
The Mathematicall Præface to *The Elements of Geometrie of the most auncient Philosopher EVCLIDE of Megara*
(London: John Daye, 1570), 2.

The word 'classic' … is often used … to indicate qualities which are the special praise of Greek and Roman work – stateliness, elegance, and the careful coordination of all the parts of the composition … It [implies] standard excellence.

RUSSELL STURGIS:
A Dictionary of Architecture and Building
(London and New York: Macmillan, 1901), 609–610.

There was a time when students of architecture were required to survey a building of quality and prepare fine measured drawings (sometimes rendered in watercolour) based on that survey: the buildings selected were usually Classical (either 18th or early 19th century), and drawings and notes were subjected to close scrutiny, criticised, and then marked. This discipline proved invaluable, and instilled in me, from my first year of study, a healthy respect for the complexities, subtleties, and qualities of the Classical language of architecture. Surveys and measured drawings oblige students to look at buildings and understand them, including the materials of which they are made: it is only by careful measuring and drawing up those surveys that a detailed knowledge can be acquired of how *materials used* (such as brick and stone) can inform *design, proportional systems, relationships of parts, mouldings*, and, above all, *how junctions are formed in a satisfactory manner*. A brick, for instance, has certain fixed dimensions, and its proper use will help to govern certain dimensions in the finished design.

I learned very early in my career (to give some examples) how a moulded skirting stops at a block above which an architrave rises; how a band of mouldings joins another band at right angles; how the features of a room (such as fireplaces, windows, niches, doors, and bays) relate to each other by means of main axes and subsidiary axes; how subtle, recessed bands or planted beads can not only disguise joints, but can help objects to look pleasing by their logical positioning and the resulting subdivision of planes; how plinths, pedestals, rails, and cornices divide and finish the designs of walls; how pilasters or lesenes can break up a long wall into a series of parts and relate to the design of entablatures and ceiling compartments; how to design a corner (inside and out); how the height of courses of brickwork can determine the exact size of, say, a window-opening or a stone quoin; and a great deal more. I discovered a rich alphabet to start with, then a vocabulary, and then a whole language capable of infinitely adaptable use. What is more, I realised that Classicism actually worked, and created buildings that functioned well in every way *as architecture*. I have always been grateful for that invaluable training, for it enabled me to look at buildings with an informed eye, and has made visiting fine cities, towns, and buildings one of the greatest of pleasures in life, and one that has never palled.

From the 1950s, however, architectural students were required to design in the manner that had become *de rigueur* after 1945: this eschewed all 'historical' references, although it was perfectly all right to crib bits from the works of 'Le Corbusier', Miës van der Rohe, Walter Gropius, and others currently fashionable. I, like many others of my generation, had to 'design' to comply with the prejudices of those who talked about 'building for our own time', the 'poetry of concrete', the 'honest expression of structure', and other doleful matters. I realised very quickly that not only was the favoured 'architecture' promoted in the indoctrination centres known as Schools of Architecture arguably not architecture at all, because it had no vocabulary, grammar, syntax, serenity, repose, quality, or beauty, but also that it was extraordinarily easy to produce, and required the minimum of effort in terms of thought or draughtsmanship. All too often it also failed, not just structurally (as many commercially available 'systems' methods failed), but leaked, grew mould inside, and could not be described as real architecture at all: in terms of detailing, too, it just did not work. And later on in my career, I witnessed the disastrous results of applying certain claddings to provide 'skins' for buildings which subsequently 'went on fire'.

Classicism required study, practice, understanding, scholarship, and thought: it was far too difficult for people who wanted the easy way out, who did not care about the environment or about the past (several joyless puritanical individuals expressed a desire to destroy all old buildings, especially cathedrals, churches, museums, country houses, and palaces, not just because they were 'irrelevant', but because they represented values, æsthetics, scholarship, learning, and craftsmanship, and so would have no place in the grim, dystopian future those individuals wished to *impose* on the rest of us), and who preferred mouthing cant and cribbing the latest clichés from pictures in one of the 'architectural' magazines to expending any effort on learning about real architecture. The greatest problem, it seemed to me, was an obsession about abstractions, and the trouble with abstraction is that if you abstract too much, there is virtually nothing left: that obsession has dehumanised architecture, and made it so remote from humanity that people can no longer relate to it. The alien, the incomprehensible, the outrageous, the threatening, have all been promoted as part of what seems uncomfortably like a fundamentalist quasi-religious cult, backed by pretentious jargon that attempts to ape the sciences without grasping the nature of true scientific thinking.

The quality of the buildings created as a result of the fashions of the 1940s through to the third decade of the 21st century is on view virtually everywhere: it has been weighed, and, for the most part, has been found wanting. Some very large structures, 'designed' without the slightest regard for quality, and hated by their inhabitants and by those who had to look at them, have already been demolished, long before their construction costs were paid off, while others are being dressed up with feeble attempts to give them architectural coherence to make them more visually acceptable.

In particular, the manner in which Modernists use materials makes no sense: brickwork is treated like wallpaper, appearing over openings with no visible means of support, and thin veneers of stone are stuck on to buildings, *even on soffits*, looking unstable, and sometimes falling off. Not only do these unsatisfactory tricks frequently fail, but they create unease in the beholder, contributing to a sense of dissatisfaction with the built environment already present because of the visual chaos which seems to get worse with each passing year. So Classical Orders, or sometimes just columns, have reappeared, not always with success: there have even been some direct Classical quotations in otherwise unClassical buildings, sometimes referred to by critics as 'witty', depending on the identity of the architect and his or her current standing in the favouritism stakes. Yet there are so many errors being perpetrated it is quite clear that knowledge of the principles of Classicism (and even of basic masonry) is less than rudimentary among far too many architects of today. One sees stones and other components made of hard materials joined at the mitre, 'keystones' that would never work, lintels that are far too small in height or too great in length, columns carrying pediments with no supporting entablatures, and uprights that are far too widely spaced. One has the feeling that silly games are being played, and that superficiality dominates the once noble world of architecture: but what is obvious is that architectural education is failing to provide students with any basic knowledge of materials and how they are used; keeps them ignorant of the possibilities of geometry; denies the necessity of respecting other buildings and the *genius loci*; and leaves them floundering and intellectually impoverished in ways that would not be tolerated in other professions.

This book is an attempt to explain what Classical architecture is, and to demonstrate the various permutations, combinations, and possibilities when the infinitely adaptable and wonderfully rich language of Classicism is employed in the creation of a real, gloriously humane architecture that lifts, rather than depresses, the spirit. It is restricted to being an introduction to the subject because to cover it as fully as possible would make a far bigger volume than my publisher is prepared to allow me. It is hoped that it will help students of architecture to begin to have a feeling for a great resource that can still be studied, not only in some of the best buildings in the world, but in thousands of decent works of architecture that serve to enhance our towns, cities, and countryside with their well-mannered reticence. What is more, Classical architecture, rooted in millennia of precedents, actually works well, at every level, *as architecture*.

A word is necessary concerning my use of Batty and Thomas Langley as a source for some of the illustrations. I chose the Langleys for their practicality and simplicity, and because their illustrations demonstrate the modules and relationships of parts very clearly. They were, after all, catering for draughtsmen and craftsmen who had to build or make artefacts in the Classical styles, and in agreeable English towns where much of the Georgian urban fabric has managed to survive, such as Ludlow in Shropshire, the enormous influence of pattern-books and instruction manuals such as those of the Langleys will be understood. Such publications were far more widely influential for ordinary provincial builders than were the grander, far more expensive architectural books of masters like James Gibbs, Colen Campbell, or Sir William Chambers, although those beautiful volumes were of great significance in the genesis of edifices such as country houses, churches, and buildings for civic and institutional uses, and not merely within these islands either, for Gibbs's influence was considerable in America. I am particularly grateful to my distant cousin, Sheila Fallon (*née* Curl), for giving me a fine copy of the Langleys' *Builder's Jewel* (1763), owned by members and friends of the family in the Kentish Weald since 1770: it is a very small pocket-book (which would fit easily unto any pocket), copiously illustrated, and stuffed full of practical information about Classical details useful to tradesmen and draughtemen.

In several countries today, Classicism in architecture is alive and well, although it gets a bashing in the public prints from time to time, usually by those with vested interests in uglification. Yet visitors to old cities in Italy are surrounded by Classical architecture (which is almost the vernacular style there), and much 20th-century modern Italian architecture is deeply rooted in Classicism (not just of the Fascist era, for Fascism actually favoured Modernism, as in the Casa del Fascio, Como [1932–6], by Giuseppe Terragni, much lauded by Modernists). Rome, for example, is a Classical city *par excellence* and offers the student an amazing range of variety in myriad manifestations of Classicism throughout the centuries. Classicism is dominant in Paris and other French cities. In its many transformations, it can enchant those who trouble to explore (for example) the exquisite Baroque and Rococo churches in Southern Germany, just as it can delight in burnished Neo-Classical garments at the hands of a von Klenze in St Petersburg or Bavaria, a Schinkel in Potsdam or Berlin, a Soane in London, or an Erdmannsdorff in Potsdam or Wörlitz. Many great public buildings of the 19th and 20th centuries, familiar to multitudes on both sides of the Atlantic, are fine Classical compositions, and it is probably reasonable to claim that Classical architecture contributes not a little to the pleasures of travel. It therefore seems sensible to provide a volume that explains what the essence of Classical architecture actually is, for, although many buildings in different places will be familiar *partly because of the Classical language of architecture employed*, the traveller misses much if he or she cannot identify the sources of designs, the stylistic aspects, and even the Classical shadow lurking behind even the most stripped and bare essay in unornamented design.

Looking back over more than two millennia, it is clear that that language has enabled the creation of great buildings, and even whole, harmonious blocks in cities, because it is infinitely adaptable, enabling rich invention and vast numbers of variations on its basic themes to blossom. Modernism, however, has discarded a great language, a mighty and expansive vocabulary, and a whole system of grammar and syntax, in favour of visual incoherence, with the predictable making of a ghastly dystopia of uninhabitable cities, incessant noise, and violent pornographic 'entertainment': so, without an alphabet (only a few images of approved exemplars), a vocabulary, or a language, Modernism only represents itself. The so-called International Style permitted a very limited range of architectural clichés (e.g. 'flat' roofs, long strips of window, buildings raised on thin columns labelled *piloti*, and white-painted flat wall-surfaces completely devoid of any mouldings or other features): it offered a poverty-stricken vocabulary compared with the riches available in Classicism, and soon palled, after which architectural illiteracy, incoherence, anarchy, and widespread destruction of the built environment inevitably ensued.

We also had inflicted on us the flimsy codification known as Deconstructivism, with its distorted, misshapen, and menacing buildings, misguidedly hailed by some as a new paradigm, but in fact devoid of language other than threatening assaults on perceptions, serenity, and repose from which all anthropomorphic resonances had been expunged, hence the unease it induces in the beholder. Deconstructivism and its misbegotten descendants have undermined harmony, unity, and perceived stability (which the 19th-century critic, Coventry Patmore, identified as *absolutely crucial* to any *successful* work of architecture): they have been correctly perceived as *intentional aggression* on human senses, abusing perceptive mechanisms in order to generate anxiety and discomfort. If this is a new paradigm, it should cause great concern: Christopher Alexander called such tendencies 'nonsensical', mindful of the impact they so obviously have on our surroundings (some scientific studies have shown they can affect human health adversely as well). And one might hazard the thought that, as there is so much chaos, unease, dislocation, ugliness, danger, and violence in the world, why is it deemed necessary to make it all so much worse?

The *tabula rasa* demanded by Modernists jettisoned a vast architectural language, with all its possibilities, in favour of fancy wordplay, empty jargon, meaningless sound bites, and the sloganising cacophony accompanying a bogus linguistic dance. It has been and is promoted by those who are self-serving, self-regarding, interested only in power and money, and is ingested by a bemused public, often too cowed and ill-educated to be able to protest or resist. One of the big problems is that a visually illiterate and desensitised public can look only with its ears, and confuses obfuscation for profundity: cults invent their own languages and liturgies, the more obscure and dark the better they serve their protagonists.

It is astonishing that Classicism has been dismissed by the ignorant as a mere style, for it encapsulates two and a half millennia of an ever-developing architecture, adaptable, functional, and resonant with meaning. To discard it in favour of something that has manifestly failed *as architecture* might be regarded as foolish, and certainly as unwise. There are definite signs today that the entire drift of an architecture held in thrall by Modernists is being questioned, internationally too, and that appreciation of historic buildings and of old towns that have not been wrecked is growing in strength. This will be touched upon at the end of the book.

I began making notes for a possible book on Classical architecture in the late 1970s, discussing the idea with numerous friends and colleagues. I also began a process of purchasing books and other material I judged might be useful when working on the project, including three leather-bound tomes containing fine 19th-century photographs of European buildings, obviously collected by persons touring the Continent in the 1880s in search of architecture worthy of study. Those three items, crammed with fine photographs, cost me the princely sum of one pound. Gradually a book began to take shape, and I was helped by several kind persons (many of whom are no longer with us) during its preparation well into the 1990s, including Kirsten Andersen, Robert Blow, Martin Charles, Colin Clarkson, Sir Howard Colvin, Iona Cruickshank, Sonia Deadman, Margaret Eborall, Simon Edwards, Lucas Elkin, Martyn Everett, John Gloag, A. Stuart Gray, Malcolm Green, John Greenacombe, Paul Grinke, Dan Holden, Dawn Humm, Ralph Hyde, Charles Jencks, Penelope Jessel, Peter Kent, Anthony F. Kersting, Karin Kryger, Cynthia Langdon-Davies, Ian Leith, James Lomax-Simpson, Claudia Mernick, Jill Palmer, Ann Perry, Rodney C. Roach, John Sambrook, Richard Sidwell, Michael Smallman, Jeremy Smith, Gavin Stamp, Christopher Stell, Alan Stevens, Peter Swallow, Trevor Todd, Roger Towe, Pamela Walker, Mary Weston, Cathy Wilson, and Kay Woollen. Sir John Summerson kindly gave permission to quote from his work (when he ran Sir John Soane's Museum, he also lugged some formidably heavy tomes up from stygian depths for me to peruse in agreeably lit surroundings). Jonathan Clark, John Gamble, Barry Ketchum, Vicky Johnson, Hugh Pagan, Jeremy Ridge, and Meaburn Staniland all helped to locate and obtain books for me.

Timothy Auger, then editorial director of B.T. Batsford Ltd, quickly saw the point of such a book as this, and I started work on it in 1989 in Rutland: throughout, Tim and his team gave unstinting support, and the book eventually appeared in 1992 during the time when I was enjoying a Visiting Fellowship at Peterhouse, University of Cambridge. I am grateful to two of my tutors from the 1950s, Bill Murray and Ferguson Sprott, who first gave me a taste for Classicism: the first edition was dedicated to their memories.

The book was very well received, and several friends wrote to me about it in generous and appreciative terms, including Stephen Dykes Bower, who encouraged me to think about a second edition, eventually published in paperback with improved illustrations in 2001, then by Norton in New York in 2003. For that edition, Karen Latimer kindly helped with the revised bibliography, Warwick Pethers made useful suggestions, Jan Gowlett provided a peaceful sanctuary in a delightful Essex valley that shelters that amazing fragment of Tilty Abbey where much of the text was drafted, and David Watkin urged me to continue with my labours when stamina was flagging: the second edition was dedicated to David, who was a good friend to me.

Eventually the book went out of print, and all rights reverted to me, but it all lay frustratingly in limbo for some time, with one or two false starts which, unhappily, just fizzled out for one reason or another. I was fortunate to meet John Hudson, of the publishing arm of English Heritage, when he worked with me on my *Georgian Architecture in the British Isles 1714–1830* (2011). When the publishing side of EH (which had become Historic England by then) was transferred to Liverpool University Press, he established his own publishing house in London. We renewed contact, and in 2022 he published my *English Victorian Churches: Architecture, Faith, & Revival* to considerable acclaim. We then decided that giving *Classical Architecture* (on which I had already spent much time and energy, reworking material, so I was concerned all that effort would be aborted) a new start would offer another suitable vehicle for collaboration, and discussed the matter at length. We would again save space by avoiding footnotes or endnotes, aiming for a general readership; dates of individuals would be given in the index rather than litter the text; we would acknowledge important publications published since the second edition came out; and we would revise the text, adding many new illustrations.

My good friend and colleague, Geoff Brandwood, discussed illustrations with me, and started tweaking images for me from the start of 2021: his sudden and unexpected death in November that year was a terrible shock and a huge loss, and stopped work on the illustrations for a time. Further help with truly generous encouragement, illustrations, and other matters, however, was forthcoming from many individuals, including Peter Aaron, Robert Adam, Charlie and Cosy Bagot Jewitt, Sue Beaumont, Tom Bilson (Head of Digital Media, The Courtauld Institute of Art), Roger Bowdler, Tim Brittain-Catlin, Leigh Brooks, Nir Buras, Francesca Cappellini, Eric Cartwright, Jonathan Clark, Giovanna Costantini, Ingrid Curl, John Daffurn, James O. Davies, Liz Faber, Anne Fairfax, Sheila Fallon, Craig Hamilton, Angelo Hornak, Martyna Jurkevičiūtė, Mark Kirby, Victoria Landeryou, Catesby Leigh, Peter McCormack, Scott McMaster, Anna McNally, Lindsay McQuarrie, Jonathan Makepeace, Luke Moloney, Jamie Mortimer, Liam O'Connor, Alex Oliver, Ben Pentreath, Hugh Petter, Phædra Phippoussis, Włodzimierz Piwkowski, Demetri Porphyrios, Alex Ramsay, Alyson Rogers, Don Ruggles, Jakub Ryng, Richard Sammons, Durston Saylor, Samina Shahzady, Justin Shubow, John Simpson, George Saumarez Smith, John Smylie, C. Stadler, Alexander Stoddart, Quinlan Terry, Mark Watson, Christopher Webster, Seth Weine, Nicola Willmot Noller, Susan Wilson, and Mark Wilson Jones. I am most grateful to all of them.

Inevitably, in a work of this nature, some quotations are necessary. The Select Bibliography contains works in which readers can follow up the points made in the present book, and texts from which this volume has drawn information have been acknowledged in this way. My gratitude, as always, must be expressed to my wife, Dorota, who has tolerated the piles of paper and drawings that eventually became this volume, as well as the considerable time I have been obliged to spend on the project. Finally, I thank John Hudson for publishing the book, Nicola Willmot for designing and setting it, and Auriol Griffith-Jones for compiling the index.

All those who wish to look at buildings old and new with informed eyes will find in this book a rich fund of material, and the basis for an understanding of a fecund source of architectural design that has been at the heart of Western culture for over two-and-a-half millennia, so I offer this revised and expanded edition of *Classical Architecture* once again in the belief that the book has some merits, and will be useful to the student of a great architectural phenomenon. It describes the fundamental principles and various aspects of Classical architecture, and includes a detailed illustrated glossary that is almost in itself a dictionary. It discusses in clear, straightforward language the origins of Classical architecture in Antiquity, and outlines its continuous development, through its various manifestations during the Renaissance, its transformations in Mannerist, Baroque, and Rococo phases, its re-emergence in the 18th, 19th, and 20th centuries, and its survival to the present day. The accessible, jargon-free chapters, with copious illustrations, celebrate the richness of the Classical architectural vocabulary, grammar, and language, and demonstrate the enormous ranges of themes and motifs that informed real architecture.

Finally, it has been a pleasure to revisit what is a huge and life-enhancing subject: such marvellous stuff elevates the spirit and enriches the mind. Æsthetic pleasure can be found aplenty in great Classically inspired buildings, and the possibilities of endless permutations and variations give one hope that they will stimulate true creativity and civilised invention in the future, given the infinite adaptability of the Classical language of architecture.

James Stevens Curl
Burley-on-the-Hill, Rutland; Peterhouse, Cambridge;
Broadfans, Dunmow; Saffron Walden, Essex;
and Holywood, County Down, 1989–2024

1

INTRODUCTION

Eighteen centuries ago one magnificent architectural tradition ruled Europe, Africa, and Asia, from the Rhine to the Sahara, from the Atlantic to the Euphrates.

DONALD STRUAN ROBERTSON:
A Handbook of Greek and Roman Architecture (Cambridge: Cambridge University Press, 1945), 1.

It is not till we come to the rise of Greek architecture that we enter on the great course of European architectural development, in which one style arises in historic succession from another – Roman from Greek, Romanesque from Roman, Gothic from Romanesque, in a steady stream of which the glorious and perfect Art of Greece is the fountainhead.

HENRY HEATHCOTE STATHAM:
A History of Architecture (London: B.T. Batsford, 1950), 43.

What is Classical Architecture? A Few Definitions

It is perhaps as well, at the very beginning, to be reminded of what is meant by Classical architecture. The *OED* (1933) definition that 'architecture is the art or science of building or constructing edifices of any kind for human use' is surely far too wide, for it includes *any* building, whatever its quality. John Ruskin (1849), in the *Seven Lamps*, proposed that architecture was the 'art which so disposes and adorns the edifices raised by man ... that the sight of them contributes to his mental health, power, and pleasure', a definition that suggests something more than utilitarianism, and indicates a spiritual, æsthetic, and beneficial content. Ruskin, however, should be read with caution, and it is arguable that his inflated reputation was responsible for a lot of harm, not least the loss of so much of Nash's marvellous scenographic architecture in London, largely on the grounds that stucco finishes were dishonest, and therefore 'immoral'. A. Trystan Edwards, for example, deplored the failure of the generation of architects working in the 1920s for 'not having assailed the authority of Ruskin, who ... moulded the architectural opinions of almost the whole class of "educated" Englishmen now arrived at middle age': he was specifically lamenting the destruction of Nash's Regent Street, especially the Quadrant.

But it was not only concerning the morality or otherwise of stucco that should make us very wary of Ruskin, who held that ornaments deriving from plants and carved by morally upright artisans were better than hated Classical ornament, and he denounced Greek Doric triglyphs because they were not based on any natural organic form, while simultaneously praising Venetian billet-mouldings as 'fit for purpose'. To detect natural forms in billet-mouldings (essentially a Romanesque ornament) indicates an outrageous bias based on wishful thinking. He also dismissed geometrical fret ornament because the type was only found in crystals of bismuth, a position that might make one question his thought processes. The English poet/essayist Coventry Patmore, an architectural critic of extraordinary perceptiveness, realised that all great architecture turns gravitational thrust to æsthetic advantage, and that this is actually expressed in the Classical Orders. He exposed fallacious arguments about ornament, 'morality' in architecture, and other red herrings, and saw clearly that any building only succeeds *as architecture* if it expresses gravitational control and stability, thereby instilling confidence in anyone who looks at it. He knew that most contemporary architectural critics (e.g. Ruskin) were hopelessly wrong: what he would have made of Modernist critics and apologists for the sundry 'isms' that have infected architecture in the 20th and 21st centuries must remain in the realms of agreeable speculation.

Sir George Gilbert Scott (1879) stated that 'architecture, as distinguished from mere building, is the decoration of construction', but few would subscribe to that view today. Architecture implies a sense of order, an organisation, a geometry, and an æsthetic experience of a far higher degree than that in a mere 'building'. Sir Henry Wotton (1624) declared that 'In *Architecture*, as in all other Operative Arts, the End must direct the Operation. *The End is to Build well*. Well Building hath three Conditions; *Commodity, Firmness,* and *Delight*.' Wotton's 'three Conditions' are derived from Vitruvius (Marcus Vitruvius Pollio), whose *De Architectura*, apparently written in the reign (27 BC–AD 14) of the Roman Emperor Augustus, probably between 16 BC and 14 BC, is one of the most important texts dealing with Classical architecture; indeed, it is the only apparently *complete* work on architecture that has come down to us from Antiquity, and probably enshrines much earlier Hellenistic material. Vitruvius's treatise is in ten books: they include observations on the education of the architect; on fundamental principles of architecture; on building types; and on four of the Orders (not, however, discussed in their 'logical' sequence of Tuscan, Doric, Ionic, and Corinthian, which seems to have been an invention of Renaissance theorists). There is a vast amount of information about architecture and building in Antiquity included in *De Architectura*, but, although Vitruvius suggested appropriate associations for each Order, he did not give them the degree of rule-book significance accorded them later by Renaissance writers.

Vitruvius stated that architecture depends on *Ordinatio* (ordering [*taxis* in Greek] or organisation); *Dispositio* (arrangement [*diathesis* in Greek] or design); *Eurythmia* (eurythmy, beauty, or shapeliness through harmony of proportion, or some kind of rhythmical order of elements: central to that concept is beauty and fitness of the elements of a building, involving relationships of height to breadth, breadth to length, and symmetrical balance); *Symmetria* (symmetry, meaning the *proportioned* correspondence of the various parts [e.g. the elements of the various parts of the Orders of architecture], and their contribution to the appearance of the entire composition); *Decor* (principles of propriety or correctness, in respect of function, tradition, and nature, notably in relation to temples dedicated to various deities, backed by authority); and *Distributio* (allocation [*oikonomia* in Greek]). These six points appear to come from an Alexandrine text, now lost. Vitruvius also states that works of architecture should be realised with due reference to durability, soundness, or strength; convenience or utility; and beauty, attractiveness, or grace ('*Ut habeatur ratio Firmitatis, Utilitatis, Venustatis*'): durability depended on foundations and a wise choice of materials; convenience on the arrangement and usability of apartments and on orientation and exposure to the sun and air; and beauty on the appearance of the finished work and on the proportion of the various parts in relation to each other and to the whole. Usefulness, spaciousness, sound construction, and strength are indeed qualities to be expected in good buildings, but the addition of delight, uplifting of the spirits, and æsthetic aspects suggests that architecture is something far more significant than building. Sir Christopher Wren stated that the principles of architecture were, in his time, 'rather the Study of Antiquity than Fancy', and that the main principles were 'Beauty, Firmness, and Convenience', the first two depending on the geometrical factors of 'Opticks and Staticks', while the third provided variety in works of architecture.

Today, the term 'Classical' implies the first rank or authority, a standard, or a model. It is therefore exemplary, but it specifically suggests derivation from Antiquity: the term 'Classical' means conforming in style or composition (or both) to the rules or models of Greek and Roman Antiquity. The Classical ideal is characterised by clarity, completeness, symmetry, deceptive simplicity, repose, and harmonious proportions; it is associated with civilised life, perfection, taste, restraint, and serenity. It is canonical, of admitted authority, excellence, or supremacy, orthodox, accepted, and a standard. The modern use of 'Classicism' to refer either to the art, architecture, and literature of a period held to represent a peak of quality or perfection, or to the deliberate imitation of works of such a period, seems to derive from Cornelius Fronto's use of *classicus* (meaning 'of the higher class of citizens') to suggest those writers of earlier times whose linguistic skills were deserving of imitation, and this was confirmed by Aulus Gellius, who wrote about *classicus ... scriptor, non proletarius* where the word means 'high-class' as opposed to 'low', as in the *proletarius sermo* of Plautus (*sermo* meaning a dialect, or style of conversation). 'Classicism', with reference both to the imitation of Antique precedents and to more general stylistic choices, has been a significant term in the cultural history of the West for the last three centuries.

The Classical language of architecture is not a free-for-all in which elements are arbitrarily thrown together; it is a sophisticated system that was in use throughout the Roman Empire, and its traces survived throughout the centuries, especially in Italy, Greece, parts of France, and the Middle East. Classical architecture has elements that can be related directly to the architectural vocabulary and language of Græco-Roman Antiquity (especially Greek temples and the ceremonial, monumental, and public architecture of ancient Rome), or that are derived as variants from that vocabulary and language: those elements include the Orders themselves (the columns or pilasters *with entablatures*), the frames and heads of window or door openings, pedimented gables, plinths, crowning cornices, string-courses, a range of mouldings, with or without enrichment, and much else.

Classical architecture, however, does not mean only the mere *application* of Orders or other details: those are only the outward and visible distinguishing marks. It suggests that the various parts of architecture are disposed in some form of harmonious relationship, both to each other and to the whole. Of course, the proportions and relationships of the various parts, including those of solids and voids, are to a very large extent determined by the Orders and by the spaces between columns or pilasters (known as *intercolumniation*), and by whether the Orders are physically present or the façades are *astylar* (i.e. without columns or pilasters). There is also, in Classical architecture, a system by which the geometry of each part is related to the geometry of the whole, giving harmonious balance and repose to the entire façade, or total building, or both. Thus units, and multiples or subdivisions of such units, have an essential role to play in the system of Classical proportion, and the purpose of proportional systems is to help to set up harmony, balance, repose, and an agreeable æsthetic throughout the whole of the building.

A building without overt Classical detail can still be a work of Classical architecture: designs by architects such as Étienne-Louis Boullée, Claude-Nicolas Ledoux, and Friedrich Gilly, for example, often eschew references to the Orders, architraves, or any other Classical motif, with the result that their buildings have a bare, primitive, stripped appearance, yet the proportions are undeniably Classical, while occasional techniques, such as the use of unfluted, primitive Doric columns, or a cornice based on that of the exterior of the Pantheon drum, suggest Antiquity by the most understated means. Certain Romanesque and Gothic buildings, or parts of buildings, such as porches or western doors, have proportional systems that unquestionably derive from Classical Antiquity, but the majority of Romanesque or Gothic details of colonnettes, capitals, tympana, and mouldings are anything but Classical, and so cannot be considered as

Classical architecture. Nevertheless, some exemplars, especially capitals, were clearly influenced by Antique precedents. Sir John Summerson, in his *The Classical Language of Architecture*, has held that Classical architecture is only recognisable 'as such when it contains some allusion, however slight, however vestigial', to the Antique Orders: such an 'allusion may be no more than' a hint of a cornice, or it could be 'a disposition of windows which suggests' the proportional relationships of pedestals, columns, and entablature. 'Some twentieth-century buildings – notably those of Auguste Perret and his imitators' – are Classical 'in this way: that is to say, they are thought out in modern materials' but in a Classical spirit 'and sealed' as Classical 'only by the tiniest allusive gestures'. In fact, it was not just Auguste Perret, but the firm of Perret Frères (there were three brothers involved) that was responsible for what was termed 'structural Classicism' in buildings erected and designed by the firm between 1905 and c.1930.

I would go even further than Summerson, and suggest that a building can be Classical in its proportions, its relationships of solids to voids, and the clarity of its expression, but need not have any allusion to an Order *per se*, although in most true, stripped Classical buildings one can superimpose an imaginary Order that will fit easily onto the basic façade. In some cases, too, an Order or parts of an Order may even be paraphrased: that is, the Order or parts of it may be expressed or suggested by other means; so the language of Classical architecture can give a designer who is fluent in all its aspects great latitude (a fact that is obvious in the works of certain masters of the Baroque and Rococo). The *sense* of Classicism can be suggested by economical means, and may be *commented* upon by a variety of methods in design. Like all great languages with a huge vocabulary and a vast range of expressive subtleties, Classical architecture is not a matter of mere imitation (although that is necessary at an early stage of study in order to learn its basic alphabet, vocabulary, syntax, and grammar): it offers enormous possibilities for expression, creative design, and composition.

Proportion

It should be emphasised that there is far, far more to Classical architecture than the treatment of surfaces or the design of elevations. It is about three-dimensional architecture: spaces, volumes, plan-shapes; the relationship of one room to another; the setting up of axes about which balance and symmetry can be achieved; proportions of solids to voids; the position of columns in relation to beams, pilasters, corners (inside and out), and design of soffits, ceilings, and floors; how one volume can rise up through others or can penetrate surrounding volumes; how axes and entrances can be signalled or emphasised; the framing and finishing of windows, doorways, fireplaces, and niches; the establishment of different planes; the emphasis given to a main floor; and a great deal else besides. It involves using a huge range of motifs, almost 'kits-of-parts', each of which is beautifully designed in itself, and each of which relates to other motifs in a literate, grammatical way: it also can involve being able to experiment with a rich language in order to create new and interesting compositions.

An integral part of Classical architecture is the rhythm set up by the dimensions between elements, which are based upon modules, multiplied or divided: so measurement, mathematical relationships, and geometrical principles are essential components. Those modules, rhythms, and proportional systems have important anchors in the Orders themselves. So, even though an Order may not be physically present in a design, its presence may still be overwhelmingly there through the proportional systems and juxtaposition of parts.

And what do we mean by proportion? Essentially it is due relation of one part to another: that relation between parts or elements can render the whole harmonious in terms of balance, symmetry, and æsthetic appeal, but if that relation is awry, the whole can become displeasing and awkward. Vitruvius observed that no building could be said to be well designed when it wanted symmetry and proportion. Proportion is dependent upon comparative relations or ratios, but that has a mathematical aspect that would confound the belief of an 18th-century commentator that it is derived from a 'Suitableness of Parts, founded on the good Taste of the Architect'. Unfortunately, in the absence of an agreed coherent architectural language today, that would not actually work. Gwilt defined *proportion* as the 'just magnitude of each part, and of each part to another, so as to be suitable to the end in view', which seems rather vague, but went on to point out that *harmonic proportion* was that which, 'in a series of quantities, any three adjoining terms being taken, the difference between the first and second is to the difference between the second and third, as the first is to the third': this suggests a musical connection, and indeed seems to have originated from the fact that a string or other sonorous body, divided into segments whose lengths are ½, ⅓, ¼, etc., of the total length, gives a definite series of musical notes whose relations are of fundamental importance in harmony. In arithmetic, proportion was the rule or process by which, three quantities being given, a fourth may be found which is in the same ratio to the third as the second is to the first. So in measurement, the term 'harmonic' is applied to the relation of quantities whose reciprocals are in arithmetic progression (e.g. 1, ½, ⅓, ¼ …); or to points, lines, functions, etc., involving such a relation.

The laws of proportion in ancient architecture were carefully investigated by Edward Cresy, and reprinted by Gwilt, while detailed work on the principles governing the proportions of Greek buildings was carried out by several authors, notably John Pennethorne, Francis Cranmer Penrose, and Thomas John Willson. However, much ancient architecture depended on geometry, notably circles (often interlacing), squares, and triangles, the last in particular when it included the isosceles triangle and its compound, the *pentalpha*. It is interesting that Spenser, in *The Færie Queene* (1589), alludes to the circle, triangle, and square, and proportion by 7 and 9. Thomas Tresham's extraordinary Triangular Lodge, Rushton Hall, Northamptonshire (1593-7), is based on the equilateral triangle, and has hexagonal principal rooms on each floor. There are three storeys each with three windows on each of the three sides, and windows themselves feature triangles and trefoils, so almost everything is dictated by the number three, a pun on Tresham's name and an allegory of the Most Holy and Undivided Trinity. The trefoil was the emblem of the Treshams, and the building, with its many allusions to the Mass and the Trinity, is a monument to Tresham's Roman Catholicism (he converted in 1580). Even the dimensions of the building have meaning (each side of the triangular plan is 33 feet 4 inches long, exactly one-third of a hundred feet). And the building is not alone, for numerals, geometrical figures (alone or interlocking), symbols, and allegories all played no small parts in the architecture of the past.

The Module

There have been several methods employed to determine the scale of equal parts by which the Orders (*see* Chapter 2) are measured for purposes of drawing them, but they are all founded on what is called a *module* based upon the dimension of the diameter of a column at the base of its shaft. It has generally been found to be convenient to take the half of such a diameter as the module, and to divide it into a given number of parts called *minutes*. In the case of the Greek and Roman Orders the module is divided into 30 parts, but in the Orders as delineated by Vignola and other masters of the Italian Renaissance, the module employed for the Tuscan and Roman Doric Orders is divided into 12, and that for the Roman Ionic, Corinthian, and Composite Orders is divided into 18 parts: this is because of the differences in character between the sturdiness of the Tuscan and Doric Orders and the more graceful and attenuated Orders which require a module divided into a greater number of parts than 12 to avoid dividing it into small and therefore awkward, cumbersome fractions.

Consideration will now be given to the Orders of architecture, one by one. But it should be realised that those are just the eight core Orders: each has many variations, and some idea of these can begin to be understood when studying great collections of Antique fragments such as those on display in the Pergamon Museum, Berlin.

2

THE ORDERS OF ARCHITECTURE AND THEIR APPLICATION

To the Orders of Architecture all buildings are indebted for the highest magnificence of decoration. To them the architect is obliged for many of the great effects in his art. The student must therefore be well acquainted with all the varieties in the work of the ancients, and acquire the fullest knowledge and most clear and correct ideas of their constituent principles. They form, as it were, his Alphabet …

SIR JOHN SOANE:
Lectures on Architecture at the Royal Academy (1809–36), Lecture **ii**,
quoted in David Watkin: *Sir John Soane: Enlightenment Thought and the
Royal Academy Lectures* (Cambridge: Cambridge University Press, 1996), 502.

Architecture aims at Eternity; and therefore is the only Thing uncapable of Modes and Fashions in its Principals, the Orders.

SIR CHRISTOPHER WREN:
Tracts on Architecture I, quoted in Stephen Wren (ed.):
Parentalia, or Memoirs of the Family of Wrens I, reprinted in
Wren Society (Oxford: Oxford University Press, 1942), **xix**, 126.

Introduction

An Order of architecture is essentially a vertical post carrying a beam or a lintel, but there is far more to it than that. It is an assembly of parts consisting of a column, with base (usually) and capital, carrying an entablature, proportioned and embellished in consistency with one of the Orders of architecture: it is, in essence, the column and the horizontal element above of a temple colonnade, and it may or may not have a pedestal. The entablature is divided into the architrave, which is the lowest part, resting directly on the abaci of the column capitals, so the architrave is properly the lintel. Above this lintel-architrave is usually a frieze (omitted in some of the Antique examples of the Orders), and above this is the cornice, which represents the eaves of the building, protects the frieze, and sheds water from the roof.

Vitruvius provided the earliest descriptions we have of the Orders of architecture in his *De Architectura*, drawn from Greek sources and from his own experiences. The first seven books of *De Architectura* deal with architecture in general (I), building materials (II), the construction of temples (III), the Orders of architecture (IV), public buildings (V), private buildings in town and country (VI), and ornamentation of buildings (VII); the remaining books cover water and waterways, sundials and water-clocks, and the building of various machines. The Orders, therefore, are described in his third and fourth books.

Unfortunately, what was clear to Vitruvius and his contemporaries is no longer familiar, and architectural descriptions are notoriously difficult to interpret in any case, so the text poses some problems. Nevertheless, Vitruvius provided descriptions of the Doric, Ionic, and Corinthian Orders, and brief notes on the Tuscan Order. He suggested the geographical areas where each Order was evolved, and associated the Orders with various deities, indicating an appropriate Order for a particular god or goddess. Thus, from the earliest of times, *the Orders had anthropomorphic associations*, some masculine, and some feminine.

Doric (a name also given to a Greek dialect), for example, gets its name from Doris, a small district in central Greece, between Mounts Œta and Parnassus, the alleged mother-country of the Dorians, who established colonies in various places after their conquest of Peloponnesus. The worship of Apollo and Heracles seems to have been widely regarded as particularly Dorian. The Doric Order derived its proportions and its sturdy appearance from the male human figure, and it is particularly associated with Attica.

Ionic refers to Ionia, the name given to a portion of the west coast of Asia Minor adjoining the Ægean sea and bounded on the east by Lydia, the cities of which included Miletus, Priene, Ephesus, and Colophon. Ionia, in Classical times, suggested one of the four divisions of the Greek world, the others being Æolic, Doric, and Achæan (or Arcado-Cypriote), mostly linguistic.

The main cult of the Ionians was that of Poseidon, although some of their finest temples were those dedicated to Artemis, notably the splendid edifice at Ephesus. As for the Ionic Order, it derived its character from the female form, the volutes suggesting locks of hair, formally arranged.

Corinthian alludes to Corinth, a city associated with luxury and licentiousness, but in architecture the term alludes to the graceful and beautiful Order with its distinctive capital, the invention of which was said to be founded on the following. A young Corinthian woman died, and after her funeral, her nurse collected in a basket those articles to which she had shown a partiality when alive, and carried them to the tomb, placing a tile on top of the basket to protect its contents. The basket had been inadvertently set on an acanthus plant, which, in springtime, grew, its leaves appearing through the wickerwork of the basket, and forming curved elements at the corners of the capping tile. The phenomenon was seen by Callimachus, who, inspired by the image, designed a capital that itself became associated with Beauty.

Much later, in 15th-century Florence, Leon Battista Alberti prepared (1452) the first treatise on the theory and practice of architecture since Antiquity in his *De Re Ædificatoria* (first published 1485), drawing on Vitruvius and on his own acute observations of Antique remnants. Like Vitruvius's *De Architectura*, Alberti's *De Re Ædificatoria* was divided into ten books, but, unlike the earlier work, Alberti's was written in stylish Latin, and gave a coherent account of the decidedly fragmented knowledge of the architecture of Antiquity that had survived through the centuries. Alberti established architecture as an intellectual and professional discipline, and gave it a respectable theoretical substance: in fact, he laid the foundations for the development of the theory and practice of architecture in the Renaissance period. To the four Orders identified by Vitruvius, Alberti added the Composite, which he had observed in extant Roman buildings, as a distinct Order, the capital of which combined Ionic volutes with Corinthian acanthus leaves.

However, the great Renaissance writers on architecture were to be concerned with *five* Orders based on Roman exemplars, for the Greek Orders were not to be published in any detail until the second half of the 18th century, and a taste for the severe Greek Doric Order was not to develop until after such details were available. Among the most influential of Renaissance writers was Sebastiano Serlio, whose *L'Architettura* appeared from 1537 to 1575, and was further embellished with his drawings in 1584. Serlio's great work was essentially practical in that it provided an illustrated textbook describing the five Roman Orders and much else in the way of Classical detail. *L'Architettura* made not only the Orders, but the architectural language of Donato Bramante and Raffaello Sanzio (Raphael) familiar throughout Europe. Serlio had inherited many drawings by Baldassare Peruzzi, which were used in the book. *L'Architettura* quickly became the pattern-book of Europe, used extensively (and often indiscriminately) in many countries. In it the five Roman Orders are shown together for the first time, arranged in the Tuscan–Doric–Ionic–Corinthian–Composite sequence, and described by the author as the *Dramatis Personæ* of his treatise. Serlio laid these down in a canonical way, giving his successors and his readers the impression that variations on these Orders were not allowed. In the Italian Renaissance, therefore, the Orders acquired great significance as the true foundations of architecture, and even seemed to be regarded as something approaching the divinely inspired. This is not surprising, given the intellectual atmosphere of the time, in which Hermeticism, alchemy, and the beginnings of speculative Freemasonry were in evidence. Columns had associations with the Divine through the Temple of Solomon, with Ancient Egyptian mysteries, and with ideas of Strength (Doric), Wisdom (Ionic), and Beauty (Corinthian), apart from Vitruvian connections with deities: Wisdom and Beauty, therefore, were seen as encapsulated in the Composite Order, which, however, to some eyes appeared somewhat overblown, and indeed it was an Order often favoured for showy monuments such as triumphal arches.

Serlio set down proportions, dimensions, sections, and the like as though they were Holy Writ: he used Vitruvius and observed extant Classical Orders, but Vitruvius can be vague or incomplete, and surviving Roman Orders displayed wide variations, so Serlio was obliged to compose his idealised Orders from a variety of sources. His Orders, therefore, were based partly on the Antique and partly on his own invention.

The five Orders, and illustrations of them, dominated most architectural introductory texts from Serlio's time for the next three centuries. Giacomo Barozzi da Vignola's *La Regola delli Cinque Ordini d'Architettura* of 1562 (with many later editions) set out a simple modular interpretation of the Orders, which provided a straightforward architectural vocabulary, and was immensely influential as well as more accurate and scholarly than Serlio's work. Andrea Palladio's *I Quattro libri dell' Architettura* of 1570 did not show the Orders together, although his book (and his use of the Orders) was very important as a source. Vincenzo Scamozzi, a gifted follower of Palladio, produced *L'Idea dell'Architettura Universale* of 1615, which set out the Orders with dimensions, and so provided the final codifying of the five Roman Orders: his book had a profound influence on northern European architects. Claude Perrault published his *Ordonnance des Cinq Espèces de Colonnes* in 1683, which was based on all the great Italian works previously published, and included a modular scale system which enabled proportions to be determined very easily. Many other texts with fine illustrations followed, including James Gibbs's *Rules for Drawing the Several Parts of Architecture* of 1732, and Sir William Chambers's *A Treatise on Civil Architecture*, originally published in 1759, republished as *A Treatise on the Decorative Part of Civil Architecture* in 1791, and brought out again in 1825 with an 'Examination of "Grecian Architecture"' added by Joseph Gwilt. The Greek Orders are described in the Select Glossary of Terms, but a few salient points need to be made here.

The Greek Orders

There are three Greek Orders: the Doric, Ionic, and Corinthian, and these are distinct from the Roman Orders of the same name. While the Doric column resembles in some respects a rare Egyptian type found, for example, in the rock-cut tombs at Beni-Hasan, it is also like Mycenæan and Minoan types: the capitals of some very early temples of Doric type closely resemble those of the so-called Treasury of Atreus at Mycenæ.

There has been a great deal of argument as to whether or not the Greek Doric Order had a stone or a timber origin. The supporters of stone, including Henry Heathcote Statham, have argued that the Doric column and capital are stone forms because the oldest examples of column are thick, fat, and squat, while the reverse would have been true had the original columns been of timber, and because the echinus of the capital, under the abacus, is essentially a stone form, and would be difficult to carve in wood. Unfortunately for this view, while it is true that many early Doric columns are thick and heavy, some of the oldest of all are extremely slender, with very widely spreading capitals, and this type closely resembles Doric columns shown in Athenian vase paintings depicting wooden structures. However, Statham did admit that there are many rock-cut tomb façades in Asia Minor, especially in Lycia, which include frank and realistic representations of wooden construction in stone, with 'hardly any attempt even at conventionalising the original timber structure into masonic forms; the beams, the half-notching of the framework, the wedges for holding it all together, are all realistically present'. The remains of 12 columns from the sanctuary of Athena Pronaia at Delphi are probably the oldest that can be called Doric (7th century BC), with a height about six and a half times their lowest diameter and a very pronounced taper. We know that Pausanias, the Lydian traveller and geographer, saw a wooden column, much decayed, and held together only by means of bands of metal, near the Temple of Zeus at Olympia; he also saw a low building with columns of carved oak in the marketplace at Elis, and there was an ancient Temple of Poseidon Hippios, near Mantinea in Arcadia, that was built of oak, carefully fitted together. The pro-stone commentators also suggest that the triglyphs of the Doric Order could not have had a timber origin because they occur on all elevations of a temple, and because it would be difficult to cut the channels across the grain of the wood. However, the form of the triglyph frieze is suggestive of a wooden origin, a suggestion reinforced by the presence of the dowel- or peg-like guttæ of the regulæ and the mutules. The triglyphs may be a free representation of the ends of beams, and the metopes could indicate spaces between the beams: it may also be that they are not beams, but

Fig. 2.1a ↑ *Elevation of one of the octastyle ends of the temple known as the Parthenon, Athens (447–438 BC), as measured and restored, although the columns are incorrectly shown without entasis (Stuart and Revett [1787], ii, ch.1, pl.iii, coll. JSC).*

Fig. 2.1b → *Reconstruction of the Greek Doric Order from the Parthenon, an octastyle temple with 17 columns on each side. The triglyphs are over the centre-lines of columns or the spaces between columns (intercolumniations), except at the corners, where the columns are moved in from the centre-lines so that the intercolumniations at the corners are smaller. In the Greek Doric Order the triglyph block has to terminate the frieze, and this creates the problem of spacing of columns at the corners. The drawing shows the relationship of triglyphs to the columns and intercolumniations, with a detail of the corner treatment where the three corner columns are closer together than elsewhere. Between the triglyphs are the sculptured metopes, and in the tympanum of the low-pitched pediment is another sculptured group. Column shafts are fluted, with sharp arrises between flutes, and rest (without bases) directly on the stylobate of the three-stepped crepidoma. Above the shaft is the capital with hypotrachelion (–um), trachelion (–um), annulets, echinus (cushion-like pad), and square abacus-block. The entablature is divided into its three parts: the low, plain architrave (on which circular medallions of bronze have been fixed); the frieze (of triglyphs and metopes separated from the architrave by the tænia, with regulæ under the tænia with guttæ); and the cornice, which overhangs, and has sloping mutules on the soffit ornamented with guttæ, or peg-like drops (there are no mutules on the soffit of the raking cornice of the pediment). At the corners of the building, and at the apex of the pediment, over the cornice, are blocks known as acroteria, on which ornaments were set. Note the antefixa set at intervals over the cornice to cover the ends of the roofing tiles: they are ornamented with the palmette, while a variation on the palmette, the honeysuckle, ornaments the acroterion at the apex. The honeysuckle also occurs on the soffit of the cornice, at the corner, between the mutules (BTB).*

THE ORDERS OF ARCHITECTURE & THEIR APPLICATION / 7

some kind of early truss-ends, and that the channels represent the joints between the horizontal beams and the sloping members following the rake of the roof. If triglyphs were stylised and conventionalised very early, even before their translation into stone, it is a short step to continue the pattern of triglyph–metope–triglyph all around the frieze, even though logically there would be no need for the beam-ends or truss-ends on the gabled façades. The fact that the soffit or underside of the cornice is inclined at the angle of the slope of the roof, and has flat blocks called mutules decorated with 18 guttæ, suggests that

Fig. 2.1c ← *Corner detail of the Greek Doric Order, with triglyphs joining at a bevel. The relationships of column capital, abacus, architrave, frieze, and cornice should be noted. The sloping mutules with guttæ on the underside of the cornice relate to the centre-lines of triglyphs and metopes. Note the antefixa (with palmette ornament), lion's mask, and guttæ under each regula (the short band or fillet under the tænia separating the architrave from the frieze) (restoration by L.P. Fenger [BTB]).*

Fig. 2.1d ← *Detail from the corner of the Athenian Parthenon showing the Doric Order (Stuart and Revett [1787], ii, ch.I, pl.vi, coll. JSC).*

Fig. 2.1e ↓ *The same detail from the corner of the Parthenon, but with extra information concerning an anta (details of which differ from the main Order), one of the other capitals in the temple, and sections through the annulets (Normand [1852], coll. JSC).*

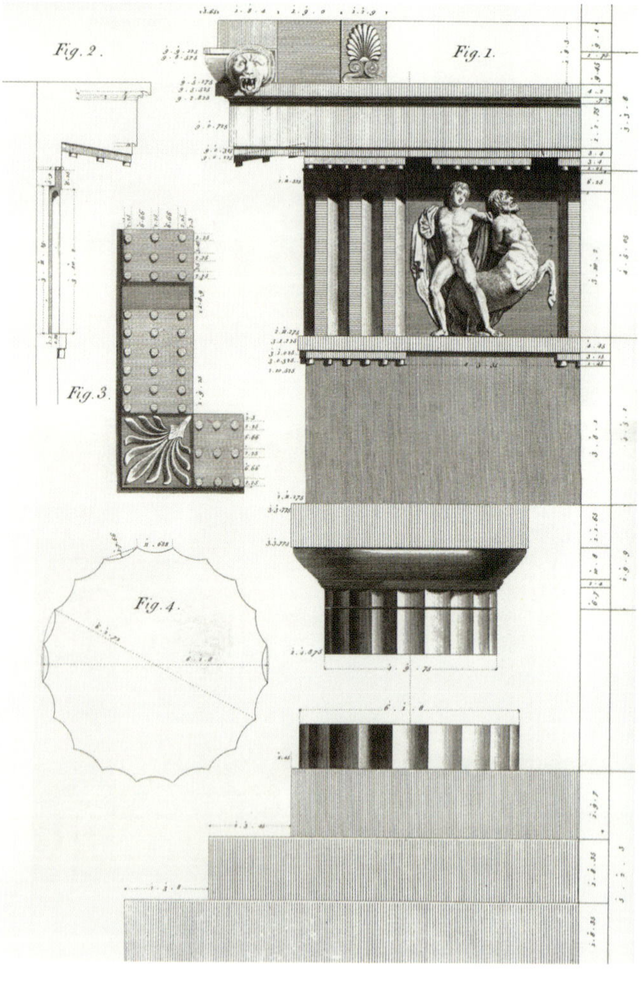

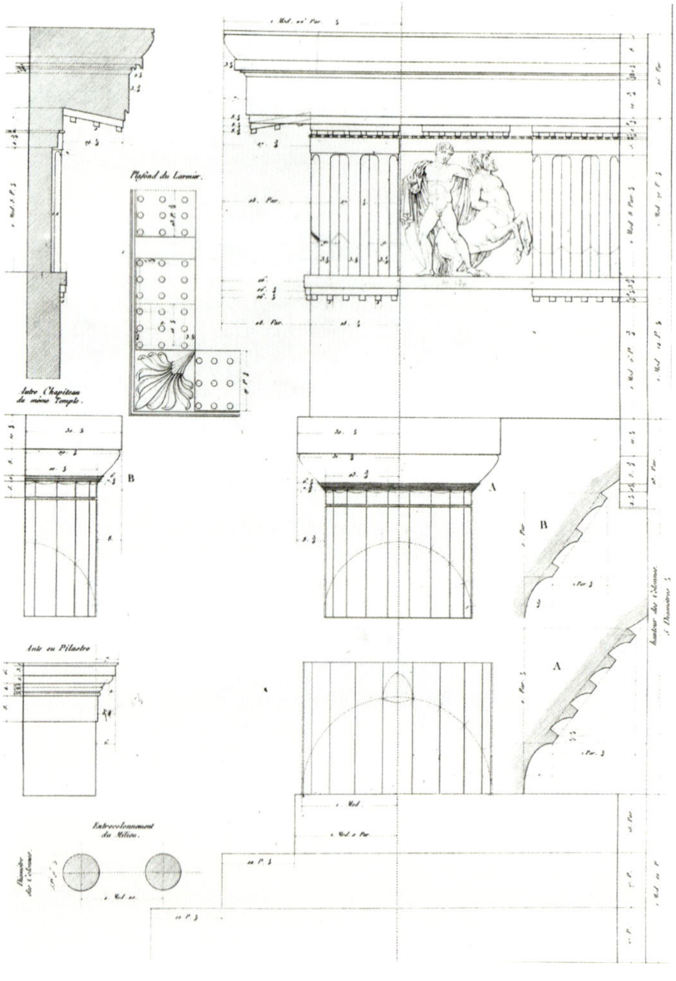

8 / Classical Architecture

the mutules may be petrified rafters. These mutules are set over each triglyph and each metope, which suggests some kind of structural origin. Occasionally, the part of the soffit between the mutules was ornamented: in the case of the Parthenon, the corner soffits had an anthemion motif (Figs 2.1a–e).

The Greek Doric Order

The Doric Order, then, might be a stylised and conventionalised petrified version of a timber prototype. The column itself could have originated as a tree-trunk, with the outside 'shaved' by means of a series of flat faces to produce a polygonal plan. The hollowing out of each flat face is a further variation and refinement. Greek Doric columns sit directly on the stylobate with no base, and have a height, including the capital, of between four and six and a half times the diameter at the base of the column. The circular form of the shaft generally has 20 shallow, concave flutes separated by arrises, but there are examples with 12, 16, 18, or 24 flutes. A choice of 20 flutes was more usual because with 20 an arris would occur under the corners of the square abacus, that is, under the diagonals of the abacus, and would permit a flute to occur in the centre of each column as viewed from the centre of each front, back, or sides.

This use of a void (as a flute appears between its arrises) in the centre of a symmetrical composition is essential to much Classical composition. Façades should have a void or a door in the centre, or a space between columns, which means that, in the most satisfactory compositions involving columns or pilasters, there must be an even number of columns (although there are examples in Greek Antiquity where odd numbers of columns create a central column, and therefore confound the normal rule).

Doric shafts are usually composed of drums jointed by means of dowels, and become more slender at the top: in fact, the diameter at the tops of such shafts will be between three-quarters and two-thirds of the base diameter. Furthermore, the shaft has a convex profile, called *entasis*, which corrects the optical illusion of concavity and apparent weakness in straight-sided tapering columns: the entasis was very obvious at the Pæstum temples (Fig. 2.2; see Fig. G83). Occasionally the shaft was unfluted, giving it a primitive look and making it look more sturdy and dumpy, as at the Temple of Apollo at Delos: there, and at Cnidos, for example, the flutes appear in a band at the base and top of the shaft (Figs 2.3a–c). Flutes serve to accentuate verticality and give the illusion of greater refinement and thinness, especially when strong shadows are cast in the flutes by the sharp arrises.

The shaft terminates at the band known as the *hypotrachelion* (or *hypotrachelium*), usually of three grooves in early examples and one in later, above which the flutes and arrises continue (the *trachelion* or necking) to the capital. This last mentioned consists of horizontal rings called annulets, above which is the circular, bulbous, cushion-like echinus (so called by Vitruvius because it is like the shell of a sea-urchin), and the plain square block called the abacus. In early Doric temples the echinus is very bulbous, like a parabolic section, and has a considerable projection, but in late examples, such as the Parthenon, it is only slightly curved from the annulets to under the abacus, when it

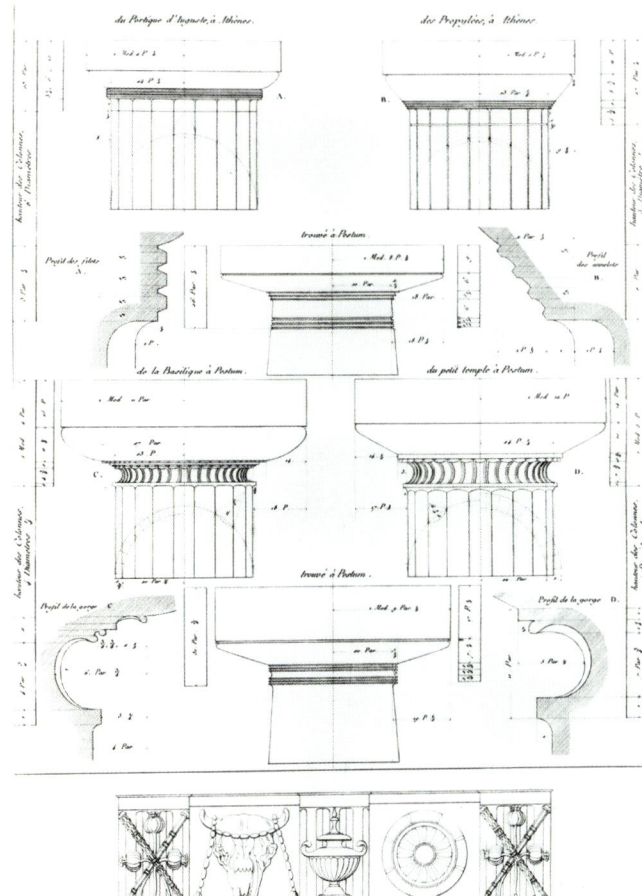

Fig. 2.2 ↑ *Greek Doric capitals: at the top are two Athenian examples; below is a capital from Pæstum showing the exaggerated entasis and the extraordinarily wide abacus and echinus associated with examples there. The remaining three capitals are variations on the Pæstum type: note the concave necking which is quite unlike the usual type of Doric trachelion. Below is a frieze of the Roman Doric type with bucranium and patera in the metopes (Normand [1852], coll. JSC).*

curves to the underside of the abacus block. The Greek Doric entablature (about a quarter the height of the total Order, which includes column *and* entablature) is carried on the abaci, and has three parts: the architrave, or beam, with a flat face in one plane, above which is a flat moulding known as the *tænia*, or *tenia*, under which, at intervals immediately under the triglyphs, are narrow bands known as *regulæ*, under which are six cones called *guttæ*; the frieze, consisting of vertical slabs known as *triglyphs* cut with vertical channels (usually two full ones and two halves at the edges), set equidistant from each other over the centre-lines of each column and over the centre-line of each space between each column, and *metopes* (the panels between each triglyph, set back from the front face of the triglyphs and often ornamented with sculpture in relief); and the *cornice*, which overhangs the *frieze*, and consists of a *cymatium* over a *corona* or vertical face to a projection, the soffit of which inclines, and has flat blocks, or *mutules*, like the ends of rafters, over each triglyph and metope, usually embellished with 18 guttæ in three rows of six for each mutule.

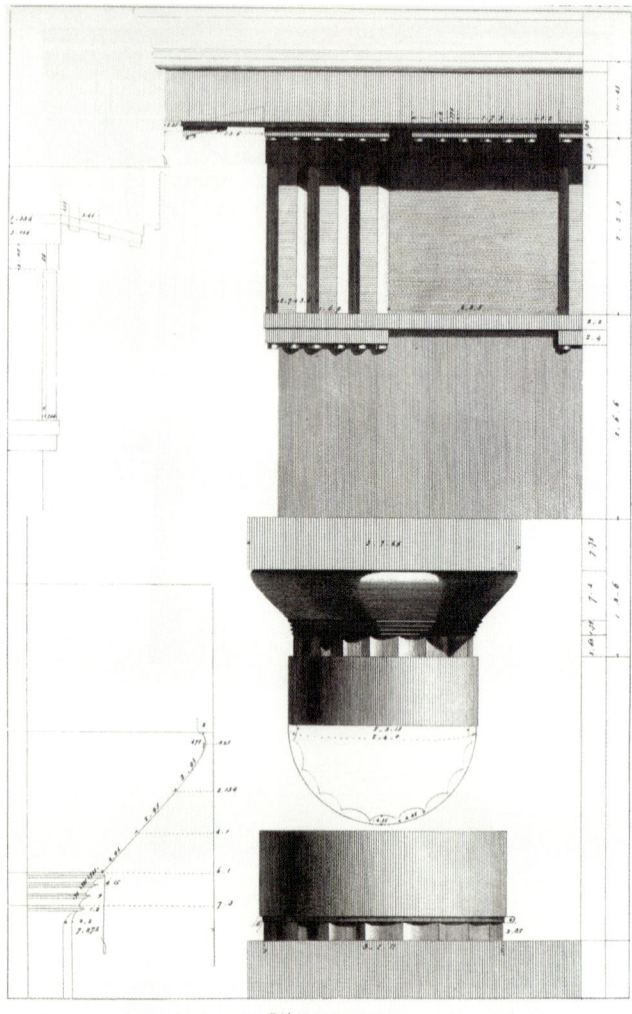

Fig. 2.3a ↑ *Detail of the Doric Order from the Temple of Apollo at Delos (late 4th–3rd century BC) (Stuart and Revett [1794], iii, ch.X, pl.ii, coll. JSC).*

Fig. 2.3b ↑ *Doric Order of the Temple of Apollo at Delos, showing the 'unfluted' shafts, but the flutes appear at the top and bottom of the shafts: it was customary to cut flutes on the remainder of the shafts* in situ, *using the flutes at the tops and bottoms as guides, but in this case the work was left incomplete, thus was perceived in the 18th century, incorrectly, as a distinct variation of the Order (Stuart and Revett [1794], iii, ch.X, pl.i, coll. JSC).*

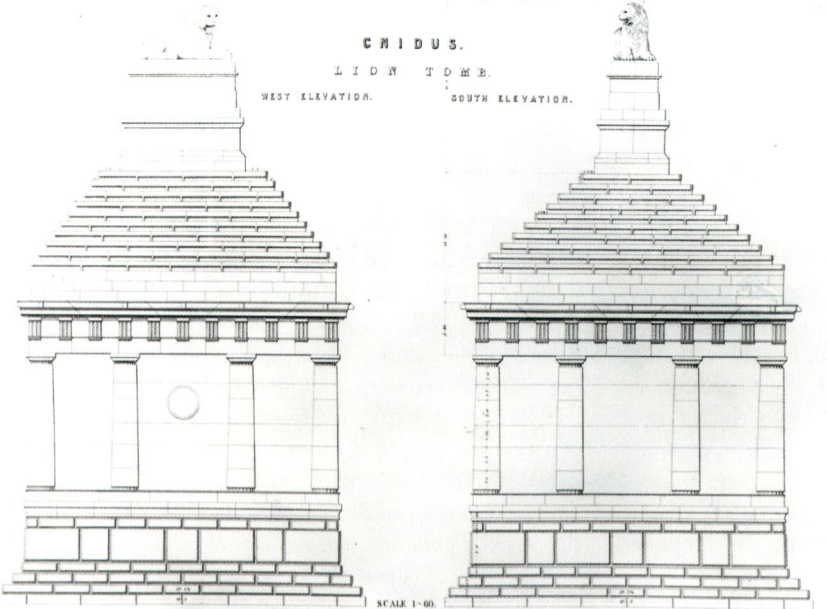

Fig. 2.3c ← *Reconstruction by Richard Popplewell Pullan of the Lion Tomb at Cnidos, with its engaged unfluted (except for vestigial fluting top and bottom) Greek Doric Order, and stepped pyramidal roof. This is an example of the so-called Hellenistic taste, dating from the middle of the 4th century BC in which the spacing (intercolumniation) of the columns became much wider; there are two and three triglyphs per intercolumniation instead of the one triglyph usual in Hellenic examples (London: Day & Son [1862], coll. JSC).*

10 / CLASSICAL ARCHITECTURE

Fig. 2.4 → *Temple of Theseus (Theseion), Athens, aka Hephæsteum or Hephæsteion (449–444 BC), a hexastyle temple with 13 columns along each of the longer sides, from the north-west (coll. JSC).*

At the corner of a Greek Doric frieze the triglyphs touch, meeting at the bevel coinciding with the half-channels, with the result that the corner column centre-line is not under the centre of the triglyph. This makes the spaces between the corner column and the columns adjacent to it on each face less than the intercolumniation elsewhere, thus giving the corner the appearance of greater stability (Fig. 2.4). In the case of the Parthenon, too, the corner columns have slightly greater diameters, so the corners are further strengthened in appearance (*see* Figs 2.1a–b).

Greek Doric channels in triglyphs are rounded at the top, and the mutules slope with the soffit, and project beneath it (*see* Figs G52a and 2.1c–e).

The Greek Ionic Order

The distinctive feature of the Ionic Order is the volute, or scroll capital, perhaps derived from shells, rams' horns, or stylised scroll forms evolved in Egyptian art, and certainly used decoratively in ancient times. Very archaic Ionic capitals have volutes that seem to derive from plant forms, with palmettes between them (*see* Fig. G7). Unlike the Doric capital, the Ionic, in its simplest form, is not based on a circle within a square (and therefore is not the same from all sides), but is rectangular, with two volutes visible on both front and back, connected at the sides by cushions (sometimes plain and sometimes ornamented) (Fig. 2.5; *see* Fig. G72). This elongated form suggests a type of bracket to support the entablature, later ornamented using a design derived from the nautilus shell. The huge archaic Temple of Artemis at Ephesus had capitals about three metres long and one metre wide.

Unlike Greek Doric, the Ionic Order has a base. It consists of an upper and lower torus (convex) separated by a scotia (concave) and fillets, with no square plinth block: this design became known as the Attic base (*see* Fig. G23). A variant was the Asiatic base, consisting of a reeded drum over which were two scotiæ and a reeded torus (*see* Fig. G22). The bases of the columns of the archaic Temple of Artemis at Ephesus were very elaborate, with many small rings of convex and concave form.

Ionic columns, therefore, had bases of varying degrees of complexity, and their heights (including bases and capitals) were approximately nine times the diameter at the bottom of the shaft. The usual treatment of the shaft was to have 24 flutes separated from each other by fillets (not sharp arrises), but in archaic examples there were as many as 40 flutes separated by arrises. Fully developed Ionic eschewed the arris and adopted the fillet, and the flutes do not terminate at the bottom of the shaft or at the annulets, but in rounded forms at the top and bottom, leaving a plain circular shaft between the terminations of the flutes and the top of the base and the bottom of the capital.

The Ionic capital, as has been stated, has two pairs of volutes, approximately two-thirds the diameter of the shaft in height, on the front and rear, connected by cushions (plain or enriched) at the sides, and by an echinus enriched with egg-and-dart on the front and back, under which is often a bead-and-reel moulding (*see* Fig. 2.5). At the acute angle between the top of the spiral form and the horizontal line above the echinus is a fragment of honeysuckle or palmette motif (Fig. 2.6). Above the subtle mouldings of the volutes and their cushions is an abacus, much smaller than the Doric, and usually moulded and enriched (Fig. 2.7).

One of the problems with the use of the Ionic capital occurred at the corners of buildings. In some instances, if there were a peristyle (rather than a prostyle portico in front of an anta arrangement), the cushions at the sides did not look well beside a colonnade with volutes, so the two faces were treated with volutes, and the corner acquired two volutes, back to back, and pulled out at an angle from the corner (*see* Figs G13, 2.6, and 2.7). A further variation occurred at the Temple of Apollo Epicurius at Bassæ in Arcadia (where all three Orders are found, the single Corinthian example being one of the earliest known): at this celebrated temple the internal walls of the naos had engaged Ionic columns attached to short cross-walls, and the capitals had corner volutes, so there were four volutes altogether (although C.R. Cockerell thought there were six). These capitals did not have the usual echinus, and the eyes of the volutes were close together. The upper lines of the channel joining the spirals were

THE ORDERS OF ARCHITECTURE & THEIR APPLICATION / 11

thrown upwards in a startling curve, and the presence of abaci is still disputed (*see* Fig. G28a). The projection of the volutes at 45° anticipates the four-sided or diagonal Ionic capital developed in Hellenistic and Roman times which had four angle volutes, so that there were eight volutes in all (*see* Fig. G28b); here the abacus acquired concave sides, thus the problem of a 'special' at the corner no longer arose. These diagonal capitals were models for the Roman Composite Order invented in the 1st century AD. The bases of the Bassæ temple were also unorthodox, for the shafts had a very wide apophyge, and a spread version of the normal torus, below which was a tall, concave moulding sweeping outwards to a shorter concave moulding under it. In the case of the Erechtheion in Athens, the very beautiful Ionic capitals had additional neckings, or a band under the capital proper at the top of the shaft, enriched with the anthemion, palmette, or honeysuckle ornament: this necking also occurs on the antæ, and is continued as a variety of decorative frieze under the architrave all around the building (Figs 2.8a–d and 2.9; *see* Fig. 2.7).

Ionic entablatures are usually about a fifth of the height of the whole Order, and do not have triglyphs or metopes. Architraves are subdivided into three fasciæ or planes, like

Fig. 2.5 ↑ *Capital from the famous mausoleum at Halicarnassus (c.353 BC), showing the three-dimensional form with volutes and pulvinated end. The flutes are separated by fillets rather than arrises (coll. JSC).*

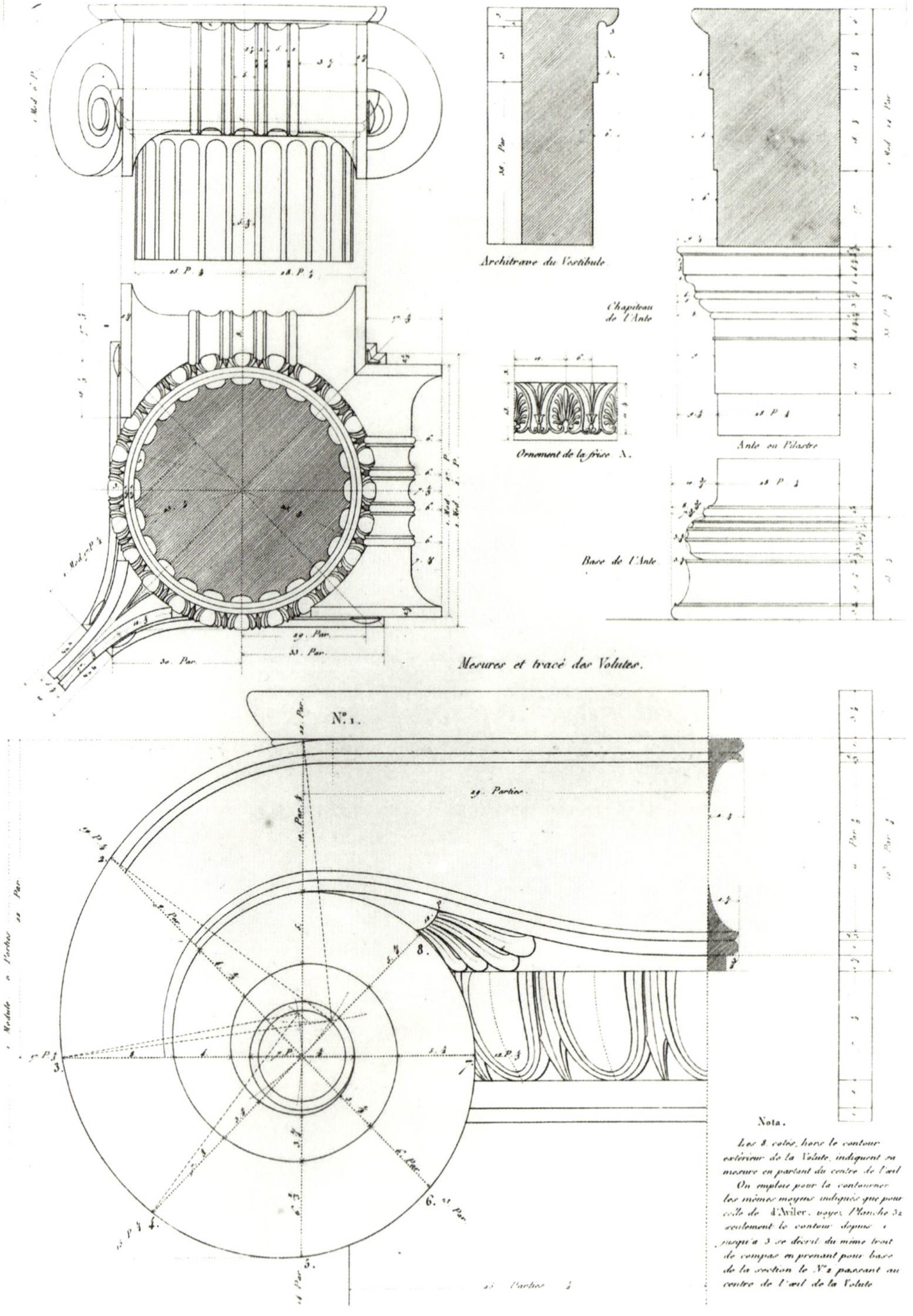

Fig. 2.6 → *Angle capital and anta of the Greek Ionic Order from the Temple on the Ilissus, Athens (c.450 BC). Note how the volute is set out and how the volutes are placed at the corner so that volutes 'read' on both outside faces. Note also how the anta differs from the columnar Order (Normand [1852], coll. JSC).*

12 / CLASSICAL ARCHITECTURE

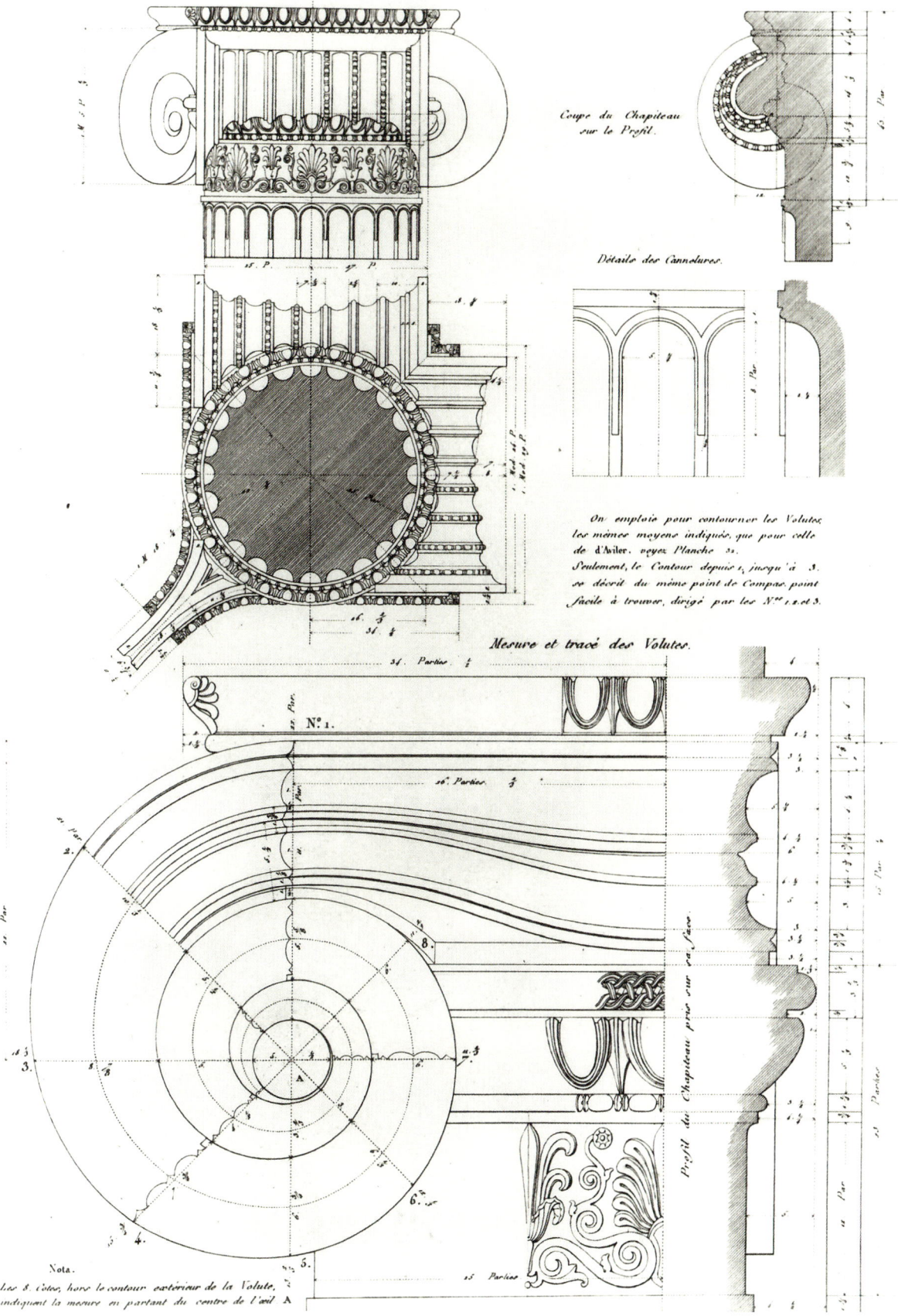

Fig. 2.7 ↑ *Detail of the Greek Ionic angle capital from the Temple of Minerva Polias (the eastern part of the Erechtheion in Athens) of c.421–407 BC. Note the extreme refinement of the enrichment. The neck is embellished with palmette and anthemion ornament. Note that the pulvinus has reeding with enrichment (Normand [1852], coll. JSC).*

THE ORDERS OF ARCHITECTURE & THEIR APPLICATION / 13

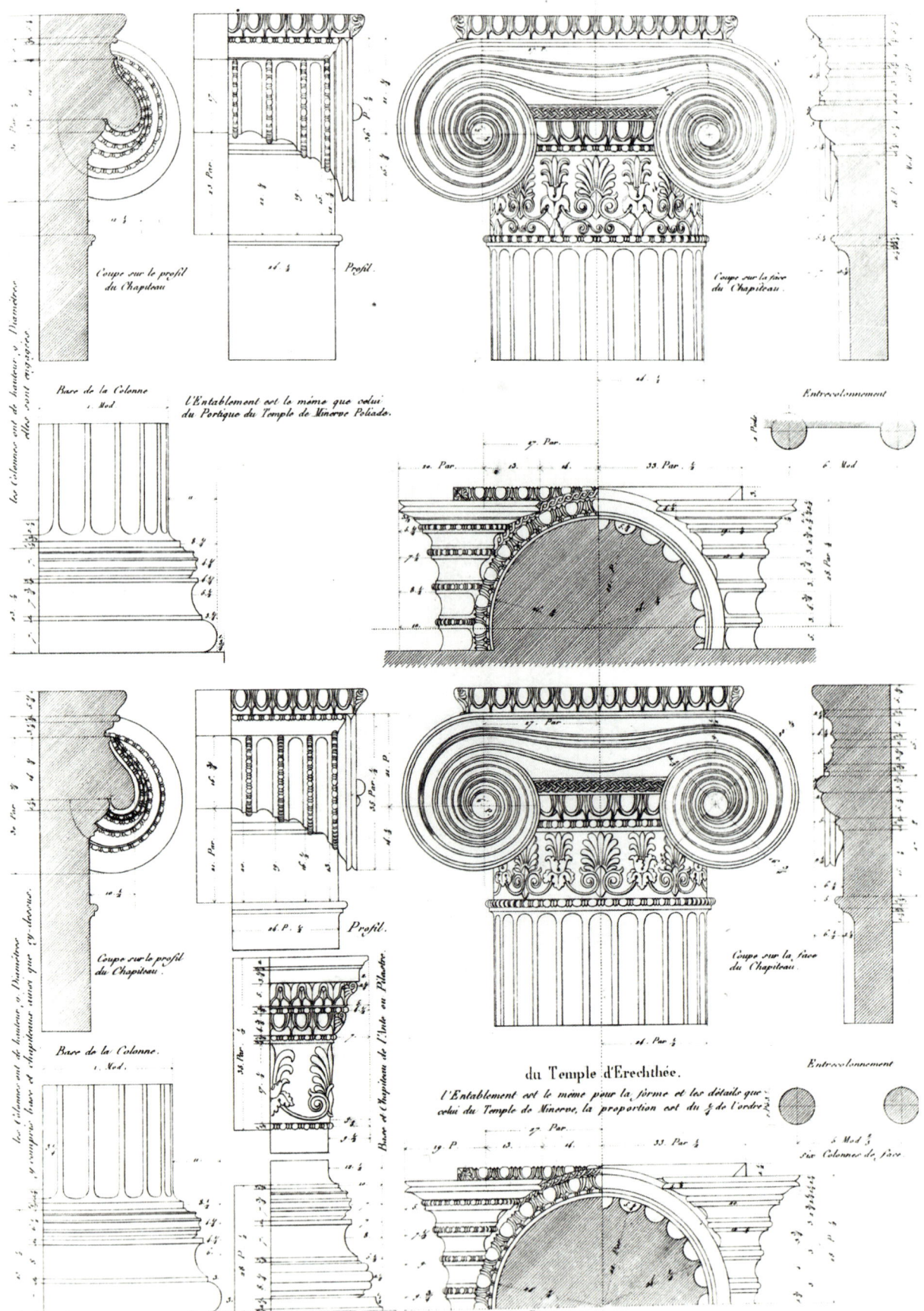

Fig. 2.8a Plans, elevations, and sections of columns from the Erechtheion in Athens. Note the elaborate enrichment of the pulvinus and base of each, and the delicate ornamentation of the neck of the column (Normand [1852], coll. JSC).

14 / Classical Architecture

Fig. 2.8b ↑ *Elements of the Erechtheion, Athens. Note the caryatid(e) porch on the right, with caryatid(e) Order (the entablature has an architrave divided into three fasciæ, but there is no frieze, and there are dentils under the cornice) and plinth. Flutes on the Ionic columns are separated by fillets, and the necks are embellished with palmette and anthemion ornament. The main entablature has three distinct parts, and the architrave is divided into three planes or fasciæ: the frieze is plain, and mutules with guttæ are no longer present. The bases of the columns have two torus and one scotia moulding, the so-called Attic base. Note the angle capitals (Stuart and Revett [1787], ii, ch.II, pl.iv, coll. JSC).*

Fig. 2.8c ↗ *South or caryatid(e) porch of the Erechtheion (AFK N14651).*

Fig. 2.8d → *Details of the caryatid(e) porch of the Erechtheion, showing the elaborate but friezeless entablature, with dentils and much enrichment of mouldings (including egg-and-dart, leaf-and-dart, bead-and-reel, etc.) (Normand [1852], coll. JSC).*

THE ORDERS OF ARCHITECTURE & THEIR APPLICATION / 15

Fig. 2.9 ← *Greek ornament*

1 and 2 Tops of Greek stelai showing variations on the anthemion and palmette ornaments;

3 Pilaster capital from Eleusis showing acanthus and other ornament;

4 Elevation and section of rosette from the architrave of the north door of the Erechtheion, Athens;

5 Anthemion and palmette ornament on the cyma recta of the cornice of the north door of the Erechtheion;

6 Detail of the egg-and-dart (top), leaf-and-tongue, and bead-and-reel from the cyma reversa moulding of the anta capital of the Erechtheion;

7 Anta capital from the Erechtheion showing the leaf-and-tongue on the Lesbian cymatium at the top, with bead-and-reel under, then another Lesbian cymatium (or cyma reversa) enriched with egg-and-dart, under which is another astragal enriched with bead-and-reel, under which is the frieze with anthemion and palmette with more bead-and-reel under;

8 and 9 Capital of anta from the Temple of Apollo Didymæus at Miletus, showing the scroll with cushion on the side elevation, and acanthus scroll decoration with anthemion on the cavetto moulding in the centre of the capital;

10 Centre panel from the same, showing acanthus scroll and anthemion in the centre;

11 Detail of the acanthus-scroll ornament from the roof of the choragic monument of Lysicrates in Athens (Spiers [1893], coll. JSC).

superimposed slabs; friezes are often unadorned, or may have a continuous band of sculpture, but in either case will have no vertical interruption; and the cornice has no mutules, but is often enriched with dentils and crowned by the corona and cyma recta moulding (frequently decorated). In many Asiatic examples of the Ionic Order the frieze is omitted altogether, giving the entablature a curiously flattened appearance.

The Greek Corinthian Order

The base and shaft of this Order resemble those of the Ionic Order, and the column (including base and capital) is about ten times the diameter at the base of the shaft in height. Corinthian shafts have flutes separated by fillets, like the Ionic Order, but the height of the capital is about one and a half times the diameter of the shaft.

The first Corinthian capital was probably the single example on the central axis of the Temple of Apollo Epicurius at Bassæ in Arcadia, although the columns on either side of it seem also to have been Corinthian. Pausanias says the temple was built by Ictinus (the architect of the Parthenon), and it appears to date from the second half of the 5th century, probably around 430 BC.

Although there are wide variations in the details of Corinthian, the capitals consisted of an inverted bell-shaped cone on top of the shaft and separated from it by a horizontal band, sometimes a recess, but more often a convex or torus moulding. The usual and developed type favoured by the Romans consisted of two tiers, each of which is formed of eight acanthus leaves; from between the leaves of the upper row rise eight stalks known as *caulicoli*, from each of which emerge helices, or volutes, that support the diagonal angles of the abacus and the

16 / CLASSICAL ARCHITECTURE

central foliated ornament. There are four of these ornaments, one on each face; in Greek examples usually of the anthemion or palmette, but sometimes a floral form.

The abacus has four concave sides curving out to a point or chamfered at the angles. An exception is the Tower of the Winds in Athens, which has one row of acanthus leaves with one row of palm leaves above, no caulicoli or volutes, and a moulded abacus square on plan (*see* Figs G85 and 6.8a–b). Extraordinarily elegant are the capitals of the choragic monument of Lysicrates in Athens, which are taller than is usual, and have several remarkable features: the flutes of the shafts terminate in projecting lotus leaves, and the lower row of capital leaves consists of 16 lotus leaves, leaving a plain channel between the base of the capital and the top of the shaft, which probably contained a ring of bronze; the upper row of capital leaves are those of the acanthus, and between each leaf is an eight-petalled flower resembling a lotus; and, above, the helices are especially elegant, supporting tall palmettes on each face and an abacus with a deep concave moulding all round (*see* Figs G46a and 6.6a–e).

The Corinthian Order has an entablature that is not unlike that of the Ionic Order. A more festive character, the elegance and beauty of the capitals (and their adaptability to any situation including colonnades, corners, and circular buildings), made this the Order favoured by the Romans.

The Roman Orders

There are five Roman Orders: the Tuscan, Doric, Ionic, Corinthian, and Composite. All, except the Tuscan, owe much to the Greek Orders.

The Tuscan Order

This has a plain, unfluted shaft with a base consisting of a square plinth, a large torus, a fillet, and an apophyge connecting the base to the shaft. At the top, the shaft is joined to a fillet by another apophyge, above which is an astragal: then comes the necking, or flat band, like a plain frieze, joined to a circular fascia or fillet with or without an apophyge. Above is an echinus carrying a square abacus, usually with a fillet over the flat sides. The entablature is divided into the usual three parts of architrave, frieze, and cornice, but the mouldings are never enriched (Figs 2.10a–d; *see* Fig. G111a). An even plainer, more primitive type of Tuscan Order eschews the frieze and cornice, and has only an architrave, over which are wide overhanging eaves carried on long plain cantilevered brackets known as mutules (*see* Figs G111b–c). The Tuscan Order was regarded by Serlio as suitable for fortifications and prisons, as it is tough, primitive, strong, and manly.

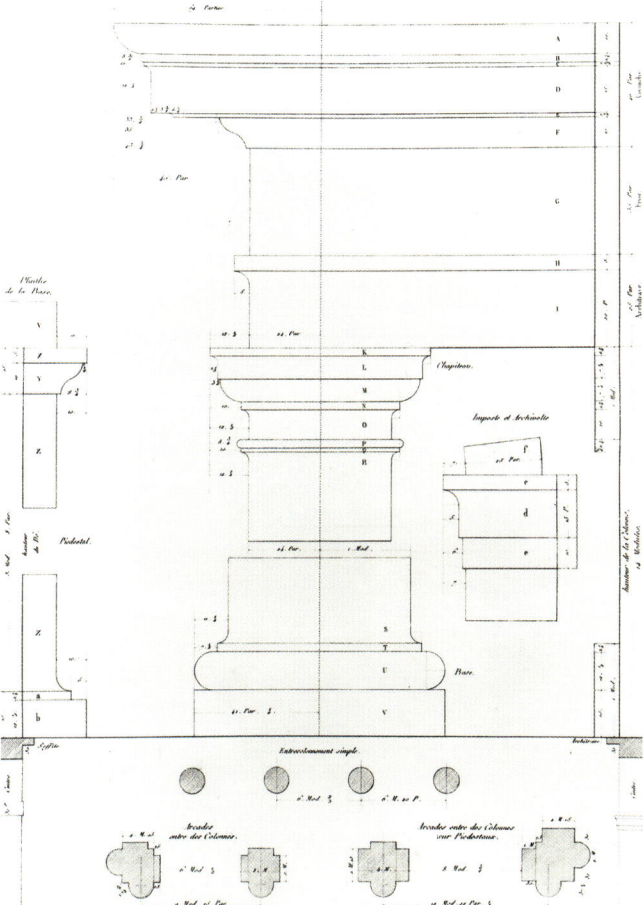

Fig. 2.10a ↑ *Renaissance Tuscan Order after Vignola: derived from Roman prototypes, it was the simplest and most severe of all the Classical Orders (Normand [1852], coll. JSC).*

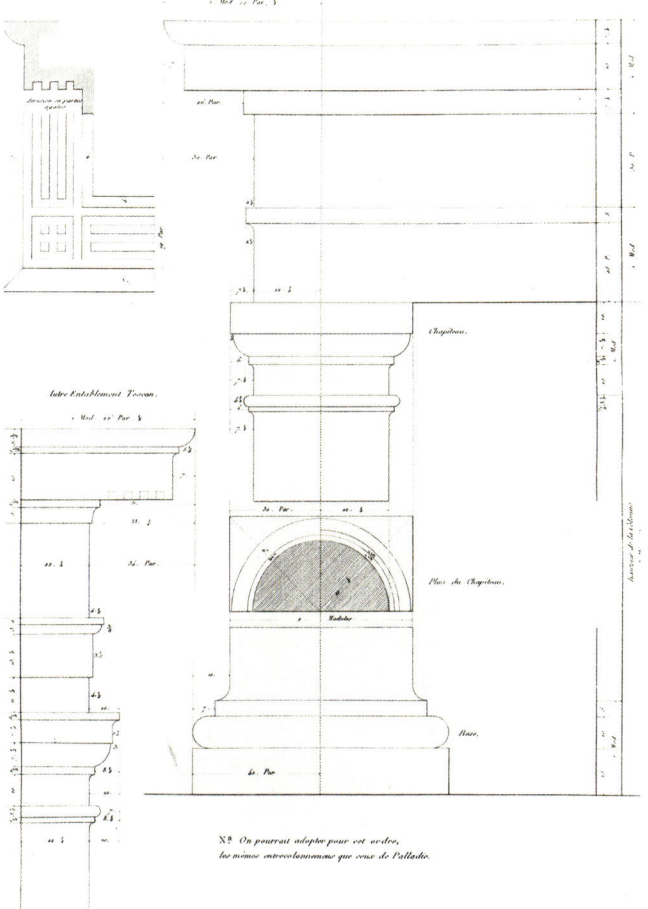

Fig. 2.10b ↑ *Tuscan Order after Serlio: note the severe, minimal treatment of the cornice soffit (Normand [1852], coll. JSC).*

THE ORDERS OF ARCHITECTURE & THEIR APPLICATION / 17

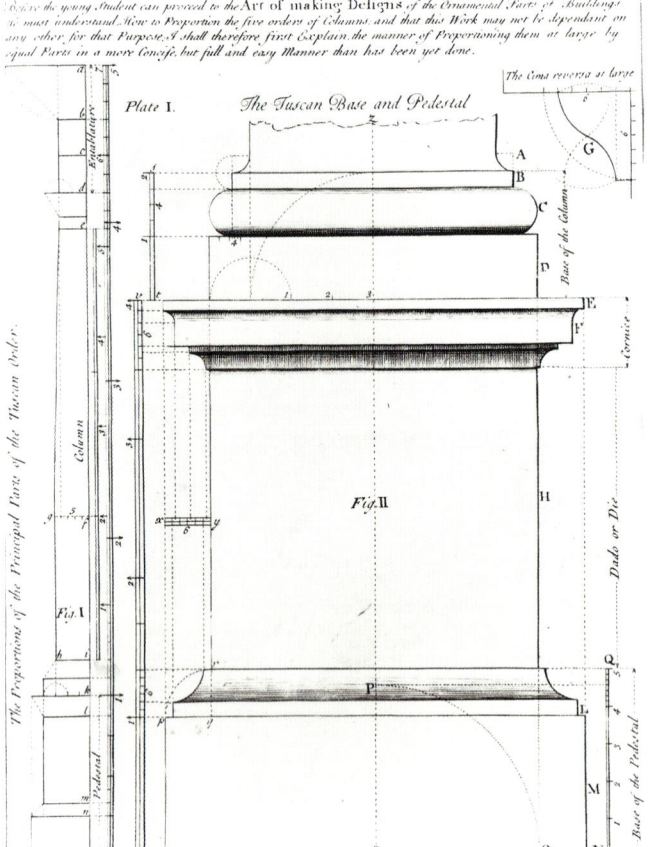

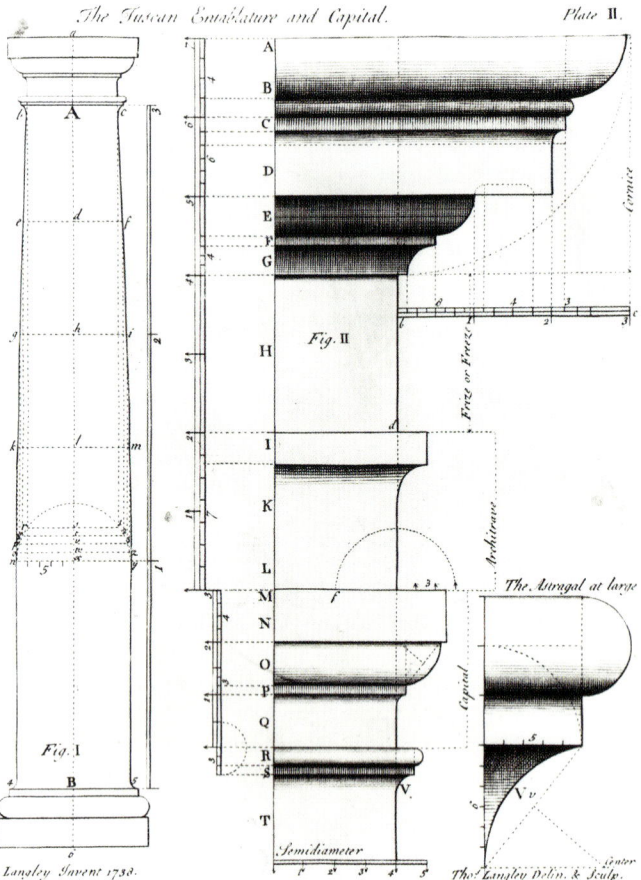

Fig. 2.10c ↑ *Tuscan base and pedestal. On the left is the Order with a pedestal, the total height divided into 5 equal parts. One part is the height of the pedestal to the top of its cornice. If the remaining 4 parts are divided into 5 parts, the upper part is the height of the entablature, and the remaining 4 the height of the column. If the height of the pedestal is divided into 4 parts, the lowest part is the height of the plinth, one third of the next part is the height of the moulding at the base of the die, and half of the upper part is the height of the pedestal cornice. Individual mouldings are plain, but can be varied (Langley [1745], coll. JSC).*

Fig. 2.10d ↗ *Tuscan Order. If the column is measured at the base of its shaft, then the height of the column (including base and capital) is 7 diameters. The heights of base and capital are each half a diameter. The capital consists of 3 equal parts: abacus, ovolo, and fillet (the last one-sixth of a part), and the neck. The astragal and its fillet are half the height of the neck. The fillet is half the height of the astragal. Note that entasis begins one-third of the way up the shaft from its cincture. At the top of the shaft, below the astragal, the diameter is four-fifths of that at the base. The semicircle described one-third of the way up the shaft is crossed by 2 parallel lines dropped from the top of the shaft, and the arcs of the circle between these positions divided into 4 equal parts. The upper two-thirds of the shaft should be divided into 4 parts, and the lines projected upwards from the circle and its crossing divisions to give the points for the thickness of the shaft rising in a gentle curve. The entablature is divided into 7 equal parts: 2 are given to the architrave, 2 to the frieze, and 3 to the cornice. Further subdivision and proportions are given (Langley [1745], coll. JSC).*

The Roman Doric Order

The Doric temple at Cori has a Doric Order similar to Greek Doric, but more slender, and with other differences, including the flutes and polygonal drums referred to below (Fig. 2.11a). The column shafts sweep by means of an apophyge to simple circular, pad-like torus bases, and the capitals are very small. A very low entablature and tall narrow triglyphs ensure that three triglyphs are placed over the intercolumniations, so the whole effect of this Order is very un-Hellenic, although the triglyphs touch at the angles of the frieze in the Greek Doric manner. Three triglyphs are also found over the intercolumniations of the lowest storey of the Theatre of Marcellus in Rome, where the engaged columns have no bases, but the columns are unfluted, and the capitals resemble those of the Tuscan Order (Fig. 2.11b). The bed-mouldings of the cornice contain dentils, however, and the soffit is elaborately enriched with guttæ and geometrical mouldings between the mutules.

The more usual type of Roman Doric always has triglyphs on the centre-lines of columns, even at corners, so a portion of metope is exposed at the angles (Figs 2.11b–c, e; *see* Fig. G52b). Columns are usually fluted with arrises, although fillets between flutes, and unfluted examples, are known. Sometimes the shaft has an apophyge terminating in a fillet, as discovered in the Alban countryside near Rome, but it can also be without a base, as in the *thermæ* of Diocletian. Capitals resemble the basic form of Tuscan types, but the necking is often enriched with four or eight rosettes or pateræ. Astragals may be enriched with bead-and-reel and echinus mouldings with egg-and-dart

Fig. 2.11a → *Roman Doric temple at Cori of the 1st century BC. It stands on a podium and has a deep prostyle tetrastyle portico, with two columns on each side between the angle columns and the antæ of the cella. Columns (much more slender than Greek versions) have bases with one convex moulding below a large apophyge, so differ from Greek examples, and lower parts of the shafts are 18-sided polygons set below 18 Doric flutes. The architrave is less tall than in Greek Doric, and the frieze has three triglyphs over each intercolumniation, so the effect is very light and elegant (BTB).*

Fig. 2.11b ↓ *Roman Doric Order from the Theatre of Marcellus, Rome (13 BC). Note that the triglyph is now centred on the corner column, leaving a piece of frieze-metope at the return. The soffit of the cornice also differs from Greek Doric, while the capital is quite different. The shaft is unfluted, and there is no base (Normand [1852], coll. JSC).*

Fig. 2.11c ↘ *Doric Order of Vignola, based on Roman exemplars, with triglyph-block placed on the centre-line of the corner column, leaving a piece of metope on the corner. The metope contains a garlanded bucranium, and the neck of the capital has rosettes. Tops of glyphs are rectangular. Note that mutules are slightly inclined and do not project below the soffit, and that there are dentils, quite unlike Greek Doric. The ornaments of the soffit have thunderbolts, lozenges, and rosettes, and the columns have bases (Normand [1852], coll. JSC).*

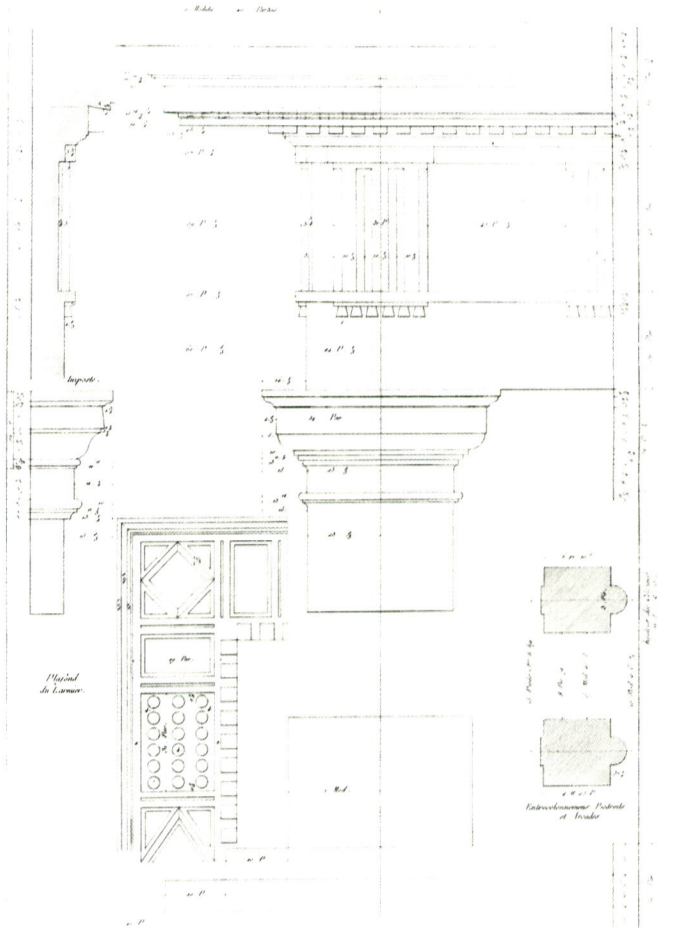

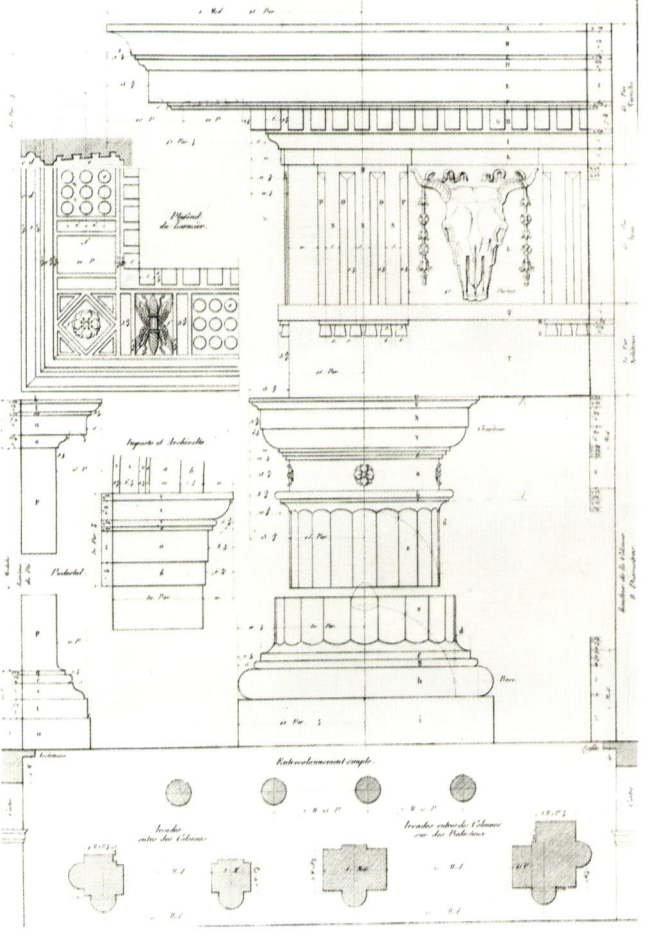

THE ORDERS OF ARCHITECTURE & THEIR APPLICATION / 19

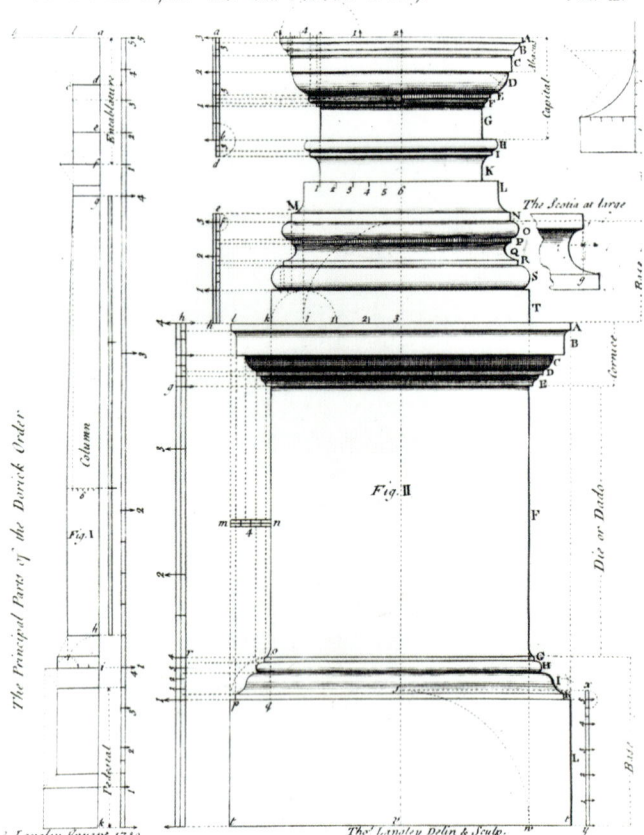

Fig. 2.11d ↑ *Doric capital, Attic base, and pedestal. The height of the Order is divided into 5 parts, the lowest of which is the height of the pedestal. The remaining 4 parts are divided into 5, the topmost part of which is the height of the entablature. The pedestal is divided into 4 vertical parts: the plinth is one part high, the base mouldings a third of a part, and the cornice a half part. The column is 8 diameters (at the base) high, and the heights of the base and capital are each half a diameter. If the base is divided into 3, one part is the height of the plinth, and the system of proportion for the rest is indicated. The capital can also be divided into 3 parts, the proportions of which are again shown (Langley [1745], coll. JSC).*

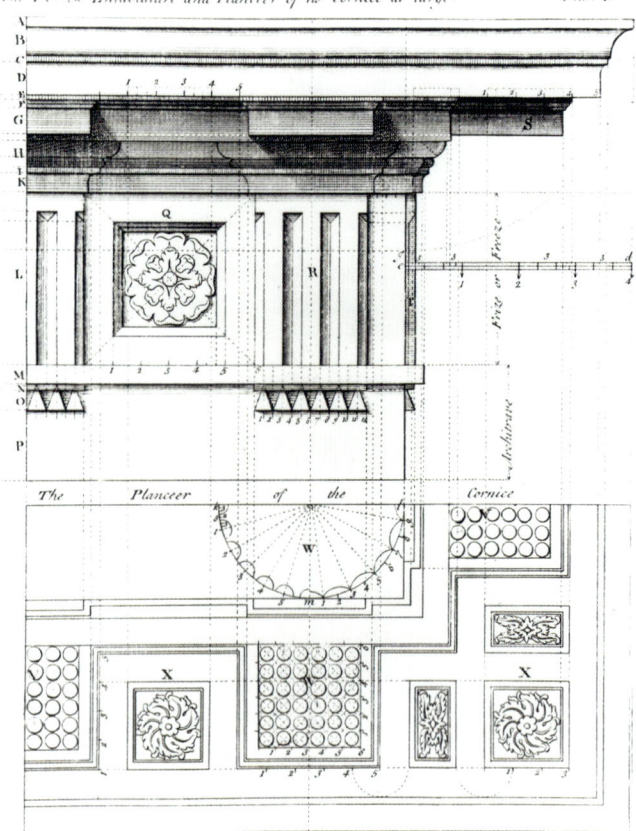

Fig. 2.11e ↑ *Details of the Roman Doric entablature. The height is divided into 8 parts, with 2 for the architrave, 3 for the frieze, and 3 for the cornice. Note the relationship of the mutules to the triglyphs. If the upper part of the 2 comprising the architrave is divided into 3, the upper subdivision is the height of the tænia, and the proportions of the guttæ are as shown. The cornice should have its 2 parts subdivided as shown. Each triglyph is half a diameter wide and each metope is the same width as the height of the frieze. Proportions of glyphs can be arrived at by dividing the triglyph into 12 verticals, which also helps to set out the 6 guttæ. Note the overhang of the cornice arrived at by striking a quarter circle as shown. This Order is based on the 'mutule' Order of Vignola, with pronounced mutules, between which are coffers (Langley [1745], coll. JSC).*

or leaf decorations. Abaci are often not plain, as in Greek Doric, but have a cyma reversa moulding at the top of the plain face, enriched with leaf-and-tongue or other ornament. Architraves are sometimes divided into two fasciæ, with mouldings, enriched or plain, between them. Metopes may be embellished with bucrania (allusions to sacrifices), pateræ (again suggesting the libations poured at sacrifices), or rosettes. More pateræ or rosettes may adorn the coffers between the mutules on the soffits, and intermediate mouldings of the entablature may be ornamented. Bed-mouldings often include dentils and other features. Mutules are usually found, but over the triglyphs only; they are slightly inclined (if at all) and do not project far below the soffits, except in the 'mutule' Order, where the mutules are given prominence. Triglyph channels are rectangular rather than curved at the top.

Doric is associated with strength and manliness: Serlio suggested it was appropriate in churches dedicated to certain male saints who were soldiers or who were militant in some other way.

The Roman Ionic Order

Roman Ionic shafts could be fluted or unfluted; Greek examples were always fluted. Bases were usually of the Attic type (Figs 2.12a, c–e; *see* Fig. G23), and capitals often had the pillows between the volutes at the sides enriched with acanthus or other ornament. Roman channels between the volutes are always shallow, and do not dip down in the centres of each face: generally, Roman Ionic capitals look small and even mean compared with the best Greek examples. Although the Romans used the angle-volute (as in the Temple of Fortuna Virilis in Rome [Figs 2.12a–b]), they also favoured the 'diagonal' type with volutes at all four corners (that is, eight volutes in all), thus avoiding awkward 'specials' for the corner details (Figs 2.12d, g; *see* Fig. G14).

Roman Ionic entablatures often had ornament on every conceivable place, and friezes with garlands, putti, and other features were sumptuous: the whole effect was luxurious, magnificent, and

Fig. 2.12a ↑ *Podium and Roman Ionic Order from the Temple of Fortuna Virilis, Rome (c.40 BC), showing how very elaborate and festive the Roman Order could be. Note the angle-volute (Normand [1852], coll. JSC).*

extremely showy. Pulvinated friezes (Fig. 2.12f) were introduced, as at the *thermæ* of Diocletian. On some of the richest examples the channels of the volutes are enriched with leaf and floral decoration (Fig. 2.12d), and in the centres, between volutes, are heads, in deep relief, of Serapis and other deities.

Serlio associated Ionic with female saints, while to Vitruvius the Order signified feminine slenderness and grace. Ionic has been associated by many writers with scholarship and with wisdom, and this is especially so in Masonic tradition.

Fig. 2.12b ↑ *Temple of Fortuna Virilis, Rome. Note that the Roman temple stands on a podium and that columns are engaged to the wall of the cella rather than carried round as a peristyle as in a Greek temple (BTB).*

Fig. 2.12c ← *Exceptionally rich Ionic Order with ornamented pulvinus, after Vignola (Normand [1852], coll. JSC).*

Fig. 2.12d → *Ionic Order after Scamozzi. Note the enriched Attic base and the modillions under the soffit of the cornice with rosettes in the coffers between them. The volutes, too, are further ornamented, and there are eight on the 'angular' or Scamozzi capital (Normand [1852], coll. JSC).*

22 / CLASSICAL ARCHITECTURE

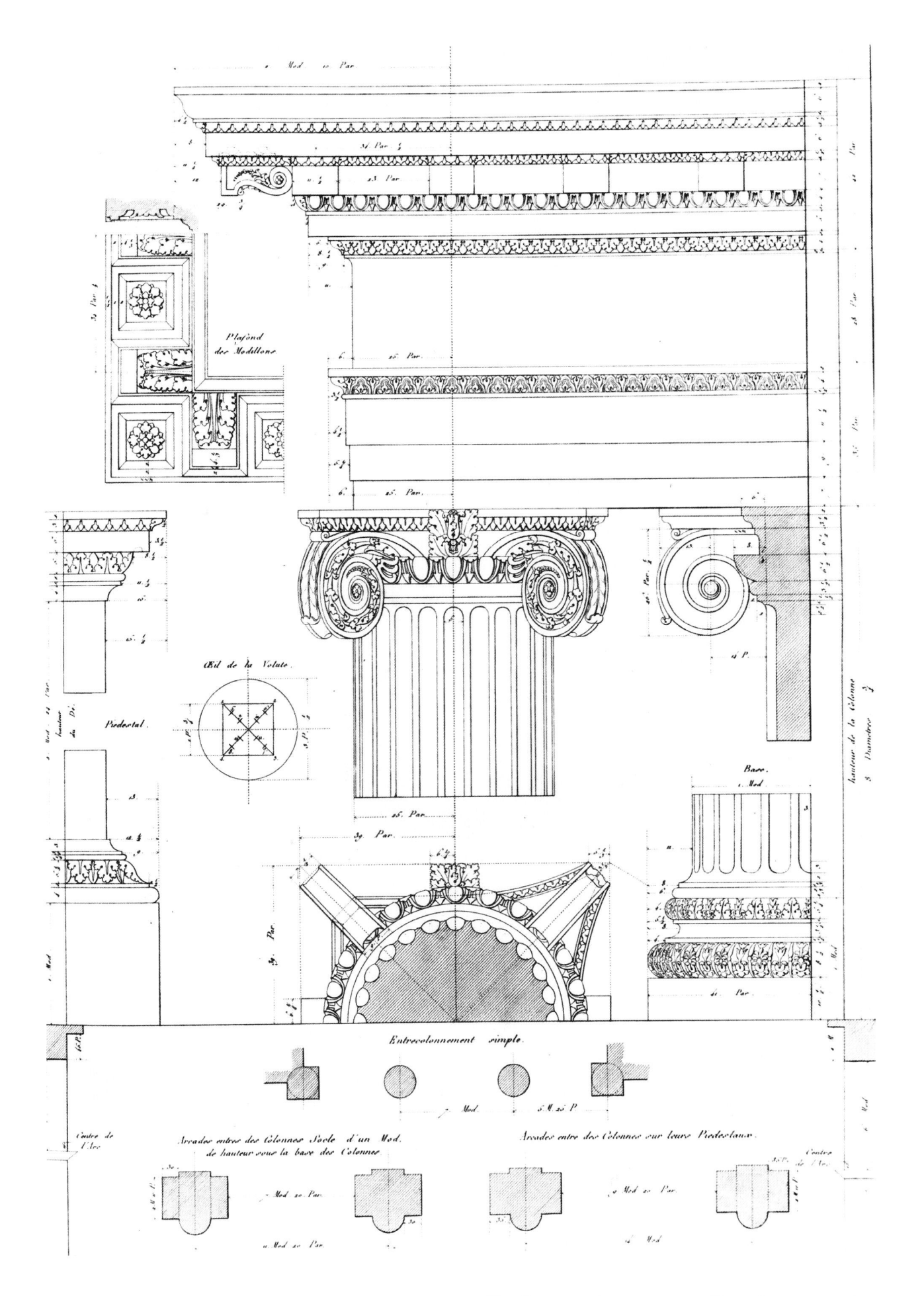

THE ORDERS OF ARCHITECTURE & THEIR APPLICATION / 23

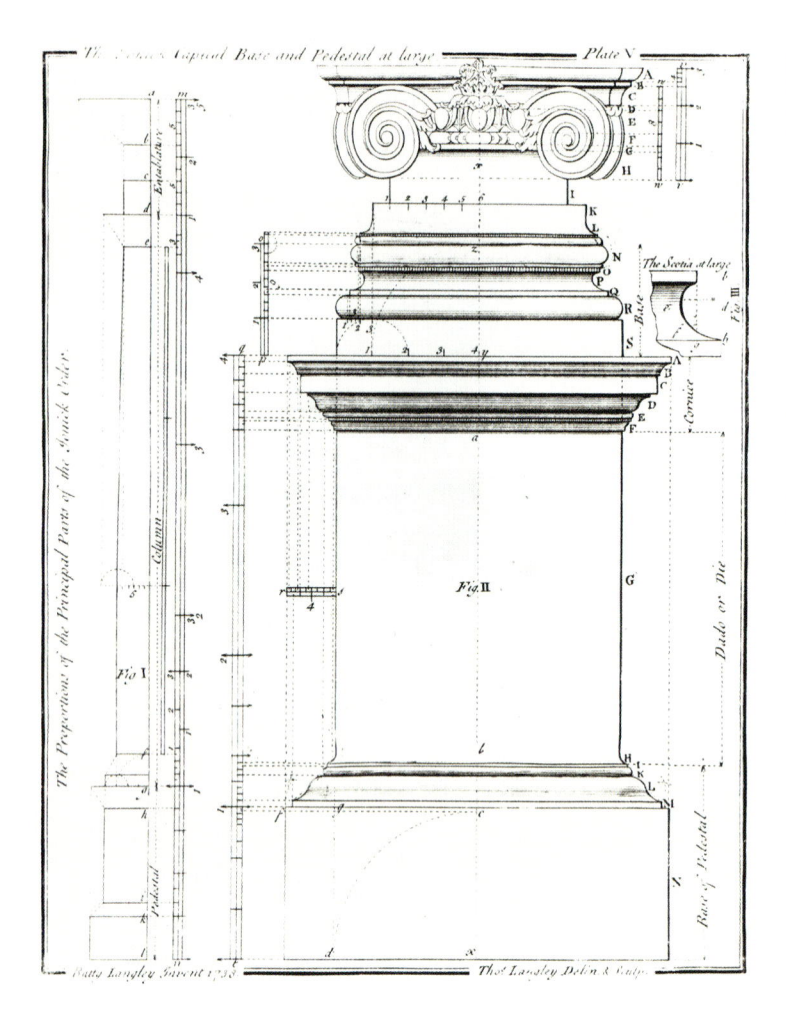

Fig. 2.12e ← Ionic Order: the whole, including the pedestal, is divided into 5 parts, and the lowest of these is the height of the pedestal. The remaining 4 parts should be divided into 6, the uppermost part of which is the height of the entablature. The height of the pedestal is divided into 4, the lowest part of which is the plinth, while the cornice is half a part high. The mouldings above the plinth, including the apophyge, are one-third of a part high. The column is 9 diameters (at the base) high, with half a diameter as the height of the capital and the height of the base. Proportions of the base mouldings and capitals are as shown. Note that the capital is of the 'diagonal', 'angular', or 'Scamozzi' type, with 8 volutes, and is identical on all 4 elevations, so this Order does not require a 'special' at the angle of a building (Langley [1745], coll. JSC).

Fig. 2.12f ← Ionic entablature. Note the position of the column and the method of subdividing it to set out the flutes, one of which is always in the centre. The frieze is pulvinated (Langley [1745], coll. JSC)

Fig. 2.12g ↓ Ionic angular capital, shown so that the volutes are visible on all sides. Circular and square columns are shown. The circumference of the column is divided into 24 equal parts, and each of those parts into 8. Using 3 of each 8 as radii the flutes can be drawn, so each fillet is 2 small parts. In the case of a square column, divide each side into 31 parts, giving 6 to each flute and 2 to each fillet. A variation is to have a bead in the angle (Langley [1745], coll. JSC)..

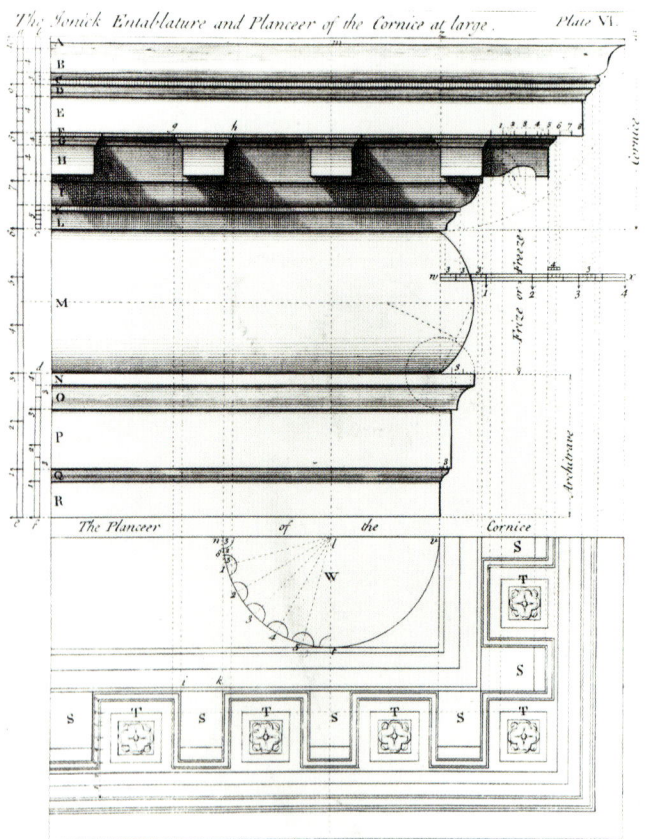

24 / Classical Architecture

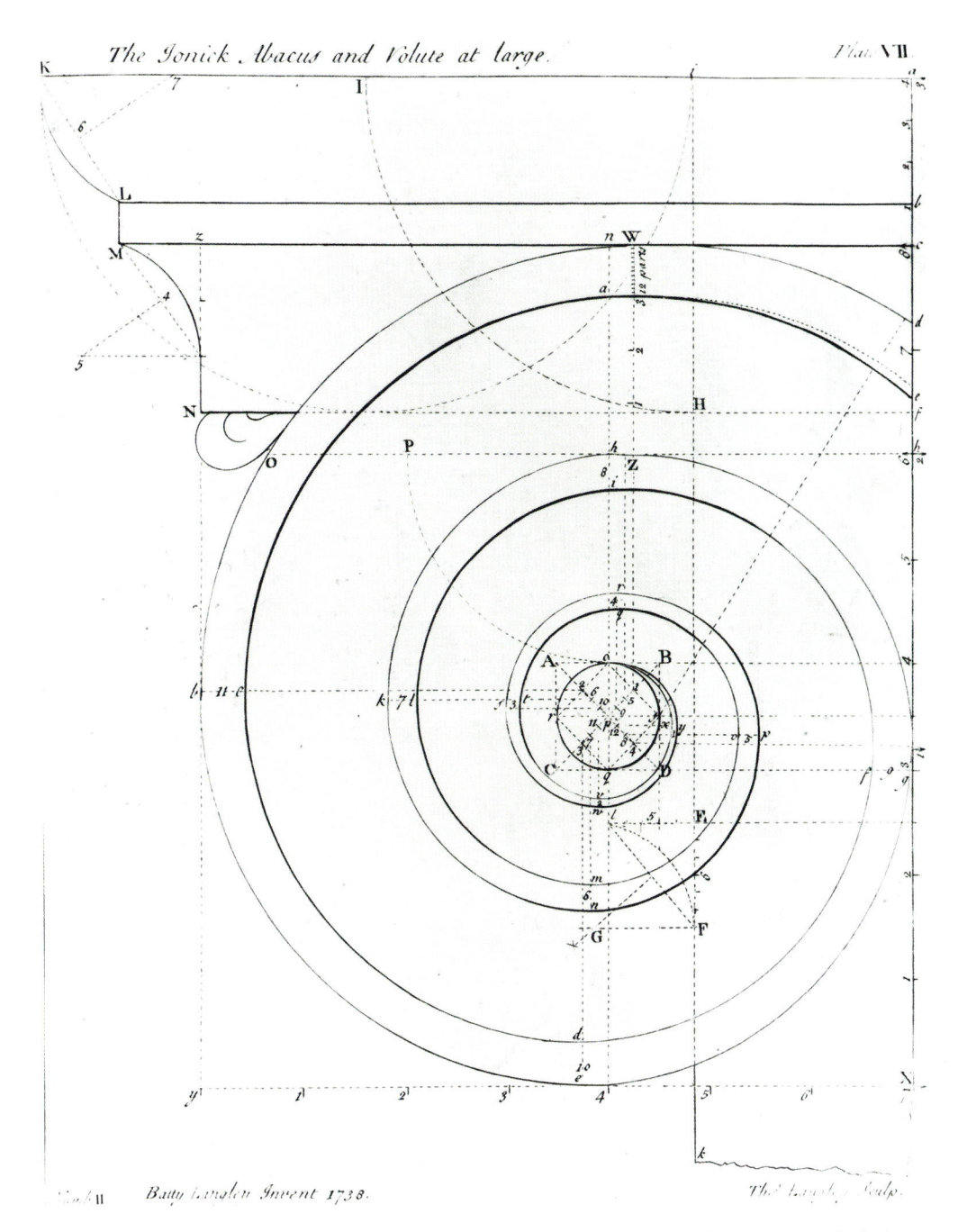

Fig. 2.12h ↑ *Ionic volute. The height of the capital (aX) is divided into 3 parts, the uppermost of which is divided in 2: this half-way line gives the position of the volute (W). A vertical line (n a p q 4) is drawn, divided into 8 parts, and p, the centre of the eye, is 0.225 column diameters from the line Mc, or 4.5 parts below line Mc, where one part is 0.25 of the dimension between Mc and AB. The eye is drawn with p as its centre, using a radius of 0.025 column diameters, or 0.5 of one of the 4 parts between AB and Mc. The horizontal diameter r p s is drawn, and the square r o x q is added within the eye. Diagonal lines are drawn through p to A B C and D, so the eye is held within a square. The arcs nb; ac; be; cd; eg; df; and gh, fi, respectively, are described as follows: the diagonals 2, 4 and 1, 3 on AD and BC are each divided into 6 parts labelled 2, 6, 10, p, 12, 8, 4 and 1, 5, 9, p, 11, 7, 3 respectively. Points 1–12 are the 12 centres from which the volute is described. Point 1 is the centre of the arc nb, point 2 of be, point 3 of eg, point 4 of gh, point 5 of hk, point 6 of kn, point 7 of np, point 8 of pr, point 9 of rs, point 10 of sw, point 11 of wy, and point 12 of yo. The line WZ (W is obtained by striking a vertical line from arc centre 1) should be divided into 4 parts, the uppermost of which, na, is the width of the list, which is subdivided into 12 parts. bc = 11 parts, ed = 10 parts, gf = 9 parts, hi = 8 parts, kl = 7 parts, and so on, diminishing by one part with each quarter circle. Subdivide the distances on AD and BC further, between 2 and 6, 6 and 10, etc., setting up 12 new centres for the inner part of the list to give the arcs ac, cd, df, fi, il, lm, mo, oq, qt, tv, vx, and xo. The main problem is the junction between the list and the eye, and if it looks uncomfortable, the diameter of the eye can be altered to give a smooth transition from list to eye (Langley [1745], coll. JSC).*

26 / Classical Architecture

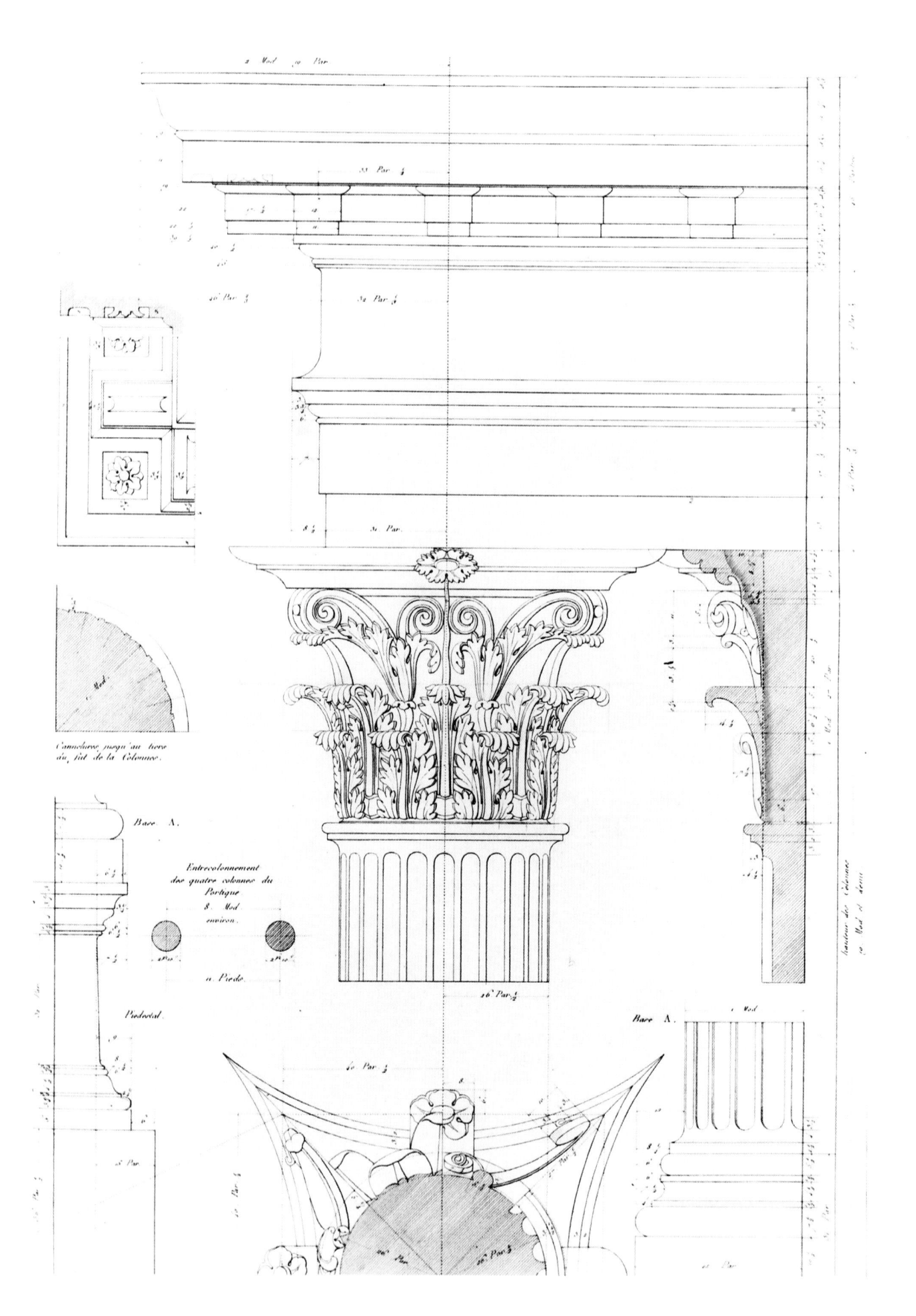

The Roman Corinthian Order

This Order was favoured by the Romans, especially during the Empire. Its grandeur, the proportions of the capital, and its elegance made it ideal for important religious (*see* Fig. 2.14h), civic, and imperial buildings.

Column shafts were fluted or unfluted, and bases were usually of the Attic type (Fig. 2.13; *see* Figs G23 and G46b). The model the Romans favoured for their Order was that of the Temple of Zeus Olympios, later the Olympieion, in Athens. Abaci and entablatures were given anything from fairly plain treatments (as at the Pantheon [Fig. 2.14b]) to the most sumptuous (as at the Forum of Nerva), where every moulding between fasciæ was enriched, friezes were treated with sculptured scenes in relief, and the modillioned cornice was embellished with a wide repertory of ornament (Fig. 2.14c). Coffers between the acanthus-covered modillions were treated with a variety of circular features. However, Roman Corinthian capitals have an important difference when compared with Greek: the acanthus leaves of Greek Orders tend to be taller and more elegant, even spikier, and were probably modelled on *Acanthus spinosus*, or prickly acanthus, while those of Roman Orders are shorter, with blunt ends to the leaves, and were probably based on *Acanthus mollis*. In some cases Roman Corinthian leaves are rather like those of the olive tree, or even resemble parsley. In addition, Greek capitals tend to have large scrolls in the centres of each face, half-way between the abacus and the top row of acanthus leaves: these scrolls support palmette ornaments which usually rise up over the face of the abacus (*see* Figs G46a and 6.6a–c). Roman volutes in the centres of each side are smaller, sit directly under the abacus, and support a fleuron in the centre of each face of the abacus (Figs 2.14a–e; *see* Figs G46b and 2.13).

Serlio associated Corinthian with virginity, especially the Blessed Virgin Mary, and Vitruvius thought of the Order as representing the figure of a girl, so it was associated with Beauty. The Corinthian Order used at the Temple of Vesta at Tivoli is unusual in its squatness, large volutes, and with a big floral device at the top, reaching upwards over the abacus (Figs 2.15a–b).

Fig. 2.13 ← *Corinthian Order from the Temple of Zeus Olympios at Athens, begun c.170 BC and completed under Hadrian c.AD 130. Note the remarkably pointed plan of the elegant abacus and the treatment of the cornice soffit (Normand [1852], coll. JSC).*

Fig. 2.14a ↗ *Corinthian Order of the Temple of Jupiter Stator, now known as the Temple of Castor and Pollux, Rome (AD 6). The capitals, with their interlocking inner helices, are exceedingly refined and beautiful, and the Order was used by James Gibbs for his London Church of St Martin-in-the-Fields (1721–6). The elaborate entablature with modillions supporting the cornice should be noted. Between the modillions are coffers with rosettes (Normand [1852], coll. JSC).*

Fig. 2.14b → *The Corinthian Order used at the great prostyle octastyle portico of the Pantheon in Rome. The shafts of the columns are unfluted monoliths of marble and granite, with capitals of marble (BTB).*

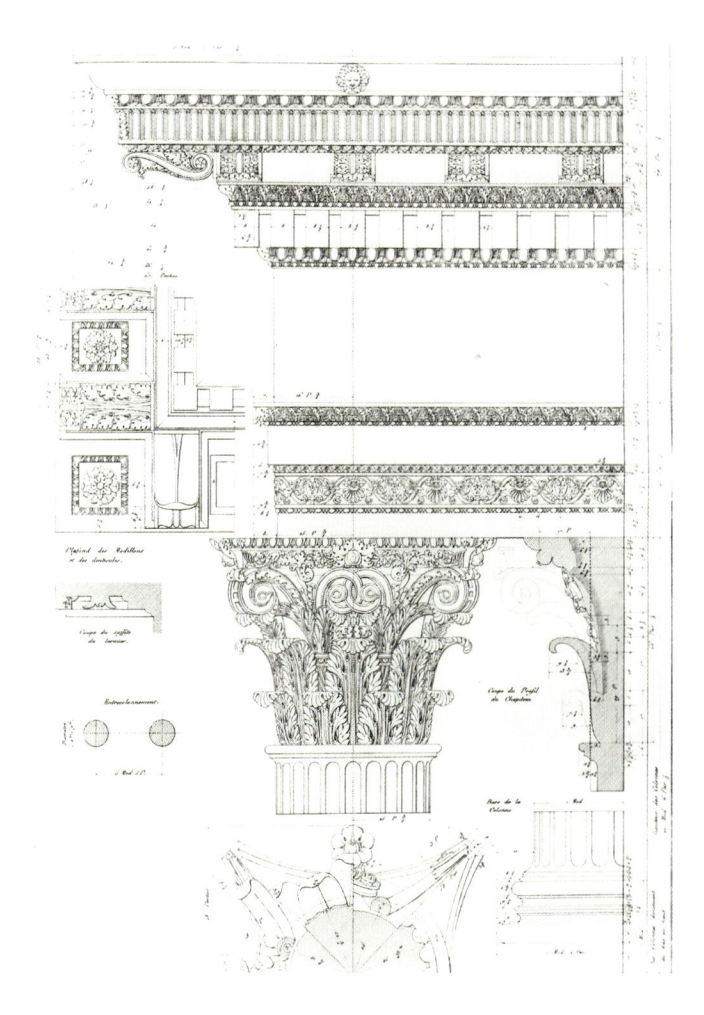

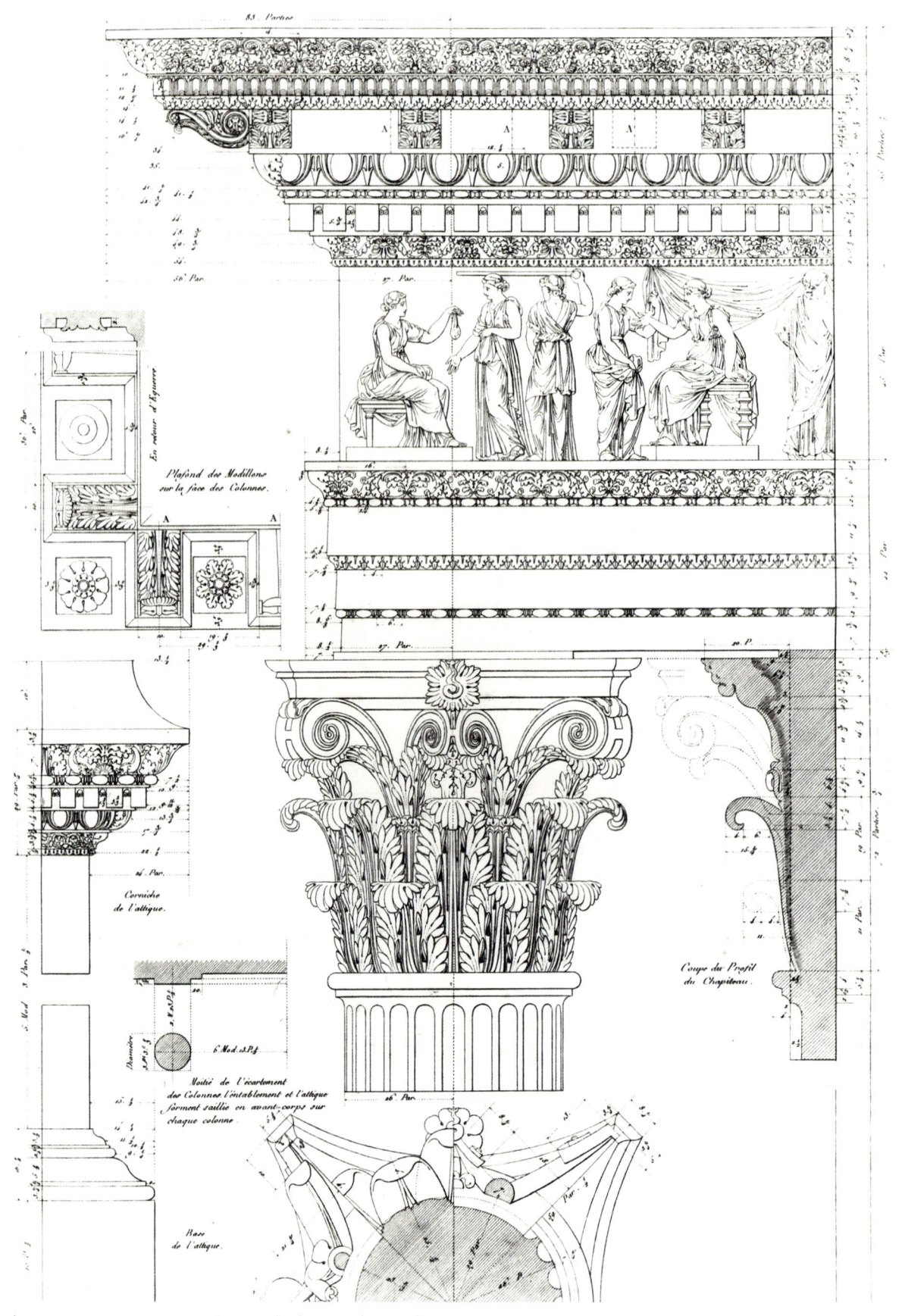

Fig. 2.14c ↑ *Roman Corinthian Order from the forum of Nerva, Rome (c.AD 90–7). A luxuriantly elaborate Order, with exquisitely sculptured frieze and crowning cornice with dentils, egg-and-dart, modillions, and coffers (Normand [1852], coll. JSC).*

28 / CLASSICAL ARCHITECTURE

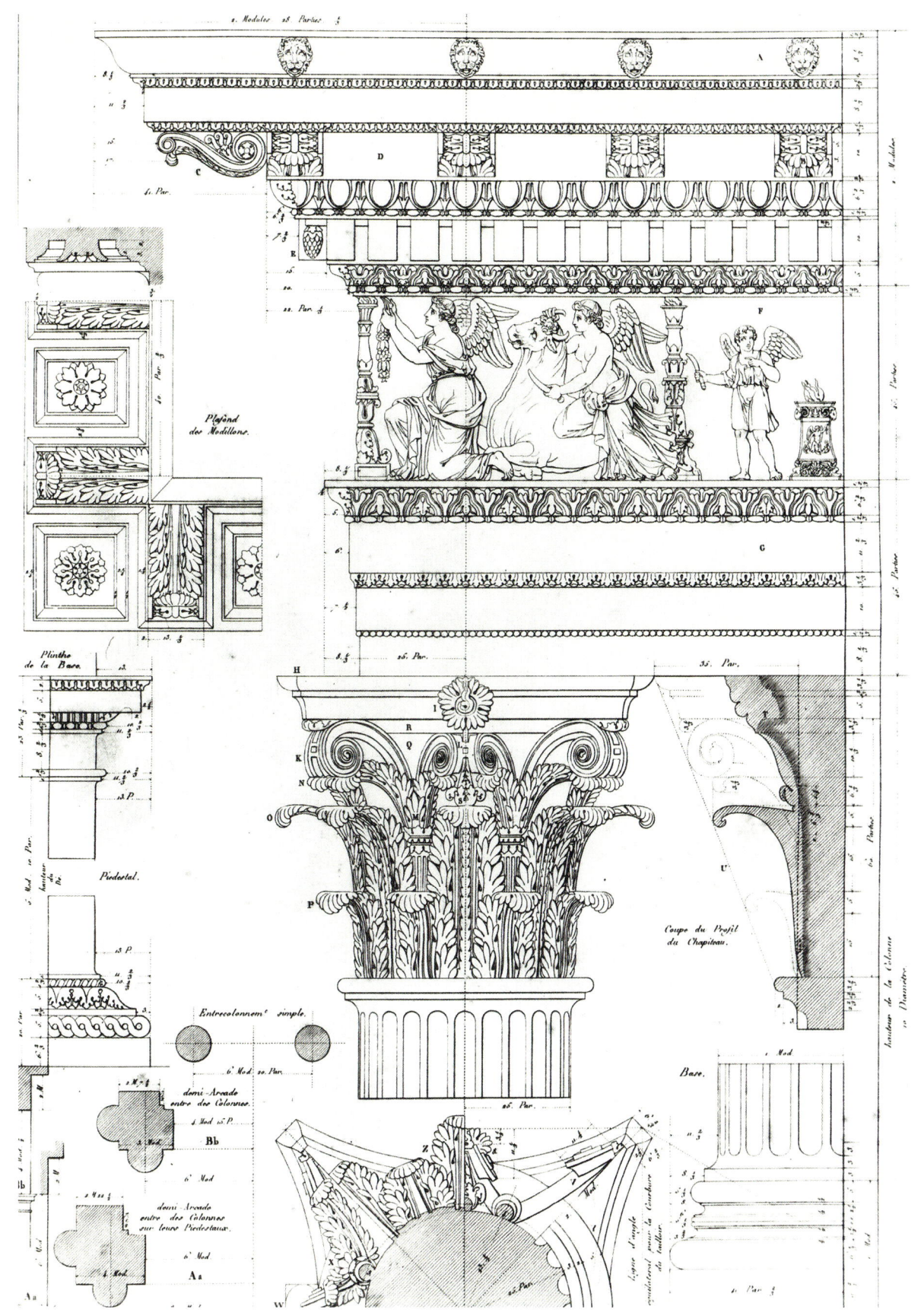

Fig. 2.14d ↑ *Corinthian Order after Vignola, showing the exceptional richness of this development of a Roman Order, the capital of which differs from Greek examples. Note the ornament of the horizontal mouldings, the elaborate modillions with coffers between them containing rosettes, and the very highly decorated frieze (Normand [1852], coll. JSC).*

THE ORDERS OF ARCHITECTURE & THEIR APPLICATION / 29

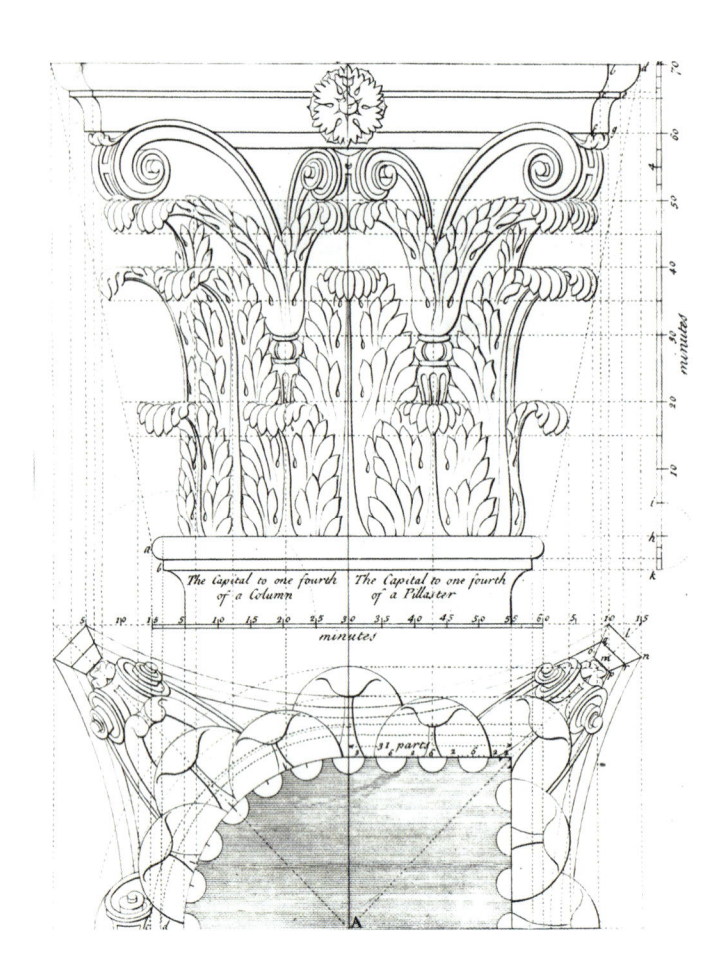

Fig. 2.14e ← *The Corinthian column is 10 diameters high, the base (including plinth), half a diameter, and the capital one-and-a-sixth diameters high: the Corinthian capital can be divided into 7 parts vertically, and each part subdivided by 10. The tops of the first range of acanthus leaves are 20 subdivisions high, the second 20, and the third 10. The total height from the astragal to the underside of the abacus is 60 subdivisions, and the abacus itself is 10 high, 5 of which are the cavetto (Langley [1745], coll. JSC).*

Fig. 2.14f ← *The Corinthian entablature is divided into 10, with 3 for the architrave, 3 to the frieze, and 4 to the cornice. An entablature height of 2.5 diameters is preferable to the 2 advocated by Gibbs. Note the system for subdividing cornice and architrave, and the method of establishing the overhang (Langley [1745], coll. JSC).*

Fig. 2.14g ↓ *Ionic and Corinthian modillion. The volute is set out on a similar system to that of the Ionic capital volute (see Fig. 2.12h). A modillion is about a sixth of a diameter in width (Langley [1745], coll. JSC).*

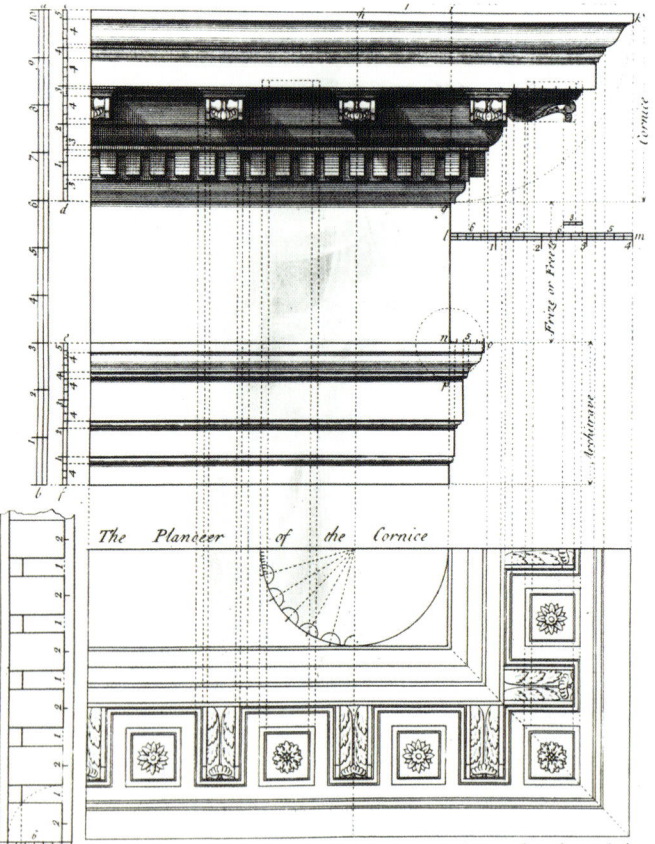

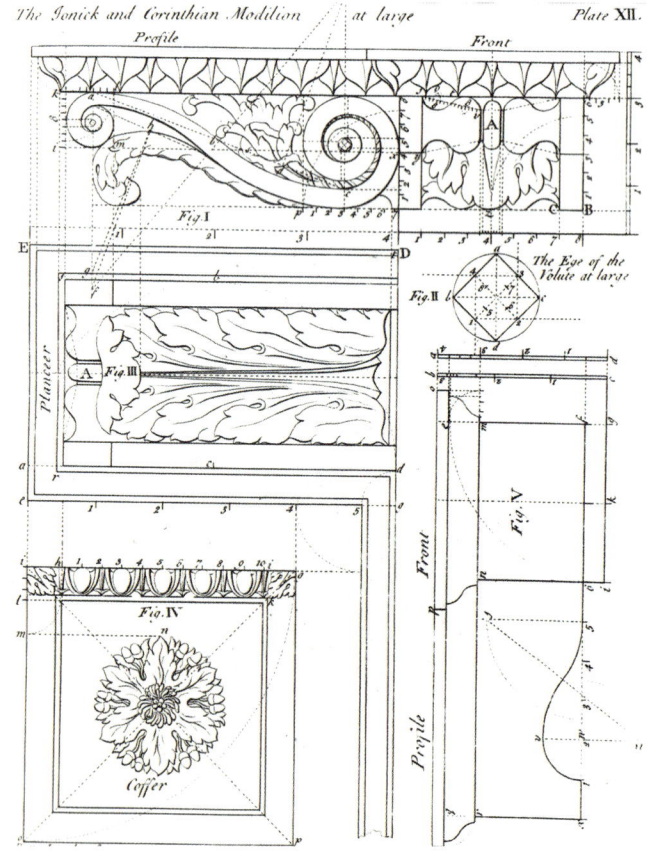

30 / Classical Architecture

Fig. 2.14h → *Roman temple known as the Maison Carrée in Nîmes of 16 BC. This is a small hexastyle pseudoperipteral Corinthian temple on a podium. Note the very deep portico. The plan is typical Græcised Roman-Tuscan, with engaged columns around the cella (AFK G13845)*

Fig. 2.15a ↓ *Roman Corinthian Order from the round temple by the waterfall at Tibur (known as the Temple of Vesta at Tivoli) of c.80 BC. This very curious Order has a somewhat squat capital 1 diameter instead of approximately 1.25 diameters in height; leaves apparently inspired by foliage differing from that found on usual Corinthian capitals; very large volutes with a big floral device in the centre; and a deep abacus of less projection than is usual, as being possibly better suited to a circular building. It looks like a tentative first attempt at a Composite Order. Note the continuous frieze of bulls' or ox heads and garlands, and the treatment of the soffit (Spiers [1893], coll. JSC).*

Fig. 2.15b ↑ *The so-called 'Tivoli Corner' of the Bank of England, London (1804–7), by Soane, showing the curved arrangement featuring the rather curious Corinthian Order derived from the Temple of Vesta (or the Sybil) at Tivoli, with its frieze of bovine heads with heavy garlands. The urns were added to the quadrant by C.R. Cockerell, but the elaborate Attic was Soane's design (unfortunately removed in 1936 when it was replaced by Baker's rotunda) (photo. c.1912, before Baker's interventions [1921–39], from Richardson [1914], coll. JSC).*

THE ORDERS OF ARCHITECTURE & THEIR APPLICATION / 31

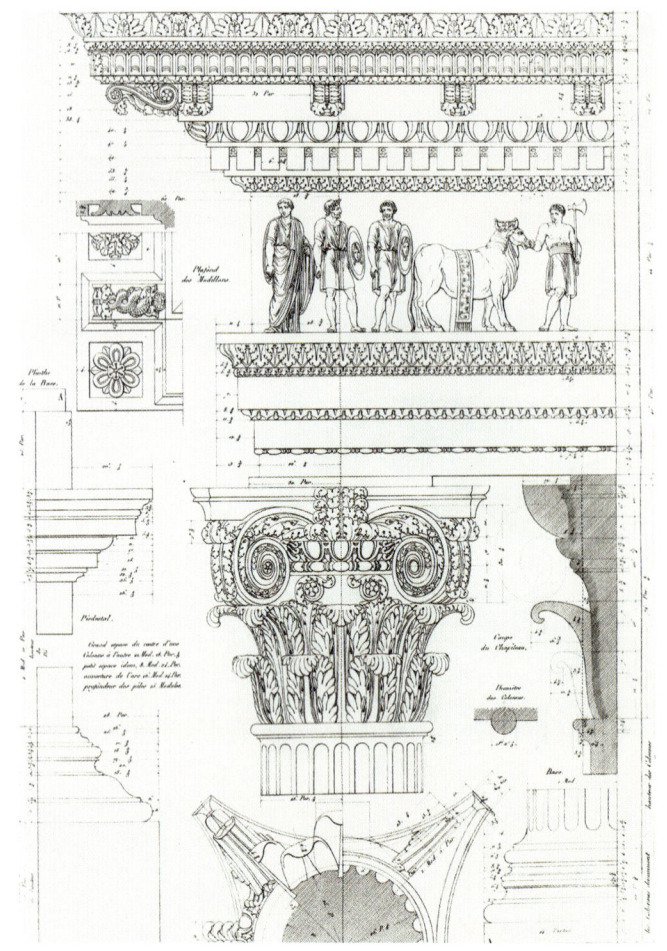

Fig. 2.16a ↑ *Composite Order from the Arch of Titus in Rome of c.AD 82. This highly elaborate Order combines Ionic and Corinthian motifs in the distinctive capital (Normand [1852], coll. JSC).*

Fig. 2.16b ↑ *Composite Order after Vignola. There are suggestions of modillions which project only partially below the cornice (Normand [1852], coll. JSC).*

The Roman Composite Order

This is very similar to the most sumptuous of the Corinthian Orders, but again, shafts can be plain or fluted. Bases were often of the Attic type (sometimes with the torus mouldings enriched), but on occasion extra mouldings were placed between the two torus rings (Figs 2.16a–b). The entablature of the Arch of Titus was exceptionally rich (Fig. 2.16a).

The characteristic feature of the Composite Order is its capital, which combines two rows of acanthus leaves (as on the Corinthian capital) with the diagonal or eight-volute Ionic capital above the top row of acanthus (see Fig. G43). Although the Romans are credited with the invention of the Composite Order in the 1st century AD, there were earlier precedents. The Temple of Athena Alea, Tegea, had two acanthus rows and corner volutes only, while the 'Corinthian-Doric' temple at Pæstum has corner volutes over a row of leaves. Composite presumably signifies the mixing of Wisdom with Beauty.

Application of the Orders

Although there are examples of engaged columns in Greek architecture (Temple of Zeus Olympios at Agrigentum (Doric), Lion Tomb at Cnidos (unfluted Doric except at the tops and bottoms of the shafts, with wide intercolumniation [see Fig. 2.3c]), Temple of Apollo Epicurius at Bassæ (four angle-voluted Ionic [see Fig. G28a]), and choragic monument of Lysicrates (Corinthian [see Figs 6.6a–c]), most Greek architecture is distinguished for its expression of a columnar and trabeated construction. When the Abbé Laugier visualised the Primitive Hut as the precedent for all subsequent architecture, he argued that the constructional integrity of such a system had been undermined by such 'abuses' as engaged columns, and so real architecture would express the columnar and trabeated form with absolute unambiguous clarity. Laugier's *Essai sur l'Architecture* of 1753 heralded a celebration of the column, a seeking for a greater purity of form and construction, and a primitivism in which stereometrical shapes and tough, robust Doric began to be used in reaction to over-refinement and Rococo frippery. Thus the rediscovery of Greek architecture occurred at a time when philosophically a return to basics was being demanded, and the uncompromising strength and severity of Greek Doric began to be admired as the direct

Fig. 2.17a ← *Merging of arcuated and columnar and trabeated forms at the Flavian amphitheatre aka the Colosseum, Rome (AD 75–82). The superimposition of Orders involves widely spaced engaged columns of the Tuscan Order, over which is an engaged Ionic Order, above which is an engaged Corinthian Order, and, finally, an Order of Corinthian pilasters. The wide spacing derives from Hellenistic and Roman examples, but the arch, which combined with the trabeated Orders, makes the spacing visually acceptable (BTB).*

Fig. 2.17b ← *Elevation of the three superimposed Orders of the Colosseum. It should be noted that a sequential superimposition of Orders (Tuscan, Doric, Ionic, Corinthian, Composite) was commonly used from Renaissance times onwards, but there is no surviving Antique monument which follows this scheme (Rosengarten [1893], coll. JSC).*

Fig. 2.18a ↓ *The columnar and trabeated form merged with the arcuated principle. The Arch of Titus in Rome of c.AD 82 showing the engaged Composite Order and the Attic storey. The Roman triumphal arch was an important precedent followed by architects of the Renaissance period. Its three divisions, the unequal spacing of the columns, and the combination of arched form and Order made it a versatile model. The very wide spacing of the central pair of columns would not work if the Order were not engaged, as it would look weak: with the arch and the background of masonry, however, the composition works (coll. JSC).*

result of the extolling of the Primitive Hut as the source of it all. Nevertheless, as scholarship revealed more and more of the refinements of Greek architecture, it was found that even the Greeks employed antæ (a species of pilaster used to terminate the side walls, with bases and capitals differing from those of adjacent columns, and, unlike pilasters, having straight sides rather than entasis), and used canephoræ and caryatid(e)s, on occasion, instead of columns.

Superimposed columns are found inside Greek temples, but using the same Order. Two or three Orders could also be employed in Greek buildings, but not superimposed. That remained true until the Hellenistic period (*see* Glossary and Chapter 3), when rules governing the syntax of the Orders were relaxed, and often a new freedom, with remarkably original and fascinating variations, enlivened and refreshed the Classical language of architecture, demonstrating renewed vigour and versatility, as well as potentially infinite applications, adaptations, and transformations to be exploited by inventive designers. Ionic colonnades over Doric (the entablature over the Ionic columns being Doric) are found at the portico of the sanctuary of Athena at Pergamon (2nd century BC), and constitute only one example of an overall loosening of practice, and a greater freedom of expression. Generally speaking, Hellenistic spacing of columns became very wide, as the one metope per intercolumniation began to seem too severe and heavy when lighter, more spacious effects were sought by architects.

This wider Hellenistic spacing was ideal for mixing the Orders with arcuated forms (Figs 2.17a–b and 2.18a–b). The Record Office (*Tabularium*) in Rome of 78 BC had concrete vaulting, and piers adorned with Doric engaged columns and entablature with four triglyphs per intercolumniation: it was a similar Order to that used at Cori (*see* Fig. 2.11a). This type of arcuated façade, to which Orders are engaged, was further developed at the Colosseum, begun by Vespasian and completed under Titus and Domitian. The outer wall of this elliptical building consisted of 80 piers connected by barrel-vaults, with the arches expressed on the outside. An engaged Order of Tuscan columns carried an entablature, over which was the storey of unfluted Ionic: above was a third arcaded storey with an engaged Corinthian Order,

THE ORDERS OF ARCHITECTURE & THEIR APPLICATION / 33

Fig. 2.18b ↑ *Arch of Constantine, Rome (c.AD 312–15), much of the relief decoration of which was somewhat inelegantly recycled from earlier monuments. However, it was a development from the single arch as in the Arch of Titus, and, with its subsidiary arches, suggested a precedent for later façade treatments (coll. JSC).*

Fig. 2.19 → *The rock-cut Khazna at Petra of c.AD 120 or later, that incorporates a considerable degree of architectural sophistication. Note the circular pavilion in the centre set between a broken pediment. The whole effect is daringly proto-Baroque (AFK H17408).*

on the entablature of which was a wall without arcades, but with every other bay pierced by a small rectangular opening. This wall was divided into bays by means of tall pilasters on pedestals of a unique, vaguely Corinthian Order (Figs 2.17a–b).

Widely spaced columns, engaged or standing before the arcuated structure behind, can also be found in Roman triumphal arches (Figs 2.18a–b), but here the intercolumniation varies: it is wider in the centre than at the sides in order to accommodate the great central arch. Thus, the Orders were further freed from Antique usage, but new proportional systems and relationships were thereby established.

The mixing of arched forms with the columnar and trabeated language of the Orders produced further variations. The traditional triangular pediment was often broken (as at the Khazna in Petra [Fig. 2.19]), and sometimes alternated with segmental pediments, a form associated with the Isiac moon and the bow of Diana. Broken-bed pediments with segmental vaults were used in the Temple of Bacchus at Baalbek, where the entrance portico to the temple complex also had a colonnade with a central arch, the entablature being carried in a semicircle over the arch, and set in a triangular pediment. A similar motif occurred at the 2nd-century temple at Termessus in Pisidia and at the palace of Diocletian at Spalato (Split), and it is probably the model for the serliana of Renaissance times (*see* Figs G100a–b).

It was but a small step to forming vaults springing from columns and entablatures, as at the *thermæ*, and to inventing complex proto-Baroque plan-forms, like the round temple at

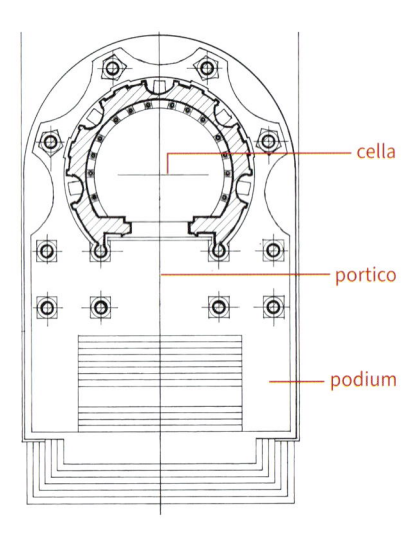

Fig. 2.20 ↑ *Plan of the 3rd-century Temple of Venus at Baalbek, showing Roman Imperial tendencies towards proto-Baroque forms (JSC).*

Baalbek, with its entablature containing five concave indentations over a circular drum (Fig. 2.20). Such variations and combinations were to form the basis for an astonishing range of further invention from the early Renaissance period.

Hellenistic and Roman exemplars, then, took over from Greece as the main sources for later Classical architecture, until Greece was once again rediscovered during the 18th century.

34 / CLASSICAL ARCHITECTURE

3

THE GRÆCO-ROMAN ROOTS OF CLASSICAL ARCHITECTURE

Greek architecture, while the fruit of all the civilisations which preceded the great period of Greek culture, did not live for itself alone; for it has sown the seed of European architecture, and has determined the future form and growth of most subsequent European art.

WILLIAM BELL DINSMOOR:
The Architecture of Ancient Greece (London: B.T. Batsford, 1950), xv.

The Greeks, it must be admitted, cultivated architecture so successfully that they left to succeeding ages only the humble task of imitating their works, works which will be ever admired but perhaps never be equalled.

SIR JOHN SOANE:
Lectures on Architecture at the Royal Academy (1809–36), Lecture **i**, quoted in
David Watkin: *Sir John Soane: Enlightenment Thought and the Royal Academy Lectures*
(Cambridge: Cambridge University Press, 1996), 497.

Greek Architecture

The lands that lie around the Mediterranean Sea produced architecture long before what we now recognise as Classicism developed into its mature forms. Millennia before Augustus, even before the maturing of the Greek Doric Order in the early 7th century BC, the Egyptians were building great works of architecture, and evolved sophisticated columnar and trabeated systems with capitals and cornices. There can be no doubt at all that the square, plain columns and simple architrave and cornice (such as those of the remarkable Temple of Queen Hatshepsut at Der el-Bahari, and in other buildings employing the square column as a peristyle around a cella, like the temple at Elephantine) influenced European architects working in Neo-Classical styles, notably Schinkel (*see* Figs 6.11f–g), von Klenze (*see* Fig. 6.12e), Kreis, Speer, and Thomson (*see* Figs 6.19a–b). Less clear is the influence of the polygonal columns of parts of the Der el-Bahari complex, or of the rock-cut tombs at Beni-Hasan (erected perhaps some two millennia before Christ) on the evolution of the Greek Doric Order. It is improbable that stone columns of circular or polygonal section were employed in the Ægean area or in Italy before the 7th century BC, even though they were not unusual in Egypt for many centuries before that. It does seem that timber was the favoured material for columns in Greece and Italy, and that wood was superseded by stone, perhaps through Egyptian influences, from the 7th century in Doric architecture, but that wood remained in use, often in combination with stone and terracotta, in Italy until much later.

Early Greek architecture from the 7th century seems to have been a development of well-established local traditions of building in timber and stone, and Egyptian influences helped to encourage an architecture primarily of masonry. Probably the most important of all the Asiatic imports to affect ancient Greece was the prototype of the Ionic capital. Early capitals, such as the Æolic type (*see* Fig. G7) from Neandria, have two volutes springing upwards and curling outwards from the top of the shaft, rather like a sapling being split at the end and the two halves bent outwards into spirals. Between the spirals is a fan-like pattern rising to a flat top that supported the beams. This type of capital is really a variety of the palmette (*see* Figs G16 and G17) pattern found in Egyptian and Cretan designs for paintings and reliefs. In true Ionic, however, the volutes do not rise from the shaft; they are quite definitely laid, like a mattress with both ends rolled up underneath to form two whorls, on top of the shaft, but separated from the shaft by the circular echinus (ornamented with egg-and-dart) which carries the central channelled portion joining the volutes (*see* Figs G72, 2.5, and 2.8a). Subsequently, of course, and certainly from the time of Alexander the Great, the process of syncretism accelerated, when Egyptian deities merged with those of the Greek civilisations. It is likely that Egyptian and Asiatic influences had an impact much earlier, even on the prehistoric architecture of Crete, but this does not mean that Cretan civilisation did not have strong native roots. The whole point to remember about the cultures of the lands in and around the Mediterranean is that the sea was the highway, and that artistic, religious, and other cross-currents were there from the very earliest of times.

What we now call Classical architecture seems to have evolved with similarities sufficient to identify it as a language, but it did have several distinct regional variations, which we might term schools, evolved for different racial, religious, geographical, and geological reasons. First of all there was the School of Greece and of its colonies in Southern Italy and Sicily, dating from around the early part of the 7th century to around 150 BC, with the Doric Order much in evidence (*see* Figs 2.1a–2.4). Then there is the School of the Greek colonies in Asia Minor, in which the Ionic Order is very much to the fore from the 6th-century temples and treasuries to those of the 2nd century BC. This does not mean, of course, that the Ionic Order was not found in mainland Greece: both the Temple on the Ilissus (*see* Fig. 2.6) and the Erechtheion (*see* Figs 2.7 and 2.8a–d) are 5th-century examples of the most refined Ionic, but the archaic Temple of Artemis at Ephesus in Asia Minor is 6th century in date. Corinthian seems to have evolved from the 5th century as a more decorated variant of Ionic, and was first used *internally* at Bassæ, Delphi, Tegea, and Epidaurus. The Corinthian Order used *externally* in temples seems first to have occurred in the 3rd-century Temple of Zeus in Cilicia, which may even be Alexandrian in date, and later at the Temple of Zeus Olympios in Athens around 170 BC. The celebrated choragic monument of Lysicrates in Athens has six engaged Corinthian columns around a hollow but inaccessible cella, and dates from the 4th century (*see* Figs G46a and 6.6a–b).

We can perhaps use the term 'Hellenic' to indicate the architecture of Greece proper and its colonies from the 7th to the middle of the 2nd century BC. Hellenic architecture, therefore, includes celebrated monuments such as the Parthenon (447–38) (*see* Figs 2.1a–b), the Temple of Aphaia at Ægina (*c*.490), the stupendous sturdy Doric temples at Pæstum (6th century), the Temple of Apollo Epicurius at Bassæ (*c*.420), the Athenian Ionic masterpieces such as the Temple on the Ilissus (*c*.450) and the Erechtheion (*c*.421–407), and the Corinthian choragic monument of Lysicrates (334).

On the other hand, the term 'Hellenistic' suggests the use of the Greek language, the adoption of Greek modes of thought, and the employment of essentials of Hellenic architecture modified by the incorporation of new or foreign non-Hellenic elements: 'Hellenistic' implies the architecture of the Greek-dominated world from the time of Alexander the Great. Hellenistic architecture is mostly associated with settlements east of the Ægean and Mediterranean Seas, especially in Asia Minor in what were known as Mysia, Lydia, Caria, and Lycia. The most obvious Hellenistic modifications in Doric, for example, include the multiplication of triglyphs, with two or even more, over the intercolumniations (a good example is the Lion Tomb at Cnidos [*see* Fig. 2.3c]): this occurred because Hellenistic taste favoured entablatures of less depth than Hellenic examples, so the shallower frieze conditioned the width of triglyphs and metopes (since proportion had to remain similar), and

because Hellenistic spacing of columns generally tended to be much wider, to give a lighter, airier, less massive effect. In addition, Hellenistic columns tend to be more slender than earlier Hellenic examples, perhaps influenced by the refinement and narrowness of Hellenistic Ionic column shafts. The Nereid monument at Xanthos (*c*.405), which is earlier than the time of Alexander, had very slender and widely spaced Ionic columns, so the tendency to wider intercolumniations, reducing the height of the entablature, and making buildings appear less robust, but lighter and more elegant, was already present in Greek architecture, but became favoured after the conquests of Alexander, especially in Asia Minor.

Hellenistic Corinthian Orders were treated very freely, and show varied local designs, often of great refinement. The Temple of Apollo Didymæus near Miletus (*c*.330) is one such example, where large acanthus leaves sweep up under the corner volutes. It was the great temple south-east of the Athenian Acropolis, however, which appears to have been among the first Corinthian temples on a grand scale. The Temple of Zeus Olbios in Cilicia, of the 3rd century, was probably the earliest, but that of Zeus Olympios at Athens, resumed in the first half of the 2nd century BC by King Antiochus Epiphanes of (significantly) Syria, was undoubtedly bigger and more splendid. Its fully developed Corinthian (completed under Hadrian) was the model for much Roman work of this Order, and therefore for standard Renaissance Corinthian, because Sulla adorned the Temple of Jupiter in Rome with columns removed from the Athenian Olympieion.

Roman Architecture

The important feature of Greek architecture (be it Hellenic or Hellenistic) was that the column and entablature were very much in evidence in most significant buildings. That is, the Greek Orders were the chief architectural expression in a wide range of structures, especially temples, where porticoes and peristyles were essential elements. All of which leads us to the various schools associated with Rome. First, there is the School of Etruria and Latium, quite distinct from the Greek schools, and dating roughly from the 6th to the 2nd century. From this derive the Tuscan Order and the Roman temple type, with its prostyle portico, bare cella, and more steeply raked roof. The Roman Republican School (150 BC to the end of the 1st century BC) has examples of Roman Doric, Ionic, and Corinthian Orders, but the appearance of buildings – temples on podia, columns engaged with cellæ, as with the Temple of Fortuna Virilis in Rome (Ionic) of *c*.40 BC – differed from that of Greek, or Greek colonial, examples, in spite of superficial similarities (*see* Figs 2.12a–b).

However, the decoration of early temples in Italy has strong affinities with Greece, although the architecture of Campania, Latium, and Etruria are similar in type, and are distinctly Italian. The temples built were mostly of timber and brick, while entablatures were of wood, often decorated with painted terracotta. The buildings stood on high podia with steps at only one end, a feature that is very rare in Greece, but was adopted universally by the Romans. Vitruvius describes an Etruscan temple (*see* Fig. G10) which consisted of three cells separated by walls, with a door each, opening to a large portico of two rows of four widely spaced columns. The eaves and gabled end had very wide projections.

It seems that strong Hellenistic influences merged with the traditions of native Italian temple architecture to produce the type favoured during the later Republic. The Doric temple at Cori (*see* Fig. 2.11a), of the 1st century BC, is one of the best preserved of all Republican temples. The plan is similar to that evolved in Etruria: it stood on a high podium approached by steps at one end, and had a deep prostyle tetrastyle portico, with two columns between each of the angle-columns and the wall of the cella, which had a central door. There were antæ at all four corners of the cella. Columns were very slender, with bases consisting of one torus below a large apophyge: the shafts had 18 Doric flutes on the upper two-thirds, but the lowest third consisted of an 18-sided polygon. Below the capital, which consisted of a small abacus and echinus, was a smooth band. The low entablature ran all the way round the building, and there were three triglyphs to each intercolumniation: like Greek Doric examples, the triglyphs at the corner met, so the corner columns were not on the centre-lines of the triglyphs. The basic form of the Temple of Fortuna Virilis (*see* Figs 2.12a–b) in Rome was similar, except that it was Ionic and had engaged columns round the cella with the same intercolumniation as that of the porticoes. With the coming of the Empire and the age of Augustus and Tiberius (31 BC–AD 37) the temple type continued, notably with the Maison Carrée in Nîmes (16 BC), a hexastyle pseudo-peripteral Corinthian temple on a podium, so the form is Hellenised Roman-Etruscan (*see* Fig. 2.14h). Many temples were of great magnificence, and the Corinthian Order was much favoured, with elaborate and deeply carved entablatures, and vigorous capitals. The Augustan Temple of Mars Ultor (2 BC) (Fig. 3.1) had a peripteral colonnade on three sides terminating in a mighty wall, into which the apse, with its concrete hemidome, was set at the end of the cella.

The most interesting innovations during the Empire included the mixing of arcuated forms with the Orders, and the development of vaults and domes, often employing concrete.

Fig. 3.2a ↑ *Triumphal-arch theme: Arc de Triomphe de l'Étoile, Paris, begun 1806 to designs by J.-F.-T. Chalgrin, and completed (1836) by G.-A. Blouet. The arch is astylar, that is without an engaged Order, but it has an extra axis running through it at right-angles to the main axis (coll. JSC).*

Under the Flavian emperors (AD 69–96), the use of superimposed Orders in storeys mixed with arcuated structure occurred in the Colosseum (*c.*AD 75–82) (*see* Figs 2.17a–b), while the Arch of Titus (*c.*AD 82) has a single arch, the early engaged Composite columns with varied intercolumniation and elaborate entablature, and a mighty Attic storey with inscription panel (*see* Figs 2.16a and 2.18a). Later triumphal arches, notably those of Septimius Severus (AD 203) and Constantine (*c.*315) (*see* Fig. 2.18b), are highly sophisticated compositions involving three arches (one central large one and two smaller flanking arches) with superimposed detached columns, entablatures, and elaborate Attic storeys, and were potent models for later such storeys of the Renaissance and later periods (Figs 3.2a–i).

From 96–138 of our era date the Pantheon (*see* Fig. 2.14c) in Rome (with its great drum, coffered brick, mortar, and concrete dome with oculus, and heroic pedimented prostyle octastyle portico [*see* Fig. G87]); the large complex of the Villa Adriana at Tivoli (involving much concrete vaulting [without metal reinforcement, of course] and convoluted allusions to various parts of the Empire); and the huge circular mausoleum of Hadrian. Massive vaults and concrete domes were being fully exploited at that time, and complicated arcuated structures, with plans of increasing geometrical intricacy, were not uncommon. At both Heliopolis (Baalbek) and the Villa Adriana there appeared a new freedom in the treatment of the Orders, involving curved entablatures and elements that are astoundingly anticipatory of 17th-century Baroque developments (*see* Fig. 2.20).

Under the Antonine emperors (138–193) architectural and structural innovations continued, but from Pertinax to Alexander Severus (193–235) the monuments associated with

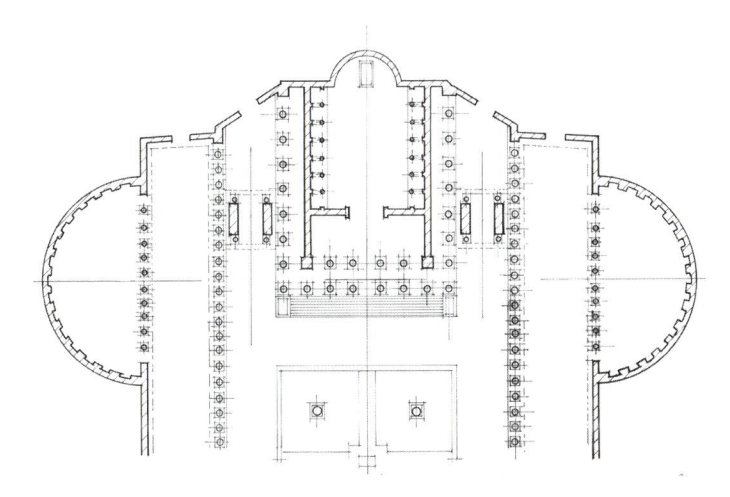

Fig. 3.1 ↑ *Plan of the Temple of Mars Ultor in the forum of Augustus, Rome (late 1st century BC to early 1st century AD) (JSC).*

THE GRÆCO-ROMAN ROOTS OF CLASSICAL ARCHITECTURE / 37

Fig. 3.2b ⭦ *Triumphal-arch theme embellished above and below: monument (dated 1533) to Jan van Dendermonde-Borgnival (d.1536) in the Grote Kerk, Breda, the Netherlands (Brindley and Weatherley [1887], coll. JSC).*

Fig. 3.2c ↑ *Triumphal-arch theme: Fontaine des Innocents, Paris (1549), by Pierre Lescot, with sculpture by Jean Goujon, reconstructed 1788 in the form of a square pavilion, with ornamentation by Pajou (coll. JSC).*

Fig. 3.2d ⭠ *Triumphal-arch theme: the Trevi Fountain, Rome (1732–7), by Nicola Salvi, influenced by Bernini, fusing the façade of the Palazzo Poli (a triumphal arch in its centre) with a fountain, the whole composition set on a rock-work base (JSC).*

38 / CLASSICAL ARCHITECTURE

Fig. 3.2e ← *Triumphal-arch theme: Canterbury Gate, Merton Street, Oxford, giving access to Canterbury Quadrangle at Christ Church (1773–83), the whole ensemble designed by James Wyatt for Richard Robinson, Archbishop of Armagh. The Order is an austere version of Roman Doric, and the primitivist bases to the columns should be noted (JSC).*

Fig. 3.2f ↖ *Triumphal-arch theme: the elegant and refined Arc de Triomphe du Carrousel, erected 1805–9 to designs by Percier and Fontaine, and based on the arch of Septimius Severus in Rome, although the Attic storey is derived from that of the Arch of Constantine (see Fig. 2.18b), but, like the Arc de Triomphe de l'Étoile, has a subsidiary axis cutting through the main one at right angles (RHB, improved by GB).*

Fig. 3.2g ↓ *Triumphal-arch theme: the Fontaine St-Michel, Place St-Michel, Paris (1858–60), designed by Gabriel Davioud, with bronze statue of the Archangel Michael and the dragon by Duret (coll. JSC).*

THE GRÆCO-ROMAN ROOTS OF CLASSICAL ARCHITECTURE / 39

Fig. 3.2h *Triumphal-arch theme: centrepiece of the Grand Palais (1896–1900) in the Avenue d'Antin, Paris, designed by Deglane, Girault, Louvet, and Thomas. Le Corbusier was planning to have the complex demolished to be replaced by one of his own creations, but he died before that could be realised (BTB).*

Fig. 3.2i *Triumphal-arch theme: the Menin Gate, Ieper, Belgium (1922–6), a memorial to British soldiers who died in the battles of the Ieper salient, and have no known graves, designed by Blomfield (JSC).*

Fig. 3.3a *Plans of Roman baths: (top) thermæ of Caracalla (AD 211–17); (bottom) thermæ of Diocletian (AD 298–306). Both demonstrate the principles of Roman Imperial planning, with vast, formal, symmetrical arrangements of elements, main axes and subsidiary axes, curved exedræ, enormous vaulted spaces, and rooms exploring circles and parts of circles (BTB).*

Septimius Severus and the enormous *thermæ* of Caracalla were built, demonstrating a complete assurance in the combinations of vaulted, arcuated, and columnar and trabeated forms (Figs 3.3a–b). The *thermæ* also demonstrate a mastery of the problems of planning very large and complicated buildings, incorporating big vaulted public rooms, gardens, and various geometries in one symmetrical composition.

From 235 to 330, that is from Maximin to the founding of Constantinople, date Diocletian's palace at Spalato (or Split) and the *thermæ* of Diocletian (Fig. 3.3a), both highly sophisticated essays in planning vast buildings housing various functions and employing many axes, systems of symmetries, and even greater freedom with the Orders. This period also saw the development of circular and polygonal structures, including various

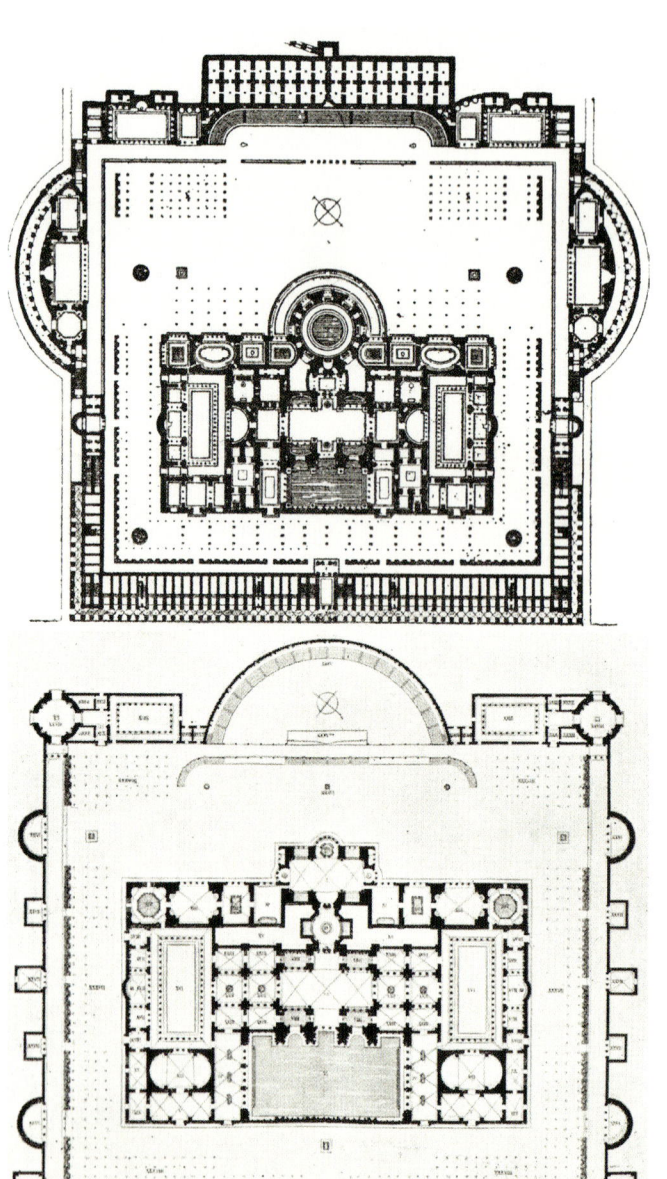

Fig. 3.3b ↑ *Restoration by George Aitchison of one of the great interiors at the* thermæ *of Caracalla, with vast concrete vaults (unreinforced with any metal), the finish of which was not bare concrete, but a covering of other materials. Note that the Composite Order is applied for æsthetic reasons, apparently supporting the springings of the vaults (coll. JSC).*

Fig. 3.4 ↓ *Mausoleum of Santa Costanza, Rome (c.AD 325 or later), showing paired Composite columns carrying an entablature with pulvinated frieze, forming an arcade supporting a drum and one side of a barrel-vault around the central space, the other outer side supported on massive walls. The barrel-vault covering the circular ambulatory, or aisle, still possesses its original mosaic decorations of geometrical motifs and intertwined vines. Engraving by Piranesi, who exaggerated the scale of what is actually not a large building (coll. JSC).*

Fig. 3.5 ↑ *Interior of Santa Maria Maggiore, Rome, a huge basilica dedicated to Sancta Maria Mater Dei shortly after the Council of Ephesus sanctioned this unquestionably Isiac appellation of the BVM in AD 431. The marble columns of the colonnade carrying the clerestorey are Antique, and the coffered ceiling dates from 1493–8, gilded with some of the first gold brought to Europe from America. The baldacchino is carried on four porphyry columns with spiral designs, a reference to the spiral columns above the tomb of St Peter in the Constantinian basilica, also associated with the Temple of Solomon (AFK H10332).*

mausolea: Santa Costanza in Rome is an example (Fig. 3.4). At the same time, increasingly complex geometries of plan-form were exploited in many projects.

The Orders were used in basilican churches, often looted from earlier structures (Fig. 3.5), and sometimes incorporating whole entablatures and occasionally arches; there are many examples, especially in Rome. The Orders employed in early basilicas tended to be colonnades supporting an entablature above which was the clerestorey (e.g. at Santa Maria Maggiore, Rome), but an important innovation was when a series of arches was substituted, the entablature reduced to small elements immediately above the capitals called dosserets (e.g. the early 4th-century Santa Costanza, Rome). An early example of an arcade carried on columns occurred at Diocletian's palace at Split, but numerous buildings with this feature followed, notably in the celebrated 6th-century churches in Ravenna (e.g. Sant'Apollinare in Classe [534–49], where the clerestorey is carried on arcades set on rows of columns on rectangular bases, and with curiously un-Classical capitals based on the Composite type above which are the dosserets). In the centrally planned octagonal Church of San Vitale, Ravenna (c.532–48), however, the beautiful block-like capitals, making the transition from circular shafts to square dosserets, are carved with delicate lace-like open-work, and have virtually no connection with Classicism, while the bases are stepped and octagonal. Capitals in the great former Church (now a mosque) of Hagia Sophia

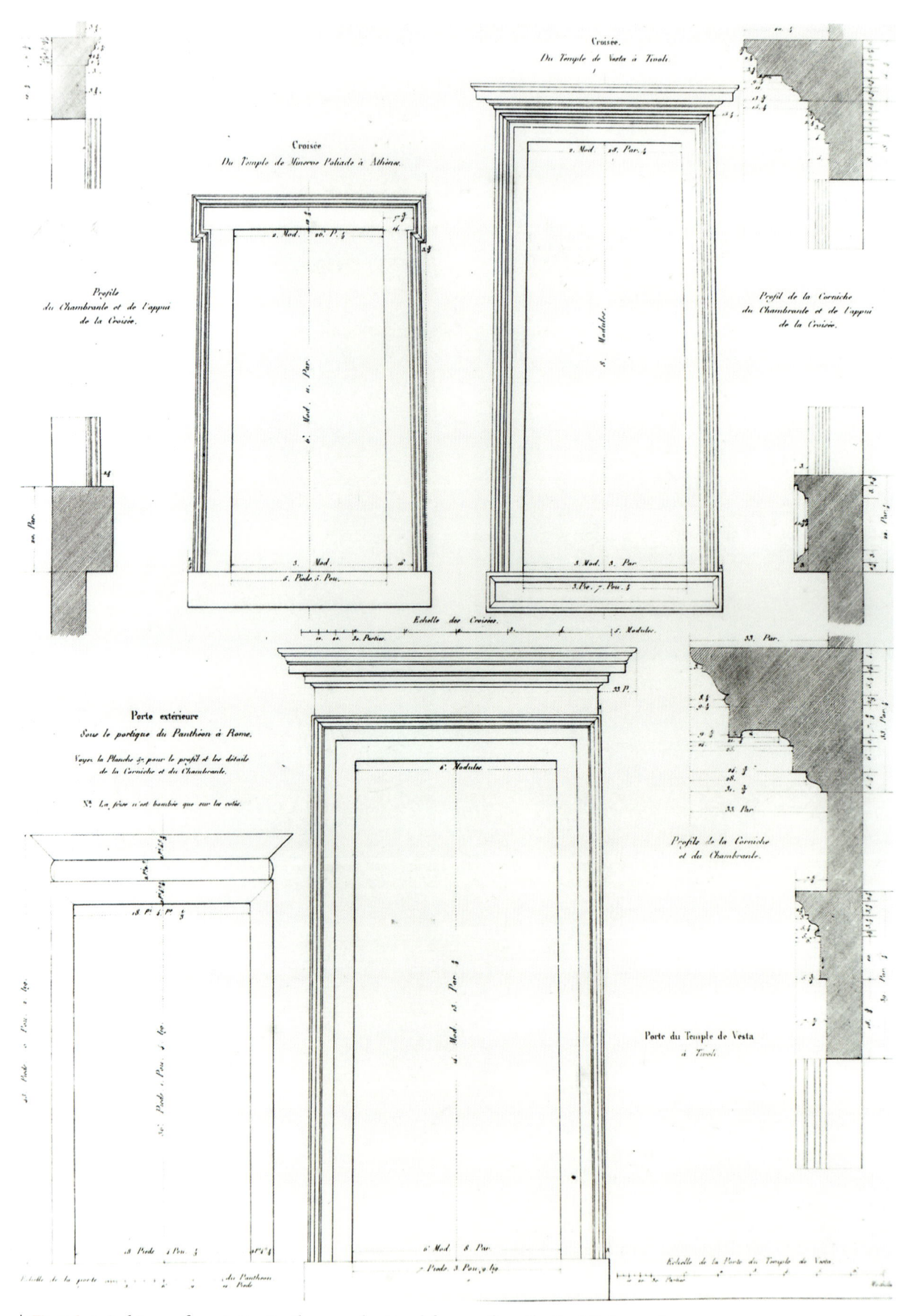

Fig. 3.6 ↑ *Architraves from Antiquity: the example at top left comes from the Erechtheion and has ears. The others are Roman: top right and bottom centre are from the Temple of Vesta at Tivoli, and that at bottom left is from the Pantheon, Rome (Normand [1852], coll. JSC).*

42 / CLASSICAL ARCHITECTURE

Fig. 3.7 → *Roman ornament:*

(a) enrichment of cyma recta moulding showing acanthus and palmette variants;

(b) (left): enrichment of cymatium or cyma recta, with anthemion and acanthus; (right): acanthus enrichment on cavetto moulding;

(c) (left): egg-and-dart over bead-and-reel; (right): variant on egg-and-dart, much enriched with acanthus. Both these examples are, essentially, enriched ovolos, the one on the left having a fillet and bead under;

(d) typical enrichment of cavetto and ogees or cyma reversa;

(e) (left): enrichment of cyma reversa. (right): The two larger examples show enrichment of cyma recta mouldings with acanthus and anthemion variants;

(f) (left): leaf-and-tongue; (right): leaf-and-tongue variant in the form of leaves and acorns;

(g) three examples of enriched cyma reversa mouldings;

(h) astragals ornamented with bead-and-reel
(Normand [1852], coll. JSC).

(532–7), in what was Constantinople (now Istanbul) were even more lavishly decorated, although traces of egg-and-dart and Ionic volutes can be detected in these remarkable confections.

Certainly, Classical elements were employed in church buildings well into the Christian era, and indeed in parts of Italy the Classical thread never seems to have been completely lost. The architecture of the Eastern Empire, which we know as Byzantine, tended to accentuate the arcuated and domed architecture developed by the Romans, and, although columns and other details sometimes suggested Classical prototypes, the pre-eminence of the Orders passed for a while into abeyance.

Concluding Comparative Remarks

Hellenic plans are often very simple, and buildings relatively small. Structure, dictated by the columnar and trabeated form, was limited in scope, and the column was pre-eminent, exploited for the beauty of its form and the expression of its function. Details, such as friezes, metopes, and sculptural elements, were often extremely refined and beautiful, in spite of the limited vocabulary of ornament employed.

Roman structural methods, employing the true arch, the dome, the vault, and concrete, enabled buildings of enormous size to be erected, while plans, employing a variety of geometrical forms, were often complex and intricate, as in the *thermæ*, palaces, and fora, and involved main and subsidiary axes. The mixing of arcuated with columnar and trabeated structural elements (the latter adapted from Hellenistic types) created an entirely new form of architectural expression, and one that was to be of great importance from Renaissance times. The Romans also superimposed different Orders on storeys, continuing a feature invented in Hellenistic times, but added the Orders to arcuated storeys.

Greek colonnades often rendered the openings in walls of lesser importance in external treatment. In the case of a few buildings such as the Erechtheion, however, the door surrounds were given exquisite treatment, with architraves, a cornice carried on consoles, and a pronounced batter, like the shape of an Egyptian pylon (Fig. 3.6; *see* Fig. G114). Roman doorcases were also framed, but the variety of treatment was greater (Figs 3.6 and 3.7).

Windows did not, on the whole, merit architectural emphasis in Greek architecture, but in grander Roman work had segmental heads, or were semicircular with two mullions, the so-called Diocletian window (*see* Fig. G50). High-level windows associated with arcuated and vaulted construction provided lighting even in highly complicated and large buildings. The uses of circular, polygonal, and other forms in plans were often responsible for creating very elaborate effects, and even suggesting swaying convex and concave entablatures over circular plans, as at Baalbek, architectural devices that are akin to 17th-century Baroque designs.

Classical mouldings were evolved as essential elements of architecture, and especially of the Orders. An entablature with no mouldings would be only a beam, while the refinements of detail, of cast shadows, and of ornament, so important in great Classical buildings, enhance the qualities of those buildings, so that their excision would be calamitous.

Mouldings help buildings to weather gracefully, and they can protect detail and sculpture from the elements. Greek mouldings had very graceful sections and were enriched with refined carvings that did not disguise the sections or profiles. Many Greek buildings were of marble, which can be cut to precise degrees of accuracy. Roman decoration is often superabundant, and mouldings are usually segments of circles in section.

Familiar ornaments such as dentils are more widely spaced in Greek than in Roman examples, and are as deep as the moulding on which they are set; Roman dentils often have a fillet below and a small fillet between the dentils at the top; Greek consoles, which are often exquisitely shaped and carved, are used vertically as supports for the cornices of openings, whereas Roman

| Fig. 3.8 ↑ *Lavish Roman ornament (Spiers [1893], coll. JSC).*

consoles also occur set horizontally as modillions on cornices, and on keystones, when they are termed *ancones*.

Honeysuckle ornament is commonly employed in Greek architecture, together with the lotus and scroll. In Roman work the acanthus is the commonest form. Egg-and-dart is taller and more elegant in Greek than in Roman work, while the profile is more subtle.

Roman ornaments, such as dolphins or bay-leaf garlands, are specifically Roman, but there are many instances in which Hellenic–Hellenistic–Roman themes mix, coalesce, and become transmogrified in subtle ways. Discussion of these permutations alone would fill a book; the present Select Glossary and illustrations must suffice to give a flavour of the range of ornament used in Classical architecture (Fig. 3.8; *see* Fig 3.7).

4

THE RENAISSANCE PERIOD

The term Renaissance (from the French renaître *[to be born again]) is given to the great revival of arts and letters under the influence of Antique precedents which began in 14th-century Italy and continued during the following two centuries, spreading to virtually all parts of Europe. It is a convenient label for the styles of architecture that developed in, and were characteristic of, that period from the time of Brunelleschi in Florence (early 15th century) to the beginnings of Mannerism (c.1520), and which were based on the architecture of Roman Antiquity. Indeed, those styles* rinascimentale *were referred to as in* maniera all'antica *[or* alla maniera antica *or* nella maniera antica*], and codified by Alberti in* De Re Ædificatoria *(begun around 1450 and completed 1452), drawing on the exemplary work of Vitruvius.*

JAMES STEVENS CURL AND SUSAN WILSON:
The Oxford Dictionary of Architecture (Oxford: Oxford University Press, 2015, 2016), 625–6.

Modern Rome subsists still, by the Ruins and Imitation of the old.

SIR CHRISTOPHER WREN:
Tracts on Architecture I, quoted in Christopher Wren:
Parentalia, or Memoirs of the Family of Wrens, Stephen Wren (ed.) (1750).
Reprinted in *Publications of The Wren Society*, Vol. **xix** (Oxford: Oxford University Press, 1942), 126.

Columns, Pilasters, Antæ, and Piers

The Orders offered architects a wide range of expression, from the primitive to the luxurious. When the Romans combined columnar and trabeated forms derived from Greek (and especially from Hellenistic [Fig. 4.1]) exemplars with arcuated and vaulted systems, even piled up in storeys, they invented a new type of architecture in which the Orders imposed a system of controlled rhythms on façades and gave a sense of decorum and celebration to the underlying structure. It is important to understand that the vertical and horizontal elements of the Roman Orders were fully integrated with the massive structure, and not simply stuck on. Arcuated and vaulted structures require mass to take the loads. In fact, massive piers carry loads and arches which could not be held by a columnar and trabeated system alone, so the two types of structure are married (*see* Figs 2.17a–2.18b).

This brings us to a consideration of the nature of columns, piers, antæ, and pilasters. Much of Greek architecture had columns supporting entablatures, but occasionally columns were engaged. It is important to distinguish between several kinds of vertical support. Associated with the Orders are columns, antæ, pilasters, and piers. A column is an upright element, circular on plan, and consists of a base (except in the Doric Order), a shaft, and a capital. It tapers towards the top, is of considerably greater length than diameter, and carries the entablature. Sometimes,

Fig. 4.1 ↑ *The temple theme: sarcophagus of the 'weepers from Sidon' in the form of a Hellenistic Ionic temple with 'weepers' in the intercolumniations (HPM, coll. JSC).*

as in the cases of Trajan's Column in Rome, Nelson's Column in Trafalgar Square, or the Downshire Column at Hillsborough, County Down, it stands alone without an entablature, and carries a statue on its abacus. A column can also be engaged, that is attached to a wall or a pier; half or less than half of the diameter of the column can be engaged with, applied to, attached to, or inserted in the mass behind it.

Greek columns were constructed of drums pegged together, and stood on a stepped crepidoma, the top of which was termed the stylobate. Pedestals were used occasionally, as in the Temple of Artemis at Ephesus. Roman columns, on the other hand, were often vast monoliths, and when hard stones like granite were used, they were unfluted (*see* Fig. 2.14c). Greek architects used superimposed Orders inside temples, Hellenistic architects used different Orders superimposed (often with the 'wrong' entablature for the Order of the columns), and the Romans used not only several storeys of different superimposed Orders, but the Orders engaged with arcuated forms (*see* Figs 2.17a–2.18b).

Then there are detached columns, which have a wall behind them (usually quite close) and an entablature connected with the wall. The Romans used this device as well as the fully engaged Order.

A pilaster is shallow, projects from a wall, and is rectangular on plan; it will resemble in all respects the columns of the Order with which it is being used. In other words, it will have a base, its shaft usually will taper and have entasis, it may or may not have flutes, and it will have a capital to match that of the column. It might be used on the wall of a gallery that is open on one side and has columns with an entablature conforming to beams that would be related to the pilasters. So, pilasters are like square columns that have had most of their volume buried in the wall.

Antæ do not necessarily have bases or capitals conforming to the Order with which they are associated: Ionic antæ, for example, do not have volutes at all. Antæ are usually on the terminating features of walls in a Greek or Greek Revival pronaos or portico. Columns set between antæ in a line are called *in antis*. The Romans used pilasters as features on the ends of walls of temple cellæ, but the Greeks used antæ to emphasise, terminate, and strengthen the ends of their naos walls. Antæ do not taper and have no entasis, so they are unlike pilasters, although they have been described as a species of pilaster.

Piers are structural elements of solid material, or the solid mass between openings in a wall. They are quite distinct from columns, although columns or pilasters may be attached to them. Piers themselves do not necessarily have capitals or bases, but they may do, and if so, usually conform to the main mouldings of the Order used in the columns and pilasters. The Colosseum is a prime example of a building with piers carrying arches with engaged superimposed Orders rising in storeys and framing the arches (*see* Figs 2.17a–b).

So, the Romans evolved a development of the Classical language of architecture, and the engaged Order/arcuated structure theme was used further, and with even more variations, by Renaissance architects. Another important Roman theme, that of the triumphal arch, with its varied intercolumniation, engaged or detached columns, entablature breaking forward over the columns, keystones touching the undersides of string-courses and architrave, coffered vaults, and richly ornamented surfaces, was widely adopted by Renaissance designers (*see* Figs 2.18a–b).

A Lingering Presence of Antiquity

There can be no doubt that all through the Middle Ages, Antiquity was never entirely submerged: it was always there, obscure perhaps, and even misinterpreted, but present nevertheless. The first conscious attempts to revive Classicism took place during the Carolingian period of the early 9th century, when some semblance of European imperial unity once more occurred under Charles the Great (Charlemagne). At Aachen, the Chapel Palatine (consecrated 805, and now the cathedral) is an astonishing achievement: derived from the octagonal plan of San Vitale, Ravenna, but with massive piers on the lowest storey, and recognisably Corinthian columns (with polished Antique shafts), it is a conscious attempt to suggest imperial grandeur and a continuation of the Roman Empire, restored in the West when the King of the Franks (from 768) and Lombards (from 774) was crowned emperor by Pope Leo III in 800. Engaged Composite columns can also be seen at the amazing late 8th-century gatehouse of what was once an abbey at Lorsch in the Rhineland. Quite a lot of Antique artefacts seem to have been recycled, though, for in the Church of San Juan Bautista de Baños de Cerrato, Palencia, central Spain (consecrated 661), the capitals (and presumably the column-shafts too) appear to have been re-used from an earlier structure, and in the celebrated and enormous Mezquita in Córdoba (786–990), the columns, with their recognisably Corinthian capitals, are obviously recycled, for some shafts have bases of various heights, while others have no bases at all.

In Italy, however, Classical elements can be found in some mediæval architecture, especially in Pisa and Pistoia cathedrals, while the 11th-century Church of San Miniato in Florence displays certain proto-Renaissance features that point to an attempt to revive Classical architectural forms (*see* Fig. 4.3). Some west fronts of 12th-century churches like those of Notre Dame at Poitiers, Saint-Gilles near Arles, Notre Dame at Échillais (Charente-Maritime), the strange confection at St-Jouin-des-Marnes, Poitou, and the celebrated porch of Saint-Trophîme, Arles, all display vestiges of the composition of a Roman triumphal arch, which is not surprising considering the many Roman remains in what is now France, and the importance of Rome as a place of pilgrimage. Such examplars are described as Romanesque, suggesting a derivation from the architecture of the Roman Empire, and indeed the Romanesque style evolved in western Europe from around 910 and continued until almost the end of the 12th century. In its maturity, it was clear and logical architecture, with thick walls, sturdy piers (usually cylindrical), semicircular arches, barrel-, groin-, and rib-vaults, clearly defined structural bays (the forms and subdivisions easily comprehensible), square or rectangular on plan, and semicircular apses. Its inherent geometrical simplicity also made it impressively powerful: its character was one of dominance. But the semicircular arch set diagonally over a vaulted compartment forced the arches over the sides of the square to be raised on straight walls called stilts, or, if the arches on the sides of the square were not to be so raised, then the diagonal ribs over the vault would have to be segments of an arch. This problem was to be overcome when the pointed arch came into use, enabling the arches to be 'hinged' at their uppermost points, as it were, and able to span compartments without recourse to such clumsy devices. And when considering details, especially capitals, the spirit of Roman Corinthian is never remote in much Romanesque work: it is present in the nave of Pisa Cathedral, in the exquisite coupled columns in the cloisters at Monreale (south-west of Palermo), in the nave arcades at Autun Cathedral (where shafts are fluted as well), and in Modena Cathedral, and in many English parish churches such traces can be found to delight the eye.

In fact, in spite of the clear stylistic differences, it is hard to imagine the development of western European Romanesque and Gothic architecture, especially in the greatest cathedrals and churches, without the precedents of so many Roman buildings; and without the Greek Orders there would not have been those of Rome, or the invention of new, developed, architectural languages that have enriched the world. Even when so-called Gothic evolved ('Pointed' is surely a better term for it), Classicism can still be detected in the overall geometries of the architecture, in details such as those of capitals in Canterbury and Noyon cathedrals and the abbey-church of St-Denis in Paris, and (stunningly) in Siena Cathedral (completed c.1264).

The 'Rediscovery' of Vitruvius

It has been repeatedly claimed that the great Augustan text on architecture by Vitruvius was unknown throughout the so-called Dark and Middle Ages, and was only 'rediscovered' by humanist scholars, notably Poggio Bracciolini in 1416, in the library of the great abbey of St Gallen, in Switzerland, thereby acting as a catalyst for the Renaissance. However, given the obvious and very visible evidence of sophisticated examples of fine architecture erected from the time of Charlemagne, it seems very unlikely that this important work was entirely forgotten, and indeed modern scholarship has revealed that most, if not all, of the early manuscripts of Vitruvius's great treatise can be traced back to a text, written probably in a Carolingian scriptorium around 800, and surviving in the British Library as the Harleian MS 2767, but we do not know what was the model from which that manuscript was copied, or from where it came.

In this respect the importance of England has been occasionally raised, for it has been claimed that an Antique copy was brought from Italy to Northumbria when searches were underway under the ægis of Benedict Biscop (founder of the monastic communities at Monkwearmouth and Jarrow) and Abbot Ceolfrith for books to fill the libraries of the newly founded monasteries there. It is possible that Cassiodorus, Roman statesman, monk, and writer, whose monastery of Vivarium on his Calabrian estates contained a hugely important collection of manuscripts, and who stressed the importance of conserving, copying, and binding ancient Classical texts, possessed a copy of Vitruvius's work, given his eminence under the Ostrogoths and during the Byzantine reconquest of Italy. Could such a copy have been brought to Northumbria? Flaccus Albinus, aka Alcuin, who was a major figure in the revival of learning and letters, spent his formative years in the Northumbrian southeast, and later became a major figure in the cultural affairs of the Carolingian court. If, in fact, collectors from England and elsewhere managed to acquire copies of Vitruvian manuscripts from Italian libraries, this might explain why they were so rare in Italy itself. It is clear, however, that some 80 copies of Vitruvius date from the mediæval period, a few of which have illustrations, including one from the first half of the 10th century, and we know copies survived in the libraries of Cluny in France, Canterbury and Oxford in England, Reichenau in Germany, and St Gallen in Switzerland, all centres from which Vitruvian theories and writings could have influenced architecture. The distinguished German, Einhard, who was educated at Fulda, and later moved to the court at Aachen, studied under Alcuin, and seems to have supervised some of the building works at Aachen: in some of his writings he demonstrated an interest in Vitruvius, and actually ordered that the bricks made to erect his abbey-church at Seligenstadt (literally 'town of the blessed'), on the river Main (831–40), should be based on dimensions recommended by Vitruvius. It should also be remembered that Vitruvius dealt with the design of basilicas in his treatise, and this would seem to have influenced the realisation of some churches. No serious student of Romanesque or early Pointed architecture can fail to detect a residual sense of Vitruvian presence in the architecture, and when we read texts such as those of the Saxon scholar Hugh of St Victor, e.g. the encyclopædic *Didascalicon de Studii Legendi*, written in Paris in the 1120s, just as the Pointed style was beginning to emerge from Romanesque, it is clear that Vitruvius was regarded as the great authority to be studied on the subject of architecture.

So, it would seem that *On Architecture* had been widely known north of the Alps during the early mediæval period, although only one copy appears to have survived in the Italian peninsula, and that was in the great Benedictine abbey at Monte Cassino. Around the middle of the 14th century, however, the Italian poet and humanist Francesco Petrarca (Petrarch) seems to have brought a copy from France and showed it to numerous persons, including Giovanni Boccaccio, so the work was known in Florence and northern Italy before its alleged 'rediscovery' in St Gallen. From that time, Vitruvius's text had a powerful influence, encouraging a view that there was a vast corpus of knowledge, principles, and laws concerning the architecture of Antiquity enshrined within it. In addition, once architecture was based on such rules, it was granted a status among the liberal arts, thereby elevating its practitioners to a social standing above that of the artisan.

However, there was much in Vitruvius, by the time his work re-emerged from comparative obscurity during the early Renaissance period, that had become very confused and obscure, not only because of his linguistic inadequacies, but because of possible errors in the transcriptions of his texts by later recorders. Leon Battista Alberti planned to write some sort of commentary on Vitruvius around 1440, but soon, realising the many problems when trying to interpret and clarify, decided to write his own book, completed in 1452, and published as *De Re Ædificatoria* in Florence in 1485, a work, as previously noted, in very much better Latin than Vitruvius could command.

Key Buildings of the Early Renaissance

Florentine Renaissance architecture of the 15th century has certain similarities at times to 11th-century architecture, but the reappearance of the Orders, complete with entablatures, great *palazzi* capped with the elaborate *cornicione*, and the evolution of astylar façades, first occurred there, with much use of arcuated forms. There can be no question that 11th-century Tuscan proto-Renaissance architecture had a profound influence on Filippo Brunelleschi, whose Foundlings' Hospital in Florence of 1419–24 (Fig. 4.2) has a loggia of arches and sail-vaults carried directly on the abaci of Classical columns; the building aims at an effect of Antiquity, but owes as much to the Church of San Miniato al Monte (Fig. 4.3). His San Lorenzo (from 1421) and Santo Spirito (from 1436) both have domes over the crossings, and both employ sail-vaults over the aisles, but the nave arches rest on a slightly clumsy version of complete Orders (Fig. 4.4), that is, the column with entablature, rather than on the abaci. In fact, the entablatures consist of a cornice, an architrave of three exaggerated fasciæ, and a frieze which is more like a dosseret.

In Brunelleschi's Pazzi Chapel of the 1430s, a Corinthian Order of pilasters is combined with vaults (both the porch and the chapel have a dome on pendentives in the centre) and arches, giving a remarkable and severe Roman effect enhanced by the cabling in the lower third of the pilasters and the gravely subdued decorative treatment. Yet the handling of the corners in the interior is weak, involving fragmentary and return pilasters. In this interesting building the grammar and discipline of Classical architecture were being re-established, not by mere imitation, but by using and reviving the language, yet there are uncertainties, clumsy and hesitant corners, and a sense that nuances of language are not fully understood (Figs 4.5a–d).

Fig. 4.2 ← *Foundlings' Hospital, Florence, arcade by Brunelleschi of 1419–24. Note the long entablature seemingly carried on pilasters, and the arcade with roundels containing sculpture in the spandrels. The columns carry the arches on heightened abaci (BTB).*

Fig. 4.3 ← *West façade of San Miniato al Monte, Florence (c.1090), expressing a basilican church with high clerestoreyed nave with lean-to aisles, features a blind arcade with Corinthian capitals, and the top of the gable is reminiscent of a pediment. The elegant marble cladding appears to have been applied in the 11th century, but subsequently restored, probably several times. In the 13th and 14th centuries this Romanesque building was thought to be a survival from the Roman past, and a model for imitation (Donald McLeish, BTB).*

Fig. 4.4 ↓ *Interior of Santo Spirito, Florence (1434–82), by Brunelleschi. The Corinthian capitals carry somewhat chunky entablatures, so a full Order supports the arches. This is more genuinely 'Antique' than the somewhat hesitant arcade of the same architect's Foundlings' Hospital (see Fig. 4.2) (BTB).*

48 / Classical Architecture

Fig. 4.5a → *Pazzi Chapel in the cloisters of Santa Croce, Florence (1429 and later), originally designed by Brunelleschi. The elegant colonnaded porch suggests a variation on the triumphal arch theme, as well as a prototype of the serliana, but as it was erected after Brunelleschi's death, it may not exactly reflect his original intentions (AH).*

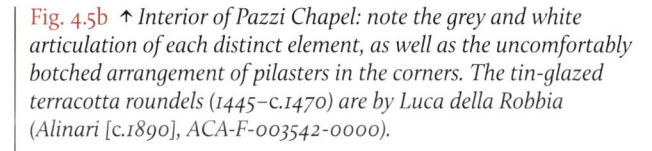

Fig. 4.5b ↑ *Interior of Pazzi Chapel: note the grey and white articulation of each distinct element, as well as the uncomfortably botched arrangement of pilasters in the corners. The tin-glazed terracotta roundels (1445–c.1470) are by Luca della Robbia (Alinari [c.1890], ACA-F-003542-0000).*

Fig. 4.5c ↗ *Pazzi Chapel: section A–A (JSC).*

Fig. 4.5d → *Pazzi Chapel: plan (JSC).*

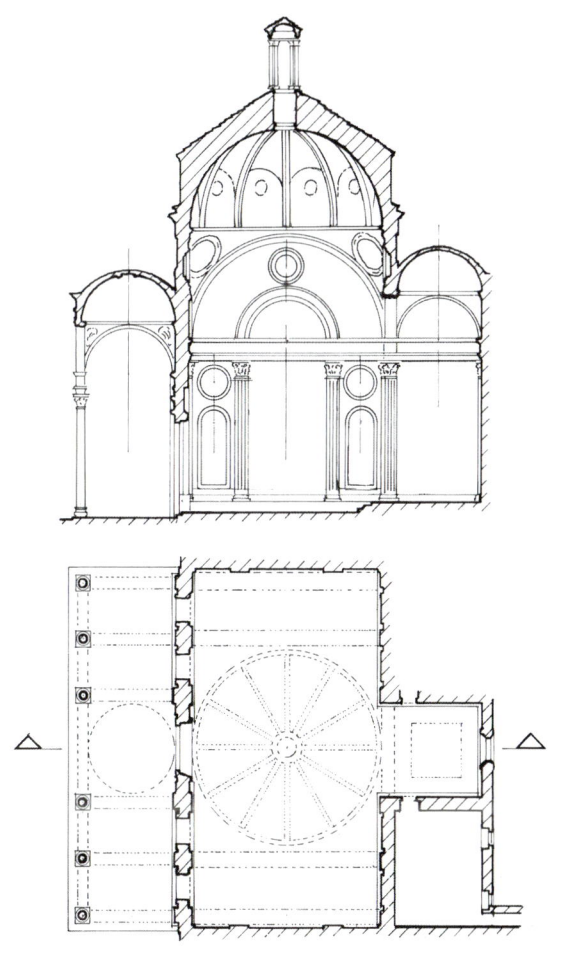

THE RENAISSANCE PERIOD / 49

Fig. 4.6 ← *Triumphal-arch theme yet again: the Church of San Francesco in Rimini, aka Tempio Malatestiano (c.1446–55), by Alberti. This was the first Renaissance example of the application of a Classical façade to a traditional church form, that is, with a high central nave and lower lean-to aisles on either side: although unfinished, its essence is based on the Roman Arch of Augustus at Rimini (27 BC), over which was to be a central arched opening flanked by pilasters, with low segmental screen walls hiding the roofs of the aisles. In the powerful arched openings at the side of the temple are sarcophagi (AFK H11916).*

Fig. 4.7 ↑ *Palazzo Rucellai in Florence (1446–52) by Alberti, the first attempt to apply the Classical Orders to a domestic façade in Renaissance times. Note the superimposed Orders of pilasters, the arches, and the powerful rustication. The executant architect was Bernardo Rossellino (Rosengarten [1893], coll. JSC).*

Fig. 4.8a → *The powerfully astylar rusticated façade of the Palazzo Medici (aka Riccardi), Florence (begun 1444), by Michelozzo Michelozzi, topped by a massive cornicione all'antica. Michelangelo filled in the arches and designed the ground-floor 'kneeling' windows with long consoles under the cills (1516–17) which became such an important feature of Tuscan window design (Rosengarten [1893], coll. JSC).*

50 / CLASSICAL ARCHITECTURE

With Leon Battista Alberti, an architect of genius, Renaissance architecture acquired its first important theorist. His first building, the extraordinary Church of San Francesco at Rimini, known as the Tempio Malatestiano (c.1446–55), incorporates a west front directly inspired by the triumphal Arch of Augustus at Rimini (Fig. 4.6) and robust, arcaded side elevations of a gravely Roman type very like the Colosseum arches *minus the Orders*. In these arches, on the cills, lie the severe Classical sarcophagi of Sigismondo Malatesta's courtiers. In his native city of Florence, Alberti designed the Palazzo Rucellai (from 1446), the first domestic Renaissance building in which each storey is defined by an Order (Fig. 4.7). The base is formed of a continuous ledge with a band carved in a diamond pattern emulating Roman *opus reticulatum*: this makes a plinth on which the Tuscan pilasters stand. The *palazzo* combines the superimposed Orders, channelled rustication of the panels bounded by pilasters and entablatures, and arched windows: the whole has a remarkably Antique feeling about it enhanced by a great *cornicione* derived from the Colosseum.

Almost exactly contemporary is the astylar Palazzo Riccardi in Florence (Fig. 4.8a) (originally the Palazzo Medici) by Michelozzo Michelozzi, aka Michelozzo di Bartolommeo. Building began in 1444, and the three storeys are indicated by string-courses which coincide with the sills of the semicircular-headed windows. The ground floor is faced with cyclopean, or rock-faced, rustication and is pierced with round-headed openings, some of which were filled in and acquired windows designed by Michelangelo in the early 16th century. Voussoirs are boldly expressed. The windows of the *piano nobile* are symmetrically disposed, but are not related to the openings below, although they are to those of the second floor. The whole composition is capped by a mighty *cornicione* that draws heavily on Roman Antiquity, while the plan, too, with its arcaded *cortile* (Figs 4.8b–c) is also derived from Antique prototypes.

Of similar astylar rusticated type with massive *cornicione* is the Palazzo Strozzi, begun in 1489 to designs by Simone del Pollaiuolo, *called* Il Cronaca, and Benedetto da Maiano. These *palazzi* allude to Antiquity in several ways, not least by the manner in which Alberti suggested *opus reticulatum* in the base, the superimposed Orders with arches, and the cornice based on that of the Colosseum in the façade of the Palazzo Rucellai. The arrangements of rooms around a central court or *cortile*, the main rooms on the *piano nobile* above the street level, and much else are not unlike Roman apartment blocks designed a millennium and a half earlier, some of which can still be seen in Ostia and elsewhere; the vestibule from the street, and the central court with rooms disposed about it and with columns at the lowest level owe much to Græco-Roman house plans; and the string-courses and *cornicione* derive directly from Roman buildings. Yet the *cornicione*, with its massive overhang, had no frieze, no architrave, and, in Riccardi and Strozzi, no columnar or pilaster system, so it had to be deliberately oversized. This in itself was a new invention of the Renaissance.

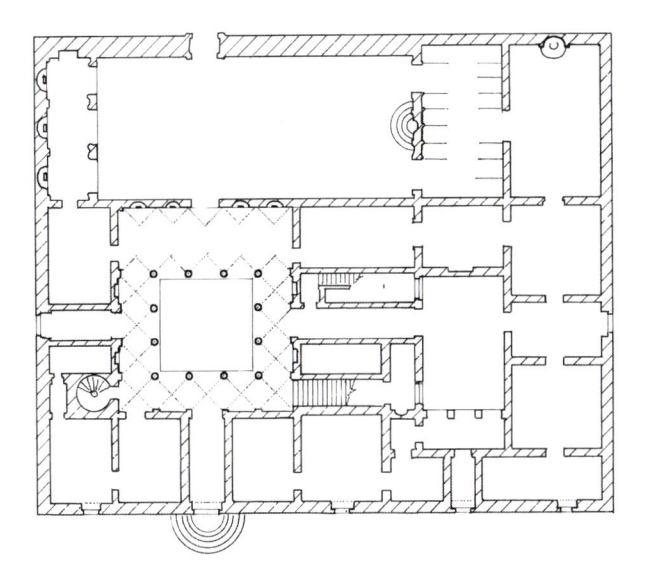

Fig. 4.8b ↑ *Palazzo Medici, Florence: plan organised around an arcaded courtyard* (cortile) *(JSC).*

Fig. 4.8c → Cortile *in the Palazzo Medici, Florence, by Michelozzo, which is basically a rather more robust Composite version of the arcade of the Foundlings' Hospital wrapped round the court, with a correspondingly weak corner detail (coll. JSC).*

THE RENAISSANCE PERIOD / 51

Later *Palazzi*

The internal *cortile* of *palazzi* became more assured in design with the Palazzo della Cancellaria of 1486–96 (Fig. 4.9) and the Palazzo Venezia of 1467–71, both in Rome. In the Venezia the two storeys of arches in the *cortile* have engaged Tuscan and Corinthian Orders and the angles, being piers, are much more confidently handled than in the Palazzo Riccardi (where Michelozzo crashed two arches, based on Brunelleschi's loggia to the Foundlings' Hospital, down on a single column [*see* Fig. 4.8c]); in the Cancellaria (Fig. 4.9) **L**-shaped piers at the corners of the *cortile* successfully terminate the arcades, allowing the arches (which are carried on columns between the piers) to rest on abaci with the archivolts intact. Even more elegant is the corner treatment of the *cortile* of the Ducal Palace at Urbino (1465–79) (Fig. 4.10a) by Luciano Laurana: there, the arcades terminate in **L**-shaped piers, taking Florentine precedent to heights of sophistication. The ends of the **L**-shaped piers have engaged half-columns terminating the arcades, and the front of the piers is faced with two pilasters in the angles, which carry the entablature (Fig. 4.10b).

Clearly related to the *insula*, or block of flats, of Classical Antiquity is a type of *palazzo* with shops set in a heavily rusticated, arcaded ground floor. The House of Raphael of *c*.1512

Fig. 4.9 ← Cortile *of the Palazzo della Cancellaria, Rome, of 1486–96, influenced by Alberti. Note the much more solid manner in which the arcades meet at the corner, although the problem has not been quite resolved (BTB).*

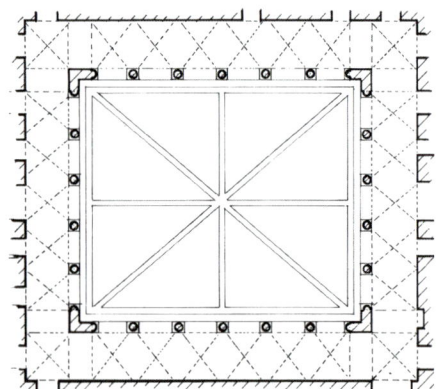

Fig. 4.10a ↑ *Urbino: Plan of the* cortile *at the Palazzo Ducale, Urbino, showing strong and æsthetically satisfactory corners (JSC).*

Fig. 4.10b → Cortile *of the Palazzo Ducale, Urbino (1465–79), by Luciano Laurana, showing the arcades terminating in* **L**-*shaped piers (Alinari [c.1915–20], ACA-F-017520-0000).*

52 / CLASSICAL ARCHITECTURE

by Donato Bramante had a façade of five bays disposed symmetrically about the central axis, with a *piano nobile* separated from the rusticated ground floor by a plain string-course: the *piano nobile* bays were divided by pairs of unfluted Tuscan columns carrying an entablature with three triglyphs over the intercolumniations. Each window had an architrave, over which was a frieze and a triangular pediment. Directly influenced by this design was the Palazzo Vidoni Caffarelli of *c*.1515, attributed to Raphael or to his assistant Lorenzetto, with its *piano nobile* treated in a similar way, but with the pediments over the windows replaced by cornices.

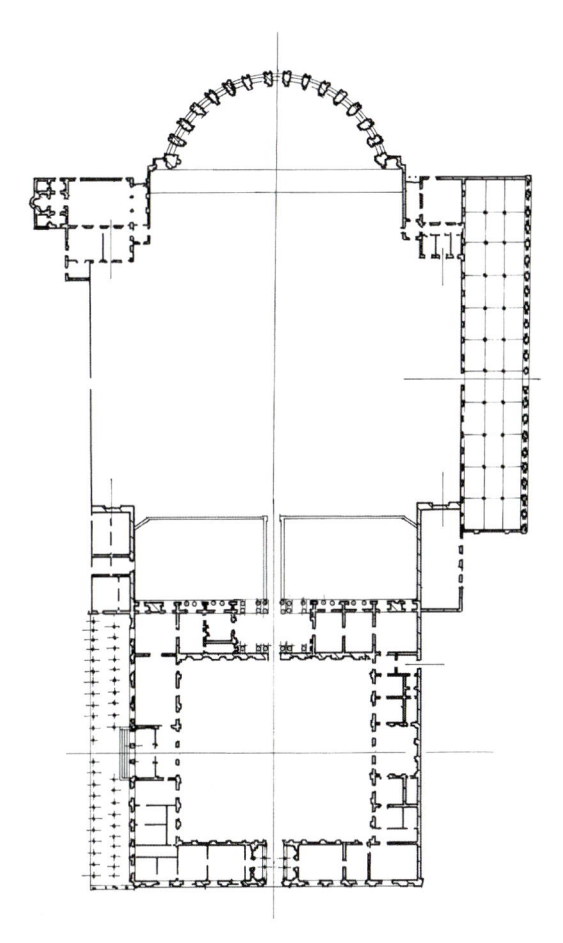

With the Palazzo del Tè in Mantua (Fig. 4.11a) (*c*.1525–34) by Giulio Romano, the plan of an Antique Roman villa is merged with that of Raphael's Villa Madama in Rome (itself much influenced by Roman *thermæ*), begun in *c*.1516, but the elevations are extraordinarily original: one has an Order of Tuscan pilasters carrying a Doric entablature, while the rusticated façade has the string-course-cum-window-sills of the plain upper windows flush with the faces of the pilasters, and tied to the huge keystones of the lower windows; another has repeated overlapping serliana motifs (Fig. 4.11b); and the inner court elevations have keystones that drop down, some triglyphs that are designed to slip below the frieze, bringing the architrave with them in places, and oversized keystones that crash upwards into pediments (Fig. 4.11c). Thus a sense of instability is created and a kind of deliberate dramatic theatricality that is one of the characteristics of Mannerism (described in the Select Glossary). Giulio's Cortile della Mostra (or Cavallerizza), in the Palazzo Ducale at Mantua of 1538–9, has tortured, engaged, irregular spiral columns above a rusticated base, but the columns sit on pedestals carried on chunky rusticated consoles: thus the theme of Raphael's house is mixed with that of the Colosseum, but rendered strangely unstable in this Mannerist creation of *c*.1539 (Fig. 4.11d). Another important Mannerist monument of the period is the Porta Palio in Verona (Fig. 4.12).

Baldassare Peruzzi's Palazzo Massimi alle Colonne, Rome, has a curved façade to the street with Tuscan columns and pilasters on the ground floor arranged in pairs (Figs 4.13a–b); the whole front is rusticated, and the *piano nobile* is separated from the ground floor by an entablature. Above the *piano nobile* are two rows of small windows, the lower of which has architraves with elaborate frames, the patterns of which were to be developed as strapwork by Serlio and disseminated through his publications all over northern Europe. The *palazzo* has two courts, designed to be similar to a Roman atrium, and arranged on two cunningly contrived axes (Fig. 4.13a).

Fig. 4.11a ← *Palazzo del Tè, Mantua: plan (JSC).*

Fig. 4.11b ↓ *Palazzo del Tè, Mantua (c.1525–34), by Giulio Romano: garden front. Repetition and overlapping of the so-called Palladian motif, or serliana (Alinari [c.1915–20], ACA-F-018683-0000).*

THE RENAISSANCE PERIOD / 53

Fig. 4.11c *Palazzo del Tè: part of the elevation of the inner court, containing many Mannerist features. Keystones seem to slip down or up, while the feeling of instability is enhanced by the 'slipping' triglyphs and architraves. However, this may have been an attempt to suggest Antiquity, for many architects had recorded ruined Roman buildings showing such slippages (Alinari [1939], ACA-F-048255-0000).*

Fig. 4.11d *Cortile della Mostra, or Cortile della Cavallerizza, Palazzo Ducale, Mantua (1538–9), by Giulio Romano, an extraordinary tour de force of rustication. The Doric columns have become grotesquely twisted and grooved, probably in reference to the 'Solomonic' columns of St Peter's in Rome. Here is Mannerism carried to extreme lengths (Alinari [1939], ACA-F-048193-0000).*

54 / CLASSICAL ARCHITECTURE

Fig. 4.12 ↑ *Porta Palio, Verona (1540s), by Michele Sanmicheli, a fortified gate that looks as though it could do its job: this impression is given because of the massive rustication, the choice of the Roman Doric Order, and the massive voussoirs and keystones. The effect is increased by the two distinct layers of rusticated masonry, set behind the engaged Order (BTB).*

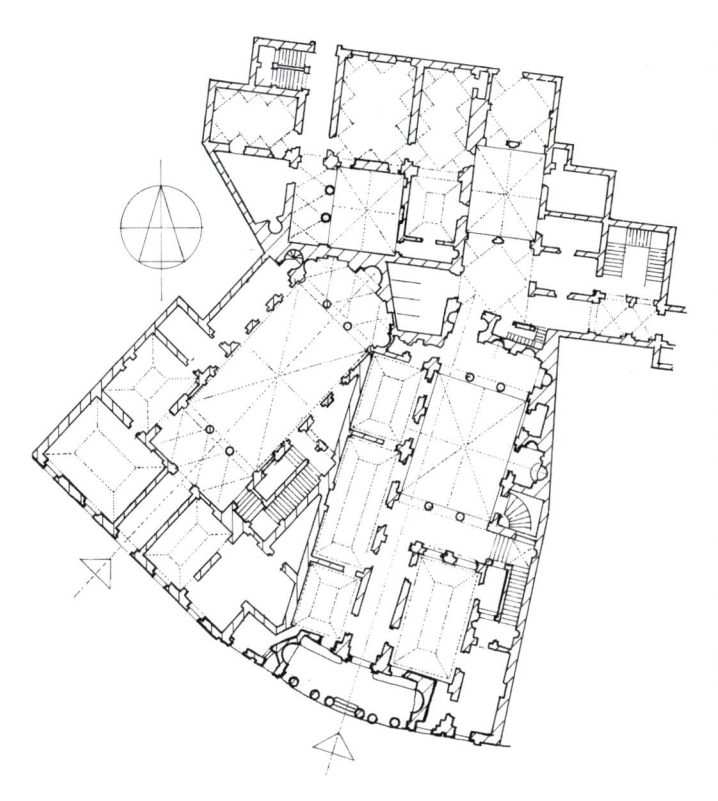

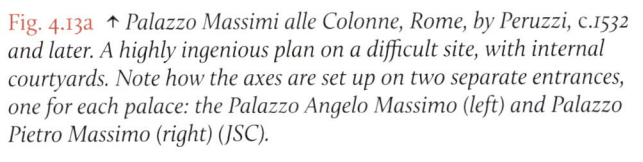

Fig. 4.13a ↑ *Palazzo Massimi alle Colonne, Rome, by Peruzzi, c.1532 and later. A highly ingenious plan on a difficult site, with internal courtyards. Note how the axes are set up on two separate entrances, one for each palace: the Palazzo Angelo Massimo (left) and Palazzo Pietro Massimo (right) (JSC).*

Fig. 4.13b ↗ *Palazzo Massimi: A unique curved façade with pilasters and columns of a severe Tuscan Order with a piano nobile and two smaller floors over it. Note the alternating rhythms of the colonnade. The elaborate frames around the upper windows have Mannerist ornament later developed by Serlio as the strapwork, which became universal in northern Europe during the late 16th and early 17th centuries (BTB).*

Contemporary with the Palazzo Massimi is the huge Roman Palazzo Farnese by Antonio da Sangallo the Younger, but finished by Michelangelo after 1546 (Fig. 4.14a). It is arranged around a central *cortile* that owes much to the Theatre of Marcellus and to the Colosseum for its arcuated superimposed storeys, with engaged Orders (Fig. 4.14b). The main elevation of the *palazzo*, however, with its ædiculated pedimented windows and huge *cornicione*, was immensely influential on later architects: Barry's Reform Club, countless stucco-faced houses in Kensington, and two important astylar buildings in Belfast (*see* Figs 6.43b–c) are directly derived from the Farnese Palace.

THE RENAISSANCE PERIOD / 55

Fig. 4.14a ↑ *The enormous Palazzo Farnese (1515–46), by Antonio da Sangallo the Younger and Michelangelo. The gigantic cornicione is Michelangelo's and the façade is astylar, that is, without columns or pilasters. Floors are separated by cornices and by bands of stone coincident with the cornices of the pedestal supporting the ædicules that frame the windows. This important design was very influential. Note the kneeling windows, especially on the ground floor (BTB).*

Fig. 4.14b ← Cortile *of the Palazzo Farnese, Rome, begun 1515. This clearly derives from the Theatre of Marcellus and the Colosseum, and consists of superimposed Orders with arches. The ground floor has a Doric Order (unfluted), and above is an Ionic Order, also with arches, and above, an Order of Corinthian pilasters. Antonio da Sangallo the Younger was the architect, but Michelangelo was responsible for filling in the arcades of the first floor and rebuilding the top storey (BTB).*

Venetian *Palazzi*, Sansovino, and Alberti

Venetian *palazzi* are quite different. The typical *palazzo* has an entrance at canal level, off which are a staircase and various storerooms above the water level. The *piano nobile* is above, and is given greater architectural expression: the main room is usually in the centre of the front, with smaller rooms on either side expressed by smaller windows, and the *gran salone* is usually indicated in the middle by very large windows. Because such *palazzi* are on restricted sites, and are built on piles, there are not always internal courts. So Venetian *palazzi* have façades that are symmetrical, and rise in distinctly expressed parts, usually three. Typical Venetian *palazzi* façades include Corner-Spinelli of *c*.1480, Vendramin-Calergi of *c*.1500–9 (Fig. 4.15), and the brilliant Palazzo Corner della Ca'Grande (Fig. 4.16), begun in 1537 to designs by Jacopo Sansovino. The last-mentioned *palazzo* has a rusticated lower floor with a triple-arched entrance and a mezzanine, then the *piano nobile* with arched windows and engaged pairs of Ionic columns, and on top a further floor treated similarly, but with paired, engaged Corinthian columns. The mezzanine windows are flanked by volutes, a Mannerist device reminiscent of Michelangelo's work in Florence.

The Palazzo Corner della Ca'Grande (*see* Fig. 4.16) is an example of Orders used above a rusticated ground floor with a mezzanine that becomes, effectively, a plinth or a podium. The Palazzo Vendramin-Calergi (*see* Fig. 4.15) has three superimposed Orders and no rustication, but the tripartite form of the façade is emphasised by flanking the single windows on either side of the façade with pairs of engaged columns. Corner-Spinelli has superimposed pilasters at each end of the front only. Sansovino's Corner della Ca'Grande was the model for later *palazzi*, such as the Palazzo Pésaro (begun 1652) (Fig. 4.17)

Fig. 4.15 ↑ *Palazzo Vendramin-Calergi, Venice, begun c.1500–9, by Pietro Lombardo. This has three storeys of Orders, and the internal arrangement is clear, with the* gran salone *in the middle. The windows, separated by single columns, are of the Venetian type, that is with two arches and a roundel overheld within a semicircular arch (Carlo Naya, Alinari [1865–75], FCC-A-000058-0016).*

Fig. 4.16 ↑ *Palazzo Corner della Ca'Grande, Venice (begun 1537), by Sansovino. The rusticated basement has a triple-arched entrance and there are two superimposed Orders with twin columns rising over (coll. JSC).*

Fig. 4.17 ← *Palazzo Pésaro, Venice, of the late 17th century, by Longhena. Note the heavily rusticated plinth and the two superimposed Orders between the columns of which is an arrangement of arched windows carried on subsidiary Orders (Carlo Naya, Alinari [1870–80], AVQ-A-002026-0013).*

THE RENAISSANCE PERIOD / 57

Fig. 4.18a *Biblioteca Marciana, Venice (begun 1536, by Sansovino, completed by Scamozzi, 1588), one of the first fully Classical buildings of the Renaissance in which superimposed Orders were convincingly used. On the right is the Loggetta, also by Sansovino, begun 1537 at the foot of the campanile, in which the triumphal-arch theme is dominant (coll. JSC).*

Fig. 4.18b *Detail of the Biblioteca Marciana, Venice. There are two superimposed Orders with reference to the Theatre of Marcellus, Rome. The corner is ingenious, for Sansovino used a Doric Order with heavy piers and got a full half-metope at the angle. The Ionic Order above is taller, of course, and the problems of proportion are solved by carrying the arches on a subsidiary Ionic Order of fluted columns (the main columns are unfluted). Notice the rich entablature with the high carved frieze that does not conform to standard rules of proportion (Rosengarten [1893], coll. JSC).*

and Palazzo Rezzonico (begun 1667) by Baldassarre Longhena, but these, with their rusticated basements, luxurious carving, and deeply recessed modelling, add Baroque extremes to the Sansovinoesque theme.

Sansovino used the superimposed Orders with arches to even sturdier effect at the great Biblioteca Marciana, begun in 1536 and completed by Vincenzo Scamozzi in 1588. The references to Antiquity are to the Theatre of Marcellus and to Vitruvius. Sansovino used heavy piers at the corners of the library, and a half-metope to turn the frieze (Figs 4.18a–b), with pilasters slightly wider than the Roman Doric columns on each face of the pier. The Ionic Order on the first floor means that this floor

58 / CLASSICAL ARCHITECTURE

Fig. 4.19 ↑ *West front of Santa Maria Novella, Florence (1456–70), by Alberti, a variation on the problem of providing a façade for the traditional basilican shape of clerestoreyed nave and lean-to aisles, and was very influential. In the centre, the Orders framing the door and the blind arcade merge the triumphal-arch theme with the San Miniato treatment. The pediment is carried on an entablature and four pilasters, suggesting a temple-front, and the huge scrolls conceal the aisle roofs (BTB).*

Fig. 4.20a ↑ *Triumphal-arch theme: west front of Alberti's Church of Sant'Andrea, Mantua (begun 1472), showing the triumphal arch with superimposed pediment instead of an Attic storey (Alinari [c.1915–20], ACA-F-018652-0000).*

is taller than the ground floor; the problem of such a difference in height is resolved by carrying the arches of the first floor on a subsidiary pair of small Ionic columns, fluted to make them even more jewel-like compared with the massive, unfluted shafts of the main Orders. The chunky entablature has an ornate frieze with swags, and is pierced with small windows; it is crowned by a balustrade with statues on the pedestals. Thus the Colosseum-Marcellus theme acquired even greater richness of expression.

Next to the library, Sansovino's La Zecca (the Mint, completed in 1545) has a rusticated astylar arcade as the ground floor, over which are two (originally one) storeys of dramatically 'Rustic Orders', that is, with banded columns, which became a common feature throughout Europe from the later 16th century, after it was made familiar by Serlio in his textbooks.

Alberti's Classical solution to the west front of the Tempio Malatestiano (*see* Fig. 4.6) was followed by his completion of the marble polychrome façade of Santa Maria Novella in Florence (begun 1458) (Fig. 4.19). There, he created a grandly Antique effect, vaguely suggestive of a remembered triumphal arch over which was a tetrastyle temple-front with pediment. There are close geometrical relationships between the various parts of the façade and the whole. Alberti's invention of large volutes on either side of the upper 'temple'-front to hide the tops of the aisles was to prove very influential in the coming three centuries.

Alberti's conscious drawing on Roman exemplars is nowhere more clear than in his great Church of Sant'Andrea in Mantua, designed 1470 and begun 1572 (Figs 4.20a–c). The plan is cruciform and the nave is roofed with a gigantic barrel vault, the largest and heaviest to be erected since Antiquity, painted to suggest it is coffered. To carry this, Alberti drew on the structural principles of Roman *thermæ*, and formed massive abutments at right angles to the axis of the nave, between which he created large and small chapels in what would have been the 'aisles'. The elevation of the nave arcades consists of three interlocked triumphal arches, and the west front combines an Antique temple with a triumphal arch that echoes the arches of the interior. So Alberti used several motifs from Roman Antiquity, and combined them in a logical and consistent manner. Bramante's designs for the Belvedere Court at the Vatican also employed repeated versions of the triumphal-arch theme.

Fig. 4.20b ↑ *Triumphal-arch theme: interior of Sant'Andrea, Mantua, by Alberti and Luca Fancelli, with its series of alternating large and small spaces opening off the barrel-vaulted nave, giving the effect of a series of overlapping triumphal arches (Alinari [c.1915–20], ACA-F-018800-0000).*

Fig. 4.20c → *Plan of Sant'Andrea, Mantua: note the massive wall-piers, hollowed out, between which are side chapels (JSC).*

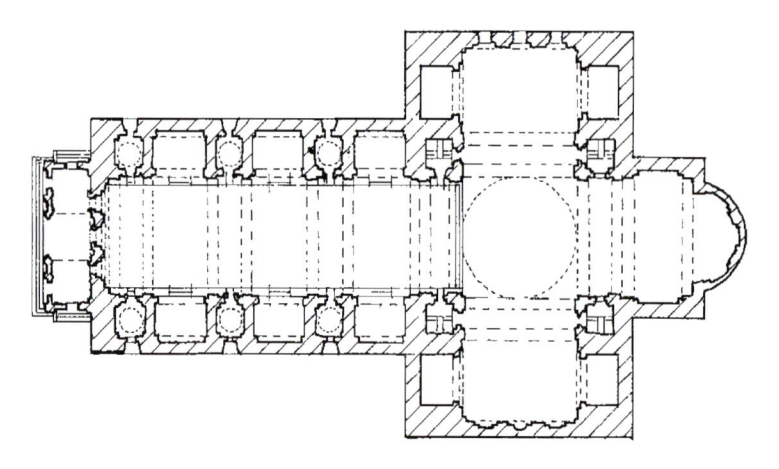

Centralised and Circular Plans

Thus, so far, the Orders, the Colosseum, the triumphal arch, *thermæ*, various vaults, domed and arched forms, the pedimented temple-front, and the house with its courtyard or atrium, all had played their parts in Renaissance architecture, together with quotations from great Roman entablatures in the *cornicione* of many a *palazzo*. However, although the rectangular Classical temple was alluded to as a pedimented temple-front in Renaissance and post-Renaissance architecture until the *whole* temple form was revived in the 18th century, the *circular* temple was of considerable importance as a model from quite early in the history of Renaissance architecture. The Pantheon was, of course, *the* great Roman circular temple, with its vast drum, dome, and Corinthian pedimented portico (Fig. 4.21; *see* Figs G87 and 2.14c).

Early in the Italian Renaissance, architects began to concern themselves with centralised, circular, or polygonal plans. Brunelleschi's octagonal dome for Florence Cathedral (relating to the freestanding octagonal baptistry which, like San Miniato, was thought at the time to be a survival from Antiquity), and his plan of *c.*1434 for Santa Maria degli Angeli in Florence (Fig. 4.22), which is related more closely to the Antique Temple of Minerva Medica in Rome (Fig. 4.23), are examples of this. Of course, the crossings of San Lorenzo and Santo Spirito, Sant'Andrea at Mantua, the old sacristy at San Lorenzo, and the Pazzi Chapel all

60 / CLASSICAL ARCHITECTURE

Fig. 4.21 ← *The prototype of large centrally planned churches is the Pantheon in Rome (c.AD 118–c.128), aka Santa Maria Rotonda, in which a great circular space is roofed by a coffered dome of brick and concrete (unreinforced with steel, of course) on a massive brick drum which probably featured three storeys of arcades corresponding to the three tiers of relieving arches which can be seen on the exterior. The coffers were originally covered with stucco with moulded edges, with gilded bronze rosettes in their centres. Note the marble columns* in antis *leading to the exedræ built into the thickness of the wall. Projecting ædicules for altars are, of course, later additions, as is much of the marble facing to the walls and floor. The upper part of the circular wall, for example, was lined with marble pilasters, redesigned with panels and pedimented recesses in the 18th century (coll. JSC).*

have domed structures, but the full expression of a circular form was still to come. Important developments of Brunelleschian ideas of centrally planned churches were Santa Maria delle Carceri at Prato (begun 1485) by Giuliano da Sangallo and Santa Maria del Calcinaio, Cortona (late 15th century), by Francesco di Giorgio.

Palladio was to recognise Donato Bramante, the first of the so-called High Renaissance architects, as the first to bring the gravity of Antiquity into the light of day, although there can be no doubt of Alberti's influence on Bramante. It was Bramante who, at Santa Maria presso San Satiro (Fig. 4.24) in Milan, built a dome with the first coffered interior since Antiquity, and made the east end appear as a deep chancel by means of theatrical perspective techniques, although it is, in fact, only a shallow recess. The dome sits over a **T**-shaped plan, and attached to the cross-arm of the **T** is the chapel of San Satiro, a Greek cross inside a square within a drum: this is the ancestor of many later churches, and has an octagonal clerestorey supporting a drum. In this chapel, Antique, Early Christian, and Brunelleschian prototypes merge. A centralised domed plan also occurs at Bramante's Santa Maria delle Grazie in Milan, of the later 1480s.

Bramante went to Rome in 1499. His first works there are of considerable importance: the elegant cloisters of Santa Maria della Pace (Fig. 4.25), begun in 1500, and the tiny *tempietto* in the *chiostro* of San Pietro in Montorio of 1502 (Fig. 4.26). The latter heralded a revival of interest in some of the circular temples of Antiquity (of which the temples of Vesta, in Rome and in Tivoli, were examples [see Figs G107c and 2.15a–b]). Circular plans were based on Antique forms it is true, but they do have important precedents in the martyria of early Christian churches. Bramante's Tempietto has a drum surmounted by a dome, and is surrounded by a peristyle of the Tuscan Doric Order, with two triglyphs over each intercolumniation; the

Fig. 4.22 → *Santa Maria degli Angeli, Florence (begun 1434): the plan is based on Roman Antique examples, e.g. the Temple of Minerva Medica, Rome (JSC).*

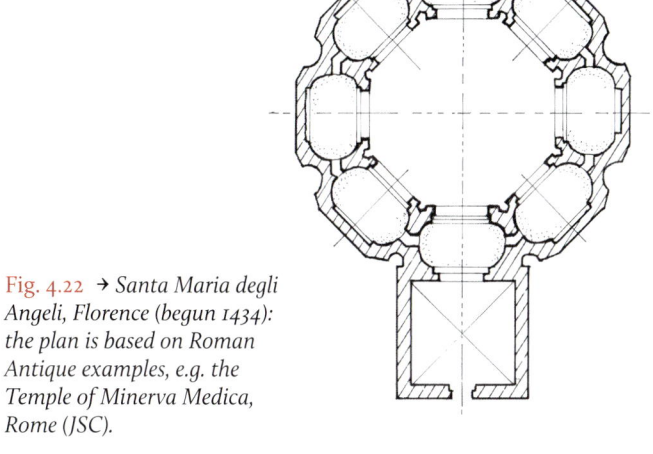

Fig. 4.23 → *(Left) Temple of Minerva Medica, Rome, c.AD 250; (right) east end of Santissima Annunziata, Florence (begun 1444), by Michelozzo di Bartolommeo. An example of a Renaissance architect evolving a solution to a problem by reference to Classical Antiquity (JSC).*

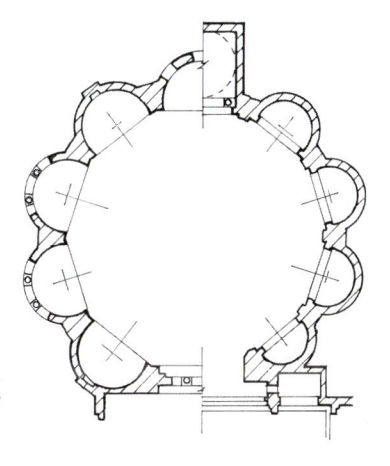

THE RENAISSANCE PERIOD / 61

Fig. 4.24 → *Plan of Santa Maria presso San Satiro, Milan, by Bramante and others, notably Giovanni Antonio Amadeo. (Top) Chapel of San Satiro, (bottom) baptistry (JSC).*

effect is graceful, serene, and Antique. Tuscan Doric was used because of its association with the strong masculine character of St Peter, whose martyrdom the building commemorates by its circular form. The Tempietto was to have had a remodelled circular cloister around it, with a concentric row of columns, and a thick wall embellished with niches and deep, chapel-like recesses: the whole design contained the essential elements of its creator's great centralised plan for the rebuilding of St Peter's in Rome.

Bramante and Pope Julius II determined in 1505 to restore, revive, and complete the choir of the Constantinian Basilica of St Peter (*see* Fig. G27a–b), which Nicholas V had begun to rebuild in the 1450s. Bramante's elaborate geometry for the east end is modelled on his Tempietto and cloisters at San Pietro in Montorio, and indicates that originally the idea was probably to create a suitable martyrium-type centralised form for the enclosure of the tomb of the Prince of the Apostles. It should

Fig. 4.25 ↑ *The Order and the arch: cloister of Santa Maria della Pace, Rome (1500–4), by Bramante. Note the columns over the centres of each arch: if the arches were not there the very wide spacing of the pilasters attached to the piers would look weak. It was a legacy of the Roman joining of columnar/trabeated and arcuated forms which produced this expression, so exploited in the Renaissance period (AFK G23926).*

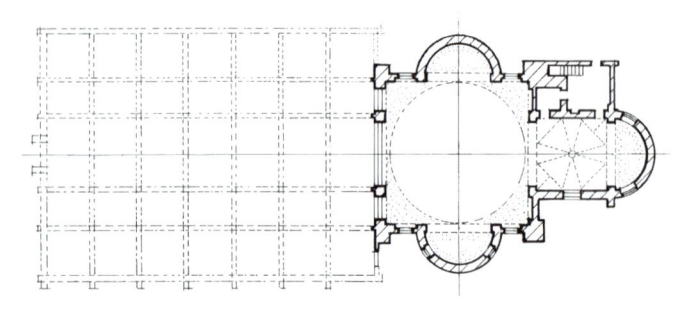

Fig. 4.26 ↑ *Bramante's Tempietto in the chiostro of San Pietro in Montorio, Rome (1502), on the traditional site of the martyrdom of St Peter. It is based on early Christian martyria which were nearly always centrally planned, and served as memorials: the Pantheon was used as a martyrium by the Church, and later became the burial place of distinguished men. Thus the Tempietto is related to circular Antique temples such as the Temple of Vesta, to the Pantheon, and to martyria. Bramante therefore re-created Antique forms, and used a central drum surrounded by an unfluted Doric peristyle and surmounted by a dome. The severity of the Doric entablature and the Tuscan columns was felt to be appropriate to the character of the saint, and Bramante used Antique shafts of granite with new marble capitals and bases. In the metopes are representations of objects used in the Christian liturgy (BTB).*

Fig. 4.27 ← *Plan of Santa Maria delle Grazie, Milan (begun 1493), showing the domed chancel, by Bramante (JSC).*

Fig. 4.28a ↑ *The Giant Order was used by Michelangelo for the apses of St Peter's Basilica in Rome, and the theme was continued by Carlo Maderno in the west front (1606–12). Note that the tetrastyle arrangement of columns under the pediment in the centre is engaged and not prostyle. Above the main entablature is an Attic storey crowned by statuary. On the left is an ancient Egyptian obelisk erected 1585–6 by Domenico Fontana. Bernini then added the huge elliptical colonnades of the Tuscan Order from 1656, part of which is visible on the right (AFK H8796).*

Fig. 4.28b → *Interior of St Peter's, Rome, showing the Giant Order of coupled Corinthian pilasters used on the piers in the nave (1607–c.1614, by Maderno), great coffered vault, domed crossing, and baldacchino (1624–33, by Bernini), with its Solomonic columns (coll. JSC).*

be remembered that Bramante had added a centralised domed form with apsidal projections to the existing Church of Santa Maria delle Grazie in Milan (Fig. 4.27), and that both the Church of the Holy Sepulchre and the Church of the Nativity in the Holy Land each had a martyrium combined with a basilica. However, the loss of the great domed Church of Hagia Sophia in Constantinople to the Ottoman Turks in 1453 probably acted as a catalyst to the idea of rebuilding the whole of the hallowed basilica rather than just the choir, east end, and bema.

The building history of St Peter's is complicated and confused; it is generally assumed that Bramante proposed a huge centralised church based on a Greek-cross plan, but this assumption mostly derives from a half-plan in the Uffizi Gallery in Florence, and on a medal of 1506 which shows a rebuilt elevation of the church. Bramante was succeeded as architect by Raphael, who, according to the evidence of Serlio, proposed a design based on a Latin cross. Bramante's dome was about the same diameter as that of the Pantheon, and was to have a similar stepped profile, but raised up on a colonnaded drum and surmounted by a lantern. Antonio da Sangallo the Elder's great Church of San Biagio at Montepulciano (1518–34) is a Greek cross on plan with a dome over the crossing, and was to have had two twin towers flanking the pedimented west front, so it is both a martyrium and very like Bramante's design for St Peter's shown on the medal. When Michelangelo succeeded Antonio da Sangallo the Younger as architect to St Peter's in 1547, he reverted to a centralised plan, raised the dome to a more pointed section than Bramante's version, and introduced a heroic Giant Order of pilasters with an Attic storey over for the scheme of the façades. The Latin cross returned when Carlo Maderno added the nave and the west front, completed in 1612 (Figs 4.28a–b).

The early Renaissance saw a rediscovery of Antiquity, and architects mixed direct quotation with a somewhat hesitant compositional technique. Even what we today call the High Renaissance was hardly easy in its use of Antique forms, but with Bramante the spirit as well as the letter of Antiquity was recalled in some of his remarkable buildings, notably the Tempietto and its great successor.

Fig. 4.29 ← *Medici Chapel (New Sacristy) in San Lorenzo, Florence (1520–34), by Michelangelo, for Cardinals Giovanni de' and Giulio de' Medici (who became popes Leo X and Clement VII respectively), intended as the mausoleum for the House of Medici. Note the sarcophagus with scrolled segmental top carrying heroic figures of Dawn and Twilight, and the blank niches with large segmental pediments. The doors have cornices but no frieze, and the oversized consoles seem to have slipped downwards, almost crushed by the massive ædicules over. The idiosyncratic detail is characteristic of Mannerism (Alinari [c.1890], ACA-F-002234-0000).*

Michelangelo

During the 16th century in Italy, after the deaths of Bramante and Raphael, the imitation of Classical details gave way to a novel disposition of elements, and even the invention of new, non-historical, vocabularies of ornament. Michelangelo Buonarrotti's design for the Medici Chapel (begun 1519), attached to the Church of San Lorenzo in Florence, is an example of the trend, with its wall surfaces treated as many-layered planes, its blind ædicules crushing the doors below (which have architraves and cornices but no friezes, so their sense of compression is increased), and its deliberate distortion of academic Classicism (Fig. 4.29).

Even more extraordinary is the stair to the library of San Lorenzo, with its columns set in recesses, above pairs of consoles fixed to the dies of the pedestals, and the strange blind ædicules with the pilasters tapering towards their bases (Fig. 4.30). Such freedom, even licence, in which motifs are used in opposition to their original meaning, significance, or even content, is known as Mannerism (*see* Select Glossary). Giorgio Vasari, in his account of Michelangelo, described the 'composite' nature of Michelangelo's 'varied and original' ornament, and praised the latter's 'licence' for freeing design from 'measure, order, and rule', thus enabling craftsmen to break from the bonds and chains of usage. But is all this 'licence' really something quite new? Does the composition not owe something to the rhythms present in the treatment of the interior of the Roman Pantheon, albeit transformed? A tribute to Antiquity, perhaps?

On occasion, however, decoration and encrustation of the architecture could get out of hand, as in the *cortile* of the Palazzo Marino, Milan, by Alessi (Fig. 4.31).

After he settled in Rome, Michelangelo designed the buildings on the Capitoline Hill in which he introduced the historically important precedent of the Giant Order, uniting

Fig. 4.30 ↑ *Vestibule to the library of San Lorenzo, Florence (1524–34), by Michelangelo. The ædicules are very odd, with their flanking pilasters like inverted obelisks. Even more curious are the pairs of columns set in recesses and standing over consoles: they are actually set on an earlier wall, so their expression is probably logical, yet the effect is unsettling and strange, as we associate columns with structure, and not as elements in recesses. The capitals, with their elongated necks, are loosely Tuscan Doric, but the abaci are anything but Doric, and owe more to the Corinthian Order. This unexpectedness and freedom with Classical motifs sum up the essence of Mannerism (Alinari [c.1890], ACA-F-001907-0000).*

the storeys within the frame of the Order (Figs. 4.32a–b). The lower storeys had smaller Orders which carried entablatures rather than arches, and the upper windows were ædiculated, with segmental pediments: a Mannerist affection for complexity of plane and detail is demonstrated in these great buildings.

Fig. 4.31 ← Cortile of Palazzo Marino, Milan (begun 1558), by Galeazzo Alessi, where decorative sculpture almost overwhelms the Orders. An example of Mannerism (BTB).

Fig. 4.32a ↓ The Capitoline palaces, Rome (begun c.1539), one of the most coherently planned ensembles of the 16th century, the three buildings disposed symmetrically around the trapezoidal Piazza del Campidoglio, in the centre of which is a Roman bronze equestrian statue of Emperor Marcus Aurelius. The piazza, designed by Michelangelo, but not completed by the Rainaldis until the mid-17th century, widens towards the central Palazzo del Senatori (completed 1600), with (left) the Palazzo Nuovo (Capitoline Museum, 1603–60), and (right) Palazzo dei Conservatori (1561–84). Of the Palazzo del Senatori façade, only the double-ramped stair was designed by Michelangelo, the rest by Martino Longhi the Elder. The façade of the Palazzo dei Conservatori was by Michelangelo, employing a Giant Order of pilasters carrying a weighty entablature over which is a balustrade crowned with statuary, and this was replicated for the Palazzo Nuova (coll. JSC).

Fig. 4.32b → The Capitoline Museum (Palazzo Nuovo), Rome, from designs erected 1644–60 under Girolamo and Carlo Rainaldi, modelled on the Palazzo dei Conservatori by Michelangelo and Giacomo della Porta, which stands across the Piazza del Campidoglio, and was completed in 1584. The most important innovation was the use of the Giant Order of Corinthian pilasters carrying the massive entablature in order to give the two-storey building the character of a mighty temple. Note the subsidiary Ionic Order on the lower level (where the span of the entablature is exceedingly wide), and the ædiculated windows on the second floor. The Antique statue of Emperor Marcus Aurelius is on the left (BTB).

THE RENAISSANCE PERIOD / 65

The Giant Order, as mentioned above, also was an important element in the design of St Peter's.

George Clarke drew on the Palazzo dei Conservatori on the Capitoline Hill for his great library, Peckwater Quadrangle, Christ Church, Oxford (1717–38), a satisfyingly robust design, in which pilasters were replaced by engaged columns, and simplification added to its success as a work of architecture (Fig. 4.32c).

Michelangelo's further inventiveness is demonstrated at the Porta Pia (Fig. 4.33) in Rome of 1561–4: in the centre a broken segmental scrolled pediment is set within a triangular pediment, and the surrounds to windows and other openings became even more complex. Michelangelo's Mannerism was to offer architects of the Baroque period many potent precedents.

Fig. 4.32c ↑ *The library, Peckwater Quadrangle, Christ Church College, Oxford, erected 1717–38 to designs derived from the Palazzo dei Conservatori, Rome, by George Clarke, who replaced the Giant Order of pilasters with engaged columns, introduced alternating triangular and segmental pediments over the upper windows, and used a subsidiary Order of Doric pilasters on the ground floor, with the spaces between the pilasters filled in and punctured with semicircular-headed windows, making the whole thing look more stable (RCR, coll. JSC).*

Fig. 4.33 ← *Porta Pia, Rome (1561–4), by Michelangelo. Mannerist tendencies present in earlier works have become extreme. A broken segmental scrolled pediment with swag sits inside a triangular pediment, while oversized guttæ hang below blocks on either side of an element which resembles a Diocletian window. Ionic capitals, freely interpreted, become copings for the crenellations, while the ædicules and frames around the windows and panels are deliberately oversized and blocky: the panels have broken scrolled ʃ-shaped pediments holding a broken segmental pediment between them, while curved crossettes sit under the ears of the architrave. The roundels above have simplified drapes over them that clearly influenced Brongniart and other French Neo-Classicists 250 years later. The side piers were to be capped by obelisks, while the Attic storey has elements of Baroque exuberance (AFK G19658).*

Serlio and Vignola

The second part of the 16th century saw not only much building, but a growing familiarity with rules, knowledge of precedents, and Antiquity. A considerable part of this familiarity was achieved through printed sources.

Sebastiano Serlio not only published his treatise on architecture, and in so doing codified the Orders and publicised the styles of Bramante and Raphael, but also established a French centre of Mannerism at Fontainebleau. Serlio's work was translated into Flemish, German, Spanish, and French, and in 1611 an English version of the Dutch edition was published; his illustrations showed Antique and modern architecture, including many elaborate and showy Mannerist features, which were copied indiscriminately and applied to what were really late-mediæval buildings in France, Germany, and England (Fig. 4.34).

Classicism was exported from Italy during the 16th century largely through two influences: the printed treatise and the important precedent of the Church of Il Gesù in Rome, by Giacomo Barozzi da Vignola and Giacomo della Porta (Figs 4.35a–c). Certainly, the influence of Serlio in northern Europe produced some very curious instances of applied ornament; while true Italian Classical architecture appeared in Spain in the palace of Charles V in Granada of 1526, it did not occur in

Fig. 4.34 ↑ *Order upon Order: five Orders piled up and superimposed on a late-Gothic gate-tower. Tuscan carries Doric, which carries Ionic, which carries Corinthian, which carries Composite, the whole capped with exuberant strapwork and other ornament framing the royal arms. On the fourth storey is a sculptured group beneath an elaborate canopy featuring King James VI and I presenting a female figure (representing the university) with a copy of his collected writings, attended by a figure of Fame blowing a trumpet: it was carved by John Clark. This Classical frontispiece is in the Schools Quadrangle, Oxford (completed 1620), and is probably by John Akroyd, with John and Michael Bentley, perhaps influenced by Sir Henry Savile. The sources are Italo-French Renaissance (JSC).*

Fig. 4.35a ↑ *West front of the Church of Santissima Nome di Gesù, called Il Gesù, Rome, the prototype of thousands of churches thereafter. It is a solution to the old problem of how to put a Classical façade on a clerestorey and nave with lean-to aisles. Designed by Vignola and begun 1568, the façade as built was modified by Giacomo della Porta from 1573. It is of two storeys, with superimposed Orders of pilasters and columns, and the roofs of the 'aisles' (they are actually chapels so we refer to this type of plan as wall-pier) are hidden behind scrolls. This device derives from Alberti's Church of Santa Maria Novella, Florence, but because Il Gesù was the mother-church of the Jesuits, the Vignola-della Porta design had far-reaching effects. Mannerist tendencies merge with the Baroque (Anderson Alinari [c.1890], ADA-F-000092-0000).*

THE RENAISSANCE PERIOD / 67

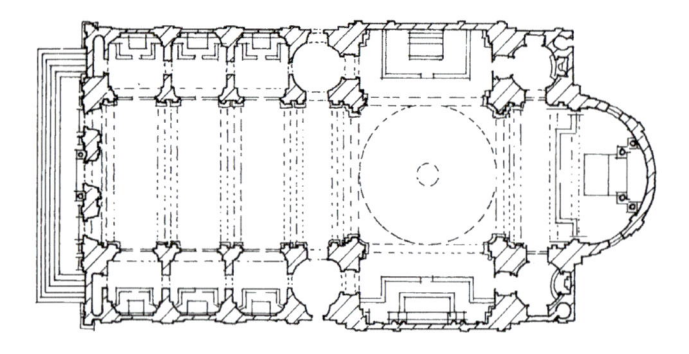

Fig. 4.35b ↑ *Il Gesù, Rome, showing the wall-pier arrangement with side chapels instead of aisles, the apsidal east end, and cupola over the crossing (JSC).*

Fig. 4.35c → *Interior of Il Gesù, Rome, showing the clear view towards the high altar: the rich Baroque illusionistic frescoes and coloured marbling were subsequently applied to Vignola's design which was originally intended to be far more austere (AH).*

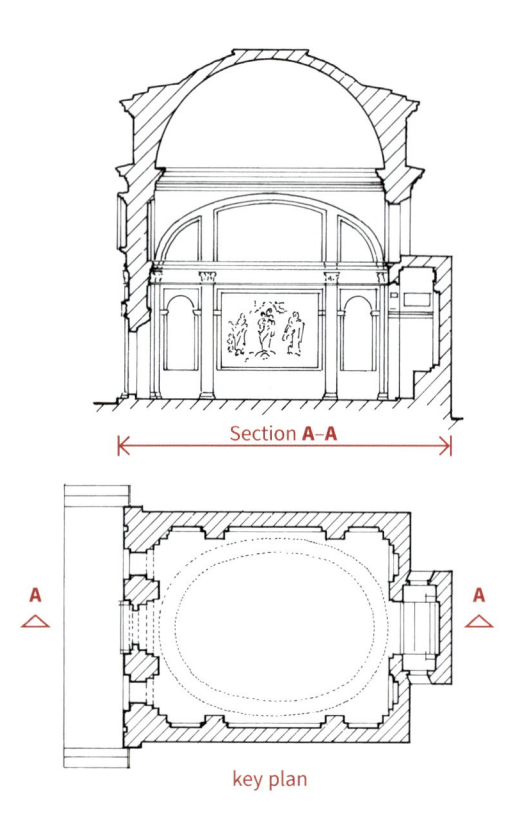

Fig. 4.36a ↑ *Sant'Andrea, Via Flaminia, Rome, by Vignola: key plan and section showing Antique style of dome and variant on Diocletian window (JSC).*

Fig. 4.36b ↗ *Vignola's church of Sant'Andrea, Via Flaminia, Rome (1550–54): the earliest example of the use of an elliptical drum and dome set on a rectangular base. Ellipses were to become important elements in Baroque design. Sant'Andrea's overall external appearance derives from Roman tombs (the suggestion of a temple-front should be noted) (Anderson Alinari [c.1940], ADA-F-040232-0000).*

Fig. 4.36c → *Plan of Vignola's later church of Sant'Anna dei Palafrenieri (begun 1572), taking the Sant'Andrea, Via Flaminia, idea a step further, uses an ellipse for the actual form of the building (JSC).*

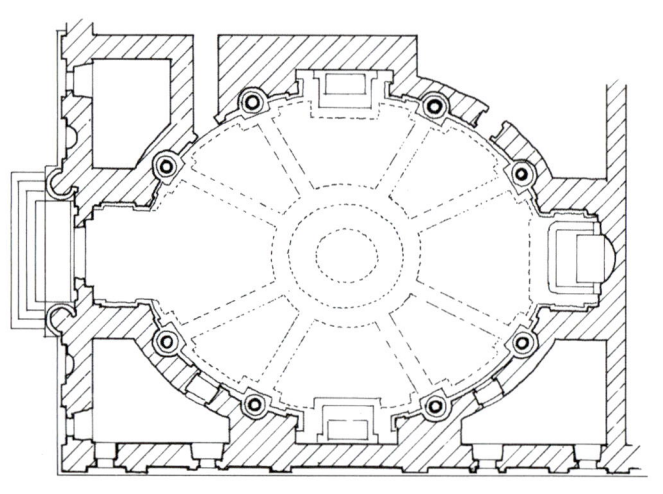

68 / CLASSICAL ARCHITECTURE

England or Germany until the second decade of the 17th century, with the works of Inigo Jones and Elias Holl respectively.

Vignola pursued the *tempietto* theme in his Sant'Andrea, Via Flaminia, Rome (Figs 4.36a–b), of 1550–54, but it is a rectangle on plan, with an elliptical dome over it based on the Pantheon form; the upper part of the rectangular volume inside has blind thermal windows above the entablature. This is the earliest example of a church with an elliptical dome on a drum. Later, from 1572, Vignola was to introduce an elliptical plan with a dome over it at the Church of Sant'Anna dei Palafrenieri in Rome (Fig. 4.36c). The elliptical theme was to become a favourite of architects of the Baroque period.

However, although these little churches with their ellipses were to be influential, Il Gesù was to be a precedent of immense importance, for it was the mother-church of the Society of Jesus, and was begun in 1568. The plan (see Fig. 4.35b), with side chapels rather than aisles, shallow transepts with an altar in each arm, apse, and great dome, is derived from the type of Sant'Andrea in Mantua (see Fig. 4.20c). Alberti had concealed the roofs of the lower aisles at Santa Maria Novella in Florence (see Fig. 4.19) behind giant scrolls, and Vignola and della Porta took up Alberti's theme at Il Gesù, designing two distinct storeys using vigorous modelling, superimposed Orders, and scrolls on either side of the upper storey. Il Gesù, despite certain hesitancies and botches in the handling of the entrance façade, was to be the model for thousands of churches all over the world, was probably the most influential ecclesiastical design in the last half millennium, and is the type par excellence associated with the Counter-Reformation.

Vignola's *La Regola delli Cinque Ordini d'Architettura* of 1562, though modelled on Serlio's work, was more scholarly and had better illustrations, but was more limited in scope. It became the standard work on the Orders and their details, and went into over 200 editions over some three centuries. The importance of Vignola's work in the context of architecture cannot be overstated.

Palladio

There can be no doubting the importance of Andrea Palladio as an architect of genius, whose works had a far-ranging influence, although he lived for almost all his life in the provincial city of Vicenza. It was not only his buildings, notably his *palazzi* and *ville* in and around Vicenza and his churches (San Giorgio Maggiore and Il Redentore in Venice) (see Figs 4.41a–c and 4.42a–b), which had international significance, but his publications, especially his *Quattro Libri dell'Architettura* of 1570: the latter stated the theoretical basis for his work, illustrated the Orders, publicised his own buildings, and showed a good selection of buildings from Antiquity. Not only were the *Quattro Libri* more scholarly and accurate than Serlio's offering, but they covered more ground than Vignola had attempted. Palladio had studied and drawn Antique remains in Rome, and was influenced by the works of both Bramante and Vignola; he also provided illustrations for one of the finest editions of Vitruvius, published in 1556.

Palladio's first great building was the case he designed for the town hall in Vicenza (the so-called Basilica) consisting of

Fig. 4.37 → *Variation on the Sansovino theme: the Basilica, Vicenza, by Palladio (1549 and later). Unlike Sansovino, Palladio brought the entablature forward over each column in ressaults, thus avoiding the strong horizontal effects of the Venetian library (AFK G12290).*

THE RENAISSANCE PERIOD / 69

Fig. 4.38a ↑ *Palazzo Porto-Breganze, aka Casa del Diavolo, Vicenza (1571), designed by Palladio, built by Scamozzi. Here Palladio used the Giant Composite Order of Michelangelo on high pedestals, with swags between the capitals. Although it is only a fragment, the two bays show a pronounced Michelangelesque influence. Once again the entablature breaks forward over each column in ressaults (Alinari [c.1900], ACA-F-012764-0000).*

an engaged Ionic Order on a Tuscan–Doric ground floor, with arches carried on smaller columns between the piers (the serliana, Palladian motif, or Venetian window) (Fig. 4.37). This theme derived from Sansovino's Biblioteca Marciano (*see* Figs 4.18a–b) of some 12 years earlier, although Palladio set the entablature back between the engaged columns, whereas Sansovino emphasised the horizontal entablatures, making the serliana motifs subservient.

At the Palazzo Porto of 1552 Palladio was influenced by Bramante, but introduced sculpture over the pediments of the windows of the centre and end bays, rather in the style of Michelangelo. His use of a Giant Order round the *cortile* is a reference to the atrium of Antiquity. The façade of the Palazzo Chiericati, begun in the 1550s, has superimposed Orders without arches, the three end bays on each side of the symmetrical five-bay front treated as *loggie*. Palladio's Palazzo Thiene, with its Mannerist textures and room plans derived from the shapes of interiors in Roman *thermæ*, merges contemporary architectural concerns with themes from Antiquity. Palladio proportioned his rooms in relation to each other, setting up cunningly contrived axes, symmetries, and balances in his interiors.

At the Palazzo Valmarano (1566) and Palazzo Porto-Breganze (1571) (Figs 4.38a–b) he used Giant Orders for the façades: the latter recalls Michelangelo's work at the Capitol in Rome. The powerful theme recurs in Palladio's *ville*, for which he designed grand entrance porticos, in the mistaken belief that Antique villas had temple-like fronts. His sources were the vague descriptions in Pliny and Vitruvius. Good examples of prostyle hexastyle porticoes on high podia, rather like temple-fronts set against plainer, massive walls, can be found at the Villa Malcontenta near Mestre (1560), and the celebrated Villa Capra (or Villa Rotonda) near Vicenza (c.1550), where there are four porticoes, one on each face (*see* Fig. G84a). The Villa Rotonda (Fig. 4.39) was completed by Vincenzo Scamozzi; it has a circular, central-domed hall with finely proportioned rooms disposed around it and, of course, the porticoes with four flights of steps, giving the villa four identical elevations. The formal symmetry of the Villa Capra and its architectonic perfection made it an important model for the 18th-century Palladians in England.

Fig. 4.38b ↑ *Intended elevation of the Casa del Diavolo, Vicenza (coll. JSC).*

Fig. 4.39 ↑ *Villa Rotonda (aka Villa Capra), Vicenza, by Palladio, begun c.1550. This* villa suburbana *has four Ionic porticoes set at* piano nobile *level over a basement, and a central domed circular space. The prostyle hexastyle temple-front porticoes were intended by Palladio to suggest Antiquity (BTB).*

70 / CLASSICAL ARCHITECTURE

Fig. 4.40 ← *Teatro Olimpico, Vicenza (1580), by Palladio, completed by Scamozzi. This is based on the Roman scheme of a fixed architectural background with the stage in front of it. The auditorium is a half-ellipse with seats rising to a colonnade with niches round the back. The flat ceiling is painted to resemble the open real sky that would have been a feature of theatres in Antiquity. Behind the proscenium is an elaborate permanent set using false perspective effects (BTB).*

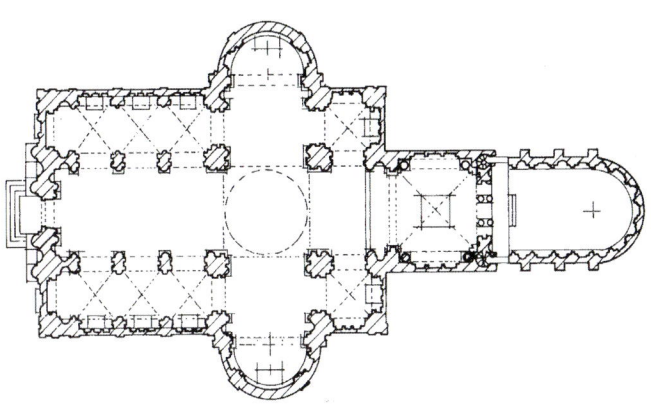

Fig. 4.41a ↑ *Palladio's Church of San Giorgio Maggiore, Venice, showing the monastic choir behind the high altar (JSC).*

Fig. 4.41b ↗ *San Giorgio Maggiore, Venice, by Palladio, of 1566, showing the architect's solution to the problem of applying a Classical façade to a clerestoreyed nave with lean-to aisles. The nave is faced with an engaged temple-front of the Composite Order on pedestals, complete with pediment and niches. The aisles are fronted using the expedient of a second, much wider and lower pediment, carried on Corinthian pilasters, which is the entire width of the church, but which is interrupted by the engaged columns of the nave 'temple'-front, and is therefore subservient. Left and right, above the low wall, are Venetian crenellations (AFK G12009).*

Fig. 4.41c → *Elevation of San Giorgio Maggiore, Venice, showing the overlapping temple-fronts (JSC).*

Palladio's Teatro Olimpico (Fig. 4.40) in Vicenza of 1580 (again, completed by Scamozzi) was strongly influenced by Antique theatres, and had a permanent architectural backdrop of elaborate 'streets' with false perspectives to give an illusion of great depth and size.

With the two great Venetian churches, San Giorgio Maggiore (from 1566) (Figs 4.41a–c) and Il Redentore (from 1576) (Figs 4.42a–b), Palladio designed Classical façades for what was still

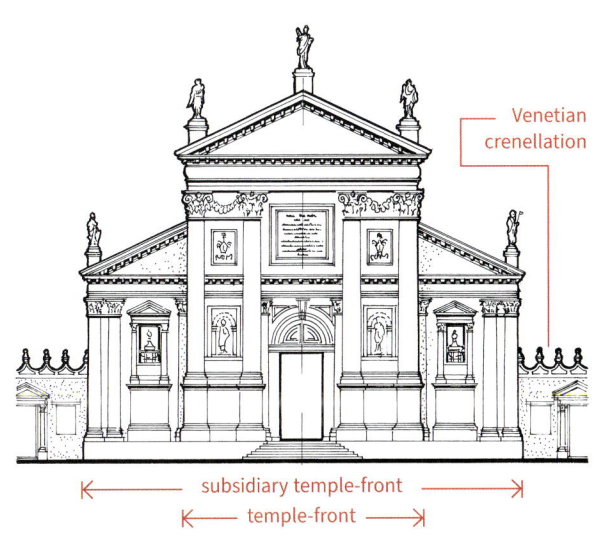

THE RENAISSANCE PERIOD / 71

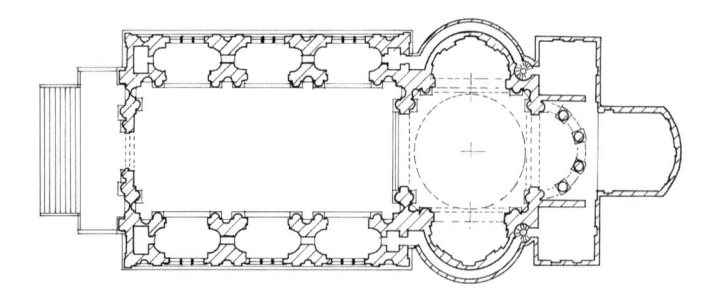

Fig. 4.42a ↑ *Il Redentore, Venice (1576–7), also by Palladio, showing the sculptured effect of the wall-piers and resulting shaped chapels. Again, the monastic choir is set behind a screen (JSC).*

Fig. 4.42b → *Il Redentore, Venice. The architectural effects differ from those of San Giorgio, although both churches have domes over the crossings, and transepts are apsidal: however, the nave is wide, and the aisles are replaced by chapels, the nave piers being altogether more massive. The apsidal form is echoed in the curved colonnade at the east separating the monastic choir from the nave so the spectator therefore seems to be looking through the apse itself. Above, the vaulted ceiling is illuminated by Diocletian windows over the entablature carried on engaged Corinthian columns. In fact, this remarkable church uses a fully articulated Corinthian Order, making a considerable departure from the massive piers with pilasters usual at the time (AFK G1II03).*

basically a basilican west front, by overlaying two temple-fronts: the nave end of San Giorgio was finished with a tall, narrow, engaged temple-front set on pedestals and capped with a pediment, while behind this front ran the lower part of what was apparently a wider pediment, the ends of which concealed the roofs of the aisles. This subsidiary wider pediment (broken at the top when the raking elements hit the tall engaged columns of the central engaged temple-front) was 'carried' on a smaller Order of pilasters (*see* Figs 4.41b–c). Inside San Giorgio, Palladio used a Corinthian Order of engaged columns and pilasters to give a much greater sense of modelling and articulation of the piers than earlier architects had achieved, while his use of a domed crossing, apsidal-ended transepts, vaults, and thermal windows recalled Antiquity in a very powerful and original way.

At Il Redentore, the temple-front sits on a podium, but the subsidiary wider pediment is completely broken by this, and an Attic storey, with subsidiary broken pediment, rises up above. The 'aisles' are side chapels, and the liturgical east end has a dome on a drum over the apsidal-ended vestigial transepts. Both churches have open screens, behind which are the monastic choirs; the architectural treatment is particularly successful in Il Redentore, with its segmental colonnade suggesting an apse beyond the crossing (*see* Fig. 4.42b). The Roman effect of the design is stunningly evocative.

Palladio's designs were free from the bustle of so much overloaded northern European work, influenced as it was by a somewhat indiscriminately eclectic use of Mannerist designs loosely interpreted from Serlio's publications. By their elegance, their serenity, and their evocation of Antique *gravitas*, Palladio's works held remarkable appeal for European sensibilities. Inigo Jones first imported the Palladian style into England in the first

Fig. 4.43 ↑ *English Palladianism: the Queen's House, Greenwich (begun 1616), by Inigo Jones. The architecture is in stark contrast to the overloaded ornament of Jacobean work. Note the rusticated base and the* piano nobile *level given extra importance by means of the Ionic loggia (AH).*

half of the 17th century (Fig. 4.43), and it was revived and further disseminated in the following century through the influence of Richard Boyle, Earl of Burlington, who saw absolute and Antique standards in the master's works.

Eighteenth-century æsthetic discernment in Britain was dominated for much of the time by Palladianism, and by the examples of Palladio's villas set in landscapes that were themselves evocative of Antiquity.

5

CLASSICAL VARIATIONS: BAROQUE, ROCOCO, PALLADIANISM, AND AFTER

The qualities of ... Baroque architecture often lack appreciation in our country by reason of national temperament, and it may be frankly admitted that we shall always regard it as the outcome of the spirit alien to our own. Unless we are able to enter into the attitude of mind that prompted its modes of expression, ... the Baroque will never, with us, be allowed its place in the long and exciting story of the development of architecture.

HENRY VAUGHAN LANCHESTER:
Fischer von Erlach (London: Ernest Benn, 1924), 7–8.

The exuberance and splendour of Baroque architecture, especially in Italy and south Germany, represent the climax of the power of the catholic church and of catholic princes before both were submerged by the rising tides of rationalism and nationalism. The Council of Trent had given the church renewed confidence in her traditional doctrines and, once the austerities associated with the initial years of the Counter-Reformation were over, she threw herself with a vigour unparalleled since the Middle Ages into the task of representing eternal truths as compellingly as possible in temporal forms. Architecturally these forms were the classical ones established by the pioneers of Renaissance design in Italy. However, they were now articulated in a more three-dimensional and forceful manner so as to create dynamic spatial effects involving an openness of structure and an imaginative control of light.

DAVID WATKIN:
A History of Western Architecture (London: Laurence King, 2005), 283.

Introduction

The Baroque (which is essentially of the 17th century) and the Rococo (which is firmly of the 18th) styles are both essentially developments and branches of Classical art and architecture. 'Baroque' means irregularly shaped, whimsical, and odd, and was a term originally applied to a rough or imperfect pearl. Germain Bazin reminded us that the belief in the absolute value of the Classical conception of art, a 'prejudice' established during the Renaissance and revived at the end of the 18th century, caused every departure from that kind of art to be considered inferior. One result has been that some of the greatest styles created by Western civilisation bear names that at first were terms of contempt: Gothic, Baroque, Rococo, but such contempt was and is wholly misplaced, for the best exemplars carried out in those styles bear comparison with the finest of any other periods.

Classical architecture implies a degree of clarity within precise boundaries, and perhaps a static quality, yet with a profound sense of order and of a continuity from Antiquity, and with a serenity, a balance, and a logic that expresses developed intellect.

Baroque architecture, on the other hand, gives an impression of always being in movement: it is expansive, and full of contrast, violence, and passion. It is expressive, seems to burst beyond its own space, and exploits illusion, appearing to defy reason and even logic; but it is in reality very much under control. It is in motion, with entablatures that sway in and out, surfaces that undulate on plan and are deeply modelled, and a sense of the theatrical seems never far away.

'Rococo' probably stems from the French *rocaille*, meaning shell- or pebble-work associated with grottoes and similar conceits. It is essentially a light, frothy, elegant style used in the 18th century, and suggesting marine-like plants, shells, and encrustations. It seems first to have appeared around 1700 at Versailles, but reached its apogee in southern Germany from the 1720s until around 1780, especially in church architecture, where it can be found in many a riot of stucco, carving, and paint.

Bernini, Borromini, Ellipses, and Western Façades

As has been mentioned above, elaborate entablatures that curved on plan were known in Antiquity; the examples from Baalbek, Petra (*see* Fig. 2.19), and Tivoli have proto-Baroque qualities. Vignola used ellipses, and during the 17th century ellipses occur in many church plans. With the works of Gianlorenzo Bernini and Francesco Borromini a new vehemence, overstatement, and disregard for convention or restraint can be found in church architecture. Bernini's Sant'Andrea al Quirinale (1658–70) (Figs 5.1a–c) and Borromini's San Carlo alle Quattro Fontane (1634–43) (Figs 5.2a–d) both exploit ellipses on plan, but in entirely different ways: the former contains an ellipsoidal space with chapels off it set in the thickness of the encompassing walls (rather like a miniature and elliptical version of the Pantheon); the latter has an elliptical, central space that merges with parts of other ellipses, with the result that the Orders are placed on contraflexed curves on plan, so that wall surfaces bow inwards and outwards, all controlled by a geometry of interconnected axes, circles, and ellipses (*see* Fig. 5.2b). Both churches exploit both the ellipse and the domed central space, but Bernini used a Giant Order of pilasters on his pedimented façade, with a smaller Ionic Order carrying a curved entablature as a porch, whereas Borromini set the whole front of San Carlo in motion by using a concave–convex–concave plan for the vaguely Ionic lower storey, and a concave-concave-concave plan for the upper free Composite façade, but with subsidiary miniature Orders for the ædicules, as on Michelangelo's Capitoline buildings, but this time exploiting curves (*see* Fig. 5.2a).

Michelangelo had heralded the Baroque in the forms of the great drum and dome of St Peter's in Rome, but Roman architects at the start of the 17th century, bored, perhaps, by the way architecture had evolved at the end of the 16th, rediscovered Michelangelo and Mannerism, and took their themes even further. One of the first true Baroque masterpieces was

Fig. 5.1a ← *Bernini's elliptical Church of Sant'Andrea al Quirinale, Rome (1658–70), expands on the elliptical theme and also recalls the Pantheon, with its chapels set into the thickness of the walls, and its great domed interior. It should be remembered that Bernini's piazza, in front of St Peter's in Rome, is also an ellipse (Anderson Alinari [c.1910], ADA-F-019746-0000).*

Fig. 5.1b ↙ *Sant'Andrea al Quirinale, with entrance façade loosely based on Michelangelo's Palazzo Capitolino, but with the subsidiary Ionic Order bursting out as a porch instead of remaining either framed or a flat plane within the larger Order (Anderson Alinari [c.1920–30], ADA-F-041600-0000).*

Fig. 5.1c ↓ *Plan of Sant'Andrea al Quirinale, showing an ellipse with short axis coinciding with that of the high altar; and the main entrance (JSC).*

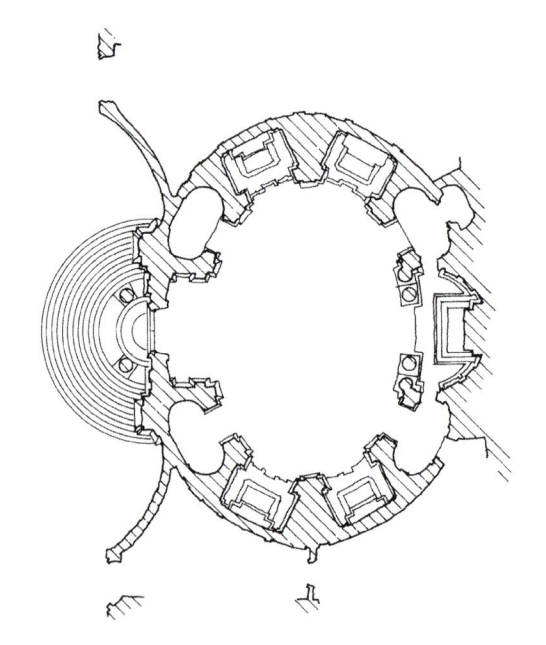

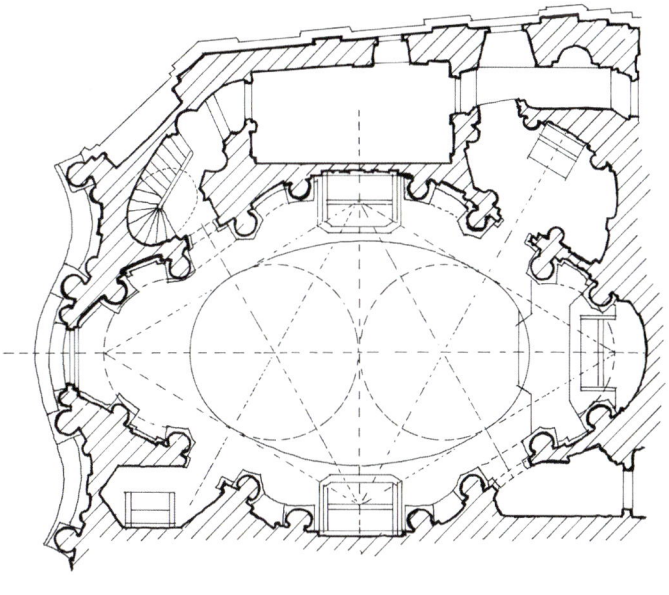

Fig. 5.2a ← *Church of San Carlo alle Quattro Fontane (aka San Carlino) by Borromini, begun in 1634, in which the ellipse is expressed in the dome, but is actually set over fragments of other ellipses that form the recesses of the chapels, the entrance chapel, and apsidal chapel. Thus, various ellipsoidal figures in plan merge. The result is that this tour de force of the Baroque, completed in 1667, seems to be in motion, rocking and swaying. The façade has two Orders superimposed, and there are subsidiary Orders for the ædicules, but the plan of the front consists of convex and concave curves. On the lower storey the plan is concave–convex–concave, but the first floor is concave–concave–concave, with a miniature elliptical pillbox set in the centre, reminiscent of the Khazna at Petra (see Fig. 2.19). Gesticulating angels hold an elliptical frame aloft between two swaying entablatures. It is a dizzy composition, but Borromini's work had considerable influence (Alinari [c.1920–30], ACA-F-027989-0000).*

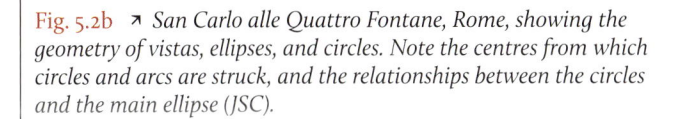

Fig. 5.2b ↗ *San Carlo alle Quattro Fontane, Rome, showing the geometry of vistas, ellipses, and circles. Note the centres from which circles and arcs are struck, and the relationships between the circles and the main ellipse (JSC).*

Fig. 5.2c → *Interior of San Carlo alle Quattro Fontane (AH).*

CLASSICAL VARIATIONS: BAROQUE, ROCOCO, PALLADIANISM, & AFTER / 75

Fig. 5.2d ↑ *The complex vaults and underside of the elliptical cupola of San Carlo alle Quattro Fontane, perhaps suggested by the fourth-century mausoleum of Santa Costanza, Rome (see Fig.3.4) (AH).*

Fig. 5.3 ↑ *Baldacchino (1624–33) over the altar set above the tomb of the Apostle in St Peter's, Rome, by Bernini, after early collaboration with Borromini. This huge bronze canopy employs the twisted 'Solomonic' columns associated with the Temple of Solomon and with the Constantinian sanctuary over the tomb of St Peter in the older basilica. Solomonic columns were used frequently in canopies over altars, in ædicules, and framing paintings or sculptures above altars set against walls. They represent not only the biblical temple but the entrance to Paradise, and are a mnemonic of these. Note the valancing hanging between the entablatures (BTB).*

the massive bronze baldacchino in St Peter's, begun in 1624 (Fig. 5.3; see Fig. 4.28b), originally conceived with Borromini as consultant, but he was superseded by Bernini after some unpleasant intrigues at the highest level. Luxuriant in its detail and employing curves and twists, even in its Composite Order, Bernini's creation is staggering in its scale, but also astounds by its technical mastery of form and material. Bernini's colonnades in front of St Peter's, begun in 1656, use severe Tuscan columns carrying an Ionic entablature, but are arranged on a vast elliptical plan (see Fig. 5.11).

Sant'Agnese in Agone, in the Piazza Navona (Figs 5.4a–b), begun in 1652 by Carlo Rainaldi on a Greek cross plan, was transformed by Borromini, who took over as architect from 1653 to 1657. The central space is an octagon in a square, over which is a drum and dome; the side chapels, with their apsidal ends lying on an axis parallel to the façade, give an illusion of an elliptical plan, while the front, with its concave plan flanked by twin towers, proved to be an important precedent. Far more extreme, even eccentric, is Borromini's treatment of other buildings, notably the façade of the Oratorio dei Filippini, Rome (1637–40): this is a strange invention, featuring subtle curves, a weird pediment, odd pilasters at the lower level, and curious canopy-pediment-hoods over some of the windows (Fig. 5.5).

Most Baroque, liturgical western façades are similar to the composition of that of Il Gesù (see Fig. 4.35a), but with more heavily modelled planes, a profusion of columns, and a riot of pediments (segmental, triangular, open, broken, and scrolled). Il Gesù's west front, though, was essentially Mannerist, and displays a curiously uneasy relationship between horizontal and vertical elements. More successful, perhaps, was Carlo Maderno's Santa Susanna in Rome of 1597 (Fig. 5.6), with its arrangement of two storeys of Orders (six engaged columns

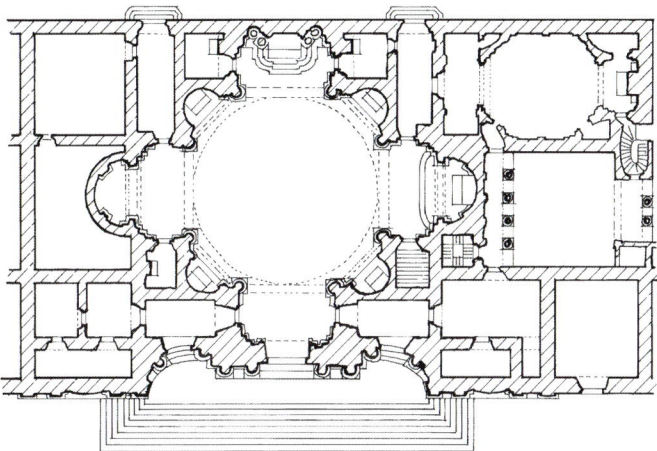

Fig. 5.4a ↑↑ *Sant'Agnese in Agone, Piazza Navona, Rome, begun (1652) by Carlo Rainaldi, worked on by Borromini (1653–7), and later completed by Rainaldi. The plan has a central octagon with niches in the corners, with choir and entrance chapels and deeper north and south transeptal chapels, which gives the effect of an ellipse with its long axis parallel to the façade. In the centre of the façade is an engaged temple-front set in a wall, concave on plan, with two towers of considerable inventive virtuosity flanking the composition. The top stages of these towers are circular on plan with projecting paired columns, set on square bases. The effect is stunningly Baroque (BTB).*

Fig. 5.4b ↑ *Plan of Sant'Agnese in Agone, showing the concave front and centralised space under the cupola (JSC).*

Fig. 5.5 ↑ *Borromini's extraordinary curved front of the Oratorio dei Filippini (oratory of the Congregation of St Philip Neri), Rome (1637–40), with its pediment fusing triangular and segmental types (JSC).*

Fig. 5.6 ↑ *Façade of the Church of Santa Susanna, Rome (1587), by Carlo Maderno. A more decisive and elegant version of the Il Gesù theme, with satisfying proportions and a more positive vertical emphasis. Here Mannerism starts to herald the Baroque (JSC).*

rather than pilasters on the lower storey, with pilasters above), and the scrolls linking the narrower upper façade to the wider front below. The emphasis was more decisive and vertical than that of the front of Il Gesù. Only a few years later, when Martino Longhi's Church of Santi Vincenzo ed Anastasio in Rome was built in 1646–50 (Fig. 5.7), the Mannerist motifs, including the mixing of segmental and triangular pediments, had been further transformed. The modelling was deeper, the columns fully

CLASSICAL VARIATIONS: BAROQUE, ROCOCO, PALLADIANISM, & AFTER / 77

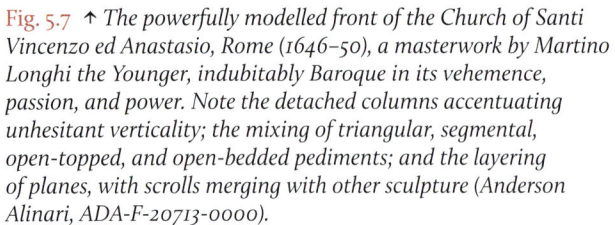

Fig. 5.7 ↑ *The powerfully modelled front of the Church of Santi Vincenzo ed Anastasio, Rome (1646–50), a masterwork by Martino Longhi the Younger, indubitably Baroque in its vehemence, passion, and power. Note the detached columns accentuating unhesitant verticality; the mixing of triangular, segmental, open-topped, and open-bedded pediments; and the layering of planes, with scrolls merging with other sculpture (Anderson Alinari, ADA-F-20713-0000).*

Fig. 5.8 ↗ *Santa Maria della Pace (1656–9), by Pietro da Cortona, with its complex concave front, out of which pushes the pedimented façade, out of which again spring two convex curved walls linked to an open-bed segmental pediment on a Composite Order, while a Tuscan semicircular portico completes an extraordinarily vivid and plastic composition (BTB).*

Fig. 5.9 → *Pietro da Cortona's façade of the Church of Santa Maria in Via Lata on the Corso, Rome (1658–62), more restrained than that of Santa Maria della Pace, employing a variety of serliana in the upper storey, but one that harks back to proto-Baroque features in Antique Roman architecture, and an in antis arrangement for the portico, perhaps suggested by Peruzzi's Palazzo Massimi (BTB).*

78 / Classical Architecture

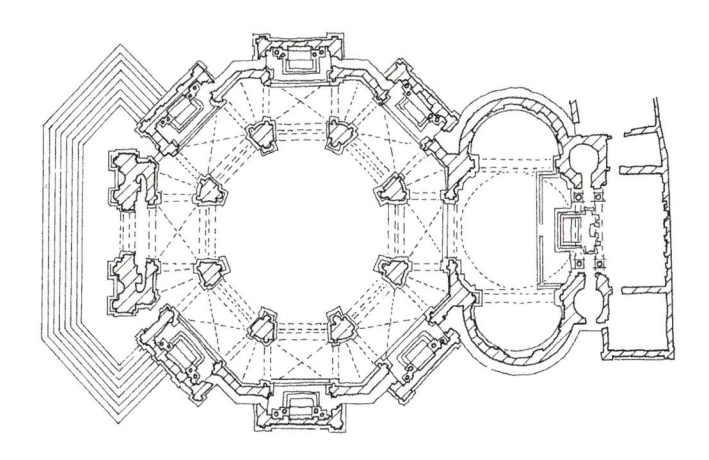

Fig. 5.10a ↑ *Church of Santa Maria della Salute, Venice: a centrally planned octagon surrounded by an ambulatory off which are small chapels and a domed sanctuary flanked by apses. The essential form featured in late Roman and Byzantine buildings in Italy, notably San Vitale, Ravenna (c.532–68) (JSC).*

Fig. 5.10b → *Longhena's great Church of Santa Maria della Salute, Venice (begun 1630), with an octagonal clerestorey supported by massive buttresses in the form of scrolls above which rises a drum and dome with lantern. Chapels illuminated by Diocletian windows project from the central body of the church, and the entrance façade facing the Grand Canal is a variation on the triumphal arch that is also used in the arrangement of bays around the interior (Carlo Naya, Alinari [1878], FCC-A-000058-0019).*

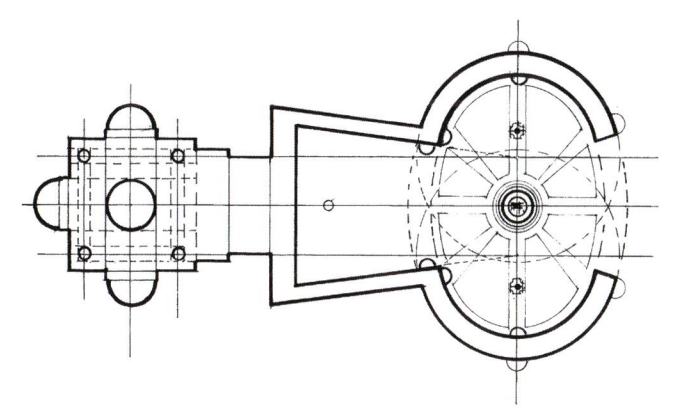

Fig. 5.11 ↑ *Diagram showing the geometry of Bernini's colonnades encircling the elliptical piazza before St Peter's Basilica, Rome (JSC).*

experienced as such, above and below, the verticality unhesitant, the scrolls merged with other sculpture; the assured rhetoric of fully developed Baroque had arrived. Nevertheless, the basic elements of the composition are those of the façade of Il Gesù, and the descendants of that design were many. The invention displayed in Roman Baroque churches was remarkable (Figs 5.8 and 5.9).

A centralised plan recurs in the brilliant Church of Santa Maria della Salute in Venice, by Baldassare Longhena, begun in 1630. The plan (Fig. 5.10a) is basically octagonal and the octagonal clerestorey is linked to the radiating chapels by means of vast buttresses in the form of scrolls; a triumphal-arch motif reappears on the entrance façade, and Diocletian windows are much in evidence in the chapels (Fig. 5.10b). In time, motifs from Antiquity were used with later inventions, such as theatrical illusionist effects, large scrolls, and swaying, undulating planes, alive with ornament.

Both illusion and perspective are invoked in Bernini's piazza of St Peter (Fig. 5.11), for the ground rises to the great front by Maderno (*see* Fig. 4.28a), and the straight arms joining the elliptical piazza to the façade are not parallel, but converge as they progress from the west front: the result is that of an illusion of greater length. Bernini employed similar tricks of perspective at the Scala Regia in the Vatican, which narrows and lowers as it rises: this has the effect of making the stair seem much longer and grander than it is. Light further increases the dramatic tension.

However, as the Baroque style found its way over the Alps it produced some interesting variants. Often, the two-storey Gesù-type front acquired flanking towers, as at Salzburg Cathedral (1614–28) by Solari (Fig. 5.12), and at the Theatine Church of St Kajetan, Munich, begun in 1663 by Barelli and Zuccalli, but completed by François Cuvilliés (Fig. 5.13). The Munich church towers have scrolled buttresses at the tops of the three-staged supporting polygonal cupolas: these scrolls resemble those of Santa Maria della Salute, but have serrated edges, like gearwheels.

The concave front with flanking towers of Santa Agnese in Agone is found again, in variance, at the Dreifaltigkeitskirche in Salzburg (Fig. 5.14) (1694–1702), by Johann Bernhard Fischer von Erlach, but combined with an elliptical plan, the long axis of which runs through the centre of the composition. The same architect's Karlskirche in Vienna of 1715–38 also exploits an

CLASSICAL VARIATIONS: BAROQUE, ROCOCO, PALLADIANISM, & AFTER / 79

Fig. 5.12 → *Cathedral of Sts Rupert and Virgil, Salzburg (1614–28), the first plans for which were by Vincenzo Scamozzi, but realised with revised designs by Santino Solari as a coherent whole. Its apsidal transepts were clearly influenced by Palladio's Il Redentore and San Giorgio Maggiore, Venice, elements which appear to have been part of Scamozzi's original proposals (JSC).*

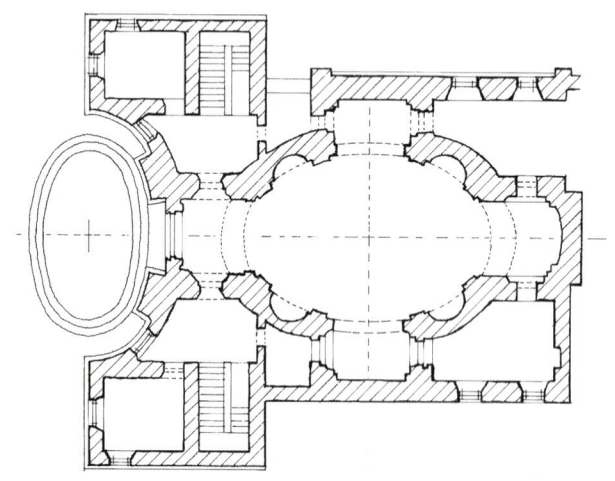

Fig. 5.14 ↑ *Plan of the Dreifaltigkeitskirche (Holy Trinity Church), Salzburg, by Fischer von Erlach, showing ellipses and the concave front suggested by Sant'Agnese in Agone, Rome (JSC).*

Fig. 5.13 ↑ *Theatinerkirche of St Kajetan, Munich, a great Baroque church (modelled on the precedent of Sant'Andrea della Valle), begun 1663 by Barelli and Zuccalli, and completed (1767) by the Walloon dwarf architect, François Cuvilliés. This is a variant of the two-storeyed west fronts of Il Gesù and Santa Susanna, both in Rome, but with the addition of twin towers capped by cupolas supported by console-buttresses (coll. JSC).*

ellipse (Figs 5.15a–b): a mighty elliptical dome sits over the central space off which are radiating chapels, and the long axis of the ellipse is again on the centre-line of the façade. The strange towers have scrolls at the tops, over the Attic storey above the second stages. In the centre of the façade is a prostyle hexastyle portico, a clear reference to Antiquity, and to the Pantheon in particular: the Antique allusions are reinforced by the two spiral columns (recalling Trajan's column in Rome), which feature scenes from the life of St Charles Borromeo, but have other significances as well. The spectacular interior is one of the finest in Vienna (Figs 5.15c–d).

Ellipse and theatre recur in the church of the Benedictine abbey of Sts George and Martin, Weltenburg an der Donau, by C.D. and E.Q. Asam (begun 1714): the central ellipse (Figs 5.16a–b)

80 / CLASSICAL ARCHITECTURE

Fig. 5.15a → *Brilliant, complex plan of the Karlskirche, Vienna (1715–38), by Fischer von Erlach, completed by his son, Joseph Emanuel Fischer von Erlach, showing the wide front with towers and Solomonic-Trajanic columns, prostyle hexastyle portico on podium, and central ellipse (JSC).*

Fig. 5.15b ↘ *The Karlskirche, Vienna. This remarkable building is a synthesis of many important ideas. The most obvious is the Temple in Jerusalem, which is shown in Mannerist prints as a Pantheon-like structure with a porch flanked by two large columns. The spiral columns, which are mnemonics of the Temple although they are based on Trajan's Column in Rome, record events in the life of St Carlo Borromeo, and signify the* Plus Ultra *of the world beyond the Pillars of Hercules, so they are gateways to Paradise, to a New World, and emblems of Habsburg supremacy. In the centre is the prostyle hexastyle temple-front, looking back to Roman Antiquity and the Temple of Concord in the Forum in Rome: there are also references to the Pantheon in the portico and dome behind (which is elliptical and therefore connected with works by Borromini and Bernini in Rome). The wide front recalls both Borromini's Sant'Agnese in Agone and the wide porch of the Solomonic Temple, which Perrault had illustrated, while the curious towers recall works of Borromini and Guarini. Fischer von Erlach also referred to the domes of François Mansart's Église des Minimes, of the Dôme des Invalides in Paris (1693–1706) by J. Hardouin-Mansart (the latter building being associated with the iconography of King Louis XIV), and of St Paul's Cathedral in London. The spiral columns also remind us of the minarets added to the great Church of Hagia Sophia in Constantinople (and therefore are references not only to Constantine and the lost Eastern Roman Empire, but to the recent invasion [1683] of Europe by Ottoman Turks). Thus the Holy Roman Emperor of the German Nation is identified with Solomon, with Roman emperors, and with the* Plus Ultra *of Charles V (BTB).*

Fig. 5.15c ↓ *Noble interior of the Karlskirche, with clear and majestic proportions, frescoes (1727–30) by Johann Michael Rottmayr, and illusory architectural painting by Gætano Fanti. Especially fine is the treatment of the elliptical dome which shows the Apotheosis of St Charles Borromeus, with the Blessed Virgin as Intercessor, making supplications for deliverance from the plague (CSB).*

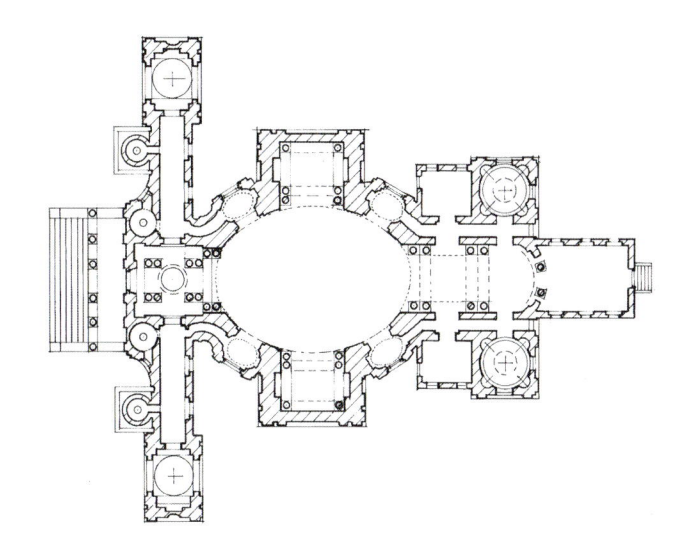

CLASSICAL VARIATIONS: BAROQUE, ROCOCO, PALLADIANISM, & AFTER / 81

Fig. 5.15d ← *The intensely dramatic high altar in the Karlskirche, where the illumination behind makes such an impact, featuring St Charles in Glory and the triangular symbol of Yahweh in a halo within a sunburst (CSB).*

has small chapels off it, and the longer axis passes through the centre-line of the high altar and western door. A statue of St George on horseback charges out of the sun, slaying the dragon, while a figure rushes off to the right: the group, rather like a scene from a Handel opera, is held within an ædicule with twisted columns set under a segmental arch. Theatrical themes are pursued in the splendours and delights of what happens above the elliptical interior (Figs 5.16c–d).

At the pilgrimage church of Vierzehnheiligen in Franconia (Figs 5.17a–d) (1742–72), the architecture of which was by Johann Balthasar Neumann, the plan is cruciform, but the nave and chancel consist of five interlocking ovals or ellipses, three of which have their long axes on the centre-line of the church, and two of which lie at right angles to the main axis. The transeptal arrangement consists of one of the two ellipses at the crossing, with intersecting circles at either end. Twin towers and a west front that bows outwards complete this extraordinary architectural ensemble (Fig. 5.17c). The enchanting Rococo decorations were almost entirely the work of F.X. and J.M. Feichtmayr and J.G. Üblhör, and the *Gnadenaltar* in the centre of the largest ellipse in the middle of the nave, a Rococo tour de force that resembles a sedan-chair (designed by J.M. Küchel), was made into something rich and strange, as though it had been immersed in the sea. Even the Rococo capitals, vaguely Corinthian in form, have sprouted upwards over the fasciæ of the entablature, and downwards over the shafts. It is as though the entire interior of this white, gold, purple, and pink building, with its vestigial aisles, had been made of Meissen porcelain;

82 / CLASSICAL ARCHITECTURE

Fig. 5.16a → *Plan of the Benedictine abbey-church of Sts George and Martin at Weltenburg an der Donau, near Kelheim, Bavaria, another use of the ellipse (JSC).*

Fig. 5.16b ↓ *Church of Sts George and Martin, Weltenburg, by the Asam brothers, showing the extraordinarily effective lighting, as St George charges with a weapon that resembles, somewhat disconcertingly, a golfing umbrella, to kill the dragon and rescue the terrified maiden who flees to the right (BSGKW).*

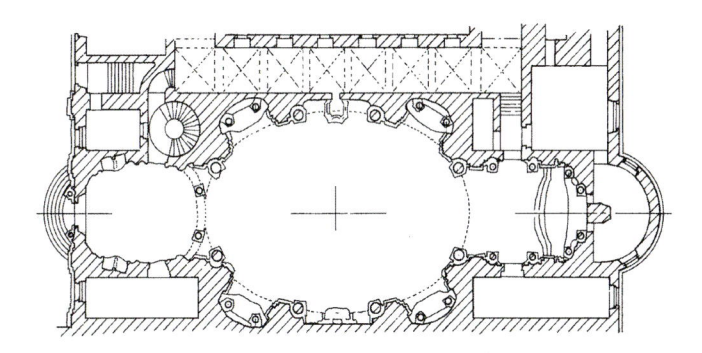

Fig. 5.16c ← *Elliptical gallery in Weltenburg, with the brilliantly illuminated ceiling fresco by Cosmas Damian Asam showing the Church Triumphant, with Coronation of the Virgin before the Holy Trinity: the delightful conceit of a life-size figure of Asam looks down to greet us as though hoping we will enjoy his glorious creation (JSC).*

Fig. 5.16d ↑ *C.D. Asam in contemporary dress looks down from the gallery at Weltenburg as we look up (JSC).*

CLASSICAL VARIATIONS: BAROQUE, ROCOCO, PALLADIANISM, & AFTER

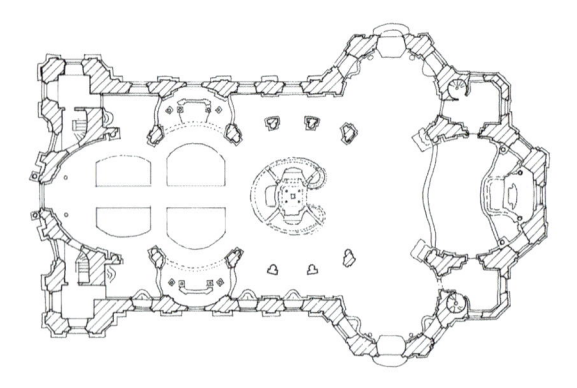

Fig. 5.17a ↑ *Plan of Wallfahrtskirche Vierzehnheiligen (pilgrimage church of the Fourteen Saints [1742–72]), near Bad Staffelstein, Lichtenfels, Upper Franconia, showing the complex geometries of interpenetrating circles, ovals, and ellipses. The* Gnadenaltar *(altar of Grace), on the site where the Fourteen Helpers-in-Time-of-Need were supposed to have been seen, is in the centre of the large ellipse (JSC).*

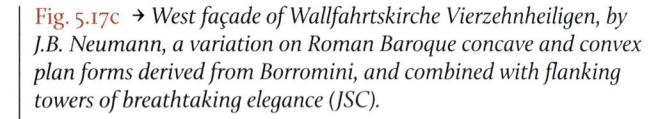

Fig. 5.17c → *West façade of Wallfahrtskirche Vierzehnheiligen, by J.B. Neumann, a variation on Roman Baroque concave and convex plan forms derived from Borromini, and combined with flanking towers of breathtaking elegance (JSC).*

Fig. 5.17d ↓ *Interior of Wallfahrtskirche Vierzehnheiligen, with the* Gnadenaltar *in the foreground. The nave consists of one large ellipse joined to two ovals, with circular transepts, a development of Borromini's ideas. All the decorative effects are Rococo, that frothy, light, and elegant surface decoration developed in the 18th century, and everything seems to be in motion, with swaying, nodding entablatures and gesticulating figures. The Rococo decorations were by Franz Xaver and Johann Michael Feichtmayr, and Johann Georg Üblhör (JSC).*

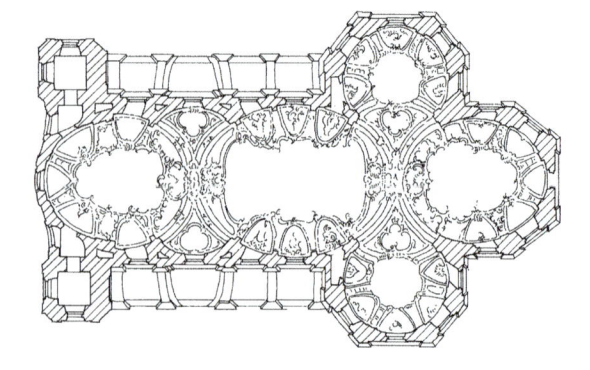

| Fig. 5.17b ↑ *Ceiling plan of Wallfahrtskirche Vierzehnheiligen (JSC).*

84 / Classical Architecture

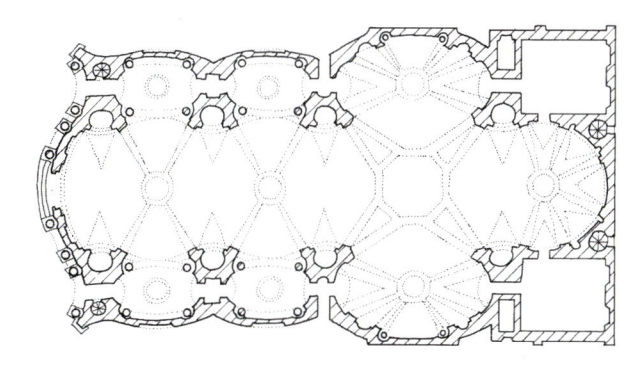

Fig. 5.18 ↑ *Plan of Santa Maria della Divina Providenza, Lisbon (1679 or 1682, destroyed 1755), by Guarino Guarini, which, in its remarkable proliferation of ellipses, has similarities to later plans in central Europe such as those of Neumann. This plan was published in Guarini's* Disegni *of 1686, so was widely disseminated (JSC).*

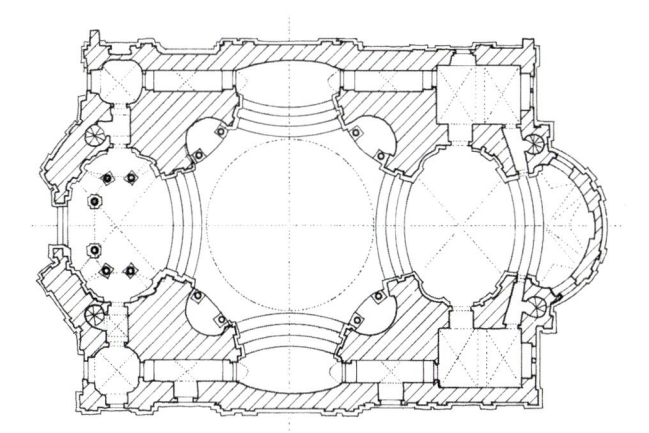

Fig. 5.19a ↑ *Plan of the Dominican Laurenzkirche, Gabel, North Bohemia (1699–1711 – now Church of Sts Laurence and Zdislawa, Jablonné v Podještědí, Czech Republic), by Lukas von Hildebrandt, demonstrating the Austrian's admiration for the work of Guarini. This plan was influential in Mitteleuropa during the 18th century (JSC).*

Fig. 5.19b ↑ *Peterskirche, Vienna, main façade with its flanking towers set at angles to the main geometry, as seen from Graben. Designed originally by Gabriele Montani (1701), from 1703 work continued under Lukas von Hildebrandt, Francesco Martinelli, and others (CSB).*

Fig. 5.19c ↓ *Peterskirche, Vienna, lavishly decorated by J.M. Rottmayr and others, including Antonio Galli-Bibiena (responsible for the presbytery, high altar, and fresco over the choir [1730–2]), M. Altomonte, and M. Steinl (pulpit of 1726). The church was consecrated in 1733 (CSB).*

it is one of the loveliest things on earth. Yet it is unquestionably Classical, derived from a great architectural language, with a vocabulary and a syntax extended and graciously expanded as only a great language can be (Fig. 5.17d).

But such things do not happen in a vacuum, spontaneously emerging, perfect, from the heads of their begetters: there were precedents galore for such wonders as Vierzehnheiligen, including the ingenious plans of Guarini which had been published as early as 1686 (Fig. 5.18) and the wonderfully integrated and clear design (1699–1711) of the Laurenzkirche at Gabel (now Jablonné v Podještědí in the Czech Republic) by Lukas von Hildebrandt (Fig. 5.19a). Hildebrandt was also involved in the design of the Peterskirche, Vienna (from 1703), begun to designs by Gabriele Montani, and planned again as a longitudinal ellipse crowned with a cupola, flanked by two rectangular compartments and an apsidal choir: the tall entrance-front is flanked by twin towers set at angles, giving great drama to the composition (Fig. 5.19b). Franz Jänggl was involved in the building's realisation, and others were Martino Altomonte, Francesco Martinelli, J.M. Rottmayr, and Matthias Steinl (Fig. 5.19c). Another splendid Viennese Baroque church is the Jesuitenkirche, transformed

CLASSICAL VARIATIONS: BAROQUE, ROCOCO, PALLADIANISM, & AFTER / 85

Fig. 5.19d ↑ *Jesuitenkirche, otherwise known as the Universitätskirche, Vienna, the main façade facing the Dr Ignaz Seipel-Platz, Vienna, as remodelled from 1703 by Andrea Pozzo, who added the twin towers (CSB).*

Fig. 5.19e ↓ *Jesuitenkirche, Vienna, as decorated 1703–9 by Andrea Pozzo, the master of* quadratura *(very realistic painted perspectives of architecture, extending the actual interior architecture as* trompe l'œil *work of breathtaking technical brilliance). Note the beautiful Composite pilasters, with cabling in the flutes of the shafts, and the glorious colour (CSB).*

theatrically (1703–9) by Andrea Pozzo, painter, architect, stage-designer, and author of the important *Perspectiva pictorum et architectorum* (1693–1700) (Figs 5.19d–e).

Ellipses recur at Neumann's abbey-church at Neresheim (Fig. 5.20); at Dominikus Zimmermann's pilgrimage churches at Steinhausen (1727–35) (Fig. 5.21a) and elsewhere (Fig. 5.21b); used as main elements (as in the piazza of St Peter in Rome [*see* Fig. 5.11], and in the church of Sant'Andrea al Quirinale [*see* Figs 5.1a–c], both by Bernini); or combined with other ellipses, circles, or figures (as in Borromini's San Carlo alle Quattro Fontane [*see* Figs 5.2a–d]). They are one of the motifs exploited to the full by Baroque and Rococo architects, especially in Central Europe, notably in Southern Germany and Bohemia.

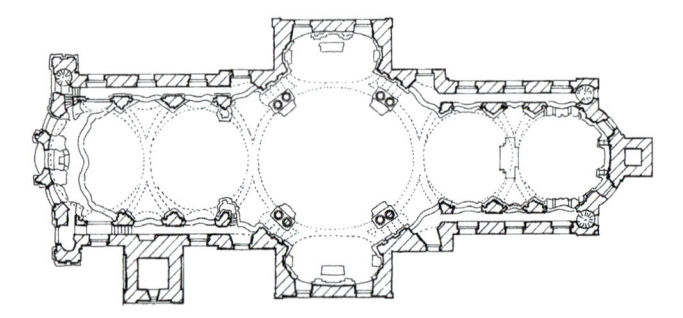

Fig. 5.20 ↑ *Plan of the abbey-church of Sts Ulrich and Afra, Neresheim, Baden-Württemberg (1747–92) (JSC).*

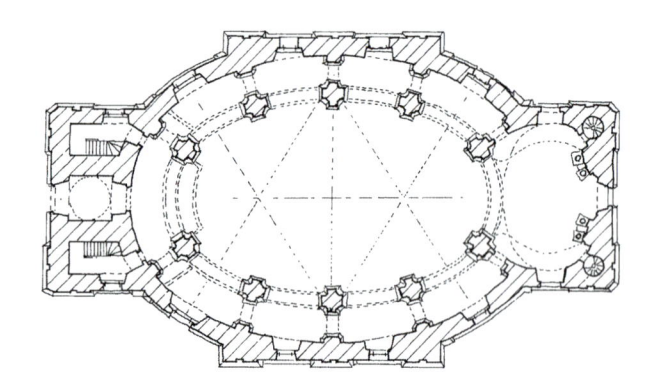

Fig. 5.21a ↑ *Plan of Wallfahrtskirche Unserer Lieben Frau (pilgrimage church of Our Lady), Steinhausen, near Bad Schussenried, Biberach, Baden-Württemberg, by Zimmermann, showing the elliptical forms (JSC).*

Fig. 5.21b ↓ *Wallfahrtskirche zum gegeißelten Heiland auf der Wies (pilgrimage church of the Scourged Saviour on the Meadow), aka Wieskirche (1744–54), near Steingaden, Bavaria, by Zimmermann, on a plan essentially two half-circles on either side of a rectangle (JSC).*

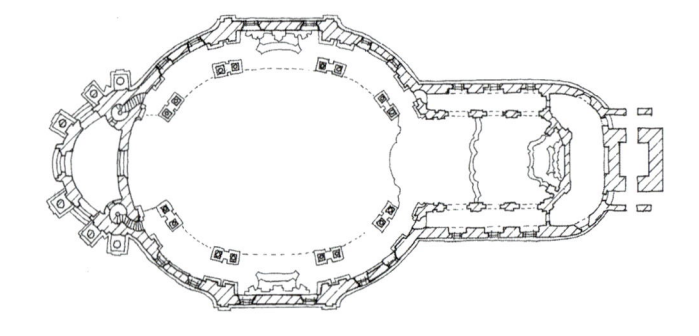

A Selection of French Examples

While the Baroque churches of Rome and the Rococo interiors of central Europe offer some of the most breathtaking and complex architectural experiences possible, a brief word is necessary concerning the design of palaces, a building type that required a specific architectural solution, not just in terms of planning, but to suggest power, the dignity of office, stability, and continuity.

The east front of the Louvre (1665–74) (Fig. 5.22) in Paris goes far beyond anything that Italian architects had achieved in terms of the exploitation of the freestanding column in the façade of a large building. The architects were Le Vau, Le Brun, and Claude Perrault, but it was probably Perrault who was mostly responsible for the design, although his brother, Charles, later claimed his was the defining influence. Bernini's work was the main influence on Perrault, who hid the roofs behind a balustrade, and who modelled the front without any great projecting wings or centrepiece: thus the design marked a departure from the elaborate style of French *château* architecture that had prevailed to that time. The smooth, ashlar face of the ground floor became, in effect, a podium in which segmental-headed windows were set, and on which the colonnade of paired Roman Corinthian columns rests. The paired columns, of course, offer a wider intercolumniation in which to place the fenestration, and there were precedents in the engaged columns used by Bramante and others, but Perrault used fully articulated freestanding columns, giving the façade something of the air of a Roman temple; this temple theme was enhanced by bringing the centre forward on four pairs of columns, carrying an entablature and pediment. This great façade, which terminates in plain projecting wings, must have looked shockingly new and plain when it was first built and when compared with French palatial architecture of the first half of the 17th century; it evoked Antiquity, severity, gravity, and serenity, yet it had majesty, and in fact looks almost like a harbinger of Neo-Classicism. It impressed Wren sufficiently for him to use the twinned columns on the west front of St Paul's Cathedral in London (mixed with Borrominiesque towers, it is true), and the segmental-headed windows at the new wing for Hampton Court Palace.

Jules Hardouin-Mansart also created, in the great domed Church of St-Louis des Invalides (c.1677–91) (Fig. 5.23a), a mixture of severe Antiquity, elegance, and grandeur, quite unlike Italian, English, or German architecture of the time. Earlier French church façades, such as those of the Sorbonne (1635–42), by Jacques Lemercier, and the Val-de-Grâce (1645–66) (Fig. 5.23b), by François Mansart, Lemercier, and others, have affinities with Roman types, but St-Gervais (1616–23), attributed to de Brosse, with contributions possibly by J.-C. Métezeau, is far more Classical, with its superimposed Orders (Roman Doric, Ionic, and Corinthian), the columns of which are not engaged, but stand before the façade proper, the topmost storey of which is crowned by a segmental pediment (Fig. 5.24).

By the time G.-N. Servandoni added the west front to St-Sulpice in Paris (from 1732) (Fig. 5.25) the effect was entirely un-Baroque, with two superimposed five-bay *loggie* set between two austerely Classical towers, while for the former Church of

Fig. 5.22 ↑ *East front of the Louvre, Paris (1665–74), by Le Vau, Le Brun, and Perrault, an astonishingly 'modern' and Classical building for its date, with a colonnade of coupled Corinthian columns (held between the pedimented centrepiece and the end pavilions with their in antis columns) set on top of a plainer podium that is punctuated by segmental-headed windows with eared architraves. This demonstrates how France was developing a clear, uncluttered architectural language which, while owing something to Bernini and Bramante (House of Raphael and Belvedere Court in the Vatican), looks forward to the Neo-Classicism of the next century (BTB).*

CLASSICAL VARIATIONS: BAROQUE, ROCOCO, PALLADIANISM, & AFTER / 87

Fig. 5.23a ← *Dôme des Invalides (c.1677–91) by J. Hardouin-Mansart: a great central space is surmounted by the dome on a drum, and the overall plan is a Greek cross with chapels filling the angles, creating a square plan. Note the severe, Classical treatment of the front, which, although having a Corinthian over a Doric Order, is very much more restrained than Roman or central European Baroque examples (JSC).*

Fig. 5.23b ← *Church of the Val de Grâce, Paris, begun 1645 under François Mansart, who was succeeded for a short time by Lemercier, then by P. Le Muet, and, finally, G. Le Duc, the last two responsible for the vaults, dome, and upper parts of the church, refining in the process the earlier designs. The full-blown Baroque front with massive scrolls (which not only help to support the front, but also act as buttresses over the aisles) is a variation on themes found at Il Gesù, Rome, and Santa Maria Salute, Venice. The mighty dome with lantern crowns this stunning Baroque composition (JSC).*

Fig. 5.24 ↓ *Order upon Order: the Church of St-Gervais, Paris (1616–23), attributed to Salomon de Brosse, but possibly partly by the contractor, J.-C. Métezeau, a remarkably sophisticated Classical design for its time (coll. JSC).*

88 / CLASSICAL ARCHITECTURE

Ste-Geneviève, the architect, Soufflot, created (1755–6) a lucid and clear Neo-Classical plan (Fig. 5.26a) with unfudged geometries and celebration of the column as a structural element, not least in the prostyle hexastyle pedimented Corinthian portico (Fig. 5.26b), the details of which were exemplary (Fig. 5.26c). After the Revolution, the church became the Panthéon, and on the advice of Quatremère de Quincy the windows were blocked up, not for purposes of strengthening the structure as has been claimed, erroneously, by some, but to give the building the character of a mausoleum fitting for its purpose as a place where the great and good of France would be commemorated.

Nevertheless, variations on the Gesù theme were powerfully inventive in French examples well into the 18th century, before Soufflot's superb essay into Neo-Classicism changed all that.

Of course, the palace of Versailles, as it had developed in the 17th century under the direction of Jules Hardouin-Mansart

Fig. 5.25 ↑ *Superimposed colonnades of Doric and Ionic Orders at the Church of St-Sulpice, Paris, influenced partly by the west front of St Paul's Cathedral, London, and partly by an earlier scheme (c.1730) by G.-M. Oppenord. The architect from 1732 was G.N. Servandoni, but J.-F.-T. Chalgrin took over in 1776, and built the north-western tower on the left, the other remaining as it was at Servandoni's death. Earlier designs included a pediment, but this was omitted, creating a more severe, Classical appearance (JSC).*

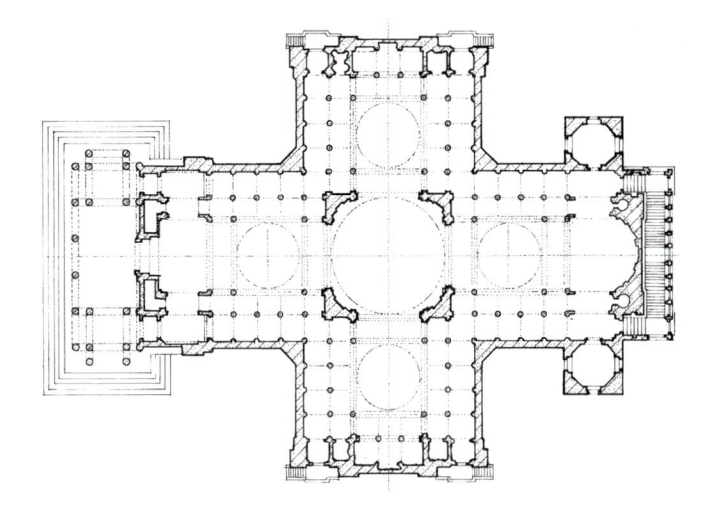

Fig. 5.26a ↑ *Soufflot's final plan for the Church of Ste-Geneviève (now the Panthéon), Paris, a model of Classical clarity (JSC).*

Fig. 5.26b ← *The Panthéon, Paris, by J.-G. Soufflot, begun 1756. The windows of what had been the Church of Ste-Geneviève, traces of which can be seen in the stonework, were blocked by order of Quatremère de Quincy after the Revolution, when the building became a national tomb for the great and good of France, so the idea was to suggest the type of a mausoleum. Wren's dome of St Paul's Cathedral, London, was the model for that of the Panthéon, while the great prostyle hexastyle portico suggests an Antique temple (BTB).*

CLASSICAL VARIATIONS: BAROQUE, ROCOCO, PALLADIANISM, & AFTER / 89

Fig. 5.26c ↑ *Detail of the return corner of the elegant Corinthian Order used in the portico at the Panthéon, Paris. In Classical architecture, the handling of corners, especially where entablatures with dentils, modillions, and other enrichments are present, is of fundamental importance: if botched, either on an external or internal angle, the results can ruin the architectural effect (JSC).*

and others, set standards for the grand axial plan, by which great house, town, park, and even country, were united in one scheme, and indeed it encapsulates the idea of centralised planning which had so occupied the minds of many early Italian Renaissance masters. The plan for Rome under Sixtus V, Scamozzi's layout for Palmanova, and the axial planning of Italian *palazzi* and French *hôtels* all proved to be potent models, but at Versailles, everything was on an enormous scale: the garden-front of the palace faces Le Nôtre's park, where its huge parterres of flowers, its vast cruciform sheets of water, its fountains, its complex layouts of parallel and radiating avenues, and its walks set between tall hedges, all suggested the taming of Nature in the service of the Sun King, Louis XIV, whose bedroom was located at the centre of the composition.

Perhaps an even better example of the centralised plan, in which the layout of a whole city consisted of avenues radiating outwards from the ducal palace, was at Karlsruhe, the Residenzstadt of Baden, designed at the beginning of the 18th century, and still remarkably readable from the air, although the place was very badly damaged in the 1939–45 war.

Classical Architecture in England

Early Classical influences from Italy first appeared in England in royal tombs in Westminster Abbey: these were the tomb-chest and effigy (1511–13) of Lady Margaret Beaufort and the entire monument (1512–18) of King Henry VII and his queen, both by Pietro Torrigiani (or Torrigiano). The latter monument is exquisitely and serenely beautiful. So royal patronage was a hugely important factor in the introduction of the new style. However, the political and cultural isolation of England after the break with Rome in 1533–4 led to knowledge of Italian Renaissance architecture being mainly acquired from Northern European sources, filtered, as it were, and altered in the process.

An outstanding funerary monument (*c.*1552 or *c.*1570) in the church of All Saints, Wing, Buckinghamshire, possibly by John Shute, demonstrates a pronounced Franco-Italian influence (it has much lavish strapwork): it consists of an altar-like sarcophagus decorated with bucrania and garlands under a massive tester set against a wall carried on paired fluted Corinthian columns with matching pilasters on the wall side, and commemorates Sir Robert Dormer.

The triumphal-arch motif appeared first at Somerset House in the Strand, London (1547–52), and later at Burghley House near Stamford in Lincolnshire (where the influences are profoundly those from the Netherlands, notably Antwerp, in the inner courtyard of *c.*1576–85), when superimposed Orders were used to great effect (Fig. 5.27). However, the sources for much late-Tudor Renaissance architecture were Shute's book on the Orders of 1563, French designs by Philibert de l'Orme, and, of course, Serlio. There are several English examples of frontispieces adorned with superimposed Orders (*see* Fig. 4.34), while a Giant Order of pilasters appears at Kirby Hall, Northamptonshire (Fig. 5.28). Until the advent of Inigo Jones's Palladianism, though, elaborate styles were derived from Northern Europe, and especially from the publications of Shute, Vredeman de Vries, and Wendel Dietterlin.

During the 16th century, Classicism was being introduced and used very freely in polite circles in England. The work at Burghley House is a prodigious example, as is that at Longleat, Wiltshire, where Alan Maynard (who was French) and Robert Smythson, working in partnership in the 1570s, produced some very impressive work (Fig. 5.29a). Smythson had worked at Somerset House, but it was Maynard who brought a more sophisticated Classical vocabulary to their joint efforts at Longleat, clothing the great house with a skin of French-inspired detail. Inside the house, in the Great Hall, is a chimneypiece by Maynard on the north wall, the lower part of which is Ionic, clearly after Philibert de l'Orme, but above the entablature is a wild Franco-Flemish concoction after Ducerceau and Vredemann de Vries.

Smythson went on to build one of the most extraordinary of houses, Wollaton Hall, Wollaton, Nottingham, from 1580 (Fig. 5.29b): he was to stay there until his death, working for Sir Francis Willoughby, who had a large library, which may have included books on architecture by Alberti, Philibert de l'Orme, Ducerceau, Palladio, Scamozzi, Serlio, Vignola, and Vitruvius (in the Venetian edition of 1567). A catalogue of Willoughby's library, dating from the latter part of the 17th century, does not

Fig. 5.27 ↑ *Inner court of Burghley House, near Stamford (c.1576–85), with frontispiece of three storeys crowned by a fantastic composition surmounted by a steep pyramidal spire. So what we have is three superimposed triumphal arches, the uppermost of which has its central arch replaced by a canted bay window, and above that is a stage containing a clock face, flanked on either side by lions and spiky obelisks. The main influences on the architecture would appear to have been from France, especially the château of Anet, Dreux (1547–55), by Philibert de l'Orme, and from Somerset House, London, which itself had been influenced by Continental work (AH).*

Fig. 5.28 ↑ *Giant Order of pilasters on the north front of the courtyard, Kirby Hall, Northamptonshire (1560, remodelled c.1630), with panels of Grotesque reliefs almost identical to the decorations on the title page of John Shute's* The First and Chief Groundes of Architecture *(1563). Similar designs occurred in northern Europe in the works of Philibert de l'Orme and Jacques Androuet Ducerceau, among others (JSC).*

Fig. 5.29a ← *South front of Longleat, Wiltshire (1567–80), by Robert Smythson, a curiously unresolved façade which lacks a strong centrepiece (JOD).*

CLASSICAL VARIATIONS: BAROQUE, ROCOCO, PALLADIANISM, & AFTER

Fig. 5.29b → *Wollaton Hall, Nottingham (1580–8), by Robert Smythson, a spectacular Elizabethan pile, symmetrical on all four sides, with storeys articulated by superimposed Classical pilasters, but the whole composition here looks back to a mediæval precedent, emphasised by the four almost free-standing towers. Above the central great hall (instead of a court), itself illuminated through a clerestorey, is a prospect room with window tracery derived from Vredeman de Vries's* Variæ Architecturæ *(1577) (AH).*

contain any mention of works by Vredeman de Vries, whose influence at Wollaton is omnipresent: the late Mark Girouard has suggested that de Vries's books may have been dismembered for use by Smythson and his associates, something not beyond the bounds of possibility. However, the versatility and enormous range of motifs found in the published books on architecture of the 16th century are demonstrated in the huge number of realised designs that enrich England.

It is often in chimneypieces (Fig. 5.30a) and funerary monuments in churches that the pronounced Classical influences from France and, particularly, the Netherlands, can be studied. In funerary monuments, especially, there are many spectacular examples, of which only a sample can be mentioned here. One of the most accomplished of mid-16th-century English craftsmen working in an early Renaissance style was John Chapman, who worked at Lacock Abbey, Wiltshire (c.1550–3), and may have been responsible for the sumptuous monument to Sir William Sharington in the north-east chapel of the Church of St Cyriac at Lacock, which is dated 1566 (Fig. 5.30b). If Chapman designed and made the so-called Holbein Porch at Wilton House, also in Wiltshire (c.1560), then he was a very sophisticated artificer in the use of accomplished Ionic and Corinthian Orders, for the building looks much later than its date might suggest.

The use of structural polychromy (differently coloured stones) frequently adds interest and vigorous colour to the lavish ensembles that often comprise the funerary monuments that grace so many churches throughout England. And many splendid examples can be found, including the towering and very sumptuous pile-up commemorating Edward Seymour in Salisbury Cathedral (Fig. 5.30c), the enchanting survivals in the Church of Sts Peter and Paul, Exton, Rutland (Figs 5.30d–e), and the Manners tombs in Bottesford, Leicestershire (Fig. 5.30f). One of the most astonishing funerary monuments (though with many parts of it missing, as it was moved at least twice from its original position) is that commemorating Lady Katherine Boyle, wife of Richard Boyle, 1st Earl of Cork, in St Patrick's Cathedral, Dublin (Fig. 5.30g), although it astonishes more by its flashiness and size than by its finesse.

Fig. 5.30a ↑ *Sumptuous drawing room, South Wraxall Manor, Wiltshire (c.1600–11), with plaster tunnel-vaulted ceiling featuring thin curved ribs and pendants, suns, moons, and other decorations, all apparently of 1611 by John Sweetman. The huge chimneypiece, the fireplace flanked by coupled terms straight from Vredeman de Vries, has a lavish overmantel with figures of Prudence, Arithmetic, Geometry, and Justice framed in shallow niches, and there much strapwork, indeed almost a surfeit of ornament, mostly from Flemish printed sources. This enormous confection, with its central figure of the overmantel a pagan deity (Pan, perhaps?), may have been the work of the Bristolian craftsmen John and Anthony Frynde: William Gryffyne, who worked at Hardwick Hall, Derbyshire, has also been suggested (JOD).*

92 / Classical Architecture

Fig. 5.30b ← Monument commemorating Sir William Sharington in the north-east chapel of the Church of St Cyriac, Lacock, Wiltshire, dated 1566, with ornament based on designs by Ducerceau. Note the Renaissance pilasters with arabesque decorations on the shafts, knotwork frieze, putti supporting Sharington's arms, and vases instead of obelisks. Possibly by John Chapman (JOD).

Fig. 5.30c ↙ Sumptuous, towering monument to Edward Seymour, 1st Earl of Hertford (d.1621), in the south choir aisle of Salisbury Cathedral, possibly by William Wright. In the centre are effigies of the Earl and his Countess (Katharine, née Grey) beneath a massive coffered arch flanked by canopies each carried on four columns. The form is in essence that of a triumphal arch, but the flanking canopies shelter kneeling figures facing north, and above each canopy is half a curved pediment topped by a female figure and an obelisk. The large central arch (at the back of which is an inscription panel) is framed by two columns supporting an entablature, and the spandrels so formed are decorated with heraldic devices: above this entablature is an upper tier with two arched inscription panels flanked by allegorical figures and obelisks. The whole is crowned with a pedestal carrying the Seymour achievement of arms. The materials are mostly alabaster, but some colour is provided it the shafts of columns and in panels of contrasting polished stone, while the rest is applied (JOD).

Fig. 5.30d ↓ Monument of Robert Kelway, his daughter, her husband, and grandchildren, in the Church of Sts Peter and Paul, Exton, Rutland. An outstanding work of the late 16th century, mostly of alabaster, but with structural colour provided by the column-shafts, obelisks, and panels of stone. The central arch is flanked by coupled columns, and shelters a recumbent effigy, two kneeling figures, and a tiny effigy of the child lying on a small pedestal. The superstructure features obelisks and an achievement of arms (JSC).

CLASSICAL VARIATIONS: BAROQUE, ROCOCO, PALLADIANISM, & AFTER / 93

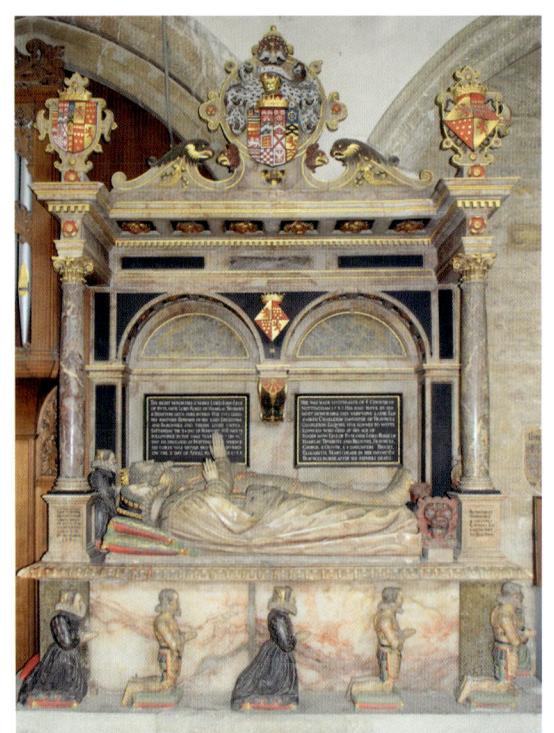

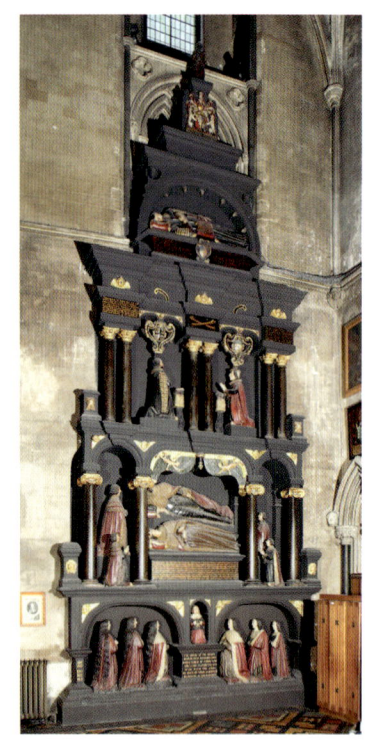

Fig. 5.30e ↑ *Another very fine funerary monument in Exton church, this time to Sir James Harington and his wife, Lucy Sidney, with kneeling figures facing each other over a prayer-desk, much of the colour provided by the stones used, and the superstructure again featuring obelisks and achievements. There is some good ribbonwork decorative carving. Like the Kelway monument, it is London work, probably by sculptors of the Southwark school (JSC).*

Fig. 5.30f ↗ *Funerary monument (completed 1591) to John Manners, 4th Earl of Rutland, in the Church of St Mary, Bottesford, Leicestershire, made in the Southwark yard of Gerard Johnson. Note the kneeling figures at the head and feet, and six smaller kneeling figures at the base (JSC).*

Fig. 5.30g ↗↗ *Prodigious monument to the Boyle family, Earls of Cork, completed 1632, in St Patrick's Cathedral, Dublin. It was designed by Alban Leverett, made by Edmund Tingham, and re-erected against the south wall of the nave in 1863. Unfortunately, much has been lost, including obelisks, allegorical figures, coronets, and even some family members (D&A).*

Fig. 5.31 ↓ *Banqueting House, Whitehall (1619–22), by Inigo Jones, a development of the Vicenzan palazzi of Palladio, with its patterns of superimposed pilasters and columns and alternating segmental and triangular pediments. An example of the first Palladian Revival in England, which must have looked almost shockingly new at the time (RHB).*

The direct influence of Italy is found in the architecture of Inigo Jones, notably the Queen's House at Greenwich (see Fig. 4.43) and the Banqueting House in Whitehall (Fig. 5.31), both exemplary buildings of what we must regard as the first English Palladian Revival. At Wilton, Wiltshire, the south front of 1636 by Isaac de Caux (with Jones's advice) incorporates many Italian features, including the central window.

John Webb designed the first pedimented temple portico for a country house in England at The Vyne, Hampshire, of 1654. Webb's very grand King Charles II block at Greenwich Hospital (1664–9) has an engaged, pedimented temple-front in the centre and two wings with Giant Orders of Corinthian pilasters at each end, one of the best of the palatial 17th-century façades in England (Fig. 5.32).

With Sir Christopher Wren, the Baroque style arrived in England, but it was a Baroque filtered through France, and not imported directly from Italy. Wren had visited Paris in 1665–66, when he saw 'esteem'd Fabricks' which influenced his future work. After the Great Fire of 1666, Wren was appointed Surveyor-General to the Office of Works in 1669, and supervised the design of the City churches. In many of these schemes Wren combined the Baroque concerns for centralised planning with some grandly Antique effects, while his inventiveness in the designs of the steeples rarely faltered.

His designs for St Paul's Cathedral owe something to French precedents, notably Mansart and Lemercier's Val-de-Grâce, and Michelangelo's St Peter's in Rome, but the version as realised incorporates the doubled columns of Perrault's east front of the Louvre; the two storeys of Inigo Jones's Banqueting House; transepts that derive from da Cortona's Santa Maria della Pace in Rome, mixed with Mansart's designs for the Louvre; western towers evolved from Borromini and Rainaldi's Santa Agnese in Agone; and a dome that is a felicitous marriage of ideas derived from Michelangelo and from French exemplars.

Wren's Trinity College library, Cambridge (1676–84), has superimposed Orders, yet, although Sansovino's St Mark's library in Venice is an obvious influence, in many respects the architectural detail seems more French than Italian (Fig. 5.33).

Hampton Court Palace's south and east wings of 1689–94 have some segmental-headed windows based on Perrault's work at the Louvre, but Wren's splendid buildings at Greenwich (1696–1716), with their Baroque domes and colonnades (again employing twinned columns) are even finer, and, with the earlier architecture of Webb and Jones, comprise one of the greatest monumental symmetrical compositions of the period (Fig. 5.34). The plan of the Invalides in Paris influenced Wren at the Greenwich and Chelsea hospitals, and the layout of Versailles was no doubt lurking at the back of his mind when he designed these remarkable ensembles. Versailles was to be a model for some of the later Baroque palaces.

William Talman was responsible for the south and east wings of Chatsworth House in Derbyshire. The south front, with its Giant Order of Ionic pilasters, owes something to Bernini's third project for the east front of the Louvre (1665). Although Talman's

Fig. 5.32 ↑ *King Charles II block at Greenwich (1664–9), by John Webb, an uncommonly grand symmetrical composition in which the Giant Order plays no small part (AFK H20758).*

Fig. 5.33 → *The library at Trinity College, Cambridge (1676–84), by Wren, in which echoes of Sansovino's library in Venice can be discerned (AFK H8242).*

Fig. 5.34 ↓ *Greenwich Hospital, with Jones's Queen's House in the centre of the composition. Completed by Wren from 1696, his work includes the colonnades (note the paired columns) and the twin domes. This is one of the finest Baroque compositions in England (AFK H11649).*

CLASSICAL VARIATIONS: BAROQUE, ROCOCO, PALLADIANISM, & AFTER / 95

Fig. 5.35a ← *Castle Howard, Yorkshire, designed 1699, and commenced on site in 1700, by Vanbrugh and Hawksmoor. This is one of the great monuments of English Baroque architecture (AFK H17559).*

Fig. 5.35b ↓ *Blenheim Palace, Oxfordshire (1705–16), erected for John Churchill, 1st Duke of Marlborough, to designs by Vanbrugh and Hawksmoor, an even more massively Baroque composition, with towers over which are Attic-storey belvederes that incorporate Antique and Baroque themes from Perrault and Borromini. Yet Blenheim also has echoes of Elizabethan and Jacobean architecture in the romantic skyline (AFK H5615).*

work at Chatsworth is grand and Baroque, it is overshadowed by the stupendous compositions of Castle Howard, Yorkshire, of 1699 (Fig. 5.35a), by Sir John Vanbrugh assisted by Nicholas Hawksmoor. At Castle Howard the precedents of Webb's work at Greenwich, Talman's at Chatsworth, and Wren's at Greenwich merge with French exemplars such as Vaux-le-Vicomte and Marly. At Blenheim Palace, Oxfordshire (1705–16 and 1722–5), Vanbrugh and Hawksmoor combined the grand centre-block, courtyard, and wings (based on Palladian and Versailles precedents) with elements from Antiquity (a Roman ruin illustrated by Perrault in his 1673 edition of Vitruvius), suggestions of Borromini's distorted skylines, and echoes of Bernini's piazza of St Peter. Blenheim combines contrasting heavy masses of masonry, Giant and subsidiary Orders, and a busy, romantic silhouette that harks back, perhaps, to early Renaissance houses of the Elizabethan period (Fig. 5.35b).

It should be remembered that Blenheim was built for John Churchill, created 1st Duke of Marlborough for his military successes, a revival of the Antique cult of heroes, emphasised by the erection of the Column of Victory in the park at Blenheim in 1727–31 to designs by Henry Herbert, assisted by Roger Morris and William Townesend. The column is surmounted by a lead statue of the duke by Robert Pit. The magnificent symbolic sculpture at Blenheim Palace is a marvellous example of how decorative carving was fully integrated within the architecture, and not stuck on as an afterthought. This, in fact, is one of Classicism's great strengths: at Blenheim, much of it was by Grinling Gibbons and his associates. It is interesting to compare Marlborough's Blenheim with the palace of his comrade-in-arms, Prince Eugen of Savoy, at the Belvedere, Vienna (1714–24), an altogether more delicate affair, by Johann Lukas von Hildebrandt (Fig. 5.35c).

Hawksmoor's London churches also mix several themes: St George's, Bloomsbury, alludes to the great Hellenistic mausoleum at Halicarnassus on top of the tower, while the noble body of the church has an Antique Roman temple-front and an interior that suggests something of the massiveness of Roman Imperial buildings (Figs 5.36a–b). At St Alphege, Greenwich, Hawksmoor used the Roman Imperial motif of an arch rising into a pediment, while at St George-in-the-East and St Anne, Limehouse, he combined Baroque exaggeration and changes of plane with Gothic lanterns composed of Classical details. Christ Church, Spitalfields, has a vast serliana as the portico, a wide triumphal-arch motif without overt Orders above, and a broach spire over the whole (Fig. 5.37).

Fig. 5.35c ↑ *The Belvedere Palace, Vienna (1714–24), designed by Lukas von Hildebrandt for Prince Eugen of Savoy, the distinguished military commander who had been a comrade-in-arms of John Churchill. The almost oriental roofs and frothy façades with shaped pediments and corner towers contrast with the infinitely more powerful composition at Blenheim Palace (CSB).*

Fig. 5.36a ← *Church of St George, Bloomsbury, London (1716–31), by Nicholas Hawksmoor, showing the prostyle hexastyle Corinthian portico, and the extraordinary steeple that alludes to the stepped pyramidal form of the Mausoleum of Halicarnassus on the tower based on Pliny's description (AFK H1768).*

Fig. 5.36b ↑ *Detail of the top of the steeple of St George's Church, Bloomsbury, showing the restored lion and unicorn alluding to the royal arms, and the composition is capped by a statue of King George I, so the building is a triumphalist statement of the recent accession of the Hanoverians to the Throne (RHB).*

CLASSICAL VARIATIONS: BAROQUE, ROCOCO, PALLADIANISM, & AFTER / 97

At Castle Howard Vanbrugh designed the Temple of the Four Winds (1724–26): it is based on the Villa Capra near Vicenza, and so, with its four identical porticoes and dome over the central body, is Palladian in inspiration, yet the appearance is anything but Palladian: it is a Baroquised version of Palladianism (Fig. 5.38). The mausoleum at Castle Howard, however, of 1728–42, was designed by Hawksmoor, and has a majestic clarity reminiscent of Bramante's Tempietto; but it is vast in size. The Tuscan columns are elongated and carry a Doric frieze: there is only one triglyph over each intercolumniation, and the effect is solemnly grand, powerful, and forbidding (Figs 5.39a–b). A mausoleum (*see* Glossary) was, of course, an Antique building type, and Hawksmoor's tremendous invention was not only a reference to Bramante's Tempietto, but a conscious re-creation of an architectural celebration of death as manifested in parts of the Antique Græco-Roman world.

James Gibbs used the circular temple theme at his Radcliffe Camera in Oxford, but with an engaged Order on a rusticated base, and references to Michelangelo and Santa Maria della Salute, among other precedents (Fig. 5.40). It is important to recognise that Bramante's Tempietto, the domes of St Paul's, St Peter's, the Val de Grâce, the Invalides, the Radcliffe Camera, and the mausoleum at Castle Howard are all related in their geometry and handling, yet they are all distinctly different as well: such were some of the infinite possibilities of the Classical language of architecture. Gibbs, of course, was responsible for other distinguished buildings, including the London churches of St Martin-in-the-Fields of 1720–6 (with its temple-front, tower, and steeple emulating Gothic form in Classical detail, and two-storey fenestration system on the sides to accommodate the gallery) (Fig. 5.41), and the masterly St Mary-le-Strand of 1714–17 (which combines a three-stage steeple derived from Wren's inventions with a powerfully Roman Baroque body) (Figs 5.42a–b). Gibbs published influential works dealing with design, rules, and methods of drawing architecture, and provided patterns for doorcases and window-surrounds that were widely copied, as with the 'Gibbs surround' (*see* Figs G64a–b). Another gifted English Baroque architect was Thomas Archer, who, more

| Fig. 5.37 ← *Serliana or Venetian window arrangement as a portico at Christ Church, Spitalfields, London (1714–29), by Nicholas Hawksmoor. The motif recurs above in the tower, capped by a Gothic broach-spire (JSC).*

| Fig. 5.38 ↓ *Temple of the Four Winds at Castle Howard, Yorkshire (1724–6), by Vanbrugh (coll. JSC).*

Fig. 5.39a ↑ *The Sublime mausoleum at Castle Howard, Yorkshire (designed 1728–9 and built 1731–42), by Nicholas Hawksmoor, based on Bramante's Tempietto at San Pietro in Montorio, Rome (but on a far grander scale), and on Hawksmoor's first proposals for the Radcliffe library, Oxford. The blending of Antiquity with Modernity is again expressed. Hawksmoor's low calotte dome and the intercolumniation of 1½ diameters (which has no Antique precedent) give the building a stern and forbidding air, enhanced by the fortress-like plinth designed by Daniel Garrett (AFK H8911).*

Fig. 5.39b ← *Noble and severe interior of the mausoleum at Castle Howard (CL).*

Fig. 5.40 ↓ *A further variation on the rotunda theme is provided by James Gibbs's Radcliffe library, Oxford (1737–48), with the paired Corinthian engaged columns set on a powerful rusticated plinth, giving a rich effect, and mixing Baroque, Antique, and Renaissance motifs (JSC).*

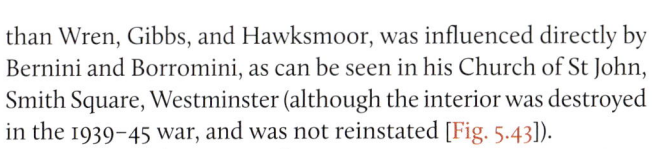

than Wren, Gibbs, and Hawksmoor, was influenced directly by Bernini and Borromini, as can be seen in his Church of St John, Smith Square, Westminster (although the interior was destroyed in the 1939–45 war, and was not reinstated [Fig. 5.43]).

However, the sense of overpowering massiveness (Fig. 5.44) found in works by Vanbrugh and Hawksmoor (both of whom knew well the language of Antiquity), the deliberate exaggeration of features such as keystones and ædicules, and the employment of Mannerist, Baroque, and other devices led to a reaction, which will be described below. There was another reason for the reaction too: Baroque was associated with Roman Catholicism and absolutism, yet was acceptable during the reign of the Stuart Queen Anne (Fig. 5.45). Gibbs was a Catholic, a Tory, a Scot, and very likely had Jacobite sympathies: his architecture, so obviously tainted with papist Roman precedent, was hardly to be endured or encouraged

CLASSICAL VARIATIONS: BAROQUE, ROCOCO, PALLADIANISM, & AFTER / 99

Fig. 5.41 ↑ *St Martin-in-the-Fields, London (1720–6), by James Gibbs, with prostyle hexastyle temple-front and spire. The body of the building has a Giant Order of Corinthian pilasters, and the window-openings above and below the galleries are surrounded with banded architraves, with massive keystones and voussoirs breaking into the tops of the architraves (a treatment known as Gibbs surrounds) (Gibbs [1728], coll. JSC).*

Fig. 5.42a ↑ *West elevation of St Mary-le-Strand, London (1714–17), by Gibbs (from Gibbs [1728], coll. JSC).*

Fig. 5.42b ↗ *Sophisticated south elevation of St Mary-le-Strand, London, by Gibbs, with a pronounced Roman influence suggested by the architect's training under Carlo Fontana (Gibbs [1728], coll. JSC).*

by the Whigs after the Jacobite Rebellion of 1715, and so it proved, for he was sacked from his surveyorship to the Commissioners for Building Fifty New Churches, possibly, as he himself believed, through the machinations of a fellow countryman, almost certainly Colen Campbell, who omitted his name from *Vitruvius Britannicus*. However, equipped as he was with a first-class architectural training gained in Rome, he was enabled to develop his connections with various grandees for whom he designed country houses (Howard Colvin called him 'the Tory architect *par excellence*'), and through the Whig Duke of Argyll he was given the post of Architect of the Ordnance (1727), a position he held for the rest of his life. His Senate House, Cambridge (1721–30), with its Giant Corinthian Order derived from the Temple of Jupiter Stator, Rome, is an elegant mix of the architectural languages of Wren, the new English Palladianism, and a tinge of the Italian architecture Gibbs had studied in his youth when he worked under Fontana (Fig. 5.46).

Gibbs advertised his work as an architect in *A Book of Architecture* (1728), which contained 150 plates of his executed and unrealised designs, a second edition of which came out in 1739, and in 1732 published the very important *Rules for Drawing the Several Parts of Architecture*, with subsequent editions of 1736, 1738, and 1753. *A Book of Architecture* was immediately successful in its time, a high-quality pattern-book in wide use on both sides of the Atlantic.

Fig. 5.43 ↑ *St John's, Smith Square, Westminster (1713–28), by Thomas Archer, a remarkable Baroque composition with four identical towers, which gave it the nickname 'Queen Anne's footstool'. Perhaps more than Wren, and certainly more than Hawksmoor, Archer was influenced by Bernini and Borromini (AFK H223).*

Fig. 5.44 ↑ *Clarendon Building, Broad Street, Oxford (1712–15), by Hawksmoor, with design advice from George Clarke. A very powerful work of architecture, full of gravitas, with massive engaged portico in the form of a Giant Order of Roman Doric, suggests Antiquity in its brooding way. Note the pediments and the oversized keystone in the segmental arches set in the wide frame around the panels (JSC).*

Fig. 5.45 ↑ *Hawksmoor's St George-in-the-East, Wapping, London (1714–29), from the south-east, showing the extraordinary Roman altars on top of the buttresses on the crowning octagon of the tower (an element perhaps derived from late mediæval exemplars such as those in Boston, Lincolnshire, or Fotheringhay, Northamptonshire: these mixes of Classical-pagan and mediæval-Christian forms are typical of Hawksmoor's interest in reconciling diverse allusions and architectural themes). Fenestration provided light above and below the galleries (accessed via the staircases on top of which were perched the inventive 'pepper-pots'). Note the immensely oversized keystones and voussoirs over openings (JSC).*

Fig. 5.46 ↑ *The Senate House, Cambridge (1721–30), by Gibbs, a subtle and refined amalgam of Baroque and Palladian themes (JSC).*

CLASSICAL VARIATIONS: BAROQUE, ROCOCO, PALLADIANISM, & AFTER / 101

Some German Buildings

One of the greatest of all European palaces was the Königliches Schloß in Berlin, designed by Nering, Schlüter, and others (totally destroyed in 1950 by the East German authorities after the Second World War, but partially reconstructed 2013–20): it owed a considerable debt to Bernini, notably his abortive scheme for the Louvre (Fig. 5.47). Nering, Schlüter, de Bodt, and others were responsible for the Zeughaus (arsenal), which still survives in the Unter den Linden, Berlin (1695–1729), a splendid realisation in Prussia of monumental Classicism (Fig. 5.48). Two of those architects' greatest contemporaries were J.B. Fischer von Erlach (whose *Entwurff einer Historischen Architektur* [1721] aroused widespread interest in a wide range of historical architecture and styles from many eras, cultures, and locations, and included several of his own projects) and Johann Lukas von Hildebrandt. The latter's Upper Belvedere in Vienna (1720–4) has exotic pavilion roofs derived from French precedents, but the detail owes much to Italian Mannerist and Baroque examples (*see* Fig. 5.35c). Fischer von Erlach's Schönbrunn Palace in Vienna was strongly influenced by French Classicism, and demonstrates how the Classical language of architecture could

Fig. 5.47 ↑ *The Königliches Schloß (royal palace), Berlin, with Schinkel's beautiful Schloßbrücke (1819–24) in the foreground, linking Unter den Linden with the Spreeinsel. Work on transforming the electoral Residenz into a grand palace for the kings of Prussia began from 1679 under Nering, then Schlüter, Eosander von Göthe, and Martin Böhme: the last completed the major works 1714–16, but the cupola was not realised until 1845–52 under F.A. Stüler (coll. JSC).*

Fig. 5.48 → *The Zeughaus (arsenal), Unter den Linden, Berlin (1695–1729), by J.A. Nering, Andreas Schlüter, Jean de Bodt, and others, a splendidly ornate realisation in Prussia of architectural sophistication derived from Italian exemplars, with its upper storey articulated by Roman Doric pilasters, and its skyline and details enriched by vigorous sculpture (coll. JSC).*

Fig. 5.49 ↑ *The pavilion principle of composition: Schloß Nymphenburg, Munich, begun 1663 by Barelli, continued from 1673 under Zuccalli, then added to by Viscardi from 1702, then resumed under Effner and others in the course of the 18th century (JSC).*

Fig. 5.50a ↓ *The extraordinary Zwinger Palace, Dresden (1711–22), by M.D. Pöppelmann for Friedrich August II, Prince-Elector of Saxony and King of Poland. This Baroque extravaganza consists of two-storey pavilions, lavishly decorated with sculpture by Balthasar Permoser, linked by single-storey galleries. The Wallpavillon (1716–17) in the centre has a festsaal within its upper level (JSC).*

Fig. 5.50b ↑ *The Kronentor at the Zwinger in Dresden, a marvellously inventive confection with all sorts of oddities, including a bulbous cupola topped by the crown of Poland rising over a veritable forest of clustered pilasters and broken pediments possibly influenced by Pozzo's book on perspective, which came out in a German edition in 1706-9 (JSC).*

be used in a long range, using a Giant Order on a plinth, repetitive elements, and emphases in the centre and ends of the composition. Very different was the system of pavilions used in Schloß Nymphenburg, Munich, designed (1663–1728) by Barelli, Zuccalli, and Viscardi, with later alterations by others (Fig. 5.49).

Even more extraordinary is the series of galleries with two-storey pavilions – part grandstand, part pleasure palace, part nymphæum, part gallery, part orangery known as the Zwinger in Dresden, designed by M.D. Pöppelmann, and built 1711-22, with sculptures by Balthasar Permoser. Here, broken segmental pediments are turned back to front, and sway apart; encrustations of figures and other decorations are piled up over every surface; and the most marvellous invention is displayed on the gate and other pavilions. Even the Italian Baroque designers seem ponderous in comparison with this Saxon masterpiece (Figs 5.50a–b).

Another fine example of Prussian palatial architecture is Schloß Charlottenburg, Berlin (begun 1695 and enlarged 1704-12 under Eosander von Göthe): its noble centrepiece sets off the entire composition (Fig. 5.51). Enchanting, too, is Frederick the Great's one-storey palace of Sanssouci at Potsdam, designed by the king and G.W. von Knobelsdorff from 1745. It has terminal atlantes on the outside (Fig. 5.52a; see Fig. G108), similar to those of the Zwinger, but the central hall, with its Corinthian columns, has a Classical simplicity in which a pronounced French influence may be detected (Fig. 5.52b). Some of the rooms, however, are still deliciously Rococo, and one is Neo-Classical, by Erdmannsdorff.

Also at Potsdam, J.G. Büring's Neues Palais of 1755–66 owes something to the south front of Castle Howard, and a further English flavour is obvious at Knobelsdorff's opera house on the Unter den Linden, Berlin, begun in 1740, the long elevations of which are based on Colen Campbell's Wanstead in Essex (Fig. 5.53). The Yorkshire and Essex houses had been published in Colen Campbell's *Vitruvius Britannicus* (1715–25), itself an important reference to veneration of the great Roman author.

Those English influences are significant, and are representative of a general reaction against Baroque and Rococo that led back first to Italian 16th-century exemplars and then, as we will see, to a search for the purity of Antiquity, and even to primitive stereometrically simple forms. However, Karl von Gontard, who arrived in Berlin from Bayreuth in 1763, and who had trained under J.-F. Blondel in Paris, brought with him a sound grasp of French Classicism in several buildings in Prussia. Perhaps his finest contribution to Berlin was the transformation of two Baroque churches in the Gendarmenmarkt which he boldly remodelled and added the twin drums and domes (Fig. 5.54): sited on either side of Schinkel's later Schauspielhaus, his work helped to create one of the grandest architectural compositions in the city (see Fig. 6.11g).

Fig. 5.51 ← *Central part of Schloß Charlottenburg, Berlin, begun (1695) under Nering and enlarged (1704–12) by Eosander, who was responsible for the tall central dome on a high drum. The equestrian statue (1696–1700) in the foreground is of the 'Great Elector', Friedrich Wilhelm, and was by Schlüter (JSC).*

Fig. 5.52a ↓ *Sanssouci Palace, Potsdam, by Knobelsdorff, of the 1740s, with the elliptical Marmorsaal projecting from the centre. Note the terms (pedestals like inverted obelisks merging with heroic male and female figures supporting the entablature) instead of pilasters (JSC).*

Fig. 5.52b → *The Marmorsaal, Sanssouci (1745–6), by Knobelsdorff. This interior is inspired by the Antique source of the Pantheon, and also suggests the coupled-column motif used by Perrault. Antiquity and Modernity merge (JSC).*

104 / CLASSICAL ARCHITECTURE

Fig. 5.53 ↑ *Knobelsdorff's opera-house on the Unter den Linden, Berlin (1740–3), the first great Neo-Palladian building in Germany. It has a temple-front, and indeed was conceived partly as a temple of the arts, with a ceremonial hall serving as vestibule and dining room. It was partly based on Colen Campbell's Wanstead (c.1714–20) (JSC).*

Fig. 5.54 ↑ *The French Church in the Gendarmenmarkt, Berlin (1701–8), originally by J.-L. Cayart and A. Quesnay, with drum and dome added 1780–85 to designs by Karl von Gontard and built under G.C. Unger (restored 1977–81 after destruction in the 1939–45 war). It mixes the clarity of Franco-Prussian Classicism with a Neo-Palladianism influenced partly by England: shades of the Villa Capra are apparent (JSC).*

CLASSICAL VARIATIONS: BAROQUE, ROCOCO, PALLADIANISM, & AFTER / 105

The Second Palladian Revival

Palladianism is a type of architecture distinguished by a style and composition derived from the buildings and publications of Andrea Palladio. Inigo Jones introduced Palladio's architecture to England in the reign of King James I and VI (*see* Figs GIIIc, 4.43, and 5.31) while Jacob van Campen and Elias Holl were the leading exponents of Palladianism in the Netherlands and in Germany.

There is one great house in England that stylistically stands between the grander Baroque palaces and the Palladian country houses. That is at Burley-on-the-Hill, Rutland (1696–1704), by the 2nd Earl of Nottingham, Henry Dormer, and John Lumley, with probable advice from others. The main house is connected by quadrants to two lower blocks which, in turn, are joined to two wings by means of great sweeping colonnades: they are Palladian villa-scale versions of the Bernini colonnades in Rome, and form a *cour d'honneur*, the grandest of such compositions to be found anywhere in England from that time. So Palladian villa design, complete with *piano nobile*, combines with Baroque bravura (Fig. 5.55a).

The true Palladian Revival took place in the first half of the 18th century, and began in Venetia (Il Veneto) and in England. One of its first manifestations was in Oxford, where Henry Aldrich designed Peckwater Quadrangle at Christ Church (1707–14), which entitles him to be regarded as one of the forerunners of the second Palladian Revival (Fig. 5.55b). Aldrich was clearly interested in Palladio's architecture, and was behind the publication of Palladio's *Antichità di Roma*, brought out by the Clarendon Press in 1709. It is significant that one of the figures associated with the second Palladian Revival was Henry Herbert, later 9th Earl of Pembroke, who was up at Christ Church in the time of Dean Aldrich, and his seat was Wilton House, Wiltshire, with which both John Webb and Inigo Jones had been associated. Herbert himself was no mean architect, and was recognised as such by several luminaries of the time. With Roger Morris he designed several fine Palladian buildings, including the very beautiful Palladian bridge at Wilton (1736–7) (Fig. 5.56), which provided a model for later such bridges at Stowe, Buckinghamshire, Prior Park, Bath, and other places.

The Revival proper was led by Colen Campbell and Lord Burlington, and was not only a reaction against the Baroque of Hawksmoor, Vanbrugh, Wren, and others, but a revival of the

Fig. 5.55a ↑↑ *Burley House, Burley-on-the-Hill, Rutland (1696–1704), probably designed by Daniel Finch, 2nd Earl of Nottingham, possibly with some help from Sir Henry Sheres (Surveyor of the Ordnance from 1685), Wren, and Thomas Poulteney (a carver who worked on several City churches, commissioned by Finch to make a model of Burley House), and built by Henry Dormer (until 1697) and John Lumley (from 1697). The enormous quadrant colonnades joining the main block to the two large service pavilions were probably suggested to Finch by Bernini's colonnades before the Basilica of San Pietro, Rome (which were under construction when he saw them in 1665), and enclose the impressive* cour d'honneur. *Two handsome gate-piers capped by gryphons support fine wrought-iron gates by Joshua Lord of 1700–4 (JSC).*

Fig. 5.55b ↑ *Peckwater Quadrangle, Christ Church College, Oxford (completed 1714), the first Palladian palace-fronted composition in England, designed by Henry Aldrich. In the centre of each façade, rising from the rusticated ground floor, is an Ionic hexastyle engaged temple-front, two storeys high (RCR, coll. JSC).*

106 / Classical Architecture

style of Inigo Jones, which the Commonwealth and the Baroque were perceived to have interrupted. Campbell's Wanstead of c.1714–20 was the first great 18th-century 'Palladian' mansion, and its building coincided with the establishment of the Hanoverian dynasty. It demonstrated immediately its anti-Baroque credentials by its austere horizontality, its prostyle hexastyle portico standing on a high podium, clearly derived from Palladio's notion of the Antique villa, and architecture that owed so much to Palladio and Jones. In 1719 Burlington sacked Gibbs as his architect, and appointed Campbell to remodel Burlington house in Piccadilly.

Burlington's adoption of the Palladian style commenced with the publication of Campbell's *Vitruvius Britannicus* and Giacomo Leoni's version of the *Quattro Libri* (1715–20): it also, significantly, coincided with the beginning of the Hanoverian Succession, and so was associated with Whiggery and with a desire to resume a style that had been interrupted in its development by the Civil War, the Commonwealth, and Baroque flirtations. It is perhaps not fanciful to see, in the adoption of Palladianism, a seeking to legitimise the Succession by association and continuity with the pre-Cromwellian period. The Baroque style was associated with the Counter-Reformation and with Continental absolutism, so Palladio, Jones, and the Palladian style seemed to offer untainted exemplars worthy of emulation. It has also been suggested that the Revival might have been connected with a hedging of bets concerning the claims of the exiled Jacobites, for the Hanoverians did not command universal loyalty as was made overt by the events of 1715–16 and 1745–6, but the fact of the matter is that the Succession came through the Stuart line,

Fig. 5.56 ↑ *Palladian bridge, Wilton House, Wiltshire (1736–7), designed by Roger Morris, with, probably, advice or collaboration with Henry Herbert, 9th Earl of Pembroke. Versions of this beautiful design were erected at Stowe, Buckinghamshire, Prior Park, Bath, Hagley, Worcestershire, and Amesbury, Wiltshire, all around the middle years of the 18th century (JSC).*

so an underscoring of legitimate descent does not seem that far-fetched in the interests of stability and continuity.

Many books appeared under the aegis of Burlington, who paid for the publication (1730) of several unknown Palladio drawings of *thermæ*, as well as an edition of works by Inigo Jones (1727) by William Kent. Burlington saw Palladianism as a means of returning to the principles of the architecture of Antiquity. His villa at Chiswick (c.1723–29) (Figs 5.57a–b; *see* Fig. G84b) is loosely based on Palladio's Villa Capra (*see* Figs G84a and 4.39) and on Scamozzi's Vettor Pisani Villa, Lonigo (1576–9):

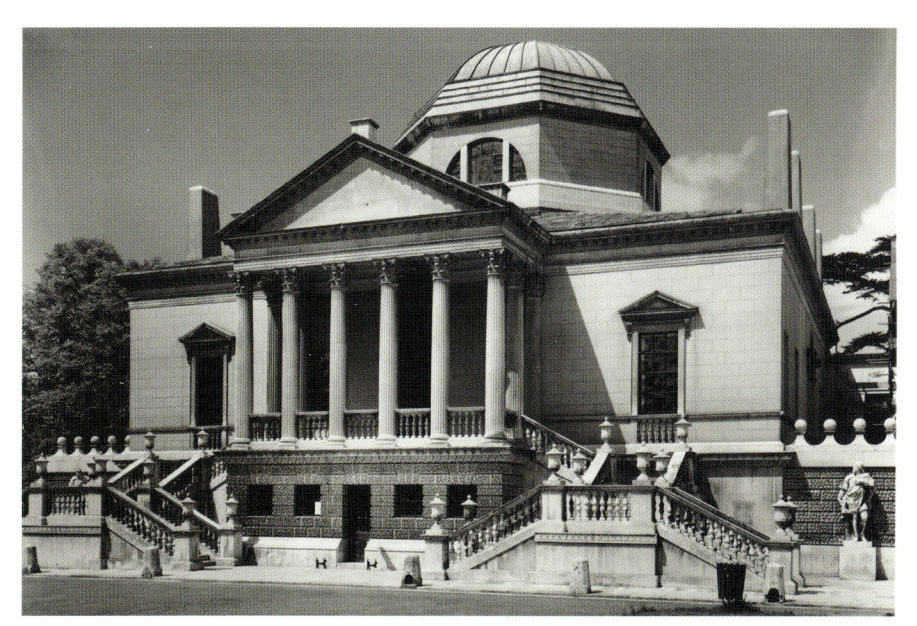

Fig. 5.57a ↑ *Palladianism: Chiswick House, west London (c.1723–9), by Lord Burlington, inspired by Palladio's Villa Capra at Vicenza, although the dome and room beneath are octagonal instead of circular. Note the Diocletian or thermal window in the octagon and the very elaborate perron (AFK H16670).*

Fig. 5.57b → *Burlington's villa at Chiswick: main elevation and plan. Note the thermal or Diocletian window in the octagon, the perron, and the prostyle hexastyle portico at* piano nobile *level. Note also the sequence of rooms in the garden front, based on Antique and Palladian precedents (from Kent [ed.] [1727], I, coll. JSC).*

CLASSICAL VARIATIONS: BAROQUE, ROCOCO, PALLADIANISM, & AFTER / 107

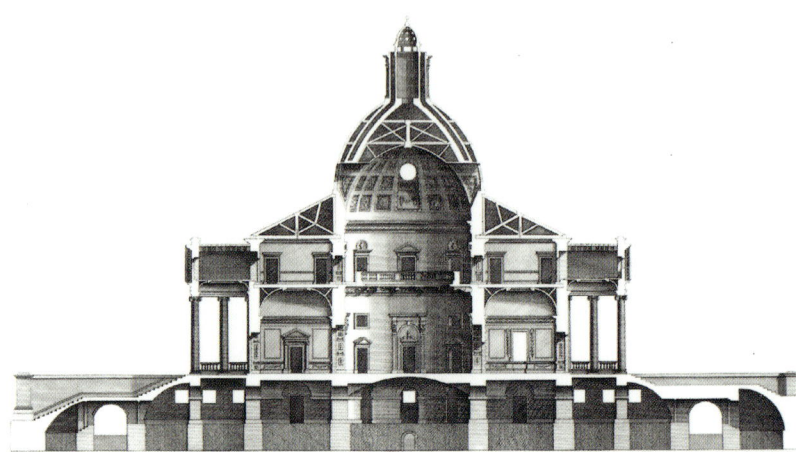

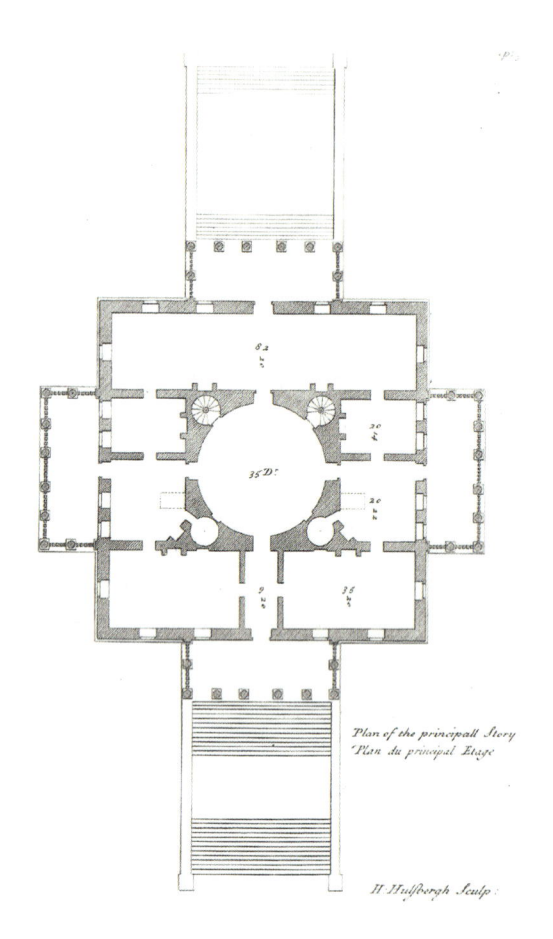

Fig. 5.58a ⤢ *Elevation of Mereworth Castle, Kent (c.1720–5), by Colen Campbell, closely modelled on the Villa Capra, and one of the major buildings of the second Palladian Revival (Campbell [1725], iii, pl.37, coll. JSC).*

Fig. 5.58b ↑ *Section through Mereworth Castle (Campbell [1725], iii, pl.38, coll. JSC).*

Fig. 5.58c ↗ *Plan of the* piano nobile *level at Mereworth Castle (Campbell [1725], iii, pl.36, coll. JSC).*

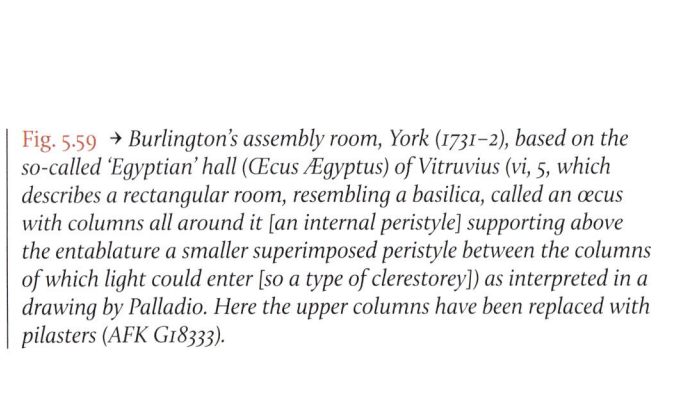

Fig. 5.59 → *Burlington's assembly room, York (1731–2), based on the so-called 'Egyptian' hall (Œcus Ægyptus) of Vitruvius (vi, 5, which describes a rectangular room, resembling a basilica, called an œcus with columns all around it [an internal peristyle] supporting above the entablature a smaller superimposed peristyle between the columns of which light could enter [so a type of clerestorey]) as interpreted in a drawing by Palladio. Here the upper columns have been replaced with pilasters (AFK G18333).*

108 / CLASSICAL ARCHITECTURE

Fig. 5.60 ↑ *South front of Houghton Hall, Norfolk (1721–6), with engaged tetrastyle portico at* piano nobile *level and the cupolas on either side, designed by Gibbs 1721–2 and built 1725–8, 'obstinately raised … in defiance of the virtuosi'. This front was published by Campbell (1725), iii, pl.33, which shows a prostyle portico and squat pedimented towers at the corners derived from Inigo Jones's work at Wilton House, Wiltshire (1636–50) (JSC).*

Fig. 5.61 → *Marble Hall at Holkham, Norfolk, looking towards the stair and apse: the impact is full of gravitas, with allusions to Roman Antiquity and to Palladio. Note the coffered ceiling, the Greek key skirting, and the Vitruvian scroll at the top of the plinth (RCHME BB66/03638).*

it contains a sequence of rooms employing circles, apses, an octagon, and a rectangle, clearly derived from Palladio's Palazzo Thiene in Vicenza, which itself owed much to Roman Antiquity, especially the *thermæ*. The importance of the Chiswick villa as a building set within a designed landscape should also be emphasised, for gardens were places with meaning, capable by means of allusion to suggest ideas, and therefore were experimental places. In this respect, Robert Castell's *The Villas of the Ancients Illustrated* (1729), dedicated to Burlington, was important, for it attempted to reconstruct Pliny's villas from the literary evidence, and was illustrated with engraved plates which showed not only the villas, but also their settings, so was yet another instance of an effort to rediscover Antiquity by going back to Antique sources, not just re-hashing the formal European canon of Classicism as then understood and accepted.

Campbell's Mereworth Castle (Figs 5.58a–c) in Kent (1722–25) is even closer to Italian precedents, and is, in some ways, an improvement on the Villa Capra. Burlington's assembly room in York of 1731–2 (Fig. 5.59) is an almost exact copy of Palladio's reconstruction of a so-called 'Egyptian Hall' (i.e. one with an internal peristyle and clerestorey) as described by Vitruvius. Holkham in Norfolk (1734–65), by Kent and others, with its great hexastyle portico, symmetrical wings, and fully expressed *piano nobile* (*see* Fig. G84c) is a good example of a Palladian country house, as is Campbell's Houghton (1721–35) (Fig. 5.60), the cubic central hall of which is modelled on Jones's Queen's House at Greenwich: Houghton has Venetian windows in the towers, which were to have been crowned with pediments, but which Gibbs altered to stone domes. Holkham was designed as a house in the Antique style, in which a collection of paintings and Classical sculpture could be set off to advantage. At the entrance hall of Holkham, set behind a prostyle hexastyle portico on a podium, Kent devised a room of stunning and severe Classical grandeur (Fig. 5.61), employing references to the screen in San Giorgio Maggiore, coffered Roman vaults, the frieze of an Antique Roman temple, and a Vitruvian peristyled interior. At Stowe, of course, he designed gardens, and buildings to adorn them, which evoked Arcady itself and the landscapes of Poussin and Claude.

CLASSICAL VARIATIONS: BAROQUE, ROCOCO, PALLADIANISM, & AFTER / 109

Fig. 5.62a ↓ *Plan of the principal floor of Kedleston Hall, Derbyshire, showing the composition, with wings (the two at the top were not built), based on Palladian precedent, the elaborate perrons, columned hall, and domed salon (Woolfe and Gandon [1767], iv, pl.46, coll. JSC).*

Fig. 5.62b ↙ *South front of Kedleston by the Adam brothers, showing the basic Palladian composition with a variation on the triumphal arch of Constantine, Rome, applied to the façade, beneath which is a perron, and above which may be seen a severely Antique dome (AFK G8585).*

Fig. 5.62c → *The hall, Kedleston, by James Paine and Robert Adam, showing the Corinthian columns with fluted monolithic shafts of pink Nottinghamshire alabaster creating a grave, Antique effect, a harbinger of Neo-Classicism (BTB).*

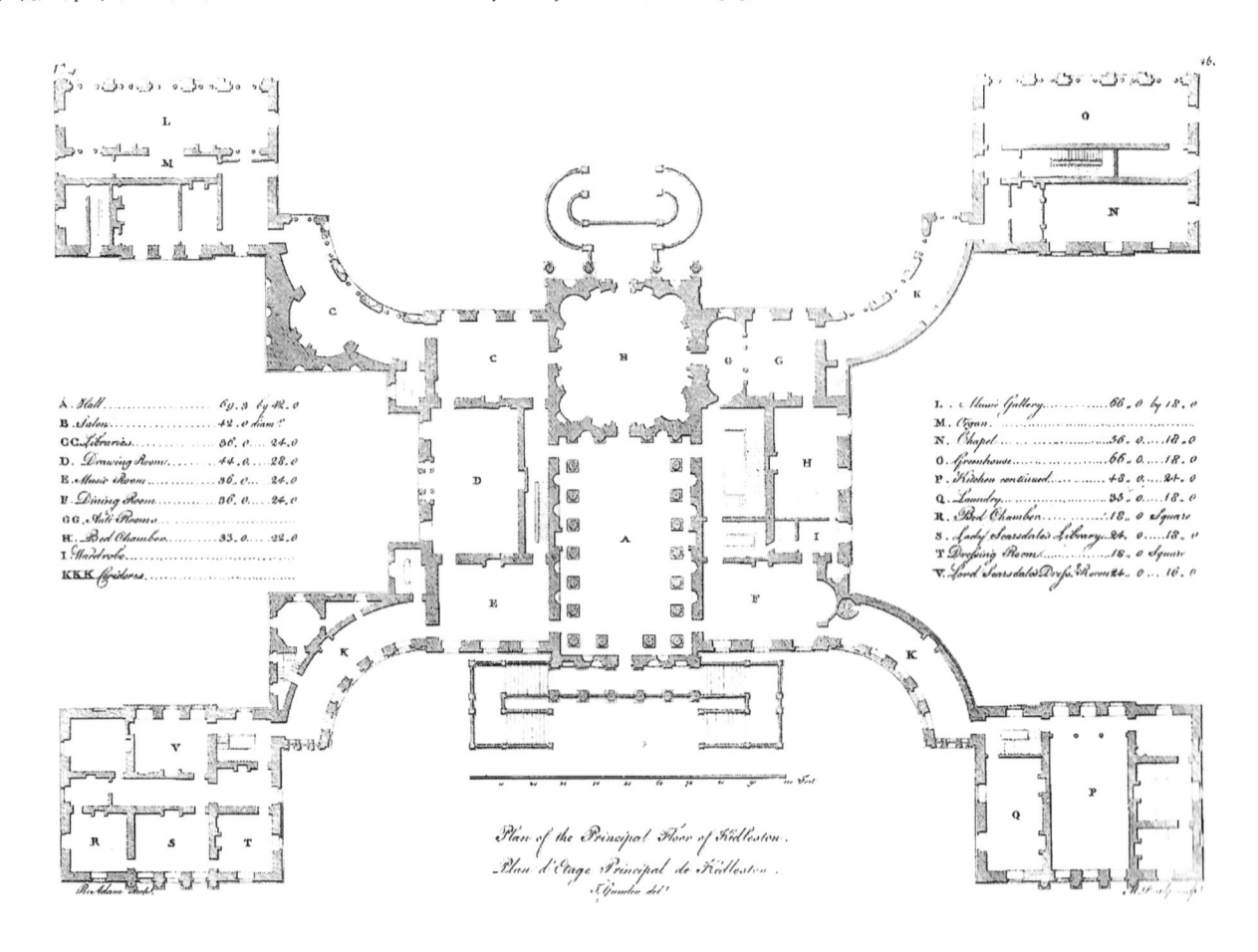

110 / CLASSICAL ARCHITECTURE

Other Palladian compositions include Kent's Horse Guards, Whitehall (1748–59), and James Paine's Kedleston in Derbyshire (1759–60), which had a central block with wings linked by curving elements (like Palladio's design for the Villa Mocenigo), but also included a Pantheon-like saloon and a hall with an internal peristyle on the main axis. Kedleston was completed, in c.1760–70, by the Adam Brothers, who replaced the bowed front on the south façade with a triumphal arch, and remodelled Paine's hall and saloon to resemble elements of Diocletian's palace at Spalato in Dalmatia (Split – now in Croatia), thus rendering a Palladian design less Palladian and more Antique (Figs 5.62a–c). In 1757, Robert Adam, accompanied by Charles-Louis Clérisseau and two other draughtsmen, had measured what remained of the vast Roman building, which led to the publication (1764) of the *Ruins of the Palace of the Emperor Diocletian at Spalatro*, a magnificent work superbly illustrated with engravings by Francesco Bartolozzi and others, which further drew attention to the monumental and superior qualities of Antique architecture, thereby tilting taste towards what was to become known as Neo-Classicism.

Fig. 5.63 ↑ *Bank of Ireland (formerly the parliament), Dublin (c.1728–39), by Sir Edward Lovett Pearce, an essay in Palladianism and in form the precedent for the British Museum (coll. JSC).*

Fig. 5.64 → *Palladianism. Castle Ward, County Down, a grand house built 1760–73 to designs by an as yet unidentified architect, although Sir Robert Taylor may have been involved at an early stage. Note the engaged Ionic Scamozzi Order with pediment set on the rusticated plinth treated as a basement (TR-S).*

CLASSICAL VARIATIONS: BAROQUE, ROCOCO, PALLADIANISM, & AFTER / 111

Fig. 5.65 ↑ *Florencecourt, County Fermanagh (mid-18th century), an example of provincial Palladianism, with some curiously botched interpretations of Gibbs surrounds and much else. The wings ending in irregular octagonal pavilions were added c.1768, possibly to designs by Davis Ducart (JSC).*

Fig. 5.66 ← *The Four Courts, Dublin (1786–1802), by James Gandon, incorporating the south and west sides of a quadrangle designed by Thomas Cooley. A severe Antique grandeur is suggested by the domed rotunda and prostyle hexastyle portico, while variations on the triumphal-arch theme lead to the two courtyards (coll. JSC).*

Sir Edward Lovett Pearce's parliament building in Dublin (Fig. 5.63), with its brilliant **E**-shaped Ionic portico and colonnade, Knobelsdorff's Berlin opera house (*see* Fig. 5.53), Friedrich Wilhelm von Erdmannsdorff's Schloß Wörlitz (1769–73), Castle Ward, County Down (Fig. 5.64), and Florencecourt, County Fermanagh (mid-18th century) (Fig. 5.65), are further fine examples of Palladian Revival architecture.

Sir William Chambers based his style on a scholarly interpretation of Palladianism, the best example of which is his Somerset House in London (1776–96), probably the grandest official building ever erected in the capital. His Casino at Marino, near Dublin (1758–76), combines a Greek cross on plan with scholarly attention to Classical detail using a Roman Doric Order. Chambers' *A Treatise on Civil Architecture* of 1759 became a standard and influential work on Classical architecture. His pupil, James Gandon, also combined Palladian compositional methods with scholarly Classical detail, as at the Four Courts in Dublin (Fig. 5.66) (with Thomas Cooley), which unites a severe Neo-Classical drum and dome, Antique hexastyle pedimented portico, and three relatively plain blocks.

Generally, Palladian townhouses had rusticated bases, applied upper Orders, and a balustrade or parapet. Three superimposed engaged Orders are found at the Circus in Bath (from 1754) by the Woods (Fig. 5.67), while at Royal Crescent (1767–75),

Fig. 5.67 ↑ *The Circus, Bath (from 1754), by John Wood the Elder, completed by Wood the Younger, following the general arrangement of a Roman amphitheatre, turned inside out, with superimposed Orders, but employing paired columns, creating a grand composition of terrace houses (coll. JSC).*

112 / CLASSICAL ARCHITECTURE

Fig. 5.68 ↑ *Royal Crescent, Bath (1767–75), by Wood the Younger, an even grander solution unifying many individual houses in one composition, but with a Giant Order of engaged Ionic columns rising from the* piano nobile *level to the crowning entablature (AFK H4241).*

Fig. 5.69 ↓ *Custom House, Dublin (1781–9), by Gandon, combining Palladian compositional method with scholarly Roman Classical detail, also drawing on elements from Wren's Chelsea and Greenwich hospitals and Chambers's Somerset House and casino at Marino, County Dublin (JSC).*

CLASSICAL VARIATIONS: BAROQUE, ROCOCO, PALLADIANISM, & AFTER / 113

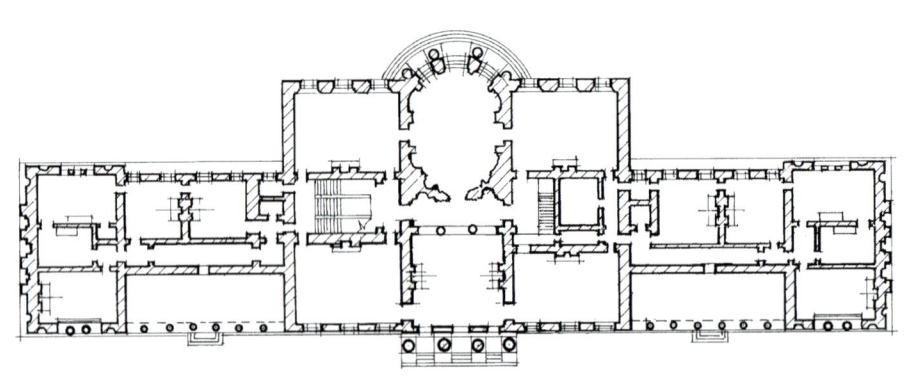

Fig. 5.70a ↑ *Castle Coole, County Fermanagh (1790–7), one of James Wyatt's finest houses: although the composition is still Palladian, the language is now Neo-Classical, and the raised* piano nobile *has been eliminated (JSC).*

Fig. 5.70b ← *Plan of Castle Coole showing how the elliptical saloon is expressed on the façade (JSC).*

by the younger Wood, a Giant Order of engaged columns rises two storeys from the ground floor over a basement (Fig. 5.68). At Bath, the Woods consciously evoked Roman plan-forms, such as the amphitheatre, while adhering to Palladian uniformity, to combine individual houses in grand unified compositions. John Wood the Elder has been claimed as the first English architect after Inigo Jones to try to make an English square a uniform Palladian composition, but, as has been pointed out above, Henry Aldrich had designed Peckwater Quadrangle, Christ Church College, Oxford, some 20 years earlier, and later, Robert Adam reintroduced the principle of the unified palatial façade to London, at the Adelphi (1768–72).

The Woods confronted the Classical ideal and Roman urban forms by combining them in unified domestic architecture, but they were also interested in arcane matters, speculating about the ancient pre-Roman history of Aquæ Sulis (as Bath was called by the Romans): in particular, Wood the Elder was obsessed by the idea that the Classical Orders were not Græco-Roman, but Divine, that Vitruvius was a pagan who had plagiarised Jewish ideas enshrined in Solomon's Temple, and that the square, terrace, forum, circus, and crescent comprised a series of mystical symbols, all adding up to a re-creation of Bath as a new Troy, a capital city of the ancient Britons, in which both Fantasy and Antiquity were applied to city-making. His was not by any means the only attempt to free Classical architecture from its perceived stigma of having pagan origins.

Most other architects of the 18th century were not concerned with speculations on the fringes of lunacy (though there were some well-known figures who, surprisingly, did just that), and their works have a serenity, sureness, and competence far-removed from such realms. James Gandon was among the best architects of his generation: his majestic Custom House in Dublin (1781–91) (where elements from the works of Wren and Chambers are quoted) combines assured Palladian compositional methods with scholarly Roman Classical detail (Fig. 5.69). Gandon published, with J. Woolfe, two further supplements to *Vitruvius Britannicus*, in 1767 and 1771, but his realised works are probably more eclectically Classical than purely Palladian.

James Wyatt still adhered to Palladian composition on occasion, notably at Castle Coole, County Fermanagh, but by its date (1781–9) a more austere Neo-Classicism was in vogue, and the *piano nobile* had been eliminated. It is one of the finest country houses in Ireland (Figs 5.70a–b).

It is a fitting note on which to end this chapter.

6

NEO-CLASSICISM AND AFTER

From the innumerable beautiful monuments of [Greek art] which remain, it is the worthiest object of study and imitation; it therefore demands a minute investigation, consisting ... in information as to its essential; an investigation in which not merely facts are communicated for instruction, but also principles for practice.

JOHANN JOACHIM WINCKELMANN:
The History of Ancient Art, first published in Dresden in 1764, Bk. IV, Ch. 1, para. 2.
G. Henry Lodge (trans.): (London: Sampson, Low, Marston, Searle, & Rivington, 1881), **i**, 285.

The Roman Palladian phase, initiated in Burlington's time, was succeeded by a Græco-Roman development mainly encouraged by the example of the Athenian researches. Hence through the remaining years of the eighteenth century until the close of the first quarter of the nineteenth the search for the sublime and lasting qualities of architecture continued.

SIR ALBERT RICHARDSON:
Monumental Classic Architecture in Great Britain and Ireland during the Eighteenth and Nineteenth Centuries
(London: B.T. Batsford, 1914), v.

Neo-Classicism and Rome

The published works of Giovanni Battista Piranesi attracted further attention to the architecture of Roman Antiquity, inflating its scale and exaggerating its impact. Certainly this architecture was revered, and the superiority of Antiquity became an 18th-century article of faith, supported not only by the images of Piranesi, but by the archæological discoveries in Rome itself and in the partially preserved towns of Herculaneum, Stabiæ, and Pompeii, excavations of which really got underway at the time, leading to important and influential publications.

Cordemoy and Laugier

When the Abbé Jean-Louis de Cordemoy published his *Nouveau Traité de Toute l'Architecture* in 1706, he was not only writing about the Orders, but was attacking Baroque styles, and arguing for a cleansed and purified architecture which, by implication, looked to Antiquity rather than to more recent times (even 16th-century architecture in Italy) for appropriate precedents. What Cordemoy was also striving for was the removal of all Mannerist and Baroque affectations, distortions, and effects: he inveighed against engaged columns, pilasters that were purely ornamental, and anything that was not 'true' to the Orders. In fact, he proposed that the Orders should be used as functional elements, that columns should be there for support only, and that the principles of Antiquity should be reappraised.

The problem with Cordemoy's notions, and indeed the whole veneration for Roman exemplars, was that the latter were not 'pure', that there were buildings erected during the Empire that were unquestionably proto-Baroque, and that Roman use of the Orders can hardly be seen as 'Primitive', rational, or always necessary. One could not examine great buildings like the *thermæ* of Diocletian or Caracalla, or Diocletian's palace at what is now Split in Croatia, with any great care and see them as 'pure' or free from very stylised use of the Orders. On the contrary, those buildings demonstrated the freedom with which the Orders could be employed, and the amazing versatility and adaptability of the Classical vocabulary in the creation of impressive architecture.

When Marc-Antoine Laugier published his *Essai sur l'Architecture* in 1753, he presented an image of the Primitive Hut with its tree-trunks, beams, and pitched roof (all of timber) as the only begetter of architecture, and he saw early Doric as directly descended from the Primitive Hut, first as a timber prototype, and then as a stone temple: from that source, Laugier argued, all architecture had evolved. Interestingly, Bramante designed columns with branches lopped off on the shafts at the cloisters of Sant'Ambrogio in Milan, a deliberate allusion to Antiquity, to Vitruvius, and to the supposed timber origins of the Orders (1492).

So, Laugier took Cordemoy's arguments, gave the Orders a rational and far more primitive origin than the Orders of Roman Antiquity, and showed that in their earliest forms they did indeed do a structural job, rather than merely decorate buildings. Laugier, in short, established that the column should be used and expressed as such, not used engaged or for decoration, and that something more primitive and more true to its origins than a mere copy of Antique Roman buildings was necessary. Laugier, in fact, promoted certain architectural ideals and principles that struck chords at a time when archæology was becoming ever more important as a source of authentic Antique details and motifs. Laugier was read all over Europe: his is the great architectural text of the Enlightenment, and it is perhaps worth pointing out that he was closely involved with Freemasonry, that columns and the Orders play no small part in Masonic iconography and systems, and that the Enlightenment was permeated with Masonic ideas.

With Jacques-Germain Soufflot's Parisian Church of Ste-Geneviève (*see* Figs 5.26a–c), begun in 1756, we find the first fruits of Laugier's ideas, and the beginnings of French Neo-Classicism. Soufflot used a dome loosely modelled on that of St Paul's Cathedral in London, but with a peristyle of Antique columns cleanly expressed around the drum, a Greek cross as the marvellously logical, clear plan, and a grave, hexastyle portico recalling the best of Roman Antiquity, correctly observed and meticulously executed. Laugier said that Ste-Geneviève was the first expression of perfect architecture: inside, the load-bearing Corinthian columns are fully expressed as such, carry straight entablatures, and give a completely different effect from that of earlier Baroque interiors with engaged columns, pilasters, and mighty piers. Soufflot combined regularity, monumental Roman detail, and elegance; and the columns, being more slender than piers, contribute to the sense of lightness judiciously mixed with gravity. Later, as has been described, when Ste-Geneviève was designated as the Panthéon in the 1790s, the windows were filled in to give the building the character of a mausoleum: this was nothing whatsoever to do with safety factors as some have misguidedly claimed.

The Rediscovery of Greece

Laugier and J.-J. Rousseau both saw virtues in the primitive. From the 1750s the search for archæological precedents and for 'purity' led back in time to the beginnings of Classicism, beyond Rome, to Greek Doric. Soufflot had visited Pæstum to see the Greek temples there in 1750, Piranesi drew them, and Richard Payne Knight found them 'Picturesque' in 1777, which helped to establish them in the realms of respectability. Johann Wolfgang von Goethe was stupefied by them in 1787, and John Soane had seen them in 1780, prompting, no doubt, his 'Barn à la Pæstum' of 1798 (Fig. 6.1). Primitive, stumpy columns were to appear in several buildings, sometimes so reduced they bore little resemblance to their Antique predecessors (Figs 6.2a–b). However, the real champion of Greek architecture was Johann Joachim Winckelmann, who published his *Reflections* on the imitation of Greek precedents in paintings and sculptures in 1755: Winckelmann's description of the noble simplicity and quiet grandeur of Greek art struck home, while his *Observations on the Architecture of the Ancients* of 1764, produced after a visit to Pæstum in 1758, helped to draw attention to the *necessity*, as he saw it, of imitating the Greeks.

Although in Italy and Sicily there were substantial and very impressive remnants of Greek architecture still standing, which could be seen by cognoscenti, Greece itself and Asia Minor (as parts of the Ottoman Empire) were not the easiest places to visit. Robert Wood, who was to become a member of the Society of Dilettanti, toured the Greek islands in 1742–43, but in 1749

Fig. 6.1 ↓ *Former 'Barn à la Pæstum' (now a dwelling-house) at 936 Warwick Road, Solihull (1798), by John Soane, who had actually been to Pæstum and measured and drawn the temples there. However, everything has been ultra-simplified, and the paired columns are very un-Greek: the design is more indebted to progressive French architecture of the 1780s and 1790s (JSC).*

Fig. 6.2a ← *Detail of the corner of the Rue de la Bourse and the Rue des Colonnes, Paris, showing primitivist unfluted baseless Greek Doric columns (based on Pæstum Doric proportions), with square columns at the corners (the square 'echinus' was a form not used by the Greeks). The combination of arcuated forms with these columns, of course, is very un-Greek, but Neo-Classical architecture tended to explore such mixes. Note the over-large anthemion ornaments over the abaci. This extraordinary street was developed 1793–5 during the Terror, to designs by Nicolas-Jacques-Antoine Vestier, based on an earlier design by Habert Thibierge, which also featured a Pæstum-derived Doric Order. An architecture of severe Neo-Classical masculinity was typical of the sober style of the Revolutionary period, and was virtuously tough and uncompromising (JSC).*

Fig. 6.2b ← *The Eben mausoleum (1798) in the Kirchhof I der Jerusalems- und Neuen Kirchengemeinde, Kreuzberg, Berlin. This remarkable design, with its primitivist interpretation of an unfluted Doric column (with vestigial flutes between the shaft and the abacus [there is no capital]), is the essence of a late 18th-century search for an architecture that was primitive, blocky, elemental, and reduced to the bare minimum. Probably by David Gilly (JSC).*

the Earl of Charlemont visited a number of sites in company with Richard Dalton, who made detailed drawings of Greek antiquities. Further interest was thus stimulated, and James Stuart and Nicholas Revett (who had become members of the Dilettanti in 1751) determined on a project which would establish a methodology of architectural archæology for Greek architecture on the lines of Antoine Desgodetz's *Édifices Antiques de Rome* of 1682. Stuart and Revett persuaded the Dilettanti to fund an expedition to Greece which the young architects, with others, having obtained the necessary permissions, carried out between 1751 and 1754. The work of surveying, measuring, and drawing the remains of Greek buildings was slow, painstaking, and often fraught with danger, but the team's heroic efforts were eventually to make Greek architecture, its Orders, and its details as familiar as those of Rome. However, the first volume of *The Antiquities of Athens* was not published until 1762, and the rest of the work was extremely slow in coming out: the second volume appeared as late as 1789, and the third, fourth, and fifth volumes were published in 1794, 1814, and 1830 respectively, largely the work of younger men. So this great sourcebook of the Greek Revival took 82 years to appear in its entirety and, as a result, its impact on architecture was spasmodic and gradual, but impressive nevertheless, and led to the creation of several major works of architecture.

The 1750s saw other, less accurate, publications on Greek architecture by Julien-David Le Roy (*Ruines des Plus Beaux Monuments de la Grèce*) in 1758 and Robert Sayer (*Ruins of Athens*) in 1759. Robert Wood brought out his *Ruins of Palmyra* in 1753 and *Ruins of Balbec* in 1757, both of which added to the store of knowledge of buildings of Classical Antiquity, while Robert Adam's sumptuous *Ruins of the Palace of the Emperor Diocletian, at Spalatro, Dalmatia*, was published in 1764.

So, in the middle of the 18th century the Primitive had been extolled, Greek architecture was being discovered, and Antique architecture generally seemed to offer more real, more pure exemplars than the second- or third-hand works of the Italian Renaissance, even when the last contained a strong dose of the Antique, or what was perceived to be the Antique, as in Palladio's work.

NEO-CLASSICISM & AFTER / 117

Fig. 6.3a ↑ *Prostyle hexastyle Greek Doric temple at Hagley Park, Worcestershire (1758–61), by James 'Athenian' Stuart, one of the first Greek Doric Revival buildings in Europe (AFK H7384).*

Fig. 6.3b ↓ *A second 'Doric temple' by Stuart (1760), this time at Shugborough, Staffordshire (JSC).*

The Greek Revival

When accurate (or reasonably accurate) illustrations of Greek architecture begin to appear, the results were visible in what began to be built. In terms of realised structures, Stuart's hexastyle Doric Temple at Hagley (Fig. 6.3a) of 1758 is probably the first manifestation of Doric Revival in Europe (it has a twin at Shugborough, Staffordshire, erected c.1760 [Fig. 6.3b]), while Revett's church at Ayot St Lawrence in Hertfordshire, with its Order based on that of the Temple of Apollo at Delos (*see* Fig. 2.3b), though slightly attenuated, dates from 1778–9, and is one of the earliest Greek Revival churches (Fig. 6.4). Important models for new buildings were provided by Stuart and Revett, not least the illustration of the choragic monument of Thrasyllus (Fig. 6.5a; *see* Fig. G15 – this gave architects a stimulus to evolve window and other openings in Greek Revival buildings, of which more anon).

In 1769 Stuart designed an orangery at Blithfield Hall, Staffordshire, which is an interesting composition, with a nine-bay colonnade of eight square columns derived from the Thrasyllus monument, stopped at each end by temple-fronted pavilions, each with four pilasters (again derived from the Thrasyllus exemplars) (Fig. 6.5b). This orangery was erected by Samuel and Joseph Wyatt, who also built an almost identical structure at Ingestre Hall, also in Staffordshire, in the 1770s. Other Athenian buildings measured, drawn, and published in *The Antiquities of Athens* included the choragic monument of Lysicrates (Figs 6.6a–b), which proved to be worthy of emulation for many years to come, and in a great many contexts and permutations: its beautiful Corinthian capital recurs (Fig. 6.6c), and the whole monument as well (Figs 6.6d–f). Apart from the hexastyle Doric 'temple', Stuart designed several Greek buildings for the gardens

Fig. 6.4 ↓ *Church at Ayot St Lawrence, Hertfordshire (1778–9), showing the temple-like church joined to two arched pavilions, a Palladian composition with Greek Revival details, including a variant on the Doric Order of the Temple of Apollo at Delos (JSC).*

118 / Classical Architecture

Fig. 6.5a ← *Choragic monument of Thrasyllus, an unusual Greek Doric building of 319–279 BC, erected as a façade to a cave in Athens. It has two antæ, between which is a single square column. The tænia between the plain architrave and frieze has a continuous row of guttæ beneath, and the frieze has no triglyphs, but is adorned with wreaths. The Attic was added in 279 BC. This monument was derived from the south-west wing of the Athenian Propylæa, which also had three square uprights and a continuous row of guttæ. The Thrasyllus monument was the inspiration of Schinkel's use of square mullions at the Berlin Schauspielhaus (1818–26), and for his continuous guttæ at the Neue Wache, Unter den Linden (1816–18), also in Berlin (Stuart and Revett [1787], ii, ch.IV, pl.iii, coll. JSC).*

Fig. 6.5b ↓ *Orangery at Blithfield Hall, Staffordshire, designed by James Stuart (1769), which drew on the choragic monument of Thrasyllus for its square columns (JSC).*

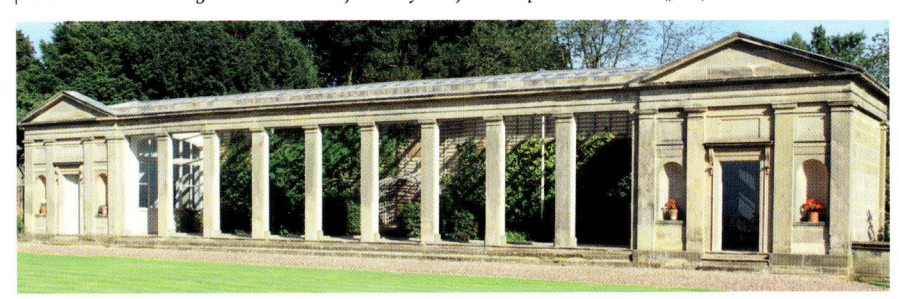

Fig. 6.6a ← *Choragic monument of Lysicrates, Athens (c.334 BC) (Stuart and Revett [1762], i, ch.IV, pl.ii, coll. JSC).*

Fig. 6.6b ↑ *Greek Corinthian Order from the choragic monument of Lysicrates, Athens. The capital has distinct differences from the Roman Corinthian Order, and is taller and more elegant. Note the helices in the centre and the honeysuckle ornament that rises up on the centre of the abacus (Stuart and Revett [1762], i, ch.IV, pl.vi, coll. JSC).*

Fig. 6.6c ↗ *A variation on the Lysicrates Corinthian Order, used in a former hotel in Stamford, Lincolnshire, of 1810–29, by J.L. Bond, a sumptuous essay in Greek Revival (JSC).*

Neo-Classicism & After / 119

Fig. 6.6d ↑ *Lanthorn of Demosthenes, aka the Dark Lanthorn, Shugborough, Staffordshire (1761–71), by James Stuart, a garden building closely resembling the choragic monument of Lysicrates, except that it lacks both the tall base and the sculptured frieze* (JSC).

Fig. 6.6e ↗ *Funerary monument of the connoisseur and collector William Weddell of Newby Hall, in the south transept of Ripon Cathedral, West Riding of Yorkshire, based on the choragic monument of Lysicrates, Athens, with a bust of Weddell by Nollekens of 1795* (JSC).

Fig. 6.6f ↗↗ *The exquisite Große Neugierde (Great Curiosity) which Schinkel added (1835–7) to the park at Schloß Glienicke, near Berlin, for Prince Karl of Prussia, who collected Antiquities. Developed from an idea of Prince Karl's brother, Crown Prince Friedrich Wilhelm, it consists of a tholos of 18 Corinthian columns, from the centre of which rises yet another version of the choragic monument of Lysicrates* (JSC).

at Shugborough in the 1760s (Fig. 6.7), including a hexagonal structure based on the Tower of the Winds in Athens which had been measured and eventually published in the book (Fig. 6.8a): variants can be found at Mount Stewart, County Down (Fig. 6.8b), and Oxford (Fig. 6.8c), among other places.

The greatest Greek Revival architecture was put up in the next century. H.W. and W. Inwood's St Pancras Church in London (1819–22) is an eclectic mix of elements from the Erechtheion, the Tower of the Winds, the choragic monument of Lysicrates, and other Athenian buildings culled from *The Antiquities of Athens* and other sourcebooks. The invention of the tower applied to a temple, with two rows of windows (one above and one below the gallery) on its long sides, was ingenious, for congregational worship and side windows were not features of Greek temples, so a degree of invention and imaginative use of Grecian elements was necessary (Figs 6.9a–b).

Fig. 6.7 ↑ *Shepherdess's Tomb at Shugborough, Staffordshire (c.1755–9), by James Stuart, featuring two primitive Doric columns (with the flutes only partially carved) supporting an elemental Doric entablature above which are shell-like antefixa: this forms an ædicule framing a rustic arch copied straight from Thomas Wright's books on grottoes within which is a carved relief by Peter Scheemakers derived from Nicolas Poussin's celebrated* Et in Arcadia Ego *(aka* Shepherds in Arcady *[c.1635–6])* (JSC).

120 / CLASSICAL ARCHITECTURE

Fig. 6.8a ↑ *Octagonal Tower of the Winds, Athens (aka Horologion of Andronikos Cyrrhestes [i.e. of Cyrrhus], c.50 BC): this version of the Corinthian Order has no base, the abacus is square on plan, and the capital consists of palm above acanthus leaves (see Fig. G85) (Stuart and Revett [1762], i, ch.III, pl.iii, coll. JSC).*

Fig. 6.8b ↗ *Tower of the Winds, a Georgian interpretation of the exemplar in Athens, transformed into an exquisite belvedere at Mount Stewart, County Down (c.1782–6), by James Stuart, one of the leading lights of the Greek Revival (ACWM).*

Fig. 6.8c ↗↗ *The Radcliffe Observatory, Oxford, begun 1772 to designs by Henry Keene, but after criticism the plans were altered by James Wyatt, and completed in 1794 by Theodosius Keene under Wyatt's direction. The design of the tower is derived from the Tower of the Winds, Athens, including the replica sculptures (1792–4) at the very top by John Bacon. Note the tall, elongated, Ionic pilasters, and the very large tripartite window with a lintel over the central window (rather than the arch found in a serliana): this type is known as a Wyatt window (see Fig. G118). The Coade stone plaques depicting the signs of the Zodiac and Morning, Noon, and Evening were modelled (c.1794) by J.C.F. Rossi (RCR, coll. JSC).*

Fig. 6.9a ← *St Pancras Church, London (1819–22), by H.W. and W. Inwood, an exquisite and scholarly work of the Greek Revival. The prostyle hexastyle Greek Ionic portico is based on the Order of the Erechtheion, while the tower is an ingenious mix of elements from the Tower of the Winds and the choragic monument of Lysicrates (AFK H4905).*

Fig. 6.9b ↓ *Caryatid(e) porch with sarcophagus at St Pancras Church, London. The figures have inverted torches and wreaths, appropriate allusions to death, as they guard the entrance to the crypt beneath the church where bodies were entombed. Note the arrangement of windows on the right to accommodate the balcony inside (AFK H15197).*

NEO-CLASSICISM & AFTER / 121

Fig. 6.10a ↑ *Charming Doric exedra bench, called the Stibadium (c.1840), at Schloß Glienicke park by Ludwig Persius. The polished bowl of Brandenburg granite was by Christian Gottlieb Cantian and the caryatid(e) centrepiece with cornucopia was based on the sculpture called* Felicitas Publica *by Christian Daniel Rauch (JSC).*

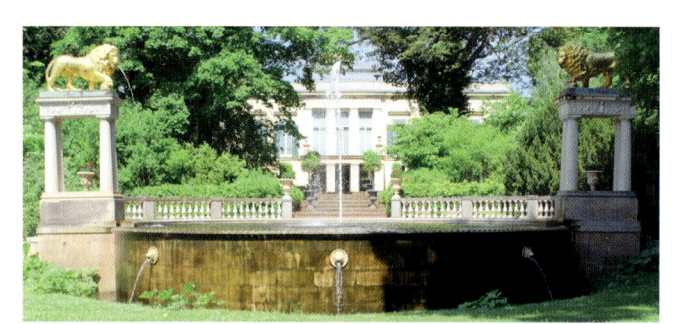

Fig 6.10b ← *The formal approach to Schinkel's Schloß Glienicke (1824–32), with fountain and lions added in 1838 (JSC).*

The Greek Revival had an enormous impact, and there are many works of architecture of the highest quality in which Greek themes are well to the fore. Gilly (*see* Fig. 6.2b), Persius (Fig. 6.10a), and Schinkel (Figs 6.10b and 6.11a–g) in Berlin; von Klenze in Bavaria (Figs 6.12a–g); Adam (Fig. 6.13), Decimus Burton, C.R. Cockerell (*see* Fig. G28b), John Griffith of Finsbury (Figs 6.14a–b), Thomas Hamilton (Fig. 6.15), Thomas Harrison, Jesse Hartley (Fig. 6.16), William Henry Playfair (Fig. 6.17), Robert Smirke (Figs 6.18a–b), Alexander Thomson (Figs 6.19a–b), and Wilkins (Fig. 6.20) in these islands; C.F. Hansen in Denmark (Fig. 6.21); Hittorff (Fig. 6.22) and Ledoux (Fig. 6.23a) in France; Thomas-Jean de Thomon in St Petersburg, Russia (Fig. 6.23b); Ehrensvärd in Sweden; and many other architects produced very interesting Neo-Classical buildings in which Greek elements were well to the fore.

Fig. 6.11a ← *The Neue Wache, Royal Guard House, Unter den Linden, Berlin (1816–18), by Karl Friedrich Schinkel, a free interpretation of Greek Doric, photographed in 1986, showing two soldiers of the former DDR on guard. As in the case of von Klenze's Propyläen in Munich, the prostyle hexastyle portico is set between massive plain pylons. The Order, however, has been adapted: gone are the triglyphs and metopes, and a continuous row of guttæ is set beneath the tænia (a motif derived from the choragic monument of Thrasyllus (see* Fig. 6.5a*) and mutules have been dispensed with. This is an example of an architect of genius unpedantically taking intelligent and informed liberties with an Order (JSC).*

Fig. 6.11b ← *The Altes Museum, Berlin (1823–8), by K.F. Schinkel, with its great* in-antis *arrangement of Greek Ionic columns, like a Hellenistic stoa, facing the Lustgarten. Here is the apparently effortless simplicity of Antiquity (it is, of course, extremely subtle and difficult to achieve such effects by means of clarity of forms and archæological correctness of detail, but Schinkel succeeded triumphantly) (Schinkel [1866], pl.39, coll. JSC).*

Fig. 6.11c ↑ *Perspective view of the main staircase gallery of the Altes Museum, Berlin, looking out through the Greek Ionic colonnades over the Lustgarten towards the royal palace and the two towers of Schinkel's Neo-Gothic Friedrich-Werderschekirche (1824–30) (Schinkel [1866], pl.43, coll. JSC).*

Fig. 6.11d ↑ *Schinkel obviously used a camera obscura or some other optical means by which he constructed his perspective view shown in Fig. 6.11c. On the left, Professors David Watkin and James Stevens Curl have avoided striking Neo-Classical attitudes while Martin Charles took the photograph from a stepladder (MC/RIBAC).*

Fig. 6.11e ↑ *Interior of the stoa-like entrance of the Altes Museum, Berlin, with its coffered ceiling and the four columns through which access to the monumental stair is gained (JSC).*

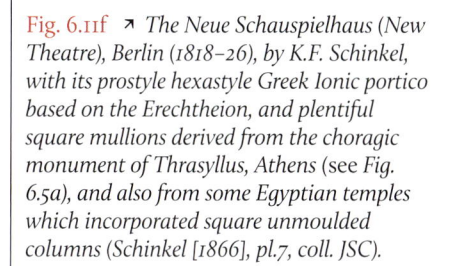

Fig. 6.11f ↗ *The Neue Schauspielhaus (New Theatre), Berlin (1818–26), by K.F. Schinkel, with its prostyle hexastyle Greek Ionic portico based on the Erechtheion, and plentiful square mullions derived from the choragic monument of Thrasyllus, Athens (see Fig. 6.5a), and also from some Egyptian temples which incorporated square unmoulded columns (Schinkel [1866], pl.7, coll. JSC).*

Fig. 6.11g → *The Gendarmenmarkt, Berlin, showing Schinkel's Schauspielhaus and the New Church beyond, with its handsome cupola by Gontard, added in 1780–5 (old postcard, c.1900, coll. JSC).*

Fig. 6.12a ← *Walhalla, near Regensburg, Bavaria (1830–42), by Leo von Klenze, modelled on the Athenian Parthenon, and set on a massive stepped podium derived from designs by Karl Haller, Freiherr von Hallerstein (GBM, coll. JSC).*

Fig. 6.12b ↓ *The Ruhmeshalle (Hall of Fame) in the Theresienwiese, Munich (1843–53), by Leo von Klenze, with colossal statue of Bavaria by Ludwig Schwanthaler cast in bronze by F. von Miller (1850). The overall stoa-like colonnade terminating at each end in projecting pedimented wings seems to have been derived from Schinkel's 1829 unrealised proposals for a monument to King Frederick II ('The Great') of Prussia in Berlin, but it is interesting in that its composition is similar to that of the Hellenistic Great Altar of Pergamon (now in Berlin), which had not been discovered when von Klenze designed the Ruhmeshalle, so he is revealed as an architect with a profound understanding of ancient Greek architecture (GBM, coll. JSC).*

Fig. 6.12c ← *Detail of the inner return of the Greek Doric entablature at the Ruhmeshalle. Note the anthemion motif on the soffit at the corner between the mutules with their guttæ (JSC).*

Fig. 6.12d ↓ *One of the temple-fronts of the Ruhmeshalle, showing the corner detail (JSC).*

124 / CLASSICAL ARCHITECTURE

Fig. 6.12e ← *The Propyläen, giving access to the Königsplatz, Munich, originally designed in 1817, erected 1847–60, with sculpture by Schwanthaler commemorating the Greek war of independence and the reign of the Bavarian Otto I as King of Greece. Note the massive pylons with the square mullions near their tops, again derived from the choragic monument of Thrasyllus (JSC).*

Fig. 6.12f ↑ *The Glyptothek (1816–31) facing the Königsplatz in Munich by Leo von Klenze, showing the prostyle octastyle Ionic portico. While the high portico is based on the Erechtheion, the lower block with its Renaissance ædiculated niches and Hellenistic pilasters introduces a syncretic note into this remarkable building, the interiors of which have been disastrously treated after war damage (JSC).*

Fig. 6.12g → *Detail of the Greek Ionic Order used by Leo von Klenze at the Glyptothek, Munich, but with unfluted shafts. Note the anta capital which differs from that of the column (JSC).*

NEO-CLASSICISM & AFTER / 125

Fig. 6.13 ← *Johnstone mausoleum in Westerkirk parish kirkyard, Bentpath, Dumfries and Galloway (1790–1), by Robert Adam: note the curious mix of Roman and Greek Doric, with bucrania oddly placed where one would expect triglyphs, and frieze of Adam's favourite motif, the scoop pattern (JSC).*

Fig. 6.14a → *The Greek Doric Order revived. The Anglican chapel at the General Cemetery of All Souls, Kensal Green, London (1836–7), by John Griffith of Finsbury, showing two sizes of Order. Note the prostyle tetrastyle portico and the antæ with capitals that are quite different from those of the columns (JSC).*

Fig. 6.14b ↓ *Dissenters' Chapel in the General Cemetery of All Souls, Kensal Green, London, completed 1834, designed by John Griffith, showing the tetrastyle portico directly derived from that of the Temple on the Ilissus, which had been illustrated in the first volume of Stuart and Revett's* Antiquities of Athens *(1762). On either side of the portico are low covered colonnades, gently curved on plan (very un-Grecian) to follow the original alignment of the boundary wall: these were a considerable innovation, marked by paired antæ derived from those of the choragic monument of Thrasyllus in Athens (see Fig. 6.5a), and they terminate in a distyle* in antis *arrangement with fluted Doric columns set between the antæ (JSC).*

126 / CLASSICAL ARCHITECTURE

Fig. 6.15 ↑↑ *Former Royal High School, Regent Road, Edinburgh (1825–9), by Thomas Hamilton, a masterly composition, one of the finest of the Greek Revival, with a central temple-like element derived from studies of the Theseion, Athens (Richardson [1914], coll. JSC).*

Fig. 6.16 ↑ *Albert Dock warehouses, Liverpool (1843–45), by Jesse Hartley, demonstrating the adaptability of Classicism for new industrial purposes. These are among the most Sublime of all 19th-century examples of commercial and industrial architecture, with their cast-iron unfluted primitive Greek Doric columns, massive undecorated brick walls, repetitive elements, and avoidance of ornament, all worthy of advanced Neo-Classicists (such as Ledoux) at their most uncompromising (JSC).*

Fig. 6.17 → *Campbell of Craigie mausoleum (1822) in the burying-ground at St Quivox, Ayrshire, designed by W.H. Playfair in the Greek Doric style. As it is now roofless it should probably fall into the category of burial enclosure rather than that of mausoleum (JSC).*

Neo-Classicism & After / 127

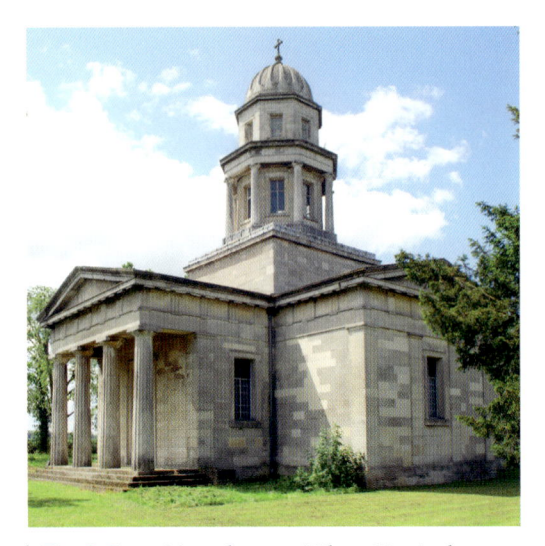

Fig. 6.18a ↑ *Mausoleum at Milton, Nottinghamshire (1831–2), designed by Robert Smirke for Henry Pelham Fiennes Pelham-Clinton, 4th Duke of Newcastle under Lyme, as the tomb of his duchess, Georgiana Elizabeth. Note the Greek Doric tetrastyle portico and the two-stage octagonal lantern, the lower stage surrounded by slender Greek Doric columns (JSC).*

Fig. 6.18b ↑ *The British Museum, Bloomsbury, London (1823–46), by Robert Smirke, featuring a Greek Ionic Order derived from that of the Antique Temple of Athene Polias, Priene, although he simplified the entablature and gave the columns Attic rather than Asiatic bases (AFK).*

Fig. 6.19a ↑ *1–10 Moray Place, Glasgow (1858–61), by Alexander 'Greek' Thomson. Here, Thomson used the continuous row of mullions which Schinkel had employed in the Berlin Schauspielhaus (see Figs 6.11f–g), derived from the choragic monument of Thrasyllus (see Fig. 6.5a). The basic composition is very similar to Stuart's design for an orangery at Blithfield Hall, Staffordshire, of 1769 (see Fig. 6.5b) (Thomas Annan, coll. JSC).*

Fig. 6.19b → *1–18 Walmer Crescent, Paisley Road West, Glasgow (1857–62), by Alexander Thomson, a powerful composition in which the Thrasyllus/Schinkel themes are magnificently and very intelligently employed (CC/HES (SNBR) SC710986).*

128 / CLASSICAL ARCHITECTURE

Fig. 6.20 ← *Grange Park, Hampshire, remodelled (c.1808–10) by William Wilkins: the Greek Doric entasis-less portico is derived from the Temple of Theseus, Athens (see Fig. 2.4), and the massive structure on the left with four square vertical elements supporting an entablature over which is an Attic storey was a variant on the choragic monument of Thrasyllus, Athens (see Fig. 6.5a) (JSC).*

Fig. 6.21 ↑ *Corner detail of the portico of the Domkirke (Vor Frue Kirke), Copenhagen, designed from 1808 to 1810 by C.F. Hansen, erected 1811–29. This is very free in its interpretation of Greek Doric: the columns have no entasis, the capital is based on the pattern from Pæstum, but, even odder, the triglyphs do not quite meet at the corner, but leave a portion of metope between them, so they are set on the centre-lines of the corner columns. Guttæ are not pegs either, but truncated pyramids. This is a Roman-Renaissance arrangement with Greek detailing. Note the anthemion at the corner of the soffit (JSC).*

Fig. 6.22 ↑ *Church of St-Vincent-de-Paul, Paris (1824–44), by Lepère and Hittorff, a fine Neo-Classical composition incorporating a prostyle hexastyle Ionic portico, with sculpture by Leboeuf-Nanteuil (commissioned 1846) in the tympanum (JSC).*

NEO-CLASSICISM & AFTER / 129

Fig. 6.23a → *Barrière de la Villette, Paris (1785–7), by C.-N. Ledoux. It is a severe square surmounted by a drum carried on pairs of primitive baseless Tuscan columns supporting plain arches directly on the abaci (a simplified, stripped version of overlapping serlianas). A rudimentary Doric entablature crowns the composition. The very stark pedimented portico has square stripped-Doric columns, combining elements of the Greek Doric Revival with an even more basic language. Here is primitive, stripped Neo-Classicism at its most sophisticated (JSC).*

Fig. 6.23b ↑ *Neo-Classical Bourse in St Petersburg, a powerful barrel-vaulted hall, illuminated at high level by semicircular-headed windows and surrounded by a Greek-Doric peristyle of the unfluted type, not unlike C.-N. Ledoux's designs for the Stock Exchange and Discount Bank at his imaginary town of Chaux, designs for which were published in his L'architecture considerée (1804). With its severe unadorned treatment, clear expression of elements, huge Diocletian windows set within great arches of rusticated voussoirs, and platform of ramps and podia, it was a major essay in Neo-Classicism as advanced as anywhere in the world for its date, and also shows some affinity with Boullée's designs. The architect was Thomas-Jean de Thomon, Swiss-born pupil of Ledoux. The huge rostral columns further add to the Neo-Classical theme and allude to naval power and the sea (JSC).*

Fig. 6.23c ← *(Left) Indian Corn, or 'Cerealian', Order in the Lower Senate Vestibule of the U.S. Capitol, Washington DC (described earlier as 'in the stairway leading to Supreme Court'), designed by Latrobe, probably c.1809, and eventually realised by Giuseppe Franzoni. The design was derived from the capital of the Tower of the Winds, Athens. Note the stalks in lieu of flutes and fillets, and the peculiarly squashed base. (Right) Latrobe's Tobacco Order in the small rotunda near the Supreme Court in the north wing of the U.S. Capitol, designed by Latrobe and carved by Iardella. This is really a Corinthian Order, very slightly adjusted (note the Attic base) with the addition of the tobacco-plant flowers (coll. JSC).*

130 / CLASSICAL ARCHITECTURE

Benjamin Henry Latrobe, who was a pupil of S.P. Cockerell, also designed a number of buildings in an advanced Neo-Classical style, including Hammerwood Lodge, East Grinstead, which employs a primitive 'Pæstum' Order. He emigrated to Virginia in 1796, and introduced a severe Neo-Classicism to the United States, giving it an American identity, beginning with his Bank of Pennsylvania of 1798. He invented 'native Orders' for the Federal Capitol in Washington (from 1814) contrasting the corncob and tobacco leaves. Corncob finials, rice plants, the bald eagle, and stars (representing the states), began to appear in American Classical design (Fig. 6.23c).

Neo-Classicism, then, included turning to the buildings of Greek and Roman Antiquity to provide exemplars, motifs, and stimuli for new architecture: this might be termed the archæological approach, and demonstrated the desire to use more original and uncorrupted sources for Classical architecture than those of the Italian Renaissance, Mannerist, and Baroque periods. Neo-Classicism was partly a reaction against what was seen as Baroque and Rococo excess. It also embraced the idea that the further back one looked to forms (the Primitive Hut) produced by Man in his primitive state, the more uncorrupted and less decadent would the architecture be. The severity, sturdiness, robustness, clarity, and 'primitiveness' of Greek Doric seemed to rise to the demand, and therefore scholarly examinations of Greek architecture were necessary in order to provide the vocabulary and language of Greek, as opposed to Roman, Classical architecture. Neo-Classicism does not imply mere copying, for, as has been pointed out, the congregational form of worship in an Anglican church of the early 19th century was quite different from the function of a Greek temple, so considerable invention had to be employed in order to adapt accurate, scholarly quotations from Ancient Greek buildings to a modern church.

Robert Adam did not adopt Grecian architecture in its entirety, although he used Greek motifs in many of his designs, judiciously mixing them quite freely with a large repertoire of decorative elements taken from many sources, mostly Roman, or from Pompeii or Herculaneum (or motifs derived from those sources). His assured use of differing room shapes in his planning derives from his studies of Roman *thermæ*. His work is lighter and more elegant than that of the earlier Palladians or the later Greek Revivalists. Very different in character, however, yet mixing Greek, Roman, and primitive elements, is Great Packington church in Warwickshire by Joseph Bonomi and the 4th Earl of Aylesford of 1789–80: the building is severely, almost aggressively, plain on the outside (Fig. 6.24a), employing semicircular lunettes and Diocletian windows in the brick walls, with no dressings or ornament, and the effect is Roman, primitive, somewhat forbidding, and Antique, with a strong hint, in the lunettes, of the *loculi* in *hypogea* or *columbaria*, both favourite devices used by French Neo-Classicist architects in designs for tombs and cemeteries. Inside, Doric columns and fragments of entablature based on the temples at Pæstum appear, almost as vestigial memories, in the corners of the central groin-vaulted space (Fig. 6.24b). To have primitive Doric carrying a square groin vault, mixed with lunettes and Diocletian windows gives a grave air to the building: a primitive, no-nonsense feel, yet a type of composite and almost painful allusion to Greek and Roman Antiquity.

Yet even Pæstum was not primitive enough for some Neo-Classicists. Carl August Ehrensvärd in Sweden, for example, produced a very stumpy version of Doric in some of his designs, which he thought of as 'Egyptian', though they were nothing of the sort. His design for a dockyard gate at Karlskrona of 1785, and his 'Egyptian Architecture in a Nordic Landscape' are examples of this ultra-primitive Doric. James Playfair used primitive, stumpy, unfluted Doric columns carrying a horizontal slab within a semicircular arch (a sort of primitive-Greek-mullioned form of the Diocletian window) at Cairness House in Aberdeenshire (1791–97) (Fig. 6.25), in which building he also designed an 'Egyptian' billiard room with primitive architraves and enlivened with bogus hieroglyphs.

Of the same period are countless designs mixing pyramids with domes, sphinxes, Greek and Roman quotations, and much else. The search for the primitive was leading beyond the Orders to an architecture that was even older: that was the architecture of ancient Egypt. In the last part of the 18th century the primitive began suggesting the stripping of all decoration, quotation, and even the Orders from buildings. A good example of the

Fig. 6.24a ↑ *Church of St James, Great Packington, Warwickshire (1789–90), showing the plain, elemental, stripped exterior with Diocletian windows (JOD).*

Fig. 6.24b ↓ *Severe Neo-Classical interior of Great Packington church showing the primitive Greek Doric Order carrying groin vaults (JOD).*

Fig. 6.25 ↑ *Detail from the service-wing, Cairness House, Aberdeenshire (1789–97), showing stumpy unfluted Doric columns and primitive lintel set within a semicircular arch forming a variation on the Diocletian window, designed by James Playfair (coll. JSC).*

primitive, with the simplest of structures for the entrance, set in a pyramid, is the cenotaph of the Archduchess Maria Christina of Austria in the Augustinerkirche, Vienna (Fig. 6.26a), although the amalgam of primitive, Egyptian, and refined Classical elements is brilliantly executed.

There were some fascinating exercises in elemental geometry among the designs by Henryk Ittar for *fabriques* in the Garden of Allusions at Arkadia, near Nieborów, Poland, for Princess Helena Radziwiłłowa: these incorporated squat Greek Doric columns, sarcophagus-lids, elementary shapes, and even nods to Egyptian motifs (Fig. 6.26b). Other garden buildings at Arkadia include the Temple of Diana, composed to be seen from several positions, each view of which would suggest a different building: from one position, for example, framed by trees, it looked like a circular structure, for a pteron of six Ionic columns led to one of the entrances, and the frieze was inscribed with words from Horace in an Italian translation, suggesting that one parts from others in order to find oneself again. However, the view across the lake revealed a tetrastyle portico flanked by an Egyptianising lion on one side and a sphinx on the other, while on the frieze was a quotation from Petrarch telling us that the temple was where its builder found peace from all tribulations (Fig. 6.26c). The architect was Simon Gottlieb Zug, a Saxon who had settled in Poland, and became known as Szymon Bogumił Zug: he collaborated with the French landscape-painter Jean-Pierre Norblin de la Gourdaine to create the magical place that is Arkadia, with its allusions to J.-J. Rousseau's tomb at Ermenonville, a grotto of the Sybil, an eclectic 'high priest's sanctuary' (Fig. 6.26d), an aqueduct, and much else.

Some other curious mixtures of quirky Classicism can be found in Stamford, Lincolnshire, and in Bourne in the same county, all by Lincolnshire-born Bryan Browning, who was active from 1817. In 1821 he designed the fine sessions house (now the town hall) in Bourne, in which the external staircase and columnar screen recall the entrance to the Rasumovsky Palace, Moscow (1801–3) (Fig. 6.27a), and in Stamford he was responsible for the Stamford Institution on St Peter's Hill (Fig. 6.27b) of 1842, and the powerful gateway (1848) to what was Grant's iron foundry (Fig. 6.27c). At Folkingham, also in Lincolnshire, Browning enlarged the House of Correction (1823–5), which was demolished in 1955 apart from the powerful gatehouse, a tremendous piece of architecture worthy of earlier masters

Fig. 6.26a ↑ *Cenotaph of the Archduchess Maria Christina of Austria in the Augustinerkirche, Vienna (1805), by Antonio Canova, erected by command of her widower, Albrecht Casimir, Duke of Saxe-Teschen. The simple, primitivist forms of pyramid and the very basic structure of the entrance (a plan lintel with slightly battered plan uprights) contrast with the sophistication of the Neo-Classical figures representing the Three Ages of Man moving in procession after a figure carrying the funerary urn (JSC).*

Fig. 6.26b ↑ *Severe Neo-Classical design by Henryk Ittar for a Tomb of Illusions at Arkadia, Poland (1799–1800), showing primitive Doric, elemental stepped elements, a sarcophagus-lid, and Egyptianising telamones (the bodies of which are inverted incomplete obelisks). Note the severe lunette (MNA.Zb.Inw.NB 3519. WP).*

Fig. 6.26c ↑ *Tetrastyle Ionic portico of the Temple of Diana at Arkadia, flanked by an Egyptianising lion and a sphinx, with steps leading down to the artificial lake: the inscription on the frieze is from Petrarch, and tells us that this is the place where its builder found peace from all tribulations. The architect was S.G. Zug, and the building was begun in 1783 (WP).*

132 / CLASSICAL ARCHITECTURE

Fig. 6.26d ↑ *One of the* fabriques *at Arkadia, erected as a 'ruined' sanctuary in 1783, with a colonnaded loggia (WP).*

Fig. 6.27a ↑ *Town hall (formerly the sessions house), Bourne, Lincolnshire (1821), with its Doric columnar screen behind which is a staircase. The composition is essentially a ghostly echo of a triumphal arch, much distorted, and was designed by Bryan Browning (JSC).*

Fig. 6.27b ←← *Former Stamford Institution, St Peter's Hill, Stamford, Lincolnshire (1842), in a Græco-Egyptian style, by Bryan Browning. Note the tapered eared frame, oddly placed consoles, and triangular pediment projecting above the string-course (JSC).*

Fig. 6.27c ← *Bryan Browning was also responsible for this monumental entrance (1845) to what was an iron foundry in Wharf Road, Stamford: it is late Classical, with a rusticated arch, quoins, and a heavy cornice (JSC).*

such as Ledoux or Vanbrugh (Fig. 6.27d). Browning's work is so stuffed full of character and originality, some other buildings in the area were tentatively associated with him, but Rock House, Stamford (Fig. 6.27e), turns out to have been by George Glover, who also designed Rock Terrace, a very distinguished group on Scotgate opposite Rock House.

Architects turned to stereometrically pure forms: the square, the circle, the cube, the sphere, the cylinder, the cone, the pyramid, and the obelisk began to appear, unadorned, in many schemes, notably those of Gilly and Weinbrenner in Germany, Bonomi and Soane in England, Latrobe in the United States, and Boullée, Ledoux, and many young French architects. Sometimes the Piranesian tendency to exaggerate scale occurs in Neo-Classical designs, notably in those of Boullée, while blank walls, primitive shapes, overpowering mass, and dark, cavernous vaults suggest the awe and terror of the Sublime. Take George Dance's Newgate gaol, London (1768–85, demolished 1902), for example:

in some ways it recalls the Carceri designs of Piranesi in its sense of oppression, bare Antiquity, and crushing weight, emphasised by the powerful rustication applied to masses of masonry and the manacles and chains over the entrances (Fig. 6.28a). Similar techniques were used in other places of incarceration such as in King's Lynn, Norfolk (Fig. 6.28b). It is worth mentioning that Newgate gaol, the massive, Piranesian, windowless, heavily rusticated walls of which were also partially based on precedents by Palladio and Giulio Romano, was one of the few works of architecture by an Englishman to be illustrated in Durand's *Recueil* (1799): it was a powerful example of *architecture parlante*, in this case a no-nonsense expression of retribution. Dance's first commission was the Church of All Hallows, London Wall (1765–7), an advanced Neo-Classical essay with a barrel-vaulted interior and a very bare exterior, with contracted entablature that perhaps demonstrates influences from Laugier and other French writers, and certainly had an impact on the subsequent work of Soane.

NEO-CLASSICISM & AFTER / 133

Fig. 6.27e ↑ *Rock House, Scotgate, Stamford (1842), a sumptuous villa, an unusual and very sophisticated example of late free Classicism, in which square columns of various sizes play no small parts. A work of the highest quality, it was erected for Richard Newcomb to designs by George Glover, of Pocock & Glover, architects, Huntingdon (JSC).*

Fig. 6.27d ↓ *Gatehouse, all that remains of the former House of Correction, Folkingham, Lincolnshire (1823–5), by Bryan Browning, a dramatically forceful composition, suggesting that breaking out of the place would not be easy (JSC).*

Boullée's importance lies in his theoretical writings and visionary drawings, for he taught generations of pupils, including Brongniart, Chalgrin, and Durand. He imbibed the French Classical traditions of the 17th and 18th centuries from Blondel and Le Geay, and with Ledoux, Peyre, and de Wailly pioneered severity in domestic architecture: he monumentalised main blocks with Giant Orders, and concealed wings behind trellises or walls to give emphasis to the composition's centrepiece. In the vanguard of the anti-Rococo decorators, he gained a reputation as an interior designer, exploiting lighting effects with considerable success. He produced (1778–88) a great range of visionary drawings, responding to Laugier's reductionist themes by stripping all unnecessary ornament from stereometrically pure forms inflated to a megalomaniac scale, repeating elements such as columns in huge ranges, and making his architecture expressive of its purpose (*architecture parlante*). His most successful

Fig. 6.28a ↓ *Front of Newgate gaol, London (1768–85, demolished 1902), by George Dance the Younger. Here, Sublime Terror is suggested in an architecture that speaks of its purpose* (architecture parlante), *with massive, rusticated walls based on precedents from Palladio and Giulio Romano, and certain elements reminiscent of Piranesi's imaginary prisons, the message being one of punishment and retribution, and that prisoners cannot get out (coll. JSC).*

Fig. 6.28b → *Detail from the centre of the former gaol, King's Lynn, Norfolk (1784), by William Tuck, showing the chains, shackles, and portcullis over the door. Note the powerful rustication (JSC).*

134 / CLASSICAL ARCHITECTURE

(though unrealised) schemes of visionary architecture are those for tombs, mausolea, cenotaphs, and cemeteries, including the huge 'Cenotaph of Newton' (a vast sphere set in a circular base topped with cypresses, echoing the enormous Imperial mausolea of Roman emperors such as Augustus and Hadrian. His 1790s treatise, *Architecture. Essai sur l'art*, was not published until the 20th century.

As for Ledoux, his extraordinarily tough Salines (salt-works) d'Arc-et-Senans (1773–8) exploited banded columns, simplified rigid geometries, and primitivist qualities emphasised by unfluted Greek Doric columns. He also published designs for a Utopian town at Chaux in *L'architecture Considerée sous le Rapport de l'Art des Mœurs, et de la Législation* (1804): it featured buildings in which a simplified, stripped Neo-Classicism was the architectural language, with allusions to all sorts of stereometrically pure geometries, including Egyptian pyramids, a phallus-shaped brothel, a hoop-shaped house for a cooper, and even spherical structures. Allied to all this were routes passing through various mnemonic devices. Although Chaux remained a strange, slightly unnerving, yet wonderfully imaginative dream, Ledoux was able to realise many of his most advanced architectural ideas in the series of *barrières*, or toll-houses, erected round Paris (1785–9), including the mighty Rotonde de la Villette (*see* Fig. 6.23a), with its drum on unfluted Greek Doric overlapping serlianas, set over a square plan to each elevation of which is attached *square* Doric columns, and the grimly powerful *barrières* of Passy, Longchamp, l'Observation, and Chopinette. Here was primitive Neo-Classicism at its starkest and most sophisticated, among the most interesting architectural creations of the 18th century.

Soane was arguably one of the greatest English architects since Vanbrugh and Hawksmoor, evolving an individual style that, while rooted in Classicism, was yet original, and consisted of certain themes, including the extensive use of segmental arches; shallow saucer-domed ceilings on segmental arches carried on piers and sometimes lit from above; cross-vaults carried on piers; top-lit volumes rising through two floors; a primitive, stripped architectural language, sometimes featuring Orders such as Pæstum Doric, but more often the replacement of Orders by a series of incised ornaments cut into unadorned simple elements; careful attention to lighting, often involving mirrors (plain and convex) and tinted glass; and, above all, an obsession with the furniture of death in the form of sarcophagi, cinerary urns and containers, and oppressive vaulted spaces. Unfortunately, his Bank of England was largely redeveloped (1921–39) under Sir Herbert Baker, apart from the screen-wall that surrounds it (*see* Fig. 2.15b), but his Dulwich Picture-Gallery and Mausoleum (1811–14, restored 1953), where the architectural language reached an unusual simplicity and refinement, survives, as does his own house in Lincoln's Inn Fields (now Sir John Soane's Museum), the exterior of which, with its plain ashlar incised front, shows how far Soane had progressed in abstracting his Neo-Classicism to the barest of minimalism (Fig. 6.29a). The building possesses one of the most complex, intricate, and ingenious series of interiors ever conceived, with much top lighting (using coloured glass), mirrors, folding walls, double-height spaces, and parts where the obsession with death and the Antique almost overwhelms. At his country house, Pitzhanger Manor, Mattock Lane, Ealing (now in north-west London), to which he moved in 1800, Soane alluded

Fig. 6.29a ↑ *Soane's applied frontage to 13 Lincoln's Inn Fields (Sir John Soane's Museum), c.1812, with sharp, simple, incised ornament, caryatid figures not actually supporting anything, and the cut stone treated in the simplest possible way (JSC).*

to the triumphal arch at the entrance (1801–3), with a detached Ionic Order like a screen set before a bare wall, and a massive Attic storey, suggesting simplified Grecianised Antiquity. The interiors are comparable with those at Lincoln's Inn Fields, for the small and intimate rooms display many of Soane's characteristic details: one of the best is the breakfast room, restored to its original colour scheme (Fig. 6.29b).

Mention should also be made of Thomas Jefferson, one of the founding fathers and third president of the United States of America, who excelled in many things, not least architecture, as demonstrated in his own house, Monticello, VA (1768–82, remodelled 1796–1809), the plans of which were a variation on a design in Robert Morris's *Select Architecture* (1755), with additional elements derived from Gibbs, and a dash of Palladio taken from Leoni's edition of the *Quattro Libri*. Indeed, the house was Palladian in layout, intelligently altered to accommodate the most convenient internal arrangements, but in its final version it suggested an Antique villa transformed by French Neo-Classicism. His greatest architectural achievement, however,

Neo-Classicism & After / 135

Fig. 6.29b ↑ *Restored colour scheme in the breakfast room, Pitzhanger Manor, Ealing, by Soane (1801–3), with a typical Soaneian dome on shallow segmental arches, seemingly floating above the room. The centre of the vault is painted to suggest a cloudy sky, while the rest of the surface is decorated with a spare fret, and winged figures in relief embellish the pendentives. In the corners are Coade stone Egyptianising figures painted a shade of bronze, and walls are marbled in slate blue-green and porphyry colours, while the fireplace is inlaid with Greek-key patterns. Niches once contained Antique sculptures collected by the architect. The overall effect is astonishingly modern, yet Soane's work is anchored in Classicism, interpreted with a powerful architectural intelligence and unusual sensitivity (MC/RIBAC).*

was the University of Virginia, Charlottesville (1817–26), a series of porticoed pavilions (each with an Order from a different Roman building), linked by colonnades, on either side of a long rectangular lawn (the so-called 'campus' plan), with a scaled-down version of the Roman Pantheon at one end of the long axis. This ensemble, also intended to be exemplary, was partly influenced by Latrobe, who advised on the design. The link between Classicism, perceived as the most appropriate style of places of learning during the Enlightenment, was clear at Charlottesville, as it was for William Wilkins's Downing College, Cambridge (1807–20), the first example of a university campus, with separate buildings disposed around a grassed area. At Downing, however, the style selected was Greek Revival, for which the connoisseur/virtuoso, Thomas Hope, was largely responsible.

In Russia, Auguste de Montferrand, a pupil of Charles Percier (of Percier & Fontaine, whose Arc de Triomphe du Carrousel perhaps epitomises their Empire style) and of A.-P. Vignon, rose to some eminence, and his St Isaac's Cathedral, St Petersburg (1818–58), merges the square domed Greek-cross plan to which porticoes are attached on all four sides: the design of the cupola and dome was influenced by Soufflot's Ste-Geneviève, Paris, a building which also impacted on Schinkel's powerful Nikolaikirche, Potsdam. Carl Ludvig Engel, who was German, and trained in Berlin under Friedrich Gilly (a contemporary at the Bauakamedie was Schinkel), was responsible for one of the great set-pieces of European Neo-Classicism, the Senate Square, Helsinki, Finland (then a Grand Duchy, and part of the Russian Empire). Dominated by the Lutheran cathedral (1818–51; similar in form to St Isaac's, though the cupola is a much more modest, smaller affair [Fig. 6.30]), the square, part of an ambitious plan by J.A. Ehrenström, is flanked by the senate building (1818–22) and the university (1828–32): both of these have very splendid Greek Doric staircases. Engel also designed the library of the university (1833–45), which has a coffered dome and very fine colonnanded reading-rooms.

Neo-Classicism is essentially restrained, and is often somewhat chilly in its imagery and severity. It is characterised by the clarity of the disposition of elements, the way in which junctions are handled, and the rigid definition of the parts of the building. Greek, Egyptian, and Roman elements can sometimes be found in the same compositions. There is another aspect of Neo-Classicism, especially its Greek-inspired branches, that should be mentioned: it was free from associations and other baggage connected with absolutism, mediæval superstitions, the Counter-Reformation, and much else, and its freshness seemed to be appropriate for modern times. It suggested a new freedom, perhaps democracy, uncorrupted Antiquity, and a great Classical past to which all should look as a paradigm.

Fig. 6.30 ← *The Lutheran cathedral, Helsinki, Finland, built as the Church of St Nicholas to designs by C.L. Engel as part of a splendid Neo-Classical town plan by J.A. Ehrenström, built 1830–40, but designed much earlier, a composition similar to that of St Isaac's Cathedral, St Petersburg, by Montferrand, although Engel's cupola is much less impressive than the exemplar in what was then the Russian capital. As Finland was at the time a Grand Duchy of the Russian Empire, the dedication may not have been unconnected with a tribute to Tsar Nicholas I (r.1801–25) (JSC).*

Fig. 6.31a ↑ *Belsay Hall, Northumberland (1806–17), designed by Sir Charles Monck, an exceptionally fine solution to the problem of adapting ancient Greek architecture to domestic purposes, and a highly original synthesis of Greek elements (MW).*

Fig. 6.31b → *Staircase-hall at Belsay, with a Greek Ionic Order below and a variety of Roman Doric above (but with anthemion necking, a Greek device), a curious inversion of the usual arrangement of Doric below and Ionic above. The very fine brass railings with acanthus scrolls between the upper columns deserve note (MW).*

Fig. 6.32a ↘ *Presbyterian church, Ballykelly, County Londonderry, erected 1826–7 on its estate by the Worshipful Company of Fishmongers of the City of London to designs by Richard Suter. It is really an astylar Roman temple (columns or pilasters could easily be added to its formal geometry, and the ghost of a triumphal arch can be detected in the entrance-front) (JSC).*

Fig. 6.32b ↘↘ *The Greek Revival Presbyterian church at Portaferry, County Down (1841 – now called Portico), designed by John Millar or Miller, an amphi-prostyle hexastyle temple on a high battered podium in which an Order similar to that of the Temple of Apollo at Delos is employed, though the triglyph blocks are plain, with no glyphs. It has also been suggested that the model for the building is the Temple of Nemesis at Rhamnus (436–432 BC), which was also hexastyle, with 12 columns on each of the longer sides. However, for the interior Millar chose the Ionic Order from the Temple of Apollo Epicurius at Bassæ (JSC).*

The Move Away from Neo-Classicism

During the 19th century taste gradually moved away from the cold and primitive images of Neo-Classicism, even though there were many great Greek Revival buildings, but the icy purity of Thomas Hamilton's Greek Doric high school in Edinburgh (*see* Fig. 6.15), the forbidding masterpieces of William Wilkins's Grange Park in Hampshire from 1809 (*see* Fig. 6.20), and Monck, Gell, and Dobson's Belsay in Northumberland of 1807–17 (Figs 6.31a–b) were all strong, perhaps too strong, meat for some. Although Greek Revival buildings continued to be built, such as Philip Hardwick's powerful Greek Doric propylæum (often called an 'arch', which it was not) at Euston railway station, London (1836–40, needlessly demolished 1961–2), taste began to favour more opulent and showy styles, prodded, perhaps, by Napoleonic and Regency fashions.

NEO-CLASSICISM & AFTER / 137

Fig. 6.33a ← *Severe and astylar is Robert Adam's monument (1777–8) to David Hume in Old Calton burying-ground, Edinburgh. This deceptively 'simple' drum, with typical Adam fluted frieze at the lower stage, crowned by a Doric entablature with pateræ in the metopes, is based in its form on the tomb of Cæcilia Metella, Via Appia, outside Rome, but the entablature is derived from that of the celebrated sarcophagus of Lucius Cornelius Scipio Barbatus (3rd century BC) (JSC).*

Fig. 6.33b ↓ *Templetown mausoleum, Castle Upton, Templepatrick, County Antrim (completed 1789), by Robert Adam, a Neo-Classical variation on the triumphal-arch theme, with typically Adam fluted friezes. The vases, roundels, and cinerary containers are of Coade stone (JSC).*

Fig. 6.33c ↑ *Yet another variation on the circular temple theme at the Pelham mausoleum, Brocklesby Park, Lincolnshire (1786–94), a masterpiece by James Wyatt, where the effect is lighter and more elegant than that of Hawksmoor's Castle Howard mausoleum because of the wider spacing of the fluted Roman Doric columns, and the use of a frieze hung with swags rather than treated with triglyphs and metopes. Wyatt's charming building is an interpretation of the temples of Vesta at Tivoli and Rome (CL).*

Fig. 6.33d → *The exquisite Pelham mausoleum, Brocklesby Park, Lincolnshire, where the Pantheon quotations are more overt in the coffered ceiling and arrangements of recesses for sculpture. In the centre is the statue of Sophia Aufrere, wife of Charles Pelham, standing on a strigillated pedestal (c.1790), carved by Nollekens (CL).*

138 / CLASSICAL ARCHITECTURE

Fig. 6.33e ↑ *Belle Isle, Windermere, Westmorland (1774–5), by John Plaw, a house based on the Roman Pantheon, with a prostyle tetrastyle portico of the Scamozzi Ionic Order (Plaw [1785], pl.xxviii, coll. JSC).*

Fig. 6.33f → *The ingenious principal floor plan of Belle Isle (Plaw [1785], pl.xxvi, coll. JSC).*

Fig. 6.33g ↘ *Mussenden Temple, Downhill, County Londonderry (c.1784–5), a delightful belvedere, erected under Michael Shanahan, with carvings by David McBlain (JSC).*

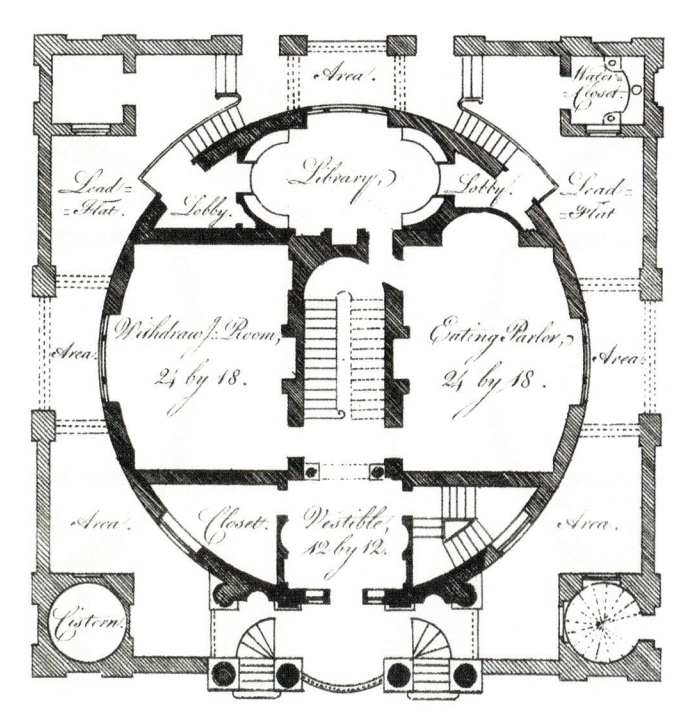

However, distinctive buildings, which obviously owed their inspiration to Classical temples, were built in certain parts: they included the Presbyterian churches at Ballykelly, County Londonderry (Fig. 6.32a), and the extraordinary Doric temple at Portaferry, County Down (1841) (Fig. 6.32b). Nevertheless, it is odd that Roman temples were not revived *in their rectangular form* until relatively recently, but the reason for this seems to have been the Renaissance models, and especially the Palladian theme, of planting 'temple-fronts' in the form of porticoes on to buildings. So Roman temples were first revived in their *circular* forms. The Tempietto of San Pietro in Montorio in Rome is an early example (*see* Fig. 4.26), and variants, such as the great dome of St Paul's Cathedral in London, the Panthéon in Paris (*see* Fig. 5.26b), the Castle Howard mausoleum in Yorkshire (*see* Figs 5.39a–b), the Radcliffe library in Oxford (*see* Fig. 5.40), and the Barrière de la Villette (*see* Fig. 6.23a), are all *derived* from early precedents, but nevertheless *transformed* by men of genius into original works of architecture. The greatest of all Roman circular temples was, of course, the Pantheon itself, but there are numerous instances of 18th- and 19th-century buildings based on a combination of *tempietto* and Pantheon themes, as well as on circular, windowless Roman tombs, such as that of Cæcilia Metella, on the Via Appia Antica, Rome (Figs 6.33a, 6.33c–g, 6.34b, and 6.35).

Roman too was the inspiration for the Arc de Triomphe (*see* Fig. 3.2a), begun in 1806 to designs by Chalgrin, but the Church of the Madeleine, started in 1804 to designs by Vignon, marks an interesting departure, for this is essentially a Roman rectangular temple (Figs 6.36a–b). The Roman temple on a high podium reappeared at Birmingham town hall (Fig. 6.37), begun in 1832 to designs by J.A. Hansom, and at Todmorden town hall (Fig. 6.38) of 1860–75, by John Gibson. Grandly Roman, too, are George Basevi's Fitzwilliam Museum (1836–45) in Cambridge, and many other major Classical buildings of the 19th century, not least the National Gallery, Berlin, a powerful composition on a high podium (Fig. 6.39). St George's Hall in Liverpool, begun in 1841 to designs by H.L. Elmes, combines the temple theme with Græco-Egyptian elements (Fig. 6.40a), while the interior has pure Greek Revival parts, but also grander rooms that are free

Neo-Classicism & After / 139

Fig. 6.34a ↓ *Tetrastyle Corinthian portico and front of St George's parish church, Belfast, originally part of the Earl-Bishop of Derry's great house at Ballyscullion, County Londonderry, built 1787 by Michael Shanahan and Francis Sandys, based on designs by Mario Asprucci, which was a smaller version of the Pantheon-rotunda theme realised at Ickworth. When Ballyscullion was demolished after the Earl-Bishop's death, the portico and a section of the curved front of the corps-de-logis were transported to Belfast and became the façade of the church when it was being erected under the direction of John Bowden. The tympanum contains the arms of the See of Down and the Town of Belfast (ACWM).*

Fig. 6.34b ↓ *Ickworth, Suffolk (from 1795), the rotunda designed by Mario Asprucci, and built under Francis and Joseph Sandys. The frieze of the crowning entablature around the rotunda and the panels between the lower columns were by Casimiro and Donato Carabelli, based on Flaxman's designs (JSC).*

Fig. 6.35 ← *The powerful Befreiungshalle, commemorating the wars of liberation against Napoléon, on the Michelsberg, near Kelheim, Bavaria (1842–63), commenced to designs by Gärtner, but completed as a completely revised work under von Klenze. The cylindrical monument has 18 great buttresses capped by female figures representing the German states, carved by Johann Halbig, and above them is a continuous Doric colonnade of 54 columns. The building has a grave, monumental appearance, worthy of a tomb, and indeed it recalls the grander mausolea of Antiquity to mind (JSC).*

140 / CLASSICAL ARCHITECTURE

Fig. 6.36a ↑ *The Roman temple theme: Church of the Madeleine, Paris (Temple de la Gloire), begun 1806 to designs by A.-P. Vignon. This grand octastyle Corinthian temple recreates a peripteral version of a Roman temple on its podium. Curiously, although the Orders are associated with Classical temples, the rectangular temple form was not revived until the 18th century, and there are several spectacular examples dating from the 19th century (AFK G5428).*

Fig. 6.36b ↑ *Detail of the richly ornamented Roman Corinthian Order of the Madeleine, Paris: note the modillions, coffers, and elaborate frieze. The resolution of detail at such significant positions as this in a Classical building is of fundamental importance (JSC).*

Fig. 6.37 ↑ *The Roman temple theme: Birmingham town hall, an octastyle peripteral temple of the Roman Corinthian Order on a podium, designed by J.A. Hansom and his partner E. Welch, in 1830–34, and built 1836–49 under Charles Edge. The design is closely based on the Temple of Castor and Pollux in the Roman Forum (AFK H3938).*

Neo-Classicism & After / 141

interpretations of parts of the *thermæ* of Caracalla (Fig. 6.40b). C.R. Cockerell's university library at Cambridge and Ashmolean Museum and Taylorian Institute at Oxford both employ the Antique Greek Ionic Order from Bassæ (*see* Figs G28a–b) mixed with arcuated elements (Fig. 6.41).

John Nash's huge scheme, transforming London from The Mall, Lower Regent Street, Piccadilly Circus, Regent Street, and through Portland Place to Regent's Park, was one of the most imaginative of its time (though much of it has been sadly mutilated), and included large palatial blocks of terrace houses treated as unified designs. A good example is the magnificent Cumberland Terrace, Regent's Park (1811-26), for which the supervising architect was James Thomson (Fig. 6.42).

In the 1820s, 1830s, and 1840s Charles Barry introduced an astylar Italian *palazzo* style with his Travellers' (1830-32) and Reform (1838-41) clubs and Bridgewater House (1846-51), all in London: this style was used on a great many buildings, including London Bridge railway terminus (1841-44) by Henry Roberts and others (Fig. 6.43a); the former headquarters of the Belfast Bank (1845) by Sir Charles Lanyon (Fig. 6.43b); and the custom house, Belfast (1854-7), by Lanyon and Lynn (Fig. 6.43c). A revival of interest in opulence as an antidote, perhaps, to the austerities of Neo-Classicism, led, not surprisingly, to renewed studies of Italian Renaissance architecture. The Barry *palazzo* style was one aspect, but even those chaste façades, capped by a *cornicione* and with ædiculated windows, proved to be rather

Fig. 6.38 ← *The Roman temple theme: Todmorden town hall, West Riding of Yorkshire (1860-75), by John Gibson, who had been a pupil of J.A. Hansom in Birmingham. The very festive Corinthian Order is engaged and set on a podium (JSC).*

Fig. 6.39 ↓ *The Roman temple theme: the National Gallery, Berlin, in the form of a Roman Corinthian temple on a high podium, with prostyle octastyle portico, designed by F.A. Stüler, who had been a principal assistant of Schinkel from 1827. The building is based on a plan devised by King Friedrich Wilhelm IV of Prussia (who is resplendent on horseback at the front of the Gallery), and the structure was erected 1866-76 by J.H. Strack. The basic idea of the building is related to F. Gilly's proposed monument (1796) to Friedrich II (Der Große) (coll. JSC).*

142 / CLASSICAL ARCHITECTURE

Fig. 6.40a ↑ *St George's Hall, Liverpool (1840–56), by H.L. Elmes, a splendid Neo-Classical celebration of civic pride, completed after 1847 under Robert Rawlinson, John Weightman, and (from 1849) C.R. Cockerell. Drawing on Roman and Greek sources, its unifying feature is the Giant Corinthian Order, although some columns, square on plan, suggest Græco-Egyptian origins, and possible influences from Schinkel and William Wilkins (MW).*

Fig. 6.40b → *The concert hall in St George's Hall, Liverpool, one of the greatest of opulent Victorian interiors, showing the pronounced Roman influence probably based on Blouet's reconstruction of the frigidarium of the thermæ of Caracalla, published 1828. The rich polychrome treatment, including the Minton tile floor, is due to Cockerell, possibly advised by Prince Albert's mentor, Ludwig Grüner (MW).*

Fig. 6.41 ↑ *Cockerell's artful combination of arcuated forms with the Greek Ionic Order from Bassæ at the Ashmolean Museum and Taylorian Institute, Oxford, accomplished, assured, and unpedantic (Richardson [1914], coll. JSC).*

Fig. 6.42 ↑ *Cumberland Terrace, Regent's Park, London (designed by Nash, 1811, built 1826 under James Thomson), the most opulent of all the terraces around the park. Sculpture by J.G. Bubb (MC/RIBAC).*

NEO-CLASSICISM & AFTER / 143

Fig. 6.43a ↑ *The markedly Italianate London terminus of the Brighton and Dover Railroads (1840–51, demolished), designed by Henry Roberts and J.U. Rastrick, although G. Smith and Thomas Turner also seem to have been involved (drawn J. Marchand, engraved by H. Adlard, coll. JSC).*

Fig. 6.43b ← *Former head office of the Belfast Bank, Belfast, remodelled 1844–6 on the Italian palazzo style by Sir Charles Lanyon. Note the ædiculated windows and massive* cornicione *(JSC).*

Fig. 6.43c ↓ *Custom house, Queen's Square, Belfast (1854–7), an opulent Italianate composition on a Palladian plan, with rich Venetian Renaissance modelling, by Lanyon and Lynn (ACWM).*

144 / CLASSICAL ARCHITECTURE

understated. Soon the Venetian verve of Sansovino at St Mark's library was being quoted in a number of instances, including Sydney Smirke's Carlton Club (Fig. 6.44) in Pall Mall (1854–6, demolished), and Parnell and Smith's Army and Navy Club, also in Pall Mall (1848–51, demolished). That is not to say the Italianate style did not continue for many years in the stucco-faced terraces of Kensington, prompted no doubt by Osborne House on the Isle of Wight (1845–53), by Thomas Cubitt and the Prince Consort. Sixteenth-century Italian styles mingled with 17th-century French motifs appear in 'Great' Scott's Foreign Office of 1868–73, while Roman Baroque was revived at Brompton Oratory, both in London.

In Scotland the Classical tradition was still strong: there were Alexander Thomson in Glasgow (mixing Græco-Egyptian elements with liberal quotations from Schinkel [*see* Figs. 6.19a–b]), the Hamiltons, Playfair, Sellars, and other robust Classicists. And it was Classicism that was to be brought south from Scotland by people like R. Norman Shaw, John Brydon, William Young, and J.J. Burnet. Baroque elements appear on Shaw's New Scotland Yard (1887–90) mixed with themes from Loire *châteaux*, but with Brydon's Chelsea town hall (1885) (Fig. 6.45) and his government offices at Whitehall (1898), architectural devices, strongly influenced by Wren, were revived. Young's city chambers in Glasgow (1883) (Fig. 6.46) quoted from Sanmichele and Sansovino, among other sources, but at the War Office in Whitehall of 1898 he used Palladian, Mannerist, and Anglo-French quotations, with a strong hint of Wren. The last building influenced the design of the former Municipal College of Technology, Belfast (1900–7), by S. Stevenson (Fig. 6.47).

The town halls of several Victorian cities aspired to considerable magnificence, starting with Birmingham, completed 1849, though designed in the reign of William IV. St George's Hall, Liverpool, was undoubtedly one of the grandest of all municipal buildings, and one used for several purposes (*see* Figs 6.40a–b),

Fig. 6.44 → *The Carlton Club, Pall Mall, London (1854–6, demolished), by Sydney Smirke, closely modelled on Sansovino's Library of San Marco in Venice (coll. JSC).*

Fig. 6.45 ↑ *Chelsea town hall, London (1885–7), by J.McK. Brydon, in a Free Classical style ('Wrenaissance') influenced by the work of Wren (JSC).*

Fig. 6.46 ← *Municipal chambers, Glasgow (1883–8), by William Young. An opulent pile of French, Flemish, Venetian, and Spanish Renaissance styles (HES [coll. A. Brown & Co.] SC 756366).*

Fig. 6.47 ↑ *The former Municipal College of Technology, Belfast (1900–7), by Samuel Stevenson, influenced by William Young's New (now Old) War Office in Whitehall, London (1898–1906), a mixture of Palladian, Mannerist, and Baroque features (JSC).*

Fig. 6.48 ← *Town hall, Headrow, Leeds, West Riding of Yorkshire (1852–8), by C. Brodrick, influenced by French Neo-Classicism, notably works by Brongniart and L.-P. Baltard, though with Baroque insinuations such as in the magnificent tower, possibly drawing on Archer's Church of St Philip, Birmingham (Richardson [1914], coll. JSC).*

146 / CLASSICAL ARCHITECTURE

Fig. 6.49 → *The Bowes Museum, Barnard Castle, County Durham (1869–79), by J.-A.-F.-A. Pellechet, an amazing manifestation of a large French château landed in a prominent position in a Dales market town (JSC).*

but Leeds town hall (1852–8), in its own way, rose to the occasion with considerable verve and elan, mixing Roman, Italianate, French, and English Baroque themes, although when it was black with the soot of 19th-century air pollution, it seemed rather more impressive than after it was cleaned (Fig. 6.48).

There were occasional outbreaks of Francophilia in architectural terms, none more startling than the apparition of the Bowes Museum, Barnard Castle, County Durham (1869–79), designed by Jules Pellechet, an incongruous pile looking like some grand *hôtel de ville* that has lost its way and ended up on a commanding site in the north of England (Fig. 6.49). It was built for John and Joséphine Bowes, who collected *objets d'art*, and, wishing to find a permanent home for their acquisitions, given France's current instability, settled on Barnard Castle, as it was near the Bowes family seat of Streatlam Castle. Pellechet's father, A.-J. Pellechet, had worked for the Bowes when they lived in France, and the building possesses recognisable elements from the Louvre, the *hôtel de ville* in Le Havre, a bit of the Tuileries for the front entrance, and at roof level some reminiscences of the Château de Cheverny. To add to the fascinating list of sources, it appears that the internal layout of the Alte Pinakothek in Munich (1826–36), by Leo von Klenze, was also considered in the process of planning. There was, of course, another extraordinary architectural re-enactment of the French Renaissance, rich with borrowings from Blois, Chambord, Azay-le-Rideau, Chenonceau, and other places, all collected together by H.-A.-G.-W. Destailleur for Baron Ferdinand de Rothschild at Waddesdon Manor, Buckinghamshire (1877–83 and later).

By the turn of the century the Baroque Revival was in full swing in the hands of architects such as John Belcher and Alfred Brumwell Thomas. Yet even as early as 1866 Joseph Poelært, in his Palais de Justice in Brussels, created a mighty pile of Baroque compositions, tempered with some Sublime chunkiness not that far removed from robust Neo-Classicism, and with a breathtaking scale. There were Baroque Revivals in Germany, Austria, France, and the United States. Berlin's Lutheran cathedral by Raschdorff, the new Hofburg in Vienna, the Paris Opéra, and the Capitol in Washington all show distinctly Baroque tendencies, but in England the Baroque Revival was closely associated with a revived interest in the work of Wren, giving it the perhaps tongue-in-cheek, though amusing label of 'Wrenaissance' (perhaps coined, it is said, by Lutyens, no less). Wren quotations can be found in Brumwell Thomas's Belfast city hall (1896–1906) (Fig. 6.50a), in the same architect's Stockport town hall (Fig. 6.50b), and at Belcher's Ashton memorial (1906) near Lancaster, to name but three great examples of distinguished late-Victorian and Edwardian Baroque.

The work of Edwin Rickards (admirably celebrated by Timothy Brittain-Catlin) should also not be discounted, for he was no mean architect, capable of tremendous elan in his ventures into a fluent use of Baroque tendencies: with H.V. Lanchester and J. Stewart, he designed the city hall and law courts, Cathays Park, Cardiff, Wales (1897–1906), with Beaux-Arts planning and lively Baroque façades. After Stewart's death, he and Lanchester won the competition to build the enormous Wesleyan Central Hall, Westminster (1905–11), one of the most exuberant monuments of its time, with more than a touch of Viennese worldliness about it (enhanced by the vigorous sculpture of Henry Poole, fully integrated with the architecture, and not treated as an afterthought). A contemporary critic described Rickards' work as 'combining opulence and taste with a touch of refined swagger', and that is exactly right. Mention of Vienna brings to mind an interesting variation on these themes. This was the impressive church which dominates the main axis of the Zentralfriedhof (Central Cemetery), Vienna: it merges Baroque power with new tendencies associated with the Vienna Secession that were present in the works of the celebrated office of Otto Wagner: the building was designed from 1899 by one of Wagner's pupils, Max Hegele, and built 1908–10 (Fig. 6.51).

As had been the case in the 18th century, there was a reaction against this florid and theatrical style. Neo-Classicism

Fig. 6.50a → *City hall, Belfast (1896–1906), a sumptuous late-Victorian essay in Baroque Revival (aka 'Wrenaissance'), heavily influenced by the works of Christopher Wren, designed by Alfred Brumwell Thomas. Three of the elevations are Neo-Palladian, with a Giant Scamozzi Order carried on a rusticated ground floor and numerous Gibbs surrounds, but the corner turrets are English Baroque derived from the western towers of St Paul's Cathedral, London, and the great central dome is partly St Paul's and partly Greenwich Hospital (ACWM).*

Fig. 6.50b ↑ *Town hall, Wellington Road South, Stockport, Cheshire (1904–8), by A.B. Thomas, an essay in Edwardian Baroque, with a touch of William and Mary, supercharged Wren, and not a little of the Palais des Beaux Arts, Lille (1892), by Bérard and Delmas, though tempered with Italian Baroque verve (JSC).*

Fig. 6.51 ↑ *The massive Church of St Karl Borromäus dominating the main axis of the Zentralfriedhof (Central Cemetery), Vienna, erected 1908–10, and designed by Max Hegele. It mingles aspects of architectural tendencies present in the work of Otto Wagner and his pupils (the so-called Wagnerschule of which Hegele had been a member) with the Baroque traditions of the Austrian capital (JSC).*

re-emerged in various guises. J.J. Burnet's extension to the British Museum (1905–14), using an engaged Ionic Order, consciously rejects Laugier's (and Smirke's) insistence on the detached column, and mixes in some judicious battered Egyptianisms with his modern Greek. Scotland's loyalty to Classicism enabled Scots architects such as Burnet, Norman Shaw, William Young, and John McK. Brydon to bring that style south to England when the time was ripe, towards the end of the 19th century. Sir Edwin Lutyens also used the Wren style (the so-called 'Wrenaissance') at the offices of *Country Life* in Tavistock Street, Covent Garden (1904), directly quoting from Hampton Court Palace. At Heathcote (1906), near Ilkley in Yorkshire, Lutyens produced a Palladian Baroque villa in which he also drew on Sanmichele, Vignola, Wren, Vanbrugh, and Hawksmoor for this essay in the 'High Game'. But after Burnet's extension to the British Museum, a more austere Classicism found favour, notably in Smith and Brewer's National Museum of Wales of 1910, Swales, Atkinson, Burnet, and Burnham's Selfridge's in Oxford Street of 1908–9, and Burnet's own Kodak House, Kingsway, London, of 1911, which eschewed the Orders altogether and, with its coved Egyptianesque cornice, seems to be using the same stripped language of Perret and others on the Continent (Fig. 6.52).

148 / CLASSICAL ARCHITECTURE

Peter Behrens, in the office block for the AEG in Berlin (1908–10), used a stripped Classical style, while Henry Bacon built a plain rectangular box surrounded by a chaste peristyle of purest Greek Doric for his Lincoln Memorial in Washington (1911–12). Very different was the work of Auguste Perret in France: it often uses Classical proportion, and suggests a Classical arrangement without overt quotation. Behrens, Perret, and some of their contemporaries *paraphrased* Classical elements, but their work is Classical nevertheless. Stripped Neo-Classicism recurs in the work of J.C.C. Petersen and I. Bentsen in 1919 for proposals in Copenhagen, and also in J.F.M. Hoffmann's Austrian pavilion and Behrens's festival hall, both at the Cologne Werkbund exhibition of 1914. At another major exhibition (1913), this time in what was then Breslau (now Wrocław, Poland), to celebrate the centenary of the battle of Leipzig (1813), a crucial and extremely bloody engagement during the 'wars of liberation' against Napoléon, the centrepiece was the enormous Jahrhunderthalle (Centenary Hall, 1911–13) by Max Berg, who held a senior position in the city's planning and building departments, and who directed the layout of the entire Jahrhundertfeier (centenary celebration). Although the Jahrhunderthalle has been the focus for the attention of architectural historians, many of the other exhibition buildings were and are of equal interest, including work by Hans Poelzig, who was director (1903–16) of the Königliche Kunst- und Kunstgewerbeschule (Royal School of Arts and Applied Arts). Poelzig, working under Berg's overall command, adopted a stumpy Greek Doric for his buildings, adapting the Order to be made of concrete (Fig. 6.53). The choice of a simplified Doric was deliberate, as Poelzig argued it was expressive of the early 19th-century period being celebrated. Besides, Berg's great hall was itself not without its stripped-Classical allusions.

After the catastrophe of 1914–18, numerous memorials were erected, most of which, especially in the British Isles, adopted the Classical language of architecture. Not all were simply monuments, though: some of the most impressive were buildings for use, none more impressive than the Masonic Peace Memorial

Fig. 6.53 ↑ *The Four Domes pavilion, Szczytnicki Park, Wrocław (formerly Breslau) (1911–13), designed by Hans Poelzig, employing a simplified Greek Doric Order, but made of concrete. The Order and general style were chosen to suggest the time in which the great battle of Leipzig was fought (1813) (JSC).*

Fig. 6.54 ↓ *Fine perspective drawing of the Masonic Peace Memorial, headquarters of the United Grand Lodge of England, and called Freemasons' Hall, Great Queen Street, London (1926–33), designed by H.V. Ashley and F. Winton Newman (UGLE).*

Fig. 6.52 ↑ *Kodak House, Kingsway, London, by John James Burnet and Thomas Tait. Designed 1910, and completed 1912, Kodak House admits to its steel frame, but it is still Classical. There is a two-storey podium on which sits a Giant Order, but it is an Order with a base and no capitals: this capital-less language was used by the ancient Egyptians (as at the mortuary temple of Queen Hatshepsut), and the Egyptian theme is further pursued in the coved cornice. The Attic storey is not original, but works well (D&C).*

NEO-CLASSICISM & AFTER / 149

Fig. 6.55a ↑ *View from the English Garden, Munich, of the Haus der Deutschen Kunst (House of German Art, 1933–7), an essay in stripped Neo-Classicism, by Paul Ludwig Troost, with pallid echoes of Schinkel's Altes Museum colonnade in Berlin (see Fig. 6.11b) (Troost [ed.] [1942–3], coll. JSC).*

Fig. 6.55b → *View along the stripped-Classical colonnade of Troost's Haus der Deutschen Kunst, showing the design's indebtedness to Schinkel's Altes Museum (see Fig. 6.11e) (JSC).*

(Freemasons' Hall), headquarters of the United Grand Lodge of England, in Great Queen Street, London, designed by H.V. Ashley and F. Winton Newman in 1926 and erected 1927–33. The complex is cleverly planned on a tapering corner site: it bewildered Pevsner in its self-possession and extremes of theatrical display, but mingled with the modern Grecianism throughout the building is a subtle Egyptian flavour, which is not surprising given the Craft's debt to the Hermetic traditions (Fig. 6.54).

With I.J. Tengbom's concert hall in Stockholm (1923–6) comes a tendency to interpret and elongate the Orders, something that occurs in the work of several architects of the era. This can also be seen in P.L. Troost's Haus der Deutschen Kunst (1933–7) in Munich (Figs 6.55a–b), a primitivist Neo-Classicism that was matched by several German architects in the 1920s and 1930s. A concern for the simple purity of form re-emerges at A.V. Shchusev's Lenin mausoleum in Moscow, which is very Egyptian in its inspiration, and in K. Fisker's Danish pavilion at the 1925 Paris international exposition. Sigurd Lewerentz, in his designs for funerary buildings (Malmö, 1926, and Enskede, 1922–5 [Fig. 6.56], for example), exploited both the Orders, blank walls, and stereometrically pure forms to create a dignified and solemn architecture. E.G. Asplund, too, interpreted Classical architecture, and during the 1920s and 1930s a simplified Classicism was pre-eminent in Scandinavian architecture.

Speer, Kreis, and others looked to Schinkel and von Klenze as well as to Roman Antiquity (the Pantheon and triumphal arches in Rome, both inflated to Boullée-esque scales). Vast buildings designed within a Classical system were not confined to National Socialist Germany, but were erected in quantities in various Eastern European countries, in the post-war era, under Stalin and his associates. Even Communist China adopted an official architecture that owes not a little to European Classicism and Neo-Classicism, and examples were still being erected in the 1970s (e.g. the memorial hall of Chairman Mao in Beijing, which although hardly subtle or refined, betrays its origins).

Fig. 6.56 ↑ *Resurrection Chapel, Woodland Cemetery, Enskede, Stockholm (1922–6), perhaps one of the most successful creations of understated Swedish Classicism, designed by Sigurd Lewerentz (JSC).*

But none of that should invalidate Classicism: its credentials and its long and honourable history are far too sound for that.

150 / CLASSICAL ARCHITECTURE

7

ASPECTS OF A CONTINUING CLASSICISM

There are some men formed with feeling so blunt, with tempers so cold and phlegmatic, that they can hardly be said to be awake during the whole course of their lives. Upon such persons, the most striking objects make but a faint and obscure impression.

EDMUND BURKE:
'Introduction: On Taste', in *A Philosophical Inquiry into the Origin of Our Ideas of the Sublime and Beautiful, with an Introductory Discourse concerning Taste, and Several Other Additions* (London: Thomas McLean, 1823), 118.

If we regard the origin of the professional architect, and the history of his evolution, it is easy to see what … has developed … His environment has moulded his characteristics … [he] cannot be excepted from the fate of every artist that essays professionalism. He loses the art fibre and must depend on make-believe and borrowing. We have no quarrel [with the RIBA] that its members have pleased the public, if they have pleased them, or that the business which they have brought into fellowship with architecture has reaped its business reward. But we protest that this business is not real architecture, but its complete negation, – really nothing but the enterprise of a tradesman, whether it is advertised as art, science, or business, or any other judicious amalgam which Presidents of the Institute may favour. Professed allegiance to art has only made betrayal of it more pernicious. Under any reasonable definition art and profession must run into different categories. The professional architect is a contradiction in terms; he … must become a dealer in wares, not a producer, a chapman, not a craftsman … But the public has not really been hoodwinked.

EDWARD SCHRÖDER PRIOR:
'The Ghosts of the Profession' in Richard Norman Shaw and Thomas Graham Jackson (eds): *Architecture – A Profession or an Art: Thirteen Short Essays on the Qualifications and Training of Architects* (London: John Murray, 1892), 99–115.

Preliminary Remarks

Looking back on the 20th century from the third decade of the 21st, it is difficult to enthuse about the vast majority of buildings erected since the Second World War. In spite of the polemics and optimistic claims for the so-called Modern Movement as the style (or non-style) of the era, there were not all that many examples of it realised until after 1945. This was especially true of the British Isles.

In the early 1900s the Baroque Revival was in full swing, but a more severe Neo-Classical manner, sometimes stripped of all but the most elemental mouldings, emerged before 1914, and continued after 1918. Classicism, in one guise or another, was undoubtedly the most significant architectural language in Europe and America, and where there were Western influences, until 1945.

The single most devastating blow given to the acceptability of Classical architecture was the fact that stripped, bare Classicism was favoured in the Third Reich *for official buildings*, and that Adolf Hitler himself was deeply interested in it. Many architects in Germany, not without talent (such as P. Baumgarten, G. Bestelmeyer, P. Bonatz, E. Haiger, W. Kreis, W. March, Arthur Reck, A. Speer, and P.L. Troost), produced numerous designs in that style under National Socialism. And, like it or not, the *planning* of the Neue Reichskanzlei (New Reich Chancellery – built 1938–9, destroyed), on an impossibly long, thin site, stretching along the Voss-straße from the Wilhelmplatz to the Tiergarten, Berlin, designed by Albert Speer, was brilliant, and the architecture did what it was supposed to do – impress: its language of simplified Classicism realised with very fine materials and competent workmanship contributed to its success.

One should judge such architecture *as architecture*, not through biased blinkers clouded with scruples of hindsight, or because Speer fell short in political or moral terms. Again, the malign influence of Ruskin and others has tended to warp æsthetic judgements. As Léon Krier, who edited a fine book (1985) on the work of Albert Speer, wrote, publishing or investigating architecture by any individual is its only justification, and such a study cannot disculpate the crimes of a regime or

151

of a person, nor would it ever wish to or attempt such a foolish and hopeless task.

This association was almost fatal to Classicism, in spite of the fact that there were very numerous and distinguished Classical buildings designed during the inter-war years in countries that were *not* under any sort of totalitarian regime, be it Italian Fascist, German National Socialist, or Soviet Communist. In the Scandinavian democracies a stripped, simplified Classicism was *de rigueur*, and hugely admired, notably in Britain: it included works by Aalto, Asplund, Bentsen, Grut, Hjorth, Kampmann, Lallerstedt, Leche, Lewerentz, Östberg, Petersen, Rafn, Tengbom, Thomsen, and many, many others. In France, too, Classicism survived, again often reduced to its bare bones, but it was Classicism nevertheless, as in the Palais de Chaillot, Paris (1935–7, by Carlu, Boileau, and Azéma), which is only one example, and it continued in the United States, where a Beaux Arts tradition of teaching continued, notably under French-born Paul Cret. This architect's public library, Indianapolis, IN (1914–17), has massive blocky pavilions on either side of a severe Doric colonnade, but with his Aisne-Marne memorial to the American dead of 1917–18, near Château-Thierry, France (1925–33), he employed exactly the same architectural language of square columns and blocky piers that is found repeated in works by Kreis, Troost, Speer, and their German contemporaries. Other American examples would have to include the noble architecture of McKim, Mead, & White (e.g. the magnificent Pennsylvania Station, New York City [1902–11, destroyed 1963–5, although it was described as dramatising the whole majestic symbolism of Classical architecture]), and that of the greatest academic American Classicist of his time, John Russell Pope (whose National Gallery of Art [1936–41] and Jefferson Memorial [1935–43], both in Washington, DC, testify to his undoubted distinction).

There was also a former member of the celebrated atelier of Otto Wagner in Vienna, an architect of genius, Jože Plečnik, who was producing remarkably original Classically based work in Slovenia right up to the year in which he died (1957, when Slovenia still was merged into Jugoslavia). His extraordinary fluency in virtuosic variations on Classicism can be seen in several buildings he designed at the Žale cemetery (1937–40) (Fig. 7.1), the wonderful market complex (1939–42), and the church of St Francis of Assisi (1924–31), all in the Slovenian capital, Ljubljana. He left considerable architectural legacies in Vienna and Prague as well. There have been several volumes about his fascinating architectural career published over the last few decades, and those demonstrate very clearly how the Classical language of architecture in the hands of a master can lend itself to an enormous variety of building types, endlessly interesting, and never dull.

The above-mentioned are only a few among very many who were producing splendid Classical architecture in the first half of the 20th century in countries untainted by 'National Socialism'. The Hitlerian association, however, gave Modernists a weapon which they did not fail to use: as one historian has noted, some still think of stormtroopers when they see columns. A curious aspect of this dismal, dishonest affair is that since Classicism was the favoured style of many democracies in the 1920s and 1930s, why can it not, therefore, be 'Democratic' rather than 'Fascist'?

Fig. 7.1 ↑ *Funerary chapel on the main axis of the Žale cemetery, Ljubljana, Slovenia (1937–40), by Jože Plečnik, a remarkably subtle design with a baldachin in front of the chapel proper, which features a Greek Doric column centrally placed (JSC).*

Even more peculiar is the fact that Lenin's mausoleum in Moscow of 1924–30 (by Alexei Shchusev) is in the most severe stripped and impeccable Neo-Classical manner, worthy of a Gilly or a Ledoux in their most 'primitive' moods: in fact, the building owes much to the square-columned arrangement of Egyptian temples, so it belongs firmly in the Neo-Classical canon. Another successful architect of the Soviet era was B.M. Iofan, whose massive Bersenevskaya Embankment apartment block in Moscow (1928–31), which incorporated shared facilities such as a laundry, shops, and a cinema (an early *Unité d'Habitation* exemplar, perhaps?), presented a front facing the river, owing much to a severely stripped Neo-Classicism. Other residents in this vast complex included N.S. Krushchev and G.K. Zhukov. Iofan, with V.A. Shchuko and V.G. Gel'freykh, was responsible for the monstrous, but unexecuted Palace of the Soviets, to be capped by a huge statue of Lenin: this design signalled the institutionalisation of a simplified Classicism, hugely inflated in scale, as the official style of the Stalinist dictatorship. Iofan also designed the Soviet Pavilion for the Paris Exposition of 1937, with its heroic personifications of Industry and Agriculture (by V.I. Mukhina), the male figure holding a hammer and the hefty farm-girl a sickle, suspended in confrontation with Albert Speer's stripped-Classical German Pavilion (capped by an impressive eagle clutching a wreath surrounding a swastika, sculpted by K. Schmid-Ehmen) situated directly opposite. The curious thing about Iofan's design is that it was far more dynamic than was Speer's static structure (details of which owed much to earlier work of P.L. Troost in Munich), and, with its heroic realistic figures, seemed to surge forward (Iofan likened it to a ship): in fact, it was not entirely innocent of themes drawn from the RCA Building at Rockefeller Center, New York (1931–40), designed by R.M. Hood.

In 1949 Iofan was denounced for his 'decadent bourgeois values', and for 'hampering the development of the architectural sciences by continuing to grovel' before the 'bourgeois models' of the USA, Paris, and Rome. In other words, he was straying from the approved 'Socialist' language of Classicism. However, unlike his mentor and erstwhile friend, A.I. Rykov, Iofan managed to escape 'liquidation', perhaps because Stalin believed he might still be of some use to him. Yet his career, like that of Speer, is a cautionary tale of how damaging it can be to come too close to political power, especially when negotiating an accommodation with tyranny: those so-called starchitects of today, their tongues hanging out with avarice as they smarm over oligarchs, dictators, and every kind of horror holding capacious moneybags, are odiously familiar. Architecture can often be an instrument of statecraft, and its practitioners can have reputations besmirched by close association with systems that fall from power and favour.

But the point here is that Classicism cannot be dismissed because it had associations with National Socialism: that does not make sense, because it was also favoured in the Soviet Union, and its more universal applications in the inter-war period of the 1920s and 1930s were in the democracies, notably Scandinavia, where many works of real distinction, such as those of Lewerentz, were realised, so to label it as 'Nazi' is both dishonest and historically untrue. It would be more accurate to perceive it as a universal architectural style.

Classicism was also the dominant architectural language of the Stalinist era throughout Eastern Europe after 1945: the former Stalinallee in Berlin, and similar developments in Magdeburg, Dresden, and throughout what used to be the Soviet Union and its satellites, all suggest (if the association with Hitler and Classicism is used to damn that language) that Classical architecture can also be a style associated with the extreme left, that is Soviet Communism and centralised Socialism. Those who promoted the Modern Movement in the post-1945 era cannot have it both ways: they cannot condemn a language for its association with Hitler on the grounds that it is 'far-right' if it is also a language widely used by both Western democracies and Stalinist regimes in Eastern Europe.

It is also worth pointing out that there were plenty of buildings erected under the ægis of the Third Reich which were impeccably 'Modern', such as service stations on the new motorways (good examples are those designed by Paul Hofer and Karl Johann Fischer), the buildings for the Heinkel aircraft factory at Oranienburg, Brandenburg (1935–6), by Herbert Rimpl and Josef Bernard, and the Opel works at Brandenburg-an-der-Havel (1935) by Heinrich Bärsch, but that indubitable fact has been deliberately concealed. It has also been claimed that some almost deified Modernist heroes and their works (because they were Modernist) were somehow connected with democracy, but many attempted to ingratiate themselves with National Socialism. Miës van der Rohe, for example, was one of several cultural leaders in Germany who, claiming to 'belong to the young Führer's followers', signed a proclamation published in the Nazi newspaper *Völkischer Beobachter* (18 August 1934) urging everyone to vote Hitler into supreme power after the death of President Hindenburg. It is very striking that the architectural language used by Mies van der Rohe in America (minus the diæresis over the ë of Mies he had given himself in the 1920s to conceal the unpleasant associations [which *Mies* has in German]) for the over-praised ITT buildings in Chicago, IL, from 1941 onwards, with its steel frames and brick infill panels, was almost identical to that employed by Hermann Brenner and Werner Deutschmann for the German Research Institute for Aviation, Berlin-Adlersdorf (completed 1936). The eager embrace of former *Bauhäusler* like Gropius, Miës van der Rohe, and others by the USA in the 1930s, and their shoehorning into influential positions where they could impose Modernist indoctrination on American education, was aptly and shrewdly described by Sibyl Moholy-Nagy as 'Hitler's Revenge'.

It is true that Hitler was uninterested in tedious doctrinal disputes between dim-witted architects: he did make it clear that service stations were not places where horses were watered, but where motor vehicles received fuel, and therefore modern styling was appropriate, as it was also for industrial buildings. So it is simply a downright, wicked lie that Modernism was banned in the Third Reich: it was not, as a huge number of industrial buildings that looked to be fully fledged products of the Modern Movement testify to all but the most wilfully myopic.

The Survival of Classicism

Neo-Classical architecture in the late 18th and early 19th centuries was infinitely varied, often brilliant, frequently stripped to its bare minimum, and usually displayed a scholarly notion of proportion, detail, and composition. Twentieth-century Classicism, especially in Scandinavia, Germany, Austria, France, and the United States, explored further the ideas of simplicity and stripped architecture which the Neo-Classicists of the period 1770 to 1830 had developed. Wagner, Behrens, Kreis, and others were actually building in an earlier tradition, while in Britain, architects such as Reginald Blomfield (with his Menin Gate at Ieper [*see* Fig. 3.2i]); Lutyens (with his Sublime memorial at Thiepval [Fig. 7.2]); Sir John Burnet (with his splendidly assured extension to the British Museum); and Thomas S. Tait of John Burnet, Tait, & Lorne (with his masterly St Andrew's House at Calton Hill in Edinburgh, of 1936–9) demonstrated that the language of Classicism was very much alive, offered an enormous vocabulary with infinite possibilities, and could be explored to marvellous effect in the hands of competent and imaginative designers. It is also worth pointing out that the architectural language used for the huge war cemeteries for the dead of the British Empire, created in the aftermath of the catastrophe of 1914–18, was Classical, as it was deemed the only such language capable of rising to the solemnity of the task: skilled architects were involved, including Blomfield, Sir Herbert Baker, Lutyens, H. Chalton Bradshaw, W.H. Cowlishaw, and many others, clearly familiar with, and at ease in, the richly adaptable mode of architectural expression.

The late Gavin Stamp, towards the end of his life, rejoiced in the fact that, although it was still rare, it was a relief to be able to carry on a discussion about the use of the Classical language of architecture at all, as the topic was very much frowned upon, and in many cases actually forbidden, by doctrinaire Modernists. In his admirable *Interwar British Architecture 1919–39* (2024), he

Fig. 7.2 ← *Thiepval Memorial raised to the 60,000 Missing of the Somme (1927–32), by Sir Edwin Lutyens, showing the transformation of the triumphal arch so that the subordinate sides become triumphal arches themselves. This is an extraordinarily eclectic work, brilliantly pulling together quotations from numerous precedents, including, perhaps, the Arco dei Quattro Venti, at the Villa Doria-Pamphilji, Rome, designed by A. Busiri Vici in memory of those who fell during the French bombardment of 1849–50. Monumental blocky masses make this one of the most Sublime memorials ever created: it is an accomplished variation on the simple two-axis arch, but interlocking the geometries in a virtuoso performance of great subtlety. Lutyens further developed variations on triumphal-arch themes explored in this master-work in his brilliant designs for the Roman Catholic Metropolitan Cathedral of Liverpool., designed from 1929, commenced in 1933, halted in 1941 after only part of the magnificent crypt had been constructed, and regrettably abandoned in the 1950s (RHB/GB).*

gave us an account of a great many wonderful buildings, including numerous exemplars with impeccable Classical credentials, and not just the 'big names'. Baker's work at Soane's Bank of England was damned by Pevsner, no less, as 'the worst individual loss suffered by London architecture in the first half' of the 20th century (1921–39), but sometimes Baker could produce fine and sensitive work: an example is the very beautiful and moving War Memorial cloister at Winchester College, of 1924 (Figs 7.3a–b).

Many memorable Classical buildings were erected in the so-called British Isles between the wars, including London's County Hall (1908–22) by Ralph Knott; the Council House (now Guildhall), Nottingham (1925–9), by T. Cecil Howitt; the Central Library, Manchester (built 1930–4), by E. Vincent Harris (Fig. 7.4); the fine front of Lloyd's of London, Leadenhall Street (1928), and the former National Provincial Bank, Poultry, both in London (completed 1932), and both by Sir Edwin Cooper; the very grand Wolseley House, Piccadilly, London (1921–2) by W. Curtis Green; the Union Bank of Scotland, St Vincent Street, Glasgow (1924–7), by Richard McL.M. Gunn; the magnificent Freemasons' Hall, Great Queen Street, London (1926–33), by H.V. Ashley and F.W. Newman (*see* Fig. 6.54); India Buildings, Water Street, Liverpool (1924–32), by Herbert J. Rowse; and the Northern Ireland parliament building, Stormont, Belfast (1927–32), by Sir Arnold Thornely, of Liverpool, who, with F.G. Briggs, F.B. Hobbs, and H.V. Wolstenholme, had earlier been responsible for the showy but admirable Baroque Wrenaissance domed and towered Mersey Docks and Harbour Offices that grace Pier Head in that city (1900–7).

It is peculiar that mainstream books on 20th-century architecture in Italy tend to concentrate on the work of people like Giuseppe Terragni, who designed the Casa del Fascio, Como (1932–6), for Benito Mussolini's Fascist Party, a building held up as a paradigm of Modernism to this day, as previously noted, but ignore distinguished Italian Classical architecture because it does not fit neatly within the authorised Grand Narrative of Modernism. Marcello Piacentini, for example, was influential in promoting a stripped Neo-Classicism, and was no mean architect, as his Hotel Ambasciatori, Rome (1926–7), shows in its powerful Mannerist façade. Other significant works include the splendid mausoleum at Palanza (1929–30) of Marshal Count Luigi Cadorna, the formal Piazza della Vittoria, Brescia (1927–32), the war memorials at Genoa (1927–34) and Bolzano (1926–8), the Casa Madre dei Mutilati, Rome (1928), the Palace of Justice, Milan (1933–40), and his work with Pagano, Piccinato, and others in the planning of the Esposizione Universale di Roma (EUR) for the projected 1942 exhibition (which did not happen because of the world war). He was no mean scholar either, and his book, *Architettura d'oggi* (1930) was greatly admired at the time. It is an indictment of architectural commentators that Piacentini has had a 'bad press', unlike the treatment given to Fascists such as Pagano and Terragni (although Pagano rejected Fascism at the end, and paid for his apostasy in Mauthausen [1945]).

Another very distinguished and interesting Italian architect who has been virtually ignored by writers promoting a Modernist agenda was Luigi 'Gino' Coppedè, whose works include the astonishingly Mannerist Palazzo Pastorino (1907)

154 / CLASSICAL ARCHITECTURE

Fig. 7.3a ↑ *War Memorial cloister, Winchester College, Hampshire (1922–4), by Herbert Baker, one of his best buildings, showing one of the entrances, constructed of flint with dressed stone (JSC).*

Fig. 7.3b ↗ *War Memorial cloister, Winchester College: the centre of the garth, showing the Portland stone Tuscan columns, two deep, carrying hefty arches (note the interesting detail just above where the arches spring). The memorial cross, with figures on the octagonal shaft, was made by Alfred Turner (JSC).*

and several family tombs as well as the entrance (1904) to the English cemetery at the Staglieno, all in Genoa. Responsible for the brilliant Quartiere Coppedè around the Piazza Mincio, Rome (1917–27), he demonstrated how new urban fabric can have a richness of decorative treatment as interesting as anything in the older parts of the city: this he achieved by a collage of features drawn from various periods and in different styles to give his buildings a kind of fictional history, as well as a human scale, which promoted sour Modernist labelling of his work as 'irrelevant' and 'not of today', despite its obvious success. His brother, Adolfo, with Dario Carbone, designed the lavishly Neo-Baroque Palazzo della Borsa Valori, Genoa (1906–12).

'Gino' Coppedè's enchanting Roman Quartiere had a comparable, albeit rural, development in Wales at Portmeirion, Merioneth (now Gwynedd), where, employing a collage of recycled architectural fragments rescued from demolished buildings, combined with colour-washed new fabric, a picturesquely playful Baroque Mediterraneanesque village was created from 1925 under the direction of Clough Williams-Ellis, inspired by a visit to Portofino in the company of Eric Kennington. Although Portmeirion has been somewhat unkindly (if wittily) referred to as a 'home for fallen buildings', Christopher Hussey was to write of the place as 'a dream citadel that had shot up out of wood and water like a fragment of Amalfi or Sorrento'.

Fig. 7.4 ↑ *The space between the Central Library (left: designed 1927 by Vincent Harris, influenced by the Roman Pantheon, and erected 1930–4) and the town hall extension (right: also designed by Harris in 1927, and built 1934–8), one of the most exciting pieces of townscape in Manchester, at once mysterious, forbidding, inviting, and architecturally thrilling. As an ensemble, the two buildings comprise perhaps the most impressive civic project realised in Britain at that time (JSC).*

ASPECTS OF A CONTINUING CLASSICISM / 155

Williams-Ellis elaborated on many of the themes explored in Portmeirion in his *Pleasures of Architecture* (1924, 1954), written with his wife, Amabel Strachey, and he was a tireless campaigner against the contemporary tendencies in architecture and planning that were ruining the urban fabrics and landscapes of these islands. Gavin Stamp reminded us that 'for all the talk of progress and modernity, neither the Picturesque tradition nor the romantic, nostalgic impulse in British architecture could easily be eradicated', but the Gwynedd volume in *The Buildings of Wales* (2009) said of the place that 'in its determination to communicate truths through architectural jesting, Portmeirion is disquietingly sophisticated as well as naive', but that is unfair: Williams-Ellis rejected much of what became acceptable in the architectural world of his time, and sought a far more cheerful way of dealing with the built environment than that accepted by the humourless puritans of doctrinaire Modernism.

Kennington was adamant that architecture and sculpture were interdependent, and insisted that sculpture should be part of a building and not stuck on afterwards, recognising that in Classicism the former was always the case, but that Modernism had actually severed the two. In fact, any decoration (if allowed at all, as Modernism was very leery about it, given that luminaries such as Adolf Loos had denounced it as a crime [1908], and in America Louis Sullivan had written [1892] that it should be eschewed for a time) tended to be an optional extra, sometimes disguised as 'ironmongery' in Bills of Quantities in post-1945 architecture. One of Classical architecture's greatest attractions was and is that sculpture is *fully integrated* with it, not applied as an optional, and therefore unnecessary, afterthought.

Lord Clark of Saltwood objected to the labelling of an artist as a *pasticheur* by those who held that the term was pejorative: indeed, he could see no reason why, at certain times when the

Fig. 7.5a ↑ *Detail of the glowing rood screen in the Church of St Mary, Wellingborough, Northamptonshire, undoubtedly among the most beautiful of English parish churches, with one of the most gloriously inventive interiors of the 20th century. Gilded and painted Tuscan columns support a Gothic loft and rood, set in a Gothic church designed by Ninian Comper (from 1908), a fine example of his 'Unity by Inclusion', mixing Classical and Gothic styles, yet creating a whole. The gilding and colour were completed in stages (MK).*

Fig. 7.5b → *Canopy or baldacchino over the high altar, St Mary's, Wellingborough, by Comper, a magnificently rich variation on a gilded Corinthian Order within a Gothic Revival church (MK).*

consciousness of historical styles might be strong and reviving, works of art should not be created in this way. Certain individuals he identified as belonging to an age which was deeply conscious of the past, and their work was all the better for it, be they poets, musicians, painters, or architects: he mentioned that glorious confection, *Ariadne auf Naxos* (1915–16), by Hugo von Hofmannsthal and Richard Strauss, as one example, and Ninian Comper's incomparably beautiful merging of Classical and Gothic, as in St Mary's, Wellingborough, Northamptonshire (1904–31), which Comper called 'unity by inclusion', as another (Figs 7.5a–b). Clark went on to remark that Lutyens, the greatest English architect since Wren, in his opinion, was a *pasticheur*. Williams-Ellis, steeped in the Arts and Crafts movement, the Italian Renaissance, the Picturesque, and English and Mediterranean vernacular architecture, with a deep love of tradition, unspoiled landscape, and beautiful things, was a *pasticheur*, in the best meaning of a word that, contrary to its misuse by Modernists, is completely devoid of anything ignoble or unworthy. He was also endowed with a fine sense of humour, obvious when visiting his creation in Gwynedd. Other architects, active today, rejoice in being *pasticheurs*, including Luke Moloney, who is based in Dumfries and Galloway, and carries out unobtrusive, well-mannered, decent, traditionally based designs which respect the *genius loci*.

In the inter-war period, many architects were fascinated by developments in Scandinavia, especially in Sweden, where the works of Gunnar Asplund and Ivar Tengbom were hugely admired: the Classical work of Tengbom, especially, was referred to as 'Swedish Grace'. He evolved a simplified Neo-Classicism, exemplified in his Concert House, Stockholm (1923–8), in which the building became a blocky mass fronted by a huge portico of attenuated stripped-Corinthian columns. His Swedish Match Company headquarters, Stockholm (1926–8), was austere, looking back to the stripped Classicism of the early 19th century. One example, and a very fine one, of Swedish-influenced architecture in England, was the headquarters of the Royal Institute of British Architects in Portland Place, London (1932–4), by G. Grey Wornum (Fig. 7.6). Hugh Casson wrote, just before the 1939–45 war began, that Wornum's R.I.B.A. was the 'most beautifully finished building in London ... unsurpassed in its feeling of internal spaciousness'. The materials used were very fine, and the detailing impeccable: in addition, the decorative art was fully integrated with the architecture. One could say the same for Speer's Neue Reichkanzlei in Berlin, if one were honest.

There were many other architects capable of doing good things, not least Sir Albert Richardson, responsible for a great book on *Monumental Classic Architecture in Great Britain and Ireland* (1914), but his own built work could be excellent: it includes Bracken House, Cannon Street (1955–9 – although today with a new core [1987–92] by Michael Hopkins), and 25–35 Grosvenor Place, Belgravia (1956–8), both in London. And the firm of McMorran & Whitby produced buildings of real architectural distinction after 1945, influenced partly by Vincent Harris and mostly by Lutyens, best described as undoctrinaire Classicism. Good examples include Devon County Hall, Exeter (1954–63), Shire Hall extensions, Bury St Edmunds, Suffolk (1957–68), various buildings for the University of Nottingham (1950s), and the police station, Wood Street, City of London

Fig. 7.6 ↑ *Headquarters of the Royal Institute of British Architects, Portland Place, London (1932–4), by G. Grey Wornum: clearly influenced by the contemporary architecture of Sweden, notably the work of Asplund, it is enlivened with sculpted figures in relief by Edward Bainbridge Copnall, and the two columns flanking the entrance, by James Woodford, suggest Jachin and Boaz, the 'pillars' associated with the Temple of Solomon, and were an allusion to Freemasonry, which was once closely connected to architecture. Wornum was himself a Freemason, initiated in 1923 and 'raised' in 1924 (AFK A83/970).*

(1959–66). Their housing estate at Lammas Green, Sydenham Hill, London (1955–7), used traditional materials and had a village-like character utterly unlike that of contemporary local authority estates elsewhere in the capital.

Two very splendid designs by English architects should be noted here, although neither was realised. Vincent Harris produced a master plan for the University of Exeter in 1931: it was a pleasing layout of 'gentlemanly symmetry' based on a formal Classical axial arrangement, but was ruined after the Modernist Holford changed it in 1953 to an incoherent grouping of buildings unrelated to each other, all too unhappily obvious when erected (1955–75). The other was the wonderful proposal by Lutyens for the Roman Catholic Metropolitan Cathedral of Liverpool, designed from 1929 under the ægis of the dynamic Richard Downey, who had been appointed archbishop in 1928: it would have been twice the size of St Paul's Cathedral in London, but, unlike Wren, Lutyens resolved the problems of combining an aisled cruciform plan with a massive central volume under a dome. He also integrated themes explored in the Thiepval arch into the design, pulling everything together in one of the finest works ever conceived by an English architect. Work on building started in 1933, but was halted by the 1939–45 war in 1941: by that time only part of the crypt had been completed. What was actually realised gives us some idea of how great and truly magnificent the final building would have been: it also incorporated some quirky Mannerist details (*see* Fig. G76). After the war, a climate that favoured Modernism, combined with loss of nerve, Downey's death in 1953, and alleged prohibitive costs, led to the abandonment of what would have been one of the greatest buildings in all England of all time. An architectural competition was held in 1959, won by Frederick Gibberd with a mediocre design, built 1962–7, but requiring major surgery in

ASPECTS OF A CONTINUING CLASSICISM / 157

the 21st century to remedy failures, largely due to the choice of 'modern' materials. It should be noted, however, that not Modernism, nor cost, nor loss of nerve managed to stop the great Anglican cathedral by Giles Gilbert Scott (1904–78) in its tracks, and for that we should be profoundly grateful, for it is a truly staggering work of real architecture, albeit largely 'Gothic', so beyond the scope of this study. It stands only half a mile away from Gibberd's spiky circular effort, which is known by local wags as 'Paddy's Wigwam' or 'The Mersey Funnel'.

However, Classicism and traditional architecture actually survived, in spite of concerted attempts to snuff them out, and in the hands of a relatively small number of courageous practitioners, they continued, even in the hostile architectural environment created after 1945. A recent book by Julian Holder and Elizabeth McKellar has chronicled how the Neo-Georgian style of architecture, which appeared on the scene around 1880, was continued until the 1970s, and Gavin Stamp, in his excellent study of *Interwar British Architecture 1919–39*, devoted a hefty chapter to it: significantly, it was virtually ignored by the architectural press in the past, because only Modernism was accepted as worthy of notice. Modernists insisted that the 'functionalists' of the 1920s and 1930s were carried on the current of that hoary old Germanic concept, the *zeitgeist*, into the 'ocean of the International style of the 1930s', but the historical reality was very different. Modernism made very little headway in Britain before 1945, largely because most people did not like it, apart from relatively wealthy persons of 'progressive' views: it became ubiquitous as part of the huge political shift to the Left after the end of the war, and was imposed (largely on what used to be called 'the working classes' who had hardly any say in the matter), with very little effective opposition until its failures became all too obvious.

Post-Modernism

In recent decades various labels have been attached to certain architectural trends, including 'Post-Modernism' (PoMo), which has been connected with a loss of faith in what were once regarded as certainties (e.g. so-called progress, supposed rationality, and alleged scientific approaches to design [in reality a search for appropriate *images* to *suggest* all of those]) and with a growing acceptance of a bewilderingly large palette of images, signs, and products promoted on a scale never experienced before in the history of the world, which some, including Robert Charles Venturi, welcomed as offering complexity, contradiction, and diversity in design as a refreshing change from the aridity and poverty-stricken language of conventional Modernism. Indeed, Venturi rejected Miës van der Rohe's dictum that 'less is more',

Fig. 7.7 ↓ *Detail of part of the Order employed at the Sainsbury Wing of the National Gallery, Trafalgar Square, London, designed by Venturi, Rauch, & Scott Brown, of 1987–91, perceived as an example of Post-Modernism, but perhaps it might also be seen as a curious late interpretation of Mannerism. The Order employed by William Wilkins in 1833–8 for the pilasters has been repeated around the shallow angles, first of all in a cluster of overlapping pilasters, then a couple more pilasters, then a solitary engaged column set partly over a single pilaster, then vanishes: somewhat disconcertingly, the entablature loses its dentils as it turns corners, and then sheds even more parts, until it just peters out at the southwest corner of the building. Two blind openings and one wraith-like suggestion of a third contribute to a curious unease, compounded by a perception that there is no coherent form behind the façade: one is reminded of something applied, like wallpaper, perhaps, that just runs out, and this façade does not hint at any architectural volumes behind it (AH).*

158 / CLASSICAL ARCHITECTURE

replacing it with 'less is a bore', and with his wife and professional partner, Denise Scott Brown, even floated the heretical notion that somewhere as noisily populist as Las Vegas might offer something from which architects could learn. Venturi's firm, Venturi, Rauch, & Scott Brown, was responsible for the extension (Sainsbury Wing) to William Wilkins's National Gallery in London (1833–8), of 1987–91, generally regarded as a paradigm of Post-Modernism (Fig. 7.7).

So there was a tendency towards Pluralism, and some architecture drew on elements that were not themselves archæologically or historically accurate, but had vague references to once-familiar motifs such as the Orders, cornices, pediments, etc., often brashly and crudely used. Post-Modernism involved fragmentation, ill-digested eclecticism, and what has been called by Jameson 'the cultural logic of late capitalism'. The label has been loosely stuck to various architects moving away from Modernism, even though their various responses widely differed: among them may be mentioned Ricardo Bofill Levi, Sir Terry Farrell, Michael Graves, Hans Hollein, Philip Johnson, Charles Moore, and R.A.M. Stern. Bofill Levi's massive housing developments, Les Espaces d'Abraxas, Noisy-le-Grand, near Paris (1978–82), and Les Arcades du Lac, Montigny-le-Bretonneux of the same period, were perceived as PoMo, with their formal geometrical layouts and remote allusions to Classicism, but they owe more, perhaps, to Soviet Socialist Realism, and in some respects to the work of Iofan, as well as to the inflated scale of proposals by a Boullée or a Speer.

Philip Johnson, with John Henry Burgee, sent shockwaves through the cosy world of orthodox Modernism with their American Telephone and Telegraph skyscraper, New York City (1978–83 – now the Sony Building – a masonry-clad structure with powerful mullions set on a stripped version of a serliana-cum-triumphal arch, and capped by a paraphrase of an open-topped pediment), described variously as 'flippant', 'simplistic', and the first Post-Modern building.

Perhaps one of the more interesting examples of eclectic Post-Modernism, shot through with informed eclecticism, wit, and scholarly, albeit with tongue-in-cheek, allusions, can be found at No. 19, Lansdowne Walk, Kensington, London, transformed 1978–83 by that indefatigable categoriser of styles and historian of Post-Modernism, the controversial and combative Charles Jencks, working with the Terry Farrell Partnership. There are contributions within by others, including fire surrounds by Michael Graves, but the whole ensemble, centred around rooms that represent the seasons, is an amusing melange of Classical,

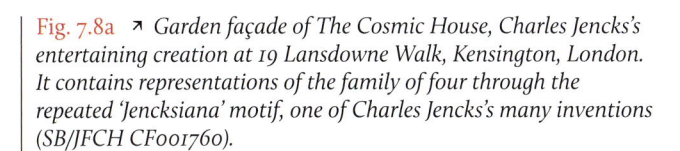

Fig. 7.8a ↗ *Garden façade of The Cosmic House, Charles Jencks's entertaining creation at 19 Lansdowne Walk, Kensington, London. It contains representations of the family of four through the repeated 'Jencksiana' motif, one of Charles Jencks's many inventions (SB/JFCH CF001760).*

Fig. 7.8b → *The 'Dome of Water', an amusing jacuzzi designed by Piers Gough in The Cosmic House of Charles Jencks, the* trompe l'œil *effect claimed to be inspired by an inversion of the dome of Borromini's church of San Carlo alle Quattro Fontane, Rome (compare Fig. 5.2d, which demonstrates, perhaps, that a Roman connection is somewhat tentative) (SB/JFCH CF006757).*

Egyptianising, and other elements, stuffed with symbolism. It is called The Cosmic House, and is on a more elevated intellectual plane than much that passed as PoMo at the time: the massive 'voussoirs' and missing, transparent 'keystone' over the arched door are jokey nods to the oversized, blocky masonry employed by Baroque architects such as Hawksmoor to create dramatic intensity, while another motif, repeated four times on the façade, was named a 'Jencksiana', a humorous allusion to the more familiar and frequently repeated serliana common in Classical architecture (Fig. 7.8a). The interiors are full of all sorts of mnemonic devices, visual jokes, and clever, sometimes distorted, images connected to ideas, elements, and fragments from the past. In the kitchen there is a hilarious take on a Doric frieze, where the glyphs of the 'triglyphs' are actually in the form of spoons (so-called *spoonglyphs*), between which, instead of metopes, are voids for storing crockery and other objects: Jencks's joke there was that if you could not stand the kitsch, then you should get out of the kitchen. The jacuzzi has playful *trompe l'œil* inverted coffering by Piers Gough, claimed to have been inspired by the dome of Borromini's San Carlo alle Quattro Fontane in Rome (Fig. 7.8b).

But what does this confection have to do with Classicism? Some might argue it is far too distorted and lightweight. It is included because it suffices to show that the subject has by no means been exhausted: even in its bizarre manifestations, its essence is still discernible, despite being bent out if shape and treated with strange whimsy.

In Italy, architects such as Rossi argued that as cities were organic phenomena, their grain, history, and context must be responded to in any architectural intervention, and in particular, that the *genius loci* should be recognised and not damaged, the complete opposite of the International-Modernist position, which did not respect the past at all. Among others who subscribed to this view were Mario Botta, Giorgio Grassi, Josef Paul Kleihues, Léon and Rob Krier, Bruno Reichlin, and Oswald Matthias Ungers. Rossi seems to have imbibed aspects of late 18th-century Neo-Classicism of the pure type advocated by Boullée and Ledoux, mingled with a kind of proto-Surrealism reminiscent of the paintings of Giorgio de Chirico. Something of this Chirico-inspired, dream-like atmosphere can be detected in the ossuary and cemetery of San Cataldo, Modena (1971–6, 1980–8), for which he collaborated with Gianni Braghieri. San Cataldo was a masterwork of stripped Neo-Classical geometry, as severe as any late 18th- or early 19th-century essay, and became a paradigm of what was termed Neo-Rationalist architecture.

However, it is debatable if much, lazily given the PoMo label, was real architecture at all: vast numbers of buildings so called were anything but Classical, and owed more to the fairground, to commercial vulgarity, or to the Modern Movement with a few illiterate nods to Classicism stuck on. One of the most worrying things was that such supposed 'Classicism' consisted, in fact, of motifs applied to façades that were unrelated to what is happening behind (the Sainsbury Wing of the National Gallery in London is an obvious example of this); rooms uneasily placed behind fenestration that would be unacceptable to any real Classicist; and a sense of buildings becoming skin-deep, with badly proportioned and uncomfortably designed spaces behind hesitant sub-Palladian Revival or indifferently understood Georgian elevations.

This was a sorry state of affairs, and had nothing whatsoever to do with real Classicism.

New Urbanism and New Classicism

Modernism produced numerous free-standing box-like buildings deliberately unrelated to their contexts or to each other: useless bits of land wastefully treated as detritus by the rigidities of Modernism (aka SLOAP [Space Left Over After Planning]) could never be made into urban spaces that meant anything or had qualities except an ability to dismay those who experienced them. Five thousand years of urban history demonstrate that the complex relationships of streets, squares, parks, monuments, buildings, etc. not only form means of communication, but help identification and orientation, giving the urban fabric a sense of character and place, but all that was jettisoned, not least because figures such as Le Corbusier denounced the street in all its diversity, mixed uses, and variety, largely disapproving of it on grounds of supposed lack of hygiene and endemic untidiness. But life is not tidy, and human beings have different needs and tastes, indulging in a great variety of activities as should be obvious in surviving streets in healthy urban organisms.

In 1948 *Sixteen Principles of Urbanism* were drawn up in East Germany (which became the German Democratic Republic [DDR]), in agreement with Moscow, as a radical alternative to the Le Corbusier-inspired dogmas so widely (and disastrously) accepted in the West after 1945. Among them was the rejection of urban motorways cutting destructive swathes through vulnerable urban fabric, the abandonment of zoning that was to play havoc in Western cities, and the re-establishment of the urban block and traditional street as essentials, all of which were re-assessed at the end of the 20th century as part of New Urbanism, which reacted against Modernism, advocating traditional urban blocks, mixed uses, and a coherent, literate, architectural language as antidotes to unpleasant, inhumane, threatening, and incoherent environments that were the direct results of Modernist theories, dogmas, and teaching. It is interesting that the essentials of what became New Urbanism may be found in the *Sixteen Principles*, so accusations by Modernists that it, and the New Classicists associated with it, are tainted with 'Fascism', 'Naziism', or the 'Far-Right', are nonsense: in fact, the truth, as is so often the case in the dishonest 'debates' concerning Modernism, is just the opposite.

Among the many promoters of New Urbanism may be cited Maurice Culot, Sir Jeremy Dixon, Andrés Duany, Edward Jones, Michael Kirkland, Léon and Rob Krier, Elizabeth Plater-Zyberk, Demetri Porphyrios, Aldo Rossi, and John Simpson, but there have been others who have made significant contributions, and many more emerging in the field. New Urbanism has been denounced by Modernists as 'escapist' and 'historicist': some would argue that, if this is the case, then we need a lot more escapism and historicism.

Luxembourg-born Léon Krier has long been a champion of rational architecture, prompted, perhaps, by the work of J.-N.-L. Durand, the French architectural theorist, and has proposed that early 19th-century Neo-Classicism provides a suitable means by which the civilised aspects of the European city might be recovered. His seductive graphics and powerful polemics have aroused new interest in the qualities of street, square, and urban district, and his work might be seen as a series of meditations on themes in a world where so much has been devalued and forgotten. His view of the city as a document of intelligence, memory, and pleasure is the antithesis of the Modernist concept of the disposable, adaptable, plug-in city, and he has been critical of Post-Modernism and stylistic Pluralism, condemning both as unserious, unintellectual kitsch. He perceives the de-zoning of activities in cities to be essential for their life, and has been fundamentally opposed to Modernist theories and dogmas concerning the planning of towns, malign influences still firmly embedded everywhere despite efforts to excise them, and despite their obvious failure to produce environments that are other than repulsively dystopian.

Krier was involved in the master plan for the Duchy of Cornwall development at Poundbury, Dorset (1988–91), and, with Gabriele Tagliaventi, produced (1988–2002) the master plan for Città Nuova, Alessandria, the provincial capital of Piedmont, drawing on the strong urban tradition of Mediterranean countries, so his credentials as a New Urbanist are impeccable. New Urbanism also heralded a rediscovery of the works of Camillo Sitte, the Austro-Hungarian architect/planner, notably his *Der Städtebau nach seinen künstlerlischen Grundsätzen* (*Town Planning according to Artistic Principles*, 1889), which emphasised the need to design urban fabric with æsthetics and composition in mind: this work was one of the first to analyse what became known as townscape.

In Belgium, too, the Atelier de Recherche et d'Action Urbaines (ARAU) was set up in 1969 to study problems posed by drastic urban redevelopments, especially arguing for conservation and restoration. The problem was particularly obvious in Brussels, where redevelopment has been extremely destructive, not respecting anything of the past. The leading light was the distinguished architect Maurice Culot, who also (with Robert-Louis Delevoy and François Terlinden) founded *Archives d'Architecture Moderne* in the same year, publishing important works on architecture, and not following the Modernist party line. Culot, especially, has made major contributions. And in France, William Pesson, who has investigated the life and work of Quatremère de Quincy (especially in relation to the Panthéon), and has organised several important exhibitions on aspects of esoteric architecture (also a concern of Delevoy), notably that connected with Freemasonry, is involved in the problems of architectural design and urbanism, again moving away from Modernist orthodoxy. The present author has had the pleasure of working with Culot, Pesson, and others on aspects of Masonic architecture, collaborating with them on a book and an exhibition (2006–7).

New Classicism is a movement involving the study of Classical architecture, something jettisoned by the Modern Movement, which discarded everything of the past, and indeed forbade aspiring architects to have anything to do with it, an extraordinary phenomenon unknown in other professions. If all the knowledge gained over the centuries in the sciences, medicine, astronomy, etc. had been suddenly dumped and deliberately rejected in the 20th century, there would have been not only questions in the air, but, one imagines, outrage expressed and the nihilists drummed out of their positions so that they could do no more damage. But in architecture the opposite was true: the iconoclasts, book-burners, enemies of tradition, and destroyers of repositories of knowledge achieved supreme power, notably in 'education', a misnomer if ever there was one. Yet, as should have been made clear in earlier chapters, Classical architecture played a hugely important historical role in the creation of humane and civilised surroundings, renewed with 18th-century Classicism and Neo-Classicism, while as a reaction to Beaux Arts Classicism, Neo-Baroque, Neo-Renaissance, and Art Nouveau, there was a further Classical Revival just before the 1914–18 war, leading to the Neo- and stripped Classicisms that were so widespread in the 1920s and 1930s, no matter what the political climate might be: it was THE universal language of architecture.

After the 1939–45 war, there were still architects capable of ploughing what was becoming an increasingly lonely architectural furrow, but they were largely either ignored or abused by critical opinion. Two English architects, Raymond Erith and Francis Johnson, refused to be cowed by aggressive Modernists or critical neglect: both produced work of quiet, civilised distinction, often understated, but agreeable and, above all, comfortable and well mannered.

And in 1952, across the Pond, Henry Hope Reed became painfully aware that most contemporary American architecture was fraudulent, ugly, and illiterate. Convinced that Classicism embraced an architectural language capable of modern use, he published his views in *The Golden City* (1959), and founded (1968) Classical America to promote Classical architecture through exemplars and publications, which merged (2002) with the Institute of Classical Architecture (founded 1991) to form the Institute of Classical Art & Architecture. The seed that he planted has grown to a strong, powerful tree.

Many young and aspiring architects responded, and today Classicism provides the basis for the outputs of practices far too numerous to list them all, which is a healthy situation though much more progress needs to be made, given the myopic hostility so prevalent in doctrinaire circles.

8

EPILOGUE

So strongly planted are the giant roots of the Classic growth that they withstood ... successive shocks and storms occasioned by ... uncertain tendencies, ... and today the tree promises a renewed blossoming. The need for the steadying influence of an academic style is [today] more than apparent. There can be no question of revivals or revivifications; such terms are erroneous; but in the continuance of the Classic tradition lies the greatest promise for the art of the future.

SIR ALBERT RICHARDSON:
Monumental Classic Architecture in Great Britain and Ireland during the Eighteenth and Nineteenth Centuries
(London: B.T. Batsford, 1914), vi.

An understanding of functional design, the study of the building and its various parts, cannot ... be satisfactorily translated into an architectural creation unless it is accomplished through a comprehension of the laws of composition, through knowledge of the grammar of design ... but even the most gifted designer will benefit by applying to his work the test of an examination of his design syntax ... Perfection of grammar... is not, however, ... sufficient by itself, and is only a means to an end.

HOWARD MORLEY ROBERTSON:
The Principles of Architectural Composition (London: Architectural Press, 1924), 1, 4.

Some Practitioners of Classical Architecture in Recent Times

The South African-born American (since 1973) Allan Greenberg confidently rejected Modernism, and this led to a re-appraisal of Classicism, in the realisation of which he has become a distinguished practitioner: his News Buildings, Athens, GA (1992), have an unfluted Greek Doric portico and an overall authority worthy of earlier Neo-Classicists. Another American, T.H. Beeby, believed that context should be a major factor in determining form and that successful architecture should show 'a decrease in the level of abstraction with the notion of an increased comprehensibility': one of his firm's (Hammond, Beeby, & Babka Inc.) most successful works is the Harold Washington Library Center, Chicago, IL (completed 1991) – a massive pile with façades of correctly used brick (set on a granite plinth) pierced by huge arched openings, drawing on historical precedents, not least from Florentine *palazzi* and ancient Greece and Rome, with a strong dash of 19th-century metal-and-glass structures, the whole crowned with an enormous cornice. Particularly successful are the huge metal acroter ornaments on the corners above the cornice.

R.A.M. Stern, also American, has been a formidable critic of Modernism, and has advocated an architecture of associations prompting mnemonic perceptions, firmly rooted in culture. He has argued robustly for the study of history and for an eclectic use of forms to give buildings meaning, and has been successful in reviving something of the severe French Neo-Classicism of the latter part of the 18th and early 19th centuries. Yet another American, Thomas Gordon Smith, author of *Vitruvius on Architecture* (2004), believed in the continuing relevance of Classicism, leading him to create buildings that engage the intellect and the emotions, achieved not without self-interested opposition. His works included the Vitruvian House, South Bend, IN (1989–90), and Bond Hall, for the School of Architecture at Notre Dame, IN (1994–70), with Greek motifs very much in evidence.

Robert Adam, who is British, blessed with a name that conjures up in mind a distinguished 18th-century predecessor, has argued that Classicism, being the common and very rich architectural language of the Western world, is accessible, has many resonances, and is capable of infinite continuing *evolution*, as he has demonstrated in numerous works, including a new country house at Ashley, Hampshire (1999–2005), and the former Sackler Library, Oxford (Fig. 8.1), which employs Greek Doric as well as incorporating allusions to the fine circular public libraries at Stockholm (1920–8, by Asplund) and Manchester (1925–38, by Vincent Harris): the Haverfield wing of the library incorporates

Fig. 8.1 ← Entrance to the former Sackler, now the Bodleian Art, Archaeology, and Ancient World Library, Oxford, by Robert Adam of ADAM Architecture (AA).

Fig. 8.2 ↓ The Millennium Gate, Atlanta, GA, with, on the right, Alexander Stoddart's personification of Justice in the Egyptianising Greek Goddess Dike, holding in her left hand the sistrum, and in her right a great key to the gates of the ways of Night and Day, for She, as Avenging Justice, is their Keeper. Before her is Horus/Harpocrates, alluding to Silence and Discretion necessary for the imparting of Knowledge and Justice (AA/DT).

Fig. 8.3 ↙↙ Proposed town square at the centre of Park View, a development on the Blenheim estate, Woodstock, Oxfordshire, with commercial space on the ground floor of the buildings and apartments above, master planned by Hugh Petter of ADAM Architecture (AA: CGI by Glass Canvas).

Epilogue / 163

a noble Classical frieze by the distinguished Scots sculptor, Alexander Stoddart, whose work and thinking are profoundly influenced by Græco-Roman Antiquity. Adam published (1990) *Classical Architecture: A Complete Handbook*, and the firm he founded, ADAM Architecture, continues under directors (which include Hugh Petter, George Saumarez Smith, and Nigel Anderson), producing distinguished and well-crafted buildings, among them 45 The Park, Cheltenham (2003–7), Bear Ash, Hare Hatch, Berkshire (2008), the Millennium Gate, Atlanta, GA (2003) (Fig. 8.2), and major developments at Nansledan and Tregunnel Hill, Newquay, Cornwall (from 2012). Such work continues, as at Park View, Woodstock, Oxfordshire (from 2015), by Petter in collaboration with other architects (Fig. 8.3). Saumarez Smith was responsible for a fine building in New Bond Street, London (Fig. 8.4).

Quinlan Terry joined Raymond Erith in 1962, having had a difficult time with Modernists when a student at a school of architecture, and became the older man's professional partner in 1967. Among his many works are the Howard (1983–6), Residential (1993–5), and Greek Revival Maitland Robinson (1989–93) buildings at Downing College, Cambridge (Fig. 8.5). His Ionic (1987), Veneto (1988), and Regency (2001) villas, Regent's Park, London, are scholarly evocations of Georgian buildings, but his Corinthian Villa (Fig. 8.6) there alludes to Borromini and the swaying motion of Italian Baroque. Terry was attracted to 17th-century Palladian models, as with Waverton House, Gloucestershire (1979–80), Ferne Park, Dorset (1998–2002), and Kilboy, County Tipperary, Ireland (completed 2013) (Fig. 8.7). In the 1980s he entered the world of major office developments, popularising Classicism at the same time, as at Richmond Riverside, Richmond-on-Thames, Surrey (1985–8), allying himself with the ideas of Léon Krier (Fig. 8.8). Terry's Roman Catholic Cathedral of Sts Mary and Helen, Brentwood, Essex (1989–91), demonstrates his familiarity with the architectural languages of Bramante, Brunelleschi, and Wren (Figs 8.9a–c). Terry has also been responsible for sensitive work in Williamsburg, VA (from 2000), Poundbury, Dorset (from 2004), and the Royal Infirmary, Chelsea Hospital, London (from 2004). He has published substantial accounts of his output, and been well served by some architectural historians, notably David Watkin, who was an effective critic of Modernism as well as a doughty champion of Classicism and Classicists. Eric Cartwright, who worked with Terry for a number of years in Dedham, Essex, acquired sophisticated skills using refined linocut in illustrating the Orders as well as details and façades designed by the practice: some of these have been published and exhibited.

Greek-born Demetri Porphyrios has argued passionately that architecture must be grounded in building technology, craftsmanship, and the use of sustainable natural materials,

Fig. 8.4 ↑ *Art gallery in New Bond Street, London, with Portland stone façade and bronze-framed shopfront, completed 2011, designed by George Saumarez Smith of ADAM Architecture. The frieze, by Alexander Stoddart, depicts the legend of the winnowing fan from Book XI of* The Odyssey, *intended as an allegory of the journey taken by modern art in the course of the 20th century (AA/MvS).*

Fig. 8.5 ↑ *The Maitland Robinson library at Downing College, Cambridge (1990–4), by Quinlan Terry. Constructed of Ketton stone, it has a fine tetrastyle Greek Doric portico partly based on the Athenian Propylæa (439–32 BC), partly on the gateway to the Roman agora at Athens (10 BC), and partly on work by William Wilkins, Downing's original architect, including his unexecuted design for a porter's lodge at the college and a demolished (1872–89) portico (probably the first pure Greek example in British domestic architecture) at Osberton Park, Nottinghamshire (c.1805–6). The metopes of the frieze are carved with symbols representing the various subjects taught at the college. Above is an octagonal lantern surmounted by a palm-leaf capital supporting a weathervane: this is a reference to the Tower of the Winds, Athens (c.50 BC) (see Fig. 6.8a). On the left is the east wing to the north range (1929–32) by Herbert Baker, with its tetrastyle Ionic portico, an undistinguished design (QT/NCP).*

Fig. 8.6 ↑ *Corinthian Villa, Regent's Park, London (2001), one of seven villas designed by Quinlan Terry from 1988 and sited between the Outer Circle and the Grand Union Canal. Envisaged as early as 1990, it demonstrates the architect's belief that the forms and ornaments of Italian Baroque could be merged with the English Palladian tradition. It this case, the swaying curves and counter-curves of the front derive from Borromini; the spiral fluting of the shafts was suggested by the 4th-century AD Temple of Clitumnus near Spoleto and by Sanmicheli's Palazzo Bevilacqua (c.1530) and Cappella Pellegrini attached to the church of San Bernardino, Verona (1527–57); the capitals were derived from Vitruvius's description of how the Corinthian Order was suggested to Callimachus by acanthus leaves growing through the weaves of a basket; and the elaborate bases were inspired by those in the baptistry of Constantine at the Basilica of San Giovanni in Laterano, Rome (c. 315–24), to which Palladio had drawn attention in Book IV of his* Quattro Libri dell'Architettura *(1570) (QT/NCP).*

and has been unafraid of returning to the principles of 'firmness, commodity, and delight' as essentials in his thoughtful architecture. At Oitiousa, Spetses, Greece (completed 1993), he created an environment firmly based on traditional European patterns, with houses drawing on Neo-Classical precedents, including paraphrases of designs by Schinkel: the scheme might be regarded as an example of New Urbanism. His house at Chepstow Villas, Kensington, London (1988), is an exquisite testament to his taste, and more recently he has carried out interesting work in the USA (Fig. 8.10) and France (Fig. 8.11). The much younger Liam O'Connor has designed several splendid Classical houses in Belgravia, London (from 1996); a fine terrace of houses in Bath, Somerset (2002–4); the Armed Forces Memorial at the National Memorial Arboretum, near Lichfield, Staffordshire (2004–10) to British servicemen and women killed on duty since 1945; the Memorial to Bomber Command, Green

Fig. 8.7 ↙ *East elevation of Kilboy, Nenagh, County Tipperary, Ireland (completed 2013), by Quinlan Terry Architects. Built on the site of an earlier house of c.1770 which was burned down during the Irish Civil War (1922), its Attic storey is a particularly Irish Palladian feature, also occurring at Bellamont Forest (Cootehill, Count Cavan [c.1730], by Sir Edward Lovett Pearce); Russborough (Blessington, County Wicklow [1741–55], by Richard Castle); and Castletown Cox (Piltown, County Kilkenny [1767–71], by Davis Ducart). The powerful engaged Roman Doric temple-front and robust detailing make this one of Terry's most successful designs for country houses, for which he specified buff-coloured limestone from County Donegal and blue limestone for the architectural details from Ballinasloe, County Galway (QT/NCP).*

Fig. 8.8 ↓ *Richmond Riverside, Richmond-on-Thames, Surrey (1983–7), by Quinlan Terry, described in a recent guide to the area as 'one of the most impressive stretches beside the Thames. Its terraced gardens and adjacent buildings, dating from the seventeenth and nineteenth centuries, were beautifully restored in the 1980s', but the whole development was built from scratch to Terry's designs in the 1980s, so the description in the guide is high praise indeed. It was the first large-scale traditionally constructed and detailed contemporary Classical mixed-use development in Britain since the 1939–45 war, and consists of shops, apartments, offices, restaurants, community facilities, underground carparks, and public open space (the last obviously very much enjoyed, as the photograph demonstrates). Terry drew on inspiration from England and Venice, notably the works of Palladio, Longhena, Sansovivo, Hawksmoor, and Chambers (QT/NCP).*

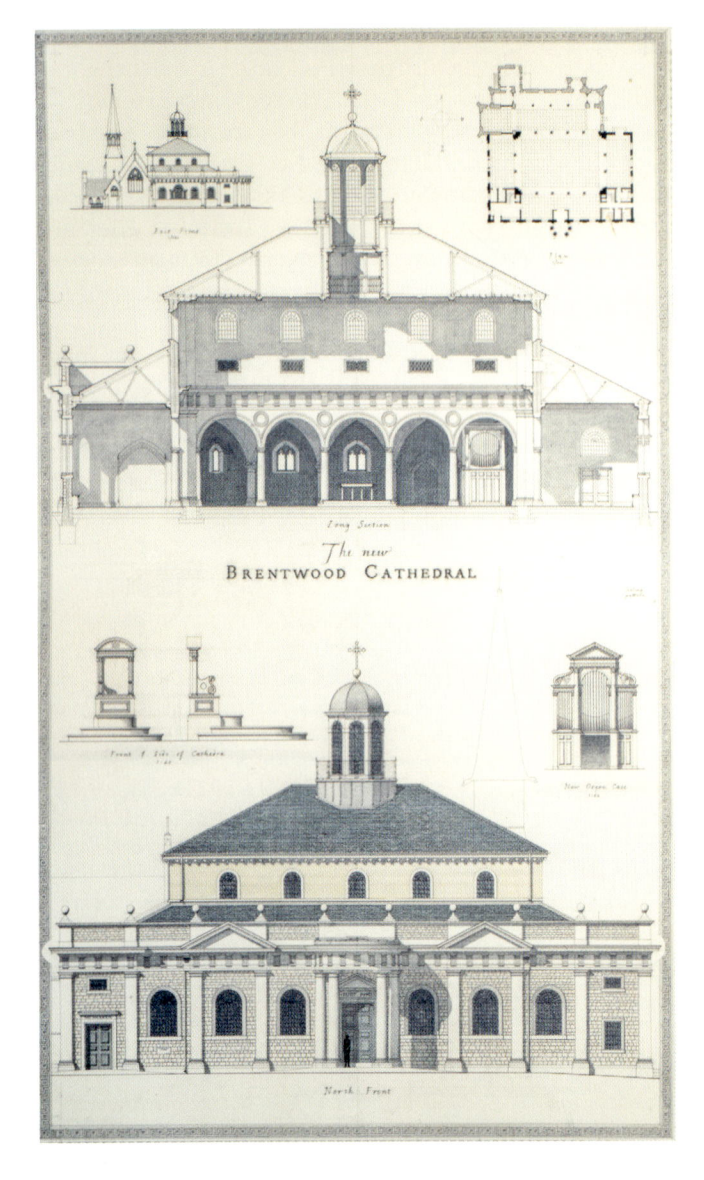

Fig. 8.9a *Plan, elevations, section, and some details (including the cathedra, shown on the left just above the main elevation) of the Roman Catholic Cathedral Church of Sts Mary and Helen, Ingrave Road, Brentwood, Essex (1989–91), by Quinlan Terry, a Classical building responding to the liturgical requirements of the Second Vatican Council, added to an undistinguished Gothic church of 1860–1 by G.R. Blount to which an even more undistinguished Modernist extension had been tacked on (1972–4, demolished). Drawing (1991, by Les Edwards) exhibited at the Royal Academy Summer Exhibition, 1992 (QT).*

Fig. 8.9b *Interior of Terry's Roman Catholic Cathedral of Sts Mary and Helen, Brentwood, Essex, showing the centrally placed altar, with ambo on the left and cathedra on the right under one of the arches. The cathedra, carved in Nabresina marble, was also designed by Terry, based on the exemplar in San Miniato al Monte, Florence. Around the main space is a Tuscan colonnade carrying a Doric entablature above which rises a clerestorey: the colonnade recalls Brunelleschi's Ospedale degli Innocenti (Foundlings' Hospital), Florence (see Fig. 4.2), but the roundels in the spandrels at Brentwood are actually Stations of the Cross made of terracotta, modelled by Raphael Maklouf (the roundels at the Ospedale were by Andrea della Robbia, of c.1487). However, the corners of the colonnades are handled with skill, satisfyingly robust compared with some Renaissance examples (see Figs 4.8c and 4.9) (QT/NCP).*

Fig. 8.9c *Brentwood Cathedral, showing the disposition of the projecting Portland stone Classical elements, contrasting with the ragstone infill. Influences from Wren, Gibbs, and Pietro da Cortona can be detected. The clerestorey is faced with Smead Dean yellow stock brick with a roof of Welsh slate surmounted by a tall glazed lantern (QT/NCP).*

166 / CLASSICAL ARCHITECTURE

Fig. 8.10 → *The Duncan art galleries at Lincoln, NE, USA (2003), by Porphyrios Associates, situated amidst a colourful quilt of green fields and thickly wooded land. Massing of the building is additive, with the principal exhibition rooms grouped around a central glazed atrium, and claims the traditional protective functions of the Classical domus, associating with and respecting the site. The architectural language owes something to the work of Schinkel at Potsdam (PorA/PA).*

Fig. 8.11 ↑ *Part of the Parkside Residential Quarter, Val d'Europe, in the new town of Marne-la-Vallée, near Paris (2006), by Porphyrios Associates, who were commissioned to design several buildings, four of which are shown in the photograph. The development consists of a series of streets, squares, avenues, and parks set in a generous, green landscape, and the urban component in the creation of the new quarters is the open perimeter block. Apartments are punctuated by pavilions, a device recalling the strategy adopted by John Nash at Regent's Park, London. The compositional permutations provided by pergolas, entrance pavilions, terraces, balconies, and gates generate a range of building-blocks that are yet stylistically and geometrically harmonious through the Classical language used in the designs. Marne-la-Vallée is laid out on the principles of New Urbanism, using a coherent architectural language. Several other distinguished practitioners have contributed designs to this interesting new town development, including Maurice Culot (PorA).*

Park, London (completed 2012, in which Greek Doric plays an important part) (Fig. 8.12); and the British Normandy Memorial near Ver-sur-Mer, France, commemorating those who died during the Normandy Landings in 1944 (2018–21) (Fig. 8.13).

Another English architect, Julian Bicknell, carried out sensitive works at the 19th-century Old Gaol, Abingdon, Oxfordshire (1972–80), but his Henbury Hall, near Macclesfield, Cheshire (1984–6), is a convincing essay in 20th-century Palladianism, its closest relative being Campbell's Mereworth Castle, Kent. He published (2000) a handsome monograph on his creations (which also drew on Arts and Crafts and vernacular traditions, as well as Classicism).

Craig Hamilton, based in Radnorshire, Wales, has specialised in progressive Classicism, notably in his garden buildings, monuments, temples, a bath-house, and Coed Mawr, his own house in the Welsh hills. In some of his realised architecture he has collaborated successfully with Alexander Stoddart. Influences from Bindesbøll and Schinkel, among others, may be detected in some of his designs. His architecture has a refinement, sureness of touch, and integrity, free from pedantry, and sometimes reminiscent of some of the better work of the 1920s and 1930s in which 'Swedish Grace' was detected (Fig. 8.14).

John Simpson is yet another English architect who rejected Modernism: he has carried out many prestigious commissions. One of his earliest works was Ashfold House, West Sussex (1985–8), informed by Soane's architecture, and he publicised New Classicism with the exhibition, provocatively entitled *Real Architecture*, at the Building Centre, London (1987). His works at Gonville and Caius College, Cambridge, including the Fellows' dining-room (where he paid tribute to Cockerell with the use of the Bassæ Order), demonstrate his mastery of colour and detail. In 1999 his firm won the competition to design the Queen's Gallery at Buckingham Palace, London, opened 2002: this has a Greek Doric entrance portico, and the entrance hall has brilliant Homeric friezes by Alexander Stoddart. Other successful works have included the tactful Carhart mansion at East 95th Street, New York City (2005–7); developments at Eton College, Buckinghamshire (from 2010) (Fig. 8.15); the new School of Architecture, University of Notre Dame, IN (2014–19) (Fig. 8.16); the Brownsword market hall, Poundbury, Dorset (2000–1); and remodelling the interior of the Royal College of Music, Kensington, London (from 2014). Very many young architects gained experience with Simpson's practice and have

Fig. 8.12 ↑ *Royal Air Force Bomber Command Memorial, London, designed by Liam O'Connor Architects: view towards Hyde Park Corner. Inaugurated 2012, it commemorates the 56,573 aircrew who died during the course of the 1939–45 war. Built of solid stone, it consists of a memorial pavilion flanked by colonnaded wings, open to both Piccadilly and Green Park, the whole employing the Greek Doric Order (LOC/NCP).*

Fig. 8.13 ↓ *British Normandy Memorial, Calvados, Normandy, France, by Liam O'Connor Architects: aerial view looking north-west towards Arromanches. Completed 2021, it is a large open cloister with 160 stone piers supporting oak beams defining the walkways, the piers carved with the names of the 22,442 servicemen and -women who died on D-Day (6 June 1944) and during the Battle of Normandy which followed. It is sited on a commanding ridge overlooking a section of the coast codenamed Gold Beach, and is set within 60 acres of newly planted parkland that was part of the battlefield (LOC/NCP).*

Fig. 8.14 ↑ *The Goldhammer mausoleum in St James's cemetery, Highgate, London (2014–17), by Craig Hamilton Architects, an interesting design that draws on the work of a wide range of architects working on both sides of the Atlantic in the first half of the 20th century, including Lutyens, C.H. Holden, and Harold Van Buren Magonigle. It also has distant echoes of 'Swedish Grace' and the work of Grey Wornum in the 1930s (compare Fig. 7.6). This severe astylar building is constructed of Indiana limestone, very accurately cut and finely jointed. Columns flanking the bronze door (embellished with pomegranates) have capitals of an original design, suggesting a funerary container with cruciform drapes, and the Diocletian window over the door (which relates to the barrel-vault within) is hidden behind a stone screen of superimposed arcades within which are bellflower motifs. Inside the mausoleum is a double sarcophagus with carved drapes, and there are three sculptures by Alexander Stoddart (CHA/PH).*

168 / CLASSICAL ARCHITECTURE

gone on to do other interesting work, including Leigh Brooks, Eric Cartwright, and John Smylie.

John Outram, in his Judge Institute of Management Studies, Cambridge (1993–5 – an extension and re-organisation of Digby Wyatt's Addenbrooke's Old Hospital), incorporated services into what he called the Ordine Robotico, or Sixth Order, not coyly hidden away, but gloriously expressed as a new polychrome Order visible throughout the building as the columns and beams were large enough to contain the services. Outram's work was hysterically denounced as 'sheer terrorism' by one defender of the Modernist faith, but it has worn well, is always interesting, and although very daring, is still rooted in historical architectural precedent A similar style to that of the Judge Institute was employed by Outram at United House, Swanley, Kent, where the stout columnar elements enclosing services and ducting, low-pitched roof, and extraordinary winged polychrome capitals suggest a kind of primitivist Græco-Egyptianising temple (Fig. 8.17), a theme he explored again in his Storm Water Pumping Station, Isle of Dogs, London (1987–8).

Many architects, aware of the damage done to the environment by wasteful, ugly, incompetently designed buildings, have turned to Classicism and traditional methods of construction with considerable success. Some used publications such as Adam's *Handbook* or Robert Chitham's excellent books on *Measured Drawing for Architects* (1980) and the *Classical Orders of Architecture* (1985) as sourcebooks, before turning to the vast

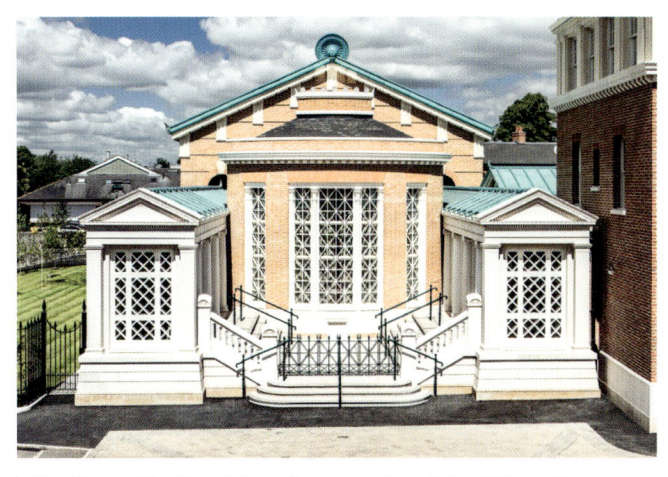

Fig. 8.15 ↑ *The Keate's Lane frontage of the Jafar Gallery, Eton College, Buckinghamshire (2010–15), by John Simpson Architects. The projecting wings on either side of the bowed front have Ionic colonnades terminating in antæ supporting pediments, and in front of the bow is a lectern, as the space can be used for lectures or debates. Behind rises the debating chamber with its acroter ornament based on a similar form that once graced the 6th-century BC Temple of Hera at Olympia, and the curious triglyph-like elements with guttæ are derived from the tripod-like ornaments around the top of the drum of the choragic monument of Lysicrates, Athens, between the capitals. The development forms part of the new McCrum Yard (JSA/AvE).*

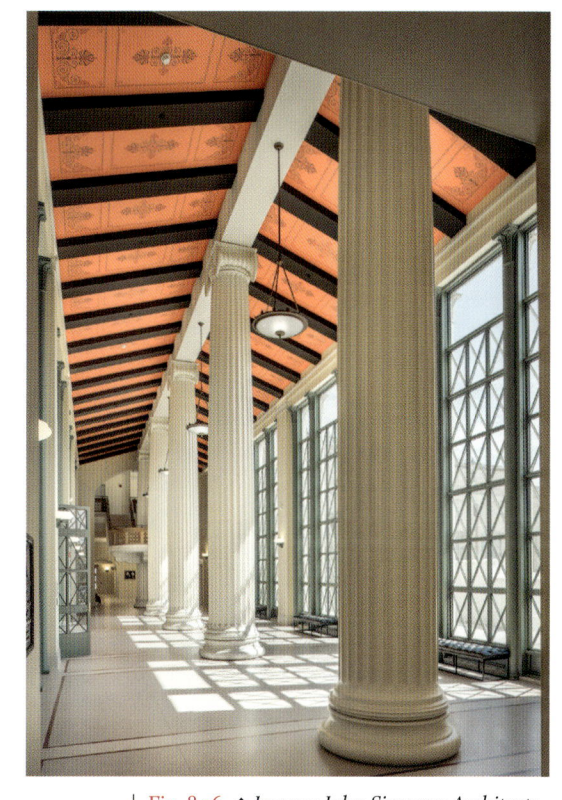

Fig. 8.16 ↑ *In 2014 John Simpson Architects won the competition to design the Walsh Family Hall for the School of Architecture, Notre Dame, IN, completed 2019. Accommodation included an auditorium, library, laboratory, classrooms, offices, studios, and various support spaces, among them the beautiful Greek Ionic stoa and gallery (PA).*

Fig. 8.17 ← *United House, Swan Mill Gardens, off Goldsel Road, Swanley, Kent (1984–5), a Græco-Egyptianising temple designed by John Outram, where the stout yellow-and-pink brindle brick columnar elements (with black engineering-brick bases topped by a band of red brick) enclose ducting and services and support the structure which leaves free open-plan interiors. Note the curious winged coloured capitals, the whole alluding to Classicism without actually quoting it (AH).*

Epilogue / 169

Fig. 8.18 ← *Royal Crescent, Truro, Cornwall, designed 2009 by Ben Pentreath for the Duchy of Cornwall. It forms part of a development that creates a new gateway into the east of this small county city. The architect was determined to create something of simple scale and substance for this dominant site, with its fine views over open country. The crescent form responds to the topography at the head of a steep valley, forms a powerful line between the edge of the city and the countryside beyond, and draws on English Classical early 19th-century precedents where understatement merges with refinement to produce a serene and pleasing whole, free from rhetoric, bombast, and architectural noise (BP/EW).*

literature that can still be found where second-hand architectural books are sold. A good library is an *essential resource* for any New Urbanist or Classicist, and it is a characteristic of most practices now working in traditional and Classical idioms that there will always be a serviceable collection of books to hand. For incompetently or ignorantly handled Classicism there is no more excuse than there is for the manifold failures in æsthetics, usability, performance, or function endemic in far too much Modernist-inspired buildings.

Ben Pentreath's creations show great sensitivity: examples can be found at Truro, Cornwall (Fig. 8.18), Poundbury, Dorset (Fig. 8.19), and Tornagrain, north-east of Inverness, Scotland (Fig. 8.20). Another architect, Mark Wilson Jones, formed Apollodorus Architecture to research and deliver an ambitious project of contemporary Classicism for a patron with an abiding interest in Greek and Roman history: this is not only a residence but a fitting home for parts of a large collection of antiquities, a scholarly emulation of a Roman maritime villa, but sited in the Caribbean, and provided with colonnades for protection from the tropical sunshine, the whole gloriously coloured (Fig. 8.21).

Wilson Jones and Jakub Ryng, appalled by the unfortunate conglomeration of 20th-century structures in Bath, and by proposals to build a new stadium which would make the problems worse, have drawn up a counter-project for the site, a vision of how things could be with sufficient will, investment, and collaboration. They believe the key is planning the new stadium in conjunction with a new leisure centre, while tying the complex into the grain of the historic fabric of the city and revitalising the riverfront. Their proposals for a new elliptical stadium, treated with allusions to the architecture of Roman theatres and amphitheatres, are thrilling, sensitive, and positive, one of the best things to have been suggested for Bath (Fig. 8.22) of late.

In Connecticut, USA, the Borough of Litchfield is known as Connecticut's 'First Historic District', and contains some

Fig. 8.19 ↑ *Corner of the Buttermarket, Poundbury, Dorset, forming the heart of the south-west quadrant of Léon Krier's master plan of the new extension of Dorchester for the Duchy of Cornwall. It was designed by Ben Pentreath, the lead architectural designer working for the Duchy at Poundbury from 2010, using a language rooted in Classicism and intended to evoke the subtle, unforced, harmonious streetscapes of the High Street in Dorchester, the heart of Bridport, and other local settlements. On the right is part of the octagonal Buttercross on a key site in Krier's plan on an intersection with the old Bridport road. The ground floor of all the buildings contains shops, including a post office, above which are apartments of varying sizes. The white-painted building at the corner, left, is affordable housing (BP/EW).*

of the finest surviving examples of late 18th-century architecture in New England. The architects Anne Fairfax and Richard Sammons were commissioned in 1993 to design a new house for a client deeply interested in the Classical language of architecture, who wanted a building that looked as though it had always been there, that utilised sustainable building methods in its construction, and paid homage to the architectural legacy of Litchfield. Completed in 1997, the house stands on a hilltop in

Fig. 8.20 ↑ *The first completed phase of the new settlement at Tornagrain, planned for the Earl of Moray and Moray Estates, situated nine miles to the east of Inverness: a view looking down Croy Road to a mix of new terrace houses and apartment buildings designed by Pentreath in a simple style evolved from the late 18th- and early 19th-century domestic architecture that had been employed in Scots estate villages. At the bottom of the hill is the first-phase village square, incorporating a shop and pharmacy, with just beyond a woodland nursery and allotments. The master plan was developed by Andrés Duany, of the Miami-based practice of DPZ, and Pentreath was the executive designer from 2011. The photograph shows the fine setting, with views across the Moray Firth to the Black Isle (an t-Eilean Dubh, which is not an island, but rather a peninsula), Ross and Cromarty (BP/EW).*

Fig. 8.21 ↑ *Caribbean villa by Mark Wilson Jones of Apollodorus Architecture (first phase completed 2022), showing part of the colonnade associated with the pool, the walls covered with a cycle of finely conceived frescoes inspired by Pompeian originals, but designed by the firm. Note the palm-leaf capitals based on the original at the Tower of the Winds, Athens (see Fig. G85) (MWJ/Ap).*

Fig. 8.22 ← *View of replacement (left) of the rather tired existing leisure centre (1970s), imagined in a more sympathetic contextual manner, with the new proposed stadium (right), an elliptical amphitheatre drawing on Roman precedents for its exterior treatment, all proposed by Apollodorus Architecture for Bath, Somerset. The new leisure centre would also feature a tower topped by an octagonal lantern, visible from various locations in the town centre, so acting as an urban way-finding marker. In the distance is the steeple (1867) of the R.C. Church of St John the Evangelist, South Parade (1861–3), by C.F. Hansom (MWJ/Ap).*

Epilogue / 171

Fig. 8.23a ↑ *Litchfield, garden front of a house standing on a hilltop in Connecticut, designed by Fairfax & Sammons, and based on Palladian influences from the work of William Adam and from Robert Morris's* Rural Architecture *(1750). It is faced with handmade bricks with a subtle interwoven diaper pattern, and the scale of the volutes, finials, etc. is enhanced, adding a Baroque touch to the rustic Palladian manner of the building. Vermont slates, graded in thickness, width, and exposure, are used for the roofs (F&S/DS).*

Fig. 8.23b ↑ *Plan of Litchfield, showing how the house, formal garden, and orangery are all conceived within one geometrical scheme. The plan of the house itself features that hallmark of the New England traditional house – the great central chimney-stack – and accommodates the entrance hall, the staircase, and the powder room on one side of the stack, with the living room on the south, the dining room and kitchen in the west, and a guest bedroom and bathroom in the east. The building is equipped with a geothermal system for heating, gains from maximum passive solar energy, and is very well insulated, making it low in maintenance and economical to run (F&S).*

Fig. 8.23c → *Detailed designs for the dining room at Litchfield, with its shallow domed ceiling and arched bookshelf recesses on four of its eight sides, showing something of the care taken concerning details of internal joinery (F&S).*

the north-western part of the Borough, and its design responds to New England's climate and to the cragginess of the landscape. The architects crafted a consciously provincial Palladian plan suggesting the transportation of civilised architecture into a rustic setting: much of its detailing and proportioning is inspired by the Scots Palladian architect, William Adam, founder of the famous Adam architectural dynasty, and its compact plan derives from Robert Morris's *Rural Architecture* (1750) (Figs 8.23a–c). Seth Weine has been connected with this firm: younger members of staff have benefited from his informed guidance, and gone on to produce sensitive work of their own.

Conclusion

There are many more architects rediscovering Classicism, who are determined to demonstrate what can be done to improve the quality of our surroundings after many years of Modernist experiments, the limitations of which are all too obvious, yet a large part of the architectural profession remains in stubborn denial. Mention of all those now working as Classicists would require another volume, so only a few can be cited here. In Scandinavia a powerful popular Architectural Uprising against Modernism began in 2014–15 (in Norway Audun Engh was very successful in promoting the cause, and others have added their weights in various ways, including Ulf Andenæs, Eskild Narum Bakken, Anders Hagalisletto, Carl Korsnes [who has edited the excellent journal, *Sivilisasjonen*], and Tor Austigard, though there are many more honourable individuals who are deeply committed), and the movement is now spreading worldwide, giving voice to a growing number of people who are appalled by what is being done to their environment by Modernist architects and planners. Today there are more than 30 countries and in excess of 300,000 members who have joined the Uprising (*Arkitektur Upproret* in Swedish, *Arkitektur Opprøret* in Norwegian, *Arkitektur Oprøret* in Danish, *Arkitektur Uppreisnin*

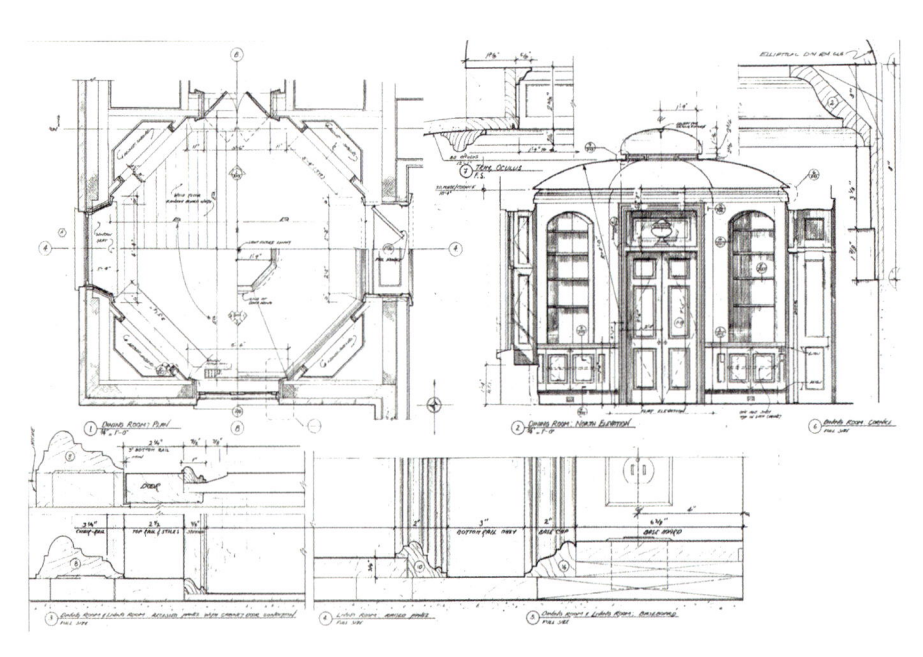

in Icelandic, and *Arkkitehtuuri Kapina* in Finnish [in Finland, Marjo Uotila has been very effective in gaining support, not only in her native land, but over a very wide geographical area]). In Germany the Uprising is called Rebellion, in the Netherlands *Omslag*, in Poland *Rewolucja*, and in Italy *In Rivolta*. In Belgium the excellent Table Ronde de l'Architecture, where the accent is largely on youth and education, has nurtured a new understanding and appreciation of traditional and Classical architecture that looks very promising.

In the United States of America the legacy of Henry Hope Reed has been immense, and the Institute of Classical Architecture & Art in the USA, which evolved from his ideas, gaining support from many who were concerned by the deterioration of the built environment, has encouraged the promotion of Classicism, presenting annual awards in recognition of important contributions to and achievements in preserving and advancing the Classical tradition in art and architecture, artisanship, community design, education, history, landscape architecture/gardening, mural painting/painting, patronage, rendering, sculpture, and stewardship/good manners (i.e. respecting the context, the *genius loci*). From 2013 the category of interior design was included in those awards. Many practitioners and others have been recognised by the Institute with the honour of an Arthur Ross Award, including those mentioned above (ADAM Architecture, Thomas H. Beeby, Andrés Duany, Fairfax & Sammons, Allan Greenberg, Craig Hamilton, Mark A. Hewitt, Léon Krier, Elizabeth Plater-Zyberk, Porphyrios Associates, John Simpson, Thomas Gordon Smith, R.A.M. Stern, Alexander Stoddart, Quinlan Terry, and HRH The Prince of Wales [now HM King Charles III]). In 2019 the author of this book also received that prestigious award for his work as an architectural historian.

In 2013 David Watkin was honoured with the Henry Hope Reed Award by the University of Notre Dame, IN, which institution was also presented with an Arthur Ross Award in 1997 for its contribution to architectural education. Two architects in England, Timothy Smith and Jonathan Taylor, who have been involved in reintroducing Classical education at Kingston School of Art, and combine teaching with their architectural practice, were recipients of an Arthur Ross Award in 2022. Another architect recognised by the Institute was David Anthony Easton, who won an Arthur Ross Award twice, in 1984 and 1988.

Although lack of space prevents inclusion of the growing number of Classicists at work today, a few more may be mentioned here for their special qualities, because of personal knowledge of their work, because of their writings, or because they have had to battle bravely in a very hostile environment. They include, for varying reasons, Steve Bass of New York, Leigh Brooks in Surrey, Luke Moloney in Dumfries and Galloway, Colum Mulhern in Luxembourg, Alex Oliver in Wiltshire, Steven W. Semes of New York and East Hampton, NY, and John Smylie in Belfast. One can only regret that the proposal for the Lincoln Center, New York City (2000), by Franck Lohsen McCrery Architects, of Washington DC and New York, was not implemented, based as it was on Michelangelo's Campidoglio, Rome: it would have been a considerable improvement on what is actually there today. Franck & Lohsen Architects, Inc., gained an Arthur Ross Award in 2011.

There have been more encouraging signs of change. One organisation grew from a research project initiated in 2000 at the Prince's Foundation for the Built Environment (another creation of the former Prince of Wales, now King Charles III) which was undertaken by Matthew Hardy: established in 2001, it is the International Network for Traditional Building, Architecture & Urbanism (INTBAU), dedicated to the support of traditional building, the maintenance of local character, and the creation of better places to live. Since 2004 INTBAU has been an independent registered charity, an active network of individuals and institutions dedicated to the creation of humane and harmonious buildings and places which respect local traditions, something to which Modernism was fundamentally opposed. INTBAU recognises the lessons of history, believing that traditional buildings and places can offer a profound modernity beyond mere novelty, and has chapters (regional subgroups) in numerous countries. It is involved in the organisation of a series of educational initiatives that promote traditional methods of designing and building, including La Table Ronde de l'Architecture (Belgium), Terrachidia Earth Building Workshop (Morocco), 'Let's Build a Beautiful City' Summer School (the Netherlands), Pono Village Workshops, Sindh (Pakistan), Rafael Manzano Summer School (Spain and Portugal), and Enduring Design Masterclass (Australia). INTBAU operates a College of Traditional Practitioners, a peer-reviewed professional organisation for architects, artists, academics, and others working in traditional styles. The trilingual *Journal of Traditional Building, Architecture and Urbanism* is aimed at providing a better understanding of the traditional building cultures of the various regions of the world, and is organised by the Spanish chapter of INTBAU, with the Rafael Manzano Martos Prize supported by the Richard H. Driehaus Charitable Trust.

Of enormous importance to traditional urbanism and architecture is the legacy of Richard H. Driehaus, the Chicago-born financier and philanthropist, who established an annual prize through the University of Notre Dame, IN. In this respect, Driehaus's benevolent support for new Classical architecture, traditional methods of building, and humane urban environments was rooted in his profound Christian faith, a factor that is conspicuously absent from the biographies of the semi-deified figures associated with Modernism, something C.F.A. Voysey pointed out in no uncertain terms when he was vociferously objecting to Pevsner's absurd classification of him as a 'pioneer of the Modern Movement'. Baillie Scott also wrote bitterly on the same subject: the essential Godlessness of Modernism. In 2012, also with the University of Notre Dame, IN, Driehaus established the Rafael Manzano Martos Award for Classical architecture and restoration of monuments. Manzano Martos, a distinguished Spanish architect, has carried out much excellent work in his native land, concerning himself with many aspects of historical architecture, not least the wonderful Islamic legacy still very much visible there. It is interesting that the career of Manzano Martos has also had a religious dimension. In 2016 the Driehaus Charitable Lead Trust, with INTBAU, established a competition to recover the partially forgotten architectural legacy of Spanish towns.

However, the Richard H. Driehaus Prize at the University of Notre Dame was established in 2003 as a global award to honour each year a major contributor in the field of contemporary traditional and Classical architecture. Laureates have been Léon Krier (2003), Demetri Porphyrios (2004), Quinlan Terry (2005), Allan Greenberg (2006), Jaquelin T. Robertson (2007), Andrés Duany and Elizabeth Plater-Zyberk (2008), Abdel-Wahed El-Wakil (2009), Rafael Manzano Martos (2010), Robert A.M. Stern (2011), Michael Graves (2012), Thomas H. Beeby (2013), Pier Carlo Bontempi (2014), David M. Schwarz (2015), Scott Merrill (2016), Robert Adam (2017), Marc Breitman and Nada Breitman-Jakov (2018), Maurice Culot (2019), Ong-ard Satrabhandhu (2020), Sebastian Treese (2021), Rob Krier (2022), and Ben Pentreath (2023). So for some time now, recognition has been given to those creative persons working outside the confines of Modernism, drawing on tradition and historical precedents for their work.

In the autumn of 2023 the first number of the *Classic Planning Herald* appeared, a journal dedicated to the discourse within the new traditional architecture community, edited by Immo Worreschk. Published by the Classic Planning Institute, a non-profit organisation based in Washington, DC, founded by Nir Haim Buras (author of *The Art of Classic Planning: Building Beautiful and Enduring Communities* [2019]), its aim is to share thoughts, encourage best practices, promote sound education, and stimulate discourse by publishing articles, showcasing projects, and advertising events. The first issue contains articles by Worreschk, Buras, Pablo Álvarez Funes (of the Spanish chapter of INTBAU), Nikos A. Salingaros (internationally recognised architectural theorist and urbanist), Nadia Naty Everard (president and co-founder of La Table Ronde de l'Architecture, who works with Colum Mulhern designing and restoring buildings in Belgium, France, and Luxembourg), Marjo Uotila (founder of INTBAU in Finland as well as of Architecture Uprising Finland), Michael Diamant (founder of the social media network, New Traditional Architecture [2013]), Ulrich Jacov Becker (founder of Architectural Uprising Israel), and the author of this book.

Intelligent students are beginning to realise that what they are being force-fed in universities is actually an outdated belief system completely irrelevant to the problems of today, and are turning to traditional architecture to study its possibilities: in many cases a realisation that Classicism can offer a way forward has begun to dawn. Several architects, realising the limitations imposed on them by the indoctrination into Modernist dogma they had received masquerading as education, turned to Classicism for the enormous possibilities it could offer, and started to produce work drawing on that rich vein of knowledge that had lain neglected by so many for so long. There are writers about architecture who have also realised that architecture and the built environment are in crisis, and have contributed articles and books to the debate. Mark Alan Hewitt has argued, correctly, that drawing, which used to be an essential part of the architectural curriculum, and which has been shamefully neglected in recent decades, should be revived, for it is really the only way in which a budding architect can understand how the various parts of a building (including its details) fit together. Christopher Alexander, Nikos Salingaros, Michael Mehaffy, and others have skewered many of the pretensions of Modernism, not least of Deconstructivism, in their many cogent writings.

Sir John Summerson, in later editions of his *The Classical Language of Architecture*, first published in 1963, observed that

> it has become the fashion to declare the Modern Movement dead ... there may be, once again, some point in discussing architectural language. ... From such speculations the classical language of architecture will never be far absent. The understanding of it will surely remain one of the most potent elements in architectural thought.

Quite so, and in that statement Summerson admits that the incoherent Modern Movement had no language at all. He had been a supporter of Modernism, but clearly had become disillusioned with it, for it had a devastating influence: it inflicted enormous damage on the image of modern architecture in the public mind.

> If, at the beginning, the mass of people regarded modern architecture as bleak and uninteresting, it was painful to discover that, as the products multiplied, people regarded them as even more bleak and less interesting and, as the years passed, about as attractive as a gorgon's head ... to all except an informed few, architecture communicated nothing but boredom.

The 'informed' few, of course, have become adept at fancy wordplay, sounding impressive to some, but actually meaning nothing at all: it is empty jargon, a meaningless, fraudulent, pseudo-language, invented by adherents of a humourless, puritanical, joyless cult. Summerson recognised that Modernism actually *attempted to kill* the language of architecture, rendering it rootless, without meaning.

Well, it tried to do just that, but the Classical language of architecture is certainly not dead, and has been kept alive by relatively small, informed, scholarly groups, working in several countries, but increasingly in touch with each other, sharing knowledge, and convinced of the relevance of tradition, of that great and adaptable language, to the problems of creating a civilised built environment today, especially as the failure of Modernism to provide it is now clear to all but those who only look with their ears.

It is all the more important to have relevant access to Classical architecture today, and this volume is offered as an attempt to provide an introduction to that enormous subject, with definitions of terms, many illustrations, and a brief narrative of its most significant features. It is hoped that it will help to foster an understanding of an immense resource, and encourage a resurgence of beauty and of a civilised architecture that has been ignored for far too long.

SELECT GLOSSARY OF TERMS

There are numbers of architects who can reproduce the beauties of antiquity ... but where is the one who ... can produce a work answering its purpose, and suitable to place and period, in the same manner and with the same freedom as did the architects of old when they produced the works which are still the marvel of the world?

These architects were familiar with the alphabet and grammar of Architecture. Ours of today, ignorant of the first principles ... collect and collate the choicest bits ..., glue them together and imagine they have made a whole. In fact, our buildings are but mere odds and ends brought together ... generally without care. At the best, this is not architecture; at the worst, it is charlatanism.

EDWARD WELBY PUGIN:
Letter in *The Times* (19 December 1871).

Every other author may aspire to praise; the lexicographer can only hope to escape reproach.

SAMUEL JOHNSON:
A Dictionary of the English Language (1755), Preface.

For a more extensive coverage of architectural styles and terms, biographies of architects, and details, readers are referred to *The Oxford Dictionary of Architecture* by James Stevens Curl and Susan Wilson (Oxford and New York: Oxford University Press, 2015, 2016).

All drawings below are by the author unless otherwise indicated.

Aaron's rod **1.** Staff with budding leaves. **2.** Rod with a serpent coiled around it. Not to be confused with **caduceus** (Fig. G1).

Fig. G1 *Unwinged Aaron's rod (left), and winged caduceus (right).*

abaciscus **1.** Small **abacus**, aka **abaculus**. **2.** Border enclosing part or the whole of a **mosaic** pavement. **3. Abaculus** or **tessera**. **4.** Small **tile**.

abaculus **Abaciscus** (**1**) or (**3**).

abacus (*pl.* **abaci**) **1.** Flat-topped slab or **tailloir** at the top of a **capital**, crowning the **column**, and supporting the **entablature**. Vitruvius confined the term to **Ionic** and **Corinthian** capitals, and called the **Doric** abacus plinthus, which indeed corresponds to the **plinth-block** under many later column-bases of other **Orders**. The **Tuscan** abacus, in the versions of Palladio and Serlio, is square on plan with flat, plain, unmoulded sides, but in the versions of Scamozzi and Vignola has a plain crowning **fillet** with **cavetto** moulding under it. The **Greek Doric** abacus is a simple square slab, unmoulded and unchamfered, but the **Roman Doric** version, while also square on plan, has plain sides surmounted by a **cyma reversa** moulding (plain or enriched) over which is a fillet. The **Greek Ionic** abacus is much thinner than the Doric or Tuscan, with an **ovolo** edge sometimes enriched, sometimes plain: in some cases (Temple of Apollo Epicurius at Bassæ) it is deeper, with concave sides on plan; usually, however, it has straight sides, although, in the case of corner capitals with volutes at 45°, it follows the plan-shape of the capital. **Roman Ionic** abaci usually have fillets over cyma reversa mouldings (the latter plain or enriched), although the ovolo-fillet-cavetto section also occurs. Usually the Corinthian (both Greek and Roman) and **Composite** abacus has four concave faces, segmental on plan, joining in points or, more often, chamfered where the concave sides meet. The four-concave-sided abacus on plan is also found in Roman Ionic Orders where there are eight volutes present instead of the usual four. In the centres of each of the four faces of the Corinthian abacus is a floral or other ornament, and the vertical section consists of ovolo, fillet, and cavetto moulding, plain or ornamented. In the Tower of the Winds, Athens (aka Horologium of Andronikos Cyrrhestes), the capitals have one row of **acanthus** leaves and a row of pointed forms resembling palm leaves (*see* Fig. G85): the abacus is, unusually for the Corinthian type, square on plan, although in vertical section it still

175

has the ovolo, fillet, and cavetto mouldings (*see* **Orders** and under the names of **Orders**) (*see* Figs 2.1a–2.10b, 2.10d–2.12e, 2.12g, 2.13–2.14e, and 2.14h–2.19). **2.** Flat slab supported on legs or a **podium**, used as a sideboard or for the display of plate, etc., in **Antiquity**. **3.** Panel on an Antique wall.

abated Stone surface cut away, leaving a design in low relief, as in a **Greek Doric metope**.

abuse Violation of established uses or corruption of form in Classical architecture. Palladio included among abuses **brackets**, **consoles**, or **modillions** supporting or appearing to support a structural load such as a **column**; **broken** or **open-topped pediments**; exaggerated projections of **cornices**; and **rusticated** or **banded** columns (*see* **band**). Perrault and others identified some more: **pilasters and columns** physically joined, esp. at the corner of a building; **coupled columns** (which Perrault himself employed at the east front of The Louvre, Paris [*see* Fig. 5.22]); distortion of **metopes** in abnormally wide **intercolumniations**; omission of the lower part of the **Ionic abacus**; **Giant** instead of an **assemblage of Orders**; an **inverted cavetto** between a column-base plinth and a pedestal-cornice; **architrave-cornices** (as in **Hellenistic Ionic**); and **entablatures** broken or interrupted above a column. Many alleged abuses featured in **Mannerist** and **Baroque** architecture.

abutment Solid part of a **pier** from which an **arch** springs, or the extremities of a bridge. Abutments must be strong enough to resist the natural tendency of an arch or **arcade** to collapse by opening outwards. Any solid structure which receives the thrust of an arch or vault (*see* Fig. G20a).

acanthus Genus of herbaceous plants, especially the species *Acanthus spinosus*, Bear's Breech, or Brank-Ursine, native to the shores of the Mediterranean, and prized among the Greeks and Romans for the elegance of its leaves. A stylised version of the thick leaf of this spiny plant, said to have been modelled first by Callimachus, is used to decorate the lower part of capitals of the **Corinthian** and **Composite Orders**, but the disposition of the leaves is different for each of these Orders. The acanthus is also found as a decorative feature elsewhere in Classical architecture. In some instances (the **triumphal arches** of Titus and Septimius Severus in Rome, for example), the leaves of the Composite Order resemble parsley, while those of the Temple of Vesta in Rome look more like the leaves of the laurel. The acanthus

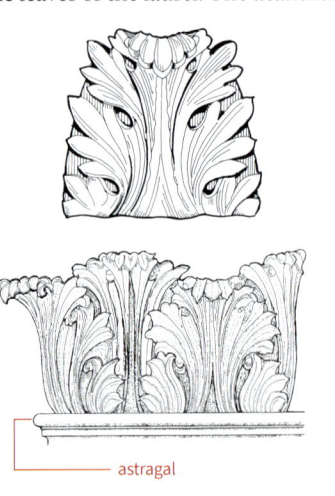

Fig. G2 *Stylised acanthus-leaf (top), with acanthus leaves over an astragal moulding (bottom).*

seems to have been used in important architecture for the first time on the **acroteria** of the **Parthenon** and in the decoration of the Erechtheion (Fig. G2; *see* Figs G43, G46a–b, 2.9, 2.13–2.14e, and 2.14g–2.16b).

achievement Collected armorial ensigns consisting of shield, **crest**, helm, mantling, and motto, with supporters and heraldic badge as appropriate. It is corrupted as **hatchment**, and this term denotes an achievement of arms painted on a diamond-shaped panel hung on a house following a death, and thereafter permanently displayed in a church.

achromatic Architecture without colour, or only with white and black, or white and gold, commonly found in early examples of the **Greek Revival** before it was realised that Greek temples were actually very brightly coloured.

acorn With **fir cones** and **pineapples**, a common **finial**, pendant, or termination representing the fruit or seed of the oak tree, often used instead of an **urn** or **pine cone**, usually on gate-piers, etc. (Fig. G3).

acrolithus, acrolith Antique or Neo-Classical statue of wood (concealed by drapery), with marble hands, feet, and face.

acropodium (*pl.* **acropodia**) **1.** Pedestal, usually elaborate and high, supporting a statue. **2. Terminal pedestal** resting on representations of feet.

acropolis Elevated part of a Greek city, esp. the Athenian acropolis (from *acro-* [highest] and *polis* [city]).

acrostolium (*pl.* **acrostolia**) Decorative upper part of the prow of an **Antique** warship, often circular, spiral, or shaped to resemble an animal: representations occur on, e.g., the **columna rostrata** (*see* Fig. G42).

acroter, acroterion, acroterium (*pl.* **acroters, acroteria**) **1.** Pedestal or

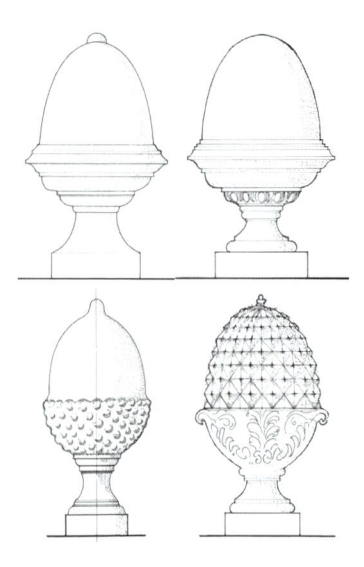

Fig. G3 *Typical finials or terminating features, all essentially variations on the acorn type: (top two) very similar, but one with egg-and-dart enrichment on the base; (bottom left) acorn-shaped cast-iron finial (c.1820), Mecklenburgh Square, London, and (bottom right) pine-cone variant.*

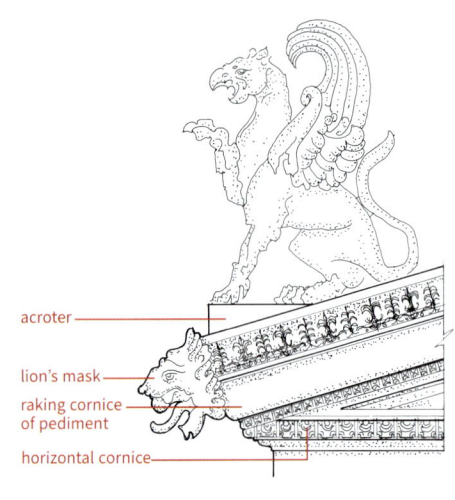

Fig. G4 *One of the two acroteria angularia from the Temple of Aphaia, Ægina (early 5th century BC).*

176 / Classical Architecture

plinth fastigium at the apex (where it is aka **ætoma**) and lower extremities of Classical **pediments** (in the latter case they are called **acroteria angularia**): they can support statuary or ornaments or can be unadorned. **Acroterium** can be interchangeable with **fastigium** in the sense of the blocks (Fig. G4). **2.** Ornament or statue with no plinth, or forming one object with its plinth, in those positions. **3.** Ridge of a Classical temple (aka **ætoma** or **ætos**). **4.** Horn or ear of an **altar**, **sarcophagus**, or **stele** (*see* Fig. G40). **5.** Erroneously used to describe the pieces of wall between **pedestals** and **balusters**.

addorsed Set back to back (Fig. G5), e.g. two identical figures facing in opposite directions (the opposite of **affronted** [*see* Fig. G8]).

Fig. G5 *Addorsed detail from an Ionic frieze according to Vignola (top), with a more elaborate version (bottom) (JSC after Normand [1852]).*

adyton, adytum Inner sanctuary, or holy of holies. Inner, unlit room of a temple.

ædes, ædis Small **Antique** shrine or other building, often circular on plan, either **monopteral** or a **rotunda** with **peristyle**.

ædicule, ædicula (*pl.* **ædicules, ædiculæ**) **1.** Shrine or **sacellum** within a temple **cella**, either a large niche or a pedestal supporting two or more columns carrying an entablature and pediment thus forming a frame or canopied housing for a cult-statue. **2.** Architectural frame around a doorway, niche, or window-aperture consisting of two columns or pilasters carrying an entablature and pediment (segmental or triangular), like a miniature distyle building: such an opening is said to be ædiculated (Figs G6a–b).

ægicrane, ægicranium (*pl.* **ægicranes, ægicrania**) Sculpted head or skull of ram

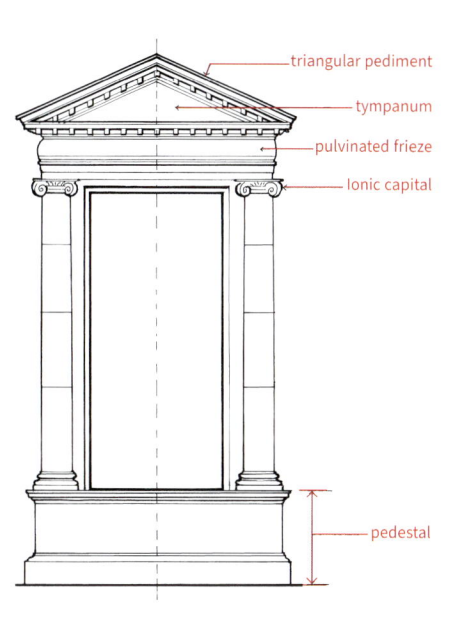

Fig. G6a *Ædicule of the Roman Ionic Order, with pulvinated frieze and triangular pediment.*

Fig. G6b (*Top*) *Tuscan and 'Dorick' ædicules, both set on pedestals or podia: note that the 'Roman Doric' version (top right) has fluted pilasters instead of columns, and the mutules are emphasised in the manner of Vignola; (bottom) 'Ionick' and Corinthian ædicules, both with plain modillions, and both set on pedestals or podia. The Ionic version has a pulvinated frieze and triangular pediment, while the Corinthian has a segmental pediment. In all four cases, the ædicules are window-surrounds (Langley [1745]).*

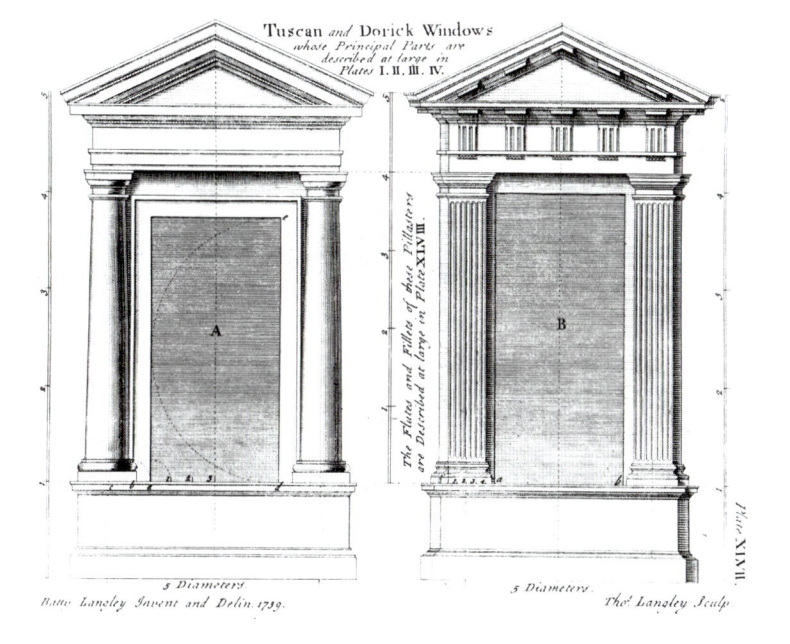

SELECT GLOSSARY OF TERMS / 177

or goat, usually associated with **festoons** or **swags** like a **bucranium** (*see* Fig. G34).

ægis Shield or breast-plate.

Æolic Early form of the **Ionic capital** having **volutes** sprouting from the column-shaft with **palmettes** filling the gap between them (Fig. G7).

Fig. G7 *Proto-Ionic Æolic capitals from Larissa (top) and Neandria (bottom).*

ætoma, ætos 1. Tympanum of a **pediment. 2.** Ridge of a Classical temple. **3.** Apex **acroter**.

affronted Opposite of **addorsed**, with identical figures or animals facing each other (Fig. G8).

Fig. G8 *Affronted detail from the tower of the St Vincent Street church, Glasgow (1857–9), by Alexander 'Greek' Thomson.*

agora Open space in a Greek city doubling as marketplace and general rendezvous: it was often surrounded by **colonnades** and important buildings.

agrafe, agraffe Keystone decorated with relief sculpture (*see* Fig. G12).

Agricultural Order Type of **Corinthian capital** with **volutes** replaced by representations of animal heads, **acanthus** eschewed for mangel-wurzel and turnip leaves, and other allusions to agriculture (e.g. the Leicester testimonial at Holkham, Norfolk [1845–50], by W.J. Donthorn) (Fig. G9).

Fig. G9 *Agricultural Order on the Leicester testimonial, Holkham, Norfolk (1844–5), by W.J. Donthorn (JSC).*

aguilla Obelisk, spire, or similar.

aisle Lateral portions of a basilican building parallel to the **nave**, choir, and chancel, and separated from the central portion of the building by **arcades** or **colonnades** carrying the **clerestorey**. Aisles are usually lower than the central, main body of the edifice (*see* **basilica** [*see* Figs G27a–b, 3.5, and 4.24]).

ala (*pl.* **alæ**) **1. Cellæ** on either side of the central **cella** of a Tuscan temple, so that there were one large central and two smaller compartments, each with its own door, set behind a deep **portico** (Fig. G10). **2.** Small room or alcove on either side of a **vestibule** in the **atrium** of a Roman house. **3.** Space between the **naos** and flanking **colonnade** of a Greek temple, or the wall of the naos itself (*see* Fig. G107b). **4. Wing** or smaller building, on either side of the

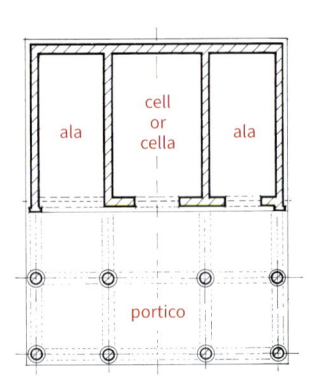

Fig. G10 *Plan of an Etruscan temple showing the alæ.*

corps-de-logis of a Classical **Palladian** composition (*see* Figs G84c–d).

albarium Opus albarium or **tectorium** was a coating applied to sun-dried brick, coarse stone, concrete, or other rough walls. The finest **stucco** was made of powdered marble.

alcove 1. Large niche or recess in the wall of any building or room. **2.** Recess or part of a chamber defined by a **balustrade**, estrade, or partition to accommodate a bed. **3.** Ornamental building in a garden, usually with a seat.

alette 1. Ala or **wing** of a building as in a **Palladian** composition (*see* Figs G84c–d). **2.** Visible parts of a **pier** to which **engaged columns** or **pilasters** are attached, often forming the **abutment** of arches. **3.** Semi-visible rear pilaster among several columnar elements.

aliform 1. Building with additions forming **wings**. **2.** Shaped like a wing.

altana Loggia, covered roof-terrace, or **belvedere**, common in **Renaissance** Rome.

altar Block, **pedestal**, stand, or **table** on which to place or sacrifice offerings to deities. In Classical Antiquity, altars had horn-like ornaments at each corner, called **acroteria** or **ears**, so their tops resembled **cinerarium** and **sarcophagus** lids, influencing the design of **Neo-Classical** gate-piers, tops of door-cases, and the like (*see* Figs G40 and G70). Christian altars, consecrated for celebration of the Eucharist, are elevated tables with a plane (usually stone) top (**mensa**), also called **altar-slab** or **altar-stone**, incised with small crosses representing the Five Wounds of Christ, and, in pre-Reformation and R.C. altars, with a Relic embedded.

178 / CLASSICAL ARCHITECTURE

Sides (**horns**) of altars are termed **Epistle** (south) and **Gospel** (north).

altar-tomb A **tomb-chest** or memorial resembling an altar (but never used as such) on which there are often recumbent effigies, sometimes with **weepers** (mourning figures) set in **niches** around the sides (*see* Fig. G117), often featuring **achievements**, and sometimes set under canopies.

alto-relievo Carved work projecting by at least half its true proportions from the background on which it is sculpted.

ambitus **1.** Area around a tomb, grave, or burial-ground attached to a church. **2.** Frame around a **loculus** for a body in a **catacomb** or **hypogæum**, or around a recess for an **urn** or **cinerarium** in a **columbarium**: it was often decorated and sealed in.

ambo, ambon (*pl.* **ambones**) Gradus, lectorium, letricium, elevated lectern, or reading-desk, frequently paired, one on the north (**Gospel**) side and the other on the south (**Epistle**), often attached to the cancelli or low screen-walls defining the sanctuary of a church.

ambulacrum **1. Atrium**, court, parvis, or xystum, often planted with trees, sometimes with a fountain in its centre, surrounded by **arcades** or **colonnades**, in front of a church. **2.** Any walk or avenue with formally arranged tree-planting.

ambulatio (*pl.* **ambulationes**) **1.** Promenade or xystum open to the sky. **2.** Covered promenade (**xystus**) defined by formal planting, a **colonnade**, or both. **3.** Walkway bounded by a **temple peristyle** and the wall of the **naos** or **cella** (*see* Fig. G107b).

American Order **Capital** resembling that of the **Corinthian Order**, but with corn cobs, corn ears, and tobacco leaves replacing **acanthus**, invented by Benjamin Latrobe for the U.S. Capitol in Washington DC (*see* Fig. 6.23c). Compare **Agricultural** (*see* Fig. G9), **Britannic, German Orders**.

Ammonite Order Variety of **Ionic** in which the **capital volutes** are modelled on a fossil genus of cephalopods, consisting of whorled chambered shells, aka snake-stones, once supposed to be coiled petrified serpents, and named from their resemblance to the Cornu Ammonis, or involuted horn of Jupiter Ammon. The Order is peculiarly English, and many examples occur in

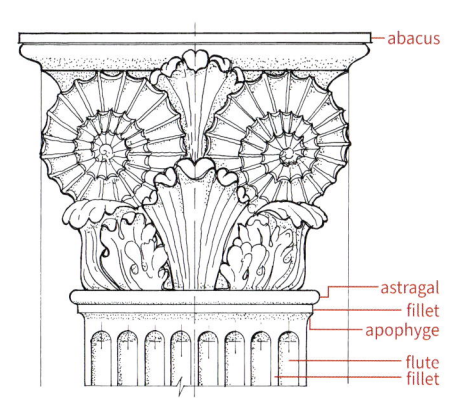

Fig. G11 *Ammonite capital of stucco, as used by the Wilds on a group of houses on the Old Kent Road, London (c.1825).*

Brighton and in South London, employed by the developers Amon and Amon Henry Wilds as a kind of 'signature' (Fig. G11).

amorino (*pl.* **amorini**) Winged male infant (unlike the wingless **putto**), often chubby and knowing, also called **amoretto**, **cherub**, **Cupid**, or **Little Love**.

amphi- Prefix, meaning on both sides, or the same on the front and rear. Compounds include **amphi-antis**: Classical temple with an **in antis** (*see* **anta**) **portico** at each end; **amphi-prostyle**: apteral temple without flanking **colonnades**, so with a **prostyle portico** at each end of the **naos** or **cella** (*see* Fig. G91); and **amphitheatre**: Greek theatres were semicircular on plan, with concentric tiers of seats rising steeply from the stage. An amphitheatre was a Roman building type resembling two theatres joined together to form an arena, elliptical on plan (*viz.* **Colosseum**, Rome).

anactoron Sacred building or part of such a building, used chiefly in connection with the Mysteries (various kinds of secret worship in Classical Antiquity which rested on the belief that, besides the general modes of honouring the deities, there was another, revealed only to the select few, or initiates).

anathyrosis Smooth dressing of the margins of ashlar masonry or of the drums comprising the shaft of a Classical column to ensure tight accurate joints. Within the edge-ring of each drum was a shallow circular depression with a deep hole in the centre for the reception of the **empolia**, or wooden blocks which contained the **poloi**, or timber dowels that connected the drums.

anchor Ornament like an arrowhead, used with an egg design to enrich mouldings: aka dart or tongue (*see* Figs G53, G74, 2.9, and 3.7 and illustrations of the **Orders**). An anchor is also a symbol of Hope (*see* Fig. G110b), as a disguised form of the Cross. An anchor fouled with rope is a symbol of death.

ancon (*pl.* **ancones**) **1. Console** ornament cut on the **keystone** of an **arch** and supporting a bust or other feature. As a feature of a keystone the ancon is wedge shaped, that is narrower at the bottom than at the top (Fig. G12, and *see* Fig. G90b). **2. Truss**, **console**, **shouldering-piece**, or **crossette** employed in the dressings or **antepagmenta** of apertures, serving as an apparent support to the **cornice** above at the topmost corners of the apertures. In this sense, an Antique ancon was often not in contact with the flanks of the **architrave**,

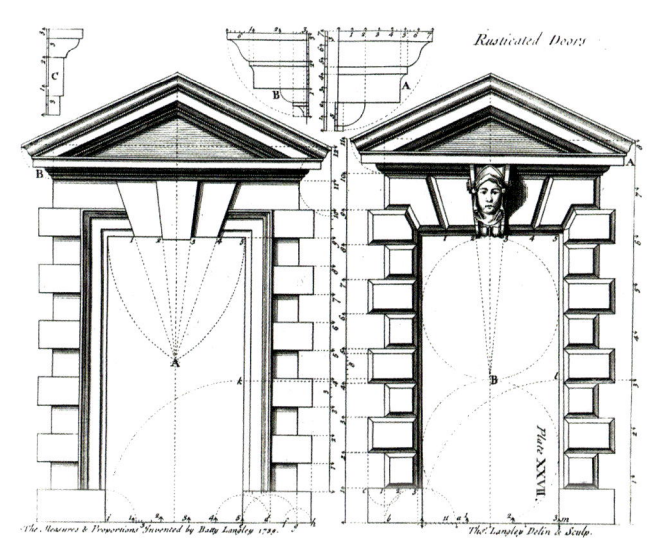

Fig. G12 *Rusticated doorways: that on the right has **V**-jointed or chamfered blocks, two crossettes at the top right and left, and a tapering ancon as a keystone (Langley [1745]).*

SELECT GLOSSARY OF TERMS / 179

but placed at a small distance from them, and was frequently wider at the top than at the bottom, like an ancon on a keystone: indeed the term ancon seems most properly to apply to this tapering type of form, as opposed to a **crossette** or **console**, which has parallel sides. Vitruvius called ancones **prothyrides** (*see* Figs G44a–c). **3.** Corner of a **quoin** of a wall.

andron Apartment reserved for men, esp. a dining room, in a Greek house.

angle capital **Capital** at the corner of a **portico**. In the **Ionic Order**, the fronts and sides of a normal capital differ, so to obtain **volutes** on both sides of the corner, those at the external angle are splayed outwards at 45° (i.e. the corner volutes are 'pulled out' at an angle of 135° to the planes of the front and returning entablatures) (Fig. G13; *see* Figs 2.6–2.7 and 2.12a). Not to be confused with **angular capitals** (Fig. G14).

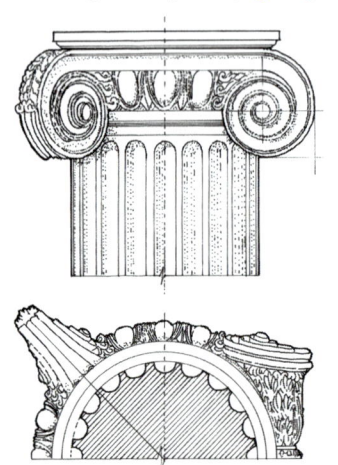

Fig. G13 *Angle or corner capital from the Temple of Fortuna Virilis, Rome (JSC after Langley [1745]).*

angle modillion **Modillion** at the mitring of a **cornice** (i.e. set diagonally at the external corner of a Classical cornice), generally regarded as an **abuse** of true Classical detail, and therefore to be avoided, even though known in **Antiquity**.

angle-volute Spiral form at the corners of **Composite**, **Corinthian**, and some **Ionic capitals**.

angoulême sprig The *barbeau* (cornflower).

angular capital Type of **Ionic** 'diagonal' capital, with four identical faces, so therefore with eight **volutes** (*see* Fig. G14). If used, no special **angle capital** (*see* Fig. G13) is needed at the return angle of a

Fig. G14 *Angular or Scamozzi capital (JSC after Langley [1745]).*

prostyle portico. Supposedly an **abuse** invented by Scamozzi, aka Modern or Scamozzian Ionic Order, it actually had Antique origins, for it was fashionable in Pompeii, is found in the upper parts of **Composite** capitals (*see* Fig. G43), and indeed was used in the Temple of Saturn, Rome (c.AD 320).

annulet **1.** Small flat **band**, **fillet**, or **shaft-ring** encircling a column, especially that repeated three to five times under the **echinus** of a Greek **Doric capital** (*see* Fig. G52a): thus **annulated** means with a ring or rings. **2. List**, **listella**, or vertical **fillet** between **flutes** in columns (*see* Fig. G59).

anta **1.** Square or rectangular **pier** formed by the thickening of the end of a wall, e.g. in Greek **temples** where the projecting

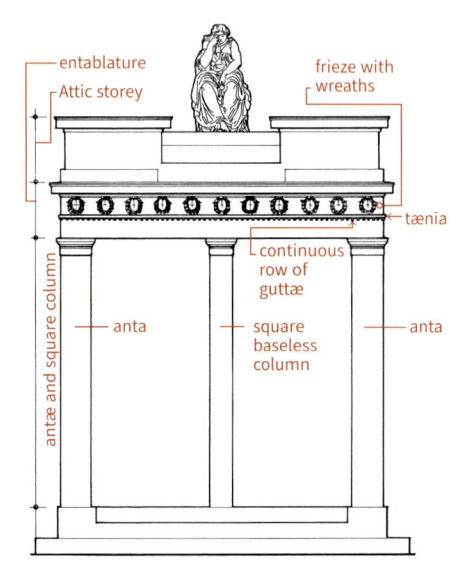

Fig. G15 *Antæ on the Bazouin mausoleum, Père-Lachaise cemetery, Paris (c.1822), designed by Blanchon, based on the choragic monument of Thrasyllus, Athens (319–279 BC): the latter provided Neo-Classical architects with a useful precedent for door-cases, window-surrounds, etc.*

lateral walls of the **naos** terminate (*see* Fig. G107a). When the **pronaos** or **porch** in front of the **cell** is formed by the projection of the walls terminated by **antæ** with columns between the antæ, the portico is said to be **in antis**: the columns in an *in-antis* arrangement, therefore, do not stand in front of the outer face of the antæ (*see* Fig. G91). Greek antæ can have capitals (and usually bases) differing from those of the Order proper, unlike Roman **pilasters**, which usually have capitals and bases identical to those of the columns with which they are associated, but have rectangular rather than circular plans. Antæ have either very slight or no entasis (Fig. G15; *see* **Orders** and Figs G52a and G107a–b). **2.** A **jamb**.

antefix (*pl.* **antefixa**) **1.** Ornamental vertical element fixed at regular intervals above the **cornice** of a Classical building at the lower edge of the roof to cover the ends of the harmi or joint-tiles (*see* Fig. G107a). Antefixa are usually ornamented with the **anthemion** or other motifs (Fig. G16) (*see* **Orders**). **2.** Term also sometimes given to ornamental heads below the eaves through the mouths of which water is cast away.

Fig. G16 *Antefix decorated with anthemion from the Parthenon, Athens.*

antepagment, antepagmentum (*pl.* **antepagments, antepagmenta**) **1.** Moulded **architrave** around an opening. More accurately the antepagmenta are the jambs of a door- or window-opening, moulded like an architrave, while the top part of the architrave (or **lintel**), returning at the ends (with similar mouldings to those of the jambs) down upon the antepagmenta, is called the **supercilium** (*see* Figs G21a–b, G44c, and G106a). **2. Anta** or **pilaster**.

anthemion Honeysuckle-like ornament found above **acroteria**, in **cornices**, on **antefixa** (*see* Fig. G16), on the neckings of some Ionic capitals (*see* Fig. 2.8a), and elsewhere in Classical architecture, often alternating with the **palmette** (Fig. G17).

180 / CLASSICAL ARCHITECTURE

Fig. G17 *Anthemion and palmette from the Erechtheion, Athens.*

antick **Grotesque** ornament.

Antiquity Period of the Classical civilisations of the Græco-Roman world.

antis, in *See* **anta**.

antithema Backing of steps, **architrave**, and **frieze**, usually separate **blocks** from those of the front.

Antonine column Monumental Tuscan-Doric column, similar to the earlier **Trajanic column**, in Rome, commemorating Emperor Marcus Aurelius Antoninus.

apodyterium Dressing-room, esp. in baths.

Apolline decoration 1. Male head surrounded by sunrays, or the **Sunburst** (*see* Fig. G105). 2. Male figure with lyre or chariot. Associated with Versailles.

apophyge Curve, **congé**, or **scape** given to the top and bottom of the shaft of a column where it expands to meet the edge of the **fillet** above the **base** and beneath the **astragal** under the **capital**: aka **apothesis** or **apophysis** (*see* Fig. G28a).

applied column Engaged column: one attached to a wall.

apron Panel below a windowsill, plain or ornamented.

apse, apsis (*pl.* **apses, apsides**) Semicircular or polygonal recess usually found at the end of the nave of a basilican building, frequently covered with a half-dome. **Apsidal** means shaped like an apse. **Apsidiole** is a subsidiary apse (*see* **basilica**).

apteral Classical building of temple form with a **portico** at one or both ends, but no **colonnades** along the sides (*see* Fig. G91).

ara (*pl.* **aræ**) Roman **altar**, it could be a large, public, commemorative structure, e.g. the sumptuous *ara pacis* erected by Emperor Augustus to mark the establishment of Imperial power and the coming of peace in 13 BC, or a small altar in a private house by which protection of the deities was invoked.

arabesque Capricious ornament found in Classical architecture, usually involving the combination of flowing lines of branches, leaves, and **scroll-work**, fancifully intertwined (Fig. G18). It does not contain human or animal figures, and it is therefore not to be confused with **Grotesque** ornament.

Fig. G18 *Arabesques (left) from a 17th-century Flemish pattern-book, and (right) 16th-century example from the Louvre, Paris.*

aræostyle *See* **intercolumniation**.

arcade Series of arches carried on **colonnettes**, **columns**, **piers**, or **pilasters**, either freestanding (Fig. G19) or attached to a wall to form a decorative rhythmic pattern: in the latter case it is referred to as a **blind arcade**. The term is applied to the arches on piers or columns that divide a **nave** from an **aisle**, in which case it is called a nave arcade.

arch Construction of blocks of material disposed in a curve or curves, and supporting one another by mutual pressure: an arch so formed over an opening is capable of carrying a superimposed weight. Each block is a **voussoir** (usually in the shape of a truncated wedge), and the block in the centre is the **keystone**. The solid extremities on or against which the arch rests are **abutments**. The lower or under curve of each stone is the **intrados**, and the upper curve the **extrados**. The distance between the piers or abutments is the **span** of the arch, and the vertical distance between the level line of the **springing** to the uppermost part of the intrados is the **height** of the arch. The springing or **impost** is the point at which an arch unites with its support. The simplest arches are **semicircular** and **segmental** arches, the former with its centre on the springing line and the latter with its centre below it. A **relieving** or **discharging arch** is one built into a wall to transfer the load of a wall from a lintel (Figs G20a–b).

architrave 1. Lowest of the divisions of an **entablature** that rests directly on the **abaci** of columns. Architraves in the **Doric Order** are plain, but in the more elaborate Orders are often divided into three **fasciæ**. In their simplest form architraves as structural beams resting on columns are called **trabes compactiles**. 2. Lintels, **jambs**, and **mouldings** surrounding a window, door,

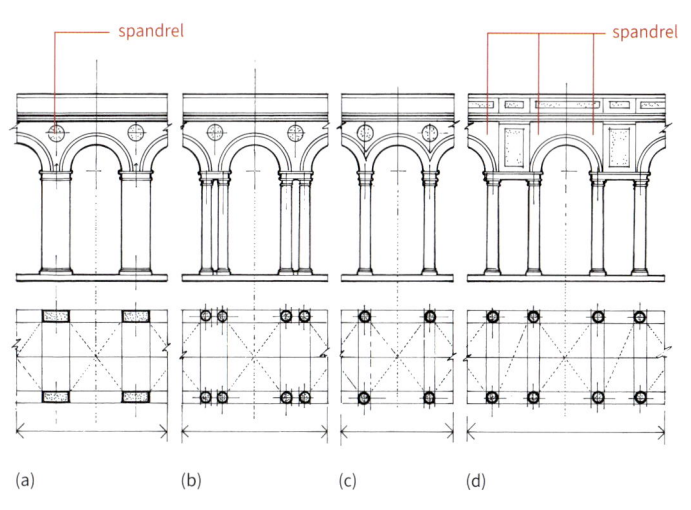

Fig. G19 *Arcades: (a) typical Classical arches on piers; (b) with coupled columns; (c) with columns; and (d) alternating, a mix of colonnade and arcade, resembling a series of overlapping serlianas.*

SELECT GLOSSARY OF TERMS / 181

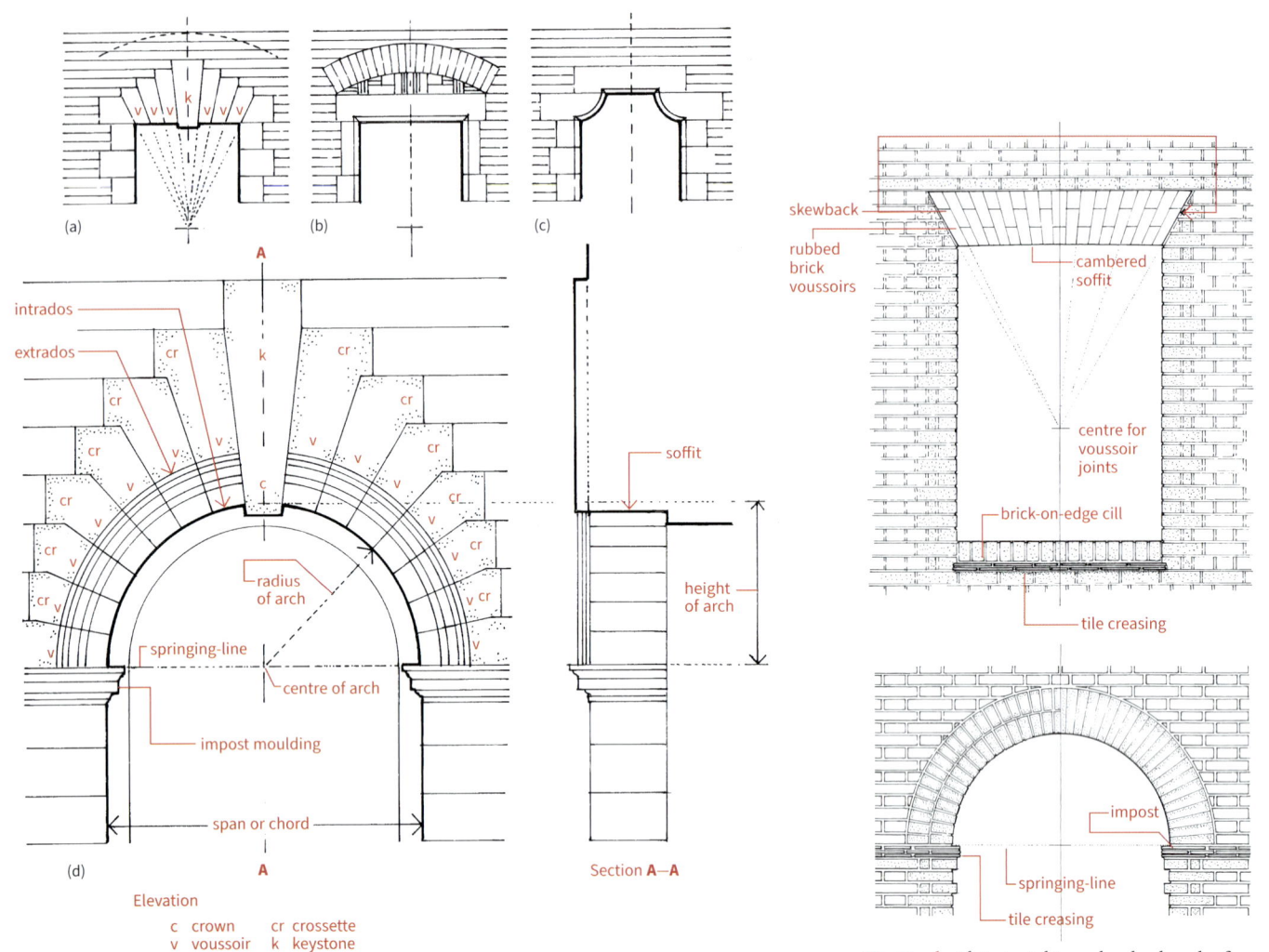

Fig. G20a *(a) Flat, aka gauged, arch with keystone and voussoirs wedged between two blocks; (b) segmental relieving, aka discharging, arch over a lintel; (c) shouldered false arch, actually a lintel carried on shaped corbels; (d) semicircular masonry arch with voussoirs cut with crossettes, and a massive keystone.*

Elevation
c crown   cr crossette
v voussoir   k   keystone

Fig. G20b *Flat, straight, or skewback arch of gauged brick rubbers (top); semicircular brick arch springing from imposts of tile creasing (bottom), that on (left) a rowlock arch of special bricks, and that on (right) of brick rubbers.*

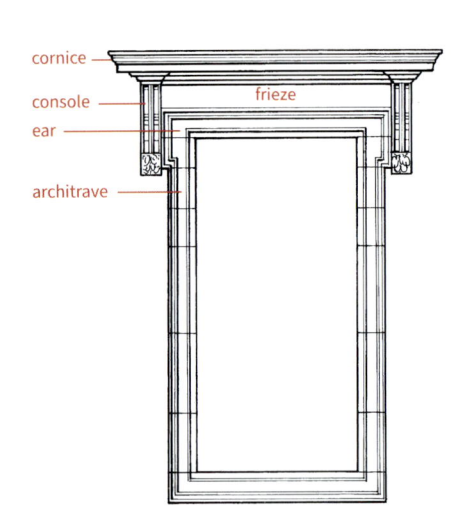

Fig. G21a *Architrave: typical Classical window-surround with consoles, cornice, and eared architrave.*

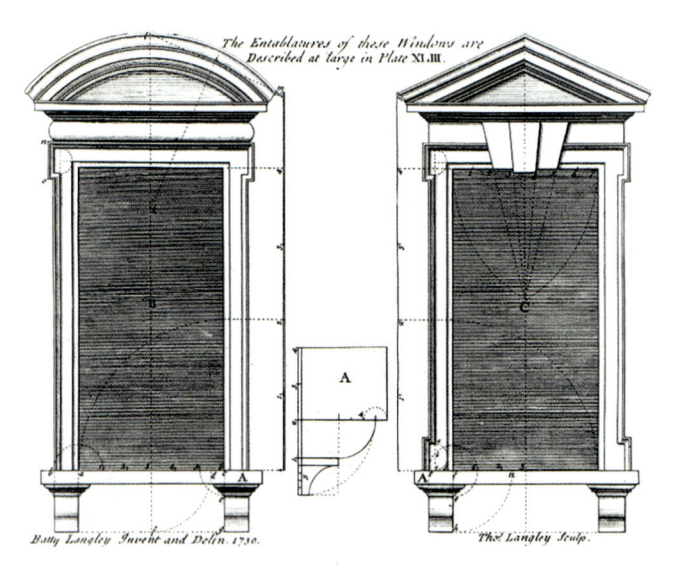

Fig. G21b *Architraves as window-surrounds: both have eared architraves and both cills are carried on brackets. That on the left has a segmental pediment and pulvinated frieze, and that on the right has a triangular pediment with keystone flanked by two voussoirs over the centre (Langley [1745]).*

182 / CLASSICAL ARCHITECTURE

panel, or **niche** (Figs G21a–b). **3.** Ornamental mouldings round the exterior curve of an **arch** (*see* **Orders** and Figs G19, G20a, G25a–b, G26, and 2.18a).

architrave cornice **Entablature** with no **frieze**.

archivolt Group of concentric **mouldings** around a Classical **arch**: an **architrave** that is curved to frame an arched opening. Not to be confused with the **soffit** of an arch (*see* **arch** and Figs G19, G20a, G25a–b, and G26).

arcuated System of construction based on the **arch** rather than on **columns** and beams (i.e. **trabeated**).

arena **1.** Central elliptical part of an **amphitheatre**. **2.** Part of a theatre used by performers.

arris Sharp crease-like edge at the junction of two surfaces, e.g. the **flutes** of a Greek Doric column meeting in a sharp arris (*see* Figs G52a–b).

arrow Found, with quiver, in **trophies**, or associated with **Cupid**. A jagged arrow is an **attribute** of Jupiter, associated with thunder and lightning.

artisan Mannerism The use of Classical motifs in a way not like their original disposition, evolved by craftsmen rather than architects.

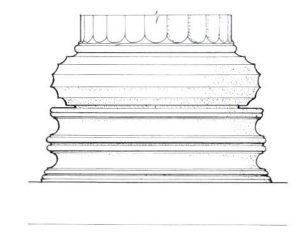

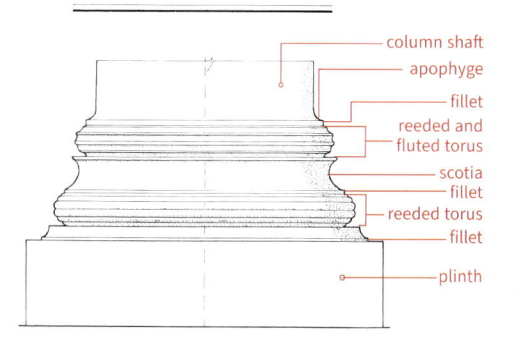

Fig. G22 *Ionic Asiatic bases: (top) an example from the Temple of Athena Polias, Priene; (bottom) from the Erechtheion, Athens.*

ash-chest *See* **cinerarium**.

ashlar Cut stone worked to even faces and right-angled **arrises**, laid in horizontal courses with vertical joints. When the resulting **façade** is smooth and finished finely, it is called **plain ashlar**; when the surface is cut regularly, with parallel incisions like miniature flutes, it is **tooled ashlar**. Other finishes are **random tooling**, or irregular texturing using a broad implement; chiselling or **boasting**, created with a fine, narrow tool; and pointed, if only the coarsest projections are removed with a pick or pointing tool. When the face of ashlar projects beyond the joints the finish is known as **rustication**. The Romans called ashlar **opus quadratum**, from the regular squared forms of the blocks (*see* **rustication** and Fig. G98a).

Asiatic base **Ionic base** developed in Asia Minor and consisting of a lower drum decorated with horizontal **reeding**, usually two **scotiæ** with separating **astragals**, and an upper **torus** decorated with reeds (Fig. G22). Compare **Attic base** (*see* Fig. G23).

assemblage of Orders Arrangement of **superimposed Orders** on a Classical façade, set one above the other with the vertical axes of the columns lining up, each Order defining a storey, aka **supercolumniation**. The **Renaissance** hierarchy places **Tuscan** at the lowest storey, then **Doric**, **Ionic**, **Corinthian**, and finally **Composite** (but there is no surviving Antique monument in Rome with the sequence Doric/Ionic/Corinthian, although the Theatre of Marcellus [23–13 BC] had Roman Doric on the lower storey, then Ionic above, as did the Basilica Julia and the Tabularium [both 1st century BC]: the last seems to have been the first instance of an arcaded structure combined with Orders). At the Roman **Colosseum**, the external arcuated walls had Tuscan, Ionic, and Corinthian engaged Orders with columns, but the topmost storey, above the Corinthian, had Corinthian pilasters (see Figs 2.17a–b). Serlio codified the Five Orders in his *L'Architettura* (1537–51) with illustrations augmenting the information (1575), and so the ensemble of Five Orders set above each other was essentially a Renaissance invention, and was widely disseminated (see Figs 4.7, 4.14b, 4.18b, and 4.34).

asser (*pl.* **asseres**) Trabiculæ are the main beams resting on the **mutuli** of a temple. On top of the **trabiculæ** are the **asseres** laid over the main beams and spanning over them at right angles.

astragal Small **moulding** with a semicircular profile, a **bead**, aka **roundel** or **baguette**. It is found as a ring separating the **capital** from the **shaft** of a Classical column, and may be ornamented. It can also be the bead that separates the **fasciæ** of **architraves**, and in such a position is usually ornamented with **bead-and-reel**. The name, meaning 'knucklebones', however, implies enrichment with bead-and-reel (*see* **Orders**).

astylar Without columns or pilasters.

atlas, atlantis (*pl.* **atlantes, atlantides**) Heroic male figures or half-figures supporting a structure, and usually shown straining against a weight. **Telamon** appears to have been an alternative name for Atlas, and so **atlantes** are also termed **telamons** or **telamones**, but these are usually straight male figures used instead of columns, and not shown in an attitude of vigorous struggle (*see* **canephora, caryatid[e], telamon**).

atrium (*pl.* **atria**) Open court surrounded by a colonnaded covered walk, found in Roman domestic architecture and in front of Early Christian churches (*see* Fig. G27b). The open roofless **compluvium** in the centre received light and rainwater, the latter collected in a cistern, aka **impluvium**.

attached column Engaged column, i.e. one attached to a wall.

Attic Storey over the main **entablature**, not to be confused with a garret. An Attic storey is closely related to the architectural arrangement below the **entablature** (as in a **triumphal arch**) (*see* Figs G110a, 2.18a–b, and 3.2c–i), and if it contains accommodation it has ceilings square with the side walls, and is quite distinct from a roof-space.

Attic base Base of a Classical column consisting of two **torus mouldings** separated by a **scotia** with **fillets** (i.e. two large convex rings between which is a concave

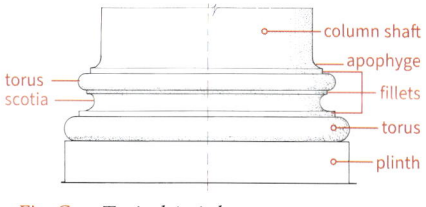

Fig. G23 *Typical Attic base.*

SELECT GLOSSARY OF TERMS / 183

moulding) (Fig. G23). This is found with all Orders except the **Greek Doric** and the **Tuscan** (*see* **Orders**). Compare **Asiatic base** (*see* Fig. G22).

Attic Order Subordinate **Order**, often of low **pilasters**, adorning the front of an **Attic storey** above the main **entablature**, lining up with the main Orders below.

attributes Motifs associated with mythological, saintly, or legendary figures. Club = Hercules, Lyre = Apollo, Grid-Iron = St Lawrence, Flaying Knife = St Bartholomew, Trident = Neptune, Spear = Pallas, Wheel = St Catherine, etc.

Bacchic ornament Decoration featuring asses, grapevines, laurels, panthers, rams, serpents, Mænades, and Thyiades, and much drunken revelry (*see* Fig. G108). Associated with sensual pleasure, it was the opposite of **Apolline decoration**.

balcony Platform projecting from the surface of a wall of a building carried on brackets, **consoles**, **corbels**, or **columns**, or cantilevered, usually placed before windows or openings, and protected by a railing or **balustrade**.

baldacchino, baldachin, or **baldaquin** Canopy over an altar, carried on columns, supported on brackets, or suspended (*see* Figs 4.28b, 5.3, and 7.5b). Compare **ciborium**.

balection *See* **bolection**.

balteus **1.** Wide step in theatres which allowed spectators to walk without disturbing those already seated. **2.** Strap which appears to bind the **cushion** or coussinet of the **Ionic capital** (*see* Fig. G72).

baluster Small colonnette or post, forming part of a **balustrade** and supporting a handrail or **coping**. It can be square, polygonal, or circular on plan, and its profile can be elaborate (Figs G24a–b). Balusters are also known as **columellæ** (*see* **balustrade**).

baluster-side Form like a rolled-up mattress, resembling a baluster laid on its side, also known as a **bolster**, **cushion**, **pulvin**, or **pulvinus**, joining the **volutes** of an **Ionic capital** (*see* Fig. G72).

balustrade Parapet composed of **balusters** with a **coping** or rail, usually found with **pedestals** or some stronger element

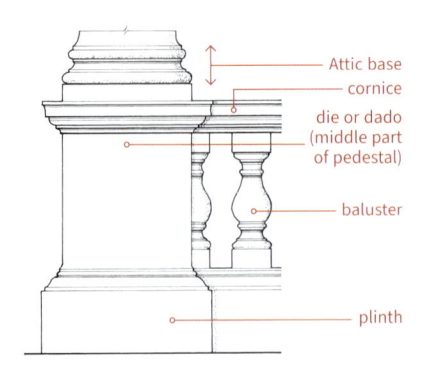

Fig. G24a *Typical Classical balustrade terminating in a pedestal supporting a column with an Attic base: note the half-baluster set against the pedestal.*

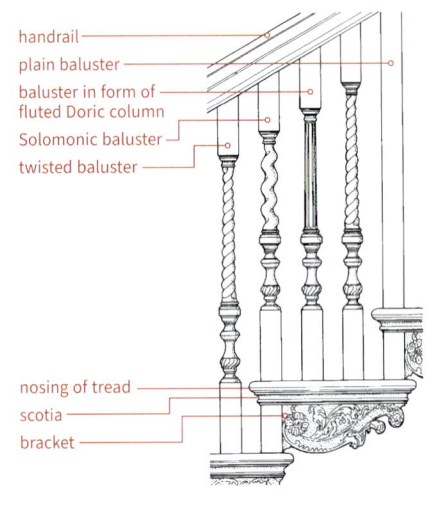

Fig. G24b *Differing turned balusters in a balustrade on a Georgian cut- or open-string stair with carved console-like brackets under the tread-ends (JSC after Osborne [1954]).*

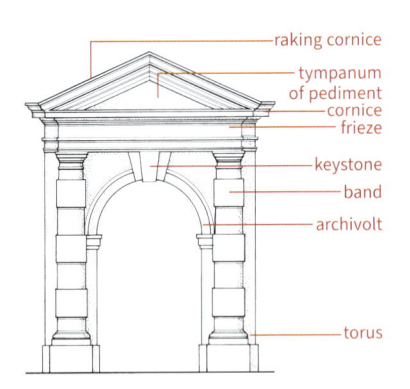

Fig. G25a *Classical gateway flanked by banded columns of the Tuscan Order, surmounted by a triangular pediment.*

Fig. G25b *Tuscan gateway, with plain (left) or banded (right) columns and pilasters. A combination of columnar and trabeated and arcuated forms derived from Roman exemplars (Langley [1745]).*

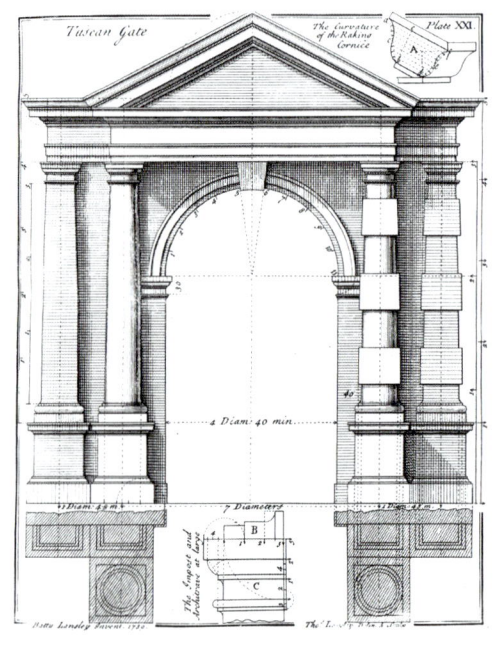

at the ends of runs of balusters (*see* Fig. G24a), or associated with the handrail of a stair (*see* Fig. G24b).

band **1.** A **face** or **fascia**. **2.** Flat, low, square-profiled **moulding** encircling a building or running across its **façade**. The strips from which **modillions** or **dentils** project are therefore termed **modillion** or **dentil bands**. **3.** A **banded column** is one where the shaft is broken by the addition of plain or rusticated blocks of stone: aka bandel column (Figs G25a–b; *see* Figs G98b–d).

bandelet Any narrow flat **moulding** such as the **tænia** between the **Doric frieze** and **architrave**.

banderole, bannerol, banner Narrow streamer or flag with a cleft end.

banister Vulgar term for a **baluster**: the plural, banisters, signifies a **balustrade**.

barley-sugar column Classical column twisted like a stick of barley-sugar, aka **Solomonic** (from its supposed use in the Temple of Solomon in Jerusalem) or **twisted** column (Fig. G26; *see* Figs G27a, G101, 5.3, 5.16b, and 5.19e).

Baroque Florid form of Classical architecture prevalent during the 17th and 18th centuries, which developed from **Mannerism**, characterised by exuberance, movement, curvaceous forms, theatrical illusionist effects, and cunningly contrived

Fig. G26 *Baroque south porch at St Mary's Church, High Street, Oxford (1637), built by John Jackson, the design of which has also been attributed to Nicholas Stone. It is a virtuoso performance, with Solomonic, spiral, twisted, or barley-sugar columns of the Composite Order, surmounted by a spectacular broken segmental pediment with scrolls, between which is a massive triangular-pedimented niche (JSC).*

and complex spatial inter-relationships (*see* Figs G26, 5.1a–5.19e, 5.34–38, and 5.47–5.52a).

barrel-vault Vault with a semicircular or segmental uniform concave ceiling and no vaults or ribs. It resembles an elongated continuous arch (*see* Fig. G112b) (*see* **vaults**).

base, basis 1. Anything on which an object rests, especially the foot or lowest member of a **colonnette**, **column**, or **pier** on which a **shaft** or mass of construction sits, so the term means a **basis**, a support, or a **pedestal**. The base of a column is that part of it between the **shaft** and the pavement, pedestal, or **plinth**. Bases differ according to the **Order** employed: the **Greek Doric Order** has no base; the **Tuscan** base has only a single **torus** with a **fillet**; the **Roman Doric** base has a torus, an **astragal**, and a fillet; the **Ionic** base has a single large torus over two slender **scotiæ** separated by two astragals (although there are many variations); the **Corinthian** base has two tori, two scotiæ, and two astragals; and the **Composite** base has a double astragal in the middle. The commonest type of base, however, is the **Attic** (*see* Fig. G23), consisting of two tori and a scotia, the top torus being smaller than the bottom, and the torus separated from the scotia by a fillet on the top of one and the bottom of the other. The Attic base appears in all Orders except the Greek Doric and the Tuscan, and even then it occasionally occurs in impure Tuscan Orders. Bases of **pilasters** are usually identical in profile to those of the columns used in the same portico or building, and may continue with the same profile when used as a continuous skirting or wall-base, but the bases of **antæ** may differ. Greek Ionic bases can sometimes be extremely elaborate, with many horizontal **flutes** called **reeds**, torus, or scotia mouldings, and fillets (*see* **Asiatic base**, **Attic base**, **Orders**). **2.** Lowest, thickest part of a wall, or the lowest visible element of a building, like a platform or podium, called the basement. The circular Ionic and Corinthian column-base is called **spira**, and can be confined to a single torus moulding, but the term can be extended to include the square plinth under the base proper, or the base of an anta, or its continuation as a wall-base or skirting.

base-block Plinth-block.

base-course Plinth.

basement Lowest storey of a building, whether partly above or below ground. For **basement-table**, *see* **stereobata**.

basilica Building divided into a **nave** flanked by two **aisles**, the former being wider and taller than the latter, with an **apse** at the end of the nave. Nave and aisles are divided from one another by means of **colonnades** or **arcades** above which is a **clerestorey** (Figs G27a–b).

basis *See* **base**.

basket 1. Bell of a **Corinthian capital**. **2. Corbeil**, a common form of ornament resembling a basket filled with fruit and flowers, often with **festoons**.

basket-weave Pattern resembling interwoven rushes, etc., found in **Rococo** decorations, especially porcelain and **stucco**.

Bassæ Order Greek Ionic Order, with a **capital** similar to the **angular** type, i.e. with **volutes** on all sides, but with a high curved join set under the **abacus** between volutes. It was developed by C.R. Cockerell

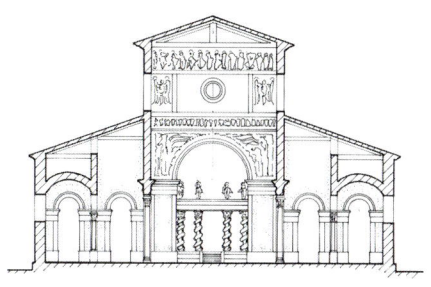

Fig. G27a *Hypothetical section through clerestoreyed nave and lean-to double aisles of the Constantinian Basilica of San Pietro, Rome (begun c.333), looking towards the high altar beyond the Solomonic columns seen through the great arch.*

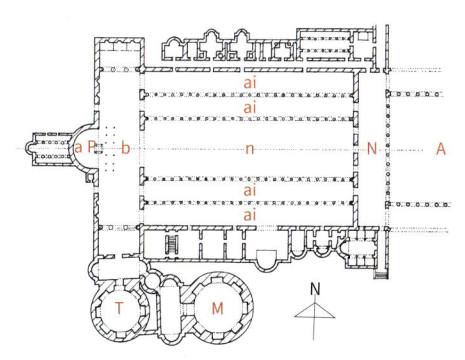

Fig. G27b *Plan of the huge Constantinian Basilica of San Pietro, Rome, consisting of nave (n) flanked by double aisles (ai) on either side; a transeptal arrangement in which stood the high altar on a bema (b) over the shrine of St Peter (P); an apse (a); a narthex (N) or entrance-porch; and an atrium (A). Attached to the church were circular mausolea of Honorius (later tomb of St Petronilla [T]) and another (later Santa Maria della Febbre [M]). This building type was the model for later mediæval churches, although orientation usually placed the high altar at the east end (JSC after an engraving of 1590).*

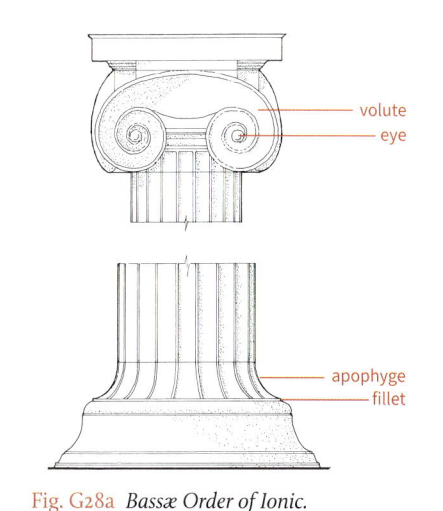

Fig. G28a *Bassæ Order of Ionic.*

from his studies of the Temple of Apollo Epicurius at Bassæ (Figs G28a–b).

SELECT GLOSSARY OF TERMS / 185

Fig. G28b *Corner of the portico of the Ashmolean Museum, Oxford (1841–5), by C.R. Cockerell, using a free interpretation of the Greek Ionic Order of the Temple of Apollo Epicurius, Bassæ (c.420 BC), with eight volutes, thus avoiding the problem at corners caused when the pulvinated ends of capitals are exposed. Cockerell's interpretation is free and unpedantic (note the drop at the corner between dentils), while the treatment of the frieze is extraordinarily rich, with an exquisite, almost Æolic, use of volute forms at the corner (JSC).*

bat's-wing 1. Half-**patera** resembling a semicircular fan, often occurring over 18th-century doors, niches, and windows, the radiating **flutes** being wide and wedge-shaped (Fig. G29). 2. **Fanlight** pattern (see Fig. G55a).

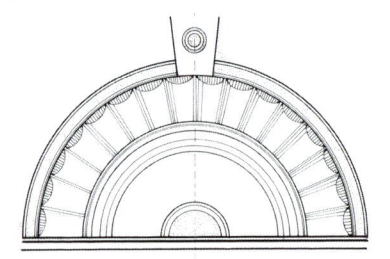

Fig. G29 *Bat's-wing by John Nash at Suffolk Place, London (1820s).*

batter Inclined face, applied to walls or openings that are sloping, thicker at the bottom than at the top, as in a **Vitruvian opening** (see Fig. G114).

bay Principal structural compartment or division of the architectural arrangement of a building, marked by **pilasters**, **piers**, or **columns**, or by the main **vaults** of the roof. It is incorrect to speak of the **façade** of a plain Georgian house as of 'five bays wide' if those 'bays' are not structural: 'five windows wide' would be more correct.

bay-leaf garland **Torus moulding** enriched with bound bay leaves (see **laurel**) (Fig. G30).

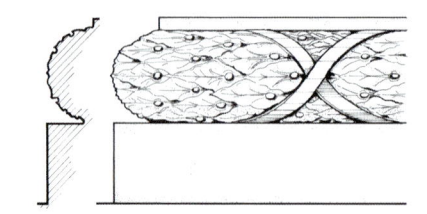

Fig. G30 *Bay-leaf garland.*

bay-window Window forming a bay or recess off a room, projecting out from the main wall in a rectangular, polygonal, or semicircular form. A bay, segmental on plan, is called a **bow**, and is associated with architecture of the **Regency** period (strictly 1810–20, but loosely applied to a period from the late 1790s to the accession of King William IV). A bay-window on an upper floor, cantilevered or corbelled out above the **naked** of the wall below, is called an **oriel**.

bead Small convex or semicircular **moulding**, often enriched. Any moulding with a convex section, an **astragal** (see Fig. 3.7).

bead-and-reel Enrichment of an **astragal** resembling a string of beads and reels (Fig. G31; see Figs 2.9 and 3.7).

Fig. G31 *Bead-and-reel.*

beak-moulding Moulding forming an **ovolo** or **ogee** with or without a **fillet** under it, followed by a hollow. It is found in the capital of an **anta** of the **Doric Order**.

bed-moulding Mouldings in the Orders under a **corona**, between it and the **frieze**, or any moulding under any projection.

bee Feature of **Renaissance** and **Neo-Classical** ornament, a symbol of order and industry.

beletion See **bolection**.

bell 1. Core of a **Corinthian capital**.
2. Bells hanging from many eaves are associated with **Chinoiserie**. 3. Term for **guttæ**.

bellflower See **husk**.

belvedere 1. **Turret**, **lantern**, or room built above a roof or on an eminence for the enjoyment of an agreeable view. 2. Summer-house, **gazebo**, or mirador, often in the form of a **temple**, or some other formal building, doubling as an **eye-catcher** in a garden.

bema Platform, **rostrum**, or raised floor in the **apse** of a **basilica** used as a sanctuary. The proto-transept of the building type based on the Constantinian Basilica of St Peter in Rome (see Figs G27a–b).

Biedermeier South-German and Austrian style of furniture and decoration from 1816 to around 1860, derived from French **Neo-Classical** and English **Regency** taste.

bifront Figure with two heads or faces looking in opposite directions. **Janus**. See **addorsed**.

bilection See **bolection**.

bipedales Large tiles used in bonding courses measuring two Roman feet each way, running at intervals through the wall.

bird's-beak Moulding, the section of which consists of an **ovolo** at the top under which is an **ogee** or hollow, forming a sharp **arris** at the junction of the two (Fig. G32).

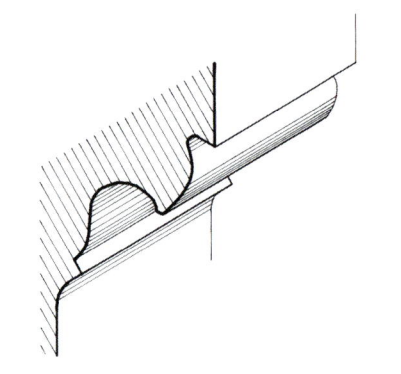

Fig. G32 *Bird's-beak moulding*

blackamoor Negroid (non-pejorative) heads or figures used in decoration.

blind Blank, as in **blind arcade**, where an arcade is engaged or fixed to a blank wall for ornamental purposes. A **blind window** is a sealed recess placed to create symmetry

186 / CLASSICAL ARCHITECTURE

in a **façade**, so any blank, blind, or dead wall has no apertures.

blind storey Heightened parapet or a fake storey, usually employed to conceal a roof or give an appearance of an **Attic storey**.

block 1. In Classical detailing, a rectangular plain element at the bottom of a door-architrave, which acts as a stop for the **architrave**, **skirt**, or **plinth**. 2. Most significant building in an architectural composition, e.g. a corps-de-logis flanked by **wings**. 3. One of a series of projecting blocks on architraves, **columns**, or **pilasters** as in a **Gibbs surround**: in such cases the architrave, etc., is said to be **banded** or **blocked**. *See* **band**. 4. Row or mass of connected buildings set against a street on the front, and bounded by other streets, often of mixed use.

block-cornice Italian Renaissance **entablature** with a series of plain undecorated **modillions** treated as **corbels** supporting a normal **cornice**, often with the **bed-mouldings** suppressed, or converted to a simple **architrave**.

blocking course 1. Plain course of stone surmounting a **cornice** at the top of a Classical building, which weights the cantilevered cornice-blocks and stabilises them. 2. Projecting course without mouldings at the base of a building, i.e. an unmoulded **plinth**. 3. Plain **band** or **string-course**.

boast To boast is to shape a stone into a simple form. Often stone carvings are boasted and built into position unfinished to be carved *in situ* at some later date. Any projection left rough on the face of a stone for the purpose of later enrichment is referred to as **boasted** or **bossage**.

bocage Densely designed leaves and flowers as backgrounds to figures, common in **Rococo** decorations.

boiserie Term commonly applied to 17th- or 18th-century timber panelling elaborately decorated with shallow-relief carvings, aka **wainscoting**.

bolection moulding Moulding that projects beyond the surface of a panel or frame, usually found in doors or in the panelling of rooms. It is used to cover the joint between the parts with different surface levels (*see* **panel mouldings**).

bolster, or **pillow** Return side of an **Ionic** **capital** resembling a horizontal **baluster**, or a **cushion** (*see* **baluster-side**, **Orders**).

bonnet top Scrolled **pediment**.

Borromini Order Variation on a **Composite capital** with **volutes** curving inwards, derived from capitals favoured by Francesco Borromini, and found in buildings of the 1730s by John and William Bastard in Blandford Forum, Dorset, in works by Thomas Archer, and in numerous **Baroque** and **Rococo** churches in Southern Germany (Fig. G33).

Fig. G33 *Borromini capital variant as employed by the Bastards of Blandford Forum, Dorset.*

bossage 1. Projecting stones laid in a wall to be carved later. 2. **Rusticated** work. 3. Can also be applied to **boasted** work.

bouleuterion Debating chamber for the senate in a Greek city-state.

boulle *See* **Buhl**.

boultin Moulding aka **egg** or **quarter-round**.

bow Projecting part of a building, semicircular or segmental on plan, as in **bow** or **bay window**.

bracketing Wooden frame to support large **cornices**. A **bracketed cornice** is one where the **modillions** have become transmogrified into large brackets, usually found in Victorian work.

brick In Antiquity bricks were often sun-dried (later *crudus*), but in later times they were baked (later *coctus* or *testaceus*). Burnt bricks used as facing to Roman concrete were called **tegulæ**.

boys and crown Crown supported by **putti** or **cherubs**.

Britannic Order Version of the **Corinthian Order** invented by Robert Adam, which incorporated winged lions and unicorns instead of the corner volutes, and the crown instead of the central **fleuron**. Because of its association with the House of Hanover, aka the **German Order**. *See* **Agricultural** and **American Order**.

buckler 1. Acrostolium (*see* Fig. G42). 2. **Pelta** ornament common on Classical **friezes** (esp. the **Roman Doric Order** according to Vignola [*see* Fig. G52b]), consisting of a wide shield-like form with its extremities returning as heads or scrolls.

bucrane, bucranium (*pl.* **bucranes, bucrania**) Carved representation of a festooned or garlanded ox-head or -skull (or **ægicrane** if ram or goat), garlanded, found in the **metopes** of the **Roman Doric frieze**, often alternating with **rosettes** or **pateræ** (Fig. G34; *see* Figs 2.11c and 2.15a).

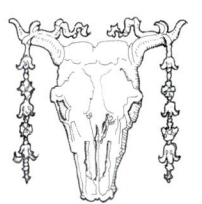

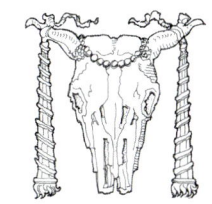

Fig. G34 *Bucranium (left) hung with bellflower or husk garlands; (right) hung with inverted flambeaux.*

bud In the **Corinthian capital**, the bud-like form at the top of the stalks out of which the **volutes** emerge.

Buhl work Aka **boule** or **boulle**, it consists of thin fretwork patterning of one or more metals (usually brass but sometimes other metals) inlaid on a ground, with polished tortoiseshell veneer surrounding the metal.

bull's eye Circular aperture for the admission of light or air, aka **œil-de-bœuf**, commonly elliptical in form.

cable moulding Moulding resembling twisted rope.

cabling Convex **mouldings** set within the **flutes** of **Classical columns** or **pilasters**, nearly filling up the hollow flutes to about one-third the total height of the shaft. Flutings thus treated are said to be **cabled** (*see* Fig. G90a). Unknown in Ancient Greek Orders.

cabriole leg Carved leg with feet in the shape of claws, paws, or hooves, based on the **monopodia** of Roman tripods.

caduceus (*pl.* **caducei**) Winged staff entwined with serpents (*see* Fig. G1).

cæmenticium Aka **structura cæmenticia**, **opus structile**, or **cæmentum**, it denotes Roman concrete.

caisson Sunken panel or **coffer** of various shapes, symmetrically disposed in **ceilings**, **vaults**, or **soffits** generally (*see* Figs G80, G87, and 4.21).

calathus As **campana**.

caldarium (*pl.* **caldaria**) That part of **thermæ** containing hot baths.

calotte Low segmental dome of the Pantheon type, like a clerical skull-cap, on a circular base (*see* Figs G87, 5.39a, and 5.66).

calyx (*pl.* **calyces**) Ornament resembling a cup-like (properly **calix**) flower, as in the **Corinthian capital**, or on the neck of the **Roman Doric capital**.

camara or **camera** Ceiling curved or **camerated** to suggest vaulted construction.

came Cast, extruded, or milled lead rods with an **H**-shaped section, used in **leaded lights** to frame and secure panes of glass.

campana Bell-shaped (**campaniform** or **campanular**) core of the **Corinthian capital**.

campanile (*pl.* **campanili**) Italian bell-tower.

campanula (*pl.* **campanulæ**) Miniature bell-like form, e.g. conic **guttæ** of the **Doric Order**.

canal 1. Flute in the **shaft** of a **column** or **pilaster**. 2. Spiral channel (**canalis**) flanked by small convex **mouldings** leading from the **eye** following the revolutions of the **volute**, and carrying over to the other volute between the **abacus** and **echinus** of the **Ionic capital**.

canalis See **canal**.

canaliculus (*pl.* **canaliculi**) Channel or groove on a **triglyph** of a **Doric Order**.

canephora (*pl.* **canephoræ**) See **caryatid(e)** (*see* Fig. G36).

cannon Often found in trophies, or the form used in bollards or parts of furniture of the **Neo-Classical** style.

canopic jar Ornament in the form of ancient Egyptian jars, with humanoid lids.

cap Capital, **cope**, **cornice**, or uppermost crowning member. A cornice on a **pedestal** is called its **cap**.

capital Chapiter, **cap**, **head**, or topmost member of an **anta**, **colonnette**, **column**, **pilaster**, **pier**, etc., set above the **shaft**, defined by distinct architectural treatment, often ornamented. The Æolic capital is an early form of **Ionic** (*see* Fig. G7). Capitals of the **Tuscan** and **Roman Doric Orders** are similar, and consist of an **abacus**, **ovolo**, **neck**, and **astragal**: the Roman Doric Order has more elaboration of the **mouldings**, and the necks are sometimes enriched with **rosettes** (*see* Fig. G52b); the Greek Doric capital has a plain **abacus**, a cushion-like **echinus** under which are **annulets**, and a groove called the **hypotrachelium** below (*see* Fig. G52a); the **Ionic** capital has coiled or scrolled elements aka **volutes**, sometimes placed between the abacus and the ovolo moulding, and sometimes springing separately from the ovolo (front and side faces of volutes normally are not the same [*see* Fig. G13), except when four volutes are set diagonally, i.e. 135° to the plane of the entablature [*see* Fig. G14]); the **Corinthian** capital (about one-and-a-sixth diameters high) is a bell-shaped object with two rows of eight **acanthus** leaves (*Acanthus spinosus* in Greek work and *Acanthus mollis* in Roman) rising above the astragal – from between the leaves of the upper row rise eight **stalks** or **caulicoli** each surmounted by a **calyx** from which emerge volutes or **helices** carrying the 'corners' of the concave-sided abacus and the central ornaments (*see* Figs. G46a–b) (a variation has one row of acanthus leaves with palm leaves above, no caulicoli or volutes, and a moulded **abacus**, square on plan, as at the Tower of the Winds in Athens [*see* Fig. G85]); and the **Composite capital** (a Roman Order) has two rows of acanthus leaves over an astragal with, instead of the caulicoli, eight Ionic volutes set at the corners (i.e. at 135° to the plane of the entablature) and **egg-and-dart** and **bead-and-reel** (*see* Fig. G43) between them. The Composite Order, a late Roman form, is not described by Vitruvius, was identified by Alberti, and was designated by Serlio as the fifth and grandest of all the Orders (although there are actually eight Orders, with many more variations).

capreolus Rafter in a roof or similar structure, but it also seems to imply a support or a strut.

caprice Decorative vignette of the **Rococo** period showing architectural ruins and emblematic figures.

cardo Main north–south street of a Roman camp, fortress, or town.

carolitic, **carolytic** Properly **corollitic**, a column with foliated **shaft** embellished with branches and leaves winding around it in spirals.

carrel 1. Alcove, or space off a larger room, used as a study. 2. Bay window. 3. Pane of glass secured by **cames** in a leaded **light**.

cartouch, cartouche 1. Modillion, usually internal, or under the **eaves** of a building, as opposed to modillions of the standard Classical **cornice**. 2. Term more commonly applied to a decorative tablet or frame for inscriptions in the form of a scroll or curling piece of parchment (Fig. G35).

Fig. G35 Baroque cartouche, possibly by Jasper Latham, commemorating Sir Walter Curl, Bart., in the 13th-century south chapel (sometimes referred to as a 'transept') of the Church of St Peter, Soberton, Hampshire.

caryatid(e) (*pl.* **caryatid(e)s** Draped, straight, standing female figure (**cora**), on its head an enriched **astragal** and square **abacus**, used instead of **columns** for the support of an **entablature** (Fig. G36; *see* Figs 2.8c–d and 6.9b). The term is also given to any support carved in the form of a human figure, but is not, strictly speaking, correct. Male figures, usually heroic in scale and proportion, and 'bent' under the weight of what they are carrying are called **atlantes**: if the male figures are unbowed and straight, they are **telamons**

Fig. G36 *(Left) caryatid(e) from the Erechtheion, Athens; (right) canephora after Piranesi*

or **telamones**. Figures of young draped women with **baskets** on their heads instead of astragal, **ovolo**, and abacus, also used instead of columns, are called **canephoræ**. **Herms** are portions of figures on quadrangular pedestals, often tapering downwards, whether carrying a weight or not (*see* Fig. G69), while **terms** (*see* Figs G108 and 5.52a) are pedestals (often inverted obelisks or parts of obelisks) which merge into the torsos and busts of humanoid or other figures. The word 'caryatid' derives from the belief by Vitruvius that the female figures of the Erechtheion represent Carian prisoners (*see* **atlas, canephora, telamon**).

case of a door   Doorcase, meaning the whole of an elaborate Classical frame to a doorway, usually of timber (*see* Fig. G44c).

casement   1. **Scotia** or deep concave **moulding**. 2. Window-frame with hinged or pivoted opening-lights or **sashes** hung from a vertical member of the fixed frame (Fig. G37).

casino   Small country house, decorative building, lodge, pleasure-pavilion, or summer-house in the grounds of a large country house.

castellated   With battlements (crenels, crenelles), turrets, etc., to give a building the appearance of a castle. The castle style was a type of 18th-century architecture intended to create the impression of being a fortified dwelling, even though the essential elements of the architecture were Classical.

catacomb   Underground public cemetery with rectangular niches (**loculi**) for the entombment of bodies.

catafalque   1. Temporary or permanent structure, decorated and usually draped, representing a tomb or **cenotaph**, and used in funeral ceremonies. 2. Altar-like structures on which coffins are placed in mortuary chapels, etc.

catenary   Curve described by anything hung from two points on the same horizontal plane (*see* Fig. G57), e.g. a **festoon** of chain-links, often used on prisons (*see* Figs 6.28a–b).

cathetus   1. Axis of an **Ionic** volute-eye. 2. Axis of any cylinder or drum, e.g. a column-shaft or colonnette.

caulicoli, caulicolæ, caulicoles   In the Corinthian capital the eight stalks that spring from the upper row of **acanthus** leaves (*see* **Corinthian Order**).

cavædium   Cavum ædium, or main room of a Roman house, aka **atrium**, and partly open to the sky by means of the **compluvium**, with an **impluvium** or tank of water in the centre.

cavetto (*pl.* cavetti)   Hollow **moulding**, principally used in **cornices**, with as profile the quadrant of a circle.

cavum ædium   See **cavædium**

cell   Part of a **temple** enclosed within the walls, otherwise the **naos** or **cella**.

cemetery   Any place where the dead are interred or deposited.

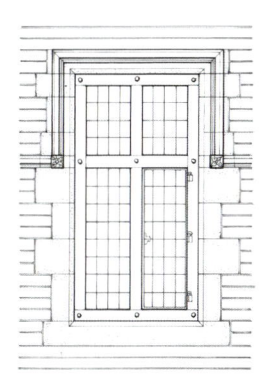

Fig. G37 *Seventeenth-century oak cross-casement with leaded lights and one wrought-iron opening sash, set in an aperture in a brick wall with stone dressings, protected by a hood-mould terminating in label-stops.*

cenotaph   Empty tomb, or a monument to commemorate a person or persons buried elsewhere.

cerquate   Arrangement of oak leaves and acorns.

chaînes   Vertical strips of pier-like masonry (often **rusticated**) of blocks of alternating width resembling **quoins** associated with door- or window-surrounds.

chains   Symbols of enslavement, usually associated with the Vices, or used in association with marine decorations, or (especially) with prisons.

chair-rail   The upper moulding of a **dado** around a room to prevent the backs of chairs from damaging the walls or their coverings. It corresponds to the **cornice** of a **pedestal** (*see* Fig. G61).

chamfering   A finish in which right-angled edges are cut off at 45° often to prevent damage, or in association with decoration, such as **rustication**.

chandelle   Decoration of lower parts of fluted columns or pilasters with plain or enriched **beading**. A form of **cabling**.

channel   As **canalis**.

chapiter, chaptrel   1. Capital. 2. Impost.

chaplet moulding   Decorative moulding resembling a string of beads, as on an **astragal**, aka **pearling** (Fig. G38).

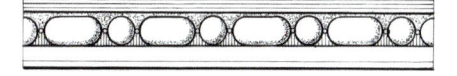

Fig. G38 *Chaplet moulding, aka pearling*

charged   A **frieze** is **charged** with ornament on it, so the term implies the dependence of one part of a work of architecture upon another.

cherub   Infantile, slightly unwholesome, podgy, male figure, winged, usually associated with clouds, funerary monuments, etc., in **Baroque** sculpture. Cherubs, aka **Cupids**, may be given to overt displays of grief. They should not be confused with **putti** (*sing.* putto) (wingless little boys, otherwise indistinguishable from cherubs).

chevron   The **zigzag**: very fluid chevron forms are called **bargello**.

chimera Creature with mane, head, and legs of a lion, the tail of a dragon, the body of a goat, and the wings of an eagle.

Chinoiserie Style of art, decoration, and architecture that evoked Cathay, reaching its finest flowering in the 18th century (Fig. G39b), associated with the **Rococo**. A Chinese fret or lattice incorporates diagonal members (Fig. G39a).

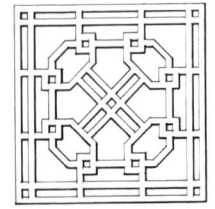

Fig. G39a *Chinese fret (Chinoiserie).*

Fig. G39b *Tea pavilion in the Sanssouci gardens at Potsdam (1754–7), designed by King Friedrich II of Prussia and Johann Gottfried Büring, a fine example of Chinoiserie, complete with magot seated under a parasol on the roof (JSC).*

ciborium (*pl.* **ciboria**) Domed canopy resembling an inverted cup, supported on columns and arches and set over a Christian altar (*see* Fig. 4.4).

cill, sill, sole, sule Horizontal member forming the bottom of a window, door, or other opening, designed to throw water away.

cimbia 1. Band or **fillet** around a column-shaft. 2. **Cornice** or band formed of fillets.

cincture Ring, list, or **fillet** that receives the **apophyge** at the top and bottom of a column- or pilaster-shaft (*see* **Orders**).

cinerarium lid Neo-Classical capping for gate-piers, **sarcophagi**, etc., often with **horns** (*see* Fig. G70) resembling **Antique** covers of receptacles (**ash-chests**) for cremated remains (Fig. G40).

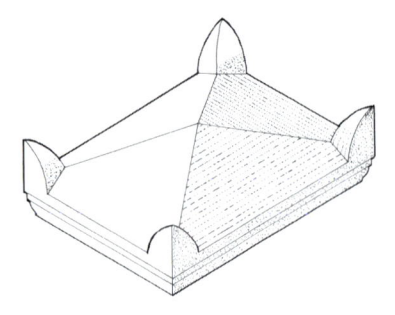

Fig. G40 *Cinerarium lid with cat's-ear horns, a common capping feature for piers, gateposts, etc.*

cinquecento Sixteenth-century Italian Renaissance art and architecture, or a later revival of that style.

cippus (*pl.* **cippi**) Small, low **column**, usually rectangular on plan, used in **Antiquity** as a direction-post or boundary-stone, sometimes employed as a grave-marker, e.g. **stele**, or as the **pedestal** for a **herm**.

circus 1. Long, rectangular space with semicircular ends in which horse or chariot races were held by the Romans. 2. Any circular or elliptical space surrounded by buildings, as in the Circus in Bath.

civic crown Garland of acorns and oak leaves used in architectural ornament.

Classical architecture Based on ancient Greek and Roman precedents, or the architecture of **Antiquity** itself. In the 18th century a scholarly return to Classical principles was led by William Kent, Lord Burlington, and Colen Campbell, who revered the works of Palladio and Inigo Jones: this movement was known as **Palladianism**, and dominated significant architecture for most of the century. Studies of the buildings of Antiquity, notably those of Rome, Greece, Spalato (Split), Palmyra, Herculaneum, and Pompeii led to the **Neo-Classical** movement, of which the **Greek Revival** was an important element.

claw Claws can appear at the bases of **herms**, **terms**, and **cabrioles**, and are any terminating figure resembling a claw.

clerestorey Any window, row of windows, or openings, in the upper part of a building, notably above the nave arcades and aisle roofs in a basilican building.

clipeus Disc-like ornament fixed to an **architrave** or **frieze** in Roman architecture.

Coade stone Artificial cast stone manufactured in London from the 1770s onwards, and used for decorative keystones, quoins, statuary, etc.

cockle stair Winding stair.

coffer **Caisson** or **lacuna**, i.e. deep panel sunk in a **ceiling**, **dome**, **soffit**, or **vault**, often decorated in the centre with a stylised flower or similar embellishment. Such sunken square compartments, often emulated in stone, concrete, or plaster, are called coffers (*see* Figs G80 and G87).

coin moulding Repeated series of overlapping discs (Fig. G41), not unlike **guilloche** (*see* Fig. G68).

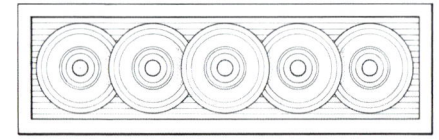

Fig. G41 *Coin moulding or money pattern.*

collarino Cylindrical part of the **capital** of the **Tuscan** and **Roman Doric Orders**, lying between the **annulets** under the **ovolo** and the **astragal**. It is termed the **neck**, and is the **hypotrachelium** of Vitruvius (*see* **Orders**).

colonnade Row of columns with entablature: if four, the range is called **tetrastyle**; if six, **hexastyle**; if eight, **octastyle**; if ten, **decastyle**, etc. When a colonnade stands before a building it is a **portico**, and if it surrounds a building it is a **peristyle**. Colonnades are further described in terms of the spaces between columns: **intercolumniation** is the distance between columns measured from the lower parts of the shafts in multiples of the diameter of a column. The main types of intercolumniation as defined by Vitruvius are **pycnostyle**, where columns are 1½ diameters apart; **systyle** (2 diameters apart); **eustyle** (2¼ diameters apart); **diastyle** (3 diameters apart); and **aræostyle** (greater than 3 diameters apart [up to a maximum of 5]), the last only used with the **Tuscan Order**. In Classical architecture, two columns between **antæ** would be described as **distyle in antis**: a front portico of four columns standing before the antæ is **prostyle tetrastyle**; and a building with four columns standing before the antæ at the front and rear is described as **amphi-prostyle tetrastyle**. A circular building with columns all round it is **peripteral** circular, while the term

peripteral octastyle means a rectangular building surrounded by columns, with eight at each end forming porticoes. **Pseudo-peripteral** means that columns are joined (**engaged**) to the walls and are not freestanding. To say that a colonnade is **dipteral** means that there are double rows of columns, so **dipteral octastyle** means a building surrounded by 2 rows of columns, with a **portico** of 16 columns at each end, 8 columns wide (*see* Figs G91 and G107a–b).

colonnette Small **baluster**, **column**, or slender circular **shaft**.

Colossal Order Order where the columns or pilasters rise from the ground or a plinth more than one storey, aka **Giant Order**.

Colosseum Huge **amphitheatre** built by Vespasian in Rome.

columbarium (*pl.* **columbaria**) Dovecote, or building with holes or **niches** in the walls, such as a structure for the reception of urns or ash-chests (**cineraria**) containing cremated remains, so called from the resemblance to the niches for pigeons or doves.

columella (*pl.* **columellæ**) **Baluster** or **colonnette**.

columen Ridge-beam of a gabled roof resting in front on the **tympanum** of the primitive **Tuscan Order**. It was therefore supported on a wall or on other timbers resting on the **trabes compactiles** or **architraves** resting on the widely spaced columns, and was cantilevered out over the line of the **colonnade** to the same projection as the **mutuli**, or secondary beams. The rafters, or **cantherii**, were supported on the **columen** and on the mutuli at the sides, producing a very deep pedimented space with overhanging roof at the ends (*see* Figs G111b–c).

column Upright member, usually circular on plan, but also polygonal or square, supporting a lintel. It consists of a **base**, **shaft**, and **capital**, except in the case of the **Greek Doric Order** which has no base. It must not be confused with a **pier**, which is more massive, and is **never** called a **pillar**.

columna cochlis Monumental **triumphal column** such as the Antonine or Trajanic examples in Rome, with an internal spiral staircase and an external spiral band of continuous sculpture.

Fig. G42 *Columna rostrata (rostral column).*

columna rostrata (*pl.* **columnæ rostratæ**) Tuscan column, usually on a pedestal, its shaft decorated with a sculpted bow (**rostrum**) of an Antique Roman warship, erected to celebrate naval victories. It was a type revived in the **Neo-Classical** period (Fig. G42).

columniation Arrangement of columns.

compactilis Term meaning fastened together, as **trabes compactiles**, or rafters.

compartment Panel or **coffer** in a ceiling.

compluvium Opening in a roof to allow sun and rain to enter, as in the **atrium** of a Roman house.

Composite Order Roman Order, aka **Compound Order**, mixing features of **Ionic** and **Corinthian Orders**. The grandest of all the Orders, it resembles the Corinthian Order except that the capitals have Ionic volutes and **echini** instead of the Corinthian **caulicoli** and **scrolls** (*see* **Orders**) (Fig. G43).

concatenation Union of composition by chaining parts together, as with separate architectural elements (each with its own roof and separate composition) in a long **façade**, the fronts being brought forward or recessed, also called **staccato** composition (*see* Figs G84c–d).

conch, concha Half dome of an **apse**, or a **niche** with a semi-dome, sometimes carved to resemble a shell, hence the term.

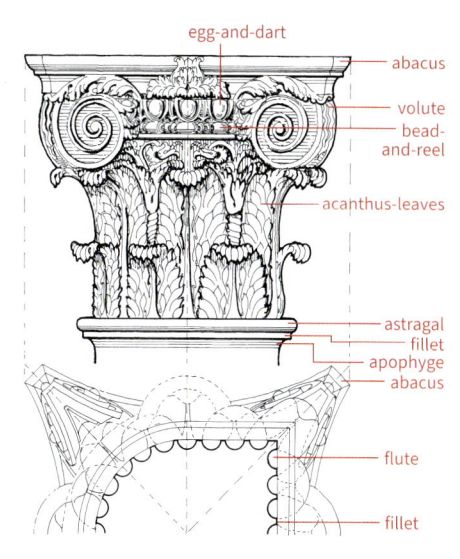

Fig. G43 *Capital of the Composite Order, with plan and elevation of circular and square examples (JSC after Langley [1745]).*

concrete, structura cæmenticia, cæmenticium, opus structile Names for Roman concrete. Broken stones or bricks were laid in courses and each course, when laid, was filled with liquid mortar made from lime and volcanic dust.

congé Echinus or quarter-round, and the **cavetto**. The former is the **swelling congé**, and the latter the **hollow congé**. Congé is the outward curve, **apophyge**, or **scape** connecting the **shaft** of a Classical **column** to the **fillets** over the **base** and under the **astragal** beneath the **capital**.

congelation Representation of water or icicles in **frosted rustication** and **grottoes**.

console *ſ*-shaped ornamented **bracket** or **corbel**, with a greater height than projection in the vertical position (aka **ancon**, **crossette**, **parotis**, or **truss**). Consoles can be placed vertically, with the smaller scroll at the base, and can support a bust or urn, or, if placed on either side of a doorcase,

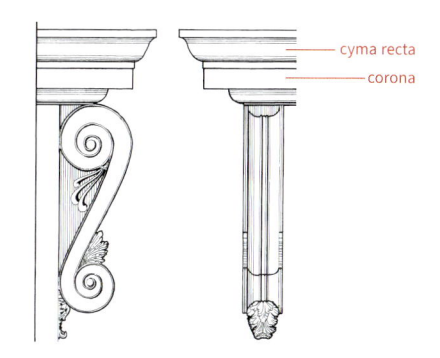

Fig. G44a *Console, front and side elevations.*

SELECT GLOSSARY OF TERMS / 191

the **cornice** over. If laid horizontally (the larger scroll nearer the wall or vertical face) it becomes a **modillion**, the expression of a **cantilever** to carry a **balcony**, cornice, etc. Consoles also occur as wedge-shaped **keystones**, aka **ancones** (Figs G44a–c; see Figs G94b and G106a. See also Figs 2.14a–b and d, 2.14f–g, and 2.16a–b).

contractura   Tapered diminution of a column-shaft from top to bottom (so wider at the top), without **entasis**, as in ancient Crete.

cope, coping   Topmost course (**capping**) of a wall, etc., formed of cap-stones or coping-stones to throw off the water (Fig. G45).

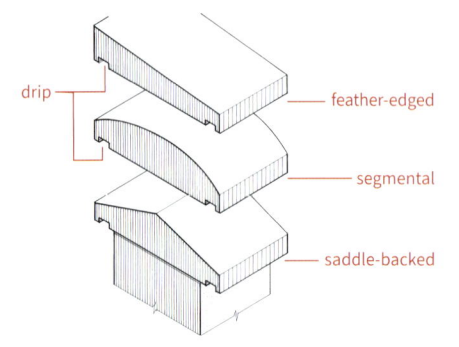

Fig. G45 *Three types of cope or copings.*

coquillage   Carved representation of shell forms, e.g. at **niche**-heads, in **grottoes**, or in **rocaille** decorations.

cora (*pl.* **coræ**)   Column in the form of a draped young woman, aka **caryatid**(e) (*see* Fig. G36).

corbeil   **1.** Carved basket with sculptured flowers and fruit. **2.** Bell-shaped core (**campana**) of the **Corinthian** capital. **3.** Basket-capital on the heads of **canephoræ** (*see* Fig. G36).

corbel   Projecting stone or timber support, or cantilever, which can be a **modillion**. Corbelling is the bridging of an opening or the roofing of a space by means of a series of overlapping horizontal courses, without using the principle of the arch.

Fig. G44b *Console, crossette, or truss. To draw it, using dividers, break down the desired height into 11 equal parts, then divide the upper 3 into 7 parts. Make ne the perpendicular line of the projection of the upper volute 8 of those latter parts out from the wall. Divide the 3rd and 4th larger vertical parts together into 7 parts, making the projection of the lower volute equal to 8 of those parts: the console will also be 8 of those parts wide. The centre of the upper eye is 4.5 and the centre of the lower is 3.5 relevant parts in from the furthest projections. Each eye is 1 relevant part in diameter, and the larger circumference of the outer eye is 1.5 relevant parts in radius. Set out the diagonal square in each smaller eye, and subdivide this square as shown, so points 1–8 are the centres to describe the volute. The face of the console has fillets each 1 lower part wide; the central astragal with its 2 fillets (A) is 1 part wide; and the cyma recta mouldings are each 2.5 parts wide (Langley [1745]).*

Fig. G44c *Classical doorcases, both with consoles. Above the architrave on the left is a suggestion of a Doric detail, with guttæ set under the raised panel. On the right is a festoon, and there are two scrolls. Note the system of proportion, again set out using dividers (Langley [1745]).*

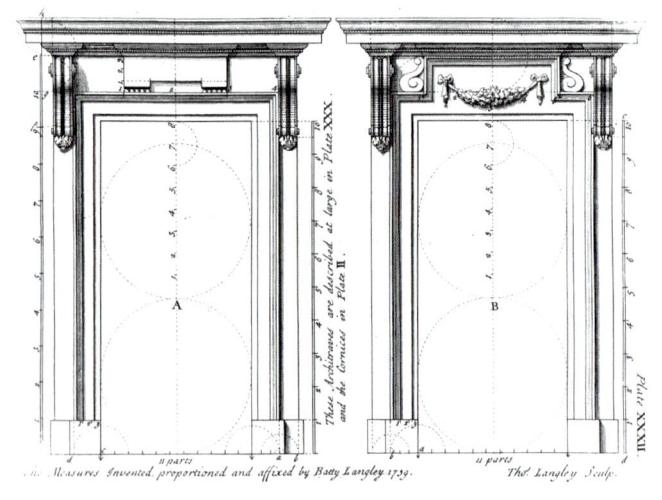

192 / CLASSICAL ARCHITECTURE

Corinthian Order Lavish **Order of architecture** used by the Greeks and Romans, and the most festive of the Greek Orders, associated with Beauty (Fig. G46a). The distinctive feature is the **capital**, which is about one-and-one-sixth diameters high, and very ornate, with **acanthus** leaves and **caulicoli**, each of which is surmounted by a **calyx** from which emerge **volutes** or **helices** supporting the **abacus** and the central foliate ornaments on each face of the abacus. Originally only the capital differentiated the Corinthian from the **Ionic Order** but in Roman work the Corinthian entablature became rich in carved ornament (Fig. G46b). The **architrave**, for example, often had many decorated **mouldings**, while the **frieze** was sometimes enriched with acanthus scroll and figured ornament. **Cornices** had sculptured **coffers** on the **soffits**, and elaborately ornamented **modillions**. Much **egg-and-dart**, **bead-and-reel**, **dentil**, and florid decoration was in evidence. **Shafts** were fluted or plain, but in the Greek version of the Order they were fluted. Abaci have moulded concave faces, meeting at points, or with chamfered 'corners' over the volutes. A simpler form of the capital, found at the Tower of the Winds in Athens, has one row of acanthus leaves over which is a row of palm leaves, but with this version the abacus is square on plan (*see* Figs G85 and 6.8a). The term Corinthian also seems to suggest an arrangement with more than four columns associated with the **cavum ædium** (**cavædium**), or inner court of a house, and supporting the roof which allowed rain to drain through the open centre (**compluvium**) into the tank or pool (**impluvium**).

corn Corn and corn cobs were introduced to **Neo-Classical** forms of the **Corinthian Order** in the USA, the so-called **American Order** (*see* Fig. 6.23c).

cornice 1. Uppermost division, consisting of several members, of a Classical **entablature**. 2. Crowning projecting moulded horizontal top of a building (if very large and topping the main **façade** of, e.g., a *palazzo*, it is termed *cornicione*). It also can crown a wall, a **moulding**, or **pedestal** (where it is termed **cap**). 3. **Crown-moulding** is a cornice at the junction of a wall and ceiling, similar in profile to a cornice on an entablature. 4. An **eaves-cornice** occurs where a roof overhangs a wall and forms eaves with a Classical profile. 5. On the sloping sides of **pediments** the cornices are **raking**.

6. A **block-cornice** has plain blocks instead of decorated modillions projecting from rudimentary bed-mouldings (*see* **Orders**).

cornicione Large elaborate crowning entablature of an Italian *palazzo*, imported by Barry and used on several buildings in the astylar **Italianate** *palazzo* style (*see* Figs 4.8a and 4.14a).

cornucopia Horn of Plenty, or Goat's Horn, overflowing with corn, fruit, and flowers, often found in Classical decoration.

corona (*pl.* **coronæ**) Part of a Classical cornice, called the **drip** or **larmier**, above the **bed-moulding** and below the **cymatium**, with a broad vertical face, usually of considerable projection, with its underside recessed and forming a drip protecting the **frieze** below it (*see* **Orders**).

corsa Plain **platband**, **square fascia**, or **string-course**, its height greater than its projection.

cortile (*pl.* **cortili**) Internal area (**cortis**) or courtyard of a *palazzo*, often with arcades or colonnades around it, rising several storeys, and open to the sky (as in various Florentine *palazzi*), or roofed (e,g, Barry's Reform Club, London [1837–41]) (*see* Figs 4.8b–4.11a, 4.13a, and 4.14b).

cottage orné Small rustic-style cottage of the **Picturesque** genre.

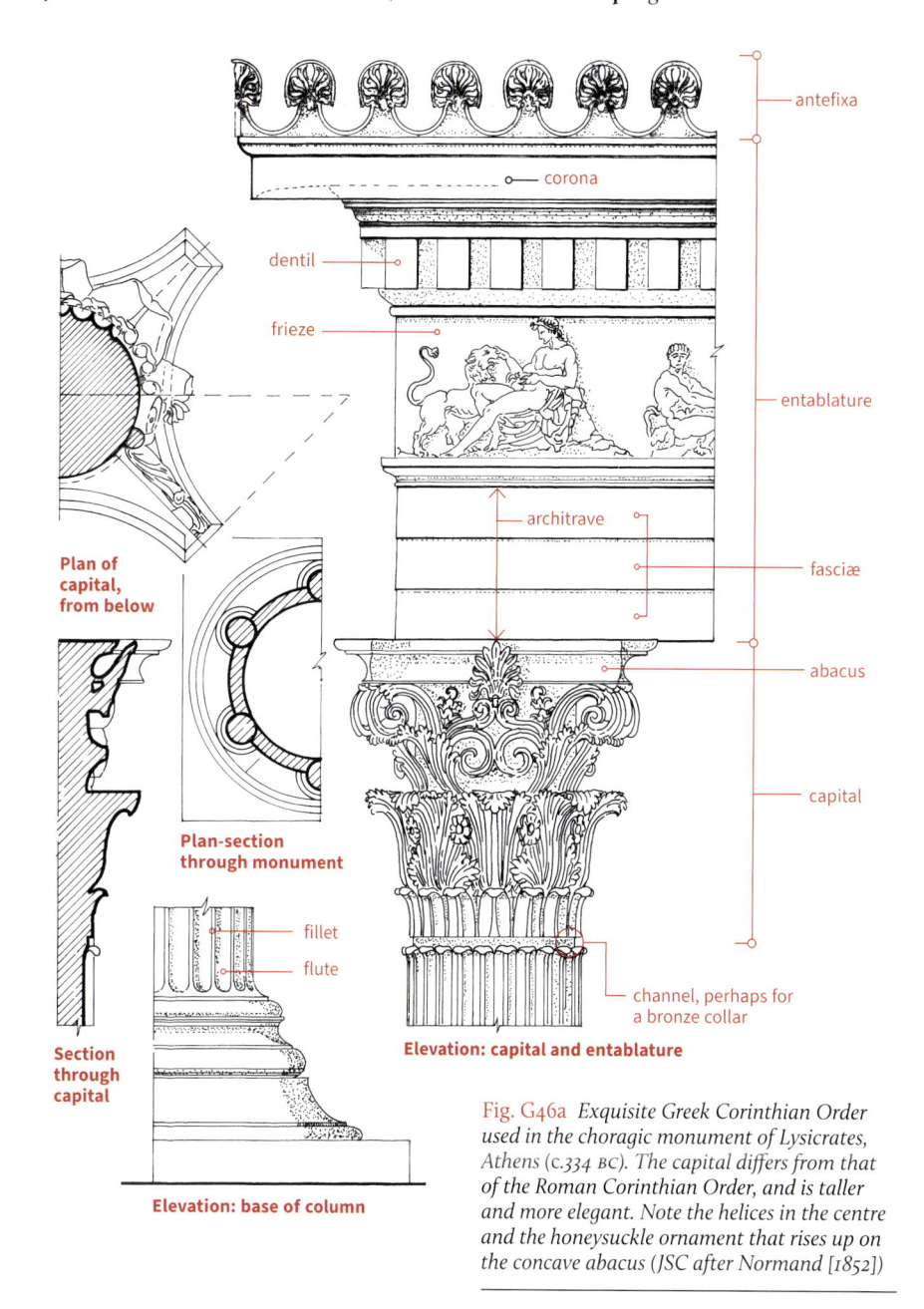

Fig. G46a Exquisite Greek Corinthian Order used in the choragic monument of Lysicrates, Athens (c.334 BC). The capital differs from that of the Roman Corinthian Order, and is taller and more elegant. Note the helices in the centre and the honeysuckle ornament that rises up on the concave abacus (JSC after Normand [1852])

SELECT GLOSSARY OF TERMS / 193

crepidoma Stepped base (**crepis**, or **crepido**) of a Greek temple (usually with three steps), the topmost platform surface of which was termed **stylobate**. These steps were usually too high to be used as a stair, so ramps or intermediate steps were introduced on main axes for use (see **Greek Orders**).

crescent 1. Series of buildings planned on the arc of a circle. 2. Attribute of Artemis-Diana-Isis.

crest Device fixed to the top of a helmet at the base of which is a coronet or wreath.

crinkle-crankle Type of garden-wall that on plan consists of alternate convex and concave curves in a continuous wavy **serpentine** line. A tall wall (one or two bricks more than the height of a man) built in a straight line without buttresses would be unstable, but the undulating plan creates a stiffening and buttressed effect making the crinkle-crankle an economical and stable structure.

criosphinx See **sphinx**.

croisée French window (see **window**).

cross Ornamental form consisting essentially of two straight or nearly straight members set at 90° to each other, one vertical and the other horizontal, but also with many variations (Fig. G47).

crossette 1. Projection called **ear**, **elbow**, **knee**, **lug**, or **shoulder** on each side of the top of a Classical architrave or casing around a door- or window-opening, at the junction of the **jamb** and **lintel**, where the **supercilium** projects beyond the **antepagments**, and the mouldings return (see

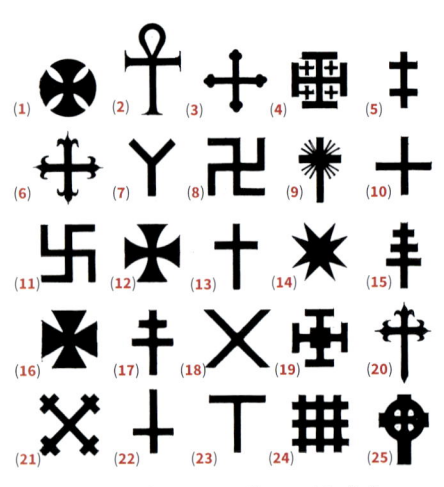

Fig. G47 *Various types of cross: (1) alisée patée or pattée; (2) ancient Egyptian Ankh; (3) botonnée or clover-leaf; (4) Crusader's or Jerusalem: if the four minor crosses are removed, it becomes potent; (5) double; (6) fleurée or fleury or flory: with the centre-leaf of each arm omitted, it is moline; (7) forked; (8) fylfot or cramponed or swastika; (9) glory or rayonnant; (10) Greek; (11) potent rotated or Hakenkreuz; (12) iron or Eiserneskreuz of Prussia, aka formée; (13) Latin or Passion; (14) Maltese; (15) Papal; (16) patée formée; (17) patriarchal; (18) St Andrew's saltire; (19) St Chad's; (20) St James's; (21) St Julian's; (22) St Peter's; (23) St Anthony's or Tau; (24) triparted; (25) Celtic or wheel-head.*

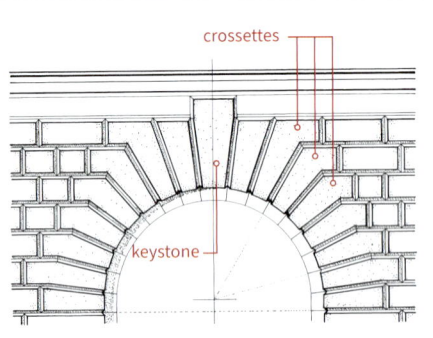

Fig. G48 **V**-*jointed masonry with crossettes.*

Figs G21a–b, G98b, and G114). **2. Console** set on each flank at the top of an **architrave** around an aperture, supporting a **cornice** (see Figs G21a, G44a–c, G94b, and G106a). **3.** Ledged or joggled **voussoir**, as in **rusticated ashlar** in an **arch**, which rests on the voussoir below, thus strengthening the construction (Fig. G48; see Fig. G20a).

crown of an arch The highest point, aka **extrados** (see **arch**) (see Fig. G20a).

C-scroll and **ʃ-scroll** Elements found in **Rococo** decorations, usually as parts of frames (see Fig. G95).

cubiculum (*pl.* **cubicula**) Large chamber in a public **catacomb**.

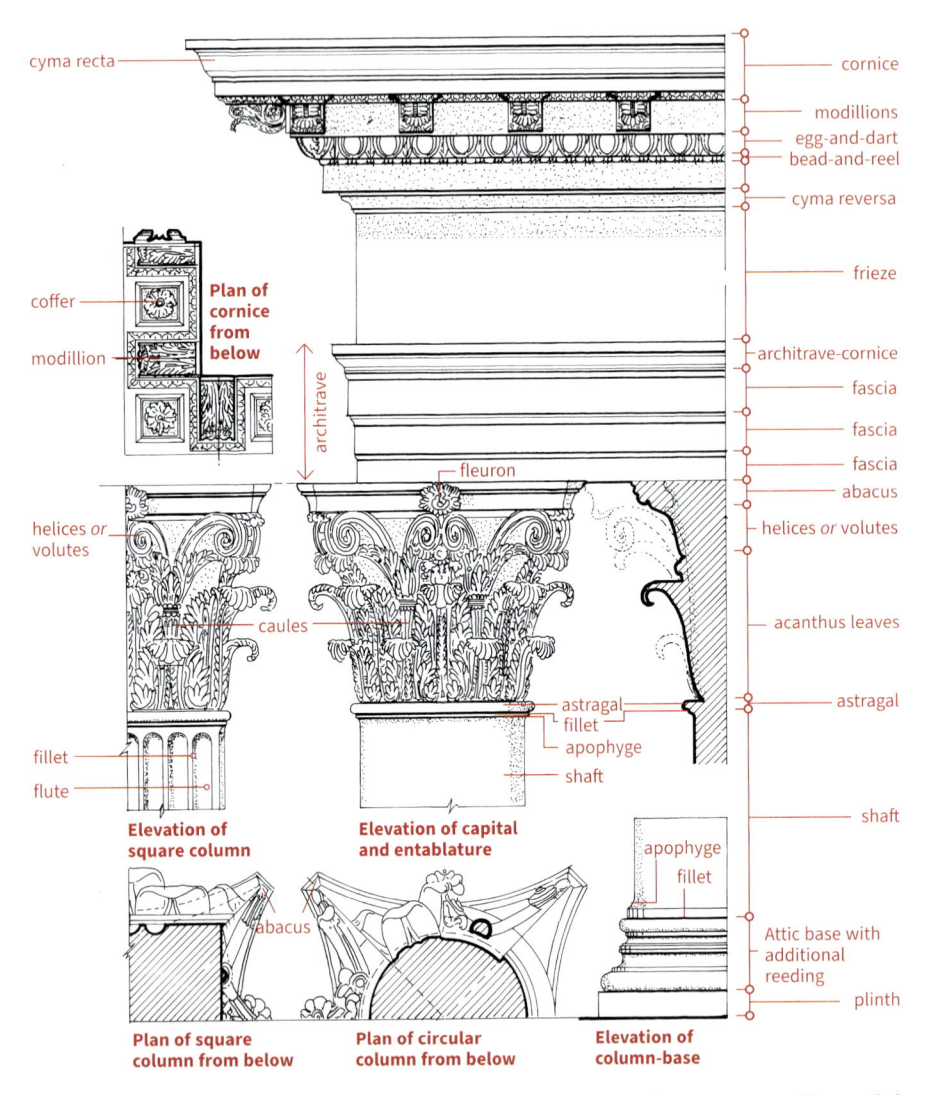

Fig. G46b *Lavish Roman Corinthian Order from the portico of the Pantheon, Rome, possibly recycled from an early 1st-century temple, and re-erected in the early 2nd century (JSC after Normand [1852]).*

cullot   String of **husks** or **bellflowers**, or the end of a **festoon** (see Figs G34, G71, and G77).

cuneus   **1.** Wedge-shaped section of the seating of a theatre bounded by stairs and passages. **2. Voussoir**.

Cupid   Similar to a **putto**, but winged, often armed with bow and arrows. A **cherub**.

cupola   **1.** Bowl-shaped roof or vault over a circular, elliptical, or polygonal plan. **2.** Underside or **soffit** of **1**. **3.** Diminutive domed form supported on columns forming a canopy over a **tomb** or an **altar**, i.e. a **ciborium**. **4.** Small **dome** on a **lantern** over the eye of a large dome, or the dome plus lantern, or any diminutive domed form visible above a roof.

curb roof   **Mansard** roof.

curia   Meeting-house for councils, usually a rectangular hall with a niche or apse at one end opposite the door.

curtail   Scroll-shaped part of the handrail of a stair and of the outer end of the lowest step.

cushion   **1.** Convex projection (**pulvinus**), e.g. a **frieze** seeming to bulge outwards as if under pressure, so termed **cushioned** or **pulvinated** (see Figs. G6a–b). **2. Corbel**, **padstone**, or **springer** in an **arch**.

cyclopean   Of masonry that is dressed to look as though the surface is naturally rough, and straight from the quarry, 'undressed' (but actually contrived to look so). Aka **rock-faced** work (see **rustication** [see Fig. G98a]).

cyclostyle   Circular **peristyle** of columns surrounding a wall-less volume, i.e. a **monopteral temple**.

cylindrical vault   **1.** Wagon-head, **barrel**, or **cradle vault** without groins resting on parallel walls (see Fig. G112b). **2.** Segmental vaults or ceilings, that is with a cross-section of less than half a circle (see **vault**).

cyma (*pl.* **cymæ**)   Ogee moulding, so called from its resemblance to a wave. Its section consists of a concave and convex line, like an elongated **S**, with a plain **fillet** above and below. There are two types: the **cyma recta** (called **Doric cyma**), usually found at the top of a **cornice**, with the concave part uppermost; and the **cyma reversa**

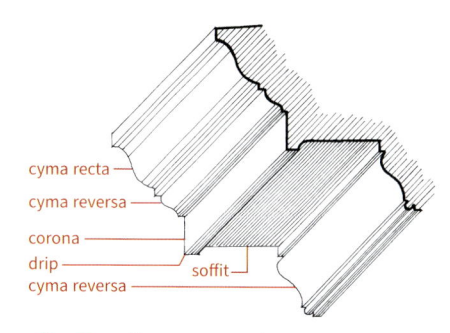

Fig. G49 *Cyma recta and cyma reversa profiles forming parts of a cornice.*

(aka **Lesbian cymatium** or **reverse ogee**, with a convex upper and concave lower part) (see **Orders**, **moulding** [Fig. G49]).

cymatium   Top member, the section of which is a curve of contrary flexure, of a group of Classical mouldings, usually the **cornice** (see **Orders**).

cymbal   Often found with musical trophies, or in **Bacchic** decorations.

cymbia   Fillet.

cyphering   Chamfering. Cyphers consist of initials interwoven to form a design, often with reversed letters for symmetry.

cyrtostyle   Curved **colonnade**.

dado   Solid block or cube forming the body of a **pedestal** or **plinth** in Classical architecture, between the **base** and the **cornice**, aka **die**. Rooms are often found decorated with a base, dado course, and cornice, resembling an elongated continuous pedestal all around the walls: in such a sense the cornice becomes the chair-rail, the plinth the skirting, and the dado the surface between the chair-rail and the skirting (see Figs G24a and G61).

damascene-work   Designs, often of the **arabesque** type, incised into metal and filled with another metal, usually gold or silver.

dancing step   Wedge-shaped step in a curved or spiral stair, the narrow end of which is almost as wide as the treads in a straight portion of a flight: aka **danced step** or **balanced winder** (see Figs G102a–c).

day   Usually symbolised by Aurora, Eos, the cock, a flame.

decastyle   Colonnade or **portico** of ten columns in a line.

declination   Angle formed between the **naked** of a wall and the **soffits** of the inclined **mutules** of the **Doric Order**.

decumanus   Main east–west street of a Roman military camp, fortress, or planned town.

demi-column   Column applied to a wall, i.e. **engaged**, as distinct from a **pilaster**.

dentil   Small block, one of a long close-set horizontal series under **cornices**, associated with the **bed-mouldings** of the **Composite**, **Corinthian**, **Ionic**, and (occasionally) the **Roman Doric Orders**. Their width should be half their height, and spaces between them should be two-thirds of their width. An **entablature** with dentils is said to be **denticulated** or **dentilated** (dentil is **denticulus** in Latin). In better work dentils should stop at the angle of a building, forming a re-entrant, and there should not be a dentil at the angle itself: they should also be spaced so that a dentil above a column should be on its centre-line (see **Orders**).

detached column   One that is **insulated**, i.e. not **engaged**, but free-standing.

diastyle   One of five species of **inter-columniation**: in this case the distance between columns is equal to three diameters of a shaft.

diazoma   Passage in a Greek theatre communicating with the radial aisles.

die   **1.** Dado (see Fig. G24a). **2. Abacus**.

diglyph   Projecting element in a **Doric frieze** in which the two half-glyphs of the **Order** are omitted, leaving only two full **glyphs** cut in the vertical block (otherwise known as **triglyph**). It is found in late-Renaissance versions of the Doric Order

diminished arch   Segmental arch, i.e. one less than a semicircle in elevation.

diminution   Contractura or reduction of the diameter of a column-shaft with height in order to give it the appearance of strength, stability, and elegance, associated with **entasis**. From the 18th century the diminution was *de rigueur* from about one-third of the height of the column, but in Greek Antique architecture it began from the bottom of the shaft.

Diocletian window Semicircular window divided into three **lights** by two **mullions**, aka **thermal window** from its use in the **baths of Diocletian** in Rome. It was revived by **Palladio**, and recurs in 18th-century architecture (Fig. G50; *see* Figs G84b, 5.57a–b, 6.23b, and 6.24a–b).

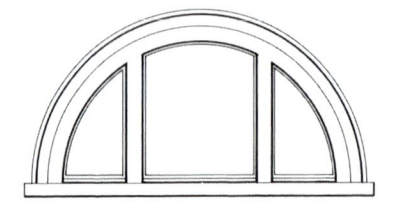

Fig. G50 *Diocletian, aka thermal, window.*

dipteral Arrangement of two rows of columns forming the **peristyle** around the **cella** in a Classical building, which meant that the **porticoes** at either end were at least **octastyle** (*see* Fig. G107b).

Directoire style **Neo-Classical** style prevalent in France from the end of the rule of Louis XVI to c.1806, often including Egyptianising elements.

diretta Cyma recta.

disappearing pilaster *See* **pilaster** (*see* Fig. G90b).

discharging arch Relieving arch, usually segmental, built into a wall over a **lintel** to relieve the latter from the weight above (*see* **arch** [*see* Fig. G20a]).

displuviate Arrangement of the **cavum ædium** known as **cavum ædium displuviatum**, with compluvium and impluvium, but with the roof sloping outwards: it permitted a better natural illumination of the room.

distyle With a **portico** of two columns: they are usually **in antis**, set between the **antæ** of the ends of projecting walls (*see* Fig. G91).

ditriglyph Interval between two columns admitting two **triglyphs** in the **frieze** above instead of the more usual single triglyph between the centre-lines of the columns of the **Doric Order**.

dodecastyle Portico or **colonnade** with 12 columns in a line.

dolphin Often found in ornament with **Nereids** and **Tritons**, dolphin ornament occurs on well-heads, embankments, and fish-markets, among other places.

dome Cupola, essentially a species of **vault**, constructed on a circular, elliptical, or polygonal plan, bulb-shaped, segmental, semicircular, or pointed in vertical section. It can be erected on top of a structure the plan of which is identical to that of the dome: if that structure's wall is circular or elliptical it is a **drum** (often pierced with windows) as in a **rotunda**. However, domes are usually found on square compartments, so adjustments are made to facilitate a transition from the square to the circular, elliptical, or polygonal base of the cupola or dome. This is achieved by means of **pendentives** (which resemble a species of concave, distorted, almost triangular **spandrels** rising from the corners of the right-angled compartment to the circular or elliptical base of the drum or cupola) or **squinches** (small arch or series of arches of increasing radius spanning the angle of the square compartment). Both the drum and the cupola will have a diameter the same dimension as the side of the square on which the whole structure stands. Types of dome include **calotte** (low cupola or saucer-dome of segmental vertical section,

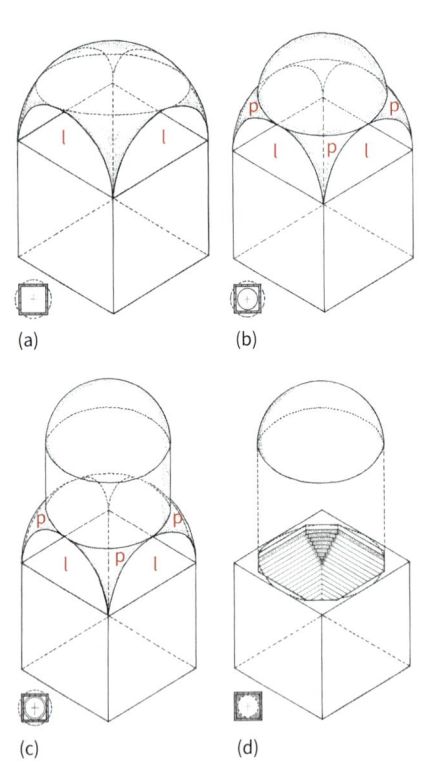

(a)   (b)

(c)   (d)

Fig. G51 *Dome treatments, all on square bases: (a) sail-dome; (b) dome on pendentives (p); (c) dome on a drum rising from pendentives; (d) dome on a drum on squinches. l = lunette.*

like a **skull-cap**); **melon** (*as* **parachute**); **Pantheon** (low dome on the exterior, often stepped, resembling that of the Pantheon in Rome, and coffered on the interior, widely copied by **Neo-Classical** architects); **parachute**, **melon**, **pumpkin**, or **umbrello** (standing on a scalloped circular base, and formed of individual webs, segmental on plan, joining in **groins**: each web has a concave interior and convex exterior, so the whole resembles a parachute rather than an umbrella); **pumpkin** (*as* **parachute**); **sail-dome** (resembles a billowing sail over a square compartment with its diameter the same dimension as the **diagonal** instead of the side of the square below, enabling the structure to rise as though on **pendentives**, but continuing without interruption. Pendentives are really parts of a sail-dome, and themselves are a species of sail-vault [*see* **vault**]) (Fig G51).

Doric drops *See* **guttæ**.

Doric Order Exists in Greek and Roman forms. In the Greek version (Fig. G52a; *see* Figs G83, G107a, and 2.1a–2.2) it consists of a **crepidoma** supporting a baseless **column** (usually fluted with sharp **arrises** between the **flutes**, but sometimes unfluted) with a pronounced **entasis**; a distinctive **capital** with **annulets** or horizontal **fillets** (from three to five in number) stopping the vertical lines of the arrises and flutes of the shaft, an **echinus** or **cushion** over them, and a plain square **abacus**; and an **entablature** (usually one-quarter the height of the Order) with plain **architrave** or principal beam over which are the **frieze** and **cornice**: Greek Doric architraves may project slightly in front of the faces of the tops of columns below, but because of the pronounced entasis, do not project beyond the faces of columns at the bases. The frieze is separated from the cornice by a plain moulding called the **tænia** under which, at intervals under each **triglyph**, is a narrow band with six **guttæ** called the **regula**. The Doric frieze is composed of alternate **metopes** (often ornamented with sculpture) and **triglyphs** (vertical elements with two **V**-shaped incised channels and two half-**V** channels at the edges producing three flat verticals and a flat band across the top). Above is the crowning **cornice** consisting of a **cyma recta** with **mutules** and guttæ on the **soffits** of the corona under the **cymatium**. Greek Doric mutules are placed over triglyphs and metopes, slope downwards with the soffit, and project beneath it. They do not

196 / CLASSICAL ARCHITECTURE

Fig. G52a *Greek Doric Order from the 5th-century BC Temple of Theseus (aka Hephæsteum), Athens (which has an arrangement of 6 × 13 columns around the naos, making it peripteral hexastyle), showing the various parts, how to set out the flutes, etc. On the left are details of an anta, the capital and base of which differ from the Order of the columns. Note the two-step crepidoma, the shaft with entasis and flutes with sharp arrises, the hypotrachelium, trachelium or neck, annulets, echinus, square abacus-block, plain architrave, frieze of triglyphs and metopes separated from the architrave by the tænia, the regula-strips with guttæ under the tænia, the sloping mutules with guttæ under the soffits of the cornice, and the cornice itself (JSC after Normand [1852]).*

Fig. G52b *Roman Doric 'mutule' Order of Vignola, showing the elaborate soffit of the cornice, ornamented with guttæ, lozenges, rosettes, and thunderbolts. Note that the triglyph block is placed on the centre-line of the corner column, leaving a piece of metope on the corner. The full metope sports a pelta, and the capital neck or hypotrachelium is decorated with rosettes. Tops of glyphs are rectangular, and columns have bases (JSC after Normand [1852])*

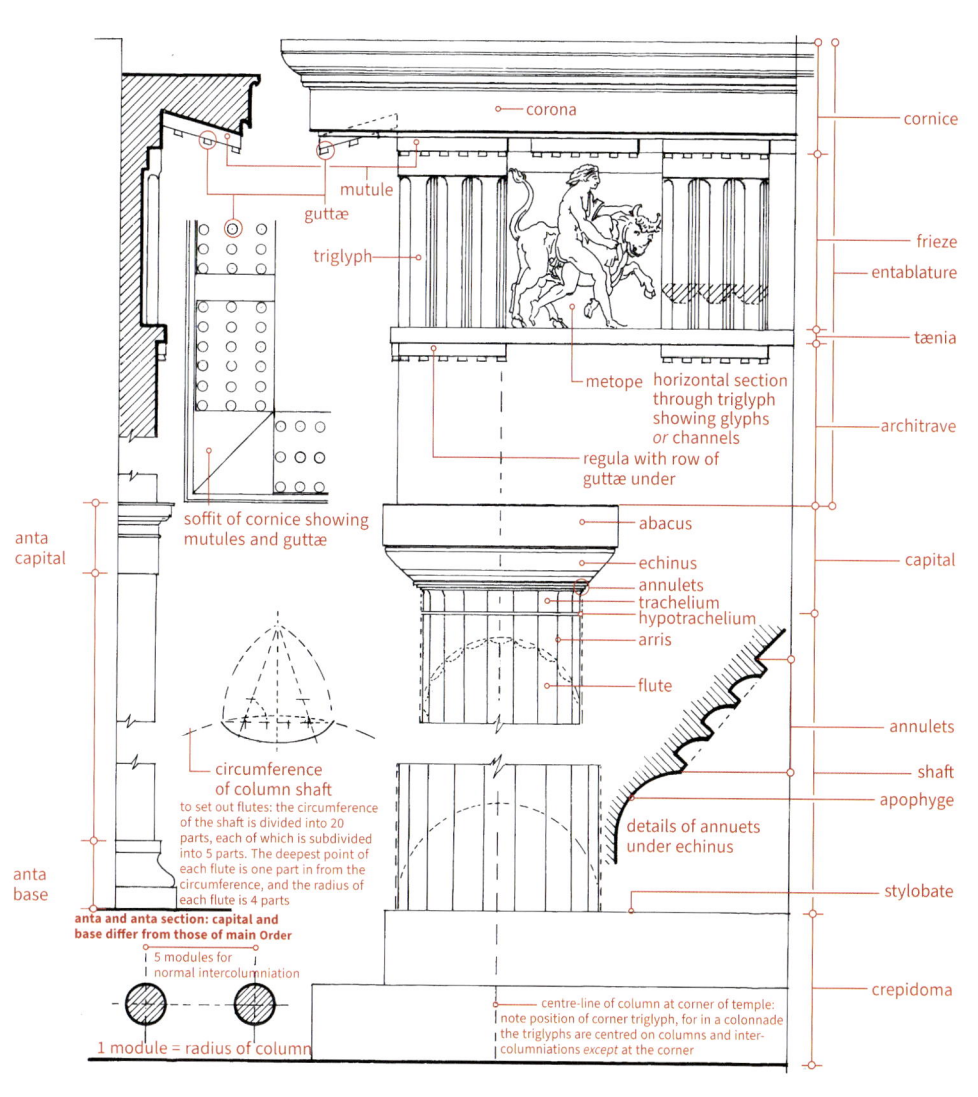

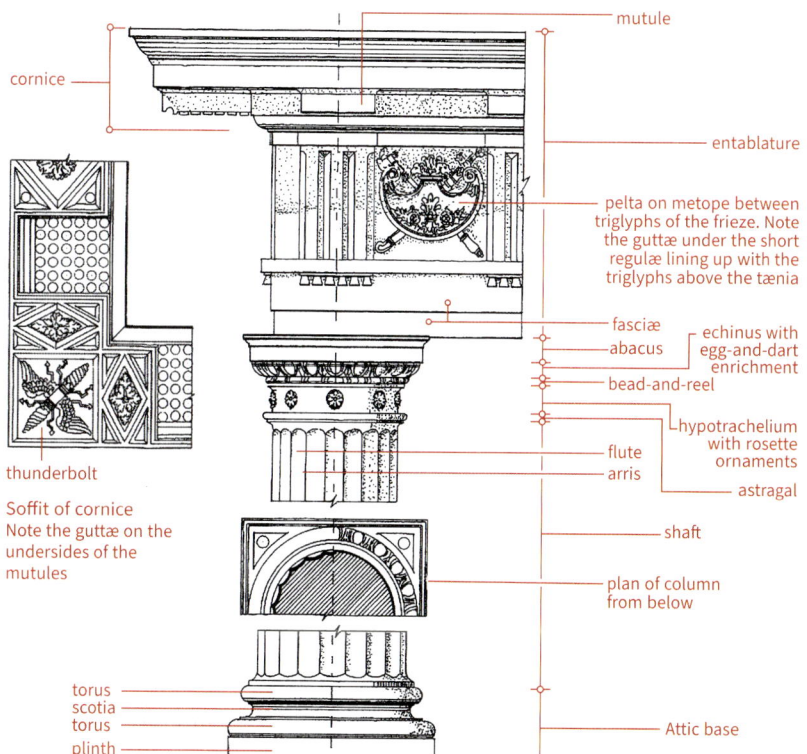

always occur under the raking cornices of pediments.

The column of the **Roman Doric Order** (Figs G52b–c) nearly always has a **base**, while the Greek version never has one. In the Roman version the **triglyphs** at the corners of the building are set on the centre-line of the columns, leaving a portion of metope on the corner, but in the Greek Doric Order the triglyphs join at the corner of the frieze, with the result that the corner columns are closer to their neighbours than elsewhere in the colonnade, so the corners of the Greek buildings appear to be more solidly proportioned. Roman Doric often has **bucrania** or **pateræ** in the metopes, and moulded **abaci**, **rosettes**, or other ornaments in the neck of the capital between the capital proper and the astragal, so the Order is quite distinct from the Greek version. Channels at the tops of Greek triglyphs are rounded, but in the Roman versions they are rectangular. Roman Doric mutules, usually set over triglyphs only, are very slightly inclined, and

SELECT GLOSSARY OF TERMS / 197

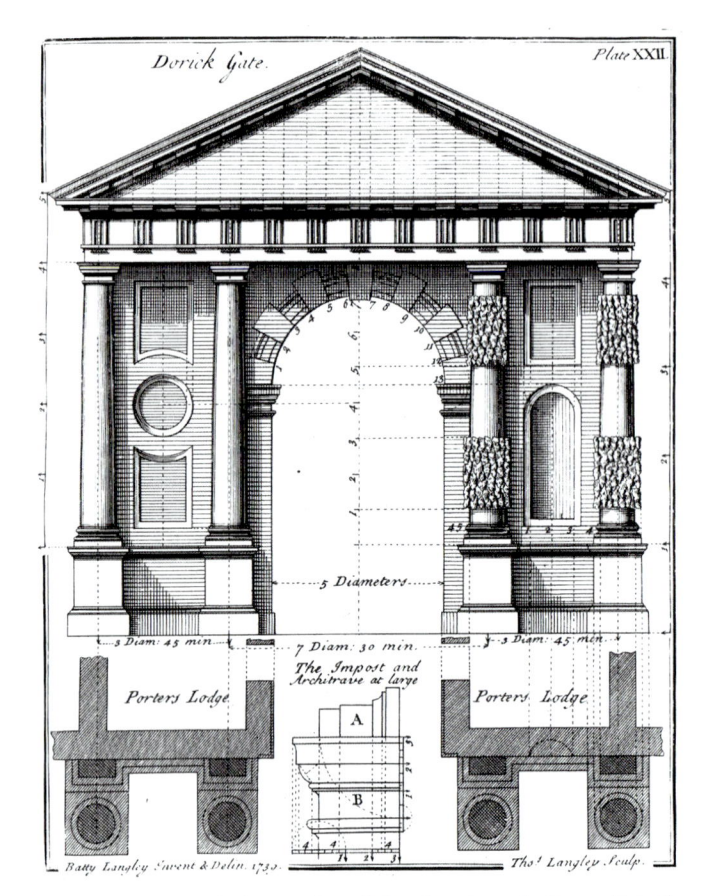

Fig. G52c *Doric gateway: a variation on triumphal-arch and temple themes. Note the mutules in the raking cornice, and the frosted rustication. In Roman Doric the triglyphs are on the centre-lines of the end columns, and two and five triglyphs are possible over the intercolumniations because the Order is combined with an arcuated form (Langley [1745]).*

do not project beneath the soffit except in the so-called 'mutule' Order of Vignola (Fig. G52b), also used by Chambers. Roman Doric Orders often feature **dentils**, but in Greek Doric these never appear. The ornaments of the Roman Doric soffit between the mutules do not drop down lower than the soffit, and are usually shallowly cut with **thunderbolts**, **rosettes**, **lozenges**, and other patterns, while guttæ are correctly conical, but are often carved as truncated pyramids. Greek Doric mutules occur over metopes as well as triglyphs, so the spaces between the mutules are usually too small for any ornamentation, except at the corners of buildings, where **anthemion** or other ornaments may sometimes be found on the soffits. Roman architraves do not project beyond the faces of the columns below (*see* Figs 2.11c and e).

dormer Window inserted vertically in a sloping roof and with its own roof and sides. If the gable over it is low-pitched and is formed into a pediment it is called a **dormer-head**. A dormer-window is placed vertically on the rafters and is not over the wall of the main **façade** below. If windows over the main **cornice** are constructed perpendicularly over the **naked** of the main façade below the **entablature** they are termed **lutherns** or **lucarnes**.

dosseret Cubical block or **super-abacus**, often taller than the capital itself, placed over the **abacus** of early Christian, Byzantine, and Romanesque capitals, really an impost-block from which arches spring. The term is also given to a short **entablature** over a **column** or **pier**, again supporting arches in an **arcade**.

dove 1. Attribute of Venus and symbol of love and constancy. 2. The Holy Spirit.

drapery Swag of drapery instead of a **festoon**, suspended from an object, e.g. **bucranium**, in Classical ornament.

dressings Mouldings, finishes, and ornaments around openings, or **quoins**, distinguished from the rest of the **naked** of a wall. A **façade** of brick with stone dressings, therefore, has most of the wall-surface of brick, but **architraves**, quoins, and the like are of **dressed stone**.

drip The projecting edge of a **moulding**, channelled or throated beneath so that water will be thrown off (*see* Fig. G45).

drop Conical **guttæ** under **triglyphs** and **mutules** of the **Doric Order**, aka **droplets**, **campanulæ**, or **lachrymæ**.

drum 1. Circular structure usually supporting a **dome**, often pierced with windows. 2. One of several cylindrical blocks from which the **shaft** of a **column** is constructed. 3. Solid **bell** or **core** of the **Corinthian** and **Composite capital** to which **foliage**, **stalks**, and **caulicoli**, etc. are attached.

duck foot, **dutch foot** Three-toed foot on a cabriole leg.

Dutch gable *See* **gable**.

eagle 1. Attribute of power or victory. 2. Gable, **pediment**, or esp. **tympanum**.

ear *See* **crossette**.

eaves Lower edge of a pitched roof projecting beyond the **naked** of the wall below. An **eaves cornice** is therefore a Classical cornice which forms the transition between the naked of the wall below and the edge of the roof above.

ecclesiasterion 1. Hall for the meeting of the sovereign assembly in a Greek city-state, hence a place for the gathering of people for purposes of serious deliberation. 2. Small theatre.

ecclesiastical hat Cardinal's hat, often found in **Baroque** decorations.

echinus 1. Sea-urchin, a genus of animals inhabiting a spheroidal shell, but the reason is obscure as to why the term has been applied to the **ovolo moulding** between the **abacus** and **annulets** of the **Greek Doric** capital; between the abacus and **hypotrachelium** of the **Tuscan** and **Roman Doric Orders**; and beneath the **pulvinus** joining the **volutes** of the **Ionic capital** where it is enriched with **egg-and-dart** (so occurs in the upper part of a **Composite** capital, always enriched). However, it should be remembered that all Classical ornament originated in some kind of formalisation of objects occurring in Nature. 2. Any convex moulding in the form of a conic section or a quarter of a

198 / CLASSICAL ARCHITECTURE

circle in Roman work. Continuous echinus mouldings are often ornamented with **egg-and-dart**, and it seems probable that the term **echinus** is only properly applied if this enrichment is present (*see* **Orders**).

eclecticism Architectural design drawing freely on a wide range of forms, motifs, details, and styles selected from historical styles and different periods.

egg-and-dart Aka **egg-and-anchor**, or **egg-and-tongue**, this is an enrichment found on **ovolo** or **echinus mouldings**, and consists of upright egg-like motifs with the tops truncated, between which are arrow-like elements, repeated alternately. This ornament may be connected with the duality of life (the egg) and death (the dart), or it might represent the shield and spear of warriors. Some have proposed it may be connected with the opium poppy and its leaves, but others, perhaps more convincingly, have suggested an origin in nuts and husks. Egg-and-dart is best confined to the late sharp arrow-head or spiked forms, which were narrower and spikier than the earlier tongue-like shapes, or leaves (*see* **Orders**, [Fig. G53; *see* Figs G74, 2.9, and 3.7]).

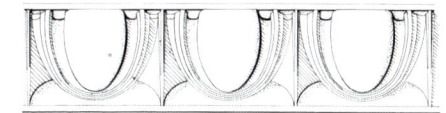

Fig. G53 *Egg-and-dart convex moulding.*

Egyptian hall Large room with an internal **peristyle** carrying a smaller superimposed upper Order or pilastered **clerestorey** over the **entablature**. It has no connection with Egyptian architecture (*see* Fig. 5.59).

Egyptian style The use of Egyptian motifs, and the simplification of form into stereometrically pure elements such as the **pyramid** and the **obelisk**, were part of the more severe, simplified phase of **Neo-Classicism**.

elbow Vertical linings of openings, such as panelled work, or the linings under shutters. *See also* **ancon**, **console**, **crossette**.

embossed Raised design, or **relievo** work, chiselled or carved.

Empire Very grand, lush, **Neo-Classical** French style associated with Napoleonic times. Roman motifs were used to identify France with Imperial Rome, and Egyptian elements also were used.

empolia Wooden blocks containing the dowels, or **poloi**, connecting the drums of Greek columns, and associated with the system of closely fitting each drum at the outer edge only (**anathyrosis**).

encarpus **Festoon** of fruit, flowers, leaves, and drapery used to decorate, e.g., a **frieze**.

endive scroll Type of **marquetry** pattern based on Moresque exemplars.

enfilade **Baroque** alignment of all the doorways (usually sited near the window-walls) connecting rooms in e.g. palaces so that long vistas through rooms are achieved: one room is therefore entered through another without any corridor.

engaged Applied, attached, **semi-engaged**, **inserted**, or seemingly partly buried in a wall or pier, such as a column with half or more of its **shaft** visible, quite distinct from a **pilaster**. True **engaged columns** have between half and three-quarters of the shafts exposed. The geometry of the **entasis** makes the junction of the shaft and the wall extremely difficult to construct if more, or less, than half the shaft is to be exposed.

enneastyle **Portico** or **colonnade** consisting of a line of nine columns.

enrichment Any elaboration of **mouldings** in Classical architecture: e.g. **egg-and-dart** on **ovolo** mouldings, **bead-and-reel** on **astragals**, and **anthemion** or **palmette** on **cyma recta** mouldings (*see* Figs 2.9 and 3.7).

entablature In **Classical Orders**, the entire horizontal mass of structure carried on **columns** and **pilasters** above the **abaci**. It usually consists of three main horizontal divisions: the **architrave** (essentially a **lintel** spanning between the columns), the **frieze** (sometimes omitted in certain examples of the **Hellenistic Ionic Order**), and the **cornice**. An entablature on the top of an **astylar façade**, as in a Florentine Renaissance *palazzo*, is termed *cornicione*. Entablatures can be found at the junction of walls and ceilings in Classical rooms (Fig. G54; *see* **Orders**).

entail Elaborate sculptured ornament.

entasis In Classical architecture **columns** are wider at the **base** than under the **capital**: the transition from the base to the top is not a straight line, but a curve, and the **diminution** usually begins from a point about a third of the height from the base. It was employed to prevent the columns from appearing concave.

entresol *See* **mezzanine**.

epicranitis Crowning **mouldings** and **enrichment** along the outer walls of a **naos** resembling the capitals of the **antæ**.

Epistle side South side of a Christian altar or church.

epistylium **Architrave** of an **entablature**, aka **epistyle**.

epithedes Upper **mouldings** of an **entablature**, or the **cymatium**.

escallop Scallop shell, often at the tops of **niches** semicircular on plan.

escape Part of the **shaft** of a **column** where it springs out of the base **mouldings**, aka **apophyge**.

escutcheon Shield on which a coat of arms is displayed.

espagnolette Female mask with ruff around head and under the chin.

estípite **Pilaster** ornament with panels containing geometrical patterns and **cartouches**, shaped like an inverted **obelisk**.

estoil Heraldic star with six wavy-sided points.

eustyle One of the five species of **intercolumniation** in which the distance between columns is equivalent to 2¼ diameters.

euthynteria Levelling-course of a Greek **temple**, connecting the buried foundation to the visible superstructure forming the **crepis** or **crepidoma**.

exedra Apse, large recess, or semicircular niche, often containing stone seats. It can be rectangular on plan, but the term means an open recess in which persons may sit.

extrados Exterior curve of an **arch** measured to the top of the **voussoirs** or **archivolt** as opposed to the **intrados** or **soffit** (*see* **arch**).

SELECT GLOSSARY OF TERMS / 199

Fig. G54 *Entablatures: (top left) block cornice, to be placed above rusticated window-surrounds, etc.; (top right) 'Ionick' entablature for doorcases, niches, or window-surrounds, with dentils and pulvinated frieze; (bottom) Tuscan and Doric entablatures for doorcases, niches, or window-surrounds (Langley [1745]).*

eye Centre of a part: the circle in the middle of an **Ionic volute** (*see* **Ionic Order**), an aperture at the summit of a **dome**, or a circular window (**oculus**) in the centre of a **pediment**. A **bull's-eye** or **œil-de-bœuf** window is a circular or elliptical opening.

eye-catcher Decorative feature (e.g. a **folly** or **temple**) in a landscape as the terminating focus of a vista.

fabrique Building in a landscaped garden, e.g. an **eyecatcher**, **folly**, or **temple**, essentially a small **Picturesque** structure intended as an ornament in a park in the English style.

façade Exterior face or main front of a building.

facettes Flat projections or **fillets** between the **flutes** of columns (*see* **Orders** and Fig. G59).

false attic **Attic storey** concealing a roof, but not containing rooms.

Fame Winged female figure blowing a trumpet, often found in **spandrels**, as in **triumphal arches**.

fanlight Window, often semicircular or segmental, over a door, and so called because of the radiating glazing-bars which suggested the shape of an open fan. The term has come to be applied to all glazed openings over doors, whether the glazing bars are in the shape of a fan or not (Figs G55a–c).

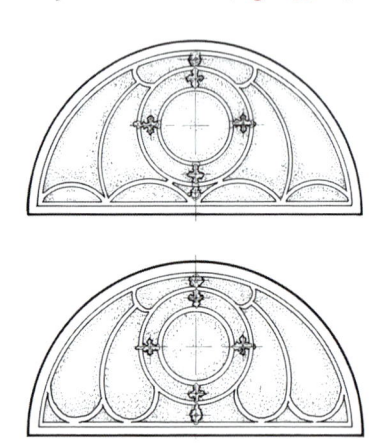

Fig. G55a *Fanlights: (top) bat's-wing pattern, c.1820; (bottom) tear-drop pattern, c.1820, both in London.*

Fig. G55b *Grander 18th-century fanlight over a door set between margent-ornamented pilasters, with margin-lights (JSC after Osborne [1954]).*

Fig. G55c *Late-Georgian fanlights in Armagh set over ædiculated Tuscan doorcases (JSC).*

fasces   Bound bundle of straight rods enclosing an axe, a Roman emblem of legal power and authority, employed in **Empire** and **Neo-Classical** architecture, and revived in Italy in the 20th century as an emblem of Fascism (Fig. G56).

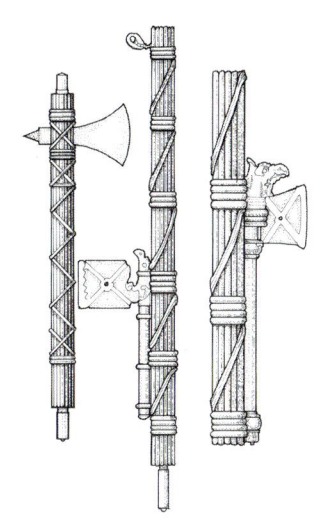

Fig. G56 *Three types of Classical fasces, with axes.*

fascia (*pl.* **fasciæ**)   **1.** One of two or three bands on a Classical **architrave**, each projecting slightly in front of the one below, often separated by enriched **mouldings** (*see* **Orders**). **2.** Broad band with a plain vertical face, e.g. a fascia-board at eaves level.

fastigium   **1.** Pediment or **gable**. **2.** Raking **mouldings** of a pediment. **3.** Apex of a pediment, or a ridge. **4.** A**croter** block.

fauces   Vestibule in a Roman house between the front door to the street and the **atrium**. If the door were to be set back from the line of the front wall the space outside the door is called **vestibulum** and the inside **prothyra**. Fauces implies a narrow space through which many pass to larger spaces.

feathers   Three or five upright feathers are common **Neo-Classical** devices.

Federal style   Style of architectural decoration prevalent in the USA from the Declaration of Independence (1776) to c.1830, drawing on aspects of **Georgian architecture**, Freemasonic symbolism, **Palladianism**, and French **Neo-Classicism**. **American Directoire** or **Directory** describes styles in America c.1805–30 influenced by French **Directoire** and **Empire** taste.

fenestration   Arrangement of windows in a **façade**.

ferme ornée   Farm designed for both utility and beauty, the buildings contributing to the æsthetic effect within a **Picturesque** landscape.

festoon   Ornament of carved wreaths, garlands of flowers or leaves, or both, suspended in **swags** on walls and **friezes**, and commonly found in Classical architecture. The swags are represented as tied, so they are narrow at each extremity, and thickest at the centre of the hanging part (Fig. G57).

Fig. G57 *Elaborate festoon with ribbons (JSC after Normand [1852]).*

fielded   Flat central raised part of a panel, thicker than the bevelled edge or margin (*see* Figs G61 and G86).

fillet   Narrow band used between **mouldings** to separate and define them, found in **cornices** and **bases**. It is not always flat, but is often found cut into two or more narrow faces with sharp edges between. Narrow flat bands are also known as **listels** or **annulets**. Small bands between the flutes of columns are also known as fillets (*see* Fig. G59).

finial   In Classical architecture surmounting any prominent **terminal**: it can represent many objects (e.g. acorn, ball, pine cone, obelisk, thin pyramid, or urn) (*see* Fig. G3).

flambeau (*pl.* **flambeaux**)   *See* **torch**.

flat tile   Rain tile or **tegula**, meaning a common flat tile, over the joints of which was fixed an **imbrex** or **covering tile**.

fleur-de-lys   Stylised lily, related to **anthemion** ornament.

Florentine arch   Arch with **intrados** and **extrados** struck from different points (Fig. G58).

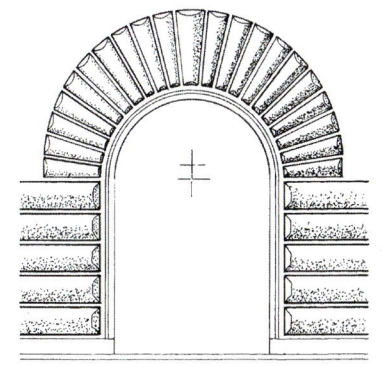

Fig. G58 *Florentine arch (note the two centres for the voussoirs of varying length).*

floriated   Carved in imitation of flowers or leaves.

flush   Even with, or on the same plane as, something else, e.g. a panel with its surface on the same plane as its surrounding frame (*see* Fig. G86), or mortar on the same plane (flush with) the face of the brickwork.

flute (*pl.* **flutes, flutings**)   Concave channel (**stria**) in the **shafts** of Classical **columns** or **pilasters**, cut perpendicularly, used in all **Orders** save **Tuscan**. There are 20 in the **Greek Doric Order**, segmental in section, meeting in sharp **arrises**, and 24 in the **Ionic**, **Corinthian**, and **Composite Orders**, deeper in section, and separated by **fillets** (Fig. G59). Sometimes (except in the Doric Order) flutes are partially filled with a convex **moulding** or **bead** to one third of the height of the shaft: this is called **cabling** (*see* Fig. G90a). Flutes most usually terminate in hemispherical forms, but in the Greek Doric Order they terminate in **annulets**. Horizontal fluting of the **torus** of an Ionic base is called **reeding** (*see* **Orders**). A **stopped flute** is one cut in the upper two-thirds of the shaft of a Classical column, below which the shaft is faceted

Select Glossary of Terms / 201

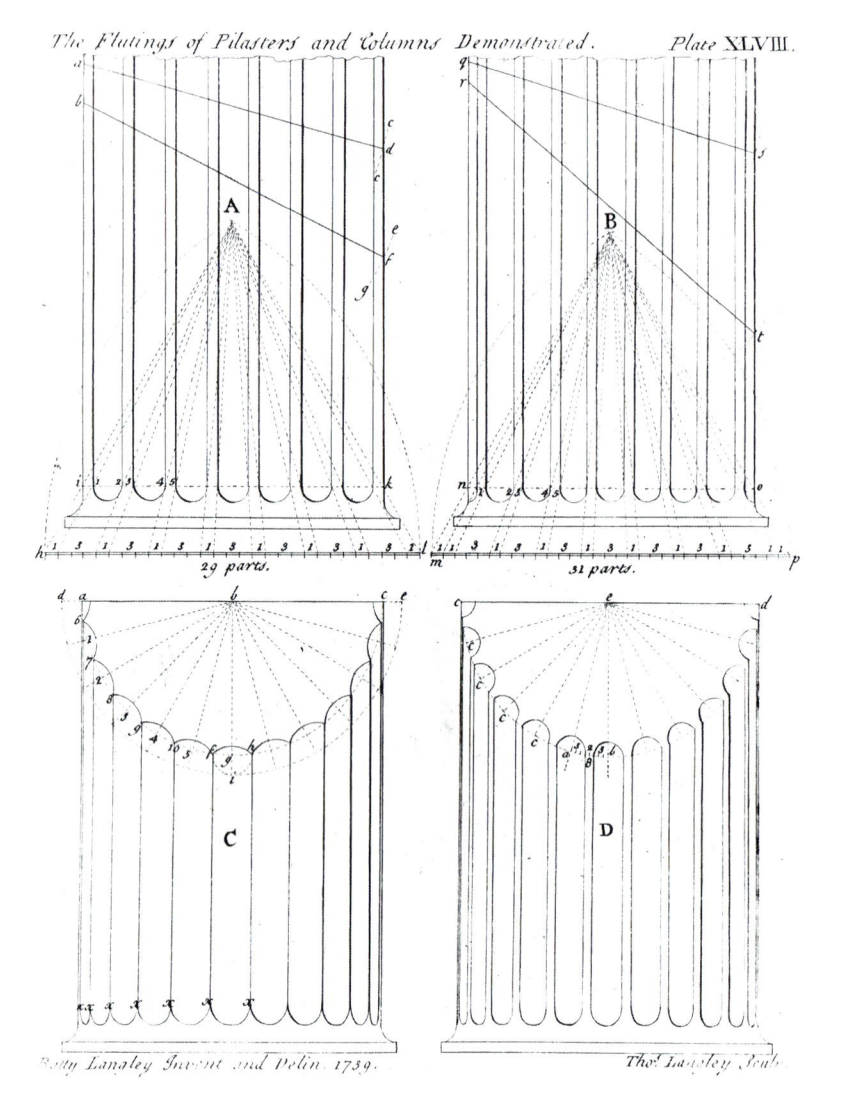

Fig. G59 *How to set out flutes and fillets of columns and pilasters (Langley [1745]).*

Fig. G60a *Triple form of the French Order (three columns on a triangular base), with garlands spiralling around the shafts, associated with French Masonic lodges, with the Solomonic temple, and with Antiquity. Plate III engraved by Pierre-Claude de la Gardette (Chamoust [1783] coll. JSC).*

Fig. G60b *(Top) Type of the French Order showing its origin; (bottom) the French Order developed, showing the triple columns used in a colonnade, and the triple, garlanded columns in the circular temple. Plate II engraved by Heinrich Schmitz (Chamoust [1783] coll. JSC).*

(i.e. polygonal), smooth, or the flutes contain cabling.

foliate mask Humanoid face surrounded by leaves, sometimes with foliage sprouting from the mouth and nostrils.

folly **Eye-catcher**, usually a building in a contrived landscape: it might be in the form of a sham ruin, a Classical **temple**, a **mausoleum**, or some other *fabrique* set in a **Picturesque** garden.

fornix **Arch** or **vault**, vaulted opening, archway, arched door, or an arch erected as a monument.

forum (*pl.* **fora**) Open space in a town serving as a marketplace and general place of rendezvous. It often was surrounded by **porticoes** or **colonnades**, and was more axially and formally planned than was the Greek **agora**.

foundation *Fundamentum* or buried substructure of a building. The Greeks called it **euthynteria**, as a levelling course joining the foundation to the **crepidoma**.

Free Classicism **1.** Late 19th-century style, not adhering strictly to historical precedents or rules, essentially a mixture of **Baroque**, **Classical**, **Mannerist**, and **Renaissance** motifs. **2.** The term **Free Classical style** was given to the **Queen Anne style** or **Revival**.

French Order **1.** Order with banded shafts, or one in which the cock and fleur-de-lys are introduced into the **capital**. **2.** Order with spirals or leaves wound round the shafts and three columns arranged on a triangular plan (∴), aka **Masonic abbreviation** (Figs G60a–b).

French window Glazed door opening in two leaves to give access to a balcony or garden.

fret, frette, fretwork Ornament consisting of **fillets** meeting at right angles arranged in bands of angular key-patterns,

202 / CLASSICAL ARCHITECTURE

aka **Greek key** or angular **guilloche** (*see* Figs G39a and G66).

frieze Middle division of an **entablature** lying between the **cornice** and **architrave**. The **Tuscan** frieze is plain, but the **Doric** is subdivided along its length by **triglyphs** and **metopes**. **Ionic**, **Corinthian**, and **Composite** friezes are often embellished with continuous sculpture, but can be plain. Sometimes friezes can be **pulvinated**, **convex**, or **cushioned**, usually in the Ionic Order. The frieze of a **capital** is called the **hypotrachelium**, as in a species of Ionic (*see* **Orders**). A **frieze panel** is the upper panel of a six-panelled door, while a **frieze rail** is the upper rail but one of a six-panelled door (Fig. G61).

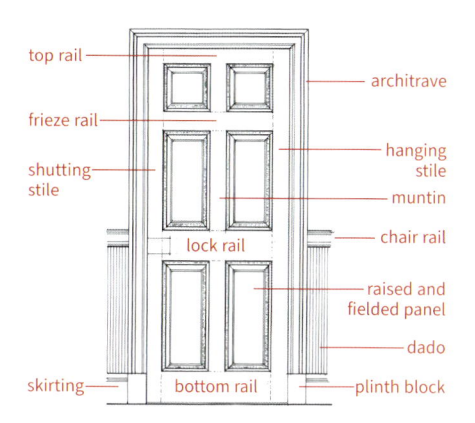

Fig. G61 *Framed door showing its various components, including frieze-rail, stiles, rails, architrave, skirting, plinth-block, dado, chair-rail, and raised and fielded panels.*

frigidarium Large, handsomely decorated room in Roman ***thermæ***, containing a large cold-water pool.

frontispiece 1. Main **façade**. 2. Entrance embellished with architectural motifs.

fronton Small **pediment** over a door-case, **niche**, etc.

frosted Type of **rustication** (*see* Fig. G98a).

fruit Used in Horns of Plenty, baskets, and **festoons**.

fusarole Ring of semicircular section, often ornamented, found under the **echinus** of the **Roman Doric**, **Ionic**, and **Composite Orders** (*see* **Orders**).

fust 1. Column-shaft or pilaster-trunk. 2. Ridge of a roof. 3. Apex of a triangular pediment.

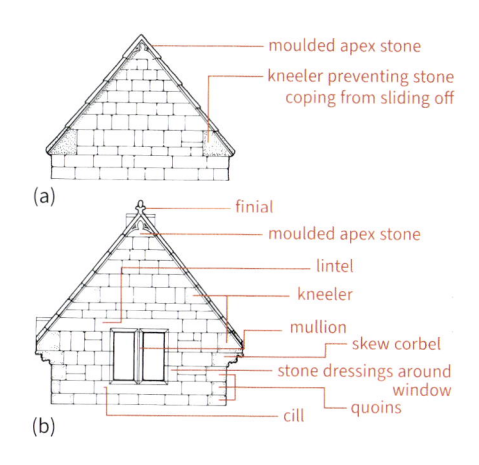

Fig. G62 *Gable: (a) triangular stone gable showing kneelers and apex stone; (b) stone gable with skew corbels; (c) elevation and section of brick corbie- or crow-stepped gable from Kent (c.1540); (d) gable with tumbled brickwork based on several East Anglian exemplars; (e) late 17th-century porch, Kent, with shaped gable; (f) brick Dutch gable based on examples from Sussex and Kent (c–f JSC after Lloyd [1925])*

fylfot *See* **cross**.

gable, gavel End wall of a building, the top of which conforms to the slope of the roof which abuts against it. In modern usage the term is applied only to the upper part of such a wall above eaves level, and the entire wall is called a **gable-end**. A **Dutch gable** is one with curved or scrolled sides (*klauwstukken*) crowned by a **pediment** or an **arch** (Fig. G62). In Classical architecture the low triangular gable, framed by the low pitches of the roof, is called a pediment (*see* Figs 2.1a and 2.4).

gadroon, godroon One of a set of convex **mouldings** joined at their extremities to form an **enrichment**: gadrooning is frequently found on the upper surface of convex mouldings, rather like fingers. **Gadrooned** means enriched with convex rods. Aka **lobes**, **(k)nulled decoration**, or **thumb mouldings** (Fig. G63).

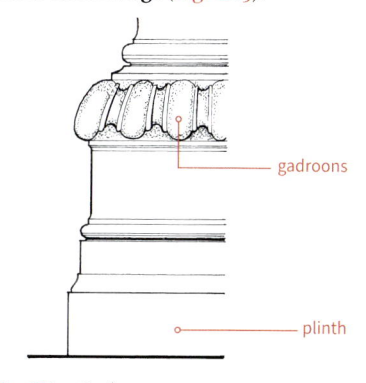

Fig. G63 *Gadroons.*

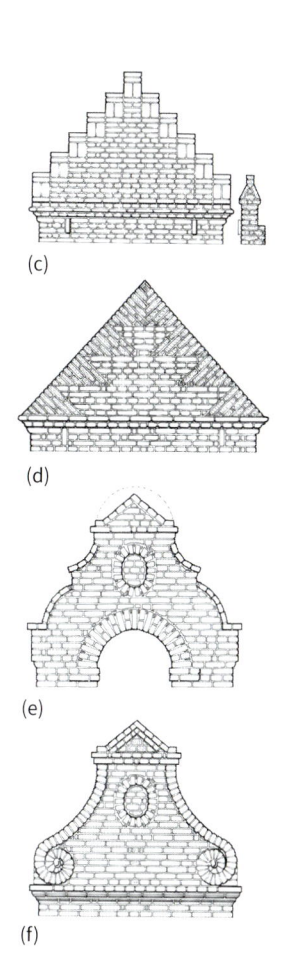

gaine **Pedestal** or lower part of a **herm** (*see* Fig. G69).

garland 1. Wreath-like ornament of flowers, fruits, leaves, etc., usually found in **friezes** or **dies** of pedestals. 2. **Festoon**.

gauged arch One with **voussoirs** radiating to a centre, with bricks finely rubbed, or stones finely cut (*see* Fig. G20b).

gazebo 1. Small apartment on a roof with a view, aka **belvedere**. 2. Summer-house, or any ornamental structure commanding a view.

geison Horizontal **cornice** on a **pediment** with shelf-like top supporting statuary in the **tympanum**.

geometrical staircase One in which the flight of stone stairs is supported by and cantilevered from the wall at only one end of the steps, each step resting on the next. There are no **newels**.

Georgian Architecture of the first four King Georges of England (1714–1830), which saw the rise of **Palladianism**, **eclecticism**, **Neo-Classicism**, the embrace

SELECT GLOSSARY OF TERMS / 203

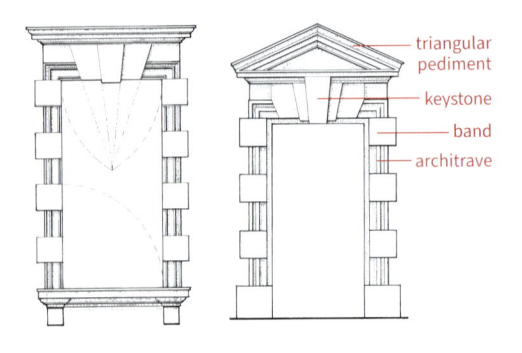

Fig. G64a *Gibbs surrounds for a window (left) and a doorway (right), in which plain ashlar blocks interrupt the architrave (JSC after Langley [1745]).*

Fig. G64b *(right) Gibbs surrounds on the façade of the White Linen Hall, Belfast (1782–5, demolished 1898), probably designed by Roger Mulholland (from an old postcard, coll. JSC).*

of **Gothic** and **Greek Revivals**, appreciation of the **Picturesque**, and flirtations with **Chinoiserie**, **Hindoo**, **Rococo**, and other exotic styles. But the term is usually applied to a very simple form of stripped Classical domestic architecture featuring plain window-openings with double-hung sashes, door-cases that vary from elaborate treatment with **consoles**, **pediments**, **columns**, and **pilasters**, to plain openings with **fanlights**.

German Order *See* **Britannic Order**.

Giant Order Order rising from the ground or from a **plinth** more than one storey, aka **Colossal Order**. *See* **Gigantic Order**.

gibbonwork Exquisite naturalistic carving in the manner of **Grinling Gibbons**.

Gibbs surround Banded **architrave** or surround of a door, **niche**, or window, usually with a massive **keystone** and **voussoirs** breaking into the top of the architrave. Named after James Gibbs (who illustrated and often employed it), it was widely used by other 18th-century and later architects (Figs G64a–b; *see* Fig. 5.41).

Gigantic Order Tuscan Order, according to Scamozzi. Not to be confused with **Giant** or **Colossal Order**.

girandole Large branched candlestick.

girdle Circular **band** or **fillet** surrounding a part of a **column**.

glacis Slope or declivity, originally falling from a fortress so that it could be raked by fire, but subsequently employed as a device in garden design.

glyph Channel, **flute**, or groove, usually vertical. The term is used to denote the perpendicular channels cut in the projecting tablets of a **Doric frieze** which are called **triglyphs** from their having two whole channels with a half-channel at each side of the tablet (*see* **Doric Order**).

glyptotheca Sculpture-gallery.

gnomon Rod or other object serving to indicate the time by casting its shadow on a marked surface: the pin or triangular plate on a sundial. A column employed in order to observe the meridian altitude of the sun. A **gnomonic column** is a cylinder on which the hour of day is indicated by the shadow cast by the stylus (fixed or moveable).

gola Ogee, or the **cymatium**.

gorge 1. Shallow **cavetto moulding** or **throating**, less recessed than a **scotia**. 2. Neck or small **frieze** (aka **collarino**,

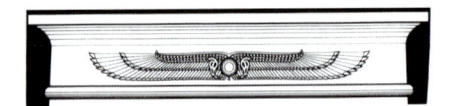

Fig. G65 *Gorge-cornice, ancient Egyptian type, with winged globe and rearing uræi, with torus below: gorge-cornices sometimes occur in the most severe Neo-Classical designs.*

gorgerin, **hypotrachelium**), at the top of **Roman Doric** and **Tuscan capitals** above the **astragal** at the top of the **shaft**. 3. Cyma. 4. Apophyge. 5. Large **cavetto** in cornices of ancient Egyptian pylon-towers, aka **gorge-cornice** (Fig. G65).

gorgerin *See* **gorge**.

gorgonela Keystones carved with the heads of Gorgons.

Gospel side North side of a Christian altar or church.

Graces Three female figures, supposedly called Aglaia, Thalia, and Euphrosyne, usually depicted holding each other's hands.

gradation 1. Rising by steps or degrees, as in a theatre. 2. Barely discernible change of colour.

gradetto (*pl.* **gradetti**) Annulet.

Greek cross Cross with arms of equal length (*see* Fig. G47).

Greek key Labyrinthine **fret** used in bands, often on **string-courses** and sometimes on **friezes** (Fig. G66). Compare **guilloche** (*see* Fig. G68).

Greek Orders Doric, Ionic, and Corinthian, each of which is distinct from Roman versions.

Greek Revival Phase of **Neo-Classicism**

Fig. G66 *Two forms of Greek key or labyrinthine fret.*

that involved using archæologically correct elements from ancient Greek architecture following the publication of a number of accurate surveys, notably Stuart and Revett's *The Antiquities of Athens*, which appeared from 1762. The adoption of Greek architecture involved considerable ingenuity on the part of designers: towers and spires involving pile-ups of Greek motifs, and churches with galleries are but two obvious examples where the style had to be used in highly original ways (*see* Figs 6.3a–6.4, 6.6c–6.7, 6.8b–6.21, 6.31a–b, and 6.32b).

griffin Animal with head, wings, and claws of an eagle, and body of a lion.

grisaille Decorative painting in grey tints to suggest bas-reliefs.

groin Intersection of two simple **vaults**, crossing each other at the same height, and forming an **arris**, or sharp edge (*see* Fig. G112c).

grotesque Light, fanciful Classical ornament consisting of foliage, figures, and animal forms, fantastically combined and interwoven (*see* Fig. 5.28). The term seems to originate from the fact that much Antique ornament of this type was found in underground apartments, and such underground volumes are called **grotte**. Compare **arabesque** (*see* Fig. G18).

grotto Artificial cave/cavern, usually decorated with shells, and often incorporating a water cascade and fountain. Grottoes were sometimes built in houses, and were fashionable in the 18th century (Fig. G67). More often, however, they were garden buildings, often adorned with '**rustick**' architecture on the outside.

ground floor Storey of a building at ground level, often containing important

Fig. G67 *Elaborate shell-work, 18th-century grotto at Schloß Pommersfelden, Germany (JSC).*

rooms. It is not always the lowest floor, and can be set over a **basement**. The best rooms are often found on the first floor, or elevated, at a *piano nobile* level.

ground tablestones Projecting course of stones above the surface of the ground, aka **plinth**.

grouped columns More than two columns grouped together on one pedestal. When only two columns are used they are called **coupled columns**. See **French Order**.

guilloche Classical ornament, aka **plait-band**, with two or more bands or strings twisting over each other so as to repeat the same figure in a continuous series, leaving circles in the centres (Fig. G68). The term

Fig. G68 *Two forms of guilloche.*

is also loosely applied to the **fret** or **Greek key** pattern, which is really an angular guilloche (*see* Fig. G66).

gula Cymatium.

gutta (*pl.* **guttæ**) Pendent ornament resembling a truncated cone hanging from the **soffits** of the **mutules** and **regulæ** of the **Doric Order**. In **Renaissance** and later versions of Doric, they are often cylindrical, like dowels, or resemble truncated pyramids. There are generally 18 under each mutule, set in three rows, each row parallel to the front, and 6 under the regula, but the number may vary. Guttæ may represent timber pegs, and thus suggest a wooden prototype for the Order. They are sometimes called **lachrymæ**, or tears, sometimes **campanulæ**, meaning bells, and sometimes **drops**, **droplets**, **nails**, or **trunnels** (*see* **Doric Order** [*see* Figs G52a–b]).

gymnasium (*pl.* **gymnasia**) Meeting-place for athletic practice, aka **palæstra**, usually several **porticoes** and rooms around a rectangular open space: it often had a type of cloistered **colonnade** around it. It must not be confused with **stadium** (racecourse for humans) or **hippodrome** (racecourse for horses), which were long and narrow on plan with rounded end or ends: the hippodrome reached its greatest development in the Roman circus with its central *spina* enriched with **trophies**, **obelisks**, and **monuments**, and many raked seats for spectators.

gynæceum, gynæcium, gynæconitis Women's quarters in a Greek or Roman house or palace, or any building set apart for women.

ha-ha Trench, consisting of a vertical or slightly battered side contained by a retaining wall or revetment of stone or brick on the side nearest a country house (or the point from which the landscape is viewed), and with the other side of the trench sloping and grassed. The ha-ha thus prevented cattle, etc. from straying to the area contained within it, but, being invisible from the vantage point or house, did not interrupt the view with a fence, wall, or hedge.

half-round Semicircular moulding, either a **bead** or **torus**.

harmonic division or **proportion** Relation of successive numbers in a series, the reciprocals of which are in arithmetical progression, the numbers being proportional to the lengths of twanged cords that sound harmonious. Rooms with measurements 1:2, 2:3, and 3:4 were held by **Renaissance** theorists to be harmonious: some, including Alberti, argued that this

SELECT GLOSSARY OF TERMS / 205

was the basis for satisfactory relationships of dimension and form in Classical architecture, and indeed the key to understanding Nature and even the Universe.

harmony An agreement, balance, or repose between all the parts of a building, having connections with **symmetry**.

harpy Monster with head and breasts of a woman and wings and claws of a bird, usually found in **Grotesque** ornament.

hatchment See **achievement**.

haunch Approximately triangular portion or **flank** between the **crown** and **abutments** of an **arch**, i.e. between the crown and the **springing** on the **piers** (see **arch** [see Fig. G20a]).

hawksbeak Crowning moulding of the **Greek Doric Order** like a **cyma recta** with the upper concave curve concealed by a beak-like overhang (see **Doric Order**).

hecatompedon Temple with a **portico** 100 Attic feet wide, or one with a **naos** 100 feet long. 101.341 English feet = 100 Attic feet. An Attic foot is derived from studies of the dimensions of the **Parthenon**.

height of an arch Dimension from the line of the **springing** to the highest point of the **intrados** (see **arch** [see Fig. G20a]).

helioscene Exterior louvered blind which protects the room from the sun yet permits a view out from that room.

helix (pl. **helices**) 1. Small **volute** or urilla under the **abacus** of the **Corinthian capital**, of which there are 16 (2 at each angle, and 2 in the centre of each face), branching from the **caulicoli** or stalks that rise between the **acanthus** leaves. Vitruvius called the eight inner spirals **helices**, terming the outer spirals at the corners **volutæ**. 2. Any volute, as on an **Ionic** or **Composite** capital, a **console**, or a **modillion** (see **Orders**). 3. Handrail of a stair **balustrade** forming a helix over the **newel**.

Hellenic Greek architecture and culture prior to c.323 BC.

Hellenistic Greek architecture and culture from the consolidation of Macedonian supremacy under Alexander III of Macedon ('the Great') in the latter part of the 4th century BC to the foundation of the Roman Empire in the eastern Mediterranean after Octavian's victory over the fleets of Mark Antony and Cleopatra VII at the Battle of Actium (31 BC). The Hellenistic period therefore coincided with the relative decline of Greece and the evolution of centres of art and patronage in the Greek kingdoms of Asia Minor and Egypt. Hellenistic architecture is characterised by a greater variation of influences than was apparent in **Hellenic** buildings, and was often more opulent, elegant, and graceful, gaining in lightness of effect through wider **intercolumniations**. The **Doric Order**, for example, became more attenuated and less severe, often with two or more **triglyphs** over each intercolumniation, and acquiring certain features from the **Ionic Order**, including the **Asiatic base** and the omission of the **frieze**, as in the Temple of Athena Polias, Priene (from c.335 BC).

hem Spiral protuberant part of an **Ionic capital** (see **Orders**).

hemi- Greek word meaning 'half', prefixing other architectural terms. Examples include **hemi-cycle**: semicircular room, part of a room, or area off a court, forum, garden, large exedra, semicircular vault, etc.; **hemi-dome**: half-dome, e.g. over an **apse** or **niche**; **hemi-glyph**: half-glyph or chamfer on each side of a **triglyph** in the **Doric Order**; **hemi-sphærium**: dome; **hemi-triglyph**: half triglyph as in an internal corner of a **frieze**, touching another.

heptastyle Colonnade or **portico** with seven columns in one line.

herm Pedestal, square on plan, terminating in a head of Hermes or some other deity. It has the generalised proportions of the human body, sometimes features feet at the base, and occasionally has the male reproductive organs protruding from the front (Fig. G69).

hermaphrodite Figure combining male and female sexual characteristics.

hermitage Small hut or dwelling in a secluded spot, usually built in a park or woodland as a resting place or **gazebo**, and constructed in the 'rustick' style, often associated with a **grotto**, **moss-hut**, or *cottage orné*. In the 18th century it was sometime inhabited by a paid 'hermit'.

heroum Shrine dedicated to a deified dead person.

Fig. G69 *Two varieties of herm: (left) Greek ithyphallic type; (right) front and side elevations, 16th-century pilaster, Villa Cambiaso, Genoa.*

hexastyle Portico of six columns in one line (see **temple**).

hieracosphinx See **sphinx**.

high relief Alto-relievo, i.e. sculpture in relief projecting more than half its form from its background.

Hindoo Exotic orientalising architectural style, part of the **eclecticism** associated with 18th-century **Picturesque**.

hippocamp Creature ('sea-horse') with the head and forelegs of a horse, and the tail of a fish.

hippodrome Racecourse for horses, as opposed to a **stadium**, a racecourse for men.

historicism 1. Attempt to understand and use the styles of the past in a correct and archæological manner. 2. Term of abuse used by Modernists to describe architecture they regard as 'irrelevant'.

hollow gorge Cavetto or Egyptian **gorge**.

honeysuckle Greek **enrichment** resembling the honeysuckle flower, called **anthemion** or **palmette**.

hoof foot, *pied de biche*, or **cloven foot** Feet of goats or sheep used to terminate **cabriole** legs.

horn 1. Composite, Corinthian, or (esp.) **Ionic volute**. 2. Projection at each corner of an **altar**, **ash-chest** (see Fig. G40), **sarcophagus**, or **stele**, aka **acroterium** or **ear** (Fig. G70).

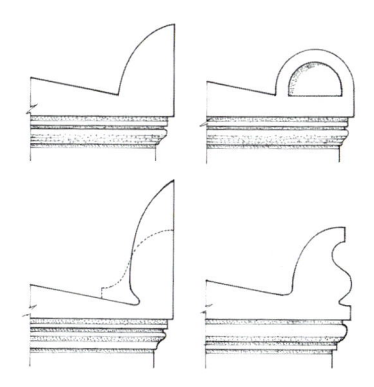

Fig. G70 *Varieties of horn: (top left) cat's ear; (top right) lion's ear; (bottom left) ass's ear (solid) and Neo-Classical (pecked); (bottom right) dog's ear.*

husk Stylised, bud-like ornament, aka **bellflower**, **nut-shell**, or **wheat-ear**, usually in series, linked together in **drops**, **festoons**, **garlands**, or **strings**. When composed to form a **husk-garland**, the vertical parts (**margents**) 'hanging' on each side have nut-shells diminishing in size towards the bottom, although, like festoons, they increase in size towards the centre of the catenary curve (Fig. G71; *see* Fig. G77).

Fig. G71 *Bellflower, husk, nut-shell, or wheat-ear garland around an elliptical Neo-Classical medallion, with margents hanging on either side (JSC after a design by Robert Adam).*

hypæthral Unroofed building, or one partly open to the sky.

hyperthyris **Lintel** or **supercilium** over a Classical doorway or other aperture.

hyperthyrum **Frieze** course between the **lintel** of a door or window and a **cornice**.

hypocaust Space under the floor of a Roman building through which hot air passes by convection to heat rooms.

hypogæum 1. All parts of a building underground. 2. Underground rock-cut or built tomb with **niches** for cremated remains or **loculi** for bodies, smaller than a **catacomb**, and usually intended for one family or group.

hypostyle 1. Covered **colonnade**. 2. Hall with many columns.

hypotrachelium (or **-on**) Lower part of the **Tuscan**, **Roman Doric**, and some **Ionic** capitals between the **astragal** at the top of the **shaft** and the **fillet** under the **ovolo**: the **frieze** of the **capital**, or the part of the shaft below the capital, or the **neck**. The **trachelium** (**-on**) in the **Greek Doric Order** is the part of the shaft between the horizontal groove or grooves circumscribing the column (aka **hypotrachelium**) and the **annulets** under the **echinus**. Thus, the hypotrachelium has a slightly different meaning for each Order, but the term seems properly to apply to the lower part of the neck (*see* **Orders**).

ice-house Building for the preservation of ice collected in the winter for use during warmer weather, usually wholly or partly underground, frequently of circular vaulted form, not uncommon on larger estates in the 18th and 19th centuries, often with *fabriques* above them to add interest to the landscape.

icicle Representation of falling water or icicles in **frosted** and **congelated rustication**, often found in fountains and **grottoes** (*see* Fig. G98a).

imbrex (*pl.* **imbrices**) Convex, half-cylindrical tile covering the joint between two adjacent concave or plain tiles, or used for gutters.

impluvium Cistern in the centre of an **atrium** used to collect water from the **compluvium** or opening in the roof: the courtyard itself.

Imperial stair Starts with one straight flight to the landing, then, turning by 180°, with two flights on either side of and parallel to the first flight, leading to the upper floor (*see* Fig. G102b).

impost Generally held to be the actual point from which an arch springs, so an **impost block** is a slab or element placed between a capital and the springing of an arch (*see* **arch** [*see* Fig. G20a]).

in antis *See* **anta**.

inband Stone laid with its length built into the return of a wall or reveal, showing only its face. **Quoin** or **jamb-stone**.

inlaid work When the surface of one material is cut away to a minimum depth in patterns, and metal, stone, cement, wood, ivory, or some other substance is inserted to fill the hollows, and finished to a **flush** surface, the result is called inlaid work. **Boule** or **Buhl** work and **marquetry** are examples. If metal is inlaid in metal it is **damascening**.

inserted column **Engaged column** or one set in a reveal, or let into a wall.

insulated Detached. An insulated column stands free from a wall: thus the columns of **peripteral temples** were said to be insulated.

intaglio Sculpture where the design is hollowed out or incised. **Intaglios** also means the carved work of an Order, or carving on any part of an edifice.

intarsia Wooden mosaic made up of different woods.

intavolata **Cymatium**.

interaxial Measurements from centre to centre, say, of adjacent columns, as opposed to **intercolumnar** measurements.

intercolumniation Distance between **columns** measured from the lower parts of the **shafts** in multiples of the shaft-diameter (d). **Greek Doric Hellenic** intercolumniation was generally that of the **monotriglyph** (i.e. having one triglyph over the space between two columns, and, of course, one on the centre-line of each column), but at the corners of Greek Doric buildings, on account of the triglyphs being placed at the angles, the extreme intercolumniation is less than that of the intermediate columns, and angle triglyphs are not on the centre-lines of columns. **Hellenistic** intercolumniation, even in the Doric Order, was generally wider than in **Hellenic** examples, often with two or more triglyphs above the spaces between columns, giving a lighter, more elegant appearance. Main types of intercolumniation, as defined by Vitruvius are **pycnostyle** (1½d), **systyle** (2d), **eustyle** (2¼d), **diastyle** (3d), and **aræostyle** (more than 3d), where d = the diameter. Aræostyle is supposed to have been an invention of Perrault, who set two columns ½d apart followed by a space of 3½d then two more columns ½d apart,

SELECT GLOSSARY OF TERMS / 207

as at the east front of the Louvre, Paris. Wren also employed this spacing on the west front of St Paul's Cathedral, London. Eustyle is the most commonly used intercolumniation, although the Doric Order intercolumniation is controlled by the triglyph/metope relationship, and triglyphs are centred on columns in **Roman Doric** at all times, so at the corners of the **frieze** there are two half-**metopes**, not triglyphs.

interdentils Spaces between **dentils**: in Roman work dentils are set closer together than in Greek exemplars.

interfenestration Space between window-openings.

intermodillion Space between **modillions**, often ornamented.

interpensivæ Cantilevers formed by the ends of joists.

interpilaster Space between **pilasters**.

intersectio Gap between dentils, described as μετόπη (**metope**) by the ancient Greeks, but metope is never used in this sense today. **Metopon** is a piece of wall between doors or windows, a Classical **trumeau** or **mullion**.

intrados Interior and lower curve of an **arch**, the **soffit** of an arch or **vault**, or its under-surface: the upper curve is called the **extrados** (see **arch** [see Fig. G20a]).

inverted arch One with the **intrados** under the centre, i.e. an arch turned upside down, used in foundations.

Ionic Order Second Greek Order, and the third Roman. The distinguishing feature is the **capital**, with its rolled-up cushion-like forms on either side, creating **volutes** on the other sides (Fig. G72). Proportions of the **column** are more slender than those of the **Doric Order**, and the Order has a **base** of the **Asiatic** or **Attic** type, the latter favoured by the Romans. The shaft is generally **fluted**, with **fillets** between the **flutes** (although **Hellenistic** columns often have the lower part of the **shaft** faceted or plain, as in the **stoa**, Priene [c.158–6 BC]), but Roman shafts are often wholly unfluted. Ionic **entablatures** do not have **triglyphs** or **metopes**, and the **frieze** can be plain or enriched. In some variations of the Order there is no frieze, but the **architrave** is usually divided into three **fasciæ**. **Abaci** are moulded, often enriched, and much smaller than Doric abaci. Cornice mouldings are often elaborate, and include **dentils**. The **echinus**, **astragal**, and **fillet** are common to both Greek and Roman Ionic capitals, and the echinus is uniformly cut into eggs surrounded with angular-sectioned borders between which are tongues or darts. Astragals are rows of **bead-and-reel** ornament. When columns are used in the flanks of the buildings as well as in the 'front', the capitals of each angular column are made to face both contiguous sides of the building, with the two adjacent volutes at the corner bending in a concave curve towards the angle (see Fig. G13). Roman Ionic capitals often have the four sides identical, with the volutes projecting diagonally at all four corners under the abacus (see Fig. G14). The Order used at the Erechtheion in Athens has a frieze of **anthemion** motifs around the necks of the columns below the astragal of the capital proper, giving it an especially rich flavour, especially as the astragal below the neck is also enriched with beads (see Figs 2.7–2.8b). The **Ammonite Order** is an English version of Ionic, found in some numbers in Kent and Sussex, and named after the whorled chambered fossil shells that are used instead of the volutes (see Fig. G11).

isodomum **1.** Masonry of stone blocks of equal length laid to courses of equal height, each vertical joint centred on the block in the course below. **2.** Masonry in which the courses are of equal height, but the alignment of vertical joints is irregular. See **pseudisodomum**.

Italianate Style based on the architecture developed in Italy from the end of the 15th century for **palazzi**, made fashionable by Barry at the Travellers' and Reform clubs (London), and later by Prince Albert at Osborne House, Isle of Wight.

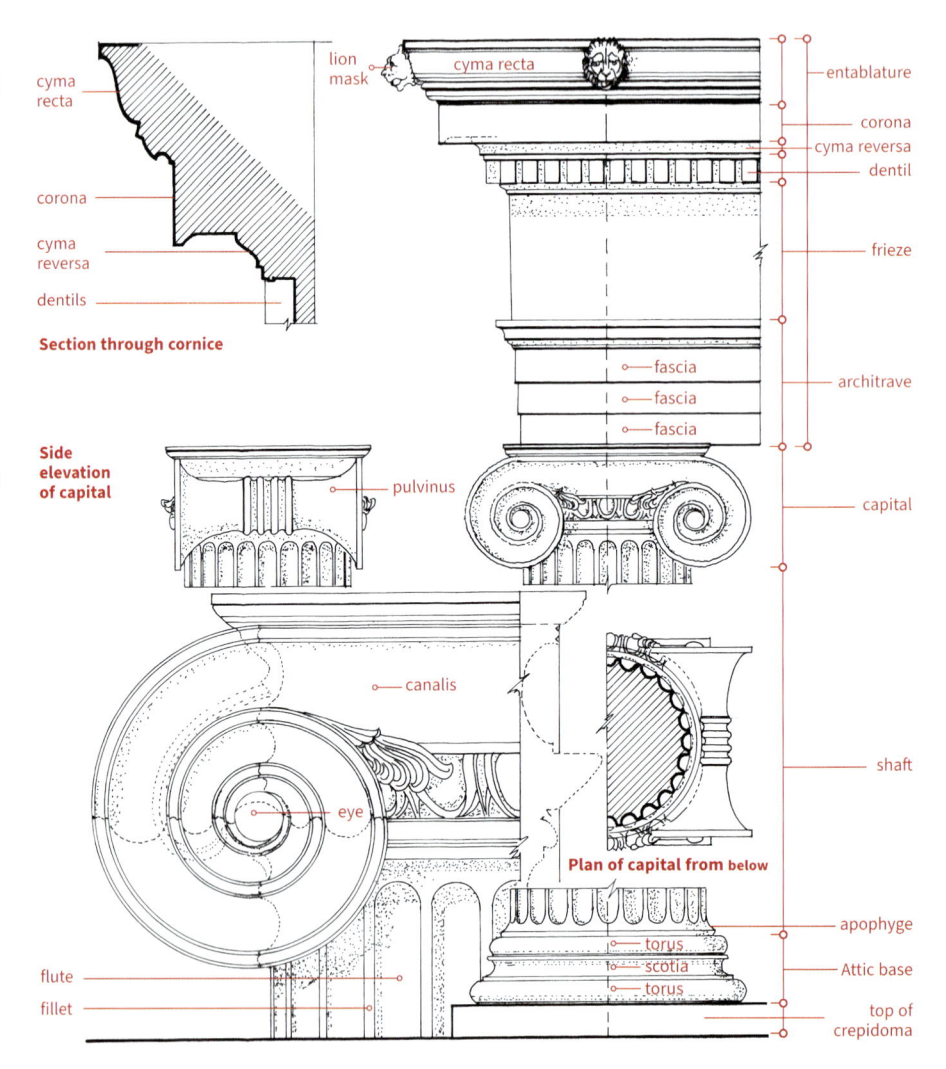

Fig. G72 *Greek Ionic Order from Eleusis (JSC after Normand [1852]).*

208 / CLASSICAL ARCHITECTURE

It is essentially **astylar**, with **ædiculated** openings, and a large *cornicione* capping the elevations (*see* Figs 6.43a–c).

Jacobean architecture Style of English architecture of the reign of King James VI and I, not differing greatly from Elizabethan architecture, and continuing for a time into the reign of Charles I. Essentially a melange of Flemish, French, and Italian Renaissance influences, it included jewelled **strapwork** and **grotesque** ornament, **assemblages of Orders**, emblems, heraldic devices, **herms**, **obelisks**, and themes drawn from Flemish **Mannerism**.

jamb Properly, the side of a window- or door-opening bearing the superincumbent weight of the wall, but more often simply the vertical lining of the opening. The **antepagmentum** supports the **lintel** or **supercilium**.

key Pattern, aka **fret** or **Greek-key** design (*see* Fig. G66).

keystone Highest and central wedge-shaped stone or **voussoir**, equidistant from the springing extremities of an **arch**, sometimes called **sagitta** (*see* Figs G12, G20a, and G90b). Often carved with human heads, or in the form of an **ancon**, it sometimes supports a bust or other ornament. In circular openings there are properly two keystones, one at the bottom and one at the top.

kiosk Open pavilion or summer-house of light construction, supported on columns and surrounded by a balustrade, often found in gardens.

knee Projection of **architrave mouldings** at the ends of the **lintel** in the dressings of a Classical door- or window-opening (*see* Figs G21a–b).

kneeler Block of stone at the top of a wall terminating the parapet, or **coping**, or **gable**, aka **padstone**, **kneestone**, and **skew-stone** (*see* Fig. G62).

kneeling window Renaissance window-surround, usually pedimented, with two long consoles under the cill, as in the additions by Michelangelo to the Palazzo Medici, Florence (1516–17), or the **façade** of the Palazzo Farnese, Rome (1515–46) (*see* Figs 4.8a and 4.14a).

knull, knulling 1. Very flat, thin, squashed **bead-and-reel** moulding. 2. **Gadroon** or **lobe** (*see* Fig. G63).

knurl foot Foot like an inward-turning scroll.

labarum Roman Imperial standard surmounted by an eagle, usually associated with **trophies** in **Neo-Classical** decoration.

label Rectangular **tablet**. Framed or plain, with wedge-shaped projections on either side, commonly found in **Neo-Classical** architecture, having its origins in Roman work, where it was often inscribed (Fig. G73).

Fig. G73 *Classical label.*

labyrinth Fret with many maze-like turnings, similar to a **key pattern** or **Greek key** (*see* Fig. G66).

lachrymæ Guttæ (*see* **Doric Order**).

laconicum Dry room for sweating in **thermæ**.

lacuna (*pl.* **lacunæ**) Classical **coffer** in a ceiling, **cornice-soffit**, etc., often elaborately ornamented with **bead-and-reel**, **egg-and-dart**, and with an ornament in its centre. A coffer under a cupola is termed **caisson**. The term **laquear** is used to express the effects of mouldings separating the margins of panels in coffering. Related terms include **lacunar**: 1. Coffer in a flat soffit, ceiling, etc., also a ceiling, cornice, etc., with coffers; 2. Beams enclosing coffers; **lacunarium** (*pl.* **lacunaria**): system of lacunæ or coffers (the plural describes the coffered ceiling of the **ambulatory** or **peridrome** between the **peristyle** and the cell walls of an **Antique temple**, as well as to the soffit of the main cornice.

lamb's tongue 1. Glazing-bar with a section of two long **ogees** separated by a **fillet**, very fine and deep compared with its width. 2. Tapering tongue-like end to a stair handrail rising in a concave curve and joining the handrail in a convex sweep.

lamp Symbol of enlightenment and immortality, often found on **urns** or **vases**.

lantern Turret, **drum**, or other structure raised above a roof or **dome** with windows around the sides to light the apartment below.

laquear *See* **lacuna**. Also perhaps a net-like form of decoration used on ceilings, etc. in Antique **grottoes**.

lararium (*pl.* **lararia**) 1. Small room or **niche** in a Roman house used as a kind of private shrine, where images of the **lares** and **penates** were placed for devotional purposes. 2. Place for the display of **Antique** statues, statuettes, etc. in a Classical house.

larmier Corona between the **cymatium** and **bed-moulding**, aka **lorimer**, acting as a **drip** (*see* **Orders**).

later (*pl.* **lateris**) Roman brick or tile. **Later crudus** is a sun-dried brick, while **later coctus** or **testaceus** is baked. Burned bricks or tiles used as facings in Roman concretes are called **tegulæ**.

lattice Openwork, often associated with **Chinoiserie** (*see* Fig. G39a).

Latin cross One with three arms of equal length and the fourth much longer (*see* Fig. G47).

laurel Bay, often used in Classical decoration, as in **bay-leaf garland** (*see* Fig. G30).

leaf-and-dart Moulding similar to **egg-and-dart** but with a leaf resembling a tongue carved on the oval shape, substituted for the egg (*see* **Orders** [Fig. G74; *see* Figs 2.9 and 3.7]).

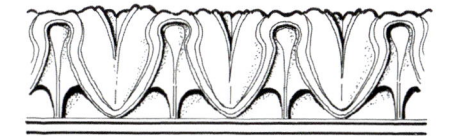

Fig. G74 *Leaf-and-dart moulding, sometimes called tongue-and-dart.*

leaf 1. Part of a door, panel, or shutter that folds, i.e. is hung on hinges or pivoted. 2. Carved, stylised ornament derived from the leaves of plants, e.g. acanthus, bay, laurel, olive, palm, or other plant (*see* **Orders**).

Lesbian cymatium What Vitruvius calls **cymatium Lesbium** seems to refer to the **cyma reversa** moulding, that is with a convex shape at the top, and a concave below, often **enriched** (*see* **Orders** and **moulding**).

SELECT GLOSSARY OF TERMS / 209

limen Lintel or threshold.

lintel Beam over an opening supporting the wall above, and spanning between **jambs** or **columns** (hence **post-and-lintel** or **trabeated** construction, as opposed to **arcuated**). A **limen superum** is specifically a lintel or **supercilium**, to distinguish it from a threshold.

lion mask Frequently found in Classical ornament, especially **keystones**, **corbels**, and **bosses**.

list or **listel** Fillet or **annulet**.

loculus (*pl.* **loculi**) **1.** In a **catacomb**, **hypogeum**, **mausoleum**, or other place of entombment, a recess large enough to receive a human corpse, with or without a coffin or **sarcophagus**. If arched it is termed **arcosolium**. **2.** Large **cinerarium** or **ollarium**. **3. Sarcophagus**.

lodge **1.** Small house at the gate of an estate (often paired with a similar structure to provide symmetry) or any small house in a park. **2.** Place where Freemasons assemble. **3. Loggia**. **4.** Building used by hunting, fishing, or shooting parties.

loggia (*pl.* **loggie**) **Lodge 1**, but more usually part of a building where one or more sides are open to the air, the opening being colonnaded or arcaded. It can be a separate building, but it is more often an open gallery or an arcaded or colonnaded large recess at ground-floor or *piano nobile* level (see Fig. 4.43).

lorymer, **lorimer**, or **larmier** Corona or any horizontal **moulding** acting as a **drip**.

lotus Common Greek and Egyptian ornament, often mixed with the **palmette**. Lotus flowers and lotus buds can sometimes be found together (see **anthemion**).

lucarne See **luthern**.

lunette Semicircular opening or blind recess.

luthern Window standing perpendicularly above the entablature and built on the **naked**, or same plane as the main **façade** below the **entablature**, to illuminate space within the roof. Lutherns can be semicircular, elliptical, segmental-headed, and of other kinds, and are associated with French Classical architecture. They are not the same as dormers, which rise vertically from the rafters of a sloping roof, and do not rise perpendicularly on the naked of the façade below.

lyre Instrument frequently found in Classical decoration, associated with Apollo.

lysis Plinth above the cornice of the podium of a Classical building.

mæander Key-pattern (see **Greek key**).

mænianum **1.** Lattice, balcony, or projecting storey. **2.** Tier of seats in a theatre.

magot Seated obese male figure, often with crossed legs, found in **Chinoiserie** decorations, aka **pagod** or **poussah**, associated with contentment (see Fig. 39b)

mandala, **mandorla** Almond-shaped figure described by two vertical arcs each passing through the other's centre, enclosing a **panel**, aka **aureole**, **halo**, or **vesica piscis** (Fig. G75).

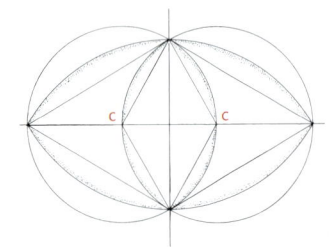

Fig. G75 *Mandala or mandorla diagram showing how an almond-shaped form related to equilateral triangles is described, c marking the centres of two circles passing through each other.*

Mannerism Style of 16th-century architecture characterised by the use of Classical motifs outside their normal context, or in a wilful, fanciful, or illogical manner. It was the precursor of **Baroque**, and is generally associated with Italian architecture from the time of Michelangelo until the beginning of the 17th century. Dropped **keystones** or **triglyphs**, **columns** inserted into recesses and apparently carried on **consoles**, and distorted **ædicules** were features of the style. Subsequently the School of Fontainebleau and the Flemish Mannerists created a lavish style of decoration with **grotesque** ornament and **strapwork** much in evidence, with **cartouches**, **herms**, **swags**, etc. It has been perceived by some as a corruption of Classicism: decadent, in other words, but others have seen it as evidence of the inexhaustible possibilities of the Classical language of architecture

Fig. G76 *Details of the external treatment of the crypt of the Metropolitan Cathedral of Christ the King, Liverpool, designed by Sir Edwin Lutyens, designed from 1929, and built from 1933 until work stopped during the 1939–45 war. The treatment of the elements flanking the doors, partly free-standing and partly subsumed into the structure, and the bent transom of the window, seemingly distorted by the downward thrust of the massive keystone, were myopically described by Pevsner as 'exasperating whimsy', but they are actually clever examples of 20th-century Mannerism, as quirkily inventive variations on Classicism as anything by Giulio Romano or Michelangelo (JSC).*

(Fig. G76; see Figs G90b, 4.11c–d, 4.29–4.31, 4.33, and 7.4).

mansard roof Roof with two inclined planes, aka **curb roof**, named after François Mansart.

mantel- or **mantlepiece** Properly, a decorative shelf in front of the **manteltree** (or **mantletree**), the horizontal beam over a fireplace. The mantelpiece is carried on the **jambs** of the chimneypiece. The term has become corrupted to mean the frame surrounding a fireplace.

marble Crystalline limestone (marmor), easily and accurately carved and polished, which can also be burned to provide **quicklime**. **Marble-stucco** is stucco with crushed marble in the mix. **Marbling** is the process, practice, craft, or finish (of considerable Antiquity) by which, using paint, a marble finish is suggested.

margent Strip of leaf and flower forms (called **wheat-ear drops** or **husks**) hanging

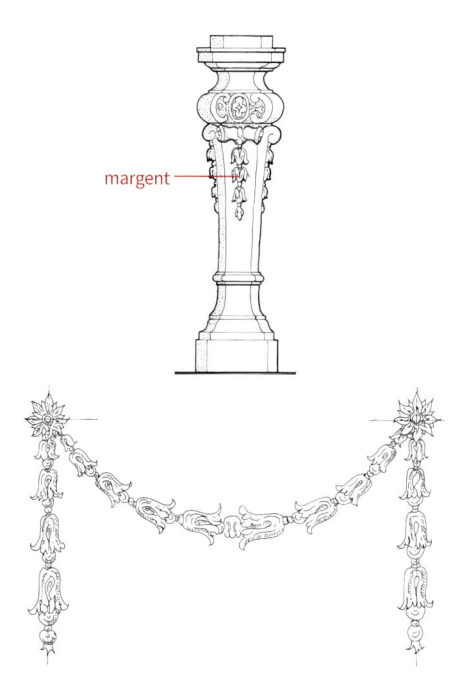

Fig. G77 *(Top) English Rococo pedestal with margents of bellflowers, husks, or wheat-ears; (bottom) festoon of bellflowers with margents on either side.*

from a **bow**, mask, **patera**, ring, or **rosette** (Fig. G77; *see* Fig. G71).

margin-draft Dressed **band** the width of a chisel all around the face of an **ashlar-block**, contrasting with the rest of the exposed stone.

margin-light 1. Tall, narrow flanking-window or wing-light on either side of a wider door or window, often found in late 18th- and early 19th-century British houses of the grander sort (*see* Fig. G55b). 2. Narrow lights defined by glazing-bars around the edges of **sash-windows**, often set with coloured glass, common in **Greek Revival** architecture, or influenced by a taste for a wider, squatter proportion of rectangular window fashionable *c*.1810 (*see* Fig. G118).

marigold Formalised circular floral decoration in Greek architecture, resembling a **rosette**, but more like a chrysanthemum or marigold, repeated in series, e.g. on the **architrave** of the north **portico** of the Erechtheion, Athens. A **marigold window** is circular, with radiating glazing-bars, often found in **gables** or **pediments**.

marine decoration Classical ornament suggesting the sea or navigation, including anchors, the **columna rostrata**, **dolphins**, fish, **frosted rustication**, **hippocamps**, mermaids, Neptune with trident, nets, ropes, sea-shells, and **Tritons**.

marmoratum opus Imitation marble, consisting of fine stuff of calcinated gypsum and crushed stones, including marble, which, when set, is rubbed down to a fine marble-like surface.

marquetry Inlaid work of thin plates of ivory, or different veneers of wood glued to a ground and forming a decorative pattern.

mascaron Representation of a human or partly human face, more or less caricatured, used as an ornament, e.g on a **keystone** over an **arch**.

masonry Craft of cutting, jointing, and laying stones for building.

mason's mitre When **mouldings** meet at an angle the joint does not (or ought not to) occur at the diagonal because the resulting acute angle of the masonry is

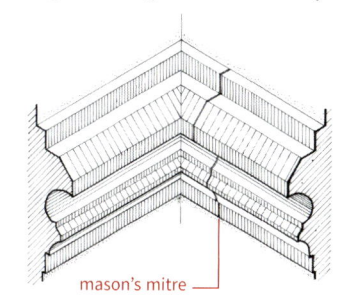

Fig. G78 *Mason's mitre.*

brittle and fragile. The moulding is therefore carried through on the return face, and the joint occurs at right angles to the face: a mason's mitre does not, therefore, have a diagonal joint (Fig. G78).

mathematical tile Facing-tiles used to clad timber-framed **façades** to make them look as though they are of fine quality brick. Good 18th-century examples can still be found in Sussex and elsewhere (Fig. G79).

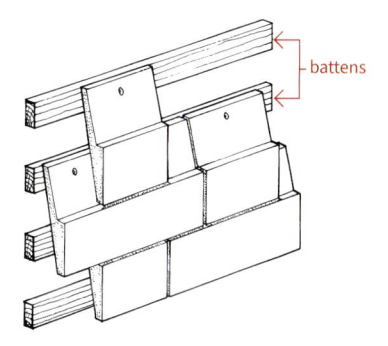

Fig. G79 *Mathematical tiles from an example in Lewes, Sussex.*

mausoleum (*pl.* **mausolea**) Built, roofed sepulchre with architectural pretensions containing **sarcophagi**, **coffins**, or **cinerary urns**, so called after the celebrated tomb of King Mausolus of Caria at Halicarnassus (*see* Figs 5.39a–b, 6.2b, 6.13, 6.17, 6.18a, 6.33a–d, and 8.14).

meander Progressive ornament on **bands**, **friezes**, **string-courses**, etc. composed of straight lines joining at right angles or cut diagonally (e.g. **fret** and **key** patterns [*see* Fig. G66]), or curving (e.g. **guilloche**, **running-dog**, **wave-**, or **Vitruvian scroll** [*see* Figs G68 and G115]).

medallion Square, elliptical, circular, or oval **tablet** on which are figures, designs, or busts, usually carved in relief.

Medusa One of the **Gorgons**, often used as a decoration on a **keystone**.

megaron Hall, **temple**, inner sanctuary, underground cavern, or a main hall or significant apartment.

memory, the art of System of mnemonic devices evolved in **Antiquity** and revived and developed in **Renaissance** times: aka the **Phoenix**. It involved the study of a building: the student would visit the rooms in a specific order, memorising that order and architectural details of each room; when memorising a speech he would revisit the building in imagination, associating the images with arguments or words that would then become the trigger for the speech.

meros Flat face between **channels** in the Doric triglyph.

metatome, metoche Space between **dentils** in Classical architecture, or the space between **triglyphs** of the **Doric Order**.

metopa, metope, metopse Square space between two **triglyphs** of the **frieze** of the **Doric Order**, either plain or decorated with **bucrania**, **trophies**, or sculptured reliefs (*see* **Doric Order**). Vitruvius also states that metope is an equivalent for **intersectio**, or the space between two dentils.

metopon The solid between doors or windows, or a **pier**, square on plan, like a **mullion**.

mews Terrace of stables or coach-houses with living quarters above, associated with grander houses.

SELECT GLOSSARY OF TERMS / 211

mezzanine Storey of medium height between two higher storeys: an **entresol**, only possible with sufficient floor-to-ceiling heights of the principal storeys.

mezzo-relievo Projection of sculptured ornaments by half their normal three-dimensional depth.

middle rail Middle rail of a door to which the lock or bolt is fixed, aka **lock-rail** (*see* Fig. G61).

military decoration Architectural ornament representing an arrangement of armour, flags, guns, helmets, swords, pikes, etc., aka **trophy**, often used on arsenals, barracks, etc., as well as on funerary monuments and memorials commemorating military men or war.

minute Sixtieth part of the diameter of a column at the base of the shaft. It is therefore a proportional measure by which the sizes of parts of an **Order** are calculated.

mitre Line formed by the meeting of two elements intersecting each other at an angle.

modillion Projecting ornament like a **console** or embellished bracket under the **corona** of the **Corinthian** and **Composite Orders**, and occasionally in the **Roman Ionic Order** (Fig. G80). Modillions are placed with intervening **coffers** or other ornaments between them. They should be regularly positioned, i.e. the centre of one should always stand over the centre-line of a **column** or **pilaster**. Corinthian modillions are usually more elaborate than those of the Ionic or Composite Orders. A **mutule**, which is confined to the **Doric Order**, is always spaced in relation to the **triglyphs**, and is very different in form compared with a modillion, although the origin is probably the same, and the architectural function, that of enriching the soffit of the corona, is identical (*see* **Orders**).

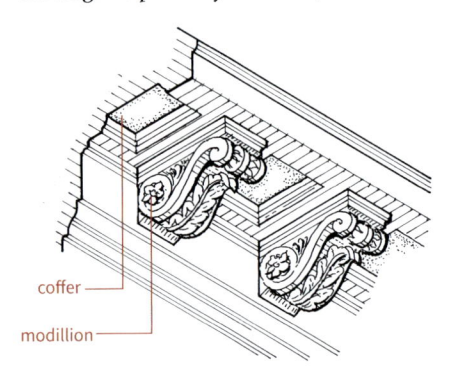

Fig. G80 *Cornice with modillions between which are coffers.*

modinature Distribution, profiles, and arrangements of the **mouldings** of an **Order**, a building, or an architectural member.

module Any measure which regulates proportion by means of its multiples or subdivisions. In Classical architecture a module is the diameter measured at the base of the **shaft**, and each module is subdivided into 60 minutes. Some authorities suggest that a module is a half-diameter of 30 minutes, and that it is only used in the **Doric Order**. However, architectural proportion always depends on some repetition of measurement, and the term refers to any system of measurement that facilitates repetition of a standard unit.

money pattern *See* **coin moulding**.

monolith Shaft of a column, an obelisk, or any part that consists of a single stone.

monopodia Representation of an animal's leg topped by a head, often of a leopard, used as a support.

monopteron, monopteros Building in which there are no walls, only columns carrying a roof to define the volume. Properly, it is circular, but Soane described his own tomb as a 'monopteral' temple although it has four square shafts carrying the monolithic lid on a square plan. It appears to mean a sacred built enclosure with no cell, but with a **peripteral** arrangement of columns.

monostyle Building of one style throughout, a **column** with a single **shaft** instead of a cluster, or with one column.

monotriglyphic Intercolumniation where only one **triglyph** and two **metopes** are introduced between the centre-lines of columns in the frieze.

monument Any edifice to commemorate a person or event.

mosaic 1. Ornamental work formed by inlaying in a cement or plaster matrix small pieces (**tesseræ**) of stone, glass, pottery, marble, etc. in a pattern which may be either geometrical or naturalistic. 2. Chequerboard pattern of black and white squares used in flooring and associated with Masonic lodges.

moulded capital Capital with mouldings, unlike a plain or block-capital.

moulding Part of an **Order** or a building shaped in profile into various curved or angular forms. Any ornamental contour given to features of a building, whether projections or cavities, e.g. an **architrave**, **astragal**, or **cornice**. Regular mouldings (Fig. G81) in Classical architecture are the **fillet** or **list**; the **astragal** or **bead**; the **cyma recta** and **cyma reversa**; the **cavetto** or **hollow**; the **ovolo** or **quarter-round**; the **scotia** or **trochilus**; and the **torus** or **round**.

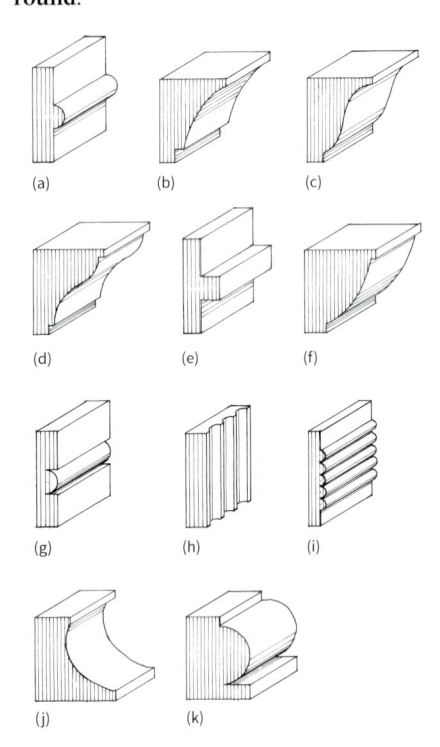

Fig. G81 *Mouldings: (a) astragal; (b) cavetto; (c) cyma recta; (d) cyma reversa, reverse ogee, or Lesbian cymatium; (e) fillet; (f) ovolo; (g) flush bead; (h) flutes and fillets; (i) reeding; (j) scotia; (k) torus.*

mouth Cavetto.

mullion Vertical member between the **lights** of a window or screen, usually moulded.

muntin Central upright framing in a door: the outer uprights are **stiles** or **styles**, and **muntins** butt into the horizontal **rails** (*see* Fig. G61).

mural Belonging to a wall, or a painting

on a wall. A **mural monument** is one fixed to a wall.

mutilated **Cornice** or **pediment** that is **broken** or **discontinued**, a device common in **Baroque** architecture.

mutule Block, like a bracket, under the **corona** of the **Doric Order**. It may have **guttæ** or **drops** on the underside, and it will be centred over the **triglyph**. In the **Tuscan Order** after Inigo Jones (*see* Fig. G111b) the mutules are like simple cantilevered brackets, but in the **Corinthian** and **Composite Orders** they are termed **modillions**, and are like **consoles** on their sides (*see* Fig. G80). The term **mutule**, or **mutulus**, suggests a structural beam, although where it is used with the Doric Order it is more like a rafter, or the top member of a primitive **truss**. Vitruvius seems to imply that in Etruscan temples the **trabes compactiles**, **architraves**, or **lintels** that were carried on the widely spaced columns supported a second set of beams at right angles to the architraves, and that these second beams were called mutuli, and were placed on the cell walls and on the centre-lines of each column of the **porch**, projecting in cantilevers forward of the line of the **colonnade** (*see* **Orders**).

naked Unornamented plain surface of a wall, **column**, or other part of a building: the main plane of a **façade**.

naos Sanctuary of a Greek temple, equivalent of the **cell** or **cella**, or the part of a temple within the walls (*see* **temple**).

narthex 1. Part of a church, screened off and situated near the west door. 2. Ante-chamber or vestibule at the west of the church, acting as a variety of **porch** (*see* Fig. G27b).

nave Part of a church west of the choir, usually a central space with two or more aisles to the north and south, and is often separated from the choir by a screen (*see* Fig. G27b).

neck Plain part of a **Roman Doric** or **Tuscan column** between the **astragal** at the top of the **shaft** and the **fillet annulets** on the **capital**. Some **Greek Ionic** columns have necks, aka **collarino** or **hypotrachelium**, usually enriched with **anthemion** ornament. A neck-moulding separates the capital from the shaft proper (*see* **Orders**).

Neo-Classicism Movement in architecture that had its beginnings in a rejection of **Baroque** and **Rococo**, and in a seeking to rediscover the architecture of Classical **Antiquity**, considered a less corrupted source than the architecture of the **Italian Renaissance**. An interest in the architecture of ancient Rome was encouraged by Piranesi's views of that city, with their exaggerated scale and Sublime visual effects, but the noble simplicity and serene grandeur of Greek architecture extolled by Winckelmann encouraged investigation of the buildings of Classical Antiquity on a new scale. Buildings were re-examined and described, so that many Renaissance sources were rejected in favour of the archæologically proven correctness of the Antique. Neo-Classicism, however, was rarely a mere copying of the works of Antiquity: although accuracy was prized in archæologically correct motifs, it was also concerned to return to first principles, basic forms, clear uncluttered geometry, and a rational approach to design, encouraged by the writings of Laugier and Lodoli. In this was an implicit faith in the superiority of primitive forms of stereometrical purity, which led designers such as Boullée, Ledoux, Ehrensvärd, Gilly, Latrobe, and Soane to experiment with an architecture from which **enrichment** was often eliminated.

Of all the Orders, **Greek Doric** was most appreciated for its severity and primitive qualities, first in the surviving remains of the Greek colonies in Sicily and at Pæstum, then in the systematic investigations of Greek architecture by Stuart and Revett which led to the publication of *The Antiquities of Athens* from 1762. The latter provided measured drawings of the architecture of Ancient Greece for designers, and had a profound effect on taste. Two years later the publication of the *Ruins of the Palace of the Emperor Diocletian at Spalatro*, based on the measurements and drawings by Robert Adam and Charles-Louis Clérisseau, gave further impetus to an understanding of the Antique, while in the 1730s and 1740s work began on the excavation of the cities of Herculaneum and Pompeii, buried since AD 79 as a result of the catastrophic eruptions of Vesuvius: the architecture, artefacts, and decorative schemes uncovered during the excavations led taste and design further towards an evocation of the Antique. Winckelmann's championing of Greek art and architecture, together with the work of Stuart and Revett, prompted a **Greek Revival** that was one of the more remarkable aspects of Neo-Classicism. Later, the publication of Denon's *Voyage dans la Basse et la Haute Égypte* in 1802, and of the monumental *Description de l'Égypte* by the Commission des Monuments d'Égypte from 1809, gave designers accurate illustrations of real ancient Egyptian buildings, and were to the Egyptian Revival what the works of Stuart and Revett had been to the Greek Revival. Egyptian architecture, with its primitive, massive elements, and its simple, pure forms, such as the **obelisk**, **pylon**, and **pyramid**, appealed to those Neo-Classical architects who sought a stereometrical purity in their designs, and a plain, tough, masculine expression of forms. Thus, certain Egyptian elements, such as the pyramid, obelisk, battered walls, and pylon-like shapes entered the vocabulary of Neo-Classical design.

Neo-Classical architecture tends to be severe, stark, serious, and even rather forbidding at times. It is very controlled, and purged of much **enrichment**, while the Orders, usually Greek and sometimes extremely primitive Greek (such as unfluted, simplified, stumpy Doric) are used to express structural ideas, and are rarely **engaged** or used as mere decoration. Forms are usually starkly defined, and volumes are expressed both inside and out (*see* Figs 6.1–6.4, 6.8b–6.40a, and 7.2).

newel 1. Central column or solid or imaginary solid around which the steps of a circular staircase wind. 2. Principal upright member set at any turning-point of a stair, or at the top of a flight, commonly forming part of the framing of a stair, and serving to connect and support the strings and handrails at a turn or end (*see* Figs G102a–d).,

niche Recess in a wall for a statue, vase, or other ornament. Niches are often semicircular on plan, and are arched. Some niches have quarter-spherical heads, often with the half-dome carved to resemble a scallop-shell, and some are treated as **ædicules**. Others are absolutely plain, without any frame (*see* Figs G89a and G110b).

nosing Prominent edge of a **moulding** or **drip**, or the projecting rounded moulding on the edge of a step (*see* Fig. G102d).

nulling Gadrooning or **lobing** (*see* Fig. G63).

nymphæum (*pl.* **nymphæa**) Grotto or structure containing pools, plants, rock-work, fountains, **shell-work**, and statues.

oak Oak leaves often appear in wreaths or on **pulvinated friezes**, with **acorns**.

obelisk Tall, tapering **shaft**, usually square on plan, with battered sides and a pyramidal top. Obelisks are normally placed on pedestals in Classical architecture, and are an instance when ancient Egyptian forms entered into the language of Classicism. Obelisks were often confused with **pyramids**, so much so that some early drawings show pyramidal forms with obelisks on top.

octastyle **Portico** of eight columns in line (*see* **temple**).

oculus (*pl.* **oculi**) **1.** Circular window. **2.** Disc, eye, or button in the centre of a volute-spiral as in the **Ionic capital**. **3.** Opening at the top of a dome, as in the Roman Pantheon.

odeum, odeon Theatre for musical performances.

œcus An odd word, with many meanings, including 'house', 'temple', 'room'. It appears to have come to mean a large and important room in a private house.

œil-de-bœuf Window of circular or elliptical form, often with four keystones.

off-set, or **set-off** Top of a wall, **buttress**, or **plinth**, sloped for weathering, aka **water-** or **weather-table**.

ogee ʃ-shaped double curve, one convex and the other concave. The **cyma moulding** (*see* Fig. G49).

ogival Ogee (as adjective).

olive Leaves often confused with bay or laurel.

ollarium (*pl.* **ollaria**) Recess, often arched, in a **columbarium** or **hypogeum** in which pairs of cinerary urns or **ash-chests** were deposited.

opæ Beds of roof-beams in a Greek building, the spaces between which are **metopes**.

opaion Lantern, or part of a roof pierced and raised for the admission of light.

open well Describes a stair which has a space or a well between the outer strings, unlike the **dog-leg** which has no space or very little space between the outer **strings** (*see* Fig. 102a).

opisthodomus **1.** Space at the rear of the **cell** of a **temple**. **2.** Open **porch**, like the **pronaos** (*see* **temple**).

optical corrections Alterations to planes or surfaces to correct possible perceptions of distortion. They include **entasis**; increasing the height of stone courses with the height of a wall so that the courses appear identical in height; and the slight convex surface of a **stylobate**.

opus (*pl.* **opera**) Latin for 'work'. The following are the commoner combinations: **opus albarium**: thin coat of burnt powdered marble, lime, sand, and water applied to a wall and polished after it had set, or a coating of pure lime on a wall; **opus Alexandrinum**: paving of coloured marbles cut in geometrical shapes, inlaid in repetitive geometrical patterns, e.g. **guilloche**, occasionally including **opus sectile**; **opus antiquum**: type of Roman masonry, aka **opus incertum**, the face of which had irregularly placed stones of different sizes (uncoursed rubble-work), with bands of brick or tile laid to provide horizontal levelling courses to bind the material together; **opus cæmenticium**: type of Roman concrete consisting of rough undressed stones placed in a mix of lime, pozzolan, sand, and water, aka **opus structile** or **structura cæmenticia**; **opus incertum**: as **opus antiquum**; **opus isodomum**: regular coursed **masonry**, with courses of equal height and the blocks of equal length with their vertical joints centred on the blocks above and below; **opus latericium** or **lateritium**: wall built of thin bricks or tiles, or of concrete faced with bricks, tiles, or a mixture of both, giving the impression that the wall is constructed of those materials rather than merely faced with them; **opus listatum**: Roman wall consisting of alternating courses of stone and brick or tiles; **opus marmoratum**: plaster or **stucco** of calcined gypsum mixed with powdered marble and water, rubbed and polished to a fine marble-like surface when dry; **opus mixtum**: wall-facing of brick (or tile) and squared **tufa** blocks laid in alternate courses; **opus pseudisodomum**: masonry laid in regular courses of broad and narrow bands, the narrow ones projecting slightly beyond the faces of the broader bands; **opus quadratum**: squared **ashlar** laid in regular courses; **opus reticulatum**: concrete wall faced with small squared stones (sometimes the bases of small pyramidal blocks), set diagonally all over the face, creating a lattice of interconnected joints, so resembling a net; **opus scalpturatum** or **sculpturatum**: inlaid work consisting of a pattern chiselled out of a solid ground, then filled in with thin slices of coloured marble (a variant was a marble slab into which a pattern was cut, then filled with coloured cement or stucco); **opus sectile**: pavement or wall-covering of differently coloured pieces (larger than **tesseræ** in mosaics) of marble, stone, and sometimes glass, cut into regular pieces of a few uniform sizes, laid in regular patterns; **opus signinum**: kind of **terrazzo** formed by mixing fragments of broken pottery or tiles with lime-mortar, then smoothing it off; **opus spicatum**: wall faced with stones or tiles arranged in herringbone patterns, usually with horizontal courses at various heights to provide bands and to bond the fabric together; **opus structile**: concrete; **opus tectorium**: as **opus albarium**; **opus tessellatum**: similar to **opus sectile**; **opus testacæum**: wall of rubble and concrete faced with whole or broken tiles, usually on both sides; **opus topiarum**: Antique mural-painting or **fresco** depicting gardens with trellis-work, trees, shrubs, etc.; **opus vermiculatum**: fine Antique mosaic, its **tesseræ** laid in curving **serpentine** lines, sometimes with emphasis added by darker tesseræ suggesting shadows.

orangery Gallery or a building with south-facing windows for the growing of oranges, or used as a conservatory for the storage in winter of trees in containers. Orangeries can be ornamental buildings in gardens (*see* Fig. 6.5b), or part of a grander composition, physically attached to a house.

oratory **1.** Small chapel or closet set apart for devotions. **2.** Religious establishment of the Congregation of St Philip Neri, aka Oratorians.

orchestra **1.** Circular area for the chorus and dancers in an ancient Greek theatre. **2.** In Roman theatres the level space between the stage and proscenium and the first semicircular row of seats.

Orders In Classical architecture, an assembly of parts making up the essential expression of a **columnar and trabeated** structure, consisting of **column**, with **base** (usually) and **capital**, and **entablature**.

There are eight distinct types of Classical Order: **Greek Doric**, **Roman Doric**, **Greek Ionic**, **Roman Ionic**, **Greek Corinthian**, **Roman Corinthian**, **Tuscan** (aka **Gigantic**), and **Composite**, although before the systematic rediscovery of Greek architecture in the 18th century the canonical five Orders (**Tuscan, Roman Doric, Roman Ionic, Roman Corinthian,** and **Composite**) were accepted, codified by Alberti, and illustrated by Serlio (1537). The Greek Doric column has no base, and sometimes (as in the **Pæstum Orders** of Doric [*see* Fig. G83]) **entasis** is exaggerated and the capital is very large, with a wide projection over the shaft; the Ionic Order has variations in the **base** (the **Asiatic** and **Attic** types [*see* Figs G22 and G23]) and **capital** (especially in relation to **angle, angular,** and **Bassæ** capitals where the problem of the corner **volute** is dealt with in different ways [*see* Figs G13, G14, and G28a–b]); and the Greek Corinthian capital (e.g. at the 4th-century BC choragic monument of Lysicrates, Athens [*see* Fig. G46a]) is taller and more elegant than its Roman counterparts (*see* Fig. G46b). In London, Kent, and Sussex there is a unique type of English Ionic capital, the **Ammonite Order** (*see* Fig. G11). At the Judge Institute of Management Studies, Cambridge (1993–5), a new polychrome Order was introduced to contain the services, named by its architect, John Outram, the **Ordine Robotico** (Robot Order). The **Tuscan** (aka **Gigantic Order**) shaft is always unfluted (*see* Figs G111a–c). A **Colossal Order** (aka **Giant Order**) is one with columns or **pilasters** rising through several storeys.

ordonnance 1. Proper disposition of the parts of a building. 2. Application of an **Order** of architecture suitable for a building and its type.

oriel Bay-window on a canted or bowed plan, cantilevered or corbelled out on an upper floor, and projecting in front of the **naked** of the wall below.

orle 1. **Fillet** under the **ovolo** or quarter-round of a **capital**. 2. **Cincture** or **fillet** at the upper and lower extremities of a column-shaft, terminating the **apophyge**. 3. **Plinth** or **pedestal** under the base of a column. 4. Face of a fillet between parallel **flutes** of a column-shaft.

orthography Elevations of a building or any part of it, showing correct relative proportions.

orthostata (*pl.* **orthostatæ**) One of several large vertical facing-slabs on the outer face of a temple wall, used as a variety of **dado** below the smaller blocks of the wall above.

orthostyle Columns set in a straight line.

oundy Vitruvian scroll, string-course decorated with a wave-like undulating motif (*see* Fig. G115).

ouroboros Snake in circular form, with its tail in its mouth, suggesting eternal recurrence, or immortality, and therefore often found on cemetery gates, funerary monuments, etc. (Fig. G82).

Fig. G82 *Ouroborus.*

ova Egg-shaped ornaments.

oversailing Courses of brick or stone corbelled out above the one below.

ovolo Convex moulding. Greek examples, aka **echinus**, are flattened, like part of the profile of an egg, while Roman ovolos are more mechanical, usually quarter-rounds. Ovolos are often ornamented with **egg-and-dart** (*see* **Orders** and **moulding**).

ovum Ovolo.

pace 1. Dais. 2. Broad raised step around an altar, tomb structure, etc. 3. Landing in a stair: **half-pace** is where one flight ends and another begins, involving a turn of 180°, and **quarter-pace** is a landing between two flights involving a turn of 90°.

packing Small stones between larger ones in rubble walls.

pad 1. Stone block aka **padstone** or **template** set on or in a wall etc. to carry a beam, **truss**, joist, or some other load. 2. **Kneeler** at the lowest point of a **gable** at the eaves to hold the **cope** in place and stop it sliding off, aka **knee-stone** or **skew**.

Pæstum Greek colony in Italy, south of Naples, of which a group of ruined **Doric temples** survives (*c.*530–*c.*460 BC). This **Doric Order** has the most exaggerated **entasis** of any **Antique** example, and the very wide, squat capitals on top of the shafts emphasise the primitive effect. The **Pæstum Order** was much admired by **Neo-Classical** architects in the late 18th and early 19th centuries (Fig. G83).

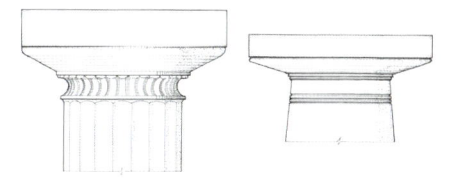

Fig. G83 *Primitive Pæstum Doric capitals (JSC after Normand [1852]).*

palace-front Classical symmetrical main elevation of a large building, or where several houses in a terrace appear to be one palatial composition, with emphases given to the centre and ends by means of **engaged porticoes**, **temple-fronts**, end-pavilions, and the like (*see* Fig. 5.55b).

palæstra Although the original meaning is narrower, suggesting a wrestling-school, it is often used in the wider sense of **gymnasium**.

palatial Italian Style applied to 19th-century banks, clubs, offices, etc. making them resemble **Italianate astylar** *palazzi* (e.g. Barry's Travellers' Club, Pall Mall, London [1829]).

palazzo (*pl. palazzi*) Grand Italian palatial residence, corresponding to a townhouse or large official residence. *See* **Italianate**, **palatial Italian**.

Palladian Style of architecture that evolved from the work of the 16th-century architect Andrea Palladio (Figs G84a–d; *see* Figs 4.37–4.43), and was brought to Britain in publications and by the works of Inigo Jones (*see* Figs 4.43 and 5.31). A revival of the style in the 18th century occurred in the area around Venice, but achieved considerable success in Britain largely through the efforts of Lord Burlington and Colen Campbell (*see* Figs 5.57a–5.59), who also revived interest in Inigo Jones's contributions. Under the ægis of the Palladians there evolved appropriate grammar and vocabulary that exercised a veritable tyranny of Taste during the reign of the first three Georges (Figs G84b–d). Palladian ideas were exported to Prussia (*see* Fig. 5.53),

SELECT GLOSSARY OF TERMS / 215

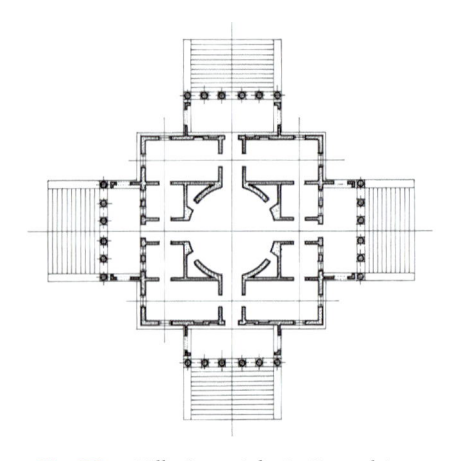

Fig. G84a *Villa Capra (aka La Rotonda), Vicenza (c.1566–70), with identical hexastyle Ionic porticoes (temple-fronts) on each of the four elevations, and a central circular two-storey room capped with a cupola, designed by Andrea Palladio.*

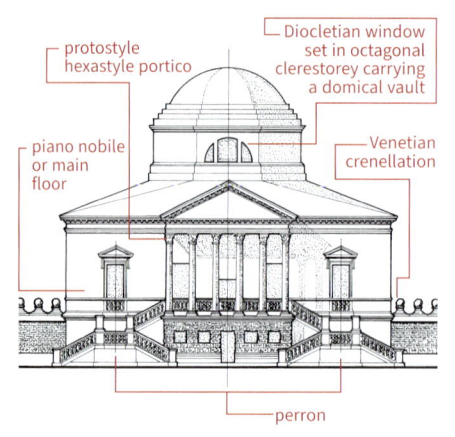

Fig. G84b *Elevation of Lord Burlington's villa at Chiswick, Middlesex (c.1723–9), inspired by Palladio's Villa Capra, Vicenza.*

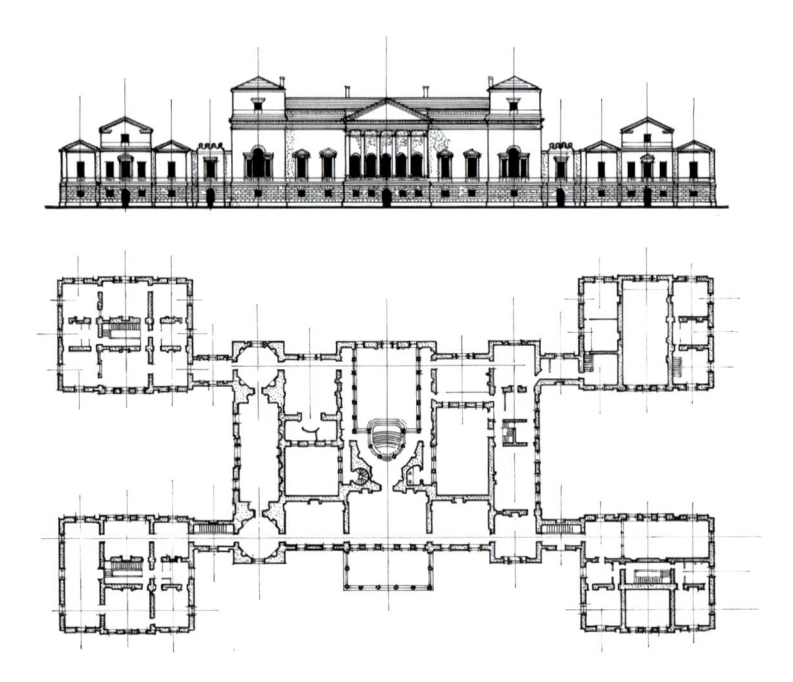

Fig. G84c *Plan and elevation of Holkham Hall, Norfolk (from 1734), by Lord Burlington, Lord Leicester, William Kent, and Matthew Brettingham, a fine example of Palladianism and concatenation. Each element of the elevations could exist as independent symmetrical compositions, and the various axes establish the order of the plan.*

Fig. G84d *Stupendous east front of Wentworth Woodhouse, West Riding of Yorkshire (c.1731–50), by Ralph Tunnicliffe and Henry Flitcroft. The 19-windows-wide central block, with its piano nobile, hexastyle Corinthian portico, and perron, was clearly inspired by the west front of Colen Campbell's Wanstead, Essex (c.1714–20), the designs of which were published in the first volume of* Vitruvius Britannicus *(1715). The flanking wings were raised a storey to designs by John Carr in 1782–4, who also added the Giant engaged Doric tetrastyle pedimented temple-fronts (JSC).*

Saxony, Russia, and the British Colonies in America. Palladian architecture was the style favoured by the Whig Oligarchy, and is associated with Anglophiles during the *Aufklärung* in German-speaking lands. A **Palladian window** is a **serliana** or **Venetian window**, and recurs in many Palladian designs (*see* Figs G100a–b and 5.37).

palm capital Variant of the Greek **Corinthian capital**, with one row of **acanthus** leaves, and an upper row of palm leaves under a square **abacus**, found at the Tower of the Winds, Athens (c.50 BC) (Fig. G85), and frequently reiterated in **Neo-Classical** work (*see* Figs 6.8a–b).

Fig.G85 *Greek Corinthian palm capital from the Tower of the Winds, Athens.*

palmette Ornament resembling a fan made up of narrow divisions or digitations, somewhat resembling a palm leaf. It is found alternating with the **lotus** (*see* **anthemion** [*see* Fig. G17]).

pampre Ornament of vine leaves and grapes, usually associated with **twisted** or **barley-sugar** columns, and often used as the **spiral** around columns, thus suggesting the twisted form (*see* Figs G60a–b and 5.3).

panache Approximately triangular surface of a **pendentive**.

pancarpi Garlands and festoons of fruit, flowers, and leaves for ornament.

panel mouldings Panels are usually held in place within a framework by means of moulded beads. These mouldings can be of various types, including **bead**, **flush**, or **bolection**, while panels can be carved, raised and fielded, or have other decorations (Fig. G86).

panier Upright basket-shaped **corbel** under a beam or **truss**.

panoply Sculptured representation of parts of a suit of armour, with various

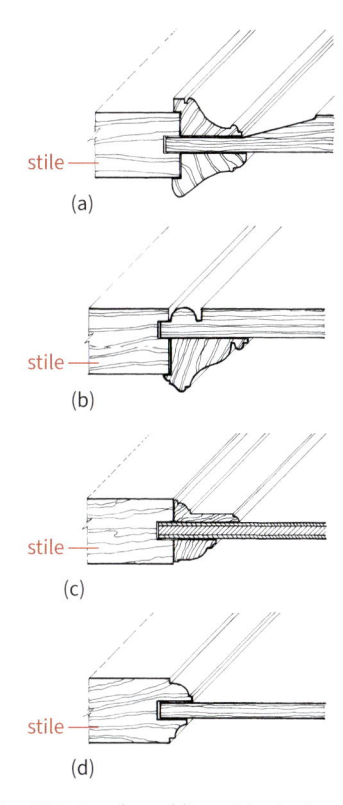

Fig. G86 *Panel mouldings: (a) raised and fielded panel secured with two variants of bolection moulding; (b) flush panel with beaded edge secured with bolection moulding; (c) ply panel secured with two types of planted moulding; (d) panel held in the stile with solid or struck ovolo (upper) and cavetto (lower) moulding.*

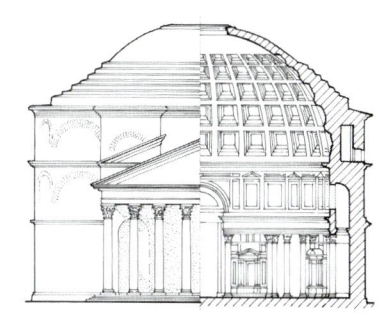

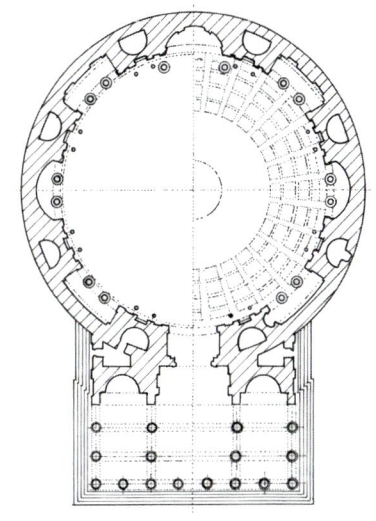

Fig. G87 *Pantheon: (top left) half-elevation showing portico and low stepped dome, a type revived by Neo-Classicism; (top right) half-section showing the oculus and coffers; (bottom) plan, with (right) the geometry of the coffers set out.*

weapons, arranged decoratively in a heap, in military decoration.

Pantheon dome Very simple dome resembling that of the Roman rotunda called the Pantheon (2nd century AD), with a series of concentric rings outside and coffers inside, sometimes with an **oculus** in the centre (Fig. G87). It was much used in the 18th and early 19th centuries as part of the severe vocabulary of **Neo-Classicism**.

pantile Tile with a section like an **S** on its side (∾) used in roofing.

parapet Low wall to protect any place where there is a drop. It may be battlemented, plain, pierced, or ornamented. In Classical architecture it may have an engaged **balustrade**, **panels**, **dies**, and other treatment.

parastas 1. Part of the flanking wall of a Greek **temple porch** projecting beyond the front wall, finished with an **anta**. 2. Space between two such flanking walls,

outside the **naos**, aka **pronaos**, so applied to a **vestibule**. 3. **Parastata**. 4. Massive **pedestal**-like element at the foot of a grand formal **stair**.

parastata, parastatica 1. Synonymous with **anta**, with only very small parts of the return-faces exposed. 2. Pilaster, again with very small return-faces.

parclose Screen separating chapels or tombs from the body of a church.

paraskenion Wing running forward from each of the ends of the **skene** of a Greek theatre.

Parker's cement Also called **Roman cement**, this was a rendering made from powdered, burnt clay nodules mixed with lime, sand, and water. It set hard, and fast, and was much used for covering **façades** with a representation of ashlar-joints scored into it.

parotis, parotides, prothyrides Ancon,

bracket, or **console**, from a Greek word associated with the human ear (*see* Figs G44a–c).

parquet Flooring of hardwood blocks laid in patterns on a base, and polished. **Parquetry** is inlaid work of thin veneers of hardwood, aka **inlaid** or plated parquet.

parterre Flat part of a garden designed with formal beds of flowers set in patterns.

Parthenon Fifth-century BC Greek Temple of Athena Parthenos on the Acropolis, Athens, widely regarded as the most refined building featuring **Hellenic Doric** architecture, and the model for much **Greek Revival** work, despite the fact that many of the details (e.g. the relationships of **columns** to **soffits**) are less than satisfactory. Subtle optical refinements (e.g. **entasis** on columns and the **stylobate**) further contributed to its stature as a canonic work, enhanced by the quality of the sculptures in the **metopes** and **pediments** (*see* Figs 2.1a–c). Within the temple was the Virgin Goddess's chamber, wherein stood four elegant **Ionic** columns.

parting bead Slip in the centre of the pulley stile of a **sash-window** to separate the two **sash-cords**.

pastas Recess off the south-facing side of the **peristyle** in a Greek house.

pastiche 1. Work that borrows from styles or historical motifs, hence an eclectic composition incorporating allusions to earlier periods, and not a mere copy, often handled with considerable *brio* and imagination. 2. Transfer of a design to another medium. In neither 1 nor 2 is the word, from the Italian, *pasticcio*, pejorative.

patera (*pl.* **pateræ**) Circular ornament, resembling a shallow **medallion**, worked in relief, with raised decorated centre. When further embellished to become a stylised representative of a flower it is aka **rosette** or **phiala** (*see* Fig. G97), occurring in **coffers**, **friezes**, and as punctuations on walls.

pattern-books Collections of published designs from which builders and craftsmen could copy architectural details and composition. They were largely the means by which Classical architecture, as well as **Chinoiserie** and **Gothick** tastes, became widespread, notably in the 18th and early 19th centuries, and explain why so many historic towns look so harmonious.

SELECT GLOSSARY OF TERMS / 217

pavilion 1. Central, flanking, or intermediate projecting subdivision of a monumental building or **façade**, accented architecturally by more elaborate treatment (e.g. **Orders**, **pediments**, or **palace-fronts**), or by greater height and distinction of skyline. 2. Detached ornamental building, e.g. a **gazebo**, **eye-catcher**, or summer-house, usually in the grounds of a larger house. 3. One of several buildings, linked by, e.g. corridors, as in a hospital or prison, for reasons of hygiene or security. 4. Feature at the angle of a building, or terminating feature of a **wing** of a larger structure, as in a symmetrical **Palladian** composition. A **pavilion roof** is one hipped equally on all sides, like a **pyramid**.

pedestal Substructure, consisting of a **base** or **plinth**, a **dado** or **die**, and a **cornice**, under a column-base in Classical architecture; used as a support for an **obelisk**, statue, **urn**, etc.; or found in **balustrades**, terminating rows of **balusters** (see Fig. G24a), and supporting **vases**, etc. A Classical **podium** is a continuous elongated pedestal, while inside a building it is expressed as a **chair-rail**, **dado**, and **skirting**. **Orders** used on **triumphal arches** have pedestals for reasons of composition and massing in the combination of **arcuated** and **columnar and trabeated** forms.

pediment In Classical architecture, a low-pitched triangular **gable** following the roof-slopes over a **portico** or **façade**, formed with **raked cornices** of the same section as that of the horizontal **entablature** at its base, and mitring with it in part. **Doric** examples often omit the **mutules** under the sloping cornices. The triangular **tympanum** framed by the raking and horizontal cornices was the **field** left plain or embellished with sculpture in high relief. Greek pediments are generally lower in pitch than Roman exemplars. Pediments may crown subordinate features, e.g. doorways, **niches**, window-openings, etc., and in such cases are called **fronton**. While **triangular pediments** are the most common, **segmental pediments** were introduced during the Roman Empire from the 1st century AD, and are associated with the cults of Isis and Artemis/Diana of Ephesus because of the shape of the crescent moon and the bow shape of the Huntress's weapon. Some Isiac temples built by the Romans had segmental pediments. Types of pediment include **broken** (with gap in the middle of the lower horizontal cornice and with raking cornices stopping before they can meet, so having no apex); **broken-apex** (with raking sides too short to meet at the apex, aka **open** or **open-topped**); **broken-base** (with the horizontal base lacking a middle section, aka **open-bed**, and often recurring in 18th-century door-cases with **fanlights** breaking upwards into the lower cornice); **scrolled** (an **open-topped segmental** pediment with segmental tops curling inwards as **scrolls** or **volutes**, or with the tops in the form of two **ogees** ending in scrolls, called **bonnet-scroll**, **goose-neck**, or **swan-neck**) (Fig. G88).

pelasgic masonry See **polygonal masonry**.

pelta Wide shield, with sides swooping up and returning as eagle- or ram-heads, often found in **Neo-Classical** design (see Fig. G52b).

pendentive Portion of a domical **vault** which descends into the corner of an angular building where a **dome** is placed on a square base. It is really a variety of concave **spandrel**, forming the junction between the corner of the square compartment and the base of a circular dome or **drum** (see Figs G51b–c).

pentastyle **Portico** of five columns in a line.

pentice Structure erected against the side of another building as a lean-to, that is, with a monopitched or **pent** roof.

perch **Bracket** or **corbel**.

pergola Two parallel rows of **columns** or **piers**, flanking a path, supporting joists, the whole to carry climbing plants.

peri- Enclosing, or surrounding. Compounds include: **peribolos** (wall or **colonnade** around a Greek temple or sacred space, or the space itself); **peridrome** (space between a colonnade and a solid wall); **peripteral** (of a building surrounded by a single range of columns); **periptery** (row of columns around a temple, aka **peristyle**); **peristyle**, **periptery**, **peristasis** (colonnades surrounding a building); **peristylium** (inner court surrounded by a colonnade) (see **temple**).

perithyride **Ancon**.

perron External landing at the *piano nobile* level, reached by symmetrically disposed stairs, common in **Palladian architecture** (see Figs G84b–d, 4.39, 5.57a–b, 5.58a–c, 5.60, and 5.62a–b).

Persian Clothed **telamon** suggestive of a Persian origin.

persienne Window-shutter with louvres.

persona **Antefix** stopping the ends of the joint-tiles of an **Antique temple**.

Fig. G88 *Pediments: (top left) triangular (with pecked and solid lines) and open-topped or broken-apex triangular (with solid lines only); (top right) open-bed or broken-base triangular (with pecked and solid lines) and true broken or open triangular (with solid lines only). The entablature at an angle is called the raking cornice; (bottom left) segmental (with pecked and solid lines), with (right) open-topped segmental (with solid lines only). The centre of the segment is obtained by drawing a line from the apex of the corona fillet of a corresponding triangular pediment to the extremities of the fillet, bisecting the line, and drawing a line at right angles to the first line through the point of bisection, as shown lightly pecked; (bottom right) scrolled pediment.*

petal Ornament suggesting overlapping scale-like shapes, representing roof-tiles, as on the top of the choragic monument of Lysicrates (4th century BC), aka **imbrication**, **petal-diaper**, or **scale-pattern**.

piano nobile Principal floor of a building, containing the main reception rooms, higher than other storeys and usually set over a basement. It is often approached by an external stair aka **perron** (see Figs G84b–d, 5.57a–b, 5.58a–c, 5.60, and 5.62b).

piazza Open space in a town, surrounded by buildings, and approached by various streets. In the 17th and 18th centuries it came to mean any covered ways or arcaded ground floors with buildings over them, as in the Covent Garden piazza, London (1631–3), by Inigo Jones, but the word also suggested a **pentice** or even **cloisters**.

Picturesque From the Italian *pittoresco*, meaning 'in the manner of the painters', this was an 18th-century æsthetic category. It defined a building, a building in a landscape, or a landscape that resembled a composition by Poussin, Claude, or Salvator Rosa as 'Picturesque'. Asymmetrical composition, natural features (whether real or contrived), and buildings that seemed to belong to the setting were important ingredients of the Picturesque.

pie Ornament resembling a stylised chrysanthemum, aka **rosette** (see Fig. G97).

piecrust Rococo scalloped, rolled, raised border around, e.g., a mirror.

piedroit Species of **pilaster** with no **base** or **capital**, aka **lesene**, often found in **Neo-Classical** work.

pier Any isolated mass of construction, such as the solid between two windows, or **gate-piers**, much more massive than a column. An arch that springs from a pier is a **pier-arch**. Piers must not be confused with **columns** or **pillars** (Figs G89a–c).

pietra dura Inlaid work with hard stones (agate, jasper, marble, etc.) aka Florentine mosaic.

pietra serena Dark greenish-grey stone used for interior **pilasters**, etc. in Florence, e.g. Pazzi Chapel.

pila Freestanding masonry **pier**, square or rectangular on plan, with no **moulding** or

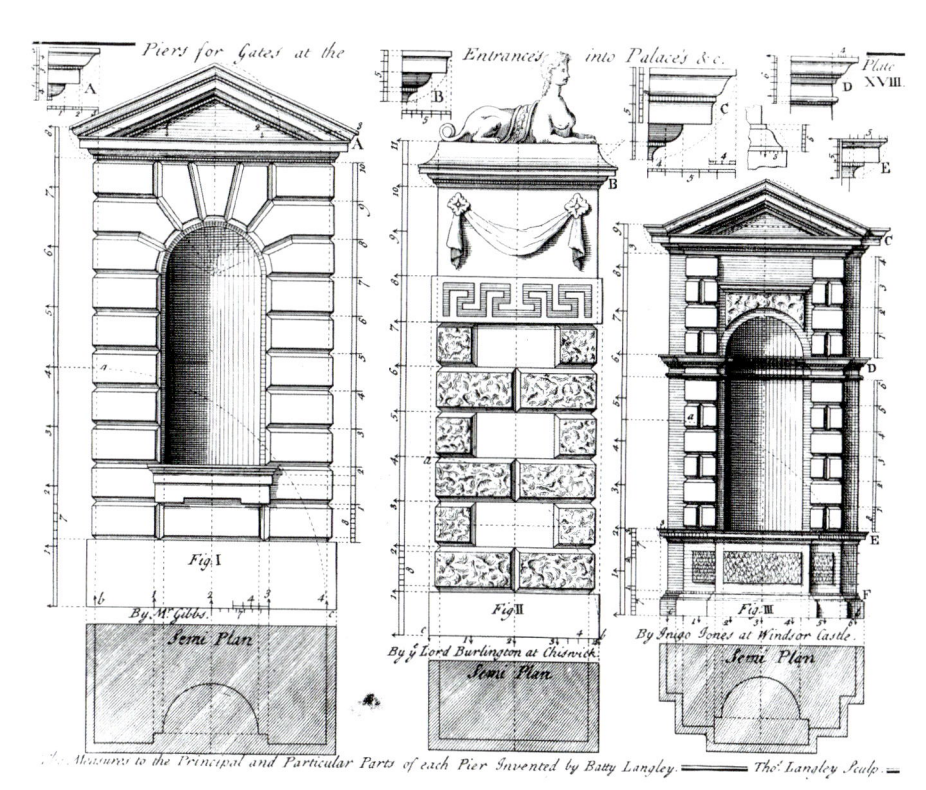

Fig. G89a *Classical piers, two with niches: (left) pier on a plain plinth, constructed with chamfered or **V**-jointed rustication, with a plain triangular pediment, and an apron under the cill; (centre) pier surmounted by a sphinx and set on a plain plinth: rock-faced rustication is chamfered or **V**-jointed. Note the Greek-key pattern and the swag; (right) the base has raised panels of frosted rustication on the die of the pedestal, while the rest of the rustication is plain chamfered or **V**-jointed, except for the panel of rock-faced work above the arch. Note the details of cornices in all cases (Langley [1745]).*

Fig. G89b *Classical gate-piers: (left) banded with frosted rustication and surmounted with an urn: (middle) with raised panels of frosted rustication, surmounted with a ball above the crowing cornice; (right two) with recessed panels in the dies containing margents, both surmounted with swagged urns. The system of proportion is indicated (Langley [1745]).*

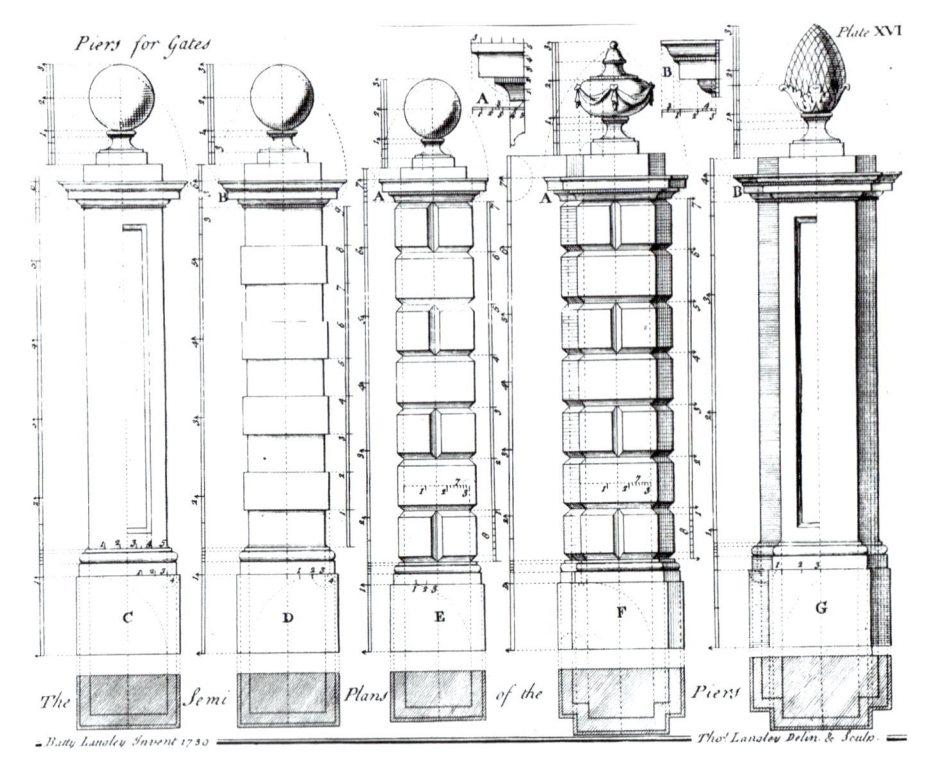

Fig. G89c *Classical gate-piers with proportional systems. C and G have a plain panel in the die or dado; D has plain, banded rustication; E and F have chamfered or **V**-jointed rustication. Note the finials in the form of balls, urn, and a pine cone (Langley [1745]).*

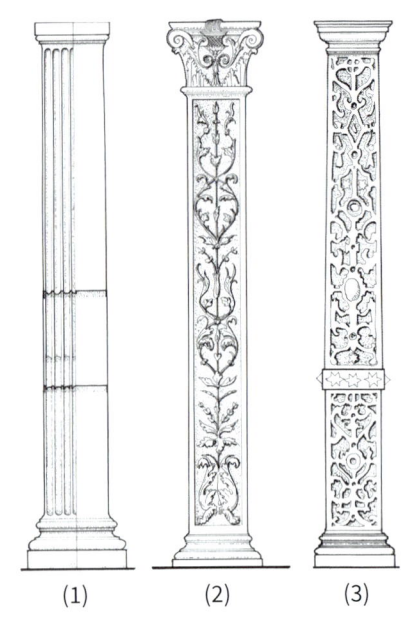

Fig. G90a *Pilasters, all with Attic bases: (1) (left) typical Classical pilaster with flutes and cabling, and (right) plain unfluted; (2) early 16th-century, from the monument of Louis XII in St-Denis, Paris, with arabesque decoration in a panel on the shaft; (3) detail from the 17th-century font-gallows in St Mary's Church, Astbury, Cheshire.*

decorations, not conforming in any way to the **Orders**, aka **pillar**.

pilaster Roman version of the **anta**, except that it conforms to the **Order** used elsewhere in a building, with **capital**, **shaft** with **entasis**, and **base**: it should not be confused with an **engaged column**. Unlike a **pier**, a pilaster has no structural purpose, and is used to respond to columns or the design of the **soffit** of a ceiling for purely æsthetic reasons. A **pilaster-strip** is one with no base or capital, aka **piedroit** or **lesene**. While an **anta** is a species of pilaster, its details differ from those of the columns of the same Order: Ionic antæ, for example, have plain capitals without volutes, but pilasters, on the other hand, conform exactly to the details of columns except that they are rectangular, projecting only slightly from the wall, and not curved on plan (Fig. G90a). The **disappearing pilaster** was a **Mannerist** feature often used by Lutyens, notably in work he carried out for the Midland Bank (Fig. G90b).

pillar Vertical, isolated, freestanding, upright element, monolithic or built up, which need not be circular on plan, and must not be confused with a **column**: aka **pila**, it does not conform to the **Orders**, and has no architectural or decorative pretensions.

pillowed Resembling a cushion, aka **pulvinated**.

pine Finials and **pendants** in Classical architecture are often in the form of **pine cones**, and sometimes resemble the skins of **pineapples**.

pineapple Symbol of hospitality, but like the **acorn**, ball, **pine cone**, **urn**, and **vase**, a common form for a **finial** on a gate-pier. At Dunmore Park, Stirlingshire, there is an **ashlar** pineapple instead of a **cupola** over an 18th-century octagonal garden **pavilion**.

pine cone Used as a **finial** or **pendant**, and frequently confused with the **pineapple** (*see* Figs G3 and G89c).

pinnacle Summit or apex, a terminating feature on buttresses, **pedestals**, **dies**, **parapets**, and other elements, often pyramidal in form.

plafond, platfond Ceiling or **soffit**.

plaisance 1. Summer-house or pleasure-pavilion. 2. Secluded part of a landscape garden laid out with lawns, shady walks, trees, and shrubs, as well as architectural elements e.g. statues, urns, fountains, seats, and gazebos.

Fig. G90b *Disappearing Doric pilaster, a favourite device of E.L. Lutyens, which much irritated Pevsner, although derived from Italian Mannerism, at the former Midland Bank headquarters, 27–35 Poultry and 5 Prince's Street, City of London (1924–39) (JSC).*

plait-band Intertwining ornament, so-called from its resemblance to plaits (*see* **guilloche**).

planceer **Soffit** or under-surface of the **corona**.

planted When a moulding, e.g. a **bead**, is shaped on a separate piece of material and subsequently fixed in place it is said to be planted.

platband 1. Flat **fascia**, **band**, or **string-course**, with a projection less than its width. 2. **Lintel**. 3. Stair-landing. 4. **Fillet** or **stria** separating the **flutes** on the **shaft** of a Classical column.

plateresque Lavish architectural ornament that is quite distinct from the structure.

plinth 1. Plain, projecting **base** of a **pedestal**, wall, etc., immediately above the ground, usually chamfered or moulded at the top, aka **quadra**. 2. Low, plain, square block below the **base** of a **column** or **pilaster**. Vitruvius also calls the **abacus** of the **Greek Doric capital** a plinthus. A **plinth-block** is the plain rectangular block at the base of an **architrave**, frame, or chimney-piece, which acts as a stop for the plinth, skirting, and architrave itself.

pluteus Low wall between Classical columns in a **colonnade**, about a third of their height.

pocket Space in the **pulley-stile** of a **sash-window**.

podium Continuous **pedestal** with base, **plinth**, **die**, and **cornice**, e.g. as used to support an **Order** of Classical columns high above ground level in a monumental building, essentially a platform on which stood a Roman temple (*see* Figs 2.12b, 2.14h, and 6.37–6.39) or a **peristyle** of columns supporting a **dome**.

polos (*pl.* **poloi**) 1. Cylindrical headdress of a **caryatid(e)** (*see* Fig. G36). 2. Dowel or centring-pin, used by the Greeks when jointing the **drums** of **column-shafts**.

polychromy Elaborate architectural decoration using colours, as in ancient Greece. **Structural polychromy** is where colour is not applied, but is provided by the materials used in the construction.

polygonal masonry Made of smooth, many-sided (i.e. with more than four angles) stone blocks closely fitted together, aka **opus polygonum**, or **cyclopean** or **pelasgic masonry** (*see* **rustication**).

polystyle With many columns.

polytriglyphal Having more than one **triglyph** to a single **intercolumniation**.

pommel Ornament on top of a **pinnacle**, **finial**, etc.: any globular ornament.

Pompeian style Derived from the decorations of Pompeii, the town engulfed by the eruption of Vesuvius in AD 79, and excavated from the 18th century.

porch Exterior adjunct over a doorway, forming a covered approach. If it has columns it is called a **portico**, perhaps more usually if it also has a **pediment** and resembles the front elevation of a **temple**.

poros Limestone coarser than marble.

porta Monumental gateway of a Roman city, or any grand entrance, aka **portal**.

porte-cochère 1. Doorway to a house or court, often quite grand, to permit wheeled vehicles to enter from a street. 2. Erroneous term for a projecting canopy large enough to shelter a carriage.

portico Structure forming a **porch** in front of a building, consisting of a roofed space open or partially enclosed at the sides, with columns, forming the entrance, and usually with a **pediment**. If it projects beyond the face of the building it is **prostyle**, but if recessed within the building so that the columns are in the same plane as the front wall, it is called **in antis** (because the columns are between the **antæ** of the walls), and if the **temple-front** is embedded in the front wall, it is **engaged**. The number of columns at the front determines whether it is **tristyle** (3), **tetrastyle** (4), **pentastyle** (5), **hexastyle** (6), **heptastyle** (7), **octastyle** (8), **enneastyle** (9), **decastyle** (10), or **dodecastyle** (12). Even numbers of columns ensure a void on the central axis for the doorway, but odd numbers are visual deterrents suggesting no entry. A projecting portico with four columns is therefore **prostyle tetrastyle**, while a recessed portico with two columns would be **distyle in antis** (Fig. G91; *see* Figs G107a–b). A portico must have a roof supported on at least one side by columns (*see* **temple**).

posticum Epinaos, or **rear porch**, or **opisthodomus**.

poyntell Pavement of small lozenge-shaped tiles or squares laid in a diagonal pattern.

præcinctio Great passage dividing the seats into two tiers in a Greek theatre.

prismatic ornament Simple geometrical forms in relief, e.g. diamond-pointed **rustication** (*see* Fig. G98a).

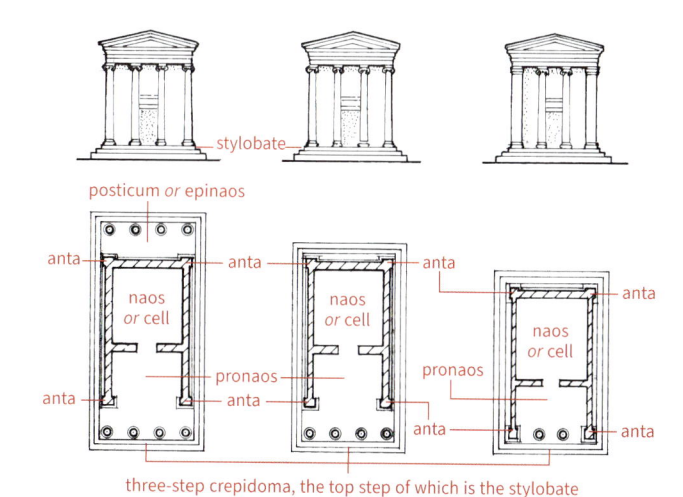

Fig. G91 Portico showing column arrangements in Classical temples: (left) amphi-prostyle tetrastyle or amphi-tetra prostyle, i.e. with four columns at each end of the cell; (middle) prostyle tetrastyle or tetra-prostyle, i.e. with four columns in front of the cell; (right) distyle in antis, i.e. two columns in front of the cell set between the antæ terminating the projecting walls, an arrangement only found in small temples, tombs, or shrines.

prodomus As **pronaos**.

profile Vertical section, esp. of a **moulding**.

pronaos Vestibule flanked by walls behind the **portico**, it is therefore partly enclosed by walls and partly by columns (*see* **temple**).

proportion The just magnitude of each part, and of each part to another, often governed by a standard unit of length called a **module**, based on half the diameter of a Classical column; the relationship existing between parts or elements that should render the whole harmonious in terms of balance, symmetry, and repose.

propylæum (*pl.* **propylæa**) Any court or **vestibule** before a building, but more usually a formal, imposing monumental entrance gateway to such court or enclosure.

proscenium Stage of a theatre, or the area between the curtain and the pit, including the arch and frame facing the audience. In a Greek theatre the **proskenion** was a stone structure, consisting of a row of columns standing on a low **stylobate** in front of the **skene** wall.

prostas As **pastas**.

prostyle With columns standing before the front of the building in a line (*see* **temple**).

prothyrides *See* **ancon**.

prothyron Porch of a Greek house open to the street outside the front door.

prow Representation of the prow of a warship as on a **rostral column** (**columna rostrata**) and in schemes of marine decoration (*see* Fig. G42).

pseudodipteral Arranged to *appear* to be **dipteral** (i.e. with two rows of columns along the flanks) but where the inner rows are omitted although the **portico** would suggest otherwise (*see* **temple**).

pseudoperipteral Disposition of columns around a Classical building in which those along the sides are **engaged** with the walls (*see* **temple**).

ptera Colonnade around the cell of a Greek temple (*see* **temple**).

pteroma Ambulatory or space between the **cell** of a Greek temple and the columns of the **peristyle** (*see* **temple**).

pteron External **peripteral colonnade** of Greek temples.

pulley stile One of the vertical side-pieces of a window **sash-frame** in which the pulleys and counterweights are housed.

pulvin, pulvinata, pulvinus (*pl.* **pulvins, pulvinatæ, pulvini**) Form resembling a pillow or cushion, such as the baluster-like side of an **Ionic capital**, aka **balteus** (*see* Fig. G72). **Pulvination** is therefore a swelling, like a squashed cushion. **Friezes** in some Classical Orders are **pulvinated**, and sometimes decorated with bound bay or oak leaves (*see* Figs G6a–b and G21b).

putto (*pl.* **putti**) Putti are unwinged, often obese, male children found in Classical and **Baroque** sculpture, especially funerary monuments, where they are found in attitudes of overt displays of grief, shedding copious tears, and clutching, e.g., inverted torches. They possess a sense of retarded physical development rendering them curiously unwholesome. Not to be confused with the winged **amorino**, **cherub**, **Cupid**, or **Love**.

pycnostyle One of the five species of **intercolumniation** defined by Vitruvius. The space in this case is 1½ diameters of a shaft.

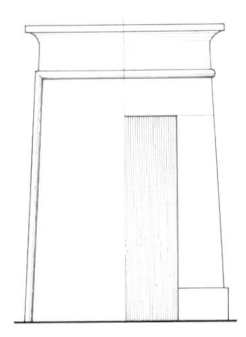

Fig. G92 *(Left) Egyptian battered pylon-form, with gorge-cornice under which is a torus moulding carried down the battered side; (right) similar pylon-form as an ædicule or door-case.*

pylon One of the vast battered towers that flanked the entrance to an Egyptian temple. Pylon-like forms became used as the supports for suspension bridges, as the section for basements, dams, and retaining walls, and as chimneypots and door-surrounds during the **Neo-Classical** period (Fig. G92).

pyramid Solid standing on a square base with steeply battered triangular sides meeting at an apex, used in **Neo-Classical** architecture. Thin pyramids are often confused with **obelisks**, and fat obelisks with pyramids, but the two forms are quite distinct although obelisks have small flattened pyramids or **pyramidions** on top of them.

pyramidion Small pyramid, or the tip of an **obelisk**.

quadra 1. Square **moulding** framing a plaque, inscription, etc. 2. **Fillet** or **list** above and below the **scotia** of an **Attic base**, esp. if used with the **Ionic Order**. 3. Plain **plinth** or **socle** of a **pedestal**, **podium**, etc.

quadrangle 1. Figure with four sides in the same plane. 2. Square or rectangular court surrounded by buildings, as in an Oxford college, where it is termed **quad** (in Cambridge it is called **court**).

quadratum, opus quadratum *See* **opus**.

quadratura *Trompe l'œil* architectural designs painted on walls and ceilings.

quadrifores Folding doors consisting of four hinged panels, i.e. folding into four leaves.

quadriga Sculptured group consisting of a chariot, driver, and four horses, found on **triumphal arches**, monuments, etc.

quarter round Convex **moulding**, the section of which is the quadrant of a circle.

quasi-reticulate Type of facing of Roman concrete formed of small regular facing-blocks creating a vaguely net-like appearance.

Queen Anne 1. Period of early 18th-century English architecture when English **Baroque** came to maturity. In domestic architecture plainness and restraint were characteristics, with red-brick **façades**, tall **sash-windows**, canopy-like timber door-cases, and roofs concealed behind **parapets**. 2. The **Queen-Anne style** or **Revival** evolved from the 1860s, with details derived from 17th- and 18th-century Flemish and English domestic architecture, but eclectic motifs were also drawn from many sources, and included rubbed-brick arches and dressings around openings, terracotta embellishments, open-bed and broken pediments, steeply pitched roofs (often rising from eaves-cornices),

Fig. G93 *Queen Anne arch: a simplified mid-18th-century variant on the serliana, with brick rubbers and keystone, in Broad Street, Ludlow, Shropshire.*

monumental chimneys, shaped and **Dutch gables**, white-painted **balustrades**, **balconies**, and **bay windows**. Planning was informal and asymmetrical, and the style incorporated elements from vernacular architecture (e.g. tile-hung gabled walls with barge-boards, clap-boarding, and casement windows with leaded lights). A **Queen Anne arch** is formed of a central semicircular-headed opening flanked by two 'flat' arches constructed of brick rubbers set over tall, thin side-lights on either side of a wider window, a variation on the **Palladian** or **Venetian** window aka **serliana**, but is commoner during the Georgian period (1714–1830) than that of Queen Anne (1702–14) (Fig. G93).

quirk   1. Piece removed from the corner of a room, or a re-entrant angle. 2. Any **V**-shaped groove between mouldings.

quoin   1. External angle of a building. 2. Dressed stones in this position, usually laid so that the faces are either long or short, or **headers** and **stretchers**, and often with chamfered edges. If they project beyond the face of the wall (as they frequently do) they are termed **rustic quoins** (*see* **rustication**).

raceme   Plant-based ornament, e.g. **anthemion** or **palmette**.

raffle leaf   Leaf in ornamental foliage with indentations at its edges, like an **acanthus**. It is usually freely flowing and asymmetrical.

rail   Horizontal piece of timber between panels in a door or in **wainscoting**.

rain-conductor   Downspout, leader, or pipe to conduct water from a gutter or **rainwater-head** to the ground, preferably a drain or gulley.

rainwater-head   Box-shaped structure of cast iron or lead, often ornamented, into which rainwater is poured from behind a **parapet** in order to convey it to a pipe. Aka hopper-head.

rake   Slope of a roof. A **raking cornice** is that on the slope of a **pediment**.

ram   Heads or skulls of rams or goats appear in Classical ornament, associated with **altars** and **festoons**: they are called ægicranes.

ramp   1. Slope to join two levels. 2. Part of a handrail of a stair that rises more steeply at a landing or where there are **winders**.

rear or **rere arch**   Internal arch aka **scoinson arch** to a window- or door-opening with a greater span than the exterior opening, because of the splayed **jambs**.

reed, reeding   Moulding consisting of three or more beads side by side, like reeds laid parallel (*see* **moulding**). Some elaborate **Ionic** bases have many horizontal flutes and mouldings called **reeding** (*see* **Asiatic base**).

Regency   Properly the period 1811–20, but includes the styles prevalent in England from around 1795 to 1830.

reglet   Flat, narrow **moulding**.

regula (*pl.* **regulæ**)   1. Band below the **tænia** and above the **guttæ** in a **Doric entablature** (*see* **Doric Order**). 2. Pedestal or **plinth** under a **column**.

reignier work   Ornamental inlaid patterns in the manner of **Buhl** work.

relief   *See* **relievo**.

relieving arch   Arch built over a **lintel** to take the weight off it, aka **discharging arch** (*see* Fig. G20a). A **relieving triangle** is a triangular mass over a lintel where masonry courses are corbelled over each other in succession, thus avoiding loading the lintel.

relievo, relief   Projection of any sculpture or ornament from its background. **Alto-relievo** stands out pronouncedly from the ground; **mezzo-relievo** projects only half the forms; **basso-relievo** projects less than half.

Renaissance   Meaning, literally, rebirth, the Renaissance suggests a rediscovery of the architecture of ancient Rome. In common usage the term implies architecture based on Italian prototypes from the early 15th century until it was superseded by **Mannerist** and **Baroque** styles: it is generally held to begin with the work of Brunelleschi in Florence.

rendering   Plastering or facing with **stucco**, pebbledash, or similar, of an outside wall.

replum   Panel in a framed door.

reprise   1. Part of a **cill** on which a **jamb** or **mullion** rests. 2. Base of an **architrave** wider than the rest (Figs G94).

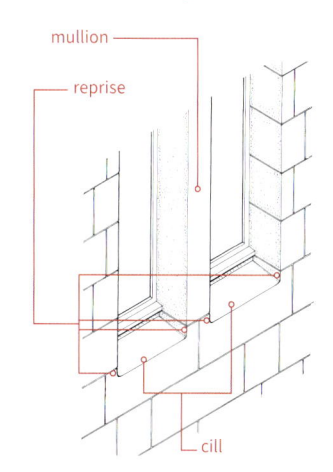

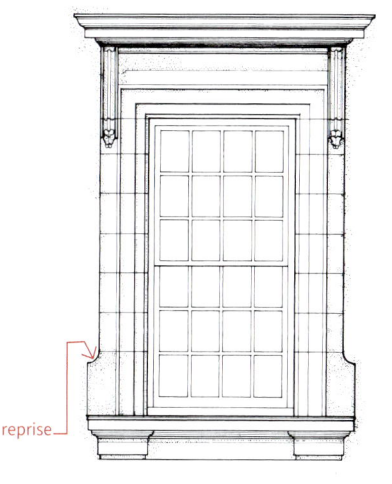

Fig. G94 *Reprise: (top) Part of a cill on which a jamb or mullion rests; (bottom) Base of an architrave wider than the rest.*

reredos   Screen or wall behind an altar, usually much ornamented, forming part of the **retable**.

respond   **Anta**, or element where an **arcade** or **colonnade** engages with a wall.

ressault   Projecting part of an **entablature**, with two returns, over a **pilaster**,

SELECT GLOSSARY OF TERMS / 223

column, or other support (*see* Figs 4.37, 4.38a, and 4.40).

ressaunt Ogee.

retable Carved structure behind an **altar**, including the **reredos**, or the shelf behind the altar, or the frame around reredos panels.

retaining wall Wall built to hold up a bank of earth, aka **revetment**, usually battered.

reticulated Like a net, as in **rustication** or in lozenge-shaped patterns.

reticulatum *See* **Opus**.

return Continuation of a moulding or projection in an opposite or different direction, with a terminating feature. The part that returns, usually at a right-angle, from the front of a building.

reveal Jamb or side of an opening between a window- or door-frame and the outer face of the wall. If it is angled it is called a **splayed reveal** or simply a **splay**.

reverse ogee *See* **cyma**.

revetment 1. **Retaining wall**. 2. Finish, cladding, or facing fixed to a wall of some other material.

rhone Half-round **gutter**.

ribbon Used with **bucrania**, **laurel** and **oak wreaths**, and **festoons**.

rinceau Continuous wave of foliate ornament, often a vine, on a band.

riparene Classical ornament associated with water, e.g. personification of rivers, **vases** pouring water, Neptune, **Tritons** and mermaids, **dolphins**, fish, reeds, seaweed, etc.

rocaille Rockwork of pebbles, shells, and other stones, used in the building of **grottoes**, **follies**, and other decorative conceits. Ornament like marine flora.

rock-work Constructions of real and imitation rocks, associated with **grottoes** and garden buildings.

Rococo Light, frothy, elegant, and playful late phase of **Baroque**, more than **rocaille**, but with much of the shell-like, coral, or marine forms associated with **grottoes** and the like. Much Rococo ornament

Fig. G95 *Typical fragment of Rococo ornament based on the work of J.-F.-V.-J. de Cuvilliés in Bavaria.*

is asymmetrical, with **S**- and **C**-shaped curves, resembling artistically draped seaweed. **Chinoiserie**, **Gothick**, 'Hindoo' (Indian), and other elements and motifs fuse in this remarkable 18th-century art form, which is more surface decoration than architectural style, although its stylistic flavour is quite distinct (Fig. G95; *see* Figs G108, G116, and 5.17d).

rod of Asclepius or **Æsculapius** Neo-Classical motif, like the **caduceus**, minus wings.

roll 1. **Bowtell** or **common round** moulding of semicircular or greater than semicircular profile (Fig. G96). 2. **Volute**, the spiral roll in **Ionic**, **Corinthian**, and **Composite capitals**.

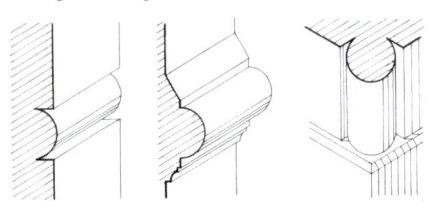

Fig. G96 *Roll-moulding: (left) flush-bead; (middle) torus or half-round; (right) angle-bead or bowtell.*

Roman cement 1. Hydraulic mortar made by mixing lime with reactive siliceous material (e.g. crushed tiles or volcanic ash). 2. **Parker's** or **Sheppey's brown cement**, a common early 19th-century rendering, made from crushed burnt calcareous clay nodules mixed with lime, sand, and water, often scored to resemble **ashlar** joints.

Roman Order **Composite Order**.

rope moulding Moulding resembling a cable or twined rope.

rose, rosette 1. Conventional representation of a flower (e.g. **fleuron** in the centre of an abacus-face of a **Corinthian capital**). 2. Circular ornament resembling a **patera**, used to decorate ceilings, etc., hence **ceiling-rose** from the centre of which a chandelier might be suspended. It is often ornamented with stylised leaves, and according to its size is termed **rosace** or **rosette**. 3. A **rosette**, essentially a patera with floral enrichment, is smaller than a rose, and decorates the centres of **coffers**, **strings**, **architraves**, etc. (Fig. G97).

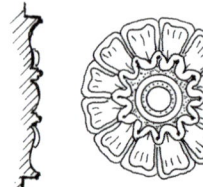

Fig. G97 *Rosette: (left) section; (right) elevation.*

rosso antico Type of fine-grained marble, deep blood-red or liver in colour, which took a high polish.

rostral column *See* **columna rostrata**.

rostrum 1. Beak (**acrostolium**) like the prow of an **Antique** warship, ornamented with an animal-head, **buckler**, or helmet, forming the projections on **columnæ rostratæ** (*see* Fig. G42). 2. Elevated platform or dais.

rotunda Cylindrical building or room, usually with a **dome** or a domed ceiling over it, with sometimes a **peristyle** inside or out, or both.

roundel 1. Large **bead** or **astragal**. 2. Circular panel or window, esp. a deep circular **niche** containing a bust. 3. Bull's-eye (œil-de-bœuf) window or **oculus**.

rubbed, rubber Brick rubbers are soft bricks made of fine loamy clay containing much sand, and baked (not burned) in a kiln, readily sawn and rubbed to the required shapes, and used to make **gauged brick** arches, etc., the extremely fine joints between the rubbers being formed of **lime-putty** rather than conventional mortar, which would be too coarse (*see* Fig. G20b).

rudenture Cabling (*see* Fig. G90a).

Rundbogenstil Eclectic round-arched style, largely derived from the Italian Early Christian, Romanesque, and

Florentine-Renaissance styles, used by important **Neo-Classical** architects such as Schinkel, von Klenze, and Gärtner in the first half of the 19th century.

running dog Repetitive Classical ornament in a **frieze**, aka **Vitruvian scroll**, with a wave-like **scroll** or **volute** form endlessly repeated.

rural architecture **Picturesque** cottage architecture often deliberately asymmetrical and derived from vernacular traditions, with materials, e.g. thatch, rough tree-trunks as columns, and a contrived attempt to appear 'rustick'.

rustic-work, rustication Ashlar masonry, the joints of which are worked with grooves or channels (moulded or plain) to emphasise the blocks, while the raised faces are roughened to form a contrast with ordinary dressed ashlar. Rustication enhances the visual impact of **keystones**, **plinths**, **quoins**, and even entire storeys. Types of rustication include **banded** (plain or textured ashlar with horizontal joints only grooved, giving the impression of a series of bands); **chamfered** (with each ashlar chamfered to create **V**-shaped joints, either all around each stone or, if at the tops and bottoms, to create banded work with chamfers); **congelated** (see **frosted**); **cyclopean** (rock- or quarry-faced ashlar with dressed projecting rough faces, designed to appear as though straight from the quarry, but, of course, dressed with precise joints, giving a massive, powerful, impregnable effect useful for piers supporting **viaducts**, **plinths**, etc.); **diamond-pointed**, aka **prismatic** or **pyramidal** (with ashlar blocks cut with chamfered faces giving the effect of a wall of a series of small **pyramids** with projecting faces terminating in points, while **quoins** will be longer and rectangular, rather than square, and so will resemble hipped roofs on their sides); **frosted** aka **congelated** (carved to look like icicles or stalactites, usually found on fountains, in **grottoes**, or other situations associated with water); **quarry-faced** (as **cyclopean**); **reticulated** (carved with indentations connected in an irregular net-like pattern); **rock-faced** (as **cyclopean**);

Fig. G98a *Types of ashlar and rusticated masonry.*

— cope
— regular coursed ashlar
— deep and narrow coursed ashlar
— pseudo-isodomic masonry
— string course
— channel-joined, frosted, or congelated rustication
— channel-joined, diamond-pointed rustication
— chamfered or **V**-jointed vermiculated rustication
— chamfered or **V**-jointed plain rustication with reticulated quoin
— chamfered or **V**-jointed rock-faced, quarry-faced, or cyclopean rustication
— plinth: pelasgic masonry, *aka* (confusingly) cyclopean masonry

Fig. G98b *Ionic rusticated doorways both with triangular pediments: (left) ædicule type with pulvinated frieze framing **V**-jointed rustication with keystone; (right) with banded pilasters, eared architrave, and keystone carved with a head (from Langley [1745]).*

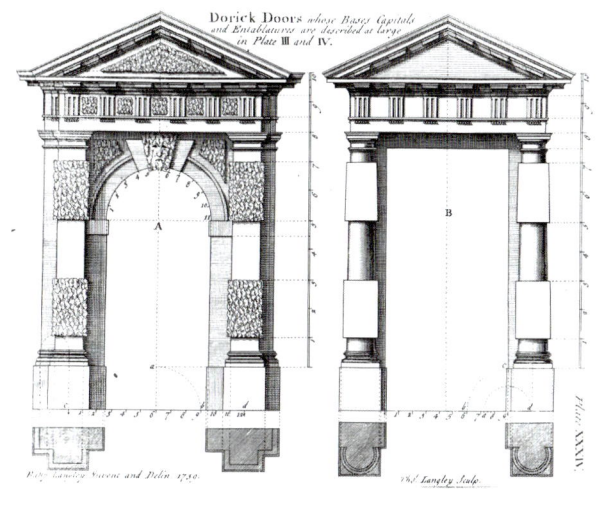

Fig. G98c *Two Doric rusticated doorways: (left) with perhaps heavily over-rustication, pilasters, and an arched centre with carved keystone flanked by plain voussoirs; (right) with banded or blocked columns (Langley [1745]).*

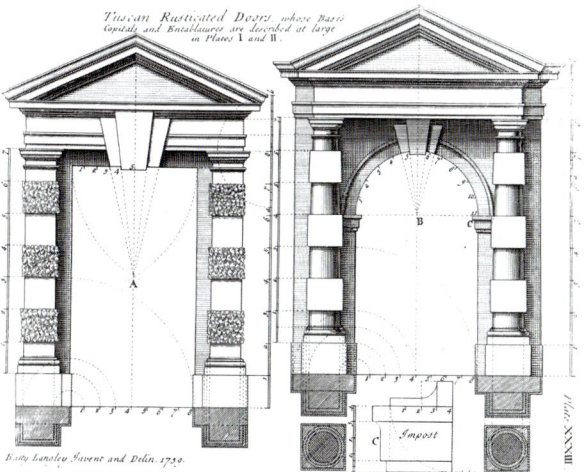

Fig. G98d *Two Tuscan rusticated doorways (Langley [1745]).*

smooth-faced (with faces flat and plain, but the joints around individual blocks clearly shown, e.g. by chamfered edges); **V-jointed** (as chamfered); and **vermiculated** (with irregular grooves, channels, and holes all over the surface, as though a section had been cut through worm-holes and worm-tracks, hence the name) (Fig. G98a). **Rustic quoins** are stones at the corners of buildings that project beyond the **naked** of the wall proper. A **rusticated column** has blocks of stone, square on plan, set at intervals up the height of the shaft and alternating with the drum-like blocks of the shaft: in a rusticated column the square blocks (rectangular on their faces) may be dressed, usually in the **vermiculated** manner, or may be plain-faced (Figs G98b–d; see Figs G25a–b and G110a).

sacellum 1. Small roofless enclosure. 2. Small enclosed space in ancient Roman houses where the **lares** and **penates** (household deities) were venerated, often treated as an **ædicule**, aka **lararium**. 3. Chapel within a church defined by a screen.

sacrarium 1. Sacred apartment, **sacellum**, or shrine. 2. **Cella** or **adytum** of a Roman temple. 3. Part of a **chancel** defined by altar-rails, i.e. the **sanctuary** in a church.

sacristy Room attached to or within a church where sacred vessels, vestments, and other items used in liturgies are kept. *See* **vestry**.

saddle 1. Board on a floor in a doorway between **jambs**. 2. Any ∧-shaped form suggesting a saddle in section, used to cap a ridge or used as a coping for a wall. 3. **Saddle-stone** is the apex stone of a **pediment** or **gable**, or is part of a **splayed coping**. 4. **Saddle-back** roof is a common pitched roof with gable-ends, on a tower. 5. **Saddle-bars** are iron or other metal bars, set into the **mullions** and **jambs** of a **leaded light**, to which lead **cames** are tied.

sagitta Keystone of an **arch**.

sala terrena Large formal room with one long side open to a garden, a kind of detached **loggia** (e.g. the fine example in the Valdštejn garden, Prague [1624–7], by Pieroni).

salamander Beast resembling a newt, lizard, and dragon.

salient Projection of any part of a building, but more usually applied to the angular projections of fortifications or garden architecture.

salomónica *See* **Solomonic**.

salon, saloon Large, spacious, tall apartment in the centre of a Classical building, sometimes circular or elliptical on plan, often vaulted or domed, usually one and a half or two storeys high, and illuminated by an **oculus**, **clerestorey**, or **lantern-light**.

sanctuary **Presbytery**, **chancel**, or eastern part of the choir of a church, where the high altar stands.

sarcophagus (*pl.* **sarcophagi**) The name, derived from the Greek, means 'flesh-eater', so it is a stone or terracotta sepulchral chest, usually ornamented, often heroic in scale, to contain a corpse. It may be given architectural form, resembling a miniature **temple**, but a common **Antique** type had a pitched roof-like lid with **horns** at the angles (*see* Figs G40 and G70). Sarcophagi-like forms were often employed in severe **Neo-Classical** designs (*see* Fig. G104).

sash, sash-window Rebated frame, fixed or opening, fitted with one or more panes of glass forming a window-light, set in a larger frame placed in the whole window-opening or aperture. **Opening sashes** can be of the vertical or horizontal sliding type in grooves, or can be hinged or pivoted at the sides, tops, bottoms, or centres. Thus **casements** have sashes. A sash capable of being moved up and down is **hung**, suspended on cords or chains from pulleys fixed in the linings of the **sash-frame**, and counterbalanced by weights attached to the concealed ends of the **sash-cords**, **-lines**, or **-chains** within the **sash-box** of the main window-frame. If only one sash moves, the window is said to be a **single-hung**, and if both sashes can be moved, it is **double-hung**. Sashes became fashionable in England in the latter part of the 17th century. **Yorkshire sliding-sashes** are moved horizontally.

satyr Creature with goat-like legs and hooves, a human male torso and face, and horns. It represents fecundity, lust, and unbridled nature.

saves, savers, saving-stones Stones built over a **lintel** to distribute the loads. They are often in the form of a **relieving-arch** (*see* Fig. G20a).

saxa quadrata Blocks of dressed squared stone for **ashlar** work.

scabellum (*pl.* **scabella**) High pedestal supporting a bust, usually shaped like the lower part of a **gaine** or **herm**.

scæna, skene Structure which faced the audience in a Classical theatre, set behind the **orchestra**.

scagliola Type of plaster or **stucco**, with colouring matter introduced so that the finished, polished material resembles marble. Although scagliola was used in interior decorative schemes in Classical times, it was widely used and perfected in the 17th and 18th centuries.

scale pattern **Imbrication** or **petal diaper**, in which the ornament resembles overlapping fish-scales.

scale steps Steps with parallel nosings and equal goings.

scallop Ornament resembling the shell of a scallop, often found at the heads of **niches**.

scalpturatum Inlaid work, the pattern being chiselled out and filled with coloured marble.

scamilli Plain blocks or sub-plinths, which, unlike **pedestals**, have no **mouldings**, and are smaller. **Scamilli impares** refers to the horizontal lines of a Classical building, which incline almost imperceptibly from the ends to the centre in order to correct the optical illusion of the centre sinking.

scandulæ Shingles.

scantling Length, breadth, and thickness of a stone.

scape, scapus (*pl.* **scapes, scapi**) 1. **Shaft** of a **column**. 2. Apophyge. 3. Stile of a door. 4. **String** of a stair.

scappling, scapling, scabbling Method of tooling the face of a stone with a small pick known as a **scappling hammer**, working it to a flat, but not smooth, surface.

scarcement Plain **band** or flat **set-off** in a wall, used as a shelf on which the ends of joists or **trusses** are carried.

scarp 1. Steep slope, aka **escarp**, below the ramparts of a fortress down which fire may be directed. **2.** Inner side of a ditch, or the battered side of an embankment. **3.** The term was also used in garden design.

scene Alley or **portico** set in rural surroundings where theatrical performances could be given.

scenography Representation of a building in **perspective**, often applied to scene-painting. Scenographic composition is where buildings were designed to be seen in perspective as a series of episodes, e.g. Nash's Regent Street, London, wrecked by subsequent developments.

scheme, skene **1.** Segmental **arch**. **2.** Structure facing the audience in a Greek theatre (**scæna**).

sciagraph Representation of a section through a building or part of it. Sciagraphy is a branch of the technique of **perspective**, dealing with the projection of shadows.

scoinson Interior edge of a window-side, so scoinson-arch is that over the interior of a window- or door-aperture, often of a much wider span than on the outside because of the splayed **jambs**.

sconce **1.** Earthwork or fortress. **2.** Screen or palisade. **3.** Arch formed across the internal corners of a room. **4.** Squinch.

sconcheon, scontion, scuntion, scuncheon **1.** Return of a **pilaster** from its face to the **naked** of a wall, or side of an aperture from the back of a **jamb** to the face of a wall. **2.** Scoinson (see **rear** or **rere**).

scoop-pattern Series of short closely spaced vertical **flutes** with curved closed ends, often used in ornamental **friezes** (Fig. G99).

Fig. G99 *Roman scoop-pattern.*

scotia (*pl.* **scotiæ**) Trochilus, or hollow concave **moulding**, found in the **Attic base** between the **fillets** of the **torus** mouldings, or under the nosing of a stair.

scouchon, skouchin Squinch.

scratch-work Type of decorative plaster-work consisting of a ground of coloured plaster, covered with a white coat: the latter is then scratched to reveal the colour below. Aka **sgraffito**.

screw-stair Newel-, vice-, or circular stair wound about a **newel** or **pier**.

scroll **1.** Convoluted or spiral ornament like **volutes**, often of double flexure, passing from one volute to another in series on a **band** or **frieze**, e.g. in **Vitruvian** or **wave-scroll**. **2.** Volute of a **console**, **modillion**, or **capital** (e.g. **Ionic**, **Corinthian**, or **Composite Orders**). **3.** Bottom curtail-step of a flight of stairs, with a rounded end or ends scrolled around the newel post, often echoing the scroll of the hand-rail. **4.** Any complex ornamental element composed of scroll-like forms, e.g. the **C** and **S** shapes in **Baroque** and **Rococo** designs, aka **scroll-work**. See **pediment**.

scutcheon **1.** As **sconcheon**. **2.** Place on a door, from the centre of which the handle projects. **3.** Plate around a keyhole. See **escutcheon**.

section Drawing of an imaginary vertical cut through a building, the convention being that all beyond the plane made by the intersection of the section is depicted in **elevation**. A **plan** is therefore a **horizontal section**.

segment **1.** Part cut off from the whole. **2.** Part of a circle, so a **segmental arch** is one struck from a centre far below its springing-line.

serliana Palladian or Venetian window: any central opening with a semicircular arch over it flanked by two rectangular openings. The rectangular openings have **pilasters** or **engaged columns** on either side of them, with **entablatures** over. The central arched opening is always wider than the rectangular openings, and its **archivolt** springs from the top of the **cornices** on either side. It is named after Sebastiano Serlio who first illustrated the form in his *Architettura* of 1537–51, although it may have originated with Bramante (Figs G100a–b).

serpent Found in Classical architecture associated with the Messenger (St John, Hermes, Harpocrates, etc.), connected with healing and wisdom, and with the **caduceus** or winged **wand** of the

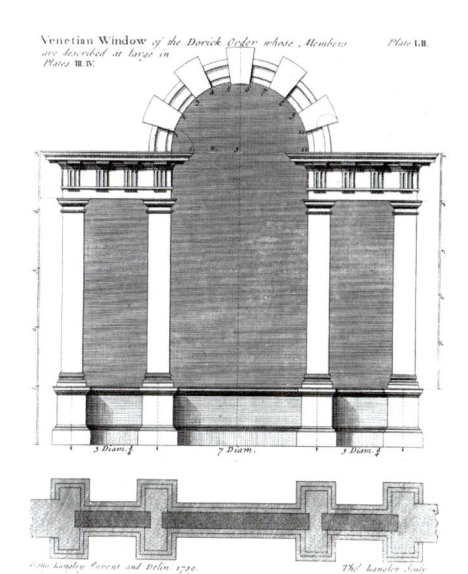

Fig. G100a *Serliana, aka Palladian or Venetian window, with Doric entablature and voussoirs interrupting the archivolt (Langley [1745]).*

Fig. G100b *Another type of serliana, employing an unfluted Ionic Order with pulvinated frieze (Langley [1745]).*

Messenger. Serpents in circular form, their tails in their mouths, denote immortality or eternity (see **ouroboros**).

serpentine **1.** Stone (sometimes called a **marble**), mainly hydrous magnesium silicate, of a dull green colour, with markings resembling a serpent's skin. **2.** Of or pertaining to a serpent, e.g. a wavy path, moulding, or stretch of water.

severans Strings or **cornices**.

severy **1.** Structural bay of a building. **2.** Top of a **ciborium**.

sgraffito See **scratch-work**.

shaft Body, **fust**, or trunk of a **column** between the **capital** and the **base**.

shank Leg or that part of a **Doric triglyph** between the **glyphs**.

shaped gable With sides formed of convex and concave curves, with a pedimented or semicircular top. See **gable**.

shed-roof Lean-to or monopitch roof abutting a higher element, e.g an **aisle-roof** under a **clerestorey**.

shell-work Arrangements of shells, minerals, mother-of-pearl, etc. in patterns, aka **coquillage** or **marine ornament**, decorating **grottoes**, **nymphæa**, etc.

shingle **1.** Wooden tiles, aka **scandulæ**. **2.** In the plural, small stones used for gravel, roughcast render, or concrete aggregate.

shoulder **1.** Bracket or **console**, aka **shoulder-** or **shouldering-piece**. **2.** Crossette. **3.** Projection narrowing the top of an aperture, as in a **shouldered arch**.

sill, cill, sole, sule See **cill**.

sima Top **moulding** of a **pediment**, placed above the **raking cornice**. Not to be confused with **cyma**.

singerie Style of 17th- and 18th-century decoration like **grotesque** (see Fig. 5.28), but with figures of monkeys imitating humans.

single-hung Sash-window in which only one sash moves.

skene See **scæna**.

skew Anything that slopes or is set obliquely, e.g. the **coping** of a **gable**, aka **skew-table**. A skew-block, -butt, -corbel, -put(t), aka **gable-springer**, **kneeler**, **springer**, or **summer-stone**, is a large block of stone set at the top of a wall at the base of a gable to stop the cope from sliding off. **Skew-back** is the sloping bed, line, **sommering**, or surface of an **abutment** from which, e.g., an **arch** springs.

skirt **1.** Projection of **eaves**. **2.** Apron-piece under a window-cill. **3.** Board (**skirting-board**) placed around the base of an internal wall at the junction of the floor and the wall, frequently moulded or chamfered at the top, and corresponding to a **plinth**.

skull **1.** Ægicrane or **bucranium** on **friezes**, etc. **2.** Human skulls represent mortality, transitory life, and vanity, so occur in funerary architecture and **monuments**, or as supports for **obelisks**.

skylight Glazed opening in a ceiling or roof.

slate Sedimentary stone capable of being split or cut into thin regular slabs, used for tombstones, roofing, or cladding. **Slate-hanging** describes a slate-clad wall.

sleeper-wall **1.** Wall, usually perforated to allow free passage of air, supporting timber joists of a ground floor where spans between walls of a room are too great. **2.** Wall placed between two structural elements, e.g. **piers**, to prevent movement.

snake Wavy-line moulding (see **serpentine**).

socle, zocle Plain block or low **pedestal** without mouldings supporting a bust, **urn**, etc., or the base-course of a wall.

soffit, soffite, soffita **1.** Ceiling. **2.** Visible underside of an **arch**, **balcony**, beam, **corona**, **cornice**, **vault**, or any exposed architectural element.

solar, solarium **1.** Loft, garret, or upper chamber opening to a terrace facing east to catch the morning sun. **2.** Balcony, terrace, or part of a building exposed to the sun. **3.** Loggia. **4.** Sundial, often with architectural pretensions.

soldier Brick with its stretcher-face set vertically.

Solomonic column Twisted, **spiral**, torso, or barley-sugar column, aka **salomónica**, so-called from its supposed use in the Temple of Solomon, much used in **Baroque** architecture. Not to be confused with the **Antonine**, **Trajanic**, or **triumphal column** with spiral bands of sculpture wound around the shaft (Fig. G101; see Figs G26, G27a, 4.11d, 5.3, 5.16b, and 5.19e).

sommering Skew-back, or the radiating joints between the **voussoirs** of an **arch**.

sopraporta Attic storey over a doorway **cornice**, often with **scrolls** and other architectural **enrichment**, sometimes forming a panel containing sculpture.

sounding-board, sound-board Canopy or **tester** over a **pulpit**.

Fig. G101 *Solomonic columns above the altar, supporting an elaborate Baroque superstructure including an open-based scrolled pediment, in the Gabrielskapelle, Friedhof St Sebastian, Salzburg, the tomb of Prince-Archbishop Wolf Dietrich von Raitenau, designed by Elia Castello (JSC).*

souse Corbel.

span of an arch Distance between the points of **springing**, or **imposts** (see **arch**).

spandrel, splandrel **1.** Quasi-triangular plane, aka hanse or **haunch**, framed by the **extrados** of an **arch**, a horizontal line projected from the **crown**, and a vertical line rising from the **springing**, often decorated. **2.** Similar plane between two arches in an **arcade**. **3.** Space between the **volutes** of an **Ionic capital**. **4.** Any approximately triangular surface-area available for decorative use.

Spanish Order Corinthian capital with lions' masks substituted for **fleurons**.

span-roof Roof with two inclined sides.

spear or **lance** Used in groups for **trophies**, **panoplies**, and military decorations, but more usually for the tops of metal railings, gates, and balconies.

speroni Anterides or **buttresses**, usually interpreted as a species of **pilaster**.

sphinx Recumbent lion with a human

head, sometimes winged. Roman sphinxes in the Egyptian style were often made, and the form later acquired female as well as male features. Other types include the **criosphinx** (ram-headed) and **hieracosphinx** (hawk-headed).

spina Barrier decorated with **obelisks** and other **monuments** along the middle of a Roman **circus** around the ends of which the contestants turned.

spira Circular column-base of an **Ionic** or **Corinthian Order**.

spiral *See* **barley-sugar**, **Solomonic**, **torso**, and **twisted column**. *See also* **stair**.

split Engaged, e.g. half-**baluster** attached to a **pedestal** (*see* Fig. G24a).

springer, springing **1.** **Springing-line** is the horizontal plane from which an **arch** begins to leave its **impost** (the point at which an arch unites with its support) by rising upwards, the bottom **voussoirs** on either side being **springers**. **2.** A **springer** can also be the **kneeler**, or **skew-block**, at the lowest end of the raking top of a **gable**. **3.** **Springing-course** is the horizontal course of stones from which an arch springs (*see* **arch**).

spur-stone Upright stone, usually circular on plan, like a short bollard, placed at the corner of a building or on either side of an entrance to prevent damage by carts or other wheeled vehicles.

square **1.** Square or rectangular open space in a town, formed at the junction of two or more streets, and surrounded by buildings, as in the **Georgian** residential squares of Britain, often with gardens in the middle. **2.** **Rubble** where the stones are roughly squared is called **squared rubble**. **3.** **Square-turned** refers to a member not carved on a lathe, but shaped on four sides, e.g. a **baluster** square on plan.

squinch Small **arch** or beam spanning across an angle of a square or rectangular plan, to support the alternate sides of octagonal spires or the base of a dome. Squinches can also be corbelled pieces built out, course by course, across a corner to carry a structure above (*see* **dome**).

stadium (*pl.* **stadia**) Racecourse for men.

staff bead Corner or angle-bead.

stage Floor or storey, especially of towers.

stair, staircase Series of **treads** and **risers**, the two making a **step**, in a **flight** of stairs, usually enclosed in a structure or cage (**staircase**, **staircase-shell**, or **stairwell**) providing access from one storey or floor to another. Parts of a staircase are as follows: **apron** (board covering the trimmer joist of a **landing**); **baluster** (one of a series of upright supports for a **handrail**, also providing protection, aka **banister**); **balustrade** (**handrail**, **string**, balusters, and **newel**, proving a barrier at the side and a grip for those ascending or descending [banister is a vulgar term for a baluster, while banisters is an equally vulgar term for a balustrade]); **bearers** (supports for **steps**); **blocks** or **brackets** (fixed to the upper edges of bearers to give additional support to the treads [blocks are also the small triangular pieces glued to the angles between treads and risers on the underside]); **cap** (top of a newel); **cappings** (cover mouldings planted on the upper edges of strings); **drop** (lower end of a newel, if visible); **easing** (junction between two strings when the flight changes direction); **flight** (continuous set of steps from one **landing** to another, or from floor to floor, or from floor to landing); **going** or **run** (of a step, distance measured horizontally between two risers, and of a flight, horizontal distance between the faces of the bottom and topmost risers): **half-pace** (landing the width of two parallel flights, one going up and the other down, involving a turn of 180°); **headroom** (distance measured vertically from the line of the nosings to the **soffit** of the flight above); **landing** (platform between flights, or the floor at the top of a stair); **line of the nosings** (line drawn through the extremities of all the nosings, so parallel to the string); **newel** (vertical member placed at the ends of the flights to support the strings, handrails, trimmers, and bearers, or a central pier of a circular stair carrying the narrower ends of each wedge-shaped step); **nosing** (front edge of a tread projecting beyond the face of the riser); **pitch** or **slope** (angle between the line of nosings and a horizontal); **quarter-pace** (landing on which a quarter-turn has to be made between the end of one flight and the beginning of the next, where flights are set at 90° to each other); **rise** (vertical dimension between the tops of consecutive treads, or between floors, or between floor and landing, defined as **rise of a step** or **rise of a flight**); **riser** (vertical part or front member of a step); **scotia** (concave moulding under the nosing); **soffit** (under-surface of the stair or flight); **spandrel** (triangular surface between outer string and floor); **strings** or **stringers** (inclined timbers [really raking beams] supporting the steps); **treads** (horizontal members forming the upper surfaces of steps); **tread-end** (part of a tread projecting over the string in a **cut-string stair**, often with a carved **console**-like bracket below it); **well** (space between the outer strings of the several flights of a stair, or the volume within which a stair rises, its inner strings against the walls of the well); and **winder** (tread wider at one end than the other, used when a stair turns).

Different types of stair include **bifurcated** (dividing into two flights or branches); **caracol** (as **cockle**, **spiral**, **vice**, or **winding**); **closed-string** (with strings of continuous raking members supporting identical balusters, the rake, slope, or inclination being parallel to the hand-rail); **cockle** (as **winding**); **cut-** or **open-string** (with strings cut to the profiles of the treads that support balusters of unequal length: in the latter case, two balusters per tread are usual in early 18th-century work, increasing to three by the middle of the century, and accompanied, in the better class of work, by elaborately carved **tread-ends** [*see* Fig. G24b]); **dog-leg** (two flights parallel to each other with a landing between them and no well between the outer strings); **double-return** (as **Imperial**); **flying**, aka **wreathed** (with stone steps cantilevered from the stair-well wall without newels at the angles or turning-points, each step resting on that below: hand-rails are usually joined by means of short curved portions called **wreaths**, hence the name); **geometrical flying** (usually circular or elliptical on plan, with stone steps with one end built into the wall and resting on the step below, the ends of the cantilevered steps forming an elegant curve); **half-turn** (with flights on three sides of the well, with landings at the corners); **Imperial** (with one straight flight, and then, after the landing, turning by 180°, with two flights parallel to the first flight, leading to the upper floor); **newel** (**1.** Circular, with steps wound round a central pier or column aka newel, thus the narrow ends of the steps are supported by the newel; **2.** Rectangular, with newels at the angles to receive the ends of the strings); **open-newel** (half-turn or other stair around a well, as distinguished from a dog-leg); **open-riser** (with no risers, the gap between treads left open); **open-well**

SELECT GLOSSARY OF TERMS / 229

(resembling a dog-leg, but with a gap or well between the outer strings, especially with a larger well, each flight terminating in a **quarter-landing**); **perron** (unenclosed external steps before the entrance to a *piano nobile* level, or the balcony-landing at the top of a double flight of steps meeting at each end of such an external landing); **spiral** (as **winding**); **straight-flight** (with one flight and no turns); **turngrece** (as **winding**); **turning** (with flights of different directions, including bifurcated, half-turn, **quarter-turn**, and **three-quarters turn** stairs); **turnpiece** (as **winding**); **vice** (as **winding**); **well** (within a well rising through more than one storey, with newel-posts forming an open well, as in a half-turn stair); and **winding** (any circular or elliptical stair, aka **caracol**, **cockle**, **spiral**, **turngrece**, **turnpiece**, or **vice**) (Figs G102a–d).

stalactites Stone or **stucco** forms resembling stalactites or icicles, aka **congelation**, found in **grottoes** and **rustication**.

stalk Stem-like ornament, sometimes fluted, in the **Corinthian capital** from which **volutes** and **helices** spring (*see* **Orders**).

stanchion Mullion.

starling Pointed **cutwater** on a bridge **pier** to divide the thrust of water.

star moulding Decoration resembling a band of stars.

starved Classicism Mean, thin, ill-proportioned, non-style, loosely based on Classicism, but displaying no feeling for rules, proportions, details, or finesse, and lacking any elan. Not to be confused with robust, powerful, confident **stripped Classicism**.

steeple Tower and spire of a church, taken together, and properly containing bells.

stele, stela (*pl.* **stelai**) Ancient Greek **monument** consisting of a vertical stone carved with reliefs, inscriptions, and ornament, often a crowning **anthemion**, commonly used as a grave-marker.

stereobata, stereobate *See* **stylobate**.

stibadium Semicircular bench in a garden from which views may be enjoyed, often associated with a fountain.

stile Upright pieces of a frame into which the ends of horizontal rails are fixed with mortices and tenons, as in a panelled door.

stillicidium Drips or eaves of a **Doric** building.

stilted arch Arch where the **springing** begins above the **impost**, i.e. with straight sides before the curve begins.

stoa 1. Colonnade of limited depth but considerable length, sometimes of two storeys, or a long **portico**. 2. **Temple portico**, with the front columns so much in advance that extra columns are needed between the colonnade in front and the structure behind.

stop Anything against which a **moulding** stops, e.g. a block of stone or wood at the base of an **architrave**, stopping both architrave and skirting (or **plinth**). For **stopped flute** see **flute**.

storey Vertical division of a building, i.e. the space between two floors, between two **entablatures**, or between any other horizontal division. Storeys are divided into **basement**, **ground** (in the USA first, in French *rez-de-chaussée*, and in German *Erdgeschoß*), **first** (or *piano nobile*, if containing the principal rooms), **second**, **third**, etc., then **Attic**, meaning above the **entablature** of the principal **façade**.

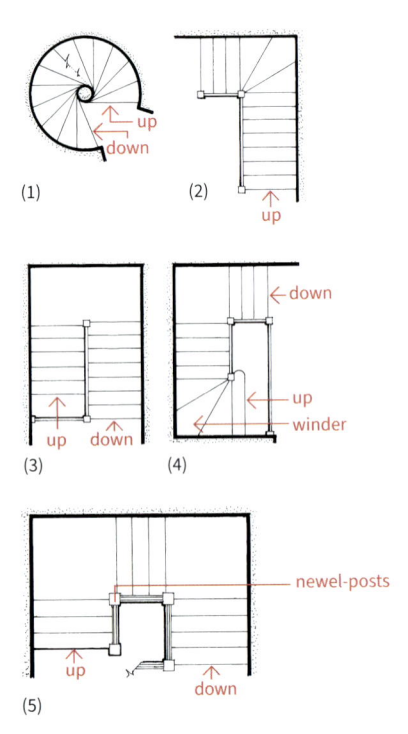

Fig. G102a *Plans of stairs: (1) circular or spiral, with winders and central newel; (2) quarter-turn with winders at the turn; (3) dog-leg with half-pace landing; (4) open-well with quarter-pace landing and winders at the first turn; (5) open-well with quarter-pace landings.*

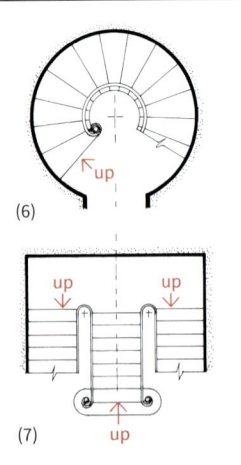

Fig. G102b *(6) geometrical, with continuous handrail: such stairs were often elliptical on plan; (7) geometrical Imperial, with scrolled handrails.*

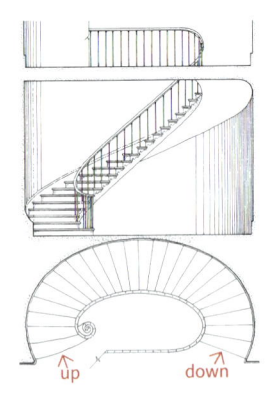

Fig. G102c *Stone geometrical or flying stair on an elliptical plan with each step resting on that below, with metal balusters and moulded continuous handrail rising from the ground to the first floor (JSC after Osborne [1954]).*

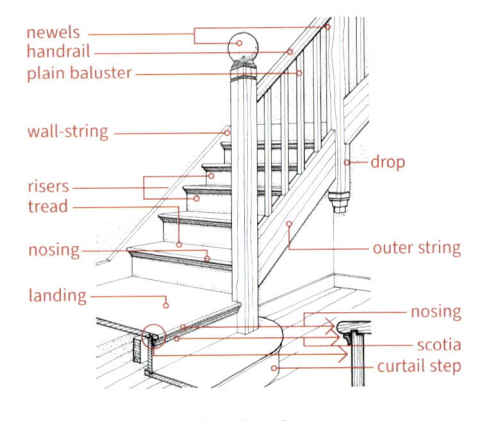

Fig. G102d *Timber closed-string stair (JSC after Osborne [1954]).*

230 / CLASSICAL ARCHITECTURE

An Attic storey may have a subsidiary entablature. **Entresols** and **mezzanines** are intermediate storeys. Vertical divisions of towers are called **stages** (e.g. **belfry-stage**).

straight arch **Lintel** of **voussoirs** based on the principle of wedges of an arch, but with a flat or slightly cambered **intrados** (or **soffit**), usually made of **brick rubbers** or finely dressed stone. It is also called a **skewback** arch (from the steeply raked **abutments** from which the arch springs).

strapwork Decoration, usually of wood, plaster, or masonry, consisting of interlaced bands like fretwork or leather straps, much used in Northern European Renaissance architecture of the 16th and early 17th centuries (Fig. G103).

Fig. G103 *Caroline strapwork from Crewe Hall, Cheshire.*

stretcher Stone or brick laid with its longer face in the surface of the wall. A **stretching**, or **stretcher course**, is a course of stretchers.

stria (*pl.* **striae**) **1.** **Fillet** separating the **flutes** of a Classical column-shaft. **2.** Flat facet in lieu of a flute on a column-shaft (*see* **flute**). **3.** Any small channel in series separated by fillets.

striges **Flutes** of a **column** or **pilaster** flanked by **lists**, **fillets**, or **striæ**.

strigil Curving flute, like an elongated *ʃ*, so **strigillation** describes repeated upright flutes, often found enriching the sides of Classical **sarcophagi**, **vases**, **urns**, etc. (Fig. G104).

Fig. G104 *Strigillation on a Roman sarcophagus.*

string **1.** Sloping or raking timber (**stringer**) carrying the ends of **treads**

and **risers** of a **stair**. **2.** Horizontal **band** (moulded or plain) on a **façade**, aka **string-course**.

stripped Classicism Classical architecture from which **mouldings**, ornament, and much detail have been removed, leaving only the main elements of the structural and proportional systems. It was a feature of late 18th- and early 19th-century **Neo-Classicism**, recurred in the 1920s and 1930s, and re-emerged later. Sometimes Classical detail was only implied, and the **Orders** were only alluded to in the most subtle ways. Not to be confused with **starved Classicism**.

strix Canal, **flute**, or **strigil**.

structura cæmenticia Concrete.

stucco Plasterwork, or calcareous cement **render**, plain or modelled. Properly, stucco is a plastered finish of lime, sand, brick-dust, stone-dust, or powdered burnt clay nodules, mixed with water, used as an external **render** instead of stone, and moulded to form architectural features i.e. **string-courses**, **cornices**, etc. It can be made to resemble **ashlar**, by means of inscribing lines on it, and it can be coloured, as in **Parker's Roman cement**, and other finishes. It is known as **opus albarium** or **opus tectorium**. Internal stucco, widely used in the 18th century, and elaborately modelled, was made of very fine sand, pulverised white Carrara marble, gypsum (hydrated calcium sulphate), alabaster dust, and water, often with other additions, e.g. colouring, provided by mixing in metallic oxides, and size and gum, which, when perfectly dry, was rubbed and polished.

stylobate, stereobata, stereobate **1.** Topmost platform surface of a three-stepped **crepidoma** on which a **colonnade** or a building with a **peristyle** is placed. **2.** In Classical architecture it has come to mean any continuous **base**, **plinth**, substructure, or solid mass of masonry on which a colonnade or wall is erected. Vitruvius defined **stereobatæ** as the walls under the columns above the ground: he was clearly thinking of the walls of temple-podia.

summer-stone Lowest stone of a gable stopping at the eaves: the first stone of the **tabling** or **coping** is supported on the summer-stone, aka **skew-corbel**.

Fig. G105 *Sunburst.*

sunburst **1.** Collection of rods, normally gilded, radiating from a centre, which is sometimes the head of a deity, usually Apollo (Fig. G105). **2.** Type of **fanlight**.

super-altar **1.** Consecrated **altar-slab**, or **mensa**. **2.** Shelf over the altar, or to the east of it.

supercilium **1.** **Lintel** above an aperture. **2.** Fillet over a **cyma** on a **cornice** forming the topmost member of an **entablature**.

superimposed When the **Orders** are used to define the storeys of a Classical **façade** and set one above the other, they have a hierarchical order. *See* **assemblage of Orders**.

surbase Topmost **moulding** of a **dado**, **pedestal**, or **stylobate**.

surbased Arch (e.g. **segmental arch**), **vault**, or **dome** of a height less than half its span.

surmounted **1.** Arch (e.g. **stilted arch**), **vault**, or **dome** rising higher than half its span. **2.** A way of stating that something is placed over part of a building: e.g. the **façade** is **surmounted** by a sculpture of **cornucopiæ** and **putti**.

swag Festoon resembling a cloth, suspended from two supports (Figs G106a–b; *see* Fig. G89a).

swan-neck **1.** Any double-curved member, or an **ogee**, e.g. the form of a stair hand-rail when it rises to join the newel-post. **2.** Scrolled pediment. **3.** Type of elegant handle found on **Georgian** furniture. **4.** Form of a rainwater-pipe connecting a gutter to a down-pipe under the eaves.

symbol Attribute or sign accompanying a statue or picture to denote identity,

SELECT GLOSSARY OF TERMS / 231

Fig. G106a *Window-surrounds with triangular pediments and swags (the swag on the left is composed of husks, or bellflowers). Note the crossettes (Langley [1745]).*

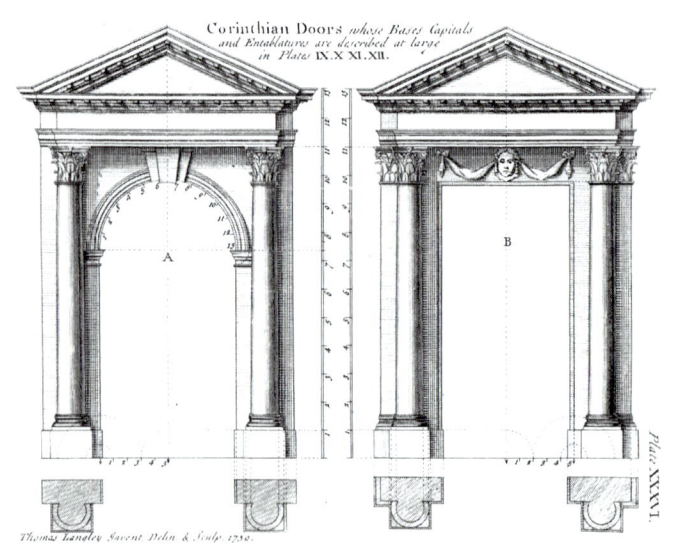

Fig. G106b *Corinthian doorways. Note the swag on the right (Langley [1745]).*

sometimes substituted for the figure. Some common attributes associated with Christianity are as follows:

Almond Tree in Flowerpot
    Blessed Virgin Mary (BVM)
Arrow Martyrdom, especially Sts Sebastian and Edmund
Asperge Purity
Book Evangelist or Doctor of the Church
Chalice Sts John the Evangelist, Benedict, Thomas Aquinas
Cross Missionary, esp. St John the Baptist
Crown, sceptre (or both)
    Royal rank, Sainthood
Dove Holy Spirit, Purity
Fountain BVM
Garden BVM
Lamp Virginity
Lily BVM
Lily among Thorns
    BVM and Confessors
Palm Victory, Martyrdom
Rose BVM
Skull St Jerome
Sword Martyrdom, especially saints decapitated
Wheel Patriarchs, St Catherine

Readers are referred to Francis Bond (1914): *Dedications and Patron Saints of English Churches. Ecclesiastical Symbolism. Saints, and their Emblems* (London: H. Milford, Oxford University Press).

symmetry 1. Harmony, proportion, or uniformity between the parts of a building and its whole. 2. Equal disposition of parts and masses on either side of an axis, as a mirror-image.

systyle See **intercolumniation**.

tab Ear, or means of securing a rainwater-pipe to a wall.

tabby Gravel, lime, and crushed oyster- or mussel-shells mixed with water, forming a type of **concrete**.

tabernacle 1. Receptacle for the Sacraments placed over the altar. 2. Any **niche** or **canopy**, esp. freestanding. 3. C**iborium** or **baldacchino**.

table 1. Any horizontal **moulding**, e.g. **band**, **cornice**, or **string-course**. 2. Flat, broad slab, as on an **altar**, where it forms the **mensa** or top.

table-tomb Flat rectangular stone carried on two or more upright stones over a grave, so that the finished object looks like a table.

tablet 1. Wall-slab or mural monument. 2. Horizontal **capping** or **coping**.

tabling Cope.

tablinum, tabulinum Room with one side open to an **atrium**, courtyard, **colonnade**, or **portico**.

tabula 1. Niche or cupboard. 2. Metal or timber altar-frontal.

tabula rasa 1. Tablet from which an inscription has been erased, enabling it to be used again. 2. Obliteration of large swathes of a town, clearing it for redevelopment, as demanded by Modernist dogma. 3. Erasure of history and collective memory.

tænia, tenia Fillet or band at the top of a **Doric architrave** separating it from the **frieze** (*see* **Doric Order**).

tailloir Abacus, esp. in the **Doric Order**.

talon As ogee.

tambour 1. Core or bell of a **Corinthian** or **Composite capital**. 2. Wall or **drum** carrying a **dome**, or a **rotunda** or any circular building. 3. Section of a column-shaft composed of drums.

taper Gradual diminution in width or thickness in any elongated object towards one extremity or another, e.g. **herm**, **obelisk**, or **term**. Column-shafts properly do not taper, as they diminish in diameter with height in a curved **entasis**.

tarras Strong cement.

tarsia Inlays of different woods, usually light on dark, often in **arabesque** or **scroll-work**.

tas-de-charge Lowest **voussoir** of an **arch** or **vault**, tied into the wall.

tassel Common ornament in Classical decoration, flags, standards, and **trophies**. The tassel also occurs as a variety of spearhead in railings.

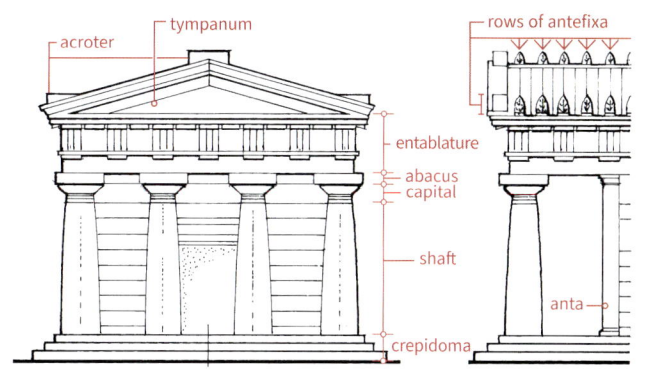

Fig. G107a *Greek Doric prostyle tetrastyle temple-front: note the anta terminating the cell wall and the series of antefixa on the ridge-crest and over the cornice.*

Fig. G107b *Various types of Greek temple plans: (1) peripteral hexastyle, i.e. with colonnades surrounding the cell, six columns at each end forming the porticoes and carrying the pediments; (2) pseudo-peripteral septostyle (or heptastyle), i.e. with all columns engaged with the temple walls, and seven columns at each end, resulting in entrances off-centre; (3A) half-plan of a dipteral octastyle, i.e. with two rows of columns surrounding the cell, eight at each end carrying the pediments; (3B) half-plan, pseudo-dipteral octastyle, i.e. with a wider pace between the walls of the cell and the peristyle, with eight columns at each end carrying the pediments.*

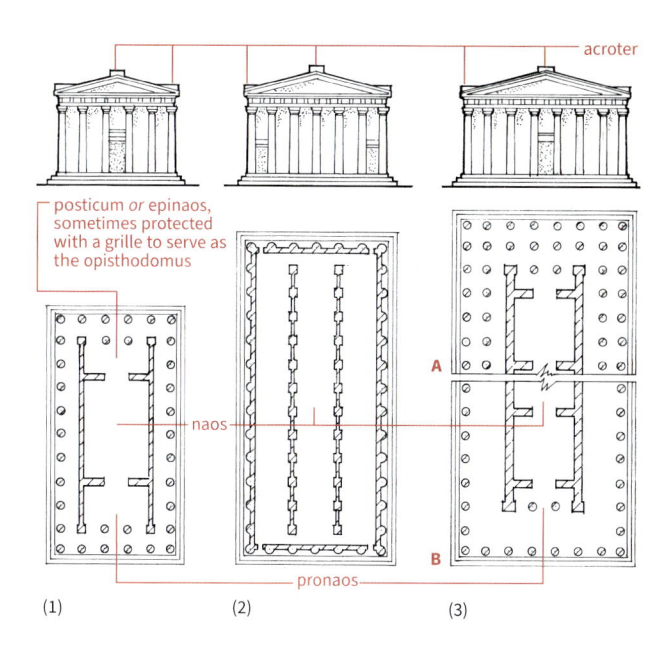

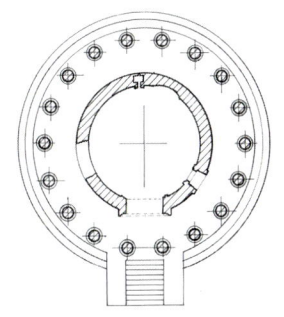

Fig. G107c *Plan of the Roman Temple of Vesta at Tivoli (c.80 BC), showing the circular peristyle.*

tauriform Bucranium (*see* Fig. G34).

tebam Rostrum or dais, esp. in a synagogue.

tectorium opus Type of plaster or stucco. *See* opus.

tegula Roof-tile, or facing-brick for walls.

telamon (*pl.* **telamones**) Upright, unbowed male whole figure acting as a column supporting an entablature on its head. *See* atlas, canephora, caryatid(e), Persian.

temenos Sacred precinct of a Classical temple.

tempietto Small Renaissance temple, often circular.

template 1. Block set under a truss, beam, etc., aka pad or padstone, providing a fixing, and distributing the load. 2. Mould, pattern, or outline to ensure accuracy when forming a profiled moulding. 3. Beam or lintel.

temple 1. Building dedicated to, or intended as the residence of, pagan deities. Classical temples were usually rectangular, and consisted of an enclosed part called the cell or naos, a portico, and a sanctuary. Greek temples were commonly surrounded by a peripteral arrangement of columns (peristyle) supporting an entablature, with a pediment at each of the shorter ends (e.g. 5th-century BC Parthenon, Athens), but sometimes had a portico at each end (amphi-prostyle) with plain walls on the longer sides (e.g. 5th-century BC Temple of Niké Apteros, Athens). Roman temples usually had a deep portico at one end (derived from Etruscan exemplars), a plain cella (sometimes with engaged columns, e.g. 1st-century BC Maison Carrée, Nîmes), and stood on high podia. Circular temples of the tholos type were erected by both the Greeks and Romans (e.g. 1st-century BC Temple of Vesta, Tivoli). For terms used to describe arrangements of columns, etc., *see* anta, colonnade, intercolumniation, portico) (Figs G107a–c; *see* Fig. G91). 2. Synagogue (alluding to the sacred edifice in Jerusalem, esp. the Temple of Solomon). 3. French Protestant church. 4. Place once occupied by a preceptory of the Knights Templars (as in London or Paris). 5. Building for special ritual use, e.g. a Freemasonic lodge (again with connections to the Temple of Solomon).

temple-front Element of a façade resembling the front of a Classical temple, with columns or pilasters carrying an entablature and pediment, applied to an elevation, as in a Palladian composition (*see* Fig. 5.55b).

tendril Architectural ornament resembling plant-like tendrils, in Classical architecture associated with acanthus, anthemion, and palmette, recurring in Renaissance and Mannerist arabesque and grotesque ornament.

tenia *See* tænia.

tepidarium Room or intermediate temperature in Roman *thermæ*.

teram Scroll at the end of a step.

term, terminal 1. Classical head and bust (often with torso) merging with a downward tapering pedestal resembling an inverted obelisk, sometimes with feet appearing beneath the pedestal (which is proportioned like the lower part of a human figure) (Fig. G108; *see* Fig. G69): **terminal figure** or **terminal** describes the bust or top part of a term, but a **terminal pedestal** has a bust set on it, rather than part of it. 2. Ornamental finish, or termination, of an object, such as a vase on a pedestal.

terrace 1. Raised space or platform adjoining a building. 2. Row of houses joined together as a unified design.

SELECT GLOSSARY OF TERMS / 233

Fig. G108 Two Rococo terms, Palace of Sanssouci, Potsdam (1745–7), Georg Wenzeslaus von Knobelsdorff, architect, Friedrich Christian Glume, sculptor. The Bacchic allusions suggest the stepped glass-houses below the palace in which vines were grown (JSC).

terracotta Baked clay, unglazed, often cast in moulds of some elaboration, used for ornament, or for facing buildings, or for parts of buildings.

terrazzo Floor or **dado** finish made of marble chips set in mortar which, when dry, is ground down and polished, providing a hard, decorative, and easily cleaned surface.

tessera (*pl.* **tesseræ**) Small square of glass, pottery, tile, brick, etc. (aka **tessella**), embedded in mortar, used to make up the pattern of a **mosaic** pavement or surface, aka **tessellation**.

testa Brick or tile, or a shard of something made of burnt clay.

tester Canopy over a pulpit, tomb, or bed.

testudo Vault over a hall, or any grand arched or vaulted roof. A **testudinate** roof is one which completely covers a building, with four sides converging to a point or a ridge and points.

tetrastyle Having four columns in one line. A **tetrastyle atrium** is one with the columns arranged around it to support the roof.

thatch Roof-covering of straw, rushes, or reeds, much favoured for the *cottage orné* or for 'rustick' buildings.

theatre Semicircular tiered structure with seats, and a stage on which plays were performed: an **amphitheatre** consists of two of these joined together, producing a circular or elliptical structure.

thermæ Roman public baths, often of great magnificence, and containing many amenities apart from baths. The complex planning and the ruins in Rome and elsewhere were sources for much **Renaissance** and later Classical architecture (*see* Figs 3.3a–b). Small baths were called **balneæ**.

thermal window Semicircular opening subdivided by means of two **mullions**, aka **Diocletian window** from its use in the **thermæ** of Diocletian (*see* Fig. G50). It was used often in **Renaissance** architecture, notably by Palladio and his followers (*see* Figs G84b, 5.57a, and 6.24a–b).

tholobate 1. Substructure for a Greek **tholos**: a circular **crepidoma** or **stylobate**. 2. Circular substructure of a **cupola**.

tholos Ancient Greek circular building, often with a **peristyle** and conical roof.

through stone 1. Stone or bond-stone, aka throughstane, in a wall that reaches through its thickness, aka parpen, parpent, or parpend. 2. Table-tomb, flat grave-stone or -slab, aka thruch.

thunderbolt Classical ornament an attribute of Jupiter, in the form of a spiral roll, pointed at both ends, often gripped in the talons of an eagle, or shown winged, with forked arrows protruding from it representing lightning (*see* Figs G52b, and 2.11c).

thyroma (*pl.* **thyromata**) A great doorway, e.g. the monumental north doorway of the Erechtheion.

thyrsus Staff with a pine cone at the end, entwined with ribbons, grapevines, and ivy leaves, found in schemes of **Bacchic decoration**.

tile Thick piece of baked clay used for flooring, or wall- or roof-covering. Flat tiles are called **plain tiles**, and curved are **pan-tiles**. Walls clad with tiles are **tile-hung**. Tiles may be glazed or unglazed (Fig. G109).

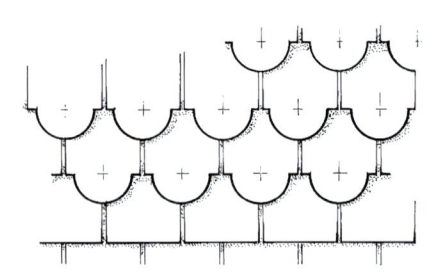

Fig. G109 Tiles: (top) fish-scale; (bottom) plain.

Tivoli window *See* **Vitruvian opening**.

tomb-chest Monument shaped like a chest or an altar, aka **altar-tomb**. A **table-tomb** is a flat slab carried on two, four, or six columns. Tomb-chests may be plain or can have effigies on top, either as sculptured figures or as incised designs, and may have standing figures, aka **weepers**, around the sides (*see* Figs G117 and 4.1).

tondo Circular **medallion** or **plaque**, often occurring in **spandrels** (*see* Fig. G19).

top rail Upper frame of a **dado** (or **wainscot**) or door (*see* Fig. G61).

torch Aka **flambeau**, often associated with **candelabra**, occurs as a decorative motif in **Neo-Classical** architecture. If inverted, it represents the extinguishing of life, and is therefore found in funerary architecture, often held by a weeping **putto**.

torso Twisted column-shaft.

torus (*pl.* **tori**) Literally a swelling or cushion-like bulge, it is a large convex **moulding** of semicircular section, used esp. at the **base** of a **column** or the top of a **plinth**, and resembles an **astragal**, but is much smaller.

tower Tall building, circular, square, or polygonal on plan, used for defence, as a landmark, for the hanging of bells, or the display of a clock. The storeys of a tower are called **stages**.

trabeation Entablature, beam, or a combination of beams in a structure. A **trabeated** building is constructed with posts or **columns** supporting **lintels** and beams (i.e. **columnar and trabeated**) rather than arches (i.e. **arcuated**).

trabes compactiles Main beams or **architraves** over the columns of Etruscan temples.

tracery Intersection of **mullions** and **transoms** of windows, screens, panels, or **vaults**. While most tracery is found in the various styles of **Gothic architecture**, early **Renaissance** variants featuring Classical **mouldings**, semicircular **arches**, and **capitals**, do exist.

trachelion, trachelium Neck of a Greek **Doric column** between the **annulets** under the **echinus** and the **hypotrachelion** (*see* **Doric Order**).

Trajanic column *See* **triumphal column**.

transenna 1. Screen of lattice-work, often of marble. 2. Beam or **transom**.

transept Large division of a building lying across its main axis at 90°, e.g. the transverse portion of a cruciform church, usually between the nave and the chancel, the arms of which are on either side of the crossing.

transition Term used to denote the passing from one style to another.

transom(e) 1. Horizontal bar dividing a window into two or more lights in height. 2. Horizontal piece of a doorway forming part of the frame, above which is a **fanlight**.

transverse arch Arch dividing one compartment of a vaulted ceiling from another.

traverse 1. Screen, with curtains to give privacy, as in an **enfilade** system of rooms, or a gallery or loft acting as a corridor or passage. 2. **Transom**, or horizontal part of an **architrave** or **door-frame**.

travertine Calcareous building stone much used in ancient Rome.

tread Horizontal part of a step of a stair.

trellis Cross-barred timber frame (**lattice-work**) used as a screen or a structure on which plants may climb. **Treillage** is trellis-work constructed with false perspectives to suggest niches, arches, or even greater length than is really the case.

tresse Interlacing ornament resembling overlapping **guilloches**, usually on a **torus moulding**, but also found on flat horizontal **bands** or **string-courses**.

tribune 1. Apse in a **basilica**, or the eastern part of a church. 2. Raised **ambo**, platform, dais, **rostrum**, pulpit, or bishop's throne. 3. Gallery in a church.

triclinium Dining room in a Roman house.

triglyph Vertical block in a **Doric frieze** comprising two **glyphs** (**V**-shaped channels) and two **half-glyphs** (hence the 'three' glyphs), separating the **metopes**. In late-Renaissance versions the two half-glyphs are often omitted, so the block becomes a **diglyph**. Triglyph blocks occur over the centre-lines of columns and spaces between columns. In the **Greek Doric Order** triglyphs at the corners of the building join, so they are not over the centre-lines of the columns at the corners, and the spaces between columns at the corners of a building are smaller: in **Roman Doric** the triglyphs are over the centre-line of the column at the corner, so that there is part of a metope at the angle of the frieze separating the triglyphs (*see* **Doric Order**).

tripod Table or bowl with three legs (often terminating in representations of the feet of animals) usually placed on high, above a crowning **cornice** on a **pedestal**.

tripteral With an external **colonnade** of three rows of **columns**.

tristyle Colonnade with three columns in the same line, usually **in antis**.

Triton Male figure, fish from the waist down, usually found in structures with a marine theme, e.g. fountains.

triumphal arch Arch erected to celebrate a person or event, usually a military victory, and often surmounted by a **quadriga**. There are two main types: those with a single arch over an axis (Titus, Rome, 1st century AD), and those with a large central arch flanked by two smaller arches (Septimius Severus, Rome, 3rd century AD). In both types a rich **Order** was applied to the **arcuated** form, and over the **entablature** the **Attic storey** was inscribed with the dedication (*see* Figs 2.18a–b). The form was revived in Renaissance times, not only for festive architecture, but in a variation, for building **façades** or parts of façades (Figs G110a–b; *see* Fig. G52c). Later triumphal arches, such as the Arc de Triomphe in Paris (1806–35) by Chalgrin, and the great Thiepval Arch by Lutyens of the 1920s, exploit more than one axis (*see* Figs 3.2a, 3.2f, and 7.2).

triumphal column Large, single, free-standing column on a pedestal, erected as a public monument. The most celebrated example is that of Trajan (2nd century AD) with its spiral bands of sculpture, and its massive base containing the tomb-chamber of the emperor (*see* Fig. 5.15b).

trochilus Scotia, or concave moulding.

trompe Vaulted structure over a part of an external angle of a building that has been removed, as when, e.g., a **niche** is placed at the corner, thus the vault is really a kind of **corbel** or **pendentive**, carrying the load above.

trompe l'œil Usually a two-dimensional painting showing an arrangement of objects that looks disconcertingly three-dimensional and real, often employed to suggest architectural elements, a texture, or a finish.

trophy Sculptured depiction of armour and arms, occasionally incorporating **wreaths**, **garlands**, and **festoons**, hung in an orderly fashion on a tree-trunk and branches. *See* **military decoration**, **panoply**.

trunnels Guttæ.

truss 1. Combination of timbers to form a frame, placed at intervals, and carrying the purlins of a roof-structure. 2. Projection from the **naked** of a wall, e.g. **corbel**, **modillion**, or **console**.

tuck pointing Lines to mark the joints in brickwork, made with ridges of lime-putty, after joints have been raked out and replaced with mortar coloured to match the brickwork. It gives an ultra-refined appearance to a **façade**.

tufa Rough, porous cellular stone, e.g. that from which Roman **catacombs** are cut.

tumbling-course Brickwork laid at 90° to the slope of a **buttress**, chimney, **gable**, or other feature, tapering into the horizontal courses (*see* Fig. G62d).

turngrece Winding stair.

turnpike stair Circular, spiral, or winding stair with a solid central post on which the narrow ends of the steps are carried.

turret Small **tower**, usually slender in form, or a large **pinnacle**.

Fig. G110a Plan and elevation of an 'Ionic gateway': an interpretation of the triumphal arch theme. The Ionic Order (shown with plain shafts on the left, and alternatively banded on the right) rises from a pedestal, and supports an entablature with pulvinated frieze above which is an Attic storey (Langley [1745]).

Fig. G110b Entrance to Der Neue Begräbnisplatz (the new burial-place), Dessau (1787–9), designed by F.W. von Erdmannsdorff as a variant on the triumphal-arch theme, crowned by a figure of Hope with her anchor and two swagged urns. In the niches are the two brothers, Sleep and Death, and the inscription assures us that Death is not Death, but only a part of the natural order of things, with reference to the ennoblement or refinement of dying Nature (Christian Friedrich Wiegand, coll. JSC).

Tuscan Order 1. Simplest of the five **Roman Orders of Classical architecture**. The shaft of the column is never fluted, and the capital has a square **abacus**. The base consists of a square **plinth** and a large **torus**, and the **entablature** is quite plain. In a primitive version of the Order the **frieze** and **cornice** are omitted, and a wide overhanging eaves carried on long **mutules** is placed directly above the **architrave** (Figs G111a–c; see Figs 2.10a–d). 2. The Tuscan **cavædium** had an inward tilt in all four directions so that rain drained through the **compluvium**.

tusk, tuss Projecting **tenon** or **toothing-stone** left in a wall to which another building is to be joined.

twisted See **barley-sugar**, **Solomonic**, **torso**.

tympanum (*pl.* **tympana**) 1. Triangular or segmental face of a **pediment** contained within the horizontal and raking (or segmental) **cornices**, often enriched with sculpture in high relief. 2. Area between a **lintel** and an **arch** over it.

type 1. **Tester** or sound-board over a **pulpit**. 2. **Capping** of a **cupola** roof or turret. 3. Exemplar, pattern, prototype, or original work serving as a model for a building. 4. Something exemplifying the ideal characteristics of, say, a temple, so some would hold that the Parthenon is the very type of a **Greek Hellenic** temple. 5. Form or character distinguishing a class or group of buildings (building type), e.g. church, mausoleum, town hall, etc.

umbraculum **Baldachin**.

umbrello Garden *fabrique*, a small structure sheltering, e.g., a seat.

uncut modillion **Mutule**, as in variants of the **Tuscan Order**, or modillion resembling a bracket or unadorned cantilevered block.

undé, undy Oundy, wave- or **Vitruvian scroll**, or any undulating, repeated, running wave-like ornament in Classical architecture.

undercroft Vaulted space or crypt under, e.g., a church, wholly or partly underground.

undulate band Ornament in a strip, in a continuous scroll of waves, the stem of which is a repeat series of **S**- or **ogee** forms, e.g. **Vitruvian scroll**.

Urbanism Approach to the design of towns taking into account the need to respond with sensitivity to urban morphologies, streets, vistas, enclosure, geometries, scale, etc., to avoid the visual chaos imposed so destructively on many cities since 1945 by slavish adherence to the tenets of the Modern Movement.

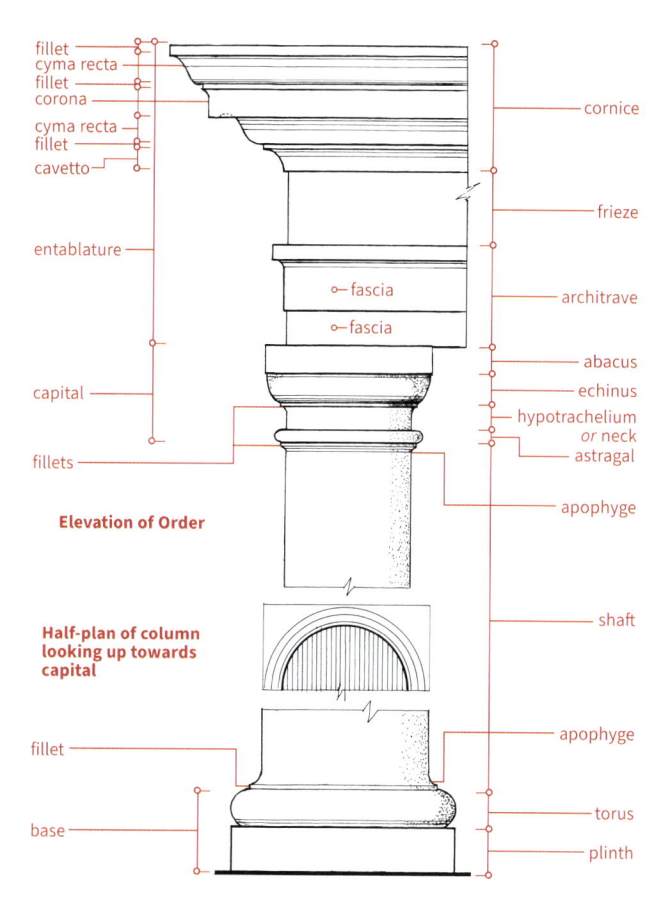

Fig. G111a *Tuscan Order (JSC after Palladio).*

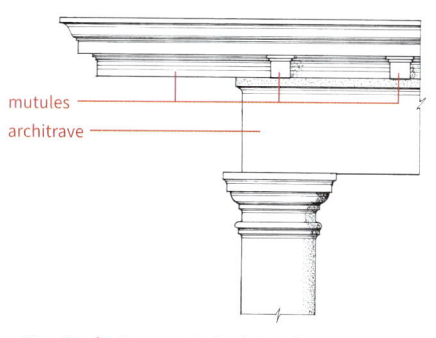

Fig. G111b *Tuscan Order (JSC after Inigo Jones).*

Fig. G111c *Tuscan portico of St Paul's Church, Covent Garden, London (1631–3), by Inigo Jones, repaired and re-cased (1788–9) by Thomas Hardwick, who again restored the building (1796–8) after a disastrous fire in 1795. Palladio had reconstructed this Order as described by Vitruvius: it has widely spaced columns, an architrave but no frieze or cornice; instead there are a wide overhanging eaves and deep pediment, both with long brackets, and really elongated mutules (JSC).*

urilla (*pl.* **urillæ**) Volute under the **abacus** of a **Corinthian capital**, aka **helix**.

urn Lidded **vase** (often draped) for cremated remains, but the form is also used for decorative motifs on top of the **dies** of **balustrades**, or on walls, or in **niches**, or as garden ornaments.

vagina Lower part of a **term** or **terminal pedestal** with which the bust merges (*see* Figs G69 and G108).

valance 1. Hung drapery or simulated drapery round a **tester**, etc. (*see* Fig. 5.3). 2. Wooden vertical boards, often pointed or curved at the lower ends, set in series at the edges of canopies.

valley Internal meeting of two slopes of a roof.

vamure Walk on top of a wall behind a **parapet**.

vane Metal banner or other motif fixed to the top of a **tower** or **cupola** to show the direction of the wind, aka **weathercock** or **-vane**.

vase 1. Ornamental unlidded vessel, distinct from an **urn**, with or without handles, occurring in a huge variety of forms in Classical Architecture. 2. Bell or core of a **Corinthian capital**.

vault 1. Arch, the depth of which exceeds its span, i.e. an **elongated arch** covering a space, constructed of brick, concrete, masonry, etc., and occasionally of wood and plaster in imitation of something heavier. Essentially a ceiling over a space, it may also be a roof, and it may carry a floor or a roof. As with an arch, it is constructed so that the stones or other materials with which it is made support and keep themselves in place. Any volume covered with a vault or **voussure** is **vaulted**, while the system of vaults over a space is termed **vaulting**. Types of vault include: **annular** (**barrel**, **cylindrical**, **tunnel**, or **wagon**, the simplest variety of vault, really an elongated arch like half a cylinder, spanning between thick parallel walls or other supports, and presenting a uniform concave **soffit** throughout its length (Fig. G112b). It can also be segmental or half-elliptical in section. If a **tunnel vault** is divided into bays by means of arches carried on piers then the arches are called **transverse**); **barrel** (as **annular**); **cloister** (as **domical**); **cross** (as **groin**); **cylindrical** (as **annular**); **domical**, aka **cloister** (not a true dome, rising from a polygonal or square base, with curved elements called **cells**, **severies**, or **webs**, meeting at **groins** [Fig. G112a]); **groin** (two identical **barrel** vaults intersecting at right angles forming **groins** [sharp arrises] at the junctions between the concave surfaces, resulting in a **groin** or **cross vault** [Fig. G112c]); **rampant** (**tunnel** vault with abutments at varying heights); **tunnel** (as **annular**); and **wagon** (as **annular**). When vaults are more than a semicircle in section they are called **surmounted vaults**, and when less than a

SELECT GLOSSARY OF TERMS / 237

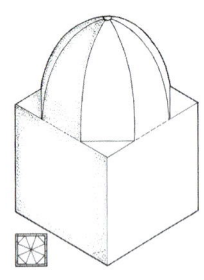

Fig. G112a *Square plan with domical vault composed of webs, severies, or cells on an octagonal base. The corners of the square are bridged by arches, called squinches, to accommodate the octagonal form.*

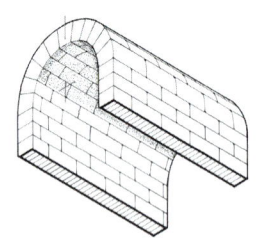

Fig. G112b *Annular or barrel-vault.*

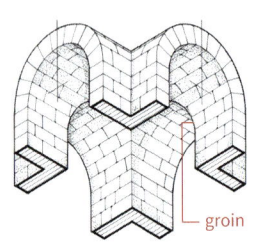

Fig. G112c *Groin-vault formed by the intersection of two barrel-vaults.*

semicircle (i.e. segmental) in section, they are **surbased**. A **dome** is a vault with a segmental, semicircular, bulbous, or pointed section rising from a circular base (*see* **dome**). **2.** Any room or enclosed space of any kind so covered. **3.** Burial-chamber or crypt, vaulted or not, e.g. a space covered by a flat slab or ledger-stone. **4.** Any strong place or place of safety. **5.** Cellar.

velarium Awning over the cavea (area occupied by spectators) in an **amphitheatre**.

vellar cupola 1. Dome over **staircases** or **salons** (saloons), that is, over any compartment that is more than one storey high. **2. Sail dome** (*see* **dome**).

Venetian arch Form of arched opening, either blind or open, consisting of a semicircular-headed arch, in the centre of which are two semicircular-headed openings separated by a **colonnette** above

Fig. G113 *Venetian arch.*

which is a **roundel** or foiled opening (Fig. G113).

Venetian crenellation **Palladian** capping to a wall consisting of balls set on a series of curved elements, resembling a row of pawns in chess (e.g. the *piano nobile* level of Burlington's villa at Chiswick) (*see* Figs G84b and 4.41b–c).

Venetian door, Venetian window *See* **serliana** and **Wyatt window**.

veranda(h) External open gallery or covered way, with a sloping or lean-to roof or canopy supported on light (usually metal) columns or posts, attached to a building, usually in front of the window of the principal rooms, with access from French windows. Verandahs were popular during the 19th century, from the **Regency** period onwards.

verge 1. Slight projection of a pitched roof over the **naked** of a gable-wall. The junction between the roof-covering and the top of the gable has to be waterproof: this is achieved by creating a tight joint, using tiles and mortar (**parged verge**), tumbled brickwork, etc. If the roof is extended over the wall it is finished with a **barge-board**, aka **verge-board. 2. Shaft** of a Classical column.

vermiculation When a surface of stonework is dressed with irregular shallow channels resembling worm-tracks it is called **vermiculated rustication** (*see* **rustic-work, rustication**).

versuræ Projecting side-walls connecting the straight walls of the cavea with the **scæna** of a theatre.

vertù 1. The fine arts as a topic of interest or study. **2.** An antique, curiosity, etc., so

a **virtuoso** is a student of objects of **vertù**, a connoisseur, a collector of antiquities.

vesica piscis Figure, aka **aureole, glory, almond,** or **mandala** (**mandorla**), formed by two segmental curves meeting in points, like an ellipse, but pointed at each end, created by the interpenetration of two equal circles, the centre of each of which is on the centre-line of each segment (*see* Fig. G75).

vestibule 1. Enclosed or partly enclosed space (**vestibulum**) in front of the main entrance of a Greek or Roman building, i.e. an entrance- or forecourt. **2.** Apartment serving as a space between rooms, usually for communication, as a waiting room, or as an antechamber. **3.** Entrance lobby or hall.

vestry, revestry Room adjacent to the chancel of a church, where vestments are kept and the clergy vested, and meetings, etc., held, aka **sacristy**.

viaduct Long bridge carrying a road, or railway, usually on a series of arches.

viæ Spaces between **mutules**.

vice, vis, vyse Spiral staircase wound around a column or pier.

villa Country house or farmstead in Classical times. In the **Renaissance** period the term meant a country house, e.g. the Villa Capra near Vicenza. During the 19th century it meant a detached house on the outskirts of a town.

Vitruvian opening Aperture, e.g. doorway or window, with battered sides, like an Egyptian **pylon**, found in **Neo-Classical** architecture with Greek and Egyptian

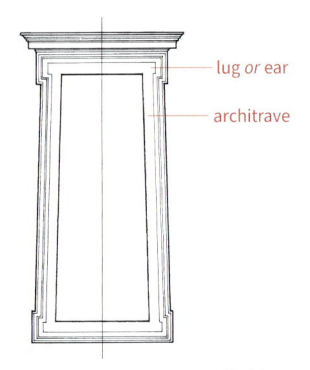

Fig. G114 *Vitruvian opening: so called because it was described by Vitruvius, and published by Palladio, it has a lugged architrave, wider at the base than at its top, and is based on an example inside the Temple of Vesta at Tivoli (c.80 BC), aka Tivoli window.*

238 / CLASSICAL ARCHITECTURE

influences. It is so called because it was described by Vitruvius (Fig. G114; *see* Fig. 3.6).

Vitruvian scroll Continuous band of ornament like a series of stylised waves, found in Classical Architecture, aka **running dog**, or **wave-scroll**, occurring in **friezes**, **dados**, etc. (Fig. G115).

Fig. G115 *Vitruvian scroll.*

vivo **Shaft** or **fust** of a **column**.

volute Spiral scroll forming the distinguishing feature of the **Ionic capital**, where there are normally four, but eight on **angular** and **Composite** capitals, and smaller types, sometimes called **helix**, on **Corinthian** capitals. It is also a distinctive element of the **ancon**, **console**, and **modillion**, where like the Ionic capital, it resembles a rolled-up mattress (*see* **Composite**. **Corinthian**, **helix**, **Ionic**, and **Orders**).

vomitorium Passage to allow ingress to or egress from an **amphitheatre**.

voussoir Wedge-shaped stone or brick, forming part of an arch, aka **cuneus** (*see* **arch**).

voussure Vault (*see* **vault**).

voutain Jointing of the web of a stone vault.

vyse *See* **vice**.

wagon ceiling, wagon vault **1.** Ceiling or vault over a rectangular space consisting of a simple half-cylinder carried on parallel walls. **2.** A **wagon-**, or **cradle-roof**, is formed of closely spaced rafters with arched braces that look like the covering of a wagon. Such roofs can be plastered or panelled.

wainscot **1.** Timber lining to walls, or timber panelling (*see* **boiserie**). **2.** Panelled **box-pews**.

wall-arcade Blind arcade.

Wallfahrtskirche Pilgrimage-church in German-speaking lands.

wall-pier *See* **wandpfeiler**.

Fig. G116 Wandpfeiler *or wall-piers in the former Benedictine abbey-church of Zwiefalten (1740–85), designed by Johann Michael Fischer, with exquisite Rococo stucco decorations by Johann Michael Feichtmayr, sculpture by Johann Joseph Christian, and frescoes by Franz Josef Spiegler (JSC).*

wandpfeiler Literally a **wall-pier**, the term is given to internal buttresses forming the walls of **side-chapels**, or pierced with arches to form **aisles** in **Baroque** churches in Central Europe (Fig. G116).

water-table Inclined surface on, e.g., a plinth or buttress **off-set**, aka **weather-table** or **weathering**.

wave-scroll *See* **Vitruvian scroll**.

weathercock *See* **weathervane**.

weathering Inclination given to horizontal surfaces to throw off water. *See* **water-table**.

weather moulding Projecting moulding with a sloping top.

weather tiling or **slating** Walls clad in tiles or slates.

weathervane Swivelling **vane**, often combined with crossed rods to indicate north, south, east, and west, frequently in the form of a cock, hence **weathercock**.

web Bay of a **vault**, between **groins**, aka **cell** or **severy**.

weeper Standing figure between the **columns** or **pilasters** or in the **niches** of an

Fig. G117 *Tomb-chest (1499–1507) of François II, Duke of Brittany, and his wife, Marguerite de Foix, in Nantes cathedral, by Michel Colombe and Jean Perréal. It represents a skilful transition from a late Gothic type to early Renaissance. Note the weepers standing in their niches and the four standing figures representing Justice, Temperance, Fortitude, and Prudence (the four Cardinal Virtues) (coll. JSC).*

altar-tomb or **sarcophagus** (Fig. G117; *see* Fig. 4.1).

weights of a sash Two weights on either side of a sash by which the moveable parts are suspended on cords or chains over pulleys or wheels.

Welsh groin Groin formed by the intersection of two cylindrical **vaults**, one of which is of lesser height than another.

well Space left beyond the ends of the steps or strings of a staircase.

wheel window Circular window with radiating spokes like a wheel.

wheeler Winder in a **newel** or **spiral stair**.

wicket Small door set within a larger one.

winder Step radiating from a centre.

winding stair *See* **stair**.

window Aperture in a wall to admit light. If the aperture is subdivided, each part is known as a **light**. Classical windows are usually vertical rectangular openings, sometimes surrounded by moulded **architraves**, and sometimes crowned with an **entablature** with or without a **pediment**. If the opening has **columns** or **pilasters** on either side supporting an **entablature**, **pediment**, **gable**, **lintel**, or plaque, it is said to be **ædiculated**.

Window-frames in Classical architecture are of two basic types: the **casement** and the **sash**. In the 17th century the frame

SELECT GLOSSARY OF TERMS / 239

was often cruciform, with **quarries** of glass in lead **cames** supported by **saddle-bars**, and the opening lights (often of iron) were hinged at the sides, opening in or out (*see* **casement**) (*see* Fig. G37). In 1685 the frames of the Palladian banqueting-house in Whitehall were replaced by wooden sash-windows, one frame of which slid vertically in grooves in front of the other. Sashes were suspended on cords over pulleys and counterbalanced by means of weights held in the surrounding frames within the **jambs**. If only one sash could be moved, it was **single-hung**, and if both, the window was **double-hung**. This type of sash-window rapidly gained in popularity, and replaced the casement types in all the better-class work. Crown glass was generally used, but sashes had to be subdivided by means of glazing-bars, which were generally thick and somewhat clumsy. During the 18th century, glazing-bars became finer, with elegant mouldings, and panes became bigger. In the first decades of the 19th century, the wider proportions of windows fashionable with the **Neo-Classical** styles produced the need to have narrow bands of glazing around the larger panes of glass: these **margin-panes** often held coloured glass. From around 1830 larger panes of glass became available at cheap rates, and it became fashionable to remove glazing-bars: this altered the vertical emphasis of windows, and the proportional relationship of the window openings to the **façade**. Repeal of taxes on glass in England (1845) and on windows (1851) gave windows greater prominence in elevations from those dates.

Other types of window associated with Classical architecture include **bay-** and **bow-windows**, canted, segmental or semi-circular on plan, and found in 18th- and 19th-century domestic architecture. The term **bay** is usually applied to the canted form on plan, while **bow** suggests the segmental or semicircular type: both bays and bows rise from the ground. A bow may also be a projection of the window-frame only, rather than part of the structure. **French** or **croisée** windows are casements carried down to the floor level and opening like doors to gardens, **verandahs**, or terraces: they are so called from their use in the 1660s at Versailles. **Dormer** windows are set on the slope of a roof and are independently roofed themselves: they are named from the fact that they usually illuminated sleeping-quarters. A dormer should not be confused with a **lucarne** or **luthern** (*see* **dormer**). A **Palladian window**, aka **Venetian window** or **serliana**, became common in English **Palladian** architecture (*see* Figs G100a–b). The **Diocletian** or **thermal window**, named after its use in the Baths of Diocletian, was also used by Palladio, and was employed in Palladian architecture in England: it is a semicircular window divided into three lights by means of two **mullions** (*see* Fig. G50).

wing **1.** Part of a building projecting from and subordinate to the main, central part. In Classical, esp. **Palladian**, composition, wings are smaller buildings on either side of the corps-de-logis, perhaps joined to it by means of quadrants and colonnades, and sometimes projecting forward to partially enclose a court or cour d'honneur. **2.** Fillet on a **moulding**. **3.** Lateral wall of a rectangular Classical temple, or the space between the **cell** wall and the **peristyle**.

withe Partition between two flues of a chimneystack.

wreath **1.** Curved portion of a handrail following a turn round each angle of a **geometrical** or **wreathed stair** (which has no **newels**), or the continuous turn of the handrail in such a circular or elliptical stair. **2.** Circular or elliptical garland of flowers, leaves, or ribbons, in Classical decoration.

wreathed column Column-shaft with spirals of vines or other plants, including ivy, wound around it in spirals. *See also* **barley-sugar**, **Solomonic**, **spiral**, **torso**, or **twisted**.

Wrenaissance Revival (*c.*1890–1914) of late 17th-century English architecture, in which themes from designs by Wren were prominent, its chief protagonists being Belcher, Macartney, and Brumwell Thomas (*see* Figs 6.50a–b).

Wyatt window Similar to a **Venetian window** or **serliana**, but with a horizontal central head instead of an arched opening (Fig. G118; *see* Fig. 6.8c).

xenodochium Room, building, or apartment for the reception of strangers.

xystus **1.** Spacious **portico**, usually

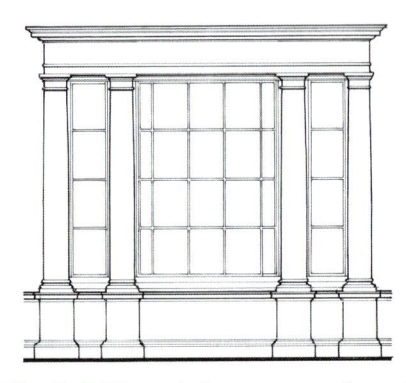

Fig. G118 *Wyatt window: a common domestic type of c.1830. Note the wide proportions of the central window, necessitating narrow margin-panes on either side.*

attached to a **gymnasium**, in which athletes could exercise during inclement weather. **2.** Long covered or open **colonnade** around a garden or court. **3. Hypæthral** walk flanked by columns, trellises, or trees. **4.** Roman garden surrounded by a colonnaded ambulatory, like a **cloister**.

yard **1.** Paved area, generally at the rear of a house, surrounded by walls or outbuildings. **2.** Enclosed utilitarian area, e.g. brick-yard, knacker's yard, tan-yard, etc.

Yorkshire light Mullioned window containing two sashes, one fixed and the other sliding horizontally in grooves.

ziggurat Series of platforms, or a temple-tower, consisting of stages, each smaller in area than the one below, found in Ancient Mesopotamia, but the name has been applied to stepped pyramidal forms, as often found in Classical designs.

zocle, zocco, zoccolo Plain block or low pedestal with no mouldings, aka **socle**.

zopf und perücke Literally 'pigtail and periwig', a style of late 18th-century German **Rococo** architecture, aka *Zopfstil*.

zophorus, zoophorus Frieze decorated with reliefs featuring animals. A **zoophoric column** is one supporting an animal sculpture, e.g. in the Piazzetta, Venice.

zotheca **1.** Small room, usually off a larger space, so a kind of **carrel** or large alcove. **2.** Niche containing a statue or **urn**.

SELECT BIBLIOGRAPHY

Books are sepulchres of thought;
The dead laurels of the dead
Rustle for a moment only,
Like the withered leaves in lonely
Churchyards at some passing tread.

HENRY WADSWORTH LONGFELLOW:
'The Wind over the Chimney' Stanza 8: from *Flower-de-Luce*
in *The Poetical Works* (London: Henry Frowde, 1893), 535.

Adam, Robert (1764) *Ruins of the Palace of the Emperor Diocletian at Spalatro in Dalmatia* (London: The Author).

Adam, Robert (1990) *Classical Architecture: A Complete Handbook* (London: Viking).

Adam, Robert (2017) *Classic Columns: 40 Years of Writing on Architecture*, Clive Aslet (ed.), with a Foreword by Sir Roger Scruton (London: Cumulus).

Adam, Robert, and Adam, James (1773–8) *Works in Architecture of Robert and James Adam* (London: The Authors). A second volume came out in 1779, and a third was published posthumously in 1822 by Priestley & Weale.

Adam, William (2011) *Vitruvius Scoticus: Plans, Elevations, and Sections of Public Buildings, Noblemen's and Gentlemen's Houses in Scotland*, with an Introduction and Annotations by James Simpson (New York: Dover).

Adjmi, Morris (ed.) (1991) *Aldo Rossi: Architecture 1981–1991* (New York: Princeton Architectural Press).

Ahlin, Janne (1987) *Sigurd Lewerentz, Architect 1885–1975* (Stockholm: Byggförlaget).

Alberti, Leon Battista (1486) *De Re Ædificatoria* (Florence: Nicolaus Laurentii, Alamani). *See* the version entitled *On the Art of Building in Ten Books*, Joseph Rykwert, Neil Leach, and Robert Tavernor (trans.) (1988) (Cambridge, MA and London: MIT Press). *See also* his *L'Architettura*, Giovanni Orlandi (ed.), with Introduction by Paolo Portoghesi (1966) (Milan: Il Polifilo).

Aldrich, Henry (1789) *The Elements of Civil Architecture, according to Vitruvius and Other Ancients, and the most approved Practice of Modern Authors, especially Palladio* (Oxford: Prince & Cooke; London: Payne et al.).

Archer, Lucy (1985) *Raymond Erith Architect* (Burford: Cygnet).

Architectural Publication Society (1852–92) *The Dictionary of Architecture*, Wyatt Angelicus Van Sandau Papworth (ed.) (London: printed by Thomas Richards [Vols. **i–vi**] and Whiting [Vols. **vii–viii**] for the Society).

Aslet, Clive (1986) *Quinlan Terry: The Revival of Architecture* (London: Viking).

Aslet, Clive (2023) *Living Tradition: The Architecture and Urbanism of Hugh Petter*, with a Foreword by the Prince of Wales and photography by Dylan Thomas (London: Triglyph).

Aurenhammer, Hans (1973) *J.B. Fischer von Erlach* (London: Allen Lane).

Aviler, Augustin-Charles D' (1694) *Cours d'Architecture qui comprend les ordres de Vignole: avec des commentaires; les figures & descriptions de ses plus beaux bâtimens & de ceux de Michel-Ange ...* etc. (Paris: Nicolas Langlois).

Baron, Hans (1966) *The Crisis of the Early Italian Renaissance* (Princeton, NJ: Princeton University Press).

Bazin, Germain (1964) *Baroque and Rococo* (London: Thames & Hudson).

Bergdoll, Barry (2000) *European Architecture 1750–1890* (Oxford: Oxford University Press).

Blondel, François (1698) *Cours d'Architecture, enseigné dans l'Académie Royale d'Architecture ...* (Paris: Mortier).

Blum, Hans (1550) *Quinque Columnarum exacta descriptio atque delinæatio cum symmetrica earum distributione ...* (Zürich: Christoffel Froschouerum). *See also* (1608) *The Booke of Five Collumnes of Architecture ... Gathered ... by H. Bloome out of Antiquities* (London: Stafford).

Bolgar, Robert Ralph (1973) *The Classical Heritage and Its Beneficiaries* (Cambridge: Cambridge University Press).

Bolton, Arthur T. (1984) *The Architecture of Robert and James Adam (1758–1794)* (Woodbridge: Antique Collectors' Club).

Bremner, G.A. (2022) *Building Greater Britain: Architecture, Imperialism, and the Edwardian Baroque Revival c.1885–1920* (London: Paul Mellon Centre for Studies in British Art).

Brindley, William, and Weatherley, W. Samuel (1887) *Ancient Sepulchral Monuments* (London: printed for the authors by Vincent Brooks, Day & Son).

Brittain-Catlin, Timothy (2023) *Edwin Rickards* (Swindon: Historic England).

Brown, Glenn (1900–3) *History of the United States Capitol* (Washington, DC: Government Printing Office).

Buras, Nir Haim (2019) *The Art of Classic Planning: Building Beautiful and Enduring Communities* (Cambridge, MA and London: Belknap).

Burckhardt, Jakob (1985) *The Architecture of the Italian Renaissance* (London: Secker & Warburg). *See also* Burckhardt's (1928) *The Civilization of the Renaissance in Italy* (Vienna: Phaidon; London: Allen & Unwin).

Campbell, Colen (1967) *Vitruvius Britannicus or The British Architect*, Vols. **i**, **ii**, and **iii**, reissued as Vol **i** of a three-volume facsimile edition, with an Introduction by John Harris (New York: Benjamin Blom), first published (1715–25) in three volumes (London: The Author). *See also* J. Badeslade and J. Rocque (1739) *Vitruvius Brittanicus* [sic], the hitherto unpublished Vol. **iv**, and John Woolfe and James Gandon (1767–71) *Vitruvius Britannicus, or The British Architect*, Vols. **iv** and **v** [actually **v** and **vi**], reissued as Vol. **ii** of a three-volume facsimile edition (New York: Benjamin Blom). *See also* George Richardson (1802–8) *The New Vitruvius Britannicus ...* (London: The Author), first published in two volumes, reissued (1970) as Vol. **iii** of a three-volume facsimile edition (New York: Benjamin Blom). *See also* Paul Breman and Denise Addis (1972) *Guide to Vitruvius Britannicus ...*, with a Foreword by John Harris, issued as Vol. **iv** of *Vitruvius Britannicus* (New York: Benjamin Blom).

Castell, Robert (1728) *The Villas of the Ancients Illustrated* (London: printed by William Bowyer for the Author).

Cerceau *see* Ducerceau

Chambers, Sir William (1759) *A Treatise on Civil Architecture, in which the Principles of that Art are laid down; and illustrated by a Great Number of Plates; accurately designed, and elegantly engraved by the best hands* (London: Haberkorn). *See also* Sir William Chambers (1825) *A Treatise on the Decorative Part of Civil Architecture, …, with Illustrations, Notes, and An Examination of Grecian Architecture, by Joseph Gwilt …* (London: Priestley & Weale). *See also* a fourth edition (1826) with an essay by John B. Papworth and nine new plates (London: J. Taylor). Chambers's great book is of considerable importance in refining and classifying the Classical language of architecture.

Chamoust, Charles-François Ribart de (1783) *L'Ordre François Trouvé dans la Nature* (Paris: The Author).

Chitham, Robert (1985) *The Classical Orders of Architecture* (London: Architectural Press).

Colvin, Howard (2008) *A Biographical Dictionary of British Architects 1600–1840* (New Haven and London: Yale University Press).

Cordemoy, Jean-Louis De (1714) *Nouveau Traité de Toute L'Architecture, ou L'Art de bastir; utile aux entrepreneurs et aux ouvriers … Avec un Dictionnaire des Termes d'Architecture …*, etc. (Paris: Coignard).

Cresy, Edward (1861) *An Encyclopædia of Civil Engineering, Historical, Theoretical, and Practical* (London: Longman, Green, Longman, & Roberts).

Crook, Joseph Mordaunt (1995) *The Greek Revival: Neo-Classical Attitudes in British Architecture 1760–1870* (London: John Murray).

Culot, Maurice, *et al.* (2006) *Architectures Maçonniques: Grande-Bretagne, France, États-Unis, Belgique* (Brussels: Archives d'Architecture Moderne).

Curl, James Stevens (2005) *The Egyptian Revival: Ancient Egypt as the Inspiration for Design Motifs in the West* (London and New York: Routledge).

Curl, James Stevens (2011) *Georgian Architecture in the British Isles 1714–1830* (Swindon: English Heritage).

Curl, James Stevens (2022) *Freemasonry and the Enlightenment: Architecture, Symbols, and Influences* (Holywood: Nerfl Press).

Curl, James Stevens, and Wilson, Susan (2015, 2016) *The Oxford Dictionary of Architecture* (Oxford: Oxford University Press).

Daffurn, John (2022) *George Glover (1812–1890): The Unfulfilled Potential of a Victorian Architect* (Stamford: Eptex).

Dietterl(e)in, Wendel (1598) *Architectura von Ausztheilung, Symmetria und Proportion der Fünff Seulen, und aller darausz folgender Kunst Arbeit, von Fenstern, Caminen, Thürgerichten, Portalen, Bronnen und Epitaphien. Wie dieselbige ausz jedweder Art der Fünff Seulen, grund, aufzureissen, zuzurichten, und ins Werck zubringen seyen, allen solcher Kunst Liebhabenden, zu einem beständigen, und ring ergreiffenden underricht, erfunden, in zwey-hundert Stuck gebracht, Geetzt, und an tag gegeben,* in five books (Nürnberg: Caymor). Another edition was published in 1655 (Nürnberg: Pauluss Fürst), again in five books with a portrait. A French version came out in 1861.

Dinsmoor, William Bell (1950) *The Architecture of Ancient Greece* (London: Batsford).

Ducerceau, Jacques-Androuet (1559–72) *Livres d'Architecture* (Paris: B. Prévost).

Ducerceau, Jacques-Androuet (1576–9) *Les plus excellents bastiments de France* (Paris: Jacques-Androuet du Cerceau).

Durand, Jean-Nicolas-Louis (1809) *Essai sur l'Histoire Générale de l'Architecture … pour servir de texte explicatif au recueil et parallèle des édifices de tout genre, anciens et modernes, remarquables par leur beauté, leur grandeur, ou leur singularité …* (Paris: Soyer). *See also* Durand (1817–21) *Précis des Leçons d'Architecture données a l'École Polytechnique* (Paris: Durand).

Engel, Carl Ludvik (1990) *Carl Ludvik Engel 1778–1840: Näyttely Helsingin Tuomiokirkon Kryptassa 7.8.–14–9.1990* (Helsinki: Helsingin kauponki, Opetusministeriö Suomen rakennustaiteen museo).

Fenger, Ludvig Peter (1886) *Dorische Polychromie: Untersuchungen über die Anwendung der Farbe auf dem dorischen Tempel* (Berlin: Asher).

Fergusson, Adam (2011) *The Sack of Bath* (London: Persephone).

Fischer Von Erlach, Johann Bernhard (1721) *Entwurff einer Historischen Architektur* (Vienna: The Author).

Franklin, Geraint (2022) *John Outram* (Swindon: Historic England).

Fréart de Chambray, Roland (1650) *Parallèle de l'Architecture Antique et de la Moderne, avec un recueil des dix principaux autheurs qui ont écrit des cinq ordres; sçavoir Palladio et Scamozzi, Serlio et Vignola, D. Barbaro et Cataneo, L.B. Alberti et Viola Bullant et De Lorme, comparez entre aux …*, etc. (Paris: Martin). This appeared in a translation by John Evelyn (1664) as *A Parallel of the Antient Architecture with the Modern, In a Collection of Ten Principal Authors who have Written upon the Five Orders, … etc.* (London: Raycroft & Place). There were many subsequent editions, including a fine one (1723) published in London by D. Browne *et al.*, which includes Wotton's *Elements of Architecture* and other matter.

Frese, Peter, *et al.* (1985) *Ein griechischer Traum. Leo von Klenze: Der Archäologe* (Munich: Staatliche Antikensammlungen und Glyptothek).

Fyfe, Theodore (1936) *Hellenistic Architecture: An Introductory Study* (Cambridge: Cambridge University Press).

Gadol, Joan (1969) *Leon Battista Alberti, Universal Man of the Early Renaissance* (Chicago: University of Chicago Press).

Gerbino, Anthony, and Johnston, Stephen (2009) *Compass and Rule: Architecture as Mathematical Practice in England 1500–1750* (New Haven and London: Yale University Press).

Gerson, Horst, and Kuile, Engelbert Hendrik Ter (1960) *Art and Architecture in Belgium 1600 to 1800* (Harmondsworth: Penguin).

Gibbs, James (1728) *A Book of Architecture, Containing Designs of Buildings and Ornaments* (London). *See also* the same author's (1732) *Rules for Drawing the Several Parts of Architecture, in a More Exact and Easy Manner than has been heretofore practised, by which all fractions, in dividing the principal members and their parts, are avoided* (London: Bowyer).

Girouard, Mark (2021) *A Biographical Dictionary of English Architecture 1540–1640* (London: Paul Mellon Centre for Studies in British Art).

Glazier, Richard (1926) *A Manual of Historic Ornament treating upon the Evolution, Tradition, and Development of Architecture & the Applied Arts prepared for the use of Students and Craftsmen* (London: Batsford).

Grafton, Anthony (1983) *Joseph Scaliger: A Study in the History of Classical Scholarship* (Oxford: Oxford University Press).

Gwilt, Joseph (1903) *An Encyclopedia of Architecture*, revised by Wyatt Papworth (London: Longmans Green).

Hegemann, Werner, and Peets, Elbert (1922) *The American Vitruvius: An Architects' Handbook of Civic Art* (New York: Architectural Book Publishing: Paul Wenzel & Maurice Krakow).

Hersey, George (1988) *The Lost Meaning of Classical Architecture* (Cambridge, MA and London: MIT Press).

Holder, Julian, and McKellar, Elizabeth (2016) *Neo-Georgian Architecture, 1880–1970: A Reappraisal* (Swindon: Historic England).

Hopkins, Andrew, and Stamp, Gavin (2002) *Lutyens Abroad: The Work of Sir Edwin Lutyens Outside the British Isles* (Rome: British School at Rome).

Houfe, Simon (1980) *Sir Albert Richardson: The Professor* (Luton: White Crescent).

Howell, Peter (2021) *The Triumphal Arch* (London: Unicorn).

Hrausky, Andrej, Koželj, Janez, and Prelovšek, Damjan (2007) *Jože Plečnik: Vienna; Prague; Ljubljana* (Ljubljana: Cankarjeva založba).

Institute of Classical Architecture (2002) *A Decade of Art and Architecture 1992–2002* (New York: The Institute).

Jencks, Charles Alexander (1978) *The Language of Post-Modern Architecture* (London: Academy Editions).

Jencks, Charles Alexander (2007) *Critical Modernism: Where is Post-Modernism Going?* (Chichester: Wiley-Academy).

Kalnein, Wend Graf, and Levey, Michael (1972) *Art and Architecture of the Eighteenth Century in France* (Harmondsworth: Penguin).

Kennon, Donald R. (ed.) (1999) *A Republic for the Ages: The United States Capitol and the Political Culture of the Early Republic* (Charlottesville and London: University of Virginia Press).

Kent, William (ed.) (1727) *Designs of Inigo Jones* (London: William Kent).

Kostof, Spiro (1995) *A History of Architecture: Settings and Rituals*, Greg Castillo (ed.) (New York and Oxford: Oxford University Press).

Krier, Léon (ed.) (1985) *Albert Speer Architecture 1932–1942* (Brussels: Archives d'Architecture Moderne).

Langley, Batty (1745) *The City and Country Builder's and Workman's Treasury of Designs: or, the Art of Drawing and Working the Ornamental Parts of Architecture* (London: S. Harding).

Langley, Batty, and Langley, Thomas (1763) *The Builder's Jewel: or, the Youth's Instructor, and Workman's Remembrancer. Explaining Short and Easy Rules, Made familiar to the meanest Capacity, For Drawing and Working, I. The Five Orders of Columns entire … II. Block and Cantilever Cornices, Rustick Quoins, etc. …* (London: C. & R. Ware).

Laugier, Abbé Marc-Antoine (1753) *Essai sur l'Architecture* (Paris: Duchesne). Another edition, augmented with a dictionary of terms and plates to explain them, was published by Duchesne (Paris: 1755). *See also* the version (1977) Wolfgang and Anni Hermann (trans.) (Los Angeles: Hennessey & Ingalls).

Lawrence, Arnold Walter (1996) *Greek Architecture* (New Haven and London: Yale University Press).

Ledoux, Claude-Nicolas (1804) *L'architecture considerée sous le rapport de l'art, des mœurs et de la législation* (Paris: The Author).

Leoni, Giacomo (1742) *The Architecture of A. Palladio, Revis'd, Design'd, & Publish'd by Giacomo Leoni, a Venetian: Architect to His Serene Highness, the Elector Palatine* (London: Leoni).

Lloyd, Nathaniel (1925) *A History of English Brickwork with Examples and Notes of the Architectural Use and Manipulation of Brick from Mediæval Times to the End of the Georgian Period* with an Introduction by Sir Edwin Lutyens, R.A. (London: H. Greville Montgomery).

Lund, Hakon, and Thygesen, Anne Lise (1995) *C.F. Hansen* (Copenhagen: Bergiafonden og Arkitektens Forlag).

McParland, Edward (2024) *The Language of Architectural Classicism: From Looking to Seeing* (London: Lund Humphries).

Martin, Thomas (1820) *The Circle of the Mechanical Arts: Containing Practical Treatises on the Various Manual Arts, Trades, & Manufactures* (London: Bumpus, Sherwood, Neely, & Jones).

Meyer, Franz Sales (1894) *A Handbook of Ornament*, Hugh Stannus (ed.) (London: Batsford).

Middleton, Robin, and Watkin, David (1987) *Neoclassical and 19th Century Architecture* (Milan: Electa; London: Faber & Faber).

Morris, Robert (1755) *Select Architecture ... etc.* (London: Robert Sayer).

Murray, James A.H., Bradley, Henry, Craigie, W.A., and Onions, C.T. (eds) (1933) *The Oxford English Dictionary* (Oxford: Clarendon).

Murray, Peter (1986) *Renaissance Architecture* (Milan: Electa; London: Faber & Faber).

Musson, Jeremy (2015) *The Country House Ideal: Recent Work by ADAM Architecture*, with Forewords by Clive Aslet and Calder Loth and photography by Paul Barker (London and New York: Merrell).

Nerdinger, Winfried (ed.) (2000) *Leo von Klenze: Architekt zwischen Kunst und Hof 1784–1864* (Munich: Prestel).

Nicholson, Peter (1835) *An Architectural and Engineering Dictionary* (London: John Weale). *See also* another edition (1852), called *Encyclopedia of Architecture* (London: Caxton).

Normand, Charles (1852) *Nouveau Parallèle des Ordres d'Architecture des Grecs, des Romains et des Autres Modernes* (Paris: Normand Aîné; and Carilian, Gœury, & Dalmont).

Onians, John (1988) *Bearers of Meaning. The Classical Orders in Antiquity, the Middle Ages, and the Renaissance* (Cambridge: Cambridge University Press).

Orme, Philibert de l' (1567) *Architecture* (Paris: Morel).

Osborne, A.L. (1954) *A Dictionary of English Domestic Architecture* (London: Country Life).

Oxford English Dictionary, The (1933) *See* Murray, James A.H. *et al.*

Paavilainen, Simo (1982) *Nordic Classicism 1910–1930* (Helsinki: Museum of Finnish Architecture).

Palladio, Andrea (1570) *I Quattro Libri dell'Architettura* (Venice: Domenico de'Franceschi). *See also* (1715–20) *The Architecture of A. Palladio in four books ... to which are added several notes and observations made by Inigo Jones ...* (London: Leoni), and (1965) *The Four Books of Architecture*, Isaac Ware (trans.) (New York: Dover).

Papadakis, Andreas, and Watson, Harriet (eds) (1990) *New Classicism*, with a Foreword by Léon Krier (London: Academy Editions).

Pausanias (1955) *Description of Greece*, W.H.S. Jones (trans.) (Cambridge, MA: Harvard University Press).

Pérouse de Montclos, Jean-Marie (1974) *Étienne-Louis Boullée (1728–1799): Theoretician of Revolutionary Architecture* (London: Thames & Hudson).

Perrault, Claude (1676) *Ordonnances des Cinq Espèces de Colonnes* (Paris: Coignard). *See also* John James (trans.) (1708) *A Treatise of the Five Orders of Columns* (London: printed by Motte and sold by Sturt).

Piacentini, Marcello (1930) *Architettura d'oggi* (Rome: Cremonesi).

Pinnegar, Anne-Noëlle, Pinnegar, David, and Pinnegar, Eileen (1992) *Hammerwood Park, East Grinstead, Sussex, 1792: First House of Benjamin Henry Latrobe* (East Grinstead: Super Form Design).

Plaw, John (1782) *Rural Architecture; or Designs from the Simple Cottage to the Decorated Villa* (London: J. Taylor).

Porphyrios, Demetri (1992) *Classical Architecture* (London: McGraw Hill).

Porphyrios, Demetri (2016) *Porphyrios Associates: The Allure of the Classical*, with a Foreword by Vincent Scully and an Essay by Kenneth Powell (New York: Rizzoli).

Raabyemagle, Hanne, and Smidt, Claus M. (eds) (1998) *Klassicisme I København: Arkitekturen på C.F. Hansens tid*, with photographs by Jens Lindhe (Copenhagen: Gyldendal).

Ramée, Daniel (ed.) (1847) *Architecture de C.-N. Ledoux* (Paris: Lenoir).

Reed, Henry Hope (2020) *Golden City*, with essays by Alvin Holm and Catesby Leigh (New York: The Monacelli Press and the Institute of Classical Architecture and Art).

Richardson, Albert Edward (1914) *Monumental Classic Architecture in Great Britain and Ireland during the Eighteenth and Nineteenth Centuries* (London: Batsford).

Ridgway, Christopher, and Williams, Robert (eds) (2004) *Sir John Vanbrugh and Landscape Architecture in Baroque England* (Thrupp, Stroud: Sutton).

Robertson, Donald Struan (1945) *A Handbook of Greek and Roman Architecture* (Cambridge: Cambridge University Press).

Robertson, Howard Morley (1924) *The Principles of Architectural Composition* (London: Architectural Press).

Robinson, John Martin (2012) *James Wyatt: Architect to George III* (New Haven and London: Yale University Press).

Robinson, John Martin, and Neave, David (2001) *Francis Johnson Architect: A Classical Statement*, with an Introduction by Giles Worsley (Otley: Oblong Creative).

Rosenau, Helen (1976) *Boullée and his Visionary Architecture* (London: Academy Editions).

Rosengarten, Albrecht (1893) *A Handbook of Architectural Styles*, William Collett-Sandars (trans.) (London: Chatto & Windus).

Ruffinière du Prey, Pierre de la (1994) *The Villas of Pliny from Antiquity to Posterity* (Chicago and London: University of Chicago Press).

Ruskin, John (1849) *Seven Lamps of Architecture* (London: Smith, Elder, & Co.).

Rykwert, Joseph (1998) *The Dancing Column: On Order in Architecture* (Cambridge, MA and London: MIT Press).

Salmon, Frank (ed.) (2008) *The Persistence of the Classical: Essays on Architecture presented to David Watkin* (London: Philip Wilson).

Salmon, William (1734) *Palladio Londinensis: or, The London Art of Building* (London: Ward & Wicksteed).

Saumarez Smith, George (2013) *A Treatise on Modern Architecture in Five Books* (Cumnor: Bardwell).

Scamozzi, Vincenzo (1582) *Discorsi sopra l'antichità di Roma* (Venice: Francesco Ziletti).

Scamozzi, Vincenzo (1615) *L'Idea dell'Architettura Universale* (Venice: The Author).

Schinkel, Karl Friedrich (1989) *Collection of Architectural Designs including Designs which have been executed and Objects whose execution was intended*, Kenneth S. Hazlett, Stephen O'Malley, and Christopher Rudolph (eds), Karin Cramer (trans.), with an Introduction by Philip Johnson, and a Prefatory Essay by Hermann G. Pundt (Guildford: Butterworth Architecture). This includes a reproduction of Schinkel (1866) *Sammlung Architektonischer Entwürfe: Neue Vollständige Ausgabe in CLXXIV Tafeln* (Berlin: Ernst & Korn).

Schuym, Joachim (1687) *The Mirror of Architecture, or, The Ground-Rules of the Art of Building exactly laid down by Vincenzo Scamozzi ... Revised and Inlarged ... Translated out of the Dutch ...* William Fisher (trans.) (London: William Fisher).

Scott, George Gilbert (1879) *Lectures on the Rise and Development of Mediæval Architecture: Delivered at the Royal Academy* (London: John Murray).

Serlio, Sebastiano (1575) *Architettura* (Venice: Francesco de'Franceschi).

Serlio, Sebastiano (1611) *The Booke of Architecture* (London: E. Stafford).

Serlio, Sebastiano (1663) *Architettura di S. Serlio Bolognese, in sei libri divisa ...* (Venice: Hertz).

Shaw, Richard Norman, and Jackson, Thomas Graham (eds) (1892) *Architecture – A Profession or an Art: Thirteen Short Essays on the Qualifications and Training of Architects* (London: John Murray).

Shute, John (1563) *The First and Chief Groundes of Architecture* (London: Thomas Marshe).

Smith, Thomas Gordon (2003) *Vitruvius on Architecture* (New York: Monacelli).

Smith, William (ed.) (1848) *Dictionary of Greek and Roman Antiquities* (London: Taylor, Walton, & Maberly; John Murray).

Smith, William (1870) *Dictionary of Greek and Roman Geography* (London: James Walton; John Murray).

Soros, Susan Weber (ed.) (2007) *James 'Athenian' Stuart, 1713-1788: The Rediscovery of Antiquity* (New Haven and London: Yale University Press).

Speltz, Alexander (1910) *The Styles of Ornament from Prehistoric Times to the Middle of the XIXth Century*, Richard Phené Spiers (ed.) (New York, Berlin, and Paris: Bruno Hessling).

Spiers, Richard Phené (1893) *The Orders of Architecture, Greek, Roman, and Italian Selected from Normand's Parallel and Other Authorities* (London: Batsford).

Stamp, Gavin (2024) *Interwar British Architecture 1919-39* (London: Profile).

Statham. Henry Heathcote (1950) *A History of Architecture*, Hugh Braun (ed.) (London: Batsford).

Steil, Lucien (2018) *In the Mood for Architecture: Tradition, Modernism, and Serendipity*, with a Foreword by Léon Krier, an Introduction by Ali Sagharchi, and an Epilogue by Maurice Culot (Berlin: Wasmuth).

Stern, Robert A.M. (1996) *Buildings* (New York: Monacelli).

Stratton, Arthur (1925) *Elements of Form and Design in Classic Architecture Shown in Exterior and Interior Motives Collated from Fine Buildings of All Time on One Hundred Plates* (London: Batsford).

Stratton, Arthur (ed.) (1926) *The Five Orders of Architecture According to Vignola*, arranged by Pierre Esquié (London: Tiranti).

Stratton, Arthur (1931) *The Orders of Architecture: Greek, Roman and Renaissance with Selected Examples of their Application shown on 80 Plates*, with an Introduction by A. Trystan Edwards (London: Batsford).

Sturgis, Russell, *et al.* (1901-2) *A Dictionary of Architecture and Building: Biographical, Historical, and Descriptive* (New York: Macmillan).

Sudjic, Deyan (2022) *Stalin's Architect: Power and Survival in Moscow: Boris Iofan (1891-1976)* (London: Thames & Hudson).

Summerson, John Newenham (1980) *The Classical Language of Architecture* (London: Thames & Hudson).

Symondson, Anthony, and Bucknall, Stephen (2006) *Sir Ninian Comper: An Introduction to his Life and Work with Complete Gazetteer* (Reading: Spire).

Tavernor, Robert (1991) *Palladio and Palladianism* (London: Thames & Hudson).

Terry, Quinlan (2022) *The Layman's Guide to Classical Architecture*, Clive Aslet (ed.), with a Foreword by HRH The Prince of Wales (Stockholm: Stolpe).

Troost, Gerdy (ed.) (1942-3) *Das Bauen im neuen Reich* (Bayreuth: Gauverlag Bayerische Ostmark).

Tyack, Geoffrey (ed.) (2013) *John Nash: Architect of the Picturesque* (Swindon: English Heritage).

Venturi, Robert (1966) *Complexity and Contradiction in Architecture* (New York: Museum of Modern Art).

Vignola, Giacomo Barozzi da (1596) *Regola delli Cinque Ordini d'Architettura* (Rome: Giovanni Battista de Rossi).

Vitruvius Pollio, Marcus (1567) *I Dieci Libri dell'Architettura di M. Vitruvio*, Daniel Barbaro (trans.) (Venice: Francesco de'Franceschi & Johann Criegher).

Vitruvius Pollio, Marcus (1826) *The Architecture of Marcus Vitruvius Pollio, in Ten Books*, Joseph Gwilt (trans.) (London: Priestley & Weale).

Vitruvius Pollio, Marcus (1960) *The Ten Books on Architecture*, Morris Hickey Morgan (trans.), with illustrations prepared under the direction of Herbert Langford Warren (New York: Dover).

Vitruvius Pollio, Marcus (1960) *Architettura*, Silvio Ferri (trans.) (Rome: Palombi).

Vitruvius Pollio, Marcus (1999) *Ten Books on Architecture*, Ingrid D. Rowland (trans.), commentary and illustrations by Thomas Noble Howe (Cambridge: Cambridge University Press).

Vitruvius Pollio, Marcus (2014) *On Architecture*, Frank Granger (trans.) (Cambridge, MA: Harvard University Press).

Vries, Paulus Vredeman de (1617) *Les cinq rangs de l'Architecture, a sçavoir, Tuscane, Dorique, Ionique, Corinthique, et Composée, – avec L'instruction fondamentale faicte par H.H.* [Henrik Hondius The Younger]. *Avec ... quelques belles ordonnances d'architecture, mises en perspective, inventées par J. Vredeman Frison et son fils* (Amsterdam: Jean Janson).

Vries, Paulus Vredeman de (1651) *L'Architecture ... avec quelques belles ordonnances d'Architecture, mises en perspective per J. Vredman Frison* (Amsterdam: Jean Janson). Many versions were published following the first Antwerp edition (1577) entitled *Architectura ...*, etc.

Ware, Isaac (1756-7) *The Complete Body of Architecture. Adorned with Plans and Elevations, from Original Designs* (London: Osborne and Shipton, Hodges, Davis, Ward, & Baldwin). One of the greatest works of the whole Palladian style.

Watkin, David (1974) *The Life and Work of C.R. Cockerell* (London: Zwemmer).

Watkin, David (1996) *Sir John Soane: Enlightenment Thought and the Royal Academy Lectures* (Cambridge: Cambridge University Press).

Watkin, David (2004) *The Architect King: George III and the Culture of the Enlightenment* (London: Royal Collection Enterprises).

Watkin, David (2006) *Radical Classicism: The Architecture of Quinlan Terry*, with a Foreword by HRH The Prince of Wales (New York: Rizzoli International).

Watkin, David (2010) *The Classical Country House from the Archives of Country Life* (London: Aurum).

Watkin, David (2016) *The Architecture of John Simpson: The Timeless Language of Classicism*, with a Foreword by HRH The Prince of Wales (New York: Rizzoli International).

Watkin, David, and Hewat-Jabor, Philip (eds) (2008) *Thomas Hope: Regency Designer* (New Haven and London: Yale University Press).

Watkin, David, and Mellinghoff, Tilman (1987) *German Architecture and the Classical Ideal 1740-1840* (London: Thames & Hudson).

Weber, Susan (ed.) (2014) *William Kent: Designing Georgian Britain* (New Haven and London: Yale University Press).

Whistler, Laurence (1938) *Sir John Vanbrugh: Architect and Dramatist 1664-1726* (London: Cobden-Sanderson).

Wiebenson, Dora (1969) *Sources of Greek Revival Architecture* (London: Zwemmer).

Wittkower, Rudolf (1974) *Palladio and English Palladianism* (London: Thames & Hudson).

Wittkower, Rudolf (1988) *Architectural Principles in the Age of Humanism* (London: Academy Editions).

Wood, John (1741) *The Origin of Building: or, the Plagiarism of the Heathens Detected* (Bath: S. & F. Farley).

Wood, John (1750) *Dissertation upon the Orders of Columns* (London: Bettenham & Leake).

Woodman, Ellis (2019) *Temples and Tombs: The Sacred and Monumental Architecture of Craig Hamilton* (London: Lund Humphries).

Worsley, Giles (2007) *Inigo Jones and the European Classicist Tradition* (New Haven and London: Yale University Press).

Wotton, Henry (1624) *The Elements of Architecture ... collected ... from the best Authors and Examples* (London: printed by John Bill).

Wragg, Brian (2000) *The Life and Works of John Carr of York*, Giles Worsley (ed.) (Otley: Oblong Creative).

Wren Society (1924-43) *Publications* Vols. **i–xx**, (Oxford: Oxford University Press): *see esp. Tracts on Architecture I: On Architecture, and Observations on Antique Temples*, etc., in the Appendix to *Parentalia*, Vol. **xix** (1942), 126.

LIST OF SUBSCRIBERS

*Sir, I have two very cogent reasons for not printing any list of subscribers;
– one, that I have lost all the names, – the other, that I have spent all the money.*[1]

SAMUEL JOHNSON:
quoted in James Boswell: *Life of Samuel Johnson, LL.D. comprehending an Account of his Studies,
and Numerous Works, in Chronological Order; with his Correspondence and Conversations.
With Copious Notes and Biographical Illustrations* by Edmond Malone
(London: Henry Washbourne, 1852), 463.

The publisher and author thank all those listed below most warmly for their generous support, without which this volume could not have been published. Fortunately, their names, given below in alphabetical order, have not been mislaid, nor have their valued subscriptions been squandered. Names are included in the manner requested by subscribers.

Acanthophyllum Books
Alastair Adair
ADAM Architecture
David Adshead
Dr Frank Albo
Nick Allen RIBA
Nigel Anderson
Sophie Andreae
Tor O Austigard
Charlie Bagot Jewitt
Professor Sir George Bain
Eskild Narum Bakken
Colin Bass
Harry Breach
John Bridges
Dr Laurence Bristow-Smith
Leigh Brooks MVO
Michael W Bruce
David Brussat
John Francis Bucknall
Nir Haim Buras
Peter Burman
Dominic Caldecott
Eric Cartwright
Ernest Chaloner
Jacob Chase
David M Child
Jonathan Clark
Paul Cockerham
Tim Cookson
The Late Lord Cormack DL FSA FRHistS

Giovanna Costantini PhD
Robert Cox
Olivia Crouch BA (Hons)
Ingrid Curl
James Stevens Curl in memory of George Stevens Curl
Curtis & Windham Architects
Clifford Dammers
James T Dean Jr
Albert M Debrunner
Kaela Diamond
Miguel Dias
Neil Dilling
Brian Dix
Pierre de la Ruffinière du Prey
Alfie Duckett
Ronald Dudley
Jonathan Edis
Dr John Edmondson
Lisbeth Ehlers
Dr Brent Elliott
David H Ellison AIA
Siegfried Engelmann
Edward Evans
John Evetts
Andrew Fane OBE
Ferguson & Shamamian Architects
Michael M Franck
Christa E Freer
Philip Gibbs
Joscelyn Godwin

Celia Greville
Eleanor Greville
Louis Greville
René Greville
Stjepan Golemac
Benedict Gummer
The Revd David Haddon-Reece
Anders Moen Hagalisletto
Bernard Hall
Craig Hamilton
Michael Harris
Wayne Hart
Adrian Hill
Karl Fredrik Honningsvåg
Anthony Horth
C J Howard
Peter Hughes KC
Professor William Hughes FRHistS FSA Scot
Brian Hurwitz and Ruth Richardson
Mike and Sue Huxley
Professor Dorota Iwaniec
Alvin Jaff and Roslyn Goldfarb
Dr Astrid James
Luca Jellinek
Patrick Keating
Robbie Kerr
Dr Mark Kirby
Bob Lane
David Lanetti
Colin and Karen Latimer

---

[1] This, according to Boswell, occurred in 1763, and is recorded in the *Life* for the year 1781.

245

Imre and Janet Leader
David Lee
Henrik Giil Liisberg
Dr Julian W S Litten
William Lock
Mandil Associates Inc
Finbar McCormick
McCrery Architects
James C McCrery II
Maryette McFarland
Murchadh McLean
W. Laurence McMinn
Edward McParland
Michael W Mehaffy PhD
Sam Merklein
Professor Rod Miller
Luke Moloney
Colum Mulhern, architecte
Rodney and Richard Munday
Casey Rutledge Nardo
Anne Noble
Toirdhealbhach O'Brien
Liam O'Connor and Annabelle Cardron
The Revd Dr Barry A Orford
Stuart Orr
Mike Osborne
Hippolyte Augustine O'Toole
Tim Payne
Alex Peacock
Ben Pentreath
Jill Pentz
Guy Peppiatt
Dr J E C Peters
Hugh Petter

The Earl of Plymouth
Celia M Potts
Ricky Craig Pound
Darren Price
Michael Grimsdell Priest
Cecil D Quillen III
Paul Rabbitts
Terence Reeves-Smyth
Bernard Richards
William J Roulston
Don Ruggles
Prof Nikos A Salingaros
Tom Sargant
Scala Architecten, The Hague
Percival Scattergoode
Reinhard W Schmidt
David Screen
Vedran Šćuric
William Seath
Steven W Semes
Andrew Shepherd
Jonathan Sidaway
George Saumarez Smith
Evan Smithers
John Smylie, Director, Space Labs Architects
Emeritus Prof Janet Myles Spencer
Friends of Spital Cemetery
Callaghan Stack
Pamela Steiner
Mary McKinney Stevenson
Alexander Stoddard, Sculptor in Ordinary to His Majesty the King in Scotland
Professor Peter Swallow

David Swarbrick
La Table Ronde de l'Architecture asbl
Simon Taylor
Jonathan Tinker
Joanna Tinworth
Malcolm T Tucker
Eskdale Turner
Cedric Unsworth
Marjo Uotila, Chair, INTBAU Finland
Professor Paul van der Lem
Cornelia van der Poll
Roger van Goethem
Mark Verma
Henry Vivian-Neal
Wolbert Vroom, architect
David M Walker
Ian James Wall
Nigel M Waring
Tom Watling
Seth Joseph Weine
Dr Philip Whitbourn OBE, FSA, FRIBA
William P Wilkins CBE
Martin Williams FSA
In memory of Hal and Gill Wilson
Primrose Wilson
Susan Wilson PhD (Bristol)
Richard Woolf MSt (Cantab) RIBA
Ron Woollacott MBE FRSA
Immo Worreschk
Patrick T Wyton
Sophia Yalland
Magnus Zetterling
Paul Zisman

Also, we thank several other subscribers who wish to remain anonymous.

INDEX

*… the best book in the world would owe the most to a good index, and the worst … ,
if it had but a single good thought in it, might be kept alive by it …*

HORACE BINNEY:
Letter to Samuel Austin Allibone (8 April 1868).

Note: Page numbers in **bold** refer to illustrations and captions. Terms in the Glossary have not been indexed.

Aachen 47
    Chapel Palatine 46
Aalto, Hugo Alvar Henrik (1898-1976) 152
Abingdon, Oxon, Old Gaol 167
Adam, James (1732-94) **110**, 111
Adam, Robert (1728-92) **110**, 111, 114, 117, **126**, 131, **138**
Adam, Robert (1948-) 162, **163**, 164, 169, 174
Adam, William (1689-1748) 172, **172**
Adlard, Henry (*fl.*1824-69) **144**
Ægina, Temple of Aphaia 36
Agrigentum, Temple of Zeus Olympios 32
Aisne-Marne memorial, Château-Thierry 152
Aitchison, George (1825-1910) **41**
Akroyd, John (1556-1613) **67**
Albert, Prince Consort (1819-61) 145
Alberti, Leon Battista (1404-72) 6, 47, **50**, 51, 59, **59**, **60**
Albrecht Casimir, Duke of Saxe-Teschen (1738-1822) **132**
Alcuin (Albinus Flaccus) (*c.*740-804) 47
Aldrich, Henry (1648-1710) 106, **106**, 114
Alessandria, Città Nuova 161
Alessi, Galeazzo (1512-72) **65**
Alexander, Christopher Wolfgang John (1936-2022) xiii, 174
Alexander III ('The Great') (*r.*336-323 BC) 35
Alexander Severus, Roman Emperor (*r.*222-35) 37
Allibone, Samuel Austin (1816-89) 247
Alrewas, near Lichfield, Armed Forces Memorial 165
Altomonte, Martino (1657-1745) 85, **85**
Amadeo, Giovanni Antonio (*c.*1447-1522) **62**
Andenæs, Ulf (1946-) 172
Anderson, Nigel (1959-) 164
Andronikos Cyrrhestes, Greek astronomer (*fl.*100 BC) **121**
Anne, Queen (*r.*1702-14) 99
Antiochus IV Epiphanes (*r.*176-164 BC) 36
Apollodorus Architecture **171**
Archer, Thomas (*c.*1668-1743) 98-9, **100**, 146
Architectural Uprising against Modernism 172
architecture
    definitions of 1–3
    see also Classical architecture; *Glossary*; Greek architecture; Roman architecture
Arkadia, Nieborów, Poland 132, **132**, **133**
Arles
    Saint-Gilles 46
    Saint-Trophîme 46
Arthur Ross Award 173
Asam, Cosmas Damian (1686-1739) 80, **83**
Asam, Egin Quirin (1692-1750) 80, **83**
Ashfold House, W Sussex 167

Ashley, Henry Victor (1872-1945) **149**, 150, 154
Ashley House, Hants 162
Asia Minor, Ionic Order 5–6, 36
Asplund, Erik Gunnar (1885-1940) 150, 152, 157, 162
Asprucci, Mario (1764-1804) **140**
Athens
    Acropolis 36
    choragic monument of Thrasyllus 118, **119**, **126**
    Erechtheion **13**, **14**, **15**, **16**, 36, **42**
    monument of Lysicrates **16**, 32, 36, 118, **119**, **120**
    Parthenon **7**, **8**, 11, 36
    Temple on the Ilissus **12**, 36, **126**
    Temple of Minerva Polias 13
    Temple of Theseus (Hephæsteion) **11**
    Temple of Zeus Olympios 27, **27**, 36
    Tower of the Winds 120, **121**
Athens, Georgia, News Building 162
Atkinson, Robert Frank (1869-1923) 148
Atlanta, Georgia, Millennium Gate **163**, 164
Attic base 11, **15**, 20, **20**, 27, 32
Aufrere, Sophia (1752/3-86) **138**
Augustus, Roman Emperor (*r.*27 BC-AD 14) 1, 37
Augustus II ('The Strong') *see* Friedrich August I
Austigard, Tor (1980-) 172
Autun, Cathedral 47
Aylesford, 4th Earl of *see* Finch
Ayot St Lawrence, Herts, church 118, **118**
Azéma, Léon (1888-1978) 152

Baalbek (Heliopolis) 37, 44, 74
    Temple of Bacchus 34
    Temple of Venus 34, **34**
Bacon, Henry (1866-1924) 149
Bacon, John (1740-99) **121**
Baker, Sir Herbert (1862-1946) **31**, 135, 153, 154, **155**, **164**
Bakken, Eskild Narum (1964-) 172
Ballykelly, County Londonderry, Presbyterian church **137**, 139
Ballyscullion, County Londonderry **140**
Baltard, Louis-Pierre (1764-1846) **146**
Barelli, Agostino (1627-79) 79, **80**, 103, **103**
Barnard Castle, Bowes Museum **147**, 147
Baroque architecture 3, **68**, 73, 74–86
    England 94–5, 96, 98–100
    France 87, **87**, **88**, 89–90, **89**, **90**
    Germany 102–4, **105**
    reaction to 99–100, 107, 115
    Revival 147, 151
Barry, Sir Charles (1795-1860) 55, 142

Bärsch, Heinrich (1899-1971) 153
Bartolozzi, Francesco (1727-1815) 111
Basevi, Elias George (1794-1845) 139
Bass, Steve (1947-) 173
Bassæ, Temple of Apollo Epicurius 11–12, 16, 32, 36
Bastard, John (1688-1770) 187, **187**
Bastard, William (c.1689-1766) 187, **187**
Bath 114, 165, 170
    leisure centre **171**
    Royal Crescent 112
    The Circus 112, **112**
Baumgarten, Paul Gotthilf Reinhold (1900-84) 151
Bazin, Germain (1901-90) 73
Bear Ash, Hare Hatch, Berks 164
Beaufort, Lady Margaret (1443-1509) 90
Beaux Arts 152
Becker, Ulrich Jacov (1982-) 174
Beeby, Thomas Hall (1941-) 162, 173, 174
Behrens, Peter (1868-1940) 149, 153
Beijing, Chairman Mao memorial hall 150
Belcher, John (1841-1913) 147
Belfast
    Belfast Bank 142, **144**
    City Hall 147, **148**
    Custom House **144**
    Municipal College of Technology 145, **146**
    St George's church **140**
    Stormont 154
Belgium
    New Urbanism 161
    Table Ronde de l'Architecture 173
Belsay Hall, Northumberland 137, **137**
Benedict Biscop aka Biscop Baducing (628-89/90) 47
Beni-Hasan, Egypt, tombs at 6, 35
Bentley, John (1574-1615) **67**
Bentley, Michael (1579-1618) **67**
Bentsen, Ivar (1876-1943) 149, 152
Bérard, Édouard (1843-1912) **148**
Berg, Max Paul Eduard (1870-1947) 149
Berlin xiii
    Altes Museum **122**, **123**
    French Church **105**
    Gendarmenmarkt **123**
    Große Neugierde **120**
    Königliches Schloß 102, **102**
    Lutheran Cathedral 147
    National Gallery 139
    Neue Reichskanzlei 151, 157
    Neue Wache, Royal Guard House **122**
    opera house, Unter den Linden 104, **105**, 112
    Pergamon Museum 4
    Schauspielhaus 104, **119**, **123**
    Schloß Charlottenburg 103–4, **104**
    Schloß Glienicke 122, **122**
    Stalinallee 153
    Zeughaus 102, **102**
Berlin-Adlersdorf, Research Institute for Aviation 153
Bernard, Josef (1902-59) 153
Bernini, Giovanni Lorenzo (1598-1680) **38**, 63, 74, **74**, 76, **76**, 79, **79**, **81**, 102
Bestelmeyer, German (1874-1942) 151
Bicknell, Julian (1945-) 167
Binney, Horace (1780-1875) 247
Birmingham
    St Philip 146
    Town Hall 139, **141**
Biscop see Benedict
Blanchon, architect of the Bazouin tomb, Père-Lachaise cemetery, Paris **108**
Blenheim Palace, Oxon 96, **96**
Blithfield Hall, Staffs 118, **119**, 128
Blomfield, Sir Reginald Theodore (1856-1942) **40**, 153

Blondel, Jacques-François (1705-74) 104, 134
Blouet, Guillaume-Abel (1795-1853) **37**
Blount, Gilbert Robert (1819-76) **166**
Boccaccio, Giovanni (1313-75) 47
Bodt, Jean de (1670-1745) 102, **102**
Bofill Levi, Riccardo (1939-2022) 159
Böhme, Martin (1676-1725) **102**
Boileau, Louis-Hippolyte (1878-1948) 152
Bolzano 154
Bonaparte, Napoléon, Emperor (r.1804-14) **140**, 149
Bonatz, Paul Michael Nikolaus (1877-1956) 151
Bond, John Linnell (1764-1837) 119
Bonomi. Joseph (1739-1808) 131, **131**, 133
Bontempi, Pier Carlo (1954-) 174
Borgnival, Jan van Dendermonde, Lord of (d.1536) **38**
Borromeo, San Carlo (1538-84) 80, **81**
Borromini, Francesco (1599-1667) 74, **75**, 76, **81**
Boswell, James (1740-95) 245
Botta, Mario (1943-) 160
Bottesford, Leics 92, **94**
Boullée, Étienne-Louis (1728-99) 2, 133, 134–5
Bourne, Lincs, Town Hall **133**
Bowden, John (fl.1798-1822) **140**
Bowes, John (1811-85) 147
Bowes (née Coffin-Chevallier), Joséphine-Benoîte (1825-74) 147
Boyle, Lady Katharine (d.1629) 92, **94**
Boyle, Richard (1566-1643), 1st Earl of Cork v, 92, **94**
Boyle, Richard (1694-1753), see Burlington
Bracciolini, Gian Francesco Poggio (1380-1459) 47
Bradshaw, Harold Chalton (1893-1943) 153
Braghieri, Gianni (1945-) 160
Bramante, Donato, aka Bramante Lazzari (c.1444-1514) 6, 53, 59, 61–3, **62**, 98, **99**, 115
Brandenburg-an-der-Havel, Opel factory 153
Breda, Grote Kerk monument **38**
Breitman, Marc (1949-) 174
Breitman-Jakov, Nada (1952-) 174
Brenner, Hermann (fl.1920s-40s) 153
Brentwood, Sts Mary and Helen RC Cathedral 164, **166**
Brescia, Piazza della Vittoria 154
Brettingham. Matthew (1699-1769) **216**
Brewer, Cecil Claude (1871-1918) 148
Briggs, Frank Gatley (1862-1921) 154
Brocklesby Park, Lincs **138**
Brodrick, Cuthbert (1821-1905) **146**
Brongniart, Alexandre-Théodore (1739-1813) 134
Brooks, Leigh (1970-) 169, 173
Brosse. Salomon de (c.1571-1626) 87, **88**
Browning, Bryan (1773-1856) 132–3, **133**, 134
Brunelleschi, Filippo (1377-1446) 48, **48**, **49**, 60, 61
Brussels 161
    Palais de Justice 147
Brydon, John McKean (1840-1901) 145, **145**, 148
Bubb, James George (1782-1853) **143**
Buckingham Palace, Queen's Gallery 167
Buras, Nir Haim (1952-) 174
Buren Magonigle, Harold Van (1867-1935) **168**
Burgee, John Henry (1933-) 159
Burghley House, Stamford 90, **91**
Büring, Johann Gottfried (1723-after 1788) 104
Burke, Edmund (1729-97) 151
Burley-on-the-Hill, Rutland 106, **106**
Burlington, Richard Boyle (1694-1753), 3rd Earl of 72, 106, 107, **107**, 109
Burnet, Sir John James (1857-1938) 145, 148, **149**, 153
Burnham, Daniel Hudson (1846-1912) 148
Burton, Decimus (1800-81) 122
Bury St Edmunds, Shire Hall 157
Busiri Vici, Andrea (1818-1911) **154**

Cadorna, Marshal Count Luigi (1850-1928) 154

Cæcilia Metella (*fl.* 1st century BC) **138**, 139
Cairness House, Aberdeenshire 131, **132**
Callimachus (*fl. c.*430-400 BC) 6
Cambridge
    Downing College 136, 164, **164**
    Fitzwilliam Museum 139
    Gonville and Caius 167
    Judge Institute 169
    Senate House 100, **101**
    Trinity College library 95, **95**
Campbell, Colen (1676-1729) xii, **105**, 106, **108**, 109, **109**
    Vitruvius Britannicus 100, 104, 107
Campbell, John (1680-1743), 2nd Duke of Argyll 100
Campen, Jacob van (1595-1657) 106
Canova, Antonio (1757-1822) **132**
Canterbury, Cathedral 47
Cantian, Christian Gottlieb (1794-1866) **122**
capitals
    Greek 6, 11-12, **13**, 16-17, **16**, 35
    Roman **19-20**, **24**, **25**, **27**, **29-30**, 32
Carabelli, Casimiro (1774-1840) **140**
Carabelli, Donato (1760-after 1840) **140**
Caracalla (Marcus Aurelius Antoninus), Roman Emperor (*r.*211-17) 40, **40**, **41**, 142
Carbone, Dario (1857-1934) 155
Cardiff
    city hall, Cathays Park 147
    National Museum of Wales 148
Carlu, Jacques (1890-1976) 152
Carr, John (1723-1807) **216**
Cartwright, Eric (1972-) **164**, 169
caryatid(e) **15**, **121**
Cassiodorus, Flavius Magnus Aurelius (*c.*485-580) 47
Casson, Sir Hugh Maxwell (1910-99) 157
Castell, Robert (*fl.*1727-8) 109
Castello, Elia (*c.*1578-1608) **228**
Castle, *aka* Cassels *or* Cassel, Richard (*c.*1690-1751) **165**
Castle Coole, County Fermanagh 114, **114**
Castle Howard, Yorks 96, **96**
    mausoleum 98, **99**
    Temple of the Four Winds 98, **98**
Castle Ward, County Down 111
Caux or Caus, Isaac (1589/90-1648) 94
Cayart, Jean-Louis (1645-1702) **105**
Ceolfrith, St (642-716), Abbot of Wearmouth & Jarrow 47
Chalgrin, Jean-François-Thérèse (1739-1811) **37**, **89**, 134, 139
Chambers, Sir William (1723-96) xii, 6, 112
Chamoust *see* Ribart de Chamoust
Chapman, John (*fl.*1541-66) 92, **93**
Charlemagne, (*r.*800-814) 46, 47
Charlemont, James Caulfeild, 1st Earl of (1728-99) 117
Charles II, King (*r.*1660-85) 94
Charles III, King (*r.*2022-) 173
    as Prince of Wales 173
Charles, Martin (1940-2012) xiii, **123**
Charles V, Holy Roman Emperor (*r.*1519-56) 67, **81**
Charlottesville, University of Virginia 136
Chatsworth House, Derbys 95-6
Cheltenham, The Park 164
Chicago
    Harold Washington Library Center 162
    ITT buildings 153
Chirico, Giorgio de (1888-1978) 160
Chitham, Robert William James (1935-2017) 169
Christian, Johann Josef (1706-77) **239**
Churchill, John (1650-1722), 1st Duke of Marlborough 96, **96**
Cilicia, Temple of Zeus Olbios 36
Clark, John (*c.*1585-1624) **67**
Clark, Kenneth Mackenzie (1903-83), Baron Clark of Saltwood 156-7
Clarke, George (1661-1736) 66, **66**, **101**

Classic Planning Herald 174
Classical architecture
    political associations of 152-3
    use of term 2-3
    see also Classicism; *Glossary*; Greek Revival; Neo-Classicism; Palladianism
Classicism
    recent practitioners 162-74
    stripped 151, 152, 153
    survival of 153-8
Claude Gellée, *called* Lorraine (1600-82) 109
Clement VII, Pope (*r.*1523-34) (Giulio de' Medici) **64**
Cleopatra VII (*r.*51-30 BC) 206
Clérisseau, Charles-Louis (1721-1820) 111
Cluny, library 47
Cnidos, Lion Tomb 9, **10**, 32, 36
Cockerell, Charles Robert (1788-1863) 11, **31**, 122, 142, **143**
Coed Mawr, Wales 167
Cologne, Werkbund exhibition (1914) 149
Colombe, Michel (*c.*1433-*c.*1514) **239**
columns 32, 37, 45-6, 115-16
    superimposed 33-4, **33**, 37, 46
Colvin, Sir Howard Montagu (1919-2007) xiii, 100
Como, Casa del Fascio xii, 154
Comper, Sir John Ninian (1864-1960) **156**, 157
Composite Order, Roman 32, **32**, 37
Connecticut, Litchfield 170, 172, **172**
Constantine I ('The Great'), Roman Emperor (*r.*324-37) **34**, 37
Constantinople 40
    Hagia Sophia 41, 43, 63, **81**
Cooley, Thomas (*c.*1740-84) 112, **112**
Cooper, Sir Thomas Edwin (1874-1942) 154
Copenhagen, Domkirke **129**
Copnall, Edward Bainbridge (1903-73) **157**
Coppedè, Adolfo (1871-1951) 155
Coppedè, Luigi 'Gino' (1866-1927) 154-5
'Corbusier, Le' (Charles-Édouard Jeanneret-Gris [1887-1965]) xi, **40**, 160
Cordemoy, Abbé Jean-Louis de (1631-1713) 115
Córdoba, Mezquita 46
Cori, Temple 18, **19**, 37
Corinthian Order 2, 6
    Greek 16-17, **16**, 36
    Hellenistic 36
    Roman **26**, 27, **27**, **28**, **29**, 30, **31**
    in Romanesque 47
Cortona, Santa Maria del Calcinaio 61
Cortona, Pietro Berrettini da (1596-1669) **78**
Cottingham, Lewis Nockalls (1787-1847) vi
Cowlishaw, William Harrison (1869-1957) 153
Cresy, Edward (1792-1858) 3
Cret, Paul-Philippe (1876-1945) 152
Crete 35, 36
Cronaca, Simone del Pollaiuolo, *called* Il (1457-1508) 51
Cubitt, Thomas (1788-1855) 145
Culot, Maurice (1939-) 160, 161, **167**, 174
Curl, Sir Walter, Bart. (*d.*1678) **188**
Cuvilliés, Jean-François-Vincent-Joseph de (1695-1768) 79, **80**

Dalton, Richard (*c.*1715-91) 117
Dance, George the Younger (1741-1825) 133, **134**
Davioud, Gabriel-Jean-Antoine (1824-81) **39**
Deconstructivism xiii, 174
Dee, John (1527-1609) xi
Deglane, Henry-Joseph-Auguste (1855-1931) **40**
Delevoy, Robert-Louis (1914-82) 161
Delmas, Fernand-Étienne-Charles (1852-1933) **148**
Delos, Temple of Apollo 9, **10**
Delphi 36
    sanctuary of Athena Pronaia 7
Der el-Bahari, Temple of Queen Hatshepsut 35

Desgodetz, Antoine (1653-1728) 117
Destailleur, Hippolyte-Alexandre-Gabriel-Walter (1822-93) 147
Deutschmann, Werner (*fl.*1920s-40s) 153
Diamant, Michael (1981-) 174
Dietrich von Raitenau, Wolf (1559-1617), Prince-Archbishop of Salzburg
    (*r.*1587-1612) **228**
Dietterlin, Wendel (1551-99) 90
Dinsmoor, William Bell (1886-1966) 35
Diocletian (Gaius Aurelius Valerius Diocletianus), Roman Emperor
    (*r.*284-305) 34, 40, 41, 111
Dixon, Sir Jeremy (1939-) 160
Dobson, John (1787-1865) 137
Domitian (Titus Flavius Domitianus), Roman Emperor (*r.*81-96) 33
Donthorn, William John (1799-1859) 178
Doric Order 2, 5, 32-3
    Greek 7, **8**, 9-11, **9**, **10**, 35, 36, **127**, **128**, 131
    Pæstum-derived 117
    Roman 18, **19**, 20, **20**, 37, **39**
    stone or timber origin 7-9, 35, 115
    Tuscan 61
Dormer, Henry (*fl.*1680-1727) 106, **106**
Dormer, Sir Robert (*d.*1552) 90
Downey, Richard Joseph (1881-1953), RC Archbishop of Liverpool 157
Dresden 153
    Zwinger Palace 103, **103**
Dreux, château of Anet 91
Driehaus, Richard Herman (1942-2021) 173
Duany, Andrés (1949-) 160, **171**, 173, 174
Dublin
    Bank of Ireland **111**
    Casino at Marino 112
    Custom House **113**, 114
    Four Courts 112, **112**
    St Patrick's Cathedral 92, **94**
Ducart or Duckart, Davis (*fl.*1761-85) **112**, **165**
Ducerceau (Du Cerceau), Jacques Androuet (1510/12-85) 90, **91**, 93
Dulwich Picture Gallery 135
Durand, Jean-Nicolas-Louis (1760-1834) 133, 134, 160-1
Duret, François-Joseph (1804-65) **39**
Dykes Bower, Stephen Ernest (1903-94) xiv

Easton, David Anthony (1937-2020) 173
Eben, Carl Ferdinand (1750-1830) 117
Eben, Ephraim (1726-1804) 117
Échillais, Notre Dame 46
Edge, Charles (*c.*1801-67) **141**
Edinburgh
    David Hume monument **138**
    Royal High School **127**, 137
    St Andrew's House 153
Edwards, Arthur Trystan (1884-1973) 1
Effner, Joseph (1687-1745) **103**
Egypt, Ancient 6
    architecture 35-6
Egyptian style **108**, 131, 148, **149**
Ehrenström, Johan Albrecht (1762-1847) 136, **136**
Ehrensvärd, Carl August (1745-1800) 122, 131
Einhard *aka* Eginhard (*c.*770-837) 47
El-Wakil, Abdel-Wahed (1943-) 174
ellipses 68, 69, 74, **74**, **75**, **76**, 80, 82, 86, **86**
Elmes, Harvey Lonsdale (1814-47) 139, **143**
Engel, Carl Ludwig (1778-1840) 136, **136**
Engh, Audun (1948-2023) 172
England, Classical architecture 90-100
entablatures 5, 9, **15**, 17, 18, 20, 24, 30, 33-4
    Renaissance 45-6
Eosander, Johann Friedrich, Freiherr von Göthe (1670-1729) 102, 103, **104**
Ephesus 5, 6
    Temple of Artemis 11, 36
Epidaurus 36

Erdmannsdorff, Friedrich Wilhelm, Freiherr von (1736-1800) xiii, 104, 112
Erith, Raymond Charles (1904-73) 161, 164
Ermenonville, Rousseau's tomb 132
Eton College, Berks 167, **169**
Etruria 36
Eugen, Prince (Eugène François), of Savoy (1663-1736) 96, **97**
Everard, Nadia Naty (1995-) 174
Exeter
    County Hall 157
    University 157
Exton, Rutland, Sts Peter and Paul 92, **93**, 94

Fairfax, Anne (1954-) 170, **172**, 173
Fancelli, Luca (*c.*1430-after 1494) 60
Fanti, Gaetano (1687-1759) 81
Farrell, Sir Terence (1938-) 159
Feichtmayr, Franz Xaver (1698-1763) 82, 84
Feichtmayr, Johann Michael (1696-1772) 82, 84
Fenger, Ludvig Peter (1833-1905) 8
Ferne Park, Dorset 164
Finch, Daniel (1647-1730), 2nd Earl of Nottingham 106, **106**
Finch, Heneage (1751-1812), 4th Earl of Aylesford 131
Fischer, Johann Michael (1692-1766) **239**
Fischer, Karl Johann (*fl.*1920s-40s) 153
Fischer von Erlach, Johann Bernhard (1656-1723) 79-80, **80**, **81**, 102
Fischer von Erlach, Joseph Emanuel (1695-1742) **81**
Fisker, Kay Otto (1893-1965) 150
Flaxman, John (1755-1826) **140**
Flitcroft, Henry (1697-1769), *aka* 'Burlington Harry' 216
Florence
    Cathedral 60
    Foundlings' Hospital 48, **48**
    Medici Chapel 64, **64**
    Palazzo Medici (Riccardi) **50**, 51, **51**, 52
    Palazzo Rucellai **50**, 51
    Palazzo Strozzi 51
    Renaissance 48, 51
    San Lorenzo 48, **64**
    San Miniato 46, 60
    San Miniato al Monte 48, **48**, 166
    San Spirito 48, **48**
    Santa Croce, Pazzi Chapel 48, **49**, 60
    Santa Maria degli Angeli 60, **61**
    Santa Maria Novella 59, **59**, 69
Florencecourt, County Fermanagh 112, **112**
Folkingham, Lincs, House of Correction 132, **134**
Fontaine, Pierre-François-Léonard (1762-1853) **39**
Fontainebleau, France, Mannerism 67
Fontana, Domenico (1543-1607) 63
France
    Baroque architecture 87, **87**, **88**, 89-90, **89**, **90**
    Neo-Classicism 87, 89, 116, 134
    New Urbanism 161
    Renaissance 147
    stripped Classicism 152
    see also Paris
Francesco Maurizio di Giorgio (Pollaiolo) (1439-1501/2) 61
Franck, Michael M. (1963-) 173
François II, Duke of Brittany (1433-88) **239**
Franzoni, Giuseppe (1780-1815) **130**
Freemasonry 6, 22, 116, **157**, 161
Friedrich August I, Prince-Elector of Saxony (*r.*1694-1733), *as* Augustus II
    ('The Strong'), King of Poland (*r.*1697-1706, 1709-33) 103
Friedrich II ('The Great'), King of Prussia (*r.*1740-86) 103-4, **142**
Friedrich Wilhelm, 'Great Elector' of Brandenburg (*r.*1640-88) 104
Friedrich Wilhelm III, King of Prussia (*r.*1797-1840) 120
Friedrich Wilhelm IV, King of Prussia (*r.*1840-61) **142**
Fronto, Marcus Cornelius (*c.*AD 95-*c.*166) 2
Frynde, Anthony (*fl.*1583-94) 92
Frynde, John (*fl.*1579-1625) 92

funerary monuments 90, 92, **93**, **94**, 150
Funes, Pablo Álvarez (1981-) 174

Gabel, Laurenzkirche 85, **85**
Galli-Bibiena, Antonio (1700-74) **85**
Gandon, James (1743-1823) 112, **112**, **113**, 114
Gardette, Pierre-Claude de la (c.1745-92) **202**
Garrett, Daniel (d.1753) 99
Gärtner, Friedrich von (1792-1847) **140**
Gel'freykh, Vladimir Georgiyevich (1885-1967) 152
Gell, Sir William (1777-1836) 137
Gellius, Aulus (c.AD 125-after 180) 2
Genoa 154
    English cemetery 155
    Palazzo della Borsa Valori 155
    Palazzo Pastorino 154
George I, King (r.1714-27) **97**
Germany 106
    Baroque architecture 102–4, **105**
    English influences 104
    National Socialist 150, 151
    see also Aachen; Berlin; Munich; Potsdam
Giant Order **63**, 64, **65**, 66, 70, **70**, 114
Gibberd, Sir Frederick Ernest (1908-84) 157-8
Gibbons, Grinling (1648-1721) 96
Gibbs, James (1682-1754) xii, 6, **27**, **30**, 98, **99**-100, **99**, **100**, **101**, 107, 109, **109**, **112**, 135
Gibson, John (1817-92) 139
Gilly, David (1748-1808) 117, 122, 133
Gilly, Friedrich (1772-1800) 2, 136, **142**
Girault, Charles-Louis (1851-1932) 40
Girouard, Mark (1931-2022) 92
Giulio Romano, (Giulio Pippi) (c.1499-1546) 53, **53**, **54**, 134
Glasgow
    Moray Place **128**
    municipal chambers 145, **146**
    Union Bank of Scotland 154
    Walmer Crescent **128**
Gloag, John Edwards (1896-1981) vi
Glover, George (1812-90) 133, **134**
Glume, Friedrich Christian (1714-52) **234**
Goethe, Johann Wolfgang von (1749-1832) 116
Gontard, Karl Philipp Christian von (1731-91) 104, **105**, **123**
Gothic architecture
    and Classical **156**, 157
    and Romanesque 2, 47
Gough, Piers (1946-) **159**, 160
Goujon, Jean (c.1510-c.1565) **38**
Grange Park, Hants **129**, 137
Grassi, Giorgio (1935-) 160
Graves, Michael (1934-2015) 159, 174
Great Packington, Warks, Church of St James 131, **131**
Greece, rediscovery of 116–17
Greek architecture
    compared with Roman 43–4
    development of 5, 35–6
    see also Glossary; Orders of Architecture
Greek Revival 118–36
Green, William Curtis (1875-1960) 154
Greenberg, Allan (1938-) 162, 173, 174
Greenwich
    Hospital 95, **95**
    King Charles II block 94, **95**
    the Queen's House **72**, 94, **95**
    St Alphege 96
Griffith, John (1796-1888) 122, **126**
Gropius, Georg Walter Adolf (1883-1969) xi
Grüner, Ludwig (1801-82) **143**
Grut, Torben (1871-1945) 152
Gryffyne, William (fl.1594-7) **92**

Guarini, Guarino (1624-83) 85, **85**
Gunn, Richard McLeod Morrison (1889-1933) 154
Gwilt, Joseph (1784-1863) 6

Hadrian (Publius Ælius Hadrianus), Roman Emperor (r.117-138) 36, 37
Hagalisletto, Anders (1969-) 172
Hagley Park, Worcs 118, **118**
Haiger, Ernst (1874-1952) 151
Halbig, Johann von (1814-82) **140**
Halicarnassus, mausoleum **12**, 37, 96
Haller, Karl Christoph Joachim, Freiherr von Hallerstein (1774-1817) **124**
Hamilton, Craig (1961-) 167, **168**, 173
Hamilton, David (1768-1843) 145
Hamilton, James (c.1826-94) 145
Hamilton, Thomas (1784-1858) 122, **127**, 137
Hammerwood Lodge, East Grinstead 131
Hampton Court Palace 95
Hansen, C.F. (1756-1845) 122, **129**
Hansom, Charles Francis (1817-88) **171**
Hansom, Joseph Aloysius (1803-82) 139, **141**
Hardouin-Mansart, Jules (1646-1708) **81**, 87, **88**, 89
Hardwick, Philip (1792-1870) 137
Hardwick, Thomas (1752-1829) **237**
Hardy, Matthew (1957-) 173
Harington, Sir James (1511-92) **94**
Harris, Emanuel Vincent (1876-1971) 154, **155**, 157, 162
Harrison, Thomas (1744-1829) 122
Hartley, Jesse (1780-1860) 122, **127**
Hawksmoor, Nicholas (1661-1736) 96, **96**, **97**, 98, **98**, 99, **99**, **101**
Heathcote, Ilkley, Yorks 148
Hegele, Maximilian (Max) (1873-1945) 147, **148**
Hellenic, Hellenistic, terms 36
Helsinki
    Cathedral 136, **136**
    Senate Square 136
Henbury Hall, Cheshire 167
Henry Hope Reed Award 173
Henry VII, King of England (r.1485-1509) 90
Herbert, Henry (c.1693-1751), 9th Earl of Pembroke 96, 106, **107**
Hervey, Frederick Augustus (1730-1803), 4th Earl of Bristol and Bishop of Derry **140**
Hewitt, Mark Alan (1953-) 173, 174
Hildebrandt, Johann Lukas von (1668-1745) 85, **85**, 96, **97**
Hillsborough, County Down, Downshire Column 45
Hindenburg, Paul von Beneckendorff und von (1847-1934), President of Weimar Republic 153
Hitler, Adolf (1889-1945) 151, 153
Hittorff, Jakob Ignaz (1792-1867) 122, **129**
Hjorth, Ragnar (1887-1971) 152
Hobbs, Frederick Brice (1862-1944) 154
Hofer, Paul (1909-95) 153
Hoffmann, Josef Franz Maria (1870-1956) 149
Hofmannsthal, Hugo Laurenz August Hofmann von (1874-1929) 157
Holden, Charles Henry (1875-1960) **168**
Holder, Julian (1957-) 158
Holford, Willian Graham, Lord (1907-75) 157
Holkham Hall, Norfolk 109, **109**
Holl, Elias (1573-1646) 69, 106
Hollein, Hans (1934-2014) 159
Honorius, Roman Emperor (r.384-423) **185**
Hood, Raymond Mathewson (1881-1934) 152
Hope, Thomas (1769-1831) 136
Hopkins, Sir Michael John (1935-2023) 157
Houghton Hall, Norfolk 109, **109**
Howitt, Thomas Cecil (1889-1968) 154
Hugh of St Victor (c.1096-1141) 47
Hume, David (1711-76) **138**
Hussey, Christopher Edward Clive (1899-1970) 155

Iardella, Francesco (c.1793-1831) **130**

Ickworth, Suffolk **140**
Ictinus (*fl.*5th century BC) 16
Ieper, Belgium, Menin Gate **40**
Indiana
    University of Notre Dame 167, **169**, 173
    Vitruvian House, South Bend 162
Indianapolis, public library 152
Ingestre Hall, Staffs 118
Institute of Classical Art & Architecture 161, 173
International Network for Traditional Building, Architecture and Urbanism 173
International Style xiii
Inwood, Henry William (1794-1843) 120
Inwood, William (*c*.1771-1843) 120
Iofan, Boris Mikhailovich (1891-1976) 152-3
Ionic Order 2, 5-6
    Greek 11-12, **12**, 13, **14**, **15**, 16, 35, 36
    Roman 20, **21**, 22, **22**, **23**, **24**, **25**
Italy
    Greek architecture 36
    modern Classicism 154-5
    Post-Modernism 160
Ittar, Henryk (1773-1850) 132, **132**

Jackson, John (*c*.1602-63) **185**
Jackson, Sir Thomas Graham (1835-1924) 151
Jacobite Rebellion (1715) 100
James, King (*r*. as James VI from 1567 as King of Scots, and *r*.1603-25 as James I of England and Ireland) 67, 106
Jameson, Frederic (1934-) 159
Jänggl, Franz (1650-1734) 85
Jefferson, Thomas (1743-1826) 135-6
Jencks, Charles Alexander (1939-2019) xiii, 159-60, **159**
Jerusalem
    Temple 81
    Temple of Solomon 6, **41**, **76**, **157**
Johnson, Francis (1911-95) 161
Johnson, Gerard (*aka* Gheerart Janssen) (*fl*.1568-1611) **94**
Johnson, Philip Cortelyou (1906-2005) 159
Johnson, Samuel (1709-84) 175
Jones, Edward (1939-) 160
Jones, Inigo (1573-1652) 69, 72, **72**, 90, 94, **94**, **95**, 106
Julius II, Pope (*r*.1503-13) 62

Kampmann, Hack (1856-1920) 152
Karl, Prince (Friedrich Karl Alexander) of Prussia (1801-83) **120**
Karlskrona, dockyard gate 131
Karlsruhe, ducal palace 90
Kedleston Hall, Derbys **110**
Keene, Henry (1726-76) **121**
Keene, Theodosius (*fl*.1770-87) **121**
Kelheim, Befreiungshalle **140**
Kelway, Robert (*c*.1504-80) **93**
Kennington, Eric Henri (1888-1960) 155, 156
Kent, William (*c*.1685-1748) 109, 111
Khrushchev, Nikita Sergeyevich (1894-1971) 152
Kilboy, County Tipperary 164, **165**
King's Lynn, Norfolk 133, **134**
Kirby Hall, Northants 90, **91**
Kirkland, Michael (1943-) 160
Kleihues, Josef Paul (1933-2004) 160
Klenze, (Franz) Leo(pold Karl) von (1784-1864) xiii, 35, 122, **122**, **124**, **125**, 150
Knight, Richard Payne (1751-1824) 116
Knobelsdorff, Georg Wenzeslaus von (1699-1754) 103-4, 112
Knott, Ralph (1879-1929) 154
Korsnes, Carl W. (1991-) 172
Kreis, Wilhelm (1873-1955) 35, 150, **151**, 152, 153
Kreuzberg, Berlin, Eben mausoleum **117**
Krier, Léon (1946-) 151, 160-1, 164, **170**, 173, 174

Krier, Rob (1938-2023) 160, 174
Küchel, Johann Jacob Michael (1703-69) 82

Lacock Abbey, Wilts 92
Lacock, Wilts, St Cyriac 92, **93**
Lallerstedt, Erik (1864-1955) 152
Lancaster, Ashton memorial 147
Lanchester, Henry Vaughan (1863-1953) 73, 147
Langley, Batty (1696-1751) xii, **18**, **20**, **24**, **25**
Langley, Thomas (1702-51) xii
Lanyon, Sir Charles (1813-89) 142, **144**
Latham, Jasper (*c*.1636-93) **188**
Latrobe, Benjamin Henry Boneval (1764-1820) **130**, 131, 133, 136
Laugier, Abbé Marc-Antoine (1713-69) 115-16
    Primitive Hut 32-3, 115
Laurana, Luciano (*c*.1420-79) 52
Le Brun, Charles (1619-90) 87, **87**
Le Duc, Gabriel (1623/5-96) **88**
Le Geay, Jean-Laurent (*c*.1710-*c*.1786) 134
Le Muet, Pierre (1591-1669) **88**
Le Nôtre, André (1613-1700) 90
Le Roy, Julien-David (1724-1803) 117
Le Vau, Louis (1612-70) 87, **87**
Lebœuf-Nanteuil, Charles-François (1792-1865) **129**
Leche, Gunnar (1891-1954) 152
Ledoux, Claude-Nicolas (1736-1806) 2, 122, **130**, 133, 134, 135
Leeds, Town Hall **146**, 147
Leicester, Thomas Coke (1697-1759), 1st Earl of **216**
Lemercier, Jacques (*c*.1585-1654) 87, **88**
Lenin, Vladimir Ilyich Ulyanov (1870-1924) 152
Leo III, Pope (*r*.795-816) 46
Leo X, Pope (*r*.1513-21) (Giovanni de' Medici) **64**
Leoni, Giacomo (*c*.1686-1746) 107, 135
Lepère, Jean-Baptiste (1761-1844) **129**
Lescot, Pierre (*c*.1500/10-78) 38
Leverett, Alban (*fl*.1630s) **94**
Lewerentz, Sigurd (1885-1975) 150, **150**, 152, 153
Lille, Palais des Beaux Arts **148**
Lincoln, New England, Duncan art galleries **167**
Lisbon, Santa Maria della Divina Providenza **85**
Liverpool
    Albert Dock warehouses **127**
    Anglican Cathedral 158
    India Buildings 154
    Mersey Docks 154
    Roman Catholic Cathedral **154**, 157
    St George's Hall 139, 142, **143**, 145
Ljubljana, Žale cemetery 152, **152**
Lodge, Giles Henry (1808-88) 115
Lodoli, Fra Carlo (Cristoforo Ignazio Antonio) (1690-1761) 213
Lohsen, Arthur C. (1967-) 173
Lombardo, Pietro Solari (*c*.1435-1515) **57**
London xiii
    Adelphi 114
    All Hallows, London Wall 133
    Army and Navy Club 145
    Bank of England **31**, 135, 154
    Banqueting House, Whitehall 94, **94**
    Belgravia 165
    Bomber Command Memorial, Green Park 165, 167, **168**
    Bracken House 157
    Bridgewater House 142
    Brighton and Dover terminus **144**
    British Museum **128**, 148
    Brompton Oratory 145
    Burlington House, Piccadilly 107
    Carlton Club 145, **145**
    Chelsea Hospital 95, 164
    Chelsea Town Hall 145, **145**
    Chepstow Villas, Kensington 165

Chiswick House 107, **107**, 109
Christ Church, Spitalfields 96, **98**
County Hall 154
Cumberland Terrace 142, **143**
Euston propylæum ('arch') 137
Freemasons' Hall 154
Goldhammer mausoleum, Highgate **168**
Grosvenor Place 157
Horse Guards, Whitehall 111
Isle of Dogs Pumping Station 169
Kensal Green Cemetery **126**
Kodak House, Kingsway 148, **149**
Lammas Green estate 157
Lansdowne Walk (Cosmic House) 159–60, **159**
Lloyd's of London 154
Masonic Peace Memorial 149–50, **149**
National Gallery, Sainsbury Wing **158**, 160
National Provincial Bank 154
Nelson's Column, Trafalgar Square 45
New Bond Street 164
New Scotland Yard 145
Newgate gaol 133, **134**
Pitzhanger Manor, Ealing 135, **136**
Reform Club 55, 142
Regent Street 1
Regent's Park 164, **165**
RIBA headquarters 157, **157**
Royal College of Music 167
St Anne, Limehouse 96
St George-in-the-East 96, **101**
St George's, Bloomsbury 96, **97**
St John's, Smith Square 99, **100**
St Martin-in-the-Fields 27, 98, **100**
St Mary-le-Strand 98, **100**
St Pancras church 120, **121**
St Paul's Cathedral 81, **89**, 95
Sir John Soane's Museum (Lincoln's Inn Fields) 135, **135**
Somerset House 90, **91**, 112
Tavistock Street 148
Travellers' Club 142
Wesleyan Central Hall, Westminster 147
Westminster Abbey 90
Whitehall 145
Wood Street police station 157
Longfellow, Henry Wadsworth (1807-82) 241
Longhena, Baldassare (1596-1682) **57**, 58, 79, **79**
Longhi, Martino the Elder (c.1534-91) 65
Longhi, Martino the Younger (1602-60) 77, **78**, 79
Longleat, Wilts 90, **91**
Lonigo, Vettor Pisani Villa 107
Loos, Adolf (1870-1933) 156
Lord, Joshua (fl. early 18th century) **106**
Lorenzetto, aka Lorenzo Lotti (1490-1541) 53
l'Orme, Philibert de (1514-70) 90, **91**
Lorne, Francis (1889-1963) 153
Lorsch, former abbey 46
Louis XII, King of France (r.1499-1515) **220**
Louis XIV, King of France (r.1643-1715) 81, 90
Louis XVI, King of France (r.1774-92) **196**
Louvet, Louis-Albert (1860-1936) **40**
Ludlow, Shropshire xii
Lumley, John (1654-1721) 106, **106**
Lutyens, Sir Edwin Landseer (1869-1944) 147, 148, 153, **154**, 157, **168**
Lynn, William Henry (1829-1915) 142, **144**
Lysicrates, Greek *choragos* (fl.335-4 BC) **16**, 32, 36, 118, **119**, 120

McBlain, David (c.1755-1847) **139**
McCrery II, James C. (1965-) 173
McKellar, Elizabeth (1962-) 158
McKim, Charles Follen (1847-1909) 152

McMorran, Donald Hanks (1904-65) 157
Maderno, Carlo (c.1556-1629) 63, **63**, 76–7, **77**, 79
Magdeburg 153
Maiano, Benedetto da (1442-97) 51
Maklouf, Raphael David (1937-) **166**
Malatesta, Sigismondo Pandolfo (1417-68) 51
Manchester, Central Library 154, **155**, 162
Mannerism 53, **54**, **55**, 64, **64**, **65**, 66, 67, **67**, 77, **158**
Manners, John, (d.1588), 4th Earl of Rutland 92, **94**
Mansart, François (1598-1666) 81, 87, **88**
Mantua
    Palazzo del Tè 53, **53**, 54
    Palazzo Ducale 53, **54**
    San Lorenzo 60
    Sant'Andrea 59, **59**, 60, **60**, 69
    Santo Spirito 60
Manzano Martos, Rafael (1936-) 174
March, Werner (1894-1976) 151
Marcus Aurelius Antoninus, Roman Emperor (r.161-180) **65**
Marguerite de Foix, Duchess of Brittany (c.1449-86) **239**
Maria Christina, Archduchess of Austria (1742-98) 132, **132**
Mark Antony (Marcus Antonius [c.83-30 BC]) 206
Marne-la-Vallée **167**
Martinelli, Francesco (1651-1708) 85, **85**
Mary II, Queen (r.1689-94) jointly with William III **148**
Massimo, Angelo (d.1550) **55**
Massimo, Pietro (d.1544) **55**
mausolea 98, 99, **117**, **126**, **127**, **128**, **138**, 150, 152, **168**
    Halicarnassus **12**, 37, 96
Mausolos or Mausolus, Satrap of Caria (r.377-353 BC) **211**
Maximin (Gaius Julius Verus Maximinus), Roman Emperor (r.235-8) 40
Maynard, Alan (fl.1563-98) 90
Mead, William Rutherford (1846-1928) 152
Mehaffy, Michael (1955-) 174
Mereworth Castle, Kent **108**, 109
Merrill, Scott (1956-) 174
Mestre, Villa Malcontenta 70
Métezeau, Jacques-Clément (1581-1652) 87, **88**
Michelangelo Buonarroti (1475-1564) 55, **56**, 63, 64, **64**, **65**, 66, **66**, 74
Michelozzo di Bartolommeo, *called* Michelozzi (1396-1472) **50**, 51, **51**, **61**
Miës van der Rohe, Maria Ludwig Michael (1886-1969) xi, 153, 158
Milan
    Palace of Justice 154
    Palazzo Marino **65**
    Santa Maria delle Grazie 61, **62**, 63
    Santa Maria presso San Satiro 61, **62**
    Sant'Ambrogio 115
Miletus, Temple of Apollo Didymæus **16**, 36
Millar or Miller, John (1810/11-76) **137**
Miller, Ferdinand von (1813-87) **124**
Milton, Notts, mausoleum **128**
Modena
    Cathedral 47
    San Cataldo cemetery 160
Modernism xi, xii, xiii, 151, 152, 154–5, 160
    rejection of 161, 162, 172–3, 174
    and sculpture 156
module 4
Moholy-Nagy (née Pietzsch), Sibyl (1903-71) 153
Moloney, Luke (1972-) 157, 173
Monck, Sir Charles Miles Lambert, Bart. (1779-1867) 137, **137**
Monreale, Sicily 47
Montani, Gabriele (fl. early 18th century) 85, **85**
Monte Cassino 47
Montepulciano, San Biagio 63
Montferrand, Henri-Louis-Auguste-Ricard de (1786-1858) 136
Montigny-le-Bretonneux, Les Arcades du Lac 159
Moore, Charles Willard (1925-93) 159
Moray, John Douglas Stuart (1966-), 21st Earl of **171**
Morris, Robert (1703-54) v, 135, 172, **172**

INDEX / 253

Morris, Roger (1695-1749) 96, 106, **107**
Moscow
    Bersenevskaya Embankment block 152
    Lenin's mausoleum 152
    Rasumovsky Palace 132
Mount Stewart, County Down 120, **121**
Mukhina, Vera Ignat'yevna (1889-1953) 152
Mulhern, Colum (1958-) 173, 174
Mulholland, Roger (1740-1818) **204**
Munich
    Alte Pinakothek 147
    Glyptothek **125**
    Haus der Deutschen Kunst **150**
    Propyläen **122**, **125**
    Ruhmeshalle **124**
    Schloß Nymphenburg 103, **103**
    Theatine Church of St Kajetan 79, **80**
Mussenden Temple, Downhill, County Londonderry **139**
Mussolini, Benito (1883-1945) 154
Mycenæ, Treasury of Atreus 6

Nansledan, Cornwall 164
Napoléon, see Bonaparte
Nash, John (1752-1835) 1, 142, **143**
Neandria 35
Nelson, Horatio (1758-1805), Viscount Nelson 45
Neo-Classicism 114, 115–50, 131
    France 87, 89, 116, 134
    move away from 137, 139, 142, 145, 147–50
    re-emergence 147–8
    stripped 148–50, **150**
Neresheim, abbey-church 86, **86**
Nering, Johann Arnold (1659-95) 102, **102**, 104
Nerva, Marcus Cocceius, Roman Emperor (r.96-98) 27, **28**
Netherlands 106
Neumann, Johann Balthasar (1687-1753) 82, **84**
New Classicism 161, 173
New Urbanism 160–1, 165, 173
New York
    ATT skyscraper (Sony building) 159
    Carhart Mansion 167
    Pennsylvania Station 152
    RCA Building 152
Newcomb, Richard (1784-1851) **134**
Newman, Francis Winton (1878-1953) **149**, 150, 154
Newton, Sir Isaac (1642-1727) 135
Nicholas I, Tsar of Russia (r.1801-25) **136**
Nicholas V, Pope (r.1447-55) 62
Nîmes, Maison Carrée **31**, 37
Nollekens, Joseph (1737-1823) 120, **138**
Norblin de la Gourdaine, Jean-Pierre (1745-1830) 132
Nottingham, 2nd Earl of, see Finch
Nottingham
    Council House 154
    University 157
Noyon, Cathedral 47

O'Connor, Liam (1961-) 165, **168**
Oliver, Alex (1964-) 173
Olympia, Temple of Zeus 7
Oppenord, Gilles-Marie (1672-1742) **89**
Oranienburg, Heinkel factory 153
Orders
    'Cerealian' **130**
    superimposed 33, **33**, **57**, 58–9, **58**, 67
    'Tobacco' **130**
Orders of Architecture 2, 5–6, 115
    application of 32–4
    Giant **63**, 64, **65**, 66, 70, **70**, 114
    Greek 6–17

Roman 17–32
    see also Composite; Corinthian; Doric; *Glossary*; Ionic; Tuscan
ornament 1
    Greek 12, **15**, 16–17, **16**
    Roman 20, 27, **29**, 43–4, **43**, **44**
    see also Glossary
Osborne House, Isle of Wight 145
Östberg, Ragnar (1866-1945) 152
Otto I, King of Greece (r.1832-62) **125**
Outram, John (1934-) 169, **169**
Oxford
    Ashmolean Museum 142, **143**
    Canterbury Gate, Christ Church **39**
    Clarendon Building **101**
    former Sackler Library 162, **163**
    library 47
    Peckwater Quadrangle, Christ Church 66, **66**, 106, **106**, 114
    Radcliffe Camera 98, **99**, **121**
    Schools Quadrangle **67**

Pæstum, Doric temples 9, **9**, 32, 36, 116, **117**, 131
Pagano Pogatschnig, Giuseppe (1896-1945) 154
Paine, James (1717-89) **110**, 111
Pajou, Augustin (1730-1809) **38**
palazzi **65**, 69, 70, 142
    Florence 48, **50**, 51, **51**
    later 52–3, **52**, **53**, **54**, 55, **55**
    Venice 56–9, **57**
Palencia, Church of San Juan Bautista de Baños de Cerrato 46
Palladianism, in England 72, 94, 98, 100, 167
    Second Revival 106–14
Palladio, Andrea *aka* Andrea di Pietro della Gondola (1508-80) 6, 61, 69–72, 104
    Antichità di Roma 106
    Quattro Libri dell'Architettura 6, 69
    in Vicenza 69–71, **69**, **70**, **71**
Paris xiii
    abbey-church of St-Denis 47
    Arc de Triomphe de l'Étoile **37**, 139
    Arc de Triomphe du Carrousel **39**
    Barrière (Rotonde) de la Villette **130**, 135
    Bazouin Family tomb, Père-Lachaise Cemetery **108**
    Church of the Madeleine 139, **141**
    Dôme des Invalides **81**, 87, **88**
    Fontaine des Innocents **38**
    Fontaine St-Michel **39**
    Grand Palais, Avenue d'Antin **40**
    Les Espaces d'Abraxas 159
    Louvre 87, **87**
    Opéra 147
    Palais de Chaillot 152
    Panthéon 89, **89**, **90**, 116
    Rue de la Bourse corner **117**
    Sorbonne 87
    St-Gervais 87, **88**
    St-Sulpice 87, **89**
    St-Vincent-de-Paul **129**
    Ste-Geneviève 89, **89**, 116, 136
    Val-de-Grâce 87, **88**
Paris Exposition (1937) 152
Parnell, Charles Octavius (1807-65) 145
pasticheur 156–7
Patmore, Coventry Kersey Deighton (1823-96) xiii, 1
Pausanias (*fl*. later 2nd century AD) 7, 16
Pearce, Sir Edward Lovett (c.1699-1733) **111**, 112, 165
Pelham, Charles Anderson (1748/9-1823), 1st Baron Yarborough **138**
Pelham-Clinton, Georgina Elizabeth (1789-1822), Duchess of Newcastle under Lyme **128**
Pelham-Clinton, Henry Pelham Fiennes (1785-1851), 4th Duke of Newcastle under Lyme **128**

254 / CLASSICAL ARCHITECTURE

Pellechet, Auguste-Joseph (1789-1871) 147
Pellechet, Jules-Antoine-François-Auguste (1829-1903) 147, **147**
Pennethorne, John (1808-88) 3
Pennsylvania, Bank of 131
Penrose, Francis Cranmer (1817-1903) 3
Pentreath, Ben (1971-) 170, **170**, **171**, 174
Percier (-Bassant), Charles (1764-1838) **39**, 136
Pergamon, sanctuary of Athena 33
Permoser, Balthasar (1651-1732) 103
Perrault, Charles (1628-1703) 87
Perrault, Claude (1613-88) 6, **81**, 87, **87**
Perréal, Jean (c.1455-after 1530) **239**
Perret, Auguste (1874-1954) 3, 149
Perret, Claude (1880-1960) 3
Perret, Gustave (1876-1952) 3
Persius, Friedrich Ludwig (1803-45) **122**
Pertinax, Publius Helvius, Roman Emperor (r.193) 37
Peruzzi, Baldassare (1481-1536) 53, **55**
Pesson, William (1977-) 161
Petersen, Johan Carl Christian (1874-1923) 149, 152
Petra 74
 Khazna 34, **34**
Petrarch (Francesco Petrarca) (1304-74) 47
Petronilla, St (1st century AD) **185**
Petter, Hugh (1966-) **163**, 164
Pevsner, Sir Nikolaus Bernhard Leon (1902-83) 154
Peyre, Marie-Joseph (1730-85) 134
Piacentini, Marcello (1881-1960) 154
Piccinato, Luigi (1899-1983) 154
Pieroni da Galiano, Giovanni Battista (1586-1654) **226**
Piranesi, Giovanni Battista (1720-78) **41**, 115, 116
Pisa 46
 Cathedral 47
Pisidia, temple at Termessus 34
Pistoia 46
Pit, Robert (fl.1730) 96
Plater-Zyberk, Elizabeth (1950-) 160, 173, 174
Plautus, Titus Maccius (fl. c.205-c.184 BC) 2
Plaw, John (c.1745-1820) **139**
Playfair, James (1755-94) 131, **132**
Playfair, William Henry (1790-1857) 122, **127**
Plečnik, Jože (1872-1957) 152, **152**
Pluralism 159
Pocock, James William (d.1847) **134**
Poelært, Joseph Philippe (1817-79) 147
Poelzig, Hans (1869-1936) 149, **149**
Poitiers, Notre Dame 46
Poitou, St-Jouin-des-Marnes 46
Pollaiuolo, Simone del see Cronaca
polychromy, structural 92, **143**
Poole, Henry (1873-1928) 147
Pope, John Russell (1873-1937) 152
Pöppelmann, Matthäus Daniel (1662-1736) 103, **103**
Porphyrios, Demetri (1949-) 160, 164-5, **167**, 173, 174
Porta, Giacomo della (1532-1602) **65**, 67, **67**
Portaferry, County Down **137**, 139
Portmeirion, Gwynedd 155-6
Post-Modernism 158-60
Potsdam xiii
 Neues Palais 104
 Nikolaikirche 136
 Sanssouci Palace 103-4, **104**
Poulteney, Thomas (fl.1679-96) **106**
Poundbury, Dorset 161, 164, 167, 170, **170**
Poussin, Gaspard Dughet, called (1615-75) 109
Poussin, Nicolas (1594-1665) 109, **120**
Pozzo, Andrea (1642-1709) 86, **86**, **103**
Prato, Santa Maria delle Carceri 61
Primitive Hut, Laugier's concept of 32-3, 115
primitivism 115-16, **116**, **117**, 131-2

Prince's Foundation for the Built Environment 173
Prior, Edward Schröder (1852-1932) 151
proportion 2, 3-4, **20**, 154
 harmonic 3
Pugin, Edward Welby (1834-75) 175
Pullan, Richard Popplewell (1825-88) 10

Quatremère de Quincy, Antoine-Chrysostôme (1755-1849) 89, **89**, 161
Quesnay, Abraham (fl. early 18th century) **105**

Radziwiłłowa, Princess Helena (1753-1821) 132
Rafael Manzano Martos Prize 173
Rafn, Aage (1890-1953) 152
Rainaldi, Carlo (1611-91) **65**, 76, **77**
Rainaldi, Girolamo (1570-1655) **65**
Raphael (Raffaelo Sanzio) (1483-1520) 6, 53, 63
Raschdorff, Julius Karl (1823-1914) 147
Rastrick, John Urpeth (1780-1856) **144**
Rauch, Christian Daniel (1777-1857) **122**, **158**
Rauch, John Keiser (1930-2022) **158**, 159
Ravenna
 Church of San Vitale 41, 46
 Sant'Apollinaire in Classe 41
Rawlinson, Sir Robert (1810-98) **143**
Reck, Artur (1882-) 151
Reed, Henry Hope (1915-2013) v, 161, 173
Regensburg, Walhalla **124**
Reichenau, Germany, library 47
Reichlin, Bruno (1941-) 160
Renaissance 6, 45-72
 Italian 142, 145
 key buildings of Early 48, 51
Revett, Nicholas (1720-1804) 117, 118
Rhamnus, Temple of Nemesis **137**
Richard H. Driehaus Charitable Trust 173-4
Richardson, Sir Albert Edward (1880-1964) **31**, 115, 157, 162
Richmond-on-Thames, Richmond Riverside 164, **165**
Rickards, Edwin Alfred (1872-1920) 147
Rimini
 Arch of Augustus **50**, 51
 San Francesco (Temple Malatestiano) **50**, 51
Rimpl, Herbert (1902-78) 153
Ripon, Cathedral **120**
Robbia, Andrea (di Marco) della (1435-1525) **49**, **166**
Robbia, Luca (di Simone) della (1399/1400-82) **49**, **166**
Roberts, Henry (1803-76) 142, **144**
Robertson, Donald Struan (1885-1961) 1
Robertson, Sir Howard Morley (1888-1963) 162
Robertson, Jaquelin Taylor (1933-2020) 174
Robinson, Richard (1709-94), Archbishop of Armagh **39**
Rococo architecture 3, 73, 82
Roman architecture 36-7, 40-1, 43
 compared with Greek 43-4
 influence in Middle Ages 46-7
 ornament 20, 27, **29**, 43-4, **43**, **44**
 recycled artefacts 46
 Republican School 36, 37
 see also Glossary; Orders of Architecture
Romanesque 2, 46
Rome xii-xiii
 Arch of Constantine **34**, 37
 Arch of Septimius Severus 37
 Arch of Titus 32, **32**, **33**, 37
 Basilica of St Peter 62, **63**, **76**
 Capitoline palaces 64, **65**
 Casa Madre dei Mutilati 154
 Church of Il Gesù 67, **67**, **68**, 69, 76
 Esposizione Universale di Roma 154
 Flavian amphitheatre (Colosseum) 33-4, **33**, 37, 46
 forum of Nerva 27, **28**

Hotel Ambasciatori 154
House of Raphael 52-3
Mausoleum of Santa Costanza 41, **41**, 76
Oratorio dei Filippini 76, **77**
Palazzo dei Conservatori **65**
Palazzo del Senatori **65**
Palazzo della Cancellaria 52, **52**
Palazzo Farnese 55, **56**
Palazzo Massimi alle Colonne 53, **55**, **78**
Palazzo Nuovo (Capitoline Museum) **65**
Palazzo Poli **38**
Palazzo Venezia 52
Palazzo Vidoni Caffarelli 53
Palmanova 90
Pantheon 2, 27, **27**, 37, **42**, 60, **61**
Piazza del Campidoglio **65**
piazza of St Peter 79, **79**
Porta Pia 66, **66**
Quartiere Coppedè 155
Record Office (*Tabularium*) 33
San Carlo alle Quattro Fontane 74, **75**, **76**, 160
San Pietro in Montorio, *tempietto* 61-2, **62**
Santa Maria della Pace 61, **62**, **78**
Santa Maria Maggiore 41, **41**
Santa Maria in Via Lato **78**
Santa Susanna 76-7, **77**
Sant'Agnese in Agone, Piazza Navona 76, **77**
Sant'Andrea al Quirinale 74, **74**
Sant'Andrea, Via Flaminia **68**, 69
Sant'Anna dei Palafrenieri **68**
Santi Vincenzo ed Anastasio 77, **78**, 79
sarcophagus of Scipio **138**
Tempietto of San Pietro **139**
Temple of Castor and Pollux (Jupiter Stator) **27**
Temple of Concord **81**
Temple of Fortuna Virilis 20, **21**, **22**, 36
Temple of Jupiter 36
Temple of Mars Ultor 36, **37**
Temple of Minerva Medica 60, **61**
Theatre of Marcellus 18, **19**, 55
thermæ of Caracalla 40, **40**, 41, 142
thermæ of Diocletian 18, 22, 40, **40**
tomb of Cæcilia Metella **138**, 139
Trajan's Column 45
Trevi Fountain **38**
Villa Madama 53
Rosa, Salvator (1615-73) 219
Ross, Arthur (1910-2007) 173
Rossellino, Bernardo di Matteo Ghambarelli, *called* (c.1409-64) **50**
Rossi, Aldo (1931-97) 160
Rossi, John Charles Felix (1762-1839) **121**
Rothschild, Baron Ferdinand de (1839-98) 147
Rottmayr, Johann Michael (1654-1730) **81**, 85
Rousseau, Jean-Jacques (1712-78) 116, 132
Rowse, Herbert James (1887-1963) 154
Rushton, Northants, Triangular Lodge 3-4
Ruskin, John (1819-1900) 1, 151
Russia, Neo-Classicism 136
Rykov, Aleksei Ivanovich (1881-1938) 153
Ryng, Jakub (1992-) 170

St Gallen, Switzerland, abbey 47
St Petersburg xiii
    Bourse **130**
    St Isaac's Cathedral 136
St Quivox, Ayrshire, Campbell of Craigie mausoleum **127**
Salines d'Arc-et-Senans 135
Salingaros, Nikos A. (1952-) 174
Salisbury, Cathedral 92, **93**
Salvi, Nicola (1697-1751) **38**

Salzburg
    Cathedral 79, **80**
    Dreifaltigkeitskirche 79-80, **80**
Sammons, Richard (1961-) 170, **172**, 173
Sandys, Francis (*fl.*1786-1814) **140**
Sandys, Joseph (c.1758-1822) **140**
Sangallo. Antonio da, 'the Elder' (c.1460-1534) 63
Sangallo, Antonio da, 'the Younger' (1484-1546) 55, **56**, 63
Sangallo, Giuliano da (1445-1516) 61
Sanmicheli or Sanmichele, Michele (c.1487-1559) 55
Sansovino, Jacopo d'Antonio (1486-1570) 56, **57**, 58-9, **58**, 70
Satrabhandhu, Ong-ard (1944-) 174
Saumarez Smith, George (1973-) 164, **164**
Savile, Sir Henry (1549-1622) **67**
Sayer, Robert (1725-94) 117
Scamozzi, Vincenzo (1548-1616) 6, **23**, 58, **58**, 70, **70**, 71, **71**, 107
Scheemakers, Peter (1691-1781) **120**
Schinkel, Karl Friedrich (1782-1841) xiii, 35, 104, **119**, 122, **122**, **123**, 136, **143**, 150
Schlüter, Andreas (c.1659-1714) 102, **102**
Schmid-Ehmen, Kurt (1901-68) 152
Schmitz, Heinrich (1758-87) **202**
Schwanthaler, Ludwig Michael, Ritter von (1802-48) **124**, **125**
Schwarz, David M. (1951-) 174
Scipio Barbatus, Lucius Cornelius (c.337 BC–270 BC) **138**
Scotland, Classicism 145, 148
Scott Brown, Denise (1931-) **158**, 159
Scott, Sir George Gilbert ('Great') (1811-78) 1, 145
Scott, Sir Giles Gilbert (1880-1960) 158
Scott, Mackay Hugh Baillie (1865-1945) 173
sculpture 9, **65**, 70, **102**, **125**, **129**
    and architecture 96, 147, 156
Seligenstadt, abbey-church 47
Sellars, James (1843-88) 145
Semes, Steven W. (1953-) 173
Septimius Severus, Lucius, Roman Emperor (r.193-211) 37, 40
serliana (Venetian window) 96, **98**
Serlio, Sebastiano (1475-1554) 6, 20, 22, 53, 63, 67, 69
Servandoni, Giovanni Niccolò Geronimo (1695-1766) 87, **89**
Seymour, Edward (c.1539-1621), 1st Earl of Hertford 92, **93**
Seymour, Katharine, Countess of Hertford **93**
Shanahan, Michael (c.1731-1811) **139**, **140**
Sharington, Sir William (c.1495-1553) 92, **93**
Shaw, Richard Norman (1831-1912) 145, 148
Shchuko, Vladimir Alekseyevich (1878-1939) 152
Shchusev, Alexei Victorovich (1873-1949) 150, 152
Sheres, Sir Henry (1641-1710) **106**
Shugborough, Staffs 118, **118**
    Lanthorn of Demosthenes 120, **120**
    Shepherdess's Tomb **120**
Shute, John (*fl.*1550-63) 90, **91**
Sicily 36
Sidney, Lucy (1520-91) **94**
Siena, Cathedral 47
Simpson, John Anthony (1954-) 160, 167, 169, **169**, 173
Sitte, Camillo (1843-1903) 161
Sixteen Principles of Urbanism, East Germany 160
Sixtus V, Pope (r.1585-90) 90
SLOAP (Space Left Over After Planning) 160
Smirke, Sir Robert (1780-1867) 122, **128**
Smirke, Sydney (1798-1877) 145, **145**
Smith, Alfred (*fl.*1843-72) 145
Smith, Arnold Dunbar (1866-1933) 148
Smith, George (1783-1869) **144**
Smith, Thomas Gordon (1948-2021) 162, 173
Smith, Timothy Mark (1979-) 173
Smylie, John (1961-) 169, 173
Smythson, Robert (c.1536-1614) 90, **91**, 92, **92**
Soane, Sir John (1753-1837) xiii, 5, **31**, 35, 116, **116**, 133, 135
    Sir John Soane's Museum (Lincoln's Inn Fields) 135, **135**

256 / CLASSICAL ARCHITECTURE

Society of Dilettanti 116–17
Solari, Santino (1576-1646) 79, **80**
Solihull, 'Barn à la Pæstum' 116, **116**
Solomon, King of Israel (c.974-937 BC) 6, **81**
Soufflot, Jacques-Germain (1713-80) 89, **89**, 116, 136
South Wraxall Manor, Wilts 92
Southwark school of sculptors 94
Soviet Union 152–3
Spalato (Split), palace of Diocletian 34, 40, 41, 111
Speer, Berthold Konrad Hermann Albert (1905-81) 35, 150, 151, 152, 157
Spenser, Edmund (c.1552-99) 3
Spetses, Greece, Oitiousa 165
Spiegler, Franz Josef (1691-1757) **239**
Stalin, Joseph Vissarionovich Dzhugashvili (1879-1953) 150
Stamford, Lincs
    former hotel **119**
    Grant's iron foundry 132, **133**
    Rock House 133, **134**
    Stamford Institution 132, **133**
Stamp, Gavin Mark (1948-2017) xiii, 153–4, 156, 158
Statham, Henry Heathcote (1839-1924) 1, 7
Steinhausen, Wallfahrtskirche 86, **86**
Steinl, Matthias (c.1644-1727) 85, **85**
Stern, Robert Arthur Morton (1939-) 159, 162, 173, 174
Stevenson, Samuel (1859-1924) 145, **146**
Stewart, James S. (1865-1904) 147
Stockholm
    Concert House 157
    public library 162
    Swedish Match Company 157
    Woodland Cemetery, Enskede 150, **150**
Stockport, town hall 147, **148**
Stoddart, Alexander (1959-) **163**, 164, **164**, 167, **168**, 173
Stone, Nicholas (c.1587-1647) **185**
Stowe, Bucks 109
Strachey, Mary Annabel Nassau (Amabel) (1894-1984) 156
Strack, Johann Heinrich (1805-80) 142
Strauß, Richard Georg (1864-1949) 157
Stuart, James 'Athenian' (1713-88) 117, 118, **118**, **119**, **120**, **121**
see also Revett
Stüler, Friedrich August (1800-65) 142
Sturgis, Russell (1836-1909) xi
Sulla, Lucius Cornelius (138-78 BC) 36
Sullivan, Louis (1856-1924) 156
Summerson, Sir John Newenham (1904-92) xiii, 3, 174
Suter, Richard (1797-1883) **137**
Swales, Francis Samuel (1879-1962) 148
Swanley, Kent, United House **169**
Sweden 157
Sweetman, John (*fl.*1611) 92

Tagliaventi, Gabriele (1960-) 161
Tait, Thomas Smith (1882-1954) **149**, 153
Talman, William (1650-1719) 95–6
Taylor, Jonathan (1975-) 173
Taylor, Sir Robert (1714-88) 111
Tegea, Temple of Athena Alea 32, 36
temple theme **45**, 87, 98, **141**, 142
Templepatrick, County Antrim, Templetown mausoleum **138**
temples
    circular 60–3, **62**, 98, **138**, 139
    Greek 9, 36
    Roman 36–7, 139
Tengbom, Ivar Justus (1878-1968) 150, 152, 157
Terlinden, François (1938-2007) 161
Terragni, Giuseppe (1904-43) xii, 154
Terry, John Quinlan (1937-) 164, **164**, **165**, 173, 174
thermæ 20, 108, 109, 115
    of Caracalla 40, **40**, **41**, 142
    of Diocletian 18, 22, 40, **40**

Thibierge, Martin-Alexandre Habert, *called* (1756-1836) **117**
Thiepval Memorial **154**, 157
Thomas, Albert-Félix-Théophile (1847-1907) **40**
Thomas, Sir Alfred Brumwell (1868-1948) 147, **148**
Thomon, Thomas-Jean de (1754-1813) 122, **130**
Thomsen, Edvard (1884-1980) 152
Thomson, Alexander 'Greek' (1817-75) 35, 122, **128**, 145
Thomson, James (1800-83) 142, **143**
Thornely, Sir Arnold (1870-1953) 154
Thrasyllus (*fl.c.*320-19 BC) 118, **119**
Tiberius (Tiberius Clauius Nero), Roman Emperor (r.14-37) 37
Tingham, Edmund (*fl.*1630s) 94
Titus (Titus Flavius Vespasianus), Roman Emperor (r.79-81) 33, 37
Tivoli 74
    Temple of Vesta 27, **31**, **42**
    Villa Adriana 37
Todmorden, Town Hall 139, **142**
Tornagrain, Inverness 170, **171**
Torrigiani, Pietro (di Torrigiano d'Antonio) (1472-1528) 90
town halls **133**, 139, **141**, **142**, 145, **145**, **146**, 147, **148**
Townesend, William (1676-1739) 96
Trajan (Marcus Ulpius Traianus), Roman Emperor (r.98-117) 45
Treese, Sebastian (1977-) 174
Tregunnel Hill, Cornwall 164
Tresham, Sir Thomas (1543-1605) 3–4
triumphal arches 6, **33**, 37, 46, **50**, 59, **91**, **154**
    theme **37**, **38**, **39**, **40**, **50**, 59, **60**, 90, 139
Troost, Paul Ludwig (1879-1934) 150, **150**, 151, 152
Truro, Cornwall, Royal Crescent 170, **170**
Tuck, William (*fl.*1741-1805) 134
Turner, Alfred (1874-1940) **155**
Turner, Thomas (*fl.*1840s) 144
Tuscan Order 2, 17, **17**, 18, 36, 61

Üblhör, Johann Georg (1703-63) 82, **84**
Unger, Georg Christian (1743-1812) **105**
Ungers, Oswald Mathias (1926-2007) 160
United States 131, 152
    New Classicism 161, 173
Uotila, Marjo (1969-) 173, 174
Urbino, Palazzo Ducale 52, **52**

Vanbrugh, Sir John (1664-1726) 96, **96**, 98, **98**, 99
Vasari, Giorgio (1511-74) 64
Vatican
    Belvedere Court 59
    Scala Regia 79
Venice
    Biblioteca Marciana 58, **58**, 70, 145
    Il Redentore 69, 71–2, **72**
    La Zecca (the Mint) 59
    palazzi 56, 58–9
    Palazzo Corner della Ca'Grande 56, **57**
    Palazzo Corner-Spinelli 56
    Palazzo Pèsaro 56, **57**
    Palazzo Rezzonico 58
    Palazzo Vendramin-Calergi 56, **57**
    San Giorgio Maggiore 69, 71–2, **71**, 109
    Santa Maria della Salute 79, **79**
Venturi, Robert Charles (1925-2018) 158–9, **158**
Ver-sur-Mer, Normandy Memorial 167, **168**
Verona, Porta Palio **54**
Versailles 73, 89–90
Vespasian (Titus Flavius Sabinus Vespasianus), Roman Emperor (r.70-79) 33, 37
Vestier, Nicolas-Jacques-Antoine (1765-1816) **117**
Vicenza 69–71
    Basilica 69–70, **69**
    Casa del Diavolo **70**
    Palazzo Porto-Breganze 70, **70**

Palazzo Thiene 109
Palazzo Valmarano 70
Teatro Olimpico 71, **71**
Villa Capra (Villa Rotonda) 70, **70**, 107, **107**, **108**, 109
Vienna
    Augustinerkirche 132, **132**
    Belvedere 96, **97**, 102
    Central Cemetery 147, **148**
    Hofburg 147
    Jesuitenkirche 85–6, **86**
    Karlskirche 79–80, **81**, **82**
    Peterskirche 85, **85**
    Schönbrunn Palace 102
Vierzehnheiligen, Wallfahrtskirche 82, **84**, 85
Vignola, Giacomo or Jacopo Barozzi da (1507-73) 67, **67**, **68**, 69
    ellipses 69, 74
    La Regola delli Cinque Ordini d'Architettura 69
    Orders 4, 6, 17, **17**, **19**, **20**, **22**, **29**
Vignon, Alexandre-Pierre (1763-1828) 136, **141**
Virginia, USA, Monticello 135
Viscardi, Giovanni Antonio (1645-1713) 103, **103**
Vitruvius (Marcus Vitruvius Pollio, *c*.80/70 BC–after 15 BC) 1–2, 114, 162
    on Etruscan temple 36–7
    Œcus Ægyptus **108**, 109
    On Architecture 1–2, 5, 6, 47
    on *Ordinatio* of architecture 2, 3, 22
    'rediscovery' of 47
Vivarium, Calabria, monastery 47
Voysey, Charles Francis Annesley (1857-1941) 173
Vries, Hans Vredeman de (1527-1606) 90, 92, **92**
The Vyne, Hants 94

Waddesdon Manor, Bucks 147
Wagner, Otto Colomann (1841-1918) 147, **148**, 152, 153
Wailly, Charles de (1730-98) 134
Wanstead House, Essex 104, **105**, 107
war memorials 154, 165, 167, **168**
Washington, DC
    Jefferson Memorial 152
    Lincoln Memorial 149
    National Gallery of Art 152
    U.S. Capitol **130**, 131, 147
Watkin, David John (1941-2018) xiv, 73, **123**, **164**, 173
Waverton House, Glos 164
Webb, John (1611-72) 94, **95**, 106
Weddell, William (1736-92) **120**
Weightman, John (1798-1883) **143**
Weinbrenner, Johann Jakob Friedrich (1766-1826) 133
Weine, Seth Joseph (1956-) 172
Welch, Edward (1806-68) **141**
Wellingborough, Northants, St Mary's **156**
Weltenburg an der Donau, Sts George and Martin 80, 82, **83**
Westerkirk, Bentpath, Dumfries, Johnstone mausoleum **126**
Whitby, George Frederick (1916-73) 157
White, Stanford (1853-1906) 152
Wiegand, Christian Friedrich (1752-1832) **236**
Wilds, Amon (1762-1833) **179**
Wilds, Amon Henry (1784-1857) **179**

Wilkins, William (1778-1839) 122, **129**, 136, 137, **143**, 159, **164**
William III (1650-1702), King [(*r*. alone from 1694)] 148
William IV, King (*r*.1830-37) 186
Williams-Ellis, Amabel *see* Strachey
Williams-Ellis, Sir (Bertram) Clough (1883-1978) 155–6, 157
Williamsburg, Virginia 164
Willoughby, Sir Francis (1546-96) 90, 92
Willson, Thomas John (1824-1903) 3
Wilson Jones, Mark (1956-) 171, **171**
Wilson, Susan 45
Wilton House, Wilts 92, 94
    Palladian bridge 106, **107**
Winchester College, War Memorial cloister 154, **155**
Winckelmann, Johann Joachim (1717-68) 115, 116
Windermere, Belle Isle 139
windows
    Diocletian 44, 72, **79**, **107**, 130, 131, **131**, **132**
    Greek and Roman 44
    serliana (Venetian) 96, **98**, 109
    Wyatt 121
Wing, Bucks, All Saints 90
Wollaton Hall, Notts 90, **92**
Wolstenholme, Henry Vernon (1863-1936) 154
Wood, John the Elder (1704-54) 112, **112**, 114
Wood, John the Younger (1728-81) 112, **112**, **113**, 114
Wood, Robert (*c*.1717-71) 116–17
Woodford, James (1893-1976) 157
Woodstock, Oxon, Park View estate **163**, 164
Woolfe, John (*fl*.1750-93) 114
Wörlitz xiii, 112
Wornum, George Grey (1888-1957) 157, **157**, **168**
Worreschk, Immo (1994-) 174
Wotton, Sir Henry (1568-1639) 1
Wren, Christopher (1675-1747) 45
Wren, Sir Christopher (1632-1723) 2, 5, 45, **106**
    Baroque architecture 94–5, **95**
    influences on 95
    St Paul's **89**, 95
Wren, Stephen (1733-83) 45
'Wrenaissance' 147, **148**
Wright, Thomas (1711-86) **120**
Wright, William (*fl*.1607-54) **93**
Wrocław, Poland
    Jahrhunderthalle 149
    Szczytnicki Park **149**
Wyatt, James (1746-1813) **39**, 114, **114**, **121**, 138
Wyatt, Joseph (1739-85) 118
Wyatt, Samuel (1737-1807) 118

Xanthos, Nereid monument 36

York, Assembly Room **108**, 109
Young, William (1843-1900) 145, **146**, 148

Zhukov, Georgy Konstantinovich (1896-1974) 152
Zimmermann, Dominikus (1685-1766) 86, **86**
Zuccalli, Enrico (1642-1724) 79, **80**, 103, **103**
Zug, Simon Gottlieb, *aka* Szymon Bogumił (1733-1807) 132, **132**